Capital Markets

Institutions and Instruments

THIRD EDITION

Frank J. Fabozzi

School of Management
Yale University

Franco Modigliani

Sloan School of Management
Massachusetts Institute of Technology

With contributions from
Frank J. Jones

The Guardian Life Insurance Company of America

Prentice
Hall

Upper Saddle River, New Jersey

Library of Congress Cataloging-in-Publication Data

Fabozzi, Frank J.
   Capital markets : institutions and instruments / Frank J. Fabozzi, Franco Modigliani.—
3rd ed.
     p. cm.
  Includes bibliographical references and index.
  ISBN 0-13-067334-X
   1. Capital market. I. Modigliani, Franco. II. Title.

HG4523 .F33 2002
332′.0414—dc21   2002016944

To our wives, Donna Marie Fabozzi and Serena Modigliani

AVP/Executive Editor: Mickey Cox
VP/Editor-in-Chief: P. J. Boardman
Managing Editor (Editorial): Gladys Soto
Assistant Editor: Beth Romph
Editorial Assistant: Kevin Hancock
Media Project Manager: Victoria Anderson
Marketing Manager: Kathleen McLellan
Marketing Assistant: Christopher Bath
Managing Editor (Production): John Roberts
Production Editor: Maureen Wilson
Production Assistant: Dianne Falcone
Permissions Coordinator: Suzanne Grappi
Associate Director, Manufacturing: Vincent Scelta
Production Manager: Arnold Vila
Manufacturing Buyer: Michelle Klein
Cover Design: Bruce Kenselaar
Cover/Photo: PhotoDisc/Don Farrall
Composition: BookMasters, Inc.
Full-Service Project Management: Jennifer Welsch
Printer/Binder: Maple-Vail

Credits and acknowledgments borrowed from other sources and reproduced, with permission, in this textbook appear on appropriate page within text.

Pearson Education LTD.
Pearson Education Australia PTY, Limited
Pearson Education Singapore, Pte. Ltd
Pearson Education North Asia Ltd
Pearson Education, Canada, Ltd
Pearson Educación de Mexico, S.A. de C.V.
Pearson Education—Japan
Pearson Education Malaysia, Pte. Ltd

10 9 8 7 6 5 4 3 2 1
ISBN 0-13-067334-X

Brief Contents

Contents

Preface

The revolution that swept through the world financial markets was aptly described in 1985 by a noted economist, Henry Kaufman:

> If a modern-day Rip Van Winkle had fallen asleep twenty years ago, or for that matter even ten years back, on awakening today, he would be astonished as to what has happened in the financial markets. Instead of a world of isolated national capital markets and a preponderance of fixed-rate financing, he would discover a world of highly integrated capital markets, an extensive array of financing instruments, and new methods of addressing market risk.

The purpose of this book is to describe the wide range of instruments for financing, investing, and controlling risk available in today's financial markets. New financial instruments are not created simply because someone on Wall Street believes that it would be "fun" to introduce an instrument with more "bells and whistles" than existing instruments. The demand for new instruments is driven by the needs of borrowers and investors based on their asset/liability management situation, regulatory constraints (if any), financial accounting considerations, and tax considerations. For these reasons, to comprehend the financial innovations that have occurred and are expected to occur in the future, a general understanding of the asset/liability management problem of major institutional investors is required. Therefore, in addition to coverage of the markets for all financial instruments, we provide an overview of the asset/liability management issues faced by major institutional investors and the strategies they employ.

We believe that the coverage provided in this book on the institutional investors and financial instruments is as up-to-date as possible in a market facing rapid changes in the characteristics of the players and those making the rules as to how the game can be played. New financial instruments are introduced on a regular basis; however, armed with an understanding of the needs of borrowers and institutional investors and the attributes of existing financial instruments, the reader will be able to recognize the contribution made by a new financial instrument.

The first edition of this book was published in 1992. At the time, the book deviated in several significant ways from the traditional capital markets textbooks, notably in its coverage of derivative markets (futures, options, swaps, etc.). These markets are an integral part of the global capital market. They are not—as often categorized by the popular press and some of our less-informed congressional representatives and regulators—"exotic" markets. These instruments provide a mechanism by which market participants can control risk—borrowers can control borrowing costs and investors can control the market risk of their portfolio. It is safe to say that without the derivative markets, an efficient global capital market would be impossible. In addition, it is important to appreciate the basic principles of options not only as a stand-alone instrument, but because many financial instruments have embedded options. Also, the liabilities of many financial institutions contain embedded options. Thus, it is difficult to appreciate the complex nature of assets and liabilities without understanding the fundamentals of option theory.

Although we recognize that many colleges offer a specialized course in derivative markets, our purpose in the first edition was not to delve deeply into the various trading strategies and the nuances of pricing models that characterize such a course. Instead, we provided the fundamentals of the role of these instruments in financial markets, the principles of pricing them, and a general description of how they are used by market participants to control risk.

A special feature of the book at the time was the extensive coverage of the mortgage market and the securitization of assets. Asset securitization refers to the creation of securities whose collateral is the cash flow from the underlying pool of assets. The process of asset securitization is radically different from the traditional system for financing the acquisition of assets. By far the largest part of the securitized asset market is the mortgage-backed securities market, where the assets collateralizing the securities are mortgage loans. Securitized assets backed by non-real estate mortgage loans were a small but growing part of the market at the time of the publication of the first edition. Now they are a major sector of the capital market where financial and non-financial corporations can raise funds.

Another key feature of this book was its emphasis on the role played by foreign investors in the U.S. market. Although the bulk of this book covers the U.S. financial markets, we discuss other major financial markets throughout.

Finally, when we decided on the topics to cover in this book we discriminated between what belongs in a course on capital markets and what is the province of investment management. Oftentimes, because the needs of institutional investors dictate the need for financial instruments with certain investment characteristics or for a particular strategy employing a capital market instrument, we had to cross the line. The approach we took in this book makes it adaptable for a course in investment banking and as a supplement for a derivative markets course.

That was our thinking in the first edition of the book. We must admit when the publisher Prentice Hall sent the initial drafts of the manuscript to ten reviewers, the reviews were mixed. Half thought that the book was so substantially different from what was traditionally taught in a capital markets or financial markets and institutions course that it would be an error for Prentice Hall to publish the book. The other five reviewers strongly endorsed the book as a major contribution and a blueprint as to how capital markets courses would be taught in the future. Of course, Prentice Hall did publish the book in 1992, and in 1996 published the second edition.

Our model or blueprint has been followed by other textbook writers since the mid-1990s. So, the unique features we claimed regarding the first edition and second edition are now common in other textbooks. However, we believe that our coverage and perspective with respect to key market sectors is still unique.

ACKNOWLEDGMENTS

We are indebted to many individuals for providing us with various forms of assistance. First and foremost is Frank J. Jones, Chief Investment Officer of The Guardian Life, who coauthored several chapters in this edition. Michael Ferri (George Mason University) provided significant assistance for several of the chapters.

Portions of the manuscript were used in our courses at MIT and in Fabozzi's courses at Yale University. We received helpful comments from many of our students. In addition, the authors would like to thank the following reviewers: K. Thomas Liaw

(St. John's University), John Spitzer (University of Iowa), Robert E. Lamy (Wake Forest University), Rita Biswas (University of Albany–SUNY), Chip Ruscher (James Madison University), and Jacobus T. Severiens (John Carroll University).

In our end-of-chapter questions, we used excerpts from *Institutional Investor* and several weekly publications of Institutional Investor Inc., *Wall Street Letter, Bank Letter, BondWeek, Corporate Financing Week, Derivatives Week, Money Management Letter*, and *Portfolio Letter*. We are grateful to Tom Lamont, editor of the weekly publications, for permission to use the material.

Frank J. Fabozzi
Franco Modigliani

CHAPTER 1

Introduction

Learning Objectives

After reading this chapter you will understand:

◆ what a financial asset is.

◆ the distinction between a debt instrument and an equity instrument.

◆ the general principles for determining the price of a financial asset.

◆ ten properties of financial assets: moneyness, divisibility and denomination, reversibility, term to maturity, liquidity, convertibility, currency, cash flow and return predictability, complexity, and tax status.

◆ the principal economic functions of financial assets.

◆ what a financial market is and the principal economic functions it performs.

◆ the different ways to classify financial markets.

◆ what is meant by a derivative instrument.

◆ the reasons for the globalization of financial markets.

◆ the classification of global financial markets.

In a market economy, the allocation of economic resources is driven by the outcome of many private decisions. Prices are the signals that direct economic resources to their best use. The types of markets in an economy can be divided into (1) the market for products (manufactured goods and services), or the *product market;* and (2) the market for the factors of production (labor and capital), or the *factor market.* In this book, we focus on one part of the factor market, the market for financial assets, or, more simply, the *financial market.* This market determines the cost of capital. In this chapter we look at the basic characteristics and functions of financial assets and financial markets.

◆ FINANCIAL ASSETS

We begin with a few basic definitions. An **asset** is any possession that has value in an exchange. Assets can be classified as tangible or intangible. The value of a **tangible asset** depends on particular physical properties—examples include buildings, land, or machinery. Tangible assets may be classified further into reproducible assets such as machinery, or nonreproducible assets such as land, a mine, or a work of art.

Intangible assets, by contrast, represent legal claims to some future benefit. Their value bears no relation to the form, physical or otherwise, in which the claims are recorded. **Financial assets**, financial instruments, or securities are intangible assets. For these instruments, the typical future benefit comes in the form of a claim to future cash. This book deals with the various types of financial assets, the markets where they are traded (i.e., bought and sold), and the principles for valuing them.

The entity that agrees to make future cash payments is called the issuer of the financial asset; the owner of the financial asset is referred to as the **investor**. Examples of financial assets include the following:

- A bond issued by the U.S. Department of the Treasury
- A bond issued by General Electric Corporation
- A bond issued by the state of California
- A bond issued by the government of France
- An automobile loan
- A home mortgage loan
- Common stock issued by Digital Equipment Corporation
- Common stock issued by Honda Motor Company

In the case of the bond issued by the U.S. Department of the Treasury, the U.S. government (the issuer) agrees to pay the investor interest until the bond matures, then at the maturity date repay the amount borrowed. For the bonds issued by General Electric Corporation and the state of California, just as with the bond issued by the U.S. Department of the Treasury, the issuer agrees to pay the investor interest until the bond matures, then at the maturity date repay the amount borrowed.

In the case of the French government bond, the cash payments are known if the French government does not default. However, the cash payments may be denominated not in U.S. dollars but in euros. Thus, while the cash payments are known in terms of the number of euros that will be received, from the perspective of a U.S. investor, the number of U.S. dollars remains unknown. The number of U.S. dollars depends on the exchange rate between euros and the U.S. dollar at the time the cash payments are received and converted into U.S. dollars.

For the automobile loan and the home mortgage loan, the issuer is the individual who borrowed the funds. The investor is the entity, such as a bank, that lent the funds to the individual. The loan agreement will include a schedule specifying how the borrower will repay the loan and how the interest will be paid.

The common stock of Digital Equipment Corporation entitles the investor to receive dividends distributed by the company. The investor in this case also holds a claim to a pro rata share of the net asset value of the company in case of liquidation.

The same applies to the cash payments of the common stock of Honda Motor Company, a Japanese corporation. In addition, because Honda makes dividend payments in Japanese yen, a U.S. investor is subject to uncertainty about the cash payments in terms of U.S. dollars. The cash payments in U.S. dollars depend on the exchange rate at the time of conversion between U.S. dollars and the Japanese yen.

DEBT VERSUS EQUITY CLAIMS

The claims of the holder of a financial asset may be either a fixed dollar amount or a varying, or residual, amount. In the former case, the financial asset is referred to as a **debt instrument**. The bond issued by the U.S. Department of the Treasury, General Electric Corporation, and the state of California are examples of debt instruments requiring fixed dollar payments to borrow the funds. The two loans are also debt instruments.

An **equity claim** (also called a **residual claim**) obligates the issuer of the financial asset to pay the holder an amount based on earnings, if any, after holders of debt instruments have been paid. Common stock is an example of an equity claim. A partnership share in a business is another example.

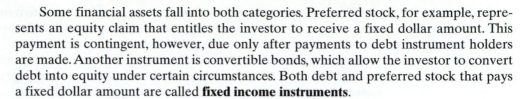

Some financial assets fall into both categories. Preferred stock, for example, represents an equity claim that entitles the investor to receive a fixed dollar amount. This payment is contingent, however, due only after payments to debt instrument holders are made. Another instrument is convertible bonds, which allow the investor to convert debt into equity under certain circumstances. Both debt and preferred stock that pays a fixed dollar amount are called **fixed income instruments**.

THE VALUE OF A FINANCIAL ASSET

Valuation is the process of determining the fair value or price of a financial asset. The fundamental principle of valuation is that the value of any financial asset is the present value of the cash flow expected. This principle applies regardless of the financial asset. Consequently, it applies equally to common stock, a bond, a loan, and real estate.

The principle is simple: just determine the cash flow and then calculate the present value. However, accomplishing the task is not simple.

Estimating the Cash Flow The first problem encountered in valuing a financial asset is interpreting what is meant by "cash flow." Accountants use a set answer: it is the net income after taxes plus noncash outlays such as depreciation. This nice definition is useless for our purposes, however. **Cash flow** is simply the cash that is expected to be received each period from investing in a particular financial asset.

The type of financial asset, whether debt instrument or equity instrument, and the characteristics of the issuer determine the degree of certainty of the cash flow expected. For example, assuming that the U.S. government never defaults on the debt instruments it issues, the cash flow of securities issued by the U.S. Department of the Treasury is known with certainty.

The cash flow of other debt instruments is not known with certainty for three reasons. First, the issuer might default. Second, provisions included in most debt instruments grant the issuer and/or the investor the right to change how the borrowed funds are repaid (these features are discussed in Section VI). Finally, as also explained in Section VI, with some debt instruments, the interest rate the issuer pays can change over the time the borrowed funds are outstanding.

The holder of common stock of a corporation faces uncertainty as to the amount and the timing of dividend payments. Dividend payments relate to corporate profits. Moreover, unlike debt instruments in which the borrowed funds are to be repaid, an investor in common stock typically must sell the stock in order to try to recover the amount invested. Whether the amount received when the stock is sold is more or less than the amount initially invested depends on the stock's price at the time of sale, another uncertainty.

Regardless of whether we talk about the cash flow of a debt or equity instrument, the preceding discussion of cash flow pertains to the nominal dollar amount, not the amount adjusted for the purchasing power of those dollars. Because of inflation, the purchasing power of the cash flow is uncertain even if the nominal dollar amount of the cash flow is certain.

The Appropriate Interest Rate for Discounting the Cash Flow Once the cash flow for a financial asset is estimated, the next step is to determine the appropriate interest rate used to calculate the present value (or discounted value). To determine the appropriate rate, the investor must address the following two questions:

1. What is the minimum interest rate the investor should require?
2. How much more than the minimum interest rate should the investor require?

The minimum interest rate that an investor should require is the interest rate available in the financial market on a default-free cash flow. Historically, in the United States the minimum interest rate coincided with the rate on U.S. Treasury securities. However, as explained in Chapter 20, the decline in the issuance of U.S. Treasury securities resulted in the search for a new benchmark that best represents the minimum interest rate. In Europe, the interest rate on government bonds of Germany provides the benchmark used for the minimum interest rate. Another benchmark used by certain institutional investors is the London interbank offered rate (LIBOR), a rate that will be discussed in Chapter 19.

The premium over the interest rate on a U.S. Treasury security or other benchmark that the investor should require should reflect the risks associated with realizing the cash flow expected. The greater the perceived risk, the larger the premium investors require. Figure 1-1 summarizes this valuation process.

Of the various types of risks discussed in this chapter and those to follow, three present themselves in our examples. The first is the risk that the issuer or borrower will default on the obligation, called **credit risk**, or **default risk**. The second is the risk attached to the potential purchasing power of the cash flow expected, called **purchasing power risk**, or **inflation risk**. Finally, financial assets whose cash flow is not denominated in U.S. dollars entail a risk that the exchange rate will change adversely resulting in fewer U.S. dollars, referred to as **foreign exchange risk**.

FINANCIAL ASSETS VERSUS TANGIBLE ASSETS

A tangible asset, such as a plant or equipment purchased by a business entity, shares at least one characteristic with a financial asset: both are expected to generate future cash flow for their owner. For example, suppose a U.S. airline purchases a fleet of aircraft for

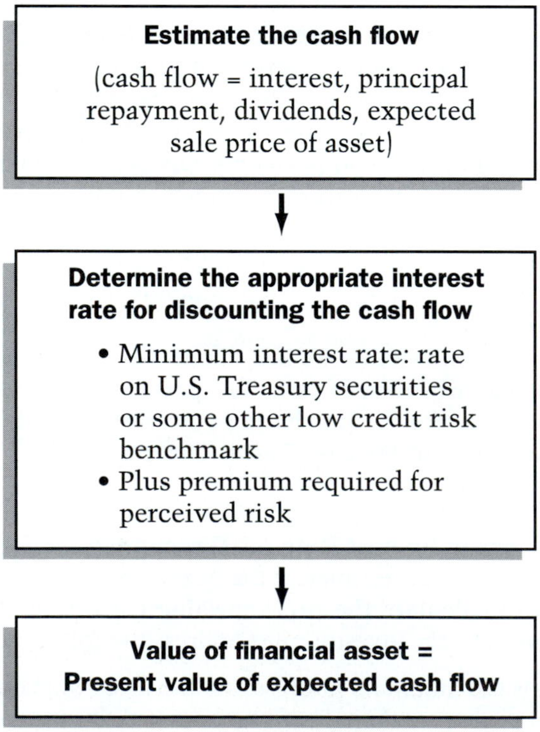

FIGURE 1-1 Summary of the Process for Valuing a Financial Asset

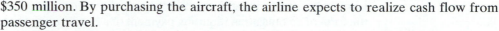

$350 million. By purchasing the aircraft, the airline expects to realize cash flow from passenger travel.

Financial assets and tangible assets are linked. Ownership of tangible assets is financed by the issuance of some type of financial asset—either debt instruments or equity instruments. For example, in the case of the airline, suppose that a debt instrument was issued to raise the $350 million to purchase the fleet of aircraft. The cash flow from the passenger travel will be used to service the obligation of the debt instrument. Ultimately, therefore, the tangible asset generates the cash flow for a financial asset.

THE ROLE OF FINANCIAL ASSETS

Financial assets serve two principal economic functions. First, financial assets transfer funds from those parties who have surplus funds to invest to those who need funds to invest in tangible assets. As their second function, they transfer funds in such a way as to redistribute the unavoidable risk associated with the cash flow generated by tangible assets among those seeking and those providing the funds. However, the claims held by the final wealth holders generally differ from the liabilities issued by the final demanders of funds because of the activity of entities operating in financial markets, called **financial intermediaries**, who seek to transform the final liabilities into different financial assets preferred by the public. Financial intermediaries are discussed in the next chapter.

To illustrate these two economic functions, consider three situations.

1. Joe Grasso obtained a license to manufacture Pooh Bear wristwatches. Joe estimates that he needs $1 million to purchase the plant and equipment to manufacture the watches. Unfortunately, he has only $200,000 to invest, his life savings, which he does not want to invest even though he feels confident a receptive market exists for the watches.
2. Susan Carlson recently inherited $730,000. She plans to spend $30,000 on some jewelry, furniture, and a few cruises, and to invest the balance of $700,000.
3. Larry Stein, an up-and-coming attorney with a major New York law firm, received a bonus check that netted him $270,000 after taxes. He plans to spend $70,000 on a BMW and invest the balance, $200,000.

Suppose that, quite by accident, Joe, Susan, and Larry meet in New York City. Sometime during their conversation, they discuss their financial plans. By the end of the evening, they agree to a deal. Joe agrees to invest $100,000 of his savings in the business and sell a 50% interest to Susan for $700,000. Larry agrees to lend Joe $200,000 for 4 years at an interest rate of 18% per year. Joe will be responsible for operating the business without the assistance of Susan or Larry. Joe now has his $1 million to manufacture the watches.

Two financial claims came out of this agreement. The first is an equity instrument issued by Joe and purchased by Susan for $700,000. The other is a debt instrument issued by Joe and purchased by Larry for $200,000. Thus, the two financial assets allowed funds to be transferred from Susan and Larry, who held surplus funds to invest, to Joe, who needed funds to invest in tangible assets in order to manufacture the watches. This transfer of funds carries out the first economic function of financial assets.

The fact that Joe is not willing to invest his life savings of $200,000 means that he wanted to transfer part of that risk. He does so by selling Susan a financial asset that gives her a financial claim equal to one-half the cash flow from the business after paying the interest expense. He further secures an additional amount of capital from

Larry, who is not willing to share in the risk of the business (except for the credit risk), in the form of an obligation requiring payment of a fixed cash flow, regardless of the outcome of the venture. This shifting of risk is the second economic function of financial assets.

PROPERTIES OF FINANCIAL ASSETS

Financial assets possess certain properties that determine or influence their attractiveness to different classes of investors. The 10 properties of financial assets are (1) moneyness, (2) divisibility and denomination, (3) reversibility, (4) term to maturity, (5) liquidity, (6) convertibility, (7) currency, (8) cash flow and return predictability, (9) complexity, and (10) tax status.[1] The following paragraphs describe each property.

Moneyness Some financial assets act as a medium of exchange or in settlement of transactions. These assets are called **money**. In the United States they consist of currency and all forms of deposits that permit check writing. Other financial assets, although not money, closely approximate money in that they can be transformed into money at little cost, delay, or risk. They are referred to as **near money**. In the United States, near money instruments include time and savings deposits and a security issued by the U.S. government with a maturity of three months called a three-month Treasury bill.[2] Moneyness clearly offers a desirable property for investors.

Divisibility and Denomination **Divisibility** relates to the minimum size at which a financial asset can be liquidated and exchanged for money. The smaller the size, the more the financial asset is divisible. A financial asset such as a deposit at a bank is typically infinitely divisible (down to the penny), but other financial assets set varying degrees of divisibility depending on their denomination, which is the dollar value of the amount that each unit of the asset will pay at maturity. Thus many bonds come in $1,000 denominations, while some debt instruments come in $1 million denominations. In general, divisibility is desirable for investors.

Reversibility **Reversibility** refers to the cost of investing in a financial asset and then getting out of it and back into cash again. Consequently, reversibility is also referred to as **round-trip cost**.

A financial asset such as a deposit at a bank is obviously highly reversible because usually the investor incurs no charge for adding to or withdrawing from it. Other transaction costs may be unavoidable, but these costs are small. For financial assets traded in organized markets or with "market makers" (discussed in Chapter 7), the most relevant component of round-trip cost is the so-called bid-ask spread, to which might be added commissions and the time and cost, if any, of delivering the asset. The **bid-ask spread** consists of the difference between the price at which a market maker is willing to sell a financial asset (i.e., the price it is asking) and the price at which a market maker is willing to buy the financial asset (i.e., the price it is bidding). For example, if a market maker is willing to sell some financial asset for $70.50 (the ask price) and buy it for $70.00 (the bid price), the bid-ask spread is $0.50. The bid-ask spread is also referred to as the bid-offer spread.

The spread charged by a market maker varies sharply from one financial asset to another, reflecting primarily the amount of risk the market maker assumes by "making" a market. This market-making risk can be related to two main forces. One is the

---

[1] Some of these properties are taken from James Tobin. "Properties of Assets," undated manuscript. New Haven: Yale.

[2] U.S. Treasury bills are discussed in Chapter 19.

variability of the price as measured, say, by some measure of dispersion of the relative price over time. The greater the variability, the greater the probability of the market maker incurring a loss in excess of a stated bound between the time of buying and reselling the financial asset. The variability of prices differs widely across financial assets. Three-month Treasury bills, for example, have a very stable price (as explained in Chapter 17), while a common stock generally tends to exhibit much larger short-run variations.

The second determining factor of the bid-ask spread charged by a market maker is what is commonly referred to as the **thickness of the market**, which is essentially the prevailing rate at which buying and selling orders reach the market maker (i.e., the frequency of transactions). A "thin market" sees few trades on a regular or continuing basis. Clearly, the greater the frequency of orders coming into the market for the financial asset (referred to as the "order flow"), the shorter the time that the financial asset must be held in the market maker's inventory, and hence the smaller the probability of an unfavorable price movement while held.

Thickness also varies from market to market. A 3-month U.S. Treasury bill easily provides the thickest market in the world. In contrast, trading in stock of small companies is said to be thin. Because Treasury bills dominate other instruments both in price stability and thickness, the bid-ask spread tends to be the smallest in the market. A low round-trip cost is clearly a desirable property of a financial asset, and as a result thickness itself is a valuable property. This attribute explains the potential advantage of large over smaller markets (economies of scale), and a market's endeavor to standardize the instruments offered to the public.

Term to Maturity   The **term to maturity** is the length of the interval until the date when the instrument is scheduled to make its final payment, or the owner is entitled to demand liquidation. Often, term to maturity is simply referred to as maturity, which is the practice that we will follow in this book.

Instruments for which the creditor can ask for repayment at any time, such as checking accounts and many savings accounts, are called **demand instruments**. Maturity is an important characteristic of financial assets such as debt instruments, and in the United States can range from one day to 100 years. For example, U.S. Treasury bills mature in one day. At the other extreme, in 1993, The Walt Disney Company issued a debt instrument that matures in 100 years, dubbed by Wall Street as "Mickey Mouse" bonds. Many other instruments, including equities, set no maturity and are thus a form of perpetual instrument.[3]

It should be understood that even a financial asset with a stated maturity may terminate before its stated maturity. An early termination may occur for several reasons, including bankruptcy or reorganization, or because of provisions entitling the debtor to repay in advance, or the investor may have the privilege of asking for early repayment.[4]

Liquidity   **Liquidity** serves an important and widely used function, although no uniformly accepted definition of liquidity is presently available. A useful way to think of liquidity and illiquidity, proposed by Professor James Tobin, is in terms of how much sellers stand to lose if they wish to sell immediately against engaging in a costly and time-consuming search.[5]

---

[3]   In the United Kingdom, one well-known type of bond promises to pay a fixed amount per year indefinitely and not to repay the principal at any time: such an instrument is called a *perpetual,* or a *consul.*

[4]   Some assets have maturities that may be increased or extended at the discretion of the issuer or the investor. For example, the French government issues a 6-year *obligation renouvelable du Tresor* that allows the investor, after the end of the third year, to switch into a new 6-year debt.

[5]   Tobin, "Properties of Assets."

An example of a quite illiquid financial asset is the stock of a small corporation or the bond issued by a small school district, for which the market is extremely thin, and one must search out the few suitable buyers. Less suitable buyers, including speculators and market makers, may be located more promptly, but will have to be enticed to invest in the illiquid financial asset by an appropriate discount in price.

For many other financial assets, liquidity is determined by contractual arrangements. Ordinary deposits at a bank, for example, are perfectly liquid because the bank operates under a contractual obligation to convert them at par on demand. In contrast, financial contracts representing a claim on a private pension fund may be regarded as totally illiquid, because they can be cashed only at retirement.

Liquidity may depend not only on the financial asset but also on the quantity one wishes to sell (or buy). Even though a small quantity may be quite liquid, a large lot may run into illiquidity problems. Note that liquidity again closely relates to whether a market is thick or thin. Thinness always increases the round-trip cost, even of a liquid financial asset. But beyond some point it becomes an obstacle to the formation of a market, and directly affects the illiquidity of the financial asset.

Convertibility   An important property of some financial assets is their convertibility into other financial assets. In some cases, the conversion takes place within one class of financial assets, as when a bond is converted into another bond. In other situations, the conversion spans classes. For example, with a corporate convertible bond the bondholder can change it into equity shares. Some preferred stock may be convertible into common stock. The timing, costs, and conditions for conversion are clearly spelled out in the legal descriptions of the convertible security at the time of issuance.

Currency   Most financial assets are denominated in one currency, such as U.S. dollars or yen or euros, and investors must choose them with that feature in mind. Some issuers, responding to investors' wishes to reduce foreign exchange risk, have issued dual-currency securities. For example, some pay interest in one currency but principal or redemption value in a second. Further, some bonds carry a currency option that allows the investor to specify that payments of either interest or principal be made in either one of two currencies.

Cash Flow and Return Predictability   As explained earlier, the return that an investor will realize by holding a financial asset depends on the cash flow expected to be received, which includes dividend payments on stock and interest payments on debt instruments, as well as the repayment of principal for a debt instrument and the expected sale price of a stock. Therefore, the predictability of the expected return depends on the predictability of the cash flow. Return predictability, a basic property of financial assets, provides the major determinant of their value. Assuming investors are risk averse, as we will see in later chapters, the riskiness of an asset can be equated with the uncertainty or unpredictability of its return.

In a world of nonnegligible inflation, it is especially important to distinguish between nominal expected return and the real expected return. The **nominal expected return** considers the dollars expected to be received but does not adjust those dollars to take into consideration changes in their purchasing power. The **real expected return** is the nominal expected return after adjustment for the loss of purchasing power of the financial asset as a result of inflation.

For example, if the nominal expected return for a 1-year investment of $1,000 is 6%, then at the end of 1 year the investor expects to realize $1,060, consisting of interest of $60 and the repayment of the $1,000 investment. However, if the inflation rate over the same period of time is expected to be 4%, then the purchasing power of $1,060 is only $1,019.23 ($1,060 divided by 1.04). Thus the return in terms of purchasing power, or real expected return, is 1.9%. In general, the real expected return can be approximated by subtracting from the nominal expected return the expected inflation rate. In our example, it is approximately 2% (6% minus 4%).

Complexity   Some financial assets are complex in the sense that they combine two or more simpler assets. To find the true value of such an asset, one must "decompose" it into its component parts and price each component separately. We will encounter numerous complex financial assets throughout this book. Indeed, many of the innovations involving debt instruments since the early 1980s resulted in complex financial assets.

Most complex financial assets involve a choice or option granted to the issuer or investor to do something to alter the cash flow. Because the value of such financial assets depends on the value of the choices or options granted to the issuer or investor, it becomes essential to understand how to determine the value of an option.

Tax Status   An important feature of any financial asset is its tax status. Governmental codes for taxing the income from the ownership or sale of financial assets vary widely if not wildly. Tax rates differ from year to year, country to country, and even among municipal units within a country (as with state and local taxes in the United States). Moreover, tax rates may differ from financial asset to financial asset, depending on the type of issuer, the length of time the asset is held, the nature of the owner, and so on.

◆ FINANCIAL MARKETS

Financial assets are exchanged (i.e., traded) in a **financial market**. Although the existence of a financial market is not a necessary condition for the creation and exchange of a financial asset, in most economies financial assets are created and subsequently traded in some type of organized financial market structure.

THE ROLE OF FINANCIAL MARKETS

The two primary economic functions of financial assets were already discussed. Financial markets provide three additional economic functions. First, the interactions of buyers and sellers in a financial market determine the price of the traded asset; or, equivalently, the required return on a financial asset is determined. The inducement for firms to acquire funds depends on the required return that investors demand, and this feature of financial markets signals how the funds in the economy should be allocated among financial assets. It is called the **price discovery process**. Whether these signals are correct is an issue that we discuss in Chapter 7 when we examine the question of the efficiency of financial markets.

Second, financial markets provide a mechanism for an investor to sell a financial asset. This feature offers liquidity in financial markets, an attractive characteristic when circumstances either force or motivate an investor to sell. In the absence of liquidity, the owner must hold a debt instrument until it matures and an equity instrument until the company either voluntarily or involuntarily liquidates. Although all financial markets provide some form of liquidity, the degree of liquidity is one of the factors that differentiates various markets.

The third economic function of a financial market reduces the search and information costs of transacting. **Search costs** represent explicit costs, such as the money spent to advertise the desire to sell or purchase a financial asset, and implicit costs, such as the value of time spent in locating a counterparty. The presence of some form of organized financial market reduces search costs. **Information costs** are incurred in assessing the investment merits of a financial asset, that is, the amount and the likelihood of the cash flow expected to be generated. In an efficient market, prices reflect the aggregate information collected by all market participants.

CLASSIFICATION OF FINANCIAL MARKETS

Of the many ways to classify financial markets, one way is by the type of financial claim. The claims traded in a financial market may be either for a fixed dollar amount or a residual amount. As explained earlier, the former financial assets are referred to as debt instruments, and the financial market in which such instruments are traded is referred to as the **debt market**. The latter financial assets are called equity instruments and the financial market where such instruments are traded is referred to as the **equity market**. Alternatively, this market is referred to as the **stock market**. Preferred stock represents an equity claim that entitles the investor to receive a fixed dollar amount. Consequently, preferred stock shares characteristics of instruments classified as part of the debt market and the equity market. Generally, debt instruments and preferred stock are classified as part of the **fixed income market**. The sector of the stock market that does not include preferred stock is called the **common stock market**. Figure 1-2 summarizes these classifications.

Another way to classify financial markets is by the maturity of the claims. For example, a financial market for short-term financial assets is called the **money market**, and the one for longer maturity financial assets is called the **capital market**. The traditional cutoff between short term and long term is one year. That is, a financial asset with a maturity of one year or less is considered short term and therefore part of the money market. A financial asset with a maturity of more than one year is part of the capital market. Thus, the debt market can be divided into debt instruments that are part of the money market, and those that are part of the capital market, depending on the number of years to maturity. Because equity instruments are generally perpetual,

FIGURE 1-2 Classification of Financial Markets by Type of Claim

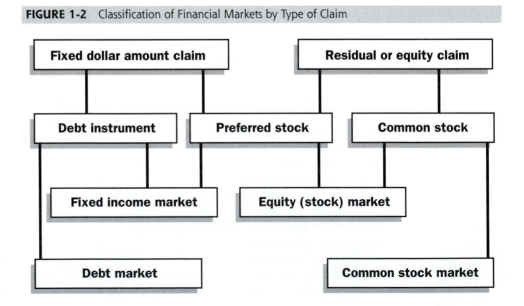

they are classified as part of the capital market. Figure 1-3 depicts financial market classifications based on maturities.

A third way to classify financial markets is by whether the financial claims are newly issued. When an issuer sells a new financial asset to the public, it is said to "issue" the financial asset. The market for newly issued financial assets is called the **primary market**. After a certain period of time, the financial asset is bought and sold (i.e., exchanged or traded) among investors. The market where this activity takes place is referred to as the **secondary market**.

Finally, a market can be classified by its organizational structure. These organizational structures can be classified as auction markets, over-the-counter markets, and intermediate markets. We describe each type in later chapters.

GLOBALIZATION OF FINANCIAL MARKETS

Globalization means the integration of financial markets throughout the world into an international financial market. Because of the globalization of financial markets, entities in any country seeking to raise funds need not be limited to their domestic financial market. Nor are investors in a country limited to the financial assets issued in their domestic market.

The factors contributing to the integration of financial markets include (1) deregulation or liberalization of markets and the activities of market participants in key financial centers of the world; (2) technological advances for monitoring world markets, executing orders, and analyzing financial opportunities; and (3) increased institutionalization of financial markets. These factors are not mutually exclusive.

Global competition forces governments to deregulate or liberalize various aspects of their financial markets so that their financial enterprises can compete effectively around the world. Technological advances increase the integration and efficiency of the global financial market. Advances in telecommunication systems link market participants throughout the world enabling orders to be executed within seconds. Advances in computer technology, coupled with advanced telecommunication systems, allow the transmission of real-time information on security prices and other key information to many participants in many places. Therefore, many investors can monitor global markets and simultaneously assess how this information affects the risk/reward profile of their portfolios. Significantly improved computing power allows the instant manipulation of

FIGURE 1-3   Classification of Financial Markets by Maturity of Claim

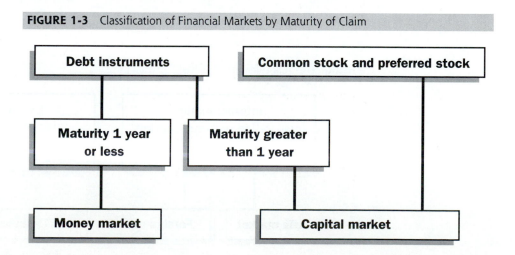

real-time market information so that attractive investment opportunities can be identified. Once these opportunities are identified, telecommunication systems facilitate the rapid execution of orders to capture them.

The shifting of the roles of the two types of investors, retail and institutional investors, in financial markets is the third factor stimulating the integration of financial markets. The U.S. financial markets shifted from domination by retail investors to domination by institutional investors. Retail investors are individuals, while institutional investors are financial institutions such as pension funds, insurance companies, investment companies, commercial banks, and savings and loan associations. These financial institutions are described in Section I.

The shifting of the financial markets in the United States and other major industrialized countries from dominance by retail investors to institutional investors is referred to as the **institutionalization of financial markets**. Unlike retail investors, institutional investors show greater willingness to transfer funds across national borders to improve the risk/reward opportunities of a portfolio that includes financial assets of foreign issuers. The potential portfolio benefits associated with global investing are documented in numerous studies, heightening investor awareness of the virtues of global investing. Moreover, investors have not limited their participation in foreign markets to those of developed economies. Participation in the financial markets of developing economies, popularly referred to as **emerging markets**, continues to increase.

CLASSIFICATION OF GLOBAL FINANCIAL MARKETS

Although no uniform system provides a classification of global financial markets, Figure 1-4 offers a schematic presentation of an appropriate classification system. From the perspective of a given country, financial markets can be classified as either internal or external. The **internal market**, also called the **national market**, can be decomposed into two parts: the **domestic market** and the **foreign market**. The domestic market is where issuers domiciled in the country issue securities and where those securities are subsequently traded.

In the foreign market of a country, securities of issuers not domiciled in the country are sold and traded. The regulatory authorities where the security is issued impose the rules governing the issuance of foreign securities. For example, securities issued by non-U.S. corporations in the United States must comply with the regulations set forth in U.S. securities law. A non-Japanese corporation that seeks to offer securities in Japan must comply with Japanese securities law and regulations imposed by the

FIGURE 1-4   Classification of Global Financial Markets

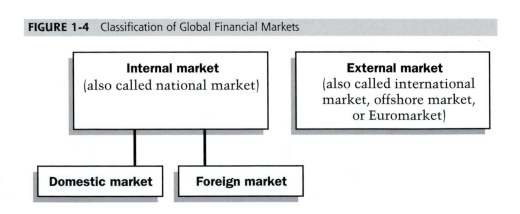

Japanese Ministry of Finance. Nicknames describe the various foreign markets. For example, the foreign market in the United States is called the "Yankee market." The foreign market in Japan is nicknamed the "Samurai market," in the United Kingdom the "Bulldog market," in the Netherlands the "Rembrandt market," and in Spain the "Matador market."

The **external market**, also called the **international market**, includes securities with the following distinguishing features: at issuance they are offered simultaneously to investors in a number of countries; and they are issued outside the jurisdiction of any single country. The external market is commonly referred to as the **offshore market**, or more popularly, the **Euromarket** (even though this market is not limited to Europe, it began there).[6]

◆ DERIVATIVE MARKETS

Some contracts give the contract holder either the obligation or the choice to buy or sell a financial asset. Such contracts derive their value from the price of the underlying financial asset. Consequently, these contracts are called **derivative instruments**. The array of derivative instruments includes options contracts, futures contracts, forward contracts, swap agreements, and cap and floor agreements. Each of these derivative instruments and the role they play in financial markets will be discussed throughout this book.

The existence of derivative instruments is the key reason why investors can more effectively implement investment decisions to achieve their financial goals and issuers can more effectively raise funds on more satisfactory terms. Several of the financial innovations and strategies discussed throughout this book rely on the market for derivative instruments.

As with any financial asset, derivative instruments can be used for speculative purposes as well as for accomplishing a specific financial or investment objective. Unfortunately, several financial fiascoes involved the use of derivative instruments. As a result, some regulators and lawmakers fear derivative instruments, viewing them as the "product of the devil."

The key role of derivative instruments in global financial markets was expressed in a May 1994 report published by the U.S. General Accounting Office (GAO) titled *Financial Derivatives: Actions Needed to Protect the Financial System:*

> Derivatives serve an important function of the global financial marketplace, providing end-users with opportunities to better manage financial risks associated with their business transactions. The rapid growth and increasing complexity of derivatives reflect both the increased demand from end-users for better ways to manage their financial risks and the innovative capacity of the financial services industry to respond to market demands.

On February 10, 2000, in testimony before the U.S. Senate Committee on Agriculture, Nutrition, and Forestry, Alan Greenspan, chair of the Federal Reserve, stated that "Over-the-counter (OTC) derivatives have come to play an exceptionally

---

[6] The classification we use is by no means universally accepted. Some market observers and compilers of statistical data on market activity refer to the external market as consisting of the foreign market and the Euromarket.

important role in our financial system and in our economy. These instruments allow users to unbundle risks and allocate them to the investors most willing and able to assume them."

To see how derivative instruments affect the American consumer, in June 2000, former Treasury Secretary Larry Summers testified concerning the Commodity Futures Modernization Act and noted that the use of derivatives "can help lower mortgage payments, insurance premiums, and other financing costs for American consumers and businesses."

The problem with derivative instruments is not with the instruments per se but the lack of understanding of their risk/return characteristics by some users. Hopefully, the discussion in this book will help dispel the misconceptions associated with derivative instruments and how they can be used to control various types of financial risk.

Summary

In this chapter we explained the characteristics of financial assets and the markets where they are traded. A financial asset (financial instrument or security) entitles the owner to future cash flows to be paid by the issuer. The claim can be either an equity or debt claim.

The value of any financial asset equals the present value of the expected cash flow. The cash flow is the cash payments (dividends, interest, repayment of borrowed funds for a debt instrument, and the expected sale price of an equity instrument). For most financial assets, the cash flow is not known with certainty. The first step to value a financial asset is to estimate the cash flow. Historically in the United States, the minimum interest rate coincided with the rate on U.S. Treasury securities. The reduction in U.S. Treasury debt issuance, however, prompted a search for a new benchmark that best represents the minimum interest rate. To that rate a premium must be added to reflect the risks associated with realizing the cash flow.

Financial assets possess certain properties that determine or influence their attractiveness to different classes of investors. The ten properties of financial assets include moneyness, divisibility and denomination, reversibility, term to maturity, liquidity, convertibility, currency, cash flow and return predictability, complexity, and tax status.

The two principal economic functions of a financial asset are (1) transferring funds from those who have surplus funds to invest to those who need funds to invest in tangible assets, and (2) transferring funds in such a way that redistributes the unavoidable risk associated with the cash flow generated by tangible assets among those seeking and those providing the funds.

Financial markets provide the following three additional functions beyond that of financial assets themselves: (1) they provide a mechanism for determining the price (or, equivalently, the required return) of financial assets; (2) they make assets more liquid; and (3) they reduce the costs of exchanging assets. The costs associated with market transactions are search costs and information costs.

Financial markets can be classified by types of financial claim (debt instrument versus equity claim), by the maturity of claims (money market versus capital market), by whether the security is newly issued or seasoned (primary market versus secondary market), or by the type of organizational structure.

Derivative instruments derive their value from an underlying financial asset. These instruments allow market players to more efficiently accomplish their financial goals.

Key Terms

- Asset
- Bid-ask spread
- Capital market
- Cash flow
- Common stock market
- Credit risk (*or* default risk)
- Debt instrument
- Debt market
- Demand instruments
- Derivative instruments
- Divisibility
- Domestic market
- Emerging markets
- Equity claim
- Equity market
- Euromarket
- External market (*or* international market)
- Financial assets
- Financial intermediaries
- Financial market
- Fixed income instruments
- Fixed income market
- Foreign exchange risk
- Foreign market
- Information costs
- Institutionalization of financial markets
- Intangible asset
- Internal market (*or* national market)
- Investor
- Liquidity
- Money
- Money market
- Near money
- Nominal expected return
- Offshore market
- Price discovery process
- Primary market
- Purchasing power risk (*or* inflation risk)
- Real expected return
- Residual claim
- Reversibility
- Round-trip cost
- Search costs
- Secondary market
- Stock market
- Tangible asset
- Term to maturity
- Thickness of the market

Questions

1. What is the difference between a financial asset and a tangible asset?
2. What is the difference between the claim of a debt holder of Ford Motor Corporation and a common stockholder of Ford Motor Corporation?
3. What is the basic principle in determining the value of a financial asset?
4. Why is it difficult to determine the cash flow of a financial asset?
5. What factors affect the interest rate used to discount the cash flow expected from a financial asset?
6. A U.S. investor who purchases the bonds issued by the Japanese government made the following comment: "Assuming that the Japanese government does not default, I know what the cash flow of the bond will be." Explain why you agree or disagree with this statement.
7. A U.S. investor who purchases the bonds issued by the U.S. government made the following statement: "By buying this debt instrument I am not exposed to default risk or purchasing power risk." Explain why you agree or disagree with this statement.
8. You just inherited 30,000 shares of a company you have never heard of, ABC Corporation. You call your broker to find out if you have finally struck it rich. After several minutes she comes back on the telephone and says: "I don't have a clue about these shares. It's too bad they are not traded in a financial market, that would make life a lot easier for you." What does she mean by her statement?
9. Explain why liquidity may depend not only on the type of financial asset but also on the quantity one wishes to sell or buy.
10. What are the two basic roles of financial assets?
11. Give three reasons for the greater integration of financial markets throughout the world.
12. In January 1992, the U.S.-based Atlantic Richfield Corporation issued $250 million of bonds with a maturity of 30 years in the United States. From the perspective of the U.S. financial market, indicate whether this issue is classified as being issued in the domestic market, the foreign market, or the offshore market.

13. In January 1992, the Korea Development Bank issued $500 million of bonds with a maturity of 10 years in the United States. From the perspective of the U.S. financial market, indicate whether this issue is classified as being issued in the domestic market, the foreign market, or the offshore market.

14. In September 1990, a study by the U.S. Congress Office of Technology Assessment, entitled "Electronic Bulls & Bears: U.S. Securities Markets and Information Technology," included this statement:

    Securities markets have five basic functions in a capitalistic economy:

    1. *they make it possible for corporations and governmental units to raise capital;*
    2. *they help to allocate capital toward productive uses;*
    3. *they provide an opportunity for people to increase their savings by investing in them;*
    4. *they reveal investors' judgments about the potential earning capacity of corporations, thus giving guidance to corporate managers; and*
    5. *they generate employment and income.*

    For each of these functions cited, explain how financial markets (or securities markets, in the parlance of this Congressional study) perform each function.

15. Indicate whether each of the following instruments trades in the money market or the capital market:
    a. General Motors Acceptance Corporation issues a financial instrument with 4 months to maturity.
    b. The U.S. Treasury issues a security with 30 years to maturity.
    c. IBM Corporation issues common stock.

16. Give three examples of derivative instruments and explain why they are called derivative instruments.

CHAPTER

2

Overview of Market Participants and Financial Innovation

Learning Objectives

After reading this chapter you will understand:

♦ the participants in financial markets: central governments, agencies of central governments, municipal governments, supranationals, nonfinancial businesses, financial businesses, and households.

♦ the business of financial institutions.

♦ what a financial intermediary is.

♦ how financial intermediaries provide at least one of four economic functions: maturity intermediation, risk reduction via diversification, reducing the costs of contracting and information processing, and a payments mechanism.

♦ the nature of the management of assets and liabilities by financial intermediaries.

♦ how different financial institutions use differing degrees of knowledge and certainty about the amount and timing of the cash outlay of their liabilities.

♦ the typical justification for governmental regulation of markets.

♦ how the government regulates financial markets through disclosure regulation, financial activity regulation, regulation of financial institutions, and regulation of foreign participants.

♦ the primary reasons for financial innovation.

♦ different ways to understand the emergence and success of financial innovations.

With an understanding of what financial assets are and the role financial assets and financial markets play, we can now identify the players in the financial markets. These players include the entities that issue financial assets and those entities that invest in financial assets. We focus on one particular group of market players, called financial intermediaries, because of the key economic functions they perform in financial markets. In addition to reviewing their economic function, we set forth the basic asset/liability problem faced by managers of financial intermediaries.

Other key players in financial markets are regulators. Because financial markets play a prominent role in any economy, governments deem it necessary to regulate certain aspects of these markets. In the United States, regulation occurs at the federal or state level, and in some cases both. We introduce specific regulatory bodies and legislation in the chapters to follow, but our objective in this chapter is to provide an overview of the various types of regulation.

We live in a time marked by an unusually rapid pace of financial innovation. This innovation reflects and responds to the needs of issuers and investors attempting to accomplish their financial goals. At the end of the chapter we provide a brief overview of some of the reasons for and benefits of financial innovation.

◆ ISSUERS AND INVESTORS

Various entities issue financial assets, both debt instruments and equity instruments, and various investors purchase these financial assets. These two groups are not mutually exclusive, however. It is common for an entity to both issue a financial asset and at the same time invest in a different financial asset. Thus, it makes little sense to discuss issuers and investors separately. Instead, we refer to both issuers and investors as entities that participate in the financial market.

CLASSIFICATION OF ENTITIES

A simple classification of these entities follows: (1) central governments, (2) agencies of central governments, (3) municipal governments, (4) supranationals, (5) nonfinancial businesses, (6) financial enterprises, and (7) households. Central governments borrow funds for a wide variety of reasons. Debt obligations issued by central governments carry the full faith and credit of the borrowing government. In the United States, the role of raising funds rests with the Department of the Treasury. Funds are raised by the issuance of debt obligations called **Treasury securities**. In Japan, the Ministry of Finance raises funds via the sale of securities.

Many central governments establish agencies to raise funds to perform specific functions. In the United States, for example, federal agencies created by Congress reduce the cost of raising funds for certain borrowing sectors of the economy deemed worthy of assistance. The entities in these privileged sectors include farmers, homeowners, and students. The two types of government agencies in the United States are **federally related institutions** and **government-sponsored enterprises**. The former are arms of the federal government, such as the Farmers Housing Administration. Government-sponsored enterprises, also called federally sponsored agencies, are privately owned, publicly chartered entities. An example is the Federal Home Loan Mortgage Corporation, popularly referred to as Fannie Mae. In Germany, two federal agencies that issue securities are the Federal Railway (Bundesbahn) and the Post Office (Bundespost). Agency obligations may or may not be guaranteed by the full faith and credit of the central government that created the agency.

In most countries, municipalities raise funds in the capital market. For example, in the United States municipal governments include states, counties, and cities. These entities also create "authorities" and special districts to raise funds for a specific purpose, an example being the Port Authority of New York and New Jersey.

A supranational institution is an organization formed by two or more central governments through international treaties. These supranational institutions promote economic development for the member countries. Two examples of supranational institutions are the International Bank for Reconstruction and Development, popularly referred to as the World Bank, and the Inter-American Development Bank. The general objective of the former is to improve the efficiency of the international financial and trading markets. The objective of the latter is to promote economic growth in the developing countries of the Americas.

Businesses are classified into nonfinancial and financial businesses. These entities borrow funds in the debt market and raise funds in the equity market. Nonfinancial businesses are divided into three categories: corporations, farms, and nonfarm/noncorporate businesses. The first category includes corporations that manufacture products (e.g., cars, steel, computers) and/or provide nonfinancial services (e.g., transportation, utilities, computer programming). In the last category businesses produce the same products or provide the same services as corporations but are not incorporated.

Financial businesses, more popularly referred to as **financial institutions**, provide one or more of the following services:

1. Transform financial assets acquired through the market and constitute them into a different, and more widely preferable, type of asset, which becomes their liability. This function is performed by **financial intermediaries**, the most important type of financial institution.
2. Exchange financial assets on behalf of customers.
3. Exchange financial assets for their own account.
4. Assist in the creation of financial assets for their customers and then sell those financial assets to other market participants.
5. Provide investment advice to other market participants.
6. Manage the portfolios of other market participants.

Financial intermediaries include depository institutions (commercial banks, savings and loan associations, savings banks, and credit unions) who acquire the bulk of their funds by offering their liabilities to the public mostly in the form of deposits; insurance companies (life and property and casualty companies); pension funds; and finance companies. Deposit accepting, or depository, institutions are discussed in Chapter 3. Other financial intermediaries are covered in Chapter 4.

The second and third services in the preceding list are the broker and dealer functions discussed in Chapters 5 and 7. The fourth service is referred to as underwriting. As will be explained in Chapters 5 and 6, typically a financial institution that provides an underwriting service also provides a brokerage and/or dealer service.

Some subsidiaries of nonfinancial businesses provide financial services. For example, many large manufacturing firms own subsidiaries that provide financing for the parent company's customer. These financial institutions are called **captive finance companies**. Examples include General Motors Acceptance Corporation (a subsidiary of General Motors) and General Electric Credit Corporation (a subsidiary of General Electric).

◆ ROLE OF FINANCIAL INTERMEDIARIES

Financial intermediaries obtain funds by issuing financial claims against themselves to market participants, then investing those funds. The investments made by financial intermediaries—their assets—can be in the form of loans and/or securities, referred to as **direct investments**. Two examples will illustrate intermediary functions. Most readers of this book are familiar with what a commercial bank does. Commercial banks accept deposits and may use the proceeds to lend funds to consumers and businesses. The deposits represent the IOU of the commercial bank and a financial asset owned by the depositor. The loan represents an IOU of the borrowing entity and a financial asset of the commercial bank. The commercial bank makes a direct investment in the borrowing entity; the depositor effectively makes an indirect investment in that borrowing entity.

As a second example, consider an investment company that pools the funds of investors and uses those funds to buy a portfolio of securities such as stocks and bonds.

Investors providing funds to the investment company receive an equity claim that entitles the investor to a pro rata share of the outcome of the portfolio. The equity claim is issued by the investment company. The portfolio of financial assets acquired by the investment company represents a direct investment. By owning an equity claim against the investment company, those who invest in the investment company make an indirect investment.

Financial intermediaries play the basic role of transforming financial assets that are less desirable for a large part of the public into other financial assets—their own liabilities—which are more widely preferred by the public. This transformation involves at least one of four economic functions: (1) providing maturity intermediation, (2) risk reduction via diversification, (3) reducing the costs of contracting and information processing, and (4) providing a payments mechanism.

MATURITY INTERMEDIATION

In our example of the commercial bank, two things should be noted. First, the maturity of at least a portion of the deposits accepted is typically short term. For example, certain types of deposit are payable upon demand; others have a specific maturity date, but most are less than two years. Second, the maturity of the loans made by a commercial bank may be considerably longer than two years. In the absence of a commercial bank, the borrower would have to borrow for a shorter term or find an entity willing to invest for the length of the loan sought, and/or investors who make deposits in the bank would have to commit funds for a longer length of time than they want. By issuing its own financial claims the commercial bank in essence transforms a longer-term asset into a shorter-term one by giving the borrower a loan for the length of time sought and the investor/depositor a financial asset for the desired investment horizon. This function of a financial intermediary is called **maturity intermediation**.

Maturity intermediation presents two implications for financial markets. First, investors have more choices concerning maturity for their investments; borrowers have more choices for the length of their debt obligations. Second, because investors are reluctant to commit funds for a long period of time, they require long-term borrowers to pay a higher interest rate than on short-term borrowing. In contrast, a financial intermediary is willing to make longer-term loans, and at a lower cost to the borrower than an individual investor would, by counting on successive deposits providing the funds until maturity (although at some risk). Thus, the second implication is that the cost of longer-term borrowing is likely to be reduced.

RISK REDUCTION VIA DIVERSIFICATION

Consider the example of the investor who places funds in an investment company. Suppose that the investment company invests the funds received in the stock of a large number of companies. By doing so, the investment company diversifies and reduces its risk. Investors with a small sum to invest would find it difficult to achieve the same degree of diversification because of their lack of sufficient funds to buy shares of a large number of companies. Yet by investing in the investment company for the same sum of money, investors can accomplish this diversification, thereby reducing risk.

This economic function of financial intermediaries—transforming more risky assets into less risky ones—is called **diversification**. Even though individual investors can do it on their own, they may not be able to do it as cost effectively as a financial intermediary, depending on the amount of funds they want to invest. Attaining cost effective diversification in order to reduce risk by purchasing the financial assets of a financial intermediary is an important economic benefit for financial markets.

REDUCING THE COSTS OF CONTRACTING AND INFORMATION PROCESSING

Investors purchasing financial assets must develop skills necessary to evaluate an investment. Once those skills are developed, investors can apply them when analyzing specific financial assets for purchase (or subsequent sale). Investors who want to make a loan to a consumer or business need to write the loan contract (or hire an attorney to do so). Although some people may enjoy devoting leisure time to this task, most of us find leisure time to be in short supply and want compensation for sacrificing it. The form of compensation could be a higher return obtained from an investment.

In addition to the opportunity cost of the time to process the information about the financial asset and its issuer, the cost of acquiring that information must also be considered. All these costs are called **information processing costs**. The costs of writing loan contracts are referred to as **contracting costs**. Another dimension to contracting costs is the cost of enforcing the terms of the loan agreement.

With these points in mind, consider our two examples of financial intermediaries— the commercial bank and the investment company. Their staffs include investment professionals trained to analyze financial assets and manage them. In the case of loan agreements, either standardized contracts can be prepared, or legal counsel can be part of the professional staff to write contracts involving more complex transactions. The investment professionals can monitor compliance with the terms of the loan agreement and take any necessary action to protect the interests of the financial intermediary. The employment of such professionals is cost-effective for financial intermediaries because investing funds is their normal business.

In other words, economies of scale can be realized in contracting and processing information about financial assets because of the amount of funds managed by financial intermediaries. The lower costs accrue to the benefit of the investor who purchases a financial claim of the financial intermediary and to the issuers of financial assets, who benefit from a lower borrowing cost.

PROVIDING A PAYMENTS MECHANISM

Although the previous three economic functions may not be immediately obvious, this last function should be. Most transactions made today are not done with cash. Instead, payments are made using checks, credit cards, debit cards, and electronic transfers of funds. Financial intermediaries provide these methods for making payments.

At one time, noncash payments were restricted to checks written against noninterest-bearing accounts at commercial banks. Similar check writing privileges were provided later by savings and loan associations and savings banks, and by certain types of investment companies. Payment by credit card was also at one time the exclusive domain of commercial banks, but now other depository institutions offer this service. Debit cards are offered by various financial intermediaries. A debit card differs from a credit card in that a bill sent to the credit cardholder periodically (usually once a month) requests payment for transactions made in the past. With a debit card, funds are immediately withdrawn (debited) from the purchaser's account at the time the transaction takes place.

The ability to make payments without the use of cash is critical for the functioning of a financial market. In short, depository institutions transform assets that cannot be used to make payments into other assets that offer that property.

◆ OVERVIEW OF ASSET/LIABILITY MANAGEMENT FOR FINANCIAL INSTITUTIONS

In Chapters 3 and 4, we will discuss the major financial institutions. To understand why managers of financial institutions invest in particular types of financial assets and the types of investment strategies employed, it is necessary to have a general understanding of the asset/liability problem.

The nature of the liabilities dictates the investment strategy a financial institution will pursue. For example, depository institutions seek to generate income by the difference between the return that they earn on assets and the cost of their funds. This difference is referred to as a **spread**. That is, they buy money and sell money seeking to realize a profit. They buy money by borrowing from depositors or through other sources of funds. They sell money when they make loans and buy securities. Their objective is to sell money for more than it costs to buy money. The cost of the funds and the return on the funds sold is expressed in terms of an interest rate per unit of time. Consequently, the objective of a depository institution is to earn a positive spread between the assets it invests in (what it has sold the money for) and the cost of its funds (what it has purchased the money for). As we shall see in Chapter 4, life insurance companies are in the spread business.

Pension funds are not in the spread business in that they do not raise funds themselves in the market. They seek to cover the cost of pension obligations at a minimum cost that is borne by the sponsor of the pension plan. Investment companies face no explicit costs for the funds they acquire and must satisfy no specific liability obligations, except in the case of one type of investment company that agrees to repurchase shares at any time.

NATURE OF LIABILITIES

The liabilities of a financial institution include the amount and timing of the cash outlays that must be made to satisfy the contractual terms of the obligations issued. The liabilities of any financial institution can be categorized according to four types, as shown in Table 2-1. The categorization in the table assumes that the entity that must be paid the obligation will not cancel the financial institution's obligation prior to any actual or projected payout date.

The descriptions of cash outlays as either known or uncertain are undoubtedly broad. When we refer to a cash outlay as being uncertain, we do not mean that it cannot be predicted. For some liabilities, the "law of large numbers" makes it easier to predict the timing and/or amount of cash outlays. This work is typically done by actuaries, but even actuaries cannot precisely predict natural catastrophes such as floods and earthquakes.

These risk categories will be further discussed in later chapters. Here we give a brief illustration of each one.

TABLE 2-1   Nature of Liabilities of Financial Institutions

Liability Type	*Amount of Cash Outlay*	*Timing of Cash Outlay*
Type I	known	known
Type II	known	uncertain
Type III	uncertain	known
Type IV	uncertain	uncertain

Type I Liabilities   With Type I liabilities both the amount and timing of the liabilities are known with certainty, such as when a financial institution knows that it must pay $50,000 in 6 months' time. For example, depository institutions know the amount that they are committed to pay (principal plus interest) on the maturity date of a fixed rate deposit, assuming that the depositor does not withdraw funds prior to the maturity date.

Type I liabilities, however, are not limited to depository institutions. A major product sold by life insurance companies is a **guaranteed investment contract**, popularly referred to as a GIC. The obligation of the life insurance company under this contract is that, for a sum of money (called a premium), it will guarantee an interest rate up to some specified maturity date.[1] For example, suppose a life insurance company, for a premium of $10 million, issues a 5-year GIC agreeing to pay 6% compounded annually. The life insurance company knows that it must pay $13.38 million to the GIC policyholder in 5 years.[2]

Type II Liabilities   With Type II liabilities the amount of the cash outlay is known, but the timing of the cash outlay is uncertain. The most obvious example of a Type II liability is a life insurance policy. The most basic of the many types of life insurance policy provides that, for an annual premium, a life insurance company agrees to make a specified dollar payment to policy beneficiaries upon the death of the insured.

Type III Liabilities   With this type of liability, the timing of the cash outlay is known but the amount is uncertain, such as when a financial institution has issued an obligation in which the interest rate adjusts periodically based on some interest rate benchmark. Depository institutions, for example, issue liabilities called certificates of deposit with a stated maturity. The interest rate paid need not be fixed over the life of the deposit but may fluctuate. If a depository institution issues a 3-year floating-rate certificate of deposit that adjusts every 3 months and the interest rate paid is the 3-month Treasury bill rate plus one percentage point, the depository institution knows its liability must be paid off in 3 years, but the dollar amount of the liability is not known. It will depend on 3-month Treasury bill rates over the 3 years.

Type IV Liabilities   Numerous insurance products and pension obligations involve uncertainty as to both the amount and the timing of the cash outlay. Probably the most obvious examples are automobile and home insurance policies issued by property and casualty insurance companies. When, and if, a payment will be made to the policyholder is uncertain. Whenever damage is done to an insured asset, the amount of the payment that must be made is uncertain.

As we discuss in Chapter 4, sponsors of pension plans can agree to various types of pension obligations to the beneficiaries of the plan. Under some plans, retirement benefits depend on the participant's income for a specified number of years before retirement and the total number of years the participant worked. These factors affect the amount of the cash outlay. The timing of the cash outlay depends on when the employee elects to retire, and whether the employee remains with the sponsoring plan until retirement. Moreover, both the amount and the timing depend on how the employee elects to take payments—over only the employee's life or those of the employee and spouse.

---

[1]   A GIC does not seem like a product we would associate with a life insurance company, because the policyholder does not have to die in order for someone to be paid. Yet, as discussed in Chapter 4, a major group of insurance company financial products are in the pension benefit area—GIC is one such product.
[2]   This amount is determined as follows: $\$10,000,000 \,(1.06)^5$.

LIQUIDITY NEEDS

Because of uncertainty about the timing and/or the amount of the cash outlays, a financial institution must be prepared with sufficient cash to satisfy its obligations. Also keep in mind that our discussion of liabilities assumes that the entity that holds the obligation against the financial institution may exercise its right to change the nature of the obligation, perhaps incurring some penalty. For example, in the case of a certificate of deposit, the depositor may request the withdrawal of funds prior to the maturity date. Typically, the deposit-accepting institution will grant this request, but assess an early withdrawal penalty. Certain types of investment companies give shareholders the right to redeem their shares at any time.

Some life insurance products provide a cash-surrender value that allows the policyholder to exchange the policy for a lump sum payment at specified dates. Typically, the lump sum payment will penalize the policyholder for turning in the policy. Some life insurance products also offer a loan value, which gives the policyholder the right to borrow against the cash value of the policy.

In addition to uncertainty about the timing and amount of the cash outlays, and the potential for the depositor or policyholder to withdraw cash early or borrow against a policy, a financial institution is concerned with possible reduction in cash inflows. In the case of a depository institution, it means the inability to obtain deposits. For insurance companies, it means reduced premiums because of the cancellation of policies. For certain types of investment companies, it means not being able to find new buyers for shares.

◆ REGULATION OF FINANCIAL MARKETS

Financial markets play a prominent role in many economies, and governments around the world have long deemed it necessary to regulate certain aspects of these markets. In their regulatory capacities, governments greatly influence the development and evolution of financial markets and institutions. It is important to realize that governments, issuers, and investors tend to behave interactively and to affect one another's actions in certain ways. Thus, it is not surprising to find that a market's reactions to regulations often prompt a new response by the government, which can cause the institutions of the market to change their behavior further, and so on. A sense of how the government can affect a market and its participants is important to an understanding of the numerous markets and securities that will be described in the chapters to come.

In this section, we discuss regulation in the United States. Our purpose is not to provide a detailed account of the U.S. regulatory structures and rules. Rather, we provide a broad view of the goals and types of regulations currently in place in the United States.

JUSTIFICATION FOR REGULATION

The standard explanation or justification for governmental regulation of a market is that the market, left to itself, will not produce its particular goods or services in an efficient manner and at the lowest possible cost. Efficiency and low-cost production are hallmarks of a perfectly competitive market. Thus, a market unable to produce efficiently must be one that is not competitive at the time and that will not gain that status by itself in the foreseeable future. Of course, it is also possible that governments may regulate markets that are viewed as competitive currently but unable to sustain competition, and thus low-cost production, over the long run. A version of this justification for regulation is that the government controls a feature of the economy that the market mechanisms of competition and pricing could not manage without help. A shorthand expression used by economists to describe the reasons for regulation is *market failure*. A market is said to fail if it cannot, by itself, maintain all the requirements for a competitive situation.

The regulatory structure in the United States is largely the result of financial crises that have occurred at various times. Most regulatory mechanisms are the products of the stock market crash of 1929 and the Great Depression in the 1930s. Some of the regulations may make little economic sense in the current financial market, but they can be traced back to some abuse that legislators encountered, or thought they encountered, at one time. Further, in addition to financial institution regulation, three other forms of regulation are most often a function of the federal government, with state governments playing a secondary role. For that reason, the present discussion of regulation concentrates on the federal government and its agencies. We will examine the role of state governments in Chapters 3 and 4.

FORMS OF FEDERAL GOVERNMENT REGULATION OF FINANCIAL MARKETS

Government regulation of financial markets takes one of four forms: (1) disclosure regulation, (2) financial activity regulation, (3) regulation of financial institutions, and (4) regulation of foreign participants. In the following sections, each is described along with a discussion of this form of regulation in the United States.

Disclosure Regulation   Disclosure regulation requires issuers of securities to make public a large amount of financial information to actual and potential investors. The standard justification for disclosure rules is that the managers of the issuing firm have more information about the financial health and future of the firm than investors who own or are considering the purchase of the firm's securities. The cause of market failure here, if indeed it occurs, is commonly described as "asymmetric information," which means investors and managers are subject to uneven access to or uneven possession of information. Also, the problem is said to be one of "agency," in the sense that the firm's managers, who act as agents for investors, may act in their own interests to the disadvantage of investors. The advocates of disclosure rules say that, in the absence of the rules, the investors' comparatively limited knowledge about the firm would allow the agents to engage in such practices.

The United States is firmly committed to disclosure regulation. The Securities Act of 1933 and the Securities Exchange Act of 1934 led to the creation of the Securities and Exchange Commission (SEC), which is responsible for gathering and publicizing relevant information and for punishing those issuers who supply fraudulent or misleading data. None of the SEC's requirements or actions constitutes a guarantee, a certification, or an approval of the securities being issued. Moreover, the government's rules do not represent an attempt to prevent the issuance of risky assets. Rather, the government's (and the SEC's) sole motivation in this regard is to supply diligent and intelligent investors with the information needed for a fair evaluation of the securities.

It is interesting to note that several prominent economists deny the need and justification for disclosure rules. Led by George Benston, they argue that the securities market would, without governmental assistance, get all the information necessary for a fair pricing of new as well as existing securities. In this view, the rules supposedly extracting key data from agent-managers are redundant.[3] One way to look at this

---

3   George J. Benston. "Required Disclosure and the Stock Market: An Evaluation of the Securities Exchange Act of 1934." *American Economic Review* 63 (March 1973), pp. 132–55.

argument is to ask what investors would do if a firm trying to sell new shares did not provide all the data investors would want. In that case, investors either would refuse to buy that firm's securities, giving them a zero value, or would discount or under-price the securities. Thus, a firm concealing important information would pay a penalty in the form of reduced proceeds from the sale of the new securities. The prospect of this penalty is potentially as much incentive to disclose as the rules of a governmental agency.

Financial Activity Regulation   Financial activity regulation consists of rules about traders of securities and trading on financial markets. A prime example of this form of regulation is the set of rules against trading by insiders who are corporate officers and others in positions to know more about a firm's prospects than the general investing public. Insider trading is another problem posed by asymmetric information. A second example of this type of regulation would be rules regarding the structure and operations of exchanges where securities are traded. The argument supporting these rules rests on the possibility that members of exchanges may be able, under certain circumstances, to collude and defraud the general investing public.

Like disclosure, financial activity regulation is also widely implemented in the United States. The SEC has the duty of carefully monitoring the trades that corporate officers, directors, or major stockholders ("insiders") make in the securities of their firms. The SEC and another federal government entity, the Commodity Futures Trading Commission (CFTC), share responsibility for the federal regulation of trading in derivative instruments.

Regulation of Financial Institutions   Regulation of financial institutions is that form of governmental monitoring that restricts these institutions' activities in the vital areas of lending, borrowing, and funding. The justification for this form of government regulation is that these financial firms have a special role to play in a modern economy. Financial institutions help households and firms to save; as depository institutions, they also facilitate the complex payments among many elements of the economy; and they serve as conduits for the government's monetary policy. Thus, it is often argued that the failure of these financial institutions would disturb the economy in a severe way.

Historically, the U.S. government imposed an extensive array of regulations on financial institutions. Most of this legislation traces its historical roots to the Great Depression in the 1930s and deals with restrictions on the activities of financial institutions. (Later chapters will explain some of the significant changes in these regulations.) In recent years, expanded regulations restrict how financial institutions manage their assets and liabilities, typically in the form of minimum capital requirements for certain regulated institutions. These capital requirements are based on the various types of risk faced by regulated financial institutions and are popularly referred to as **risk-based capital requirements**.

Regulation of Foreign Participants   Government regulation of foreign participants limits the roles foreign firms can play in domestic markets and their ownership or control of financial institutions. Many countries regulate participation by foreign firms in domestic financial securities markets. Like most countries, the United States extensively reviews and changes it policies regarding foreign firms' activities in the U.S. financial markets on a regular basis.

◆ FINANCIAL INNOVATION

Competition among financial institutions brings forth and fosters the development of new products and markets. Regulations that impede the free flow of capital and competition among financial institutions (particularly interest rate ceilings) motivate the development of financial products and trading strategies to get around these restrictions. Finally, the global pattern of financial wealth transforms financial markets from local markets into globally internationalized financial markets. Through technological advances and the reduction in trade and capital barriers, surplus funds in one country can be shifted more easily to those who need funds in another country. As a result, a need arises for financial products and trading strategies to more efficiently protect against the adverse movements of foreign currencies.

CATEGORIZATIONS OF FINANCIAL INNOVATION

Since the 1960s, there has been a surge in significant financial innovations. Observers of financial markets categorize these innovations in different ways. Here are just three ways suggested to classify these innovations.

The Economic Council of Canada classifies financial innovations into the following three broad categories:[4]

- *Market-broadening instruments,* which increase the liquidity of markets and the availability of funds by attracting new investors and offering new opportunities for borrowers
- *Risk-management instruments,* which reallocate financial risks to those who are less averse to them or who have offsetting exposure, and who are presumably better able to shoulder them
- *Arbitraging instruments and processes,* which enable investors and borrowers to take advantage of differences in costs and returns between markets, and which reflect differences in the perception of risks, as well as in information, taxation, and regulations

Another classification system of financial innovations based on more specific functions has been suggested by the Bank for International Settlements: *price-risk-transferring innovations, credit-risk-transferring instruments, liquidity-generating innovations, credit-generating instruments,* and *equity-generating instruments.*[5] Price-risk-transferring innovations provide market participants with more efficient means for dealing with price or exchange rate risk. Reallocating the risk of default is the function of credit risk-transferring instruments. Liquidity-generating innovations do three things: (1) they increase the liquidity of the market; (2) they allow borrowers to draw upon new sources of funds; and (3) they allow market participants to circumvent capital constraints imposed by regulations. Instruments to increase the amount of debt funds available to borrowers and to increase the capital base of financial and nonfinancial institutions are the functions of credit-generating and equity-generating innovations, respectively.

---

[4] *Globalization and Canada's Financial Markets* (Ottawa, Canada: Supply and Services Canada, 1989), p. 32.
[5] Bank for International Settlements, *Recent Innovations in International Banking* (Basle: BIS, April 1986).

Finally, Professor Stephen Ross suggests two classes of financial innovation: (1) new financial products (financial assets and derivative instruments) better suited to the circumstances of the time (e.g., to inflation) and to the markets in which they trade; and (2) strategies that primarily use these financial products.[6]

One of the purposes of this book is to explain these financial innovations. First, we will discuss why financial innovation takes place.

MOTIVATION FOR FINANCIAL INNOVATION

Two extreme views seek to explain financial innovation.[7] At one extreme are those who believe that the major impetus for innovation comes out of the endeavor to circumvent (or "arbitrage") regulations and find loopholes in tax rules.[8] At the other extreme are those who hold that the essence of innovation is the introduction of more efficient financial instruments for redistributing risks among market participants.

Many of the innovations that pass the test of time provide more efficient mechanisms for redistributing risk. Other innovations may just represent a more efficient way of doing things. If we consider the ultimate causes of financial innovation,[9] the following emerge as the most important:

1. Increased volatility of interest rates, inflation, equity prices, and exchange rates
2. Advances in computer and telecommunication technologies
3. Greater sophistication and educational training among professional market participants
4. Financial intermediary competition
5. Incentives to get around existing regulation and tax laws
6. Changing global patterns of financial wealth

With increased volatility comes the need for certain market participants to protect themselves against unfavorable consequences, which means new or more efficient ways of risk sharing in the financial market. Many of the financial products require the use of computers to create and continually monitor them. To implement trading strategies using these financial products also requires computers, as well as telecommunication networks. The advances in computer and telecommunication technologies make many of the innovations possible. Although financial products and trading strategies created by some market participants may be too complex for other market participants to use, the level of market sophistication, particularly in terms of mathematical understanding, continues to rise, permitting the acceptance of some complex products and trading strategies.

As you read the chapters on the various sectors of the financial markets that we review in this book, it is important to understand the factors behind any innovations in that market.

ASSET SECURITIZATION AS A FINANCIAL INNOVATION

The major financial innovations are discussed throughout this book; however, we conclude this chapter with a key financial innovation in the 1980s that dramatically influences the role of financial intermediaries—asset securitization. The process of asset

---

[6] Stephen A. Ross. "Institutional Markets, Financial Marketing, and Financial Innovation," *Journal of Finance* (July 1989), p. 541.

[7] Ian Cooper, "Financial Innovations: New Market Instruments," *Oxford Review of Economic Policy* (November 1986).

[8] Merton H. Miller, "Financial Innovation: The Last Twenty Years and the Next," *Journal of Financial and Quantitative Analysis* (December 1986), pp. 459–71.

[9] Cooper, "Financial Innovations," Table 9. We add inflation to the first category described.

allocation involves the collection or pooling of loans and the sale of securities backed by those loans. This system differs radically from the traditional system for financing the acquisition of assets, which called for one financial intermediary, such as a commercial bank, to (1) originate a loan, (2) retain the loan in its portfolio of assets, thereby accepting the credit risk associated with the loan, (3) service the loan by collecting payments and providing tax or other information to the borrower, and (4) obtain funds from the public with which to finance its assets (except for the small amount representing the institution's equity).

Asset securitization means that more than one institution may be involved in lending capital. Consider loans for the purchase of automobiles. A lending scenario can look like this: (1) A commercial bank originates automobile loans; (2) the commercial bank issues securities backed by these loans; (3) the commercial bank obtains credit risk insurance for the pool of loans from a private insurance company; (4) the commercial bank sells the right to service the loans to another company that specializes in the servicing of loans; and (5) the commercial bank uses the services of a securities firm to distribute the securities to individuals and institutional investors.

Besides the original lending bank, an insurance company, another institution that services loans, a securities firm, an individual, and other institutional investors participate. The commercial bank in our example does not absorb the credit risk, service the loan, or provide the funding. Although we use automobile loans as an example, this system can be applied to residential and commercial mortgage loans, home equity loans, boat loans, credit card loans, credit sales by finance companies and manufacturing firms, and lease receivables.

Asset securitization provides various benefits for borrowers and presents far-ranging implications for the U.S. financial system. In Chapter 27, we will explain the securitization process in greater detail and explain why corporate issuers may find it more cost-effective to raise funds via asset securitization rather than offering a typical corporate bond. In later chapters we will discuss risk-based capital requirements for certain financial institutions. Asset securitization can be used as a tool to manage risk-based capital requirements and directly affects U.S. financial institutions such as banks, thrifts, and insurance companies. However, the concept of using asset securitization as a means of attaining optimal capital adequacy standards is also of direct relevance to European financial institutions, for which growing competition due to deregulation and changing regulatory and environmental trends increases interest in asset securitization in the context of asset/liability management. As we will see in later chapters, financial institutions are exposed to interest rate risk—the risk that a change in interest rates will adversely affect the financial institution. With respect to the management of interest rate volatility, the securitization of assets fulfills a dual role. The dual role stems from the fact that the institution can securitize assets that expose the institution to higher interest rate risk and retain certain customized parts of the asset securitization transaction to attain an improved asset/liability position. In this respect, the financial institution serves the dual role of issuer and investor.

Summary

Entities in the financial market can both raise funds (debt or equity) by issuing financial obligations, and invest in financial assets. These entities can be classified into one of the following categories: (1) central governments, (2) agencies of central governments, (3) municipal governments, (4) supranationals, (5) nonfinancial businesses, (6) financial enterprises, and (7) households.

Financial institutions provide various types of financial services: broker and dealer functions and underwriting functions. A special group of financial institutions are called financial intermediaries. These entities obtain funds by issuing claims to market participants and use these funds to purchase financial assets. Intermediaries transform assets they acquire into assets (their liabilities) that are more attractive to the public in four ways, by (1) providing maturity intermediation, (2) providing risk reduction via diversification at lower cost, (3) reducing the cost of contracting and information processing, and (4) providing a payments mechanism.

The nature of their liabilities, as well as regulatory and tax considerations, determines the investment strategy pursued by all financial institutions. The liabilities of all financial institutions will generally fall into one of the four types shown in Table 2-1.

Regulation of the financial system and its various component sectors occurs in almost all countries. A useful way to organize the many instances of regulation is through four general forms: (1) disclosure regulation, (2) financial activity regulation, (3) regulation of financial institutions, and (4) regulation of foreign participants.

Financial innovation increased dramatically since the 1960s, particularly in the late 1970s. Although financial innovation can be the result of arbitrary regulations and tax rules, innovations that persist after changes in regulations or tax rules, designed to prevent exploitation, are frequently those that offer a more efficient means for redistributing risk. A key financial innovation with far-reaching implications is the securitization of assets.

Key Terms ▪

- Asset securitization
- Captive finance companies
- Contracting costs
- Direct investments
- Diversification
- Federally related institutions

- Financial institutions
- Financial intermediaries
- Government-sponsored enterprises
- Guaranteed investment contract
- Information processing costs

- Maturity intermediation
- Risk-based capital requirements
- Spread
- Treasury securities

Questions ▪

1. Explain how the household sector participates as both a borrower and lender of funds in the financial market.
2. What entities are included in the nonfinancial business sector of the financial market?
3. Explain why some subsidiaries of a nonfinancial business may be classified as financial businesses.
4. Why were government agencies created in the United States?
5. The European Investment Bank was established by the European Economic Community and charged with the role of promoting balanced regional development, serving the common interest of member states, and furthering industrial modernization. The member states include certain European countries. Would the European Investment Bank be classified as a municipal government or a financial business entity? If neither, how would it be classified?
6. a. Explain why an individual's account at a financial intermediary may be called an indirect investment in a firm that has borrowed money from the intermediary.
   b. Explain why the intermediary's loan to the firm is a direct investment.

7. Referring to Table 2-1, match the types of liabilities to these four assets that an individual might own:
   a. Car insurance policy
   b. Variable rate certificate of deposit
   c. Fixed rate certificate of deposit
   d. A life insurance policy that allows the holder's beneficiary to receive $100,000 when the holder dies, or $150,000 for an accidental death.
8. A bank issues an obligation to depositors in which it agrees to pay 8% guaranteed for 1 year. With the funds it obtains, the bank can invest in a wide range of financial assets. What is the risk if the bank uses the funds to invest in common stock?
9. Explain how financial intermediaries provide maturity intermediation.
10. How do financial intermediaries reduce the cost of contracting?
11. a. What is the economic rationale for the widespread use of "disclosure regulation"?
    b. Why do some economists believe that disclosure regulation is unnecessary?
12. What is meant by financial activity regulation?
13. A 1989 study entitled "Globalization and Canada's Financial Markets," a research report prepared for the Economic Council of Canada, reported the following:

    An important feature of the increasing significance of some aspects of financial activity is the greater use of financial markets and instruments that intermediate funds directly—a process called "market intermediation," which involves the issuance of, and trading in, securities such as bonds or stocks—as opposed to "financial intermediation," in which the financial institution raises funds by issuing a claim on itself and provides funds in the form of loans.

    a. Commercial banks are financial institutions that raise funds by issuing claims against themselves and then use the funds to provide loans. What do you think are the implications of the shift from financial intermediation to market intermediation for commercial banks?
    b. What do you think some of the obstacles are in market intermediation?

CHAPTER 3

Depository Institutions

Learning Objectives

After reading this chapter you will understand:

- what a depository institution is.
- how a depository institution generates income.
- differences between commercial banks, savings and loan associations, savings banks, and credit unions.
- the asset/liability problem all depository institutions face.
- what is meant by funding risk.
- who regulates commercial banks and thrifts and the types of regulations imposed.
- the funding sources available to commercial banks and thrifts.
- reserve requirements imposed on banks.
- the risk-based capital requirements imposed on commercial banks and savings and loan associations.

Depository institutions include commercial banks (or simply banks), savings and loan associations (S&Ls), savings banks, and credit unions. These financial intermediaries accept deposits. Deposits represent the liabilities (debt) of the deposit-accepting institution. With the funds raised through deposits and other funding sources, depository institutions make direct loans to various entities and also invest in securities. Their income is derived from two sources: the income generated from the loans they make and the securities they purchase, and fee income.

S&Ls, savings banks, and credit unions are commonly called "thrifts," which are specialized types of depository institutions. Traditionally, thrifts were not permitted to accept deposits transferable by check (negotiable) through checking accounts. Instead, they obtained funds primarily by tapping the savings of households. Since the early 1980s, however, thrifts offer negotiable deposits entirely equivalent to checking accounts, although they bear a different name (NOW accounts, share drafts).

Depository institutions are highly regulated because of the important role they play in the financial system. Demand deposit accounts provide the principal means that individuals and business entities use for making payments. Also, government implements monetary policy through the banking system. Because of their important role, depository institutions are afforded special privileges such as access to federal deposit insurance and access to a government entity that provides funds for liquidity or emergency needs. For example, most depository institutions currently insure deposits up to $100,000 per account.

In this chapter, we look at depository institutions—the nature of their liabilities, where they invest their funds, and how they are regulated. Before we examine the specific institutions, we begin with an overview of the asset/liability problem faced by the manager of a depository institution.

◆ ASSET/LIABILITY PROBLEM OF DEPOSITORY INSTITUTIONS

The asset/liability problem that depository institutions face is quite simple to explain, although not necessarily easy to solve. A depository institution seeks to earn a positive spread between the assets in which it invests (loans and securities) and the cost of its funds (deposits and other sources). The spread is referred to as **spread income** or **margin**. The spread income allows the institution to meet operating expenses and earn a fair profit on its capital.

In generating spread income a depository institution faces several risks, including credit risk, regulatory risk, and funding (or interest rate) risk. **Credit risk**, also called **default risk**, refers to the risk that a borrower will default on a loan obligation to the depository institution or that the issuer of a security that the depository institution holds will default on its obligation. **Regulatory risk** is the risk that regulators will change the rules and affect the earnings of the institution unfavorably.

FUNDING RISK

Funding risk can be explained best by illustration. Suppose that a depository institution raises $100 million by issuing a deposit account with a maturity of 1 year and by agreeing to pay an interest rate of 7%. Ignoring for the time being the fact that the depository institution cannot invest the entire $100 million because of reserve requirements, which we discuss later in this chapter, suppose that $100 million is invested in a U.S. government security that matures in 15 years, paying an interest rate of 9%. Because the funds are invested in a U.S. government security, the depository institution faces no credit risk in this case.

At first, the depository institution appears to lock in a spread of 2% (9% minus 7%). This spread can be counted on only for the first year, though, because the spread in future years depends on the interest rate this depository institution will have to pay depositors in order to raise $100 million after the 1-year time deposit matures. If interest rates decline, the spread increases because the depository institution locked in the 9% rate. If interest rates rise, however, spread income declines. In fact, if this depository institution must pay more than 9% to depositors at any time during the next 14 years, the spread becomes negative. That is, it costs the depository institution more to finance the government securities than it earns on the funds invested in those securities.

In our example, the depository institution borrowed short (borrowed for 1 year) and lent long (invested for 15 years). This policy benefits from a decline in interest rates but suffers if interest rates rise. Suppose the institution could borrow funds for 15 years at 7% and invest in a U.S. government security maturing in 1 year earning 9%—that is, borrow long (15 years) and loan short (1 year). A rise in interest rates benefits the depository institution because it can then reinvest the proceeds from the maturing 1-year government security in a new 1-year government security offering a higher interest rate. In this case a decline in interest rates reduces the spread. An interest rate falling below 7% results in a negative spread.

All depository institutions face this funding problem. Managers of a depository institution with particular expectations about the future direction of interest rates will seek to benefit from these expectations. Those who expect interest rates to rise may pursue a policy to borrow funds for a long time horizon (borrow long) and lend funds for a short time horizon (lend short). If interest rates are expected to drop, managers may elect to borrow short and lend long.

The problem of pursuing a strategy of positioning a depository institution based on expectations is that considerable adverse financial consequences will result if those expectations are not realized. The evidence on interest rate forecasting suggests that it is a risky business. No manager of a depository institution can accurately forecast interest rate moves so consistently that the institution can benefit in the long run. The goal of management is to lock in a spread as best as possible, not to wager on interest rate movements.

Funding risk exposure is inherent in any balance sheet of a depository institution. Managers must be willing to accept some exposure, but they can take various measures to address the interest rate sensitivity of the institution's liabilities and its assets. The asset/liability committee of a depository institution assumes responsibility for monitoring the interest rate risk exposure. Several financial instruments developed to help managers of depository institutions more effectively deal with their asset/liability problem are described in later chapters.

LIQUIDITY CONCERNS

Besides facing credit risk and interest rate risk, a depository institution must be prepared to satisfy withdrawals of funds by depositors and to provide loans to customers. A depository institution can accommodate withdrawal and loan demand in several ways: (1) attract additional deposits, (2) use existing securities as collateral for borrowing from a federal agency or other financial institution, (3) sell securities that it owns, or (4) raise short-term funds in the money market.

The first alternative is self-explanatory. The second concerns the privilege allowed to banks to borrow at the discount window of the Federal Reserve Banks. The fourth alternative primarily includes using marketable securities owned as collateral for raising funds in the repurchase agreement market (see Chapter 20).

The third alternative, selling securities that it owns, requires that the depository institution invest a portion of its funds in securities that are both liquid and have little price risk. By price risk we refer to the prospect that the selling price of the security will be less than its purchase price, resulting in a loss. For example, as we explain in Chapter 18, even though a 30-year U.S. government security is a highly liquid security, its price changes dramatically with increases in interest rates. A price decline of, say, 25% would not be uncommon in a volatile interest rate environment. A 30-year government bond is therefore highly liquid, but exposes the depository institution to substantial price risk.

In general, as we explain in Chapter 18, short-term securities entail little price risk. It is therefore short-term, or money market, debt obligations in which a depository institution will invest in order to satisfy withdrawals and customer loan demand, chiefly by lending federal funds, an investment vehicle that we discuss later in this chapter. The term to maturity of the securities it holds affects the amount that depository institutions can borrow from some federal agencies because only short-term securities are acceptable collateral.

Securities held for the purpose of satisfying net withdrawals and customer loan demands are sometimes referred to as *secondary reserves.*[1] A disadvantage of holding secondary reserves is that securities with short maturities offer a lower yield than securities with a longer maturity in most interest rate environments. The percentage of a depository institution's assets held as secondary reserves depends both on the institution's ability to raise funds from other sources and on its management's risk preferences for liquidity (safety) versus yield.

Depository institutions hold liquid assets not only for operational purposes, but also because of the regulatory requirements that we discuss later.

◆ COMMERCIAL BANKS

As of March 2001, 8,237 commercial banks were operating in the United States. A commercial bank can be chartered either by the state (state-chartered banks) or by the federal government (national banks). Of the 8,237 commercial banks, 6,036 were state chartered.[2] All national banks must be members of the Federal Reserve System and must be insured by the Bank Insurance Fund (BIF), which is administered by the Federal Deposit Insurance Corporation (FDIC). Federal depository insurance began in the 1930s, and the insurance program is administered by the FDIC. BIF was created by the Financial Institutions Reform, Recovery, and Enforcement Act of 1989 (FIRREA).

State-chartered banks may elect to join the Federal Reserve System. Their deposits must be insured by the BIF. A minority of state-chartered banks elect to be members of the Federal Reserve System. As of March 2001, of the 6,036 state-chartered banks, only 980 elected membership. In spite of the large number of banks that choose not to be members of the Federal Reserve System, banks that are members hold more than 75% of all deposits in the United States. Moreover, with the passage of the Depository Institutions Deregulation and Monetary Control Act of 1980 (DIDMCA), the reserve requirements that we shall discuss for member banks apply also to state-chartered banks.

The size of banks in the United States varies greatly as can be seen from Table 3-1, which shows the distribution for FDIC-insured banks as of March 2001. Shown in the same table are total assets for each asset size. As can be seen, although less than 5% of the banks have total assets in excess of $1 billion, these banks hold more than 85% of the total assets. The five largest U.S. commercial bank holding companies, based on assets as of the end of 2001, were Citigroup ($1,051 billion), JP Morgan Chase ($694 billion), Bank of America ($622 billion), Wachovia ($330 billion), and Wells Fargo ($308 billion).

BANK SERVICES

Commercial banks provide numerous services in the U.S. financial system. The services can be broadly classified as follows: (1) individual banking, (2) institutional banking, and (3) global banking. Of course, different banks generate more activity in certain

---

[1]   Roland I. Robinson. *The Management of Bank Funds* (New York: McGraw-Hill, 1962), p. 15. The term *secondary reserves* is used because primary reserves are the reserves required by the Federal Reserve Board. The balance sheet of a depository institution will not use the term *secondary reserves* because a depository institution invests in short-term or money market instruments for reasons other than liquidity and does not report the purpose for which it acquires securities.

[2]   These data were obtained from the FDIC Web site: www.fdic.gov.

TABLE 3-1 Distribution of FDIC-Insured Commercial Banks by Size

Asset Size	Number of Banks	Percent of Banks	Assets ($billions)	Percent of Assets
Less than $25 million	1,016	12.33	16,903	0.27
$25 to 50 million	1,636	19.86	61,068	0.97
$50 to 100 million	2,107	25.58	151,517	2.40
$100 to 300 million	2,307	28.01	388,908	6.16
$300 to 500 million	459	5.57	174,586	2.77
$500 to 1 billion	322	3.91	217,623	3.45
$1 to 3 billion	219	2.66	366,722	5.81
$3 to 10 billion	92	1.12	517,332	8.20
$10 billion or more	79	0.96	4,416,155	69.98
Total institutions	8,237	100.00	6,310,814	100.00

Source: Data to construct this table were obtained from www.fdic.gov, March 21, 2001.

areas than others. For example, money center banks (defined later) are more active in global banking.

Individual banking encompasses consumer lending, residential mortgage lending, consumer installment loans, credit card financing, automobile and boat financing, brokerage services, student loans, and individual-oriented financial investment services such as personal trust and investment services. Mortgage lending and credit card financing generate interest and fee income. Mortgage lending is often referred to as "mortgage banking" (see Chapter 25). Brokerage services and financial investment services also generate fee income.

Loans to nonfinancial corporations, financial corporations (such as life insurance companies), and government entities (state and local governments in the United States and foreign governments) fall into the category of institutional banking. Also included in this category are commercial real estate financing, leasing activities, and factoring.[3] In the case of leasing, a bank may be involved in leasing equipment either as lessors,[4] as lenders to lessors, or as purchasers of leases. Loans and leasing generate interest income, and other services that banks offer institutional customers generate fee income. These services include management of the assets of private and public pension funds, fiduciary and custodial services, and cash management services such as account maintenance, check clearing, and electronic transfers.

In the area of global banking, banks now compete head-to-head with another type of financial institution—investment banking firms (see Chapter 5). Global banking covers a broad range of activities involving corporate financing and capital market and foreign exchange products and services. Most global banking activities generate fee income rather than interest income.

Corporate financing involves two components. The first is the procuring of funds for a bank's customers, which can go beyond traditional bank loans to involve the underwriting of securities, though the Glass-Steagall Act limits bank activities in this area. In assisting its customers in obtaining funds, banks also provide bankers' accep-

---

3 The factoring business involves a bank's purchase of accounts receivable.
4 The bank buys the equipment and leases it to another party. The bank is the lessor and the party that uses the leased equipment is the lessee.

tances, letters of credit, and other types of guarantees for their customers. That is, if a customer borrows funds backed by a letter of credit or other guarantee, its lenders can look to the customer's bank to fulfill the obligation. The second area of corporate financing involves advice on such matters as strategies for obtaining funds, corporate restructuring, divestitures, and acquisitions.

Capital market and foreign exchange products and services involve transactions where the bank may act as a dealer or broker in a service. Some banks, for example, are dealers in U.S. government or other securities. Customers who wish to transact in these securities can do so through the government desk of the bank. Similarly, some banks maintain a foreign exchange operation, where foreign currency is bought and sold. Bank customers in need of foreign exchange can use the services of the bank.

In their role as dealers, banks generate income in three ways: (1) the bid-ask spread, (2) capital gains on the securities or foreign currency used in transactions, and (3) in the case of securities, the spread between interest income earned by holding the security and the cost of funding the purchase of that security.

The financial products developed by banks to manage risk also yield income. These products include interest rate swaps, interest rate agreements, currency swaps, forward contracts, and interest rate options. We discuss each of these in later chapters. Banks generate either commission income (that is, brokerage fees) or spread income from selling such products.

BANK FUNDING

In describing the nature of the banking business, we focused on how a bank can generate income. We now look at how a bank can raise funds. The three sources of funds for banks are (1) deposits, (2) nondeposit borrowing, and (3) common stock and retained earnings. Banks are highly leveraged financial institutions, which means that most of their funds come from borrowing—the first two sources. Included in nondeposit borrowing are borrowing from the Federal Reserve through the discount window facility, borrowing reserves in the federal funds market, and borrowing by the issuance of instruments in the money and bond markets.

Deposits   Several types of deposit accounts are available. **Demand deposits** (checking accounts) pay no interest and can be withdrawn upon demand. Savings deposits pay interest (typically below market interest rates), do not have a specific maturity, and usually can be withdrawn upon demand.

Time deposits, also called **certificates of deposit**, set a fixed maturity date and pay either a fixed or floating interest rate. Some certificates of deposit can be sold in the open market prior to their maturity if the depositor needs funds (see Chapter 20). Other certificates of deposits cannot be sold. If a depositor elects to withdraw the funds from the bank prior to the maturity date, the bank imposes an early withdrawal penalty. A **money market demand account** is one that pays interest based on short-term interest rates. The market for short-term debt obligations is called the money market, which is how these deposits get their name. They are designed to compete with money market mutual funds described in Chapter 4.

Reserve Requirements and Borrowing in the Federal Funds Market   A bank cannot invest $1 for every $1 it obtains in deposit. All banks must maintain a specified percentage of their deposits in a noninterest-bearing account at one of the 12 Federal Reserve Banks. These specified percentages are called **reserve ratios**, and the dollar amounts based on them that are required to be kept on deposit at a Federal Reserve Bank are called **required reserves**. The reserve ratios are established by the Federal

Reserve Board (the Fed). The reserve ratio differs by type of deposit. The Fed defines two types of deposits: transactions and nontransactions deposits. Demand deposits and what the Fed calls "other checkable deposits" are classified as transactions deposits. Savings and time deposits are nontransactions deposits. Reserve ratios are higher for transactions deposits relative to nontransactions deposits.

To arrive at its required reserves, a bank does not simply determine its transactions and nontransactions deposits at the close of each business day and then multiply each by the applicable reserve ratio. The determination of a bank's required reserves is more complex. Here we give a rough idea of how it is done. First to compute required reserves, the Federal Reserve uses an established two-week period called the **deposit computation period**. Required reserves are the average amount of each type of deposit held at the close of each business day in the computation period, multiplied by the reserve requirement for each type.

Reserve requirements in each period are to be satisfied by **actual reserves**, which are defined as the average amount of reserves held at the close of business at the Federal Reserve Bank during each day of a two-week reserve maintenance period, beginning on Thursday and ending on Wednesday two weeks later. For transactions deposits, the deposit computation period leads the reserve period by two days. For nontransactions deposits, the deposit computation period is the two-week period four weeks prior to the reserve maintenance period.

If actual reserves exceed required reserves, the difference is referred to as **excess reserves**. Because reserves are placed in noninterest-bearing accounts, an opportunity cost is associated with excess reserves. At the same time, the Federal Reserve imposes penalties on banks that do not satisfy the reserve requirements, giving banks an incentive to manage their reserves so as to satisfy reserve requirements as precisely as possible.

Banks temporarily short of their required reserves can borrow reserves from banks with excess reserves. The market where banks borrow or lend reserves is called the **federal funds market**. The interest rate charge to borrow funds in this market is called the **federal funds rate**.

Borrowing at the Fed Discount Window   The Federal Reserve Bank is the banker's bank—or, to put it another way, the bank of last resort. Banks temporarily short of funds can borrow from the Fed at its discount window. Collateral is necessary to borrow, but not just any collateral will do. The Fed establishes (and periodically changes) the types of eligible collateral. Currently it includes: (1) Treasury securities, federal agency securities, and municipal securities, all with a maturity of less than 6 months, and (2) commercial and industrial loans with 90 days or less to maturity.

The interest rate that the Fed charges to borrow funds at the discount window is called the **discount rate**. The Fed changes this rate periodically in order to implement monetary policy. Bank borrowing at the Fed to meet required reserves is quite limited in amount, despite the fact that the discount rate generally is set below the cost of other sources of short-term funding available to a bank. The Fed views borrowing at the discount window as a privilege to be used to meet short-term liquidity needs and not a device to increase earnings.

Continual borrowing for long periods and in large amounts is thereby viewed as a sign of a bank's financial weakness or as exploitation of the interest differential for profit. If a bank appears to be going to the Fed frequently to borrow relative to its previous borrowing pattern, the Fed will make an "informational" call to ask for an explanation for the borrowing. If no subsequent improvement in the bank's borrowing pattern occurs, the Fed then makes an "administrative counseling" call in which it tells the bank that it must stop its borrowing practice.

Other Nondeposit Borrowing   Most deposits have short maturities. Bank borrowing in the federal funds market and at the discount window of the Fed is short-term. Other nondeposit borrowing can be short-term in the form of issuing obligations in the money market, or intermediate to long-term in the form of issuing securities in the bond market. An example of the former is the repurchase agreement (or "repo") market, which we discuss in Chapter 20. An example of intermediate or long-term borrowing is floating rate notes and bonds.

Banks that raise most of their funds from the domestic and international money markets, relying less on depositors for funds, are called **money center banks**. A **regional bank**, by contrast, is one that relies primarily on deposits for funding and makes less use of the money markets to obtain funds. In recent years, the mergers of larger regional banks with other regional banks have formed so-called "superregional banks." With their greater size, these superregional banks can compete in certain domestic and international financial activities that were once the domain of money center banks.

REGULATION

Because of the special role that commercial banks play in the financial system, banks are regulated and supervised by several federal and state government entities. At the federal level, supervision is undertaken by the Federal Reserve Board, the Office of the Comptroller of the Currency, and the Federal Deposit Insurance Corporation. Although much of the legislation defining these activities dates back to the late 1930s, the nature of financial markets and commercial banking has changed in the past 20 years.

Here we review some of the major regulations concerning the activities of commercial banks. The regulations historically cover four areas:

1. Ceilings imposed on the interest rate that can be paid on deposit accounts
2. Geographical restrictions on branch banks
3. Permissible activities for commercial banks
4. Capital requirements for commercial banks

Regulation of Interest Rates   Even though regulation of the interest rates that banks can pay was eliminated for accounts other than demand deposits, we discuss it because of its historical relevance. Federal regulations prohibit the payment of interest on demand (checking) accounts. Regulation Q at one time imposed a ceiling on the maximum interest rate that could be paid by banks on deposits other than demand accounts.

Until the 1960s, market interest rates stayed below the ceiling (except those on checking deposits), so Regulation Q had virtually no impact on the ability of banks to compete with other financial institutions to obtain funds. As market interest rates rose above the ceiling and ceilings were extended to all depository institutions after 1966, these institutions found it difficult to compete with other financial institutions—such as money market funds—to attract funds. This difficulty resulted in "disintermediation"—funds flowed out of commercial banks and thrift institutions and into the other financial institutions.

To circumvent the ceilings on time deposits and recapture the lost funds, banks developed the negotiable certificate of deposit, which in effect had a higher ceiling, and eventually no ceiling at all. They also opened branches outside the United States, where no ceilings were imposed on the interest rate they could offer. As all depository institutions found it difficult to compete in the 1970s, federal legislation in the form of the Depository Institutions Deregulation and Monetary Control Act of 1980 gave banks relief. With a few exceptions, the 1980 act phased out the ceilings on interest rates on time deposits and certificates of deposit. The Garn-St. Germain Act of 1982 permitted banks to offer money market accounts that were similar to those offered by money market funds.

Geographical Restrictions   The McFadden Act of 1927 allowed each state the right to set its own rules on intrastate branch banking. This legislation was intended to prevent large banks from expanding geographically and thereby forcing out or taking over smaller banking entities, possibly threatening competition. In some states, banks cannot establish branches statewide. Other states known as unit-banking states, limit branch banking, and still others impose virtually no restrictions on statewide branching.

In 1994 Congress passed the Riegle-Neal Interstate Banking and Branching Efficiency Act permitting adequately capitalized and managed *bank holding companies* to acquire banks in any state subject to certain limitations and approval by the Federal Reserve. Starting in June 1997, this legislation allowed interstate mergers between adequately capitalized and managed banks, subject to concentration limits and state laws.

Permissible Activities for Commercial Banks   The sweeping legislation in bank regulation in recent years changed the permissible activities for banks and bank holding companies. The key legislation is the Gramm-Leach-Bliley Act of 1999. To appreciate the major impact of this legislation, we must first review the regulations on permissible bank activities prior to the passage of this legislation.

The activities of banks and bank holding companies are regulated by the Federal Reserve Board, which was charged with the responsibility of regulating the activities of bank holding companies by the Bank Holding Company Act of 1956, subsequently amended in 1966 and 1970. This act states that the permissible activities of bank holding companies are limited to those viewed by the Fed as "closely related to banking."

Early legislation governing bank activities developed against the following background:

1. Certain commercial bank lending was believed to have reinforced the stock market crash of 1929.
2. The stock market crash itself led to the breakdown of the banking system.
3. Transactions between commercial banks and their securities affiliates led to abuses. For example, it was discovered that banks were underwriting securities and then selling those securities to customers whose investment accounts they managed or advised. (We'll discuss the underwriting of securities in Chapter 5).

Against this background, Congress passed the Banking Act of 1933, which, among other provisions, created the Federal Deposit Insurance Corporation. Four sections of the 1933 act barred commercial banks from certain investment banking activities—Sections 16, 20, 21, and 32. These four sections are popularly referred to as the **Glass-Steagall Act.**

For banks that are members of the Federal Reserve System, Section 16 provided that:

> business of dealing in securities and stock by a national bank shall be limited to purchasing and selling such securities and stock without recourse, solely upon the order, and for the account of customers, and in no case for its own account, and the (national bank) shall not underwrite any issue of securities or stock.

Banks could neither (1) underwrite securities and stock, nor (2) act as dealers in the secondary market for securities and stock, although Section 16 does provide two exceptions. Banks were permitted to underwrite and deal in U.S. government obligations and "general obligations of any state or any political subdivisions thereof." (The latter securities are municipal bonds, which we shall discuss in Chapter 24. The exemption applies to one type of municipal security, general obligation bonds, and not another type, revenue bonds.) Section 16 also restricted the activities of banks in connection with corporate securities such as corporate bonds and commercial paper, and securities such as mortgage-backed and asset-backed securities (which we discuss in Chapters 26 and 27).

Under Section 20 of the Glass-Steagall Act, commercial banks that were members of the Federal Reserve System were prohibited from maintaining a securities firm. Section 20 states that no member bank shall be affiliated "with any organization, association, business trust, or other similar organization engaged principally in the issue, flotation, underwriting, public sale, or distribution at wholesale or retail or through syndicate participation of stocks, bonds, debentures, notes or other securities."

Section 21 prohibited any "person, firm, corporation, association, business trust, or other similar organization" that receives deposits—that is, depository institutions—from engaging in the securities business as defined in Section 16. Section 32 further prevented banks from circumventing the restrictions on securities activities. It did so by prohibiting banks from placing bank employees or board members in positions with securities firms so that they can obtain indirect but effective control.

The Glass-Steagall Act also imposed restrictions on bank activities in the insurance area. Specifically, it imposed restrictions on the underwriting and selling of insurance. As explained in Chapter 4, regulation of insurance activities was left to the states.

Subsequent legislation, court rulings, and regulatory decisions prior to the passage of the Gramm-Leach-Bliley Act of 1999 did erode the barriers against commercial banks' engagement in investment banking activities. The barrier was finally destroyed by the Gramm-Leach-Bliley Act of 1999. Specifically, this act did the following:

1. It modified parts of the Bank Holding Company Act so as to permit affiliations between banks and insurance underwriters.
2. It created a new financial holding company authorized to engage in underwriting and selling securities.
3. Although the act preserved the right of states to regulate insurance activities, it did prohibit state actions that adversely affect bank-affiliated firms from selling insurance on an equal basis with other insurance agents.

Consequently, the underwriting activities described in Chapter 6 and the secondary securities market described in Chapter 7 that were primarily the domain of financial entities referred to as *investment banking firms* were now opened to banks. As a result, subsequent to the act several large bank holding companies merged with investment banking firms. In Chapter 4 we discuss the impact of the Gramm-Leach-Bliley Act of 1999 on the insurance industry.

Supporters of this legislation argue that it ensures to financial institutions in the United States the ability to effectively compete in the increasingly global financial marketplace and that the resulting efficiencies will lower costs to consumers and businesses. Alan Greenspan, chair of the Federal Reserve Board, in testimony on February 11, 1999, in support of the legislation stated:

> U.S. financial institutions are today among the most innovative and efficient providers of financial services in the world. They compete, however, in a marketplace that is undergoing major and fundamental change driven by a revolution in technology, by dramatic innovations in the capital markets, and by the globalization of the financial markets and the financial services industry.

For these reasons, we support, as we have for many years, major revisions, such as those included in H.R. 10, to the Glass-Steagall Act and the Bank Holding Company Act to remove the legislative barriers against the integration of banking, insurance and securities activities. There is virtual unanimity among all concerned—private and public alike—that these barriers should be removed. The technologically driven proliferation of new financial products that enable risk unbundling have been increasingly combining the characteristics of banking, insurance, and securities products into single financial instruments. These changes, which are occurring all over the world, have also dramatically altered the way financial services providers operate and the way they deliver their products.

Upon the passage of this legislation, then U.S. Treasury Secretary Lawrence Summers stated:

> Today Congress voted to update the rules that have governed financial services since the Great Depression, and replace them with a system for the 21st century.

Capital Requirements for Commercial Banks   The capital structure of banks, like that of all corporations, consists of equity and debt (i.e., borrowed funds). Commercial banks, like some other depository institutions and like investment banks, which we discuss in Chapter 5, are highly leveraged institutions. That is, the ratio of equity capital to total assets is low, typically less than 8% in the case of banks. This level gives rise to regulatory concern about potential insolvency resulting from the low level of capital provided by the owners. An additional concern is that the amount of equity capital is even less adequate because of potential liabilities that do not appear on the bank's balance sheet. These so-called "off-balance sheet" obligations include commitments such as letters of credit and obligations on customized interest rate agreements (such as swaps, caps, and floors).

Prior to 1989, capital requirements for a bank were based solely on its total assets. No consideration was given to the types of assets. In January 1989, the Federal Reserve adopted guidelines for capital adequacy based on the credit risk of assets held by the bank. These guidelines are referred to as **risk-based capital requirements**. The guidelines are based on a framework adopted in July 1988 by the Basle Committee on Banking Regulations and Supervisory Practices, which consists of the central banks and supervisory authorities of G-10 countries.[5]

The two principal objectives of the guidelines are as follows. First, regulators in the United States and abroad sought greater consistency in the evaluation of the capital adequacy of major banks throughout the world. Second, regulators tried to establish capital adequacy standards that take into consideration the risk profile of the bank. Consider two banks, A and B, with $1 billion in assets. Suppose that both invest $400 million in identical assets, but the remaining $600 million in different assets. Bank A invests $500 million in U.S. government bonds and $100 million in business loans. Bank B invests $100 million in U.S. government bonds and $500 million in business loans. Obviously, the exposure to default losses is greater for Bank B. Even though the capital adequacy standards take this greater credit risk into account, they do not recognize liquidity factors or the market price sensitivity to which a bank may be exposed. Capital adequacy standards do give explicit recognition to off-balance sheet items.

---

[5] The eleven countries referred to as the G-10 include Belgium, Canada, France, Germany, Italy, Japan, Netherlands, Sweden, Switzerland, United Kingdom, and United States.

The risk-based capital guidelines attempt to recognize credit risk by segmenting and weighting requirements. First, capital consists of Tier 1 and Tier 2 capital, and minimum requirements are established for each tier. Tier 1 capital is considered **core capital**; it consists basically of common stockholders' equity, certain types of preferred stock, and minority interest in consolidated subsidiaries. Tier 2 capital, called **supplementary capital**, includes loan-loss reserves, certain types of preferred stock, perpetual debt (debt with no maturity date), hybrid capital instruments and equity contract notes, and subordinated debt.

Second, the guidelines establish a credit risk weight for all assets. The weight depends on the credit risk associated with each asset. The four credit risk classifications for banks in the United States are 0%, 20%, 50%, and 100%, arrived at on no particular scientific basis. Table 3-2 shows a few examples of assets that fall into each credit risk classification.[6]

The way the credit risk weights work is as follows. The book value of the asset is multiplied by the credit risk weight to determine the amount of core and supplementary capital that the bank will need to support that asset. For example, suppose that the book values of the assets of a bank are as follows:

Asset	Book Value (in millions)
U.S. Treasury securities	$ 100
Municipal general obligation bonds	100
Residential mortgages	500
Commercial loans	300
Total book value	$1,000

The risk-weighted assets are calculated as follows:

Asset	Book Value (in millions)	Risk Weight	Product (in millions)
U.S. Treasury securities	$100	0%	$ 0
Municipal general obligation bonds	100	20	20
Residential mortgages	500	50	250
Commercial loans	300	100	300
Risk-weighted assets			$570

The risk-weighted assets for this bank would be $570 million.

The minimum core (Tier 1) capital requirement is 4% of the book value of assets; the minimum total capital (core plus supplementary capital) is 8% of the risk-weighted assets. To see how this determination is made, consider the hypothetical bank we used earlier to illustrate the calculation of risk-weighted assets. For that bank the weighted risk assets are $570 million. The minimum core capital requirement is $40 million (0.04 × $1 billion); the minimum total capital requirement is $45.6 million (0.08 × $570 million).[7]

---

[6] Special rules are used for determining the amount of capital required for off-balance sheet items. An off-balance sheet item is a position in an interest-sensitive contract and/or foreign exchange-related product that is not reported on the balance sheet.

[7] Other minimum standards imposed by the guidelines cover limitations on supplementary capital elements.

TABLE 3-2   Risk Weight Capital Requirement for Various Assets

Risk Weight	Examples of Assets Included
0%	U.S. Treasury securities
	Mortgage-backed securities issued by the Government National Mortgage Association
20%	Muncipal general obligation bonds
	Mortgage-backed securities issued by the Federal Home Loan Mortgage Corporation or the Federal National Mortgage Association
50%	Municipal revenue bonds
	Residential mortgages
100%	Commercial loans and commercial mortgages
	LDC loans
	Corporate bonds
	Municipal IDA bonds

One implication of the new capital guidelines is that it encourages banks to sell their loans in the open market. By doing so, the bank need not maintain capital for the loans (assets) sold. Although the secondary market for individual bank loans continues to grow, it has not reached the stage where a bank can efficiently sell large amounts of loans. An alternative is for a bank to pool loans and issue securities collateralized by the pool of loans.

The risk-based capital requirements mentioned previously deal with credit risk. Bank regulators address ways in which interest rate risk should be incorporated into capital requirements. The Federal Depository Insurance Corporation Improvement Act of 1991 mandates that banking regulators take into consideration interest rate risk in setting capital requirements. Subsequently, banking regulators proposed several measures for quantifying interest rate exposure. In August 1995 banking regulators amended the capital requirements for banks based on a bank's exposure to interest rate risk. Exposure was measured in terms of the decline in a bank's economic value due to a change in interest rates. About a year later, a joint policy statement issued by bank regulators set forth sound practices for managing interest rate risk. Although the policy statement does not standardize how interest rate risk exposure should be measured nor quantify how an adjustment should be made to a bank's capital requirements given its interest rate exposure, the policy statement does guide how bank regulators evaluate both the adequacy and effectiveness of a bank's interest rate management policy.[8]

FEDERAL DEPOSIT INSURANCE

Because of the important economic role played by banks, the U.S. government sought a way to protect them against depositors who, because of what they thought were real or perceived problems with a bank, would withdraw funds in a disruptive manner. Bank panics occurred frequently in the early 1930s, resulting in the failure of banks that might have survived economic difficulties except for massive withdrawals. As the

---

[8] Federal Deposit Insurance Corporation, "Differences in Capital and Accounting Standards Among the Federal Banking and Thrift Agencies; Report to Congressional Committees," *Federal Register* 65, no. 127 (June 30, 2000), p. 40665.

mechanism devised in 1933 to prevent a "run on a bank," the U.S. government created federal deposit insurance. The insurance was provided through a new agency, the Federal Deposit Insurance Corporation. A year later, federal deposit insurance was extended to savings and loan associations with the creation of the Federal Savings and Loan Insurance Corporation. In 1933, federal deposit insurance covered accounts up to $2,500. This amount was raised in 1980 to its current level of $100,000 per account.

Even though federal deposit insurance achieved its objective of preventing a run on banks, it unfortunately created incentives that encouraged managers of depository institutions to take on excessive risks. If highly risky investments work out, the benefits accrue to the stockholders and management; however, if they do not, it is the depositors who are supposed to absorb the losses. Yet, depositors feel little concern about the risk that a depository institution is assuming because their funds are insured by the federal government. From a depositor's perspective, as long as the amount deposited does not exceed the insurance coverage, one depository institution is as good as another.

The Federal Deposit Insurance Corporation Improvement Act of 1991 (FDICIA) included a number of significant reforms to improve the deposit insurance system. Despite the improvements, some major flaws remained, including two of particular concern. First is the increase in the amount of the deposit coverage to $100,000. This coverage was set in 1980. The basic coverage increased five times since 1934, from $5,000 to $100,000. With the exception of the increase from $40,000 to $100,000 in 1980, historically, these increases fundamentally reflected cost-of-living adjustments. In contrast, the $60,000 increase in coverage in 1980 was really intended to retain current depositors and attract new depositors to insured institutions at a time that depository institutions were losing deposits to money market funds. However, as of 2001, in terms of real dollars (i.e., the purchasing power of a dollar), coverage is less than $50,000. The FDIC is considering additional coverage.

The second flaw is the payment of insurance coverage—the premiums charged by the FDIC for insurance coverage. The conflict with respect to premiums is that on the one hand FDICIA mandates that deposit insurance premiums should be priced according to the risk posed by a depository institution; on the other hand, FDICIA mandates that the FDIC maintain a target level of reserves. To counter these conflicts came the passage of the Deposit Insurance Funds Act of 1996 (DIFA), which severely restricted the FDIC's ability to establish premiums based on a depository institution's risk profile.

The pricing of premiums imposed by the FDIC for its first 50 years in operation differs significantly from the current system. Basically, during the 50-year period all depository institutions paid a premium for insurance coverage based on the institution's size. More specifically, an annual premium rate of 3.3 to 8.3 cents was paid for every $100 of insured deposits. Legislation in the 1980s and 1990s altered this system, effectively turning such premiums into penalties for violating risk-based capital requirements or acts violating the supervisory process rather than for insurance coverage per se. Specifically, in the absence of any violations, the FDIC charges no premiums for deposit insurance coverage regardless of the risk profile of an institution. These depository institutions carry the best rating. Table 3-3 shows the current risk-based premium system used by the FDIC. A depository institution is assigned to one of nine categories based on a two-step process. The first is a capital group assignment based on capital ratios, and the second is a supervisory subgroup assignment based on other relevant information. As of the end of 1999, 93% of depository institutions that carry FDIC insurance were not charged a premium for the coverage.[9]

---

9   FDIC, "Option's Paper" (August 2000).

TABLE 3-3 FDIC's Risk Ratings Assigned to Depository Institutions

Capital Group Descriptions

Group 1:	Group 2:	Group 3:
"Well capitalized."	"Adequately capitalized."	"Undercapitalized."
Total risk-based capital ratio equal to or greater than 10%	Not well capitalized	Neither well capitalized nor adequately capitalized
Tier 1 risk-based capital ratio equal to or greater than 6%	Total risk-based capital ratio equal to or greater than 8%	Supervisory subgroup assignments for members of the BIF and the SAIF are made in accordance with section 327.4(a) (2) of the FDIC's Rules and Regulations
Tier 1 leverage capital ratio equal to or greater than 5%	Tier 1 risk-based capital ratio equal to or greater than 4%	See following Supervisory Subgroup descriptions
	Tier 1 leverage capital ratio equal to or greater than 4%	

[handwritten margin notes: "Higher costs pay ins. premium" and "only way to get better is take risky PRO to get more equity"]

Supervisory Subgroup Descriptions

Subgroup A: This subgroup consists of financially sound institutions with only a few minor weaknesses and *generally* corresponds to the primary federal regulator's composite rating of "1" or "2."

Subgroup B: This subgroup consists of institutions that demonstrate weaknesses, which, if not corrected, could result in significant deterioration of the institution and increased risk of loss to the BIF or SAIF. This subgroup assignment *generally* corresponds to the primary federal regulator's composite rating of "3."

Subgroup C: This subgroup consists of institutions that pose a substantial probability of loss to the BIF or the SAIF unless effective corrective action is taken. This subgroup assignment *generally* corresponds to the primary federal regulator's composite rating of "4" or "5."

Source: Attachment C in FDIC, "Option's Paper," August 2000.

The FDIC is reviewing a system for charging premiums to those institutions that presently pay no premiums—the 1A rated institutions—based on the institution's risk profile. Under a current proposal being entertained by the FDIC, a depository institution would pay an amount equal to the expected loss the FDIC faces from providing deposit insurance to that institution. In order to deal with the conflict noted earlier with respect to setting deposit insurance premiums, an "expected loss" pricing system would take into consideration (1) the differences in risk across depository institutions and (2) the ability to generate revenue sufficient to pay for the costs of insuring deposits. The expected loss price for a depository would depend on three factors: (1) the probability of default for that bank, (2) exposure, and (3) loss severity (or loss given default).

The expected loss pricing system for insurance premiums would effectively result in assigning every depository institution a rating similar to the credit rating that we will discuss in later chapters for the rating of corporate bond issuers. The rating would be associated with a range of default probabilities derived from historical experience. By combining these default probabilities with customized assumptions about loss severity, the FDIC's formula would compute an expected loss per dollar of assessable deposits and, in turn, derive the appropriate premium for that depository institution.

◆ **SAVINGS AND LOAN ASSOCIATIONS**

S&Ls represent a fairly old institution. The provision of funds for financing the purchase of a home motivated the creation of S&Ls. The collateral for the loans would be the home being financed.

S&Ls are either mutually owned or operate under corporate stock ownership. "Mutually owned" means no stock is outstanding, so technically the depositors are the owners. To increase the ability of S&Ls to expand the sources of funding available to bolster their capital, legislation facilitated the conversion of mutually owned companies into a corporate stock ownership structure.

Like banks, S&Ls may be chartered under either state or federal statutes. At the federal level, the primary regulator of S&Ls is the director of the Office of Thrift Supervision (OTS), created in 1989 by FIRREA. Prior to the creation of OTS, the primary regulator was the Federal Home Loan Bank Board (FHLBB). The FHLLB no longer exists. The Federal Home Loan Banks, which along with the FHLLB comprised the Federal Home Loan Bank System, still exist and make advances to member institutions.

Like banks, S&Ls are now subject to reserve requirements on deposits established by the Fed. Prior to the passage of FIRREA, federal deposit insurance for S&Ls was provided by the Federal Savings and Loan Insurance Corporation (FSLIC). The Savings Association Insurance Fund (SAIF) replaced FSLIC and is administered by the FDIC.

ASSETS

Traditionally, the only assets in which S&Ls were allowed to invest were mortgages, mortgage-backed securities, and government securities. Mortgage loans include fixed-rate mortgages and adjustable-rate mortgages (i.e., loans whose interest rate is periodically changed). Although most mortgage loans are for the purchase of homes, S&Ls do make construction loans.

As the structures of S&L balance sheets and the consequent maturity mis-match (i.e., lending long and borrowing short) led to widespread disaster and insolvency, the Garn-St. Germain Act of 1982 expanded the types of assets in which S&Ls could invest. The acceptable list of investments now includes consumer loans (loans for home improvement, automobiles, education, mobile homes, and credit cards), nonconsumer loans (commercial, corporate, business, or agricultural loans), and municipal securities.

Although S&Ls enjoyed a comparative advantage in originating mortgage loans, they lacked the expertise to make commercial and corporate loans. Rather than make an investment in acquiring those skills, S&Ls took an alternative approach and invested in corporate bonds because these bonds were classified as corporate loans. More specifically, S&Ls became one of the major buyers of noninvestment-grade corporate bonds, more popularly referred to as "junk" bonds or "high-yield" bonds. Under FIRREA, S&Ls are no longer permitted to invest new money in junk bonds.

S&Ls invest in short-term assets for operational (liquidity) and regulatory purposes. All S&Ls with federal deposit insurance must satisfy minimum liquidity requirements. These requirements are specified by the Office of Thrift Supervision. Acceptable assets include cash, short-term government agency and corporate securities, certificates of deposit of commercial banks,[10] other money market assets (described in Chapter 20), and federal funds. In the case of federal funds, the S&L lends excess reserves to another depository institution that is short of funds.

---

[10] The S&L is an investor when it holds the certificate of deposit of a bank, but the certificate represents the liability of the issuing bank.

FUNDING

Prior to 1981, the bulk of the liabilities of S&Ls consisted of passbook savings accounts and time deposits. The interest rate that could be offered on these deposits was regulated. S&Ls were given favored treatment over banks with respect to the maximum interest rate they could pay depositors—they were permitted to pay an interest rate 0.5% higher, later reduced to 0.25%. With the deregulation of interest rates discussed earlier in this chapter, banks and S&Ls now compete head-to-head for deposits.

Deregulation also expanded the types of accounts that may be offered by S&Ls. Traditionally, S&Ls had not been permitted to offer demand accounts. Since the early 1980s, however, S&Ls can offer accounts that look similar to demand deposits and that do pay interest called **negotiable order of withdrawal (NOW) accounts**. Unlike demand deposits, NOW accounts pay interest. S&Ls were also allowed to offer money market deposit accounts (MMDA).

Since the 1980s, S&Ls more actively raised funds in the money market. They can borrow in the federal funds market and they have access to the Fed's discount window. S&Ls can also borrow from the Federal Home Loan Banks. These borrowings, called **advances,** can be short-term or long-term in maturity, and the interest rate can be fixed or floating.

REGULATION

Federal S&Ls are chartered under the provision of the Home Owners Loan Act of 1933. Federally chartered S&Ls are supervised by the OTS, while state-chartered S&Ls are supervised by the respective state. A further act in 1933 established the Federal Savings and Loan Insurance Corporation, which at that time insured the deposits of federally chartered S&Ls up to $5,000 and allowed state-chartered S&Ls that could qualify to obtain the same insurance coverage.

As in bank regulation, S&Ls historically were regulated with respect to the maximum interest rates on deposit accounts, geographical operations, permissible activities (types of accounts and types of investments), and capital adequacy requirements. In addition, they faced restrictions on the sources of nondeposit funds and liquidity requirements.

The maximum interest rate permitted on deposit accounts was phased out by the Depository Institutions Deregulation and Monetary Control Act of 1980 (DIDMCA). Although it allowed S&Ls to compete with other financial institutions to raise funds, it also raised their funding costs. For reasons to be described later, banks' balance sheets were better constituted than those of S&Ls to cope with the higher funding costs resulting from interest rate deregulation.

Besides phasing in the deregulation of interest rates on deposit accounts, DIDMCA was significant in several other ways. First, it expanded the Fed's control over the money supply by imposing reserve deposit requirements on S&Ls. In return, S&Ls were permitted to offer NOW accounts.

Subsequent legislation, the Garn-St. Germain Act, not only granted S&Ls the right to offer money market demand accounts so that S&Ls could compete with money market funds, but also broadened the types of assets in which S&Ls could invest. Permission to raise funds in the money market and the bond market was granted by the Federal Home Loan Bank Board in 1975. FHLLB permission to form finance subsidiaries was granted in 1984. Through these subsidiaries, S&Ls were able to broaden their funding sources by the issuance of mortgage-related securities.

Two sets of capital adequacy standards apply to S&Ls, as they do for banks. S&Ls are also subject to two ratio tests based on "core capital" and "tangible capital." The risk-based capital guidelines are similar to those imposed on banks. Instead of two tiers of capital, however, S&Ls deal with three: Tier 1, tangible capital; Tier 2, core capital; and Tier 3, supplementary capital.

As with commercial banks, in addition to risk-based capital requirements based on credit risk, risk-based requirements depend on interest rate risk. For S&Ls, regulators take a different approach to measuring interest rate risk than do regulators of commercial banks. In December 1988, the Federal Home Loan Bank Board, the predecessor to the Office of Thrift Supervision (OTS), stated that it intended to consider interest rate risk exposure in establishing capital requirements. In December 1990, the OTS proposed a rule for dealing with interest rate risk exposure in setting capital requirements. In August 1993 the OTS finally adopted a rule that incorporates interest rate risk into risk-based capital requirements. The rule specifies that if a thrift shows greater than "normal" interest rate risk exposure (where normal is defined by the rule), then the OTS would impose a deduction of the thrift's total capital for purposes of calculating its risk-based capital requirements. Interest rate risk exposure was specified in the rule as a decline in the net portfolio value (the value of the portfolio after deducting liabilities) resulting from a 200 basis point change (up or down) in market interest rates. What is deducted from the thrift's total capital is one-half the difference between the thrift's measured exposure and the "normal" level of exposure, defined as 2% of the estimated economic value of the assets.[11]

THE S&L CRISIS

The details of the growth of the S&L industry since the late 1960s and the ensuing S&L crisis cannot be described in one chapter, so only the basics of the downfall of this industry will be presented here. Until the early 1980s, S&Ls and all other lenders financed housing through traditional mortgages at interest rates fixed for the life of the loan. The period of the loan was typically long, frequently up to 30 years. Funding for these loans, by regulation, came from deposits having a maturity considerably shorter than the loans. As explained earlier, this situation creates the funding risk of lending long and borrowing short. It is extremely risky, although regulators took a long time to understand it.

No problem arises, of course, if interest rates are stable or declining, but if interest rates rise above the interest rate on the mortgage loans, a negative spread results, which must lead eventually into insolvency. Regulators at first endeavored to shield the S&L industry from the need to pay high interest rates without losing deposits by imposing a ceiling on the interest rate that would be paid by S&Ls and by their immediate competitors, the other depository institutions. However, the approach did not and could not work.

With the high volatility of interest rates in the 1970s, followed by the historically high level of interest rates in the early 1980s, all depository institutions began to lose funds to competitors exempt from ceilings, such as the newly formed money market funds; this development forced some increase in ceilings. The ceilings in place since the middle of the 1960s did not protect the S&Ls; they began to suffer from diminished profits and increasingly from operating losses. A large fraction of S&Ls became technically insolvent as rising interest rates eroded the market value of their assets to the point where they fell short of the liabilities.

---

[11] Federal Deposit Insurance Corporation, "Differences in Capital and Accounting Standards Among the Federal Banking and Thrift Agencies; Report to Congressional Committees."

The regulators, anxious to cover up the debacle of their empire, let them continue to operate, worsening the problem by allowing them to value their mortgage assets at book value. Profitability worsened with deregulation of the maximum interest rate that S&Ls could pay on deposits. Even though deregulation allowed S&Ls to compete with other financial institutions for funds, it also raised funding costs. Banks were better equipped to cope with rising funding costs because bank portfolios were not dominated by old, fixed-rate mortgages as S&Ls were. A larger portion of bank portfolios consisted of shorter-term assets and other assets whose interest rates reset to market interest rates after short time periods.

The difficulty of borrowing short and lending long was only part of the problem faced by the industry. As the crisis progressed and the situation of many S&Ls became hopeless, fraudulent management activities were revealed. Many S&Ls facing financial difficulties also pursued strategies that exposed the institution to greater risk in the hope of recovering if these strategies worked out. What encouraged managers to pursue such high-risk strategies was that depositors were not concerned with the risks associated with the institution where they deposited funds because the U.S. government, through federal deposit insurance, guaranteed the deposits up to a predetermined amount. Troubled S&Ls could pay existing depositors through attracting new depositors by offering higher interest rates on deposits than financially stronger S&Ls. In turn, to earn a spread on the higher cost of funds, they had to pursue riskier investment policies.

◆ SAVINGS BANKS

As institutions, savings banks are similar to, although much older than, S&Ls. They can be either mutually owned (in which case they are called mutual savings banks) or stockholder owned. Most savings banks operate under the mutual form. Only 16 states in the eastern United States charter savings banks. In 1978, Congress permitted the chartering of federal savings banks.

Although the total deposits at savings banks are less than those of S&Ls, savings banks are typically larger institutions. Asset structures of savings banks and S&Ls are similar. Residential mortgages provide the principal assets of savings banks. Because states permitted more portfolio diversification than federal regulators of S&Ls, savings bank portfolios weathered funding risk far better than S&Ls. Savings bank portfolios include corporate bonds, Treasury and government agency securities, municipal securities, common stock, and consumer loans.

The principal source of funds for savings banks is deposits. Typically, the ratio of deposits to total assets is greater for savings banks than for S&Ls. Savings banks offer the same types of deposit accounts as S&Ls, and deposits can be insured by either the BID or SAIF.

◆ CREDIT UNIONS

Credit unions are the smallest of the depository institutions. Credit unions can obtain either a state or federal charter. Their unique aspect is the "common bond" requirement for credit union membership. According to the statutes that regulate federal credit unions, membership in a federal credit union "shall be limited to groups having a common bond of occupation or association, or to groups within a well-defined neighborhood, community, or rural district." They are either cooperatives or mutually owned. No corporate stock ownership is permitted. The dual purpose of credit unions is, therefore, to serve their members' saving and borrowing needs.

Of the 10,628 credit unions in operation at the end of 1999, 6,566 were federally chartered and 4,062 state chartered. Although the number of credit unions is greater than commercial banks, their assets total only a small percentage of the assets of commercial banks.

Technically, because credit unions are owned by their members, member deposits are called shares. The distribution paid to members is, therefore, in the form of dividends, not interest. The National Credit Union Share Insurance Fund (NCUSIF) established in 1970, insures the shares of all federally chartered credit unions for up to $100,000, the same as other depository institutions. State-chartered credit unions may elect to have NCUSIF coverage; for those that do not, insurance coverage is provided by a state agency.

Federal regulations apply to federally chartered credit unions and state-chartered credit unions that elect to become members of NCUSIF. Most states, however, specify that state-chartered institutions must be subject to the same requirements as federally chartered ones. Effectively, therefore, most credit unions are regulated at the federal level. The principal federal regulatory agency is the National Credit Union Administration (NCUA).

Credit unions obtain their funds primarily from deposits of their members. With deregulation, they can offer a variety of accounts, including share drafts, which are similar to checking accounts but pay interest. The Central Liquidity Facility (CLF), which is administered by NCUA, plays a role similar to the Fed as the lender of last resort. CLF provides short-term loans to member credit unions with liquidity needs.

Credit union assets consist of small consumer loans, residential mortgage loans, and securities. Regulations 703 and 704 of NCUA set forth the types of investments in which a credit union may invest. They can make investments in *corporate credit unions*.

What is a corporate credit union? One might think that a corporate credit union is a credit union set up by employees of a corporation. It is not. Federal and state-chartered credit unions are referred to as "natural person" credit unions because they provide financial services to qualifying members of the general public. In contrast, corporate credit unions provide a variety of investment services, as well as payment systems, only to natural person credit unions. As of 2000, 36 corporate credit unions ranged in size from $5 million to $30 billion. All but three corporate credit unions are federally insured. The U.S. Central Credit Union acts as the chief liquidity center for corporate credit unions by investing surplus funds from the other corporate credit unions.

Summary

Depository institutions accept various types of deposits. With the funds raised through deposits and other funding sources, they make loans to various entities and invest in securities. The deposits usually are insured by a federal agency. Income is derived from investments (loans and securities) and fee income. Thrifts (savings and loan associations, savings banks, and credit unions) are specialized types of depository institutions.

A depository institution seeks to earn a positive spread between the assets in which it invests and the cost of its funds. In generating spread income, a depository institution faces credit risk and funding or interest rate risk. A depository institution must be prepared to satisfy net withdrawals of funds by depositors and provide loans to customers. It can accommodate withdrawals or loan demand by attracting additional deposits, using existing securities as collateral for borrowing from a federal agency, selling securities that it owns, or raising short-term funds in the money market.

The services provided by commercial banks can be broadly classified as individual banking, institutional banking, and global banking. The three sources of funds for banks include deposits, nondeposit borrowing, and retained earnings and sale of equity. Banks are highly leveraged financial institutions, meaning that most of their funds are obtained from deposits and nondeposit borrowing, including borrowing from the Fed through the discount window facility, borrowing reserves in the federal funds market, and borrowing by the issuance of instruments in the money and bond markets.

Banks must maintain reserves at one of the 12 Federal Reserve Banks, according to reserve requirements established by the Fed. Banks temporarily short of their required reserves can borrow reserves in the federal funds market or borrow temporarily from the Fed at its discount window.

Regulation of banks occurs at both federal and state levels. At the federal level, supervision of banks is the responsibility of the Federal Reserve Board, the Office of the Comptroller of the Currency, and the Federal Deposit Insurance Corporation. The major regulations involve capital requirements and the activities that are permissible for commercial banks. Until the passage of the Gramm-Leach-Bliley Act of 1999, the key legislation regulating bank activities was the Glass-Steagall Act, which effectively separated commercial banking and investment banking activities. The Gramm-Leach-Bliley Act tore down the walls between commercial banks and investment banks, as well as within commercial bank activity in the insurance industry.

Like banks, S&Ls may be chartered under either state or federal statutes. At the federal level, the primary regulator of S&Ls is the Director of the Office of Thrift Supervision. S&Ls are subject to reserve requirements on deposits established by the Fed. The Savings Association Insurance Fund provides federal deposit insurance for S&Ls.

Much as in the case of bank regulation, S&Ls are regulated with respect to geographical operations, permissible activities, and capital adequacy requirements. S&Ls invest principally in mortgages and mortgage-related securities. Deregulation expanded the types of investments that S&Ls are permitted to make, as well as broadened the types of deposit accounts that may be offered and the available funding sources.

The asset structures of savings banks and S&Ls are similar. Some states permit greater portfolio diversification than permitted by federal regulators of S&Ls, which is reflected in savings bank portfolios. The principal source of funds for savings banks is deposits. Deposits can be federally insured by either the BIF or SAIF.

Credit unions are depository institutions that have a "common bond" requirement for membership and are owned by those members. Although they can be federally or state-chartered, most credit unions effectively are regulated at the federal level by the National Credit Union Administration. The assets of credit unions consist primarily of small consumer loans to their members and credit card loans.

Key Terms

- Actual reserves
- Advances
- Bank holding companies
- Certificates of deposit
- Core capital
- Corporate credit unions
- Credit risk
- Default risk
- Demand deposits
- Deposit computation period
- Discount rate

- Excess reserves
- Federal funds market
- Federal funds rate
- Funding risk
- Glass-Steagall Act
- Individual banking
- Investment banking firms
- Margin
- Money center banks
- Money-market demand account

- Negotiable order of withdrawl (NOW) accounts
- Regional bank
- Regulatory risk
- Required reserves
- Reserve ratios
- Risk-based capital requirements
- Spread income
- Supplementary capital
- Time deposits

Questions

1. Explain the ways in which a commercial bank can accommodate withdrawal and loan demand.
2. Why do you think a debt instrument whose interest rate is changed periodically based on some market interest rate would be more suitable for a depository institution than a long-term debt instrument with a fixed interest rate?
3. What is meant by: a. individual banking? b. institutional banking? c. global banking?
4. Explain each of the following: a. reserve ratio; b. required reserves; c. excess reserves.
5. Explain each of the following types of deposit accounts: a. demand deposits; b. certificates of deposit; c. money market demand accounts; d. share deposits; e. negotiable order of withdrawal accounts.
6. Alan Greenspan, the chair of the Federal Reserve Board, told the U.S. Senate on July 12, 1990:

   As you know, the Board has long supported repeal of the provisions of the Glass-Steagall Act that separated commercial and investment banking. We still strongly advocate such repeal because we believe that technology and globalization have continued to blur the distinctions among credit markets, and have eroded the franchise value of the classic bank intermediation process. Outdated constraints will only endanger the profitability of banking organizations and their contribution to the American economy.

   a. What does Mr. Greenspan mean when he says that the value of the bank intermediation process has been eroded by technology and globalization?
   b. What are some of the major benefits and risks of repealing key provisions of the Glass-Steagall Act?
7. a. Explain how bank regulators incorporate risk into capital requirements.
   b. Explain how S&L regulators incorporate interest rate risk into capital requirements.
8. How did the Gramm-Leach-Bliley Act of 1999 expand the activities permitted by banks?

Asset	Book Value (in millions)
U.S. Treasury securities	$ 50
Municipal general obligation bonds	50
Residential mortgages	400
Commercial loans	200
Total book value	$700

Asset	Risk Weight
U.S. Treasury securities	0%
Municipal general obligation bonds	20
Residential mortgages	50
Commercial loans	100

9. In a discussion with you about the savings and loan crisis, a friend states that "the whole mess started in the early 1980s. When short-term rates skyrocketed, S&Ls got killed—their spread income went from positive to negative. They were borrowing short and lending long."
   a. What does your friend mean by "borrowing short and lending long"?
   b. Are higher or lower interest rates beneficial to an institution that borrows short and lends long?
10. The following is the book value of the assets of a bank:
   a. Calculate the risk-weighted assets using the following information:
   b. What is the minimum core capital requirement?
   c. What is the minimum total capital requirement?
11. When the manager of a bank's portfolio of securities considers alternative investments, she is also concerned about the risk-weight assigned to the security. Why?
12. Describe the current system for charging premiums for federal deposit insurance and how it differs from the way premiums were charged up until 1980.
13. Explain the proposal currently under consideration by the FDIC for charging premiums on federal deposit insurance.
14. Explain why you agree or disagree with the following statement "Regulators of banks and S&Ls have formulated the same methodology for measuring the interest rate risk for a depository institution."
15. Consider this headline from the *New York Times* of March 26, 1933: "Bankers will fight Deposit Guarantees. . . . Bad Banking would be encouraged."
   a. What do you think this headline is saying?
   b. Discuss the pros and cons of whether deposits should be insured by the U.S. government.
16. The following quotation is from the October 29, 1990, issue of *Corporate Financing Week*:

   Chase Manhattan Bank is preparing its first asset-backed debt issue, becoming the last major consumer bank to plan to access the growing market. Street asset-backed officials said. . . . Asset-back offerings enable banks to remove credit card or other loan receivables from their balance sheets, which helps them comply with capital requirements. What capital requirement is this article referring to?

   What capital requirement is this article referring to?
17. An article on bank funding in the October 15, 1990, issue of *Bank Letter* states:

   The steep rise in deposit insurance next year may trigger a growing preference for note issuance over wholesale deposits by top-tier banks, according to treasurers and a recent report by Keefe, Bruyette & Woods. . . . Investor skittishness over credit quality has kept most banks out of the wholesale funding note issuance market, but when investor sentiment improves, higher quality issuers will make increased use of uninsured vehicles such as note issuance.

   Discuss this quotation. In your answer be sure to mention the three sources of bank funding.
18. What are the primary assets in which savings and loans associations invest?
19. Who regulates the activities of credit unions?

CHAPTER 4

Nondepository Institutions

Learning Objectives

After reading this chapter you will understand:

◆ the nature of the business of insurance companies and the different types of insurance companies.

◆ the different types of life insurance policies and property and casualty insurance policies.

◆ the different types of investment companies: mutual funds, closed-end investment companies, and unit trusts.

◆ how the share prices of mutual funds and closed-end funds are determined.

◆ how investment companies differ, depending on their investment objectives.

◆ the economic benefits that investment companies provide, including diversification and reduced costs of investing.

◆ what exchange-traded funds are.

◆ the similarities and differences between exchange-traded funds and closed-end funds.

◆ what a pension plan sponsor does.

◆ the different types of pension plans, including defined contribution plans, defined benefit plans, and cash balance plan.

◆ what a 401(k) plan is.

◆ what an insured plan is.

◆ the principal provisions of the Employee Retirement Income Security Act (ERISA) of 1974.

◆ what the Pension Benefit Guaranty Corporation does.

◆ the various financial services provided to pension funds.

◆ what foundations do.

◆ the goals of managing money for foundations.

In this chapter we continue our coverage of financial institutions, specifically life insurance companies, property and casualty companies, pension funds, and investment companies.

Insurance companies provide (sell and service) insurance policies, which are legally binding contracts. According to the insurance contract, insurance companies promise to pay specified sums contingent on the occurrence of future events, such as death or an automobile accident. Thus, insurance companies are **risk bearers**. They accept or underwrite the risk in return for an **insurance premium** paid by the policyholder or owner of the policy.

A major task for the insurance company is deciding which applications for insurance they should accept and which ones they should reject. They must also determine how much to charge for the insurance if they accept the application. This decision making is called the **underwriting process**.

Because insurance companies collect insurance premiums initially and make payments later *when* or *if* an insured event occurs, insurance companies maintain the initial premiums collected in an investment portfolio that generates a return. Thus, the two sources of income for insurance companies include the initial underwriting income (the insurance premium) and the investment income that occurs over time. The investment returns from the investment of the insurance premiums accumulate until the funds are paid out on the policy. The premium provides a fairly stable type of revenue. Investment returns may vary considerably with the performance of the financial markets.

Insurance company's profits, thus, result from the difference between their insurance premiums and investment returns on the one hand, and their operating expense and insurance payments or benefits on the other. The type of risk insured against, which determines the level of premium collected and benefit paid, defines the insurance company.

The two major forms of life insurance companies are stock and mutual. A **stock insurance company** is similar in structure to any corporation or public company. Shares (of ownership) are owned by independent shareholders and are traded publicly. The shareholders care only about the performance of their shares, that is the stock appreciation and the dividends. Their holding period and, thus, their view, may be short term. The insurance policies are simply the products or business of the company.

In contrast, **mutual insurance companies** have no stock and no external owners. Their policyholders are also their owners. The owners, that is the policyholders, care primarily or even solely about the performance on their insurance policies, notably the company's ability to pay on the policy. Because these payments may occur considerably into the future, the policyholders' view may be long term. Thus, while stock insurance companies answer to two constituencies, their stockholders and their policyholders, mutual insurance companies deal with only one because their policyholders and their owners are the same. Traditionally the largest insurers operated as mutual insurance companies but in a number of **demutualizations**, mutual companies converted to stock companies.

TYPES OF INSURANCE

A large number of insurance products and contracts are available.

- *Life Insurance*. The risk insured against is death. The insurance company pays the beneficiary of the life insurance policy in the event of the death of the insured. Several types of life insurance are discussed later in this chapter.
- *Health Insurance*. The risk insured is the cost of medical treatment for the insured. The insurance company pays the insured (or the provider of the medical service) all or a portion of the cost of medical treatment by doctors, hospitals, or

ing off off

others. This type of insurance experienced significant changes in the past decade. As a result, significant restructurings of the health industry include a shift whereby the largest health insurance companies specialize in health insurance rather than sell health insurance in addition to other products, such as life insurance.

- *Property and Casualty Insurance.* The risk insured by property and casualty insurance (P&C) companies is the damage to various types of property. Specifically, it is insurance against financial loss caused by damage, destruction, or loss to property as the result of an identifiable event that is sudden, unexpected, or unusual. The major types of such insurance are (1) a house and its contents against risks such as fire, flood, and theft (home owners insurance and its variants), and (2) vehicles against collision, theft, and other damage (automobile insurance and its variants).

- *Liability Insurance.* The risk insured against is litigation, the risk of lawsuits against the insured due to actions by the insured or others.

- *Disability Insurance.* Disability insurance insures against the inability of an employed person to earn an income in either his or her own occupation ("own occ" disability insurance) or any occupation ("any occ"). Typically, "own occ" disability insurance is written for professionals and "any occ" for blue-collar workers. Another distinction in disability insurance is the sustainability of the policy. Disability insurance also distinguishes between short-term disability and long-term disability, with 6 months being the typical dividing time.

- *Long-Term Care Insurance.* Because individuals now live longer, they face issues of potentially outliving their assets and being unable to care for themselves as they age. In addition, the expense of custodial care for the aged continues to increase, creating a greater demand for insurance to provide custodial care for those no longer able to care for themselves. This care may be provided in either the insured's own residence or a separate custodial facility.

- *Structured Settlements.* Structured settlements provide fixed guaranteed periodic payments over a long period of time, typically resulting from a settlement on a disability or other type of policy. For example, an individual hit by an automobile and unable to work for the rest of his or her life may sue the P&C company for future lost earnings and medical care. To settle the suit, the P&C company may then purchase a policy from a life insurance company to make the agreed-upon payments.

- *Investment-Oriented Products.* Insurance companies increasingly offer products with a significant investment component in addition to their insurance component. The first major investment-oriented product developed by life insurance companies was the **guaranteed investment contract (GIC)**. According to a GIC, a life insurance company agrees, in return for a single premium, to pay the principal amount and a predetermined annual crediting rate over the life of the investment, with the total amount paid at the maturity date of the GIC. For example, a $10 million, 5-year GIC with a predetermined credit rate of 10% means that at the end of 5 years the insurance company pays the guaranteed crediting rate and the principal. The return of the principal depends on the ability of the life insurance company to satisfy the obligation, just as in any corporate debt obligation. The insurer faces the risk that the portfolio of supporting assets earns less than the guaranteed rate. The maturity of a GIC can vary from 1 year to 20 years. The interest rate guaranteed depends on market conditions and the credit rating of the life insurance company. Pension plan sponsors often purchase these policies as a pension investment.

A GIC is nothing more than the debt obligation of the life insurance company issuing the contract. The word *guarantee* does not mean any other guarantor in addition to the life insurance company. Effectively, a GIC acts as a zero-coupon bond issued by a life insurance company and, as such, exposes the investor to the same credit risk. The default of several major issuers of GICs highlights this credit risk. The two most publicized were Mutual Benefit, a New Jersey-based insurer, and Executive Life, a California-based insurer, both seized by regulators in 1991.

• *Annuity.* Another insurance company investment product is an annuity. An **annuity** is often described as "a mutual fund in an insurance wrapper." (Mutual funds are discussed later in this chapter.) To understand this description, assume that an insurance company investment manager has two identical common stock portfolios, one a mutual fund and the other an annuity. For the mutual fund, all income (that is, the dividend) is taxable, and the capital gains (or losses) realized by the fund are also taxable, although at potentially different tax rates. The income and realized gains are taxable whether they are withdrawn by the mutual fund holder or not. A mutual fund offers no guarantees—its performance depends solely on the portfolio performance.

Because of its insurance wrapper, the tax laws treat the annuity as an insurance product, resulting in preferential rates. Specifically, the income and realized gains are not taxable if not withdrawn from the annuity product. Thus, the "inside buildup" of returns is not taxable on an annuity, just as it is not on other insurance products.

The "insurance wrapper" on the mutual fund that makes it an annuity can take various forms. The most common "wrapper" is the guarantee by the insurance company that the annuity policyholder will get back no less than the amount invested in the annuity, although a minimum waiting period may be required before withdrawal to get this benefit. Thus, if an investor invests $100 in a common stock-based annuity and at the time of withdrawal (or at the time of death of the annuity holder) the annuity value is only $95, the insurance company will pay the annuity holder (or its beneficiary) $100.

Insurance companies continue to develop many other types of protection or insurance features to their annuities. Of course, insurance companies impose a charge for this benefit—an insurance premium for the insurance component of the annuity. Thus, while mutual funds impose an expense fee on the fund's performance, an annuity imposes a **mortality and expense fee.** Thus, annuities are more expensive to the investor than mutual funds. In return, annuity policyholders get the insurance wrapper, which provides the tax benefit. Such annuities can be either fixed annuities, similar to GICs, or variable annuities whose performance is based on the return of a common stock or bond portfolio. Mutual funds and annuities distributed by insurance companies may be managed by the insurance company investment department or by external investment managers, as discussed later in this chapter.

INSURANCE COMPANIES VERSUS TYPES OF PRODUCTS

In concept, these various types of insurance could be combined in different ways in actual companies. Traditionally, however, they generally are packaged in companies in similar ways. Most commonly, life insurance and health insurance occur together in a **life and health insurance company (L&H company).** Insurance for property and casualty is combined in a **P&C (property and casualty) insurance company.** Companies that provide insurance in both insurance products are called **multiline insurance.** Investment products tend to be sold by life insurance companies, not P&C companies.

Some recent changes affect the combinations of products by type of company, however. Health insurance, predominantly separated from life insurance, now operates as a separate industry. This change resulted mainly from federal regulation of the health insurance industry. Life insurance companies increasingly offer investment-oriented products, variable and fixed annuities and mutual funds. Disability insurance is now sold primarily by pure disability companies, but is also offered by some life insurance companies. Long-term care insurance, a fairly new line of business, is offered by different types of companies. Most companies are unique with respect to the combination of products they offer and how they offer them.

FUNDAMENTALS OF THE INSURANCE INDUSTRY

A fundamental aspect of the insurance industry results from the relationship between the revenues and costs. A bread manufacturer purchases its ingredients, uses these ingredients to make bread, and then sells the bread, all over a fairly short time frame. Therefore, a bread manufacturer's profit margin can be easily calculated.

An insurance company, on the other hand, collects its premium income initially and invests these receipts in its portfolio. The payments on the insurance policy occur later and, depending on the type of insurance, often in an unpredictable manner. Consequently, the payments are *contingent* on potential future events. For example, with respect to life insurance, it is certain that everyone will die. However, it is not known *when* any individual will die. The timing of the payment on any specific life insurance company is, thus, uncertain. However, although the payments on any single life insurance policy are uncertain, statisticians or actuaries can predict the pattern of deaths on a large portfolio of life insurance policies, making the aggregate much less uncertain.

At the other extreme, not only are payments on home insurance against hurricanes singularly uncertain, but the payments on a portfolio of homes remain uncertain as well. If one house in South Florida is destroyed by a hurricane, it is likely that many others will also be destroyed.

Thus, two important differences distinguish between calculating profitability of bread manufacturers and insurance companies. The first is that the timing and magnitude of the payments are much less certain for an insurance company. The second is the long lag between the receipts and payments for an insurance company, which introduces the importance of the investment portfolio.

These differences in the providers of bread and insurance lead to differences in the way consumers of bread and insurance view their providers. Purchasers of bread are not harmed if the bread manufacturer goes bankrupt the day after they buy the bread. The purchaser of bread receives the bread immediately, but the purchaser of insurance receives the payment on his or her insurance policy in the future and, thus, must be concerned about the continued viability of the insurance company. Therefore, the credit rating of an insurance company is important to a purchaser of insurance, especially for the types of insurance that may be paid well into the future, such as life insurance.

REGULATION OF THE INSURANCE INDUSTRY

According to the McCarran Ferguson Act of 1945, the individual states, and not the federal government, regulate the insurance industry. However, more and more attention is focused on a discussion of federal regulation. Insurance companies whose stock is publicly traded are also regulated by the Securities and Exchange Commission (SEC).

Model laws and regulations developed by the National Association of Insurance Commissioners (NAIC), a voluntary association of state insurance commissioners, apply to insurance companies in all states. Adoption of a model law or regulation by the NAIC is not, however, binding on any state. However, states typically use these guidelines when writing their own laws and regulations.

Insurance companies may also be rated by the rating agencies (Moody's Investor Services, Standard & Poor's, A.M. Best Company, Fitch, and others) for both their ability to pay claims and their outstanding debt, if any. Equity analysts who work at investment banks and broker/dealers also evaluate the attractiveness of outstanding common stock of public insurance companies.

The relationship between the premium revenues and the eventual contingent contractual insurance policy payments affects an important aspect of evaluating insurance companies. Accountants/auditors, rating agencies, and government regulators all monitor insurance companies. These monitors watch the financial stability of the insurance companies based on, among other issues, the level of synchronicity between the premiums and insurance policy payments and also the volatility of the payments. To assure financial stability, these monitors require insurance companies to maintain reserves or surplus, consisting of the excess of assets over liabilities. Regulators and accountants differently define these reserves or surpluses and call them by different names. Because state statutes establish the treatment of both assets and liabilities for insurance companies, a surplus is also known as **statutory surplus** (or **reserves**) or STAT surplus. Generally accepted accounting principles (GAAP) surplus (or reserves) is defined by accountants for their purposes. Statutory and GAAP reserves are measured differently, but their purposes are similar, although not identical.

Defining assets is straightforward; defining liabilities is more difficult. The complication in determining the value of liabilities arises because the insurance company commits to make payments at some time in the future, which are recorded as contingent liabilities on its financial statement. The reserves are simply an accounting entry, not an identifiable portfolio.

Statutory surplus is important because regulators view it as the ultimate amount that can be drawn upon to pay policyholders. The growth of this surplus for an insurance company also determines how much future business it can underwrite.

STRUCTURE OF INSURANCE COMPANIES

Insurance companies are really a composite of three companies. First, the "home office" or actual insurance company designs the insurance contract ("manufactures" the contract) and provides the backing for the financial guarantees on the contract. It assures the policyholder that the contract will pay off under the conditions of the contract. This company is called the *manufacturer* and *guarantor* of the insurance policy. Second, the investment component invests the premiums collected in the investment portfolio. It is the *investment company*. The third is the *distribution component* or the salesforce. In the wake of deregulation, commercial banks become a natural means of distribution for insurance company insurance and investments products. This relationship is called **bankassurance**.

These three components of insurance companies traditionally were combined as one overall company, but now the separate functions are often provided by different companies. First, many insurance companies use independent brokers or producer groups to distribute their products rather than their own agents. Second, insurance companies may outsource parts of their investment portfolio or even the entire portfolio to external independent investment managers. Third, even as the core component of an insurance company, some home offices use external actuarial firms to design their contracts. And more importantly, they may *reinsure* some or all of the liabilities they incur in providing insurance. According to the reinsurance transaction, the initial insurer transfers the risk of the insurance to another company, the "reinsurer." An industry of reinsurers exists to accept the risk incurred by the primary insurance company. The financial guarantee on the insurance policy is, thus, provided by the reinsurer rather than the insurance company that originally provided or "wrote" the policy.

TYPES OF LIFE INSURANCE

The two fundamentally different types of life insurance are term insurance and cash value life insurance.

Term Insurance   **Term insurance** is pure life insurance. If the insured dies while the policy is intact, the beneficiary of the policy receives the death benefit. If the insured does not die within the period, the policy is invalid and holds no value. No cash value or investment value accrues to a term insurance policy. In addition, the policyholder cannot borrow against the policy.

Cash Value or Permanent Life Insurance   A broad classification of life insurance includes cash-value or permanent or investment-type life insurance, usually called **whole life insurance**. In addition to providing pure life insurance (as does term insurance), whole life insurance builds up a cash value or investment value inside the policy. This cash value can be withdrawn and can also be borrowed against by the owner of the policy. Or, if the owner wishes to let the policy lapse, he or she can withdraw the cash value. Growth in the cash value of the life insurance policy is referred to as the "inside buildup." A major advantage of this and other insurance products that offer a cash or investment value is that the inside buildup is not subject to taxation.

Life insurance and life insurance products are complex. Only an overview is provided in this chapter. The first of the two categories of cash value life insurance policies defines whether the cash value is guaranteed or variable. The second category deals with whether the required premium payment is fixed or flexible. The four possible combinations (see Table 4-1) are discussed here.

1. *Guaranteed Cash Value Life Insurance.* Traditional cash value life insurance, usually called whole life insurance, provides a guaranteed buildup of cash value based on the general account portfolio of the insurance company. The insurance company guarantees a minimum cash value at the end of each year. This guaranteed cash value is based on a minimum dividend paid on the policy. In addition, the policy can be either *participating* or *nonparticipating*. For **nonparticipating policies**, the dividend and the cash value on the policy are the guaranteed amounts. For the **participating policy**, the dividend paid on the policy is based on the realized actuarial experience of the company and its investment portfolio. The cash value may be above but not below the guaranteed level for participating policies. Thus, the actual performance of the policy may be substantially affected by the actual policy dividends over the guaranteed amount.
2. *Variable Life Insurance.* Contrary to the guaranteed or fixed cash value policies based on the general account portfolio of the insurance company, variable life insurance policies allow the policy owners to, within limits, allocate their premium payments to and among separate investment accounts maintained by the insurance company, and also be able to shift the policy cash value among the separate

TABLE 4-1   Classification of Cash Value Insurance

	Guaranteed Cash Value Policies	Variable Life Policies
Fixed Premium	Whole life insurance	Variable life insurance
Flexible Premium	Universal life insurance	Variable universal life insurance

accounts. As a result, the amount of the policy cash value and the death benefit depend on the investment results of the separate accounts selected by the policy owner. Thus, this policy offers no guaranteed cash value or death benefit, but depends instead on the performance of the selected investment portfolio.

The types of separate account investment options offered vary by insurance company. Typically the insurance company offers a selection of common stock and bond fund investment opportunities, managed by the company itself and other investment managers. If the investment options perform well, the cash value buildup in the policy will be significant. However, if the policyholder selects investment options that perform poorly, the variable life insurance policy will perform poorly, resulting in little or no cash value buildup, or, in the worst case, the termination of the policy. This type of life insurance is called **variable life insurance**. Variable life insurance, typically designed with common stock investment options, grew substantially with the stock market rally of the 1990s.

3. *Universal Life*. The key element of **universal life** is the flexibility of the premium for the policyowner. This flexible premium concept separates pure insurance protection (term insurance) from the investment (cash value) element of the policy. The policy cash value is set up as the cash value fund (or accumulation fund) to which the investment income is credited and from which the cost of term insurance for the insured (the mortality charge) is debited. Expenses are also debited.

This separation of the cash value from the pure insurance is called the **unbundling** of the traditional life insurance policy. Premium payments for universal life are at the discretion of the policyholder, except for a minimum initial premium to begin the coverage and then at least enough cash value in the policy each month to cover the mortality charge and other expenses. If not, the policy will lapse. Both guaranteed cash value and variable life can be written on a flexible premium or fixed premium basis.

4. *Variable Universal Life Insurance*. Variable universal life insurance combines the features of variable life and universal life policies. During the 1990s, term and variable life insurance grew in popularity at the expense of whole life insurance.

Survivorship (Second to Die) Insurance   Most whole life insurance policies pay death benefits when one specified insured dies. An added dimension of whole life policies insures two people (usually a married couple) jointly and pays the death benefit not when the first person dies, but when the second person (usually the surviving spouse) dies. This type of policy is called **survivorship insurance**, or **second-to-die insurance**. The survivorship feature can be added to standard cash value whole life, universal life, and variable universal life policies. Thus, each of the four policies in Table 4-1 could also be written on a survivorship basis. Survivorship insurance is typically sold for estate planning purposes.

GENERAL ACCOUNT AND SEPARATE ACCOUNT PRODUCTS

The general account of an insurance company refers to the investment portfolio of the overall company. Products "written by the company itself" generally carry a "general account guarantee," that is they are a liability of the insurance company. When the rating agencies (Moody's, Standard & Poor's, Fitch) provide a credit rating (discussed in Chapter 22), they do so on products written by or guaranteed by the general account. Such ratings are on the "claims paying ability" of the company. Typical products written by and guaranteed by the general account are whole life, universal life, and fixed annuities (including GICs). Insurance companies must support the guaranteed performance of their **general account products** to the extent of their solvency.

Other types of insurance products receive no guarantee from the insurance company's general account, and their performance is not based on the performance of the insurance company's general account, but solely on the performance of an account separate from the general account of the insurance company, often an account selected by the policyholder. These products are called **separate account products**. Variable life insurance and variable annuities are separate account products. The policyholder chooses specific portfolios to support these products. The performance of the insurance product depends almost solely on performance of the portfolio selected, adjusted for the fees or expenses of the insuring company.

PARTICIPATING POLICIES

The performance of separate account products depends on the performance of the separate account portfolio chosen and is not affected by the performance of the overall insurance company's general account portfolio. In addition, the performance of some general account products is not affected by the performance of the general account portfolio. For example, disability income insurance policies may be written on a general account, and even though their payoff depends on the solvency of the general account, the policy performance (for example, its premium) does not participate in the investment performance of the insurance company's general account investment portfolio.

Other general account insurance products participate in the performance of the company's general account performance. For example, a life insurance company provides the guarantee of a minimum dividend on its whole life policies, but the policies' actual dividend may increase if the investment portfolio performs well. This "interest component" of the dividend exists in tandem with the expense and mortality components. Thus, the performance of the insurance policy participates in the overall company's performance. Such a policy is called a *participating policy,* in this case a participating whole life insurance policy.

Stock and mutual insurance companies write both general and separate account products. However, most general account products are written in mutual companies. And all participating policies are written in general accounts, although general accounts also write nonparticipating products.

INSURANCE COMPANY INVESTMENT STRATEGIES[1]

In general, the characteristics of insurance company investment portfolios should reflect their liabilities, or the insurance products they underwrite. The various types of insurance policies differ in the following ways:

- The expected time at which the average payment will be made by the insurance company (technically, the "duration" of the payments)
- The statistical or actuarial accuracy of estimates of *when* the event insured against will occur and the *amount* of the payment (that is, the overall risk of the policy)
- Other factors

In addition, tax treatment for the various types of insurance policies and companies differs.

---

[1] For a more detailed discussion of investment strategies, see Frank J. Jones, "An Overview of Institutional Fixed Income Strategies," in Frank J. Fabozzi (ed.), *Professional Perspectives on Fixed Income Portfolio Management: Volume 1* (New Hope, PA: Frank J. Fabozzi Associates, 2000), pp. 1–13.

The key distinction between life insurance and property and casualty insurance companies lies in the difficulty of projecting whether a policyholder will be paid off and how much the payment will be. Although this task is not easy for either a life or a P&C insurance company, it is easier from an actuarial perspective for a life insurance company. The amount and timing of claims on property and casualty insurance companies are more difficult to predict because of the randomness of natural catastrophes and the unpredictability of court awards in liability cases. This uncertainty about the timing and amount of cash outlays to satisfy claims affects investment strategies for the funds of property and casualty insurance companies compared to life insurance companies.

Without investigating the details for the differences in the portfolios of different types of insurance products, we can state that the portfolios of L&H companies and P&C companies differ in a number of major ways. L&H companies on average have less common stock, more private placements, more commercial mortgages, less municipal bonds, and longer maturity bonds. (These securities and financial assets are discussed in later chapters). The difference in municipal bond holdings is due to the tax-exempt characteristic of these securities. The larger holdings of private placements and commercial mortgages indicate the yield orientation of L&H companies. This yield orientation is also consistent with the low holding of common stock for life insurance companies.

Of the differences in investment strategy between public (or stock) and mutual insurance companies of the same type, the major one is that stock companies tend to have less common stock than mutual companies. Common stock analysts, who make buy-hold-sell recommendations on all public companies for institutional and individual investors, consider mainly regularly recurring operating income in their calculation of income, not volatile returns. Coupon and dividend income tend to be stable, and capital gains tend to be unstable. Thus, these analysts favor bonds, which offer higher interest income, over stocks with their higher capital gains, and over the long term, total returns. As a result, mutual insurance companies, which are not rated by common stock analysts, can focus on total return rather than just yield and have more common stock than public companies.

TAXATION OF LIFE INSURANCE

As mentioned earlier in this chapter, the inside buildup of cash value life insurance policies is not taxed as either income or capital gains. Neither is the beneficiary of the death benefit of life insurance policy subject to an income tax. Finally, the death benefit of the policy may or may not be subject to estate tax, depending on how the beneficiary status is structured. Consequently, life insurance products offer considerable tax advantages.

DEREGULATION OF THE INSURANCE INDUSTRY

In 1933, the Glass-Steagall Act, discussed in Chapter 3, separated commercial banking, investment banking, and insurance. That is, a company could be involved in only one of these three types of business. One of the main intended purposes of this act was to prevent a single organization from gaining complete control over the sources of corporate funding, specifically lending to and underwriting the securities of a company.

Over time, due to the evolution of the financial system, the implementation of the Glass-Steagall Act became more ambiguous, more difficult to implement, and, in the view of many, counterproductive. As explained in the previous chapter, a recent landmark financial event revoked the Glass-Steagall Act. On November 12, 1999, the Gramm-Leach-Bliley Act (GLB), called the Financial Modernization Act of 1999, was signed into law. This act removed the 50-year-old "anti-affiliation restrictions" among commercial banks, investment banks, and insurance companies.

The GLB facilitated and accelerated affiliations among these three types of institutions. The first mega-institution of this type combined Salomon Brothers and Smith Barney, both investment banks, with Travelers, an insurance company, and Citicorp, a commercial bank. This merged firm is now simply called Citigroup and is involved in insurance, commercial banking, investment banking, and security brokerage.

GLB is also one reason given for the accelerated demutualization of insurance companies. Demutualization permits insurance companies to acquire not only insurance companies but other types of financial institutions. By demutualizing, insurance companies can acquire capital for acquisitions. The act also certainly accelerates bankassurance.

◆ INVESTMENT COMPANIES

Investment companies are financial intermediaries that sell shares to the public and invest the proceeds in a diversified portfolio of securities. Each share sold represents a proportional interest in the portfolio of securities managed by the investment company on behalf of its shareholders. The type of securities purchased depends on the company's investment objective.

TYPES OF INVESTMENT COMPANIES

The three types of investment companies consist of those that offer open-end funds, closed-end funds, and unit trusts.

Open-End Funds (Mutual Funds)   **Open-end funds**, commonly referred to simply as **mutual funds**, are portfolios of securities, mainly stocks, bonds, and money market instruments. Investors in mutual funds own a pro rata share of the overall portfolio, which is managed by an investment manager of the mutual fund who buys some securities and sells others.

Additionally, the value or price of each share of the portfolio, called the **net asset value (NAV)**, equals the market value of the portfolio minus the liabilities of the mutual fund divided by the number of shares owned by the mutual fund investors:

$$NAV = \frac{\text{Market value of portfolio} - \text{Liabilities}}{\text{Number of shares outstanding}}$$

For example, suppose that a mutual fund with 10 million shares outstanding has a portfolio with a market value of $215 million and liabilities of $15 million. The NAV is

$$NAV = \frac{\$215,000,000 - \$15,000,000}{10,000,000} = \$20$$

The NAV or price of the fund is determined only once each day, at the close of the day. For example, the NAV for a stock mutual fund is determined from the closing stock prices for the day. Business publications provide the NAV each day in their mutual fund tables. The published NAVs are the closing NAVs. Finally, all new investments into the fund or withdrawals from the fund during a day are priced at the closing NAV (investments after the end of the day or a nonbusiness day are priced at the next day's closing NAV).

The total number of shares in the fund increases if more investments than withdrawals are made during the day, and vice versa. For example, assume that at the beginning of a day a mutual fund portfolio is valued at $1 million, with no liabilities, and 10,000 shares outstanding. Thus, the NAV of the fund is $100. Assume that during the day investors deposit $5,000 into the fund and withdraw $1,000, and the prices of all the securities in the portfolio remain constant. These transactions mean that 50 shares were issued for the $5,000 deposited (because each share is valued at $100) and 10 shares redeemed for $1,000. The net number of new shares issued equals 40. Therefore, at the end of the day the fund contains 10,040 shares with a total value of $1,004,000. The NAV remains at $100.

If, instead, the prices of the securities in the portfolio change, both the total size of the portfolio and, therefore, the NAV will change. In the previous example, assume that during the day the value of the portfolio doubles to $2 million. Because deposits and withdrawals are priced at the end-of-day NAV, which is now $200 after the doubling of the portfolio's value, the $5,000 deposit will be credited with 25 shares ($5,000/$200) and the $1,000 withdrawn will reduce the number of shares by 5 shares ($1,000/$200). Thus, at the end of the day the fund contains 10,020 shares (25 − 5) with an NAV of $200, for a total fund value of $2,004,000. (Note that 10,020 shares × $200 NAV = $2,004,000, the portfolio value.)

Overall, the NAV of a mutual fund increases or decreases due to an increase or decrease in the prices of the securities in the portfolio. The number of shares in the fund increases or decreases due to the net deposits into or withdrawals from the fund. And the total value of the fund increases or decreases for both reasons.

Closed-End Funds   The shares of a **closed-end fund** are similar to the shares of common stock of a corporation. The new shares of a closed-end fund are initially issued by an underwriter for the fund. And after the new issue, the number of shares remains constant. After the initial issue, no sales or purchases of fund shares are made by the fund company as in open-end funds. Instead, the shares are traded on a secondary market, either on an exchange or in the over-the-counter market.

Investors can buy shares at the time of the initial issue or in the secondary market. Shares are sold only on the secondary market. The price of the shares of a closed-end fund are determined by the supply and demand in the market in which these funds are traded. Thus, investors who transact closed-end fund shares must pay a brokerage commission at the time of purchase and at the time of sale.

The NAV of closed-end funds is calculated in the same way as for open-end funds. However, the price of a share in a closed-end fund is determined by supply and demand, so the price can fall below or rise above the net asset value per share. Shares selling below NAV are said to be "trading at a discount," while shares trading above NAV are "trading at a premium." Newspapers list quotations of the prices of these shares under the heading "Closed-End Funds."

Consequently, two important differences distinguish open-end funds from closed-end funds. First, the number of shares of an open-end fund varies because the fund sponsor sells new shares to investors and buys existing shares from shareholders. Second, by doing so, the share price is always the NAV of the fund. In contrast, closed-end funds have a constant number of shares outstanding because the fund sponsor does not redeem shares and sell new shares to investors except at the time of a new underwriting. Thus, supply and demand in the market determine the price of the fund shares, which may be above or below NAV, as previously discussed.

Although the divergence of the price from NAV is often puzzling, in some cases the reasons for the premium or discount are easily understood. For example, a share's price may be below the NAV due to the fund's large built-in tax liabilities and because investors discount the share's price for that future tax liability.[2] This tax liability issue is discussed later. A fund's leverage and resulting risk may be another reason for the share's price trading below NAV. A fund's shares may trade at a premium to the NAV because the fund offers relatively cheap access to, and professional management of, stocks in another country about which information is not readily available to small investors.

The relatively new exchange-traded funds (ETFs), which are discussed later in this chapter, pose a threat to both mutual funds and closed-end funds. ETFs are essentially hybrid closed-end vehicles that trade on exchanges but typically trade very close to NAV.

Because closed-end funds are traded like stocks, the cost to any investor of buying or selling a closed-end fund is the same as that of a stock. The obvious charge is the stockbroker's commission. The bid-ask spread of the market on which the stock is traded is also a cost.

Unit Trusts   A **unit trust** is similar to a closed-end fund in that the number of unit certificates is fixed. Unit trusts typically invest in bonds. They differ in several ways from both mutual funds and closed-end funds that specialize in bonds. First, no active trading of the bonds takes place in the portfolio of the unit trust. Once the unit trust is assembled by the sponsor (usually a brokerage firm or bond underwriter) and turned over to a trustee, the trustee holds all the bonds until redeemed by the issuer. Typically, the only time the trustee can sell an issue in the portfolio is when a dramatic decline occurs in the issuer's credit quality. As a result, the cost of operating the trust will be considerably less than costs incurred by either a mutual fund or a closed-end fund. Second, unit trusts set a fixed termination date, while mutual funds and closed-end funds do not.[3] Third, unlike the mutual fund and closed-end fund investor, the unit trust investor knows that the portfolio consists of a specific portfolio of bonds and has no concern that the trustee will alter the portfolio. Unit trusts are common in Europe, but not in the United States.

FUND SALES CHARGES AND ANNUAL OPERATING EXPENSES

Investors in mutual funds bear two types of costs. The first is the **shareholder fee**, usually called the **sales charge**. This cost is a "one-time" charge debited to the investor for a specific transaction, such as a purchase, redemption, or exchange. The type of charge is related to the way the fund is sold or distributed. The second cost is the annual fund operating expense, usually called the **expense ratio**, which covers the fund's expenses, the largest of which is for investment management. This charge is imposed annually and occurs on all funds and for all types of distribution.

Sales Charge   Sales charges on mutual funds are related to their method of distribution. The two types of distribution are sales force (or wholesale) and direct. **Salesforce (wholesale) distribution** occur via an intermediary such as an agent, a stockbroker, insurance agent, or other entity who provides investment advice and incentive to the client, actively "make the sale," and provides subsequent service. The other approach is **direct distribution** (from the fund company to the investor). The client approaches the mutual fund company, most likely by a toll-free telephone contact, in response to media advertisements or general information, and opens the account. Little or no investment counsel or service is provided either initially or subsequently.

---
2   Harold Bierman, Jr. and Bhaskaran Swaminathan, "Managing a Closed-End Investment Fund," *Journal of Portfolio Management* (Summer 2000), p. 49.
3   This statement is subject to some exceptions. Target term closed-end funds have a fixed termination date.

For the service provided in the salesforce distribution method, the customer bears a sales charge paid to the agent. The sales charge is called a **load**. The traditional type of load is called a **front-end load**, because the load is deducted initially or "up front." That is, the load is subtracted from the amount invested by the client and paid to the agent/distributor. Directly placed mutual funds require no sales agent and, therefore, no sales charge. Funds with no sales charges are called **no-load mutual funds**.

Recent adaptations of the sales load are back-end loads and level loads. Front-end loads are imposed at the time of the purchase of the fund, but the **back-end load** is imposed at the time fund shares are sold or redeemed. Level loads are assessed uniformly each year. These two alternative methods both provide ways to compensate the agent. However, unlike the front-end load, both of these distribution mechanisms permit the client to buy a fund at NAV, that is, not have any of their initial investment debited as a sales charge before it is invested in their account. The most common type of back-end load currently is the **contingent deferred sales charge (CDSC)**. This approach imposes a gradually declining load on withdrawal. For example, a common "3,3,2,2,1,1,0" CDSC approach imposes a 3% load on the amount withdrawn after one year, 3% after the second year, 2% after the third year, and so on. No sales charge for withdrawals applies after the seventh year.

Another type of load is neither a front-end load at the time of investment nor a (gradually declining) back-end load at the time of withdrawal, but a constant load each year (e.g., a 1% load every year). This approach is called a **level load**. This type of load appeals to the types of financial planners who charge annual fees rather than commissions, such as sales charges.

Many mutual fund families often offer their funds with all three types of loads—that is, front-end loads (usually called "A shares"); back-end loads (called "B shares"); and level loads (called "C shares")—and permit the distributor and its client to select the type of load they prefer.[4]

The sales charge is, in effect, paid by the client to the distributor. How does the fund family, typically called the sponsor or manufacturer of the fund, cover its costs and make a profit? This second type of "cost" to the investor covers the fund annual operating expense.

Annual Operating Expenses (Expense Ratio)   The **operating expense**, also called the **expense ratio,** is debited annually from the investor's fund balance by the fund sponsor. The three main categories of annual operating expenses are the management fee, distribution fee, and other expenses.

The **management fee**, also called the **investment advisory fee**, is charged by the investment advisor for managing a fund's portfolio. If the investment advisor works for a company separate from the fund sponsor, some or all of this investment advisory fee is passed on to the investment advisor by the fund sponsor. In this case, the fund manager is called a **subadvisor**. The management fee varies by the type of fund, specifically by the difficulty of managing the fund.

In 1980, the SEC approved the imposition of a fixed annual fee, called the **12b-1 fee**, which is, in general, intended to cover distribution costs, including continuing agent compensation and manufacturer marketing and advertising expenses. Such 12b-1 fees are now imposed by many mutual funds. By law, 12b-1 fees cannot exceed 1% of the fund's assets per year. The 12b-1 fee may include a service fee of up to 0.25% of assets

---

4   Edward S. O'Neal, "Mutual Fund Share Classes and Broker Incentives," *Financial Analysts Journal* (September/October 1999), pp. 76–87.

per year to compensate sales professionals for providing services or maintaining share-holder accounts. The major rationale for the component of the 12b-1 fee, which accrues to the selling agent, is to provide an incentive to selling agents to continue to service their accounts after they receive a transaction-based fee such as a front-end load. As a result, a 12b-1 fee of this type is consistent with salesforce-sold load funds, not with directly sold no-load funds. The rationale for the component of the 12b-1 fee that accrues to the manufacturer of the fund is to provide incentive and compensate for continuing advertising and marketing costs.

Other expenses include primarily the costs of (1) custody (holding the cash and securities of the fund), (2) the transfer agent (transferring cash and securities among buyers and sellers of the securities and the fund distributions, etc.), (3) independent public accountant fees, and (4) directors' fees.

The sum of the annual management fee, the annual distribution fee, and other annual expenses is called the expense ratio. All the cost information on a fund, including selling charges and annual expenses, are included in the fund prospectus.

ECONOMIC MOTIVATION FOR FUNDS

Recall from Chapter 2 that financial intermediaries obtain funds by issuing financial claims against themselves and then investing these funds. An investment company is a financial intermediary in that it pools the funds of individual investors and uses these funds to buy portfolios of securities. Recall the special role in financial markets played by financial intermediaries. Financial intermediaries provide some or all of the following six economic functions: (1) risk reduction via diversification, (2) lower costs of contracting and processing information, (3) professional portfolio management, (4) liquidity, (5) variety, and (6) a payments mechanism. Consider these economic functions as provided by mutual funds.

Consider first the function of risk reduction through diversification. By investing in a fund, an investor can obtain broad-based ownership of a sufficient number of securities to reduce portfolio risk. (We will be more specific about the type of risk that is reduced in Chapter 8.) Although an individual investor may be able to acquire a broad-based portfolio of securities, the degree of diversification will be limited by the amount available to invest. By investing in an investment company, however, the investor can effectively achieve the benefits of diversification at a lower cost even if the amount of money available to invest is not large.

The second economic function is the reduced cost of contracting and processing information, because an investor purchases the services of a presumably skilled financial advisor at less cost than if the investor directly and individually negotiated with such an advisor. The advisory fee is lower because of the larger size of assets managed, as well as the reduced costs of searching for an investment manager and obtaining information about the securities. Also, the costs of transacting in the securities are reduced because a fund is better able to negotiate transactions costs; and custodial fees and record-keeping costs are less for a fund than for an individual investor. For these reasons, investment management enjoys economies of scale.

Third, and related to the first two advantages, is the advantage of the professional management of the mutual fund. Fourth is the advantage of liquidity. Mutual funds can be bought or liquidated any day at the closing NAV. Fifth is the advantage of the variety of funds available, in general, and even in one particular family of funds.

Finally, money market funds and some other types of funds provide payment services by allowing investors to write checks drawn on the fund, although this facility may be limited in various ways.

TYPES OF FUNDS BY INVESTMENT OBJECTIVE

Mutual funds developed out of a need to satisfy the various investment objectives of investors. In general, within the main categories—stock funds, bond funds, money market funds, and others—several subcategories of funds exist. Other funds are U.S.-only, international (no U.S. securities), or global (both U.S. and international securities). Still other funds are considered passive or active funds. **Passive** (or **indexed**) **funds** are designed to replicate an index, such as the S&P 500 Stock Index, the Lehman Aggregate Bond Index, or the Morgan Stanley Capital International EAFE (Europe, Australasia, and the Far East) Index. **Active funds**, on the other hand, attempt to outperform an index and other funds by actively trading the fund portfolio. The objective of numerous other categories of funds is stated in the specific fund's prospectus, as required by the SEC and the "1940 Act."

Stock funds differ in the following ways:

- The average market capitalization ("market cap"; large, mid, and small) of the stocks in the portfolio
- Style (growth, value, and blend)
- Sector specialization, such as technology, health care, or utilities

As of late 2000, the categories for market capitalization were as follows:

- Small: $0 to $2 billion
- Mid: $2 billion to $12 billion
- Large: Over $12 billion

With respect to style, stocks with high price-to-book and price-to-earnings ratios are considered "growth stocks," and stocks with low price-to-value and price-to-earnings ratios are considered value stocks, although other variables are also considered. Some styles can be considered blend stocks.

Bond funds differ by the creditworthiness of the issuers of the bonds in the portfolio (for example, U.S. government, investment grade corporate, and high-yield corporate) and by the maturity (or duration) of the bonds (long, intermediate, and short). Another category of bond funds called municipal bond funds offer tax-exempt coupon interest. Municipal funds may also be single state (that is, all the bonds in the portfolio were issued by issuers in the same state) or multi-state.

Asset allocation, hybrid, or balanced funds categories all hold both stocks and bonds. Convertible bond funds provide another option for investors.

A category of money market funds with maturities of 1 year or less provides protection against interest rate fluctuations. These funds may have some degree of credit risk, except for the U.S. government money market category. Many of these funds offer check-writing privileges. In addition to taxable money market funds, tax-exempt municipal money market funds are available as well.

Among the other fund offerings are index funds and funds of funds. Index funds, as already discussed, attempt to passively replicate an index. A **fund of funds** invests in other mutual funds. Compare the 16 funds of funds with $1.4 billion in assets in 1990 to the 213 funds of funds with $48 billion in assets in 1999.[5]

Several organizations provide data on mutual funds. The most popular ones are Morningstar and Lipper, which provide data on fund expenses, portfolio managers,

---

[5] Brian Reid, *The 1990s: A Decade of Expansion and Changes in the U.S. Mutual Fund Industry*, Investment Company Institute, 6, No. 3 (July 2000), pp. 14–15.

fund sizes, and fund holdings. But perhaps most importantly, they provide performance (that is, rate of return) data and rankings among funds based on performances and other factors. To compare fund performance on an "apples to apples" basis, these firms divide mutual funds into several categories intended to be fairly homogeneous by investment objective. The categories provided by Morningstar and Lipper are similar but not identical. Mutual fund data are also provided by the Investment Company Institute, the national association for mutual funds.

THE CONCEPT OF A FAMILY OF FUNDS

A concept that revolutionized the fund industry and benefited many investors is what the mutual fund industry calls a **family of funds**, a group of funds or a complex of funds. Many fund management companies offer investors a choice of numerous funds with different investment objectives in the same fund family. In many cases, investors may move their assets from one fund to another within the family at little or no cost via a phone call. Of course, if these funds are in a taxable account, tax consequences may accompany the sale. Although the same policies regarding loads and other costs may apply to all the members of the family, a management company may have different fee structures for transfers among different funds under its control.

Large fund families usually include money market funds, U.S. bond funds of several types, global stock and bond funds, broadly diversified U.S. stock funds, U.S. stock funds that specialize by market capitalization and style, and stock funds devoted to particular sectors such as health care, technology, or gold companies. Well-known management companies, such as Fidelity, Vanguard, and American Funds, the three largest fund families, sponsor and manage varied types of funds in a family. Fund families may also use external investment advisors along with internal advisors in their fund families. The number of family funds grew from 123 in 1980 to 433 in 1999. Fund data provided in newspapers group the various funds according to their families. For example, all the Fidelity funds are listed under the Fidelity heading, all the Vanguard funds are listed under their name, and so on.

TAXATION OF MUTUAL FUNDS

Mutual funds must distribute at least 90% of their net investment income earned (bond coupons and stock dividends) exclusive of realized capital gains or losses to shareholders (along with meeting other criteria) to be considered a **regulated investment company (RIC)** and, thus, not be required to pay taxes at the fund level prior to distributions to shareholders. Consequently, funds make these distributions. Taxes on distributions are paid only at the investor level, not the fund level. Even though many mutual fund investors choose to reinvest these distributions, the distributions are taxable to the investor, either as ordinary income or capital gains (long term or short term), whichever is relevant.

Capital gains distributions must occur annually, and typically occur late during the calendar year. The capital gains distributions may be either long-term or short-term capital gains, depending on whether the fund held the security for a year or more. Mutual fund investors have no control over the size of these distributions and, as a result, the timing and amount of the taxes paid on their fund holdings is largely out of their control. In particular, withdrawals by some investors may necessitate sales in the fund, which in turn cause realized capital gains and a tax liability to accrue to investors who maintain their holding.

New investors in the fund may assume a tax liability even though they realized no gains, that is, all shareholders as of the date of record receive a full year's worth of dividends and capital gains distributions, even if they have owned shares for only one day. This lack of control over capital gains taxes is regarded as a major limitation of mutual funds. In fact, this adverse tax consequence is one of the reasons suggested for a closed-end company's price selling below par value. Also, this adverse tax consequence is one reason for the popularity of the exchange-traded funds discussed later.

Of course, the investor must also pay ordinary income taxes on distributions of income. Finally, when the fund investors sell the fund, they realize long-term or short-term capital gains or losses, depending on whether they held the fund for at least a year.

REGULATION OF FUNDS

Four major laws or acts relate either indirectly or directly to mutual funds. The Securities Act of 1933 provides purchasers of new issues of securities with information regarding the issuer and, thus, helps prevent fraud. Because open-end investment companies issue new shares on a continuous basis, mutual funds must also comply with the 1933 Act. The Securities Act of 1934 is concerned with the trading of securities after issuance, with the regulation of exchanges, and with the regulation of broker/dealers. Mutual fund portfolio managers must comply with the 1934 Act in their transactions.

All investment companies with 100 or more shareholders must register with the SEC according to the Investment Company Act of 1940. The primary purposes of the 1940 Act are to reduce investment company selling abuses and to ensure that investors receive sufficient and accurate information. Investment companies must provide periodic financial reports and disclose their investment policies to investors. The 1940 Act prohibits changes in the nature of an investment company's fundamental investment policies without the approval of shareholders. This act also provides some tax advantages for eligible regulated investment companies (RIC). The purchase and sale of mutual fund shares must meet the requirements of fair dealing that the SEC 1940 Act and the National Association of Securities Dealers (NASD), a self-regulatory organization, established for all securities transactions in the United States.

Finally, the Investment Advisors Act of 1940 specifies the registration requirements and practices of companies and individuals who provide investment advisory services. This act deals with registered investment advisors (RIAs). Overall, even though an investment company must comply with all aspects of the 1940 Act, it is also subject to the 1933 Act, the 1934 Act, and the Investment Advisors Act of 1940.

An important feature of the 1940 Act exempts any company that qualifies as a "regulated investment company" from taxation on its gains, either from income or capital appreciation. As stated earlier, to qualify as an RIC, the fund must distribute to its shareholders 90% of its net income excluding capital gains each year. Furthermore, the fund must follow certain rules about the diversification and liquidity of its investments, and the degree of short-term trading and short-term capital gains.

ALTERNATIVES TO MUTUAL FUNDS

Due to the success of mutual funds, investment management companies developed several alternatives to mutual funds. The major alternatives include exchange-traded funds, segregated accounts, and folios.

Exchange-Traded Funds Although the popularity of mutual funds grew with individual investors during the 1980s and 1990s, mutual funds are often criticized for two reasons. First, mutual funds shares are priced at, and can be transacted only at, the end-of-the-day or closing price. Specifically, transactions (i.e., purchases and sales) cannot be made at intraday prices, but only at closing prices. The second issue relates to taxes and the investors' control over taxes. As noted earlier, withdrawals by some fund shareholders may cause taxable realized capital gains for shareholders who maintain their positions.

During 1993, a new investment vehicle with many of the same features of mutual funds but that responded to these two limitations was introduced. This investment vehicle, called **exchange-traded funds (ETFs)**, consists of investment companies that are similar to mutual funds but trade like stocks on an exchange. Even though they are open-end funds, ETFs are, in a sense, similar to closed-end funds, which have small premiums or discounts from their NAV. Through 2000, these ETFs were based only on U.S. and international stock indexes and subindexes, not actively managed portfolios or funds. In addition to broad stock indexes, ETFs are also based on style, sector, and industry-oriented indexes.

In an ETF, the investment advisor assumes responsibility for maintaining the portfolio such that it replicates the index and the index's return accurately.[6] Because supply and demand determine the secondary market price of these shares, the exchange price may deviate slightly from the value of the portfolio and, as a result, may provide some imprecision in pricing. Deviations remain small, however, because arbitrageurs can create or redeem large blocks of shares on any day at NAV, significantly limiting the deviations.

Along with being able to transact in ETFs at current prices throughout the day comes the flexibility to place limit orders, stop orders, and orders to short sell and buy on margin, none of which can be done with open-end mutual funds. These types of orders are discussed in Chapter 7.

The other major distinction between open-end mutual funds and ETFs relates to taxation. For both open-end funds and ETFs, dividend income and capital gains realized when the funds or ETFs are transacted are taxable to the investor. However, in addition, in the case of redemptions, open-end mutual funds may have to sell securities (if the cash position is not sufficient to fund the redemptions), thus causing a capital gain or loss for those who held their shares. ETFs, on the other hand, do not have to sell portfolio securities because redemptions are effected by an in-kind exchange of the ETF shares for a basket of the underlying portfolio securities—not a taxable event to the investors. Therefore, investors in ETFs are subject to significant capital gains taxes only when they sell their ETF shares (at a price above the original purchase price). However, ETFs do distribute cash dividends and may distribute a limited amount of realized capital gains and these distributions are taxable. Overall, ETFs, like index mutual funds, avoid realized capital gains and the taxation thereof due to their low portfolio turnover. But unlike index mutual funds (or other funds for that matter), they do not cause potentially large capital gains tax liabilities that accrue to those who held their positions in order to meet shareholder redemptions due to the unique way in which they are redeemed.

The earliest and currently the most popular ETFs include the following:

- *SPDRS*—pronounced "Spiders" for Standard and Poor's Depository Receipts; ticker symbol: SPY; tracks the S&P500
- *DIAMONDS*—diamonds; ticker symbol: DIA; tracks the Dow Jones Industrial Average

---

[6] Early investment advisors in ETFs include State Street Global Advisors and Barclays Global Investors.

- *WEBS*—World Equity Benchmarks; tracks the Morgan Stanley Capital International indexes of various countries; recently renamed *iShares MSCI*
- *QQQs*—often called Qubes; ticker symbol: QQQ; tracks the Nasdaq 100 index
- *i Shares*—provided by Barclays Global Investors; tracks 42 different stock indexes

Segregated (Separately Managed) Accounts   Many high net worth individuals object to mutual funds because of their lack of control over taxes, their lack of any input into investment decisions, and the absence of "high touch" service. The use of separate accounts respond to all these limitations of mutual funds, although they are more expensive. Previously, money managers managed separate accounts for only large portfolios, typically $1 million and more. Currently, however, many money managers are significantly decreasing the minimum size of their separately managed accounts. As a result, many investors with mid-sized portfolios use segregated, individually managed accounts provided by many companies and other investment managers. Typically, asset managers earn higher fees on separately managed accounts but also have higher service costs relative to mutual funds.

Folios   A recent Internet-based product offers a variety of preselected portfolios consistent with any particular investment strategy investors may desire. For instance, it offers a preselected large cap equity growth portfolio, a small cap equity value portfolio, and so on. These preselected portfolios are called **folios**. Investors can also alter the portfolio selections if they choose. After an investor selects and alters one of these portfolios, the portfolio can be transacted through an Internet service at a discount price. Folios are being marketed as an alternative to mutual funds.[7]

◆ PENSION FUNDS

Pension funds, which exist in some form in all developed economies, are major institutional investors and participants in the financial markets. A pension plan fund is established for the eventual payment of retirement benefits. The entities that establish pension plans—called **plan sponsors**—may be private business entities acting for their employees (called corporate or private plans); federal, state, and local entities on behalf of their employees (called *public plans*); unions on behalf of their members (called *Taft-Hartley plans*); and individuals for themselves (called *individually sponsored plans*). The two largest government-sponsored funds are California Public Employees Retirement System and New York State Common Retirement Fund with assets of approximately $156 billion and $111 billion, respectively.

Pension funds are financed by contributions from the employer. In some plans, employers match employee contributions to some degree. The great success of private pension plans is somewhat surprising because the system involves investing in an asset—the pension contract—which for the most part is very illiquid. It cannot be used, not even as collateral, until retirement. The key factor explaining pension fund growth is that the employer's contributions and a specified amount of the employee's contributions, as well as the earnings of the fund's assets, are tax exempt. In essence, a pension is a form of employee remuneration for which the employee is not taxed until funds are withdrawn. This tax exemption results from meeting many federal requirements (such plans are called *qualified* pension plans). Pension funds also traditionally

7   Jim McTague, "Basket Weaver," *Barron's* (August 7, 2000), pp. F6–8; and Patrick McGeehan and Danny Hakim, "Online Funds, Built to Order," *New York Times* (August 13, 2000), Money & Business section 3, p. 1.

serve to discourage employees from quitting, because the employer, until vested, could lose at least the accumulation resulting from the employer contribution.

TYPES OF PENSION PLANS

Two basic and widely used types of pension plans are defined benefit plans and defined contribution plans. In addition, a hybrid type of plan, called a cash balance plan, combines features of both pension plan types.

Defined Benefit Plan   In a **defined benefit (DB) plan**, the plan sponsor agrees to make specified dollar payments annually to qualifying employees beginning at retirement (and some payments to beneficiaries in case of death before retirement). These payments typically occur monthly. The retirement payments are determined by a formula that usually takes into account the length of service of the employee and the employee's earnings. The pension obligations are effectively a debt obligation of the plan sponsor. The plan sponsor, thus, assumes the risk of having insufficient funds in the plan to satisfy the regular contractual payments that must be made to retired employees.

A plan sponsor establishing a defined benefit plan can use the payments made into the fund to purchase an annuity policy from a life insurance company. Defined benefit plans that are guaranteed by life insurance products are called insured plans. An insured plan is not necessarily safer than a noninsured plan, because it depends on the ability of the life insurance company to make the contractual payments, whereas the uninsured plan depends on the ability of the plan sponsor. Whether a private pension plan is insured or noninsured, a federal agency, the Pension Benefit Guaranty Corporation (PBGC), which was established in 1974 by the ERISA legislation, insures the vested benefits of participants.

Benefits become vested when employees reach a certain age and complete enough years of service so that they meet the minimum requirements for receiving benefits upon retirement. The payment of benefits is not contingent upon a participant's continuation with the employer or union.

Defined Contribution Plan   In a **defined contribution (DC) plan**, the plan sponsor is responsible only for making specified contributions into the plan on behalf of qualifying participants, not specified payments to the employee after retirement. The amount contributed is typically either a percentage of the employee's salary and/or a percentage of the employer's profits. The plan sponsor does not guarantee any specific amount at retirement. The payments that will be made to qualifying participants upon retirement depend on the growth of the plan assets. That is, retirement benefit payments are determined by the investment performance of the funds in which the assets are invested and are not guaranteed by the plan sponsor. The plan sponsor gives the participants various options as to the investment vehicles in which they may invest. Defined contribution pension plans come in several legal forms: 401(k) plans, money purchase pension plans, and employee stock ownership plans (ESOPs).

By far the fastest-growing sector of the defined contribution plan is the 401(k) plan, or its equivalents in the nonprofit sector, the 403(b) plan, and in the public sector, the 457 plan. To the firm, this kind of plan offers the lowest costs and the least administrative problems. The employer makes a specified contribution to a specific plan/program, and the employee chooses how it is invested.[8] To the employee, the plan is attractive because it offers some control over how the pension money is managed. In

---

8   "Calling It Quits," *Institutional Investor* (February 1991), p. 125.

fact, plan sponsors frequently offer participants the opportunity to invest in one or more of a family of mutual funds. More than half of all defined contribution plans in public institutions such as state governments use mutual funds, and the percentage of private corporations that use this approach is even higher. By the end of 1999, more than $1 trillion had been placed in 401(k) accounts, and the big mutual funds were attracting the bulk of the new money flowing into these accounts.

Employees in the public and corporate sectors responded favorably, and almost half of all assets in DC pensions are now invested in mutual funds, with the bulk of the money placed in funds emphasizing equities and growth.[9] Regulations issued by the U.S. Department of Labor require firms to offer their employees a set of distinctive choices, a development that has further encouraged pension plans to opt for the mutual fund approach because families of mutual funds can readily provide investment vehicles offering different investment objectives.[10]

Several fundamental differences separate defined benefit plans from defined contribution plans. In the defined benefit plan, the plan sponsor guarantees the retirement benefits, makes the investment choices, and bears the investment risk if the investments do not earn enough to fund the guaranteed retirement benefits. On the other hand, in a defined contribution plan, the employer does not guarantee any retirement benefits, but the employer does agree to make specified contributions to the employee's account; the employee selects the investment options; and the employee retirement payments come from the return on the investment portfolio plus, of course, the employee and employer contributions.

Hybrid Pensions Plans   Defined benefit pension plans are cumbersome for the plan sponsor to administer and are not portable from one job to another by employees in an increasingly mobile workforce. Defined contribution plans put the investment choices and investment risk on the employee. In response to these and other limitations, forms of **hybrid pension plans**, or combinations of defined benefit and defined contribution plans developed. Although several types of hybrid plans include pension equity, floor-offset, and others, the most common hybrid form is the cash balance plan.

Cash Balance Pension Plan   A **cash balance pension plan** is basically a defined benefit with some of the features of a defined contribution plan. A cash balance plan defines future pension benefits, not employer contributions. Retirement benefits are based on a fixed-amount annual employer contribution and a guaranteed minimum annual investment return. Each participant's account in a cash balance plan is credited with a dollar amount that resembles an employer contribution and is generally determined as a percentage of pay. Each participant's account is also credited with interest linked to some fixed or variable index such as the consumer price index (CPI). The plan usually provides benefits in the form of a lump sum distribution such as an annuity. Interest is credited to the employee's account at a rate specified in the plan and is unrelated to the investment earnings of the employer's pension trust. The employee's benefit does not vary based on the interest credit. The promised benefits are fixed, and the investment gains or losses are borne by the employer. However, like in a defined contribution plan, an individual employee can monitor his or her cash balance plan "account" in a regular statement.

Also like a defined contribution plan, and important to today's job-changing workforce, many cash balance plans allow the employee to take a lump sum payment of

9 "Taking a Fancy to Mutual Funds," *Institutional Investor* (May 1992), p. 119.
10 "The Communication Cloud over 401(k)s," *Institutional Investor* (September 1991), p. 189.

vested benefits when terminating, which can be rolled over into an IRA or to the new employer's plan. That is, cash balance plans are portable from one job to another.

REGULATION

Because pension plans are so important for U.S. workers, Congress passed comprehensive legislation in 1974 to regulate pension plans. This legislation, the Employee Retirement Income Security Act of 1974 (ERISA), is fairly technical in its details. For our purposes, it is necessary only to understand its major provisions.

First, ERISA established **funding standards** for the minimum contributions that a plan sponsor must make to the pension plan to satisfy the actuarially projected benefit payments. Prior to the enactment of ERISA, many corporate plan sponsors followed a pay-as-you-go funding policy. That is, when an employee retired, the corporate plan sponsor took the necessary retirement benefits out of current cash flow. Under ERISA, such a practice is no longer allowed, rather the program must be funded; that is, regular contributions to an investment pool along with investment earnings must be sufficient to pay the employee retirement benefits.

Second, ERISA established **fiduciary standards** for pension fund trustees, managers, or advisors. Specifically, all parties responsible for the management of a pension fund are guided by the judgment of what is called a "prudent man" in seeking to determine which investments are proper. Because a trustee is responsible for other people's money, it is necessary to make sure that the trustee takes the role seriously. To fulfill their responsibilities, trustees must act as a reasonably prudent person to acquire and use the information pertinent to making an investment decision.

Third, ERISA establishes minimum **vesting standards**. For example, the law specifies that, after 5 years of employment, a plan participant is entitled to 25% of accrued pension benefits. The percentage of entitlement increases to 100% after 10 years. Additional vesting requirements are noted in ERISA.

Finally, ERISA created the Pension Benefit Guaranty Corporation (PBGC) to insure vested pension benefits. The insurance program is funded from annual premiums that must be paid by pension plans.

Responsibility for administering ERISA is delegated to the Department of Labor and the Internal Revenue Service. To ensure that a pension plan is in compliance with ERISA, periodic reporting and disclosure statements must be filed with these government agencies. It is important to recognize that ERISA does not require that a corporation establish a pension plan. If a corporation does establish a defined benefit plan, however, it must comply with the numerous and complex regulations set forth in ERISA.

MANAGERS OF PENSION FUNDS

A plan sponsor chooses one of the following to manage the defined benefit pension assets under its control: (1) use in-house staff to manage all the pension assets itself; (2) distribute the pension assets to one or more money management firms to manage; or (3) combine alternatives 1 and 2. In the case of a defined contribution pension plan, the plan sponsor typically allows participants to select how to allocate their contributions among funds managed by one or more fund groups.[11]

We discussed earlier insurance company involvement in the pension business through their issuance of GICs and annuities. Insurance companies also operate

---

[11] Keith Ambachtsheer, Ronald Capelle, and Tom Scheibelhut, "Improving Pension Fund Performance," *Financial Analysts Journal* (November/December 1998), pp. 15ff; and Francis Gupta, Eric Stubbs, and Yogi Thambiah, "U.S. Corporate Pension Plans," *The Journal of Portfolio Management* (Summer 2000), pp. 65ff.

subsidiaries that manage pension funds. The trust departments of commercial banks, affiliates of investment banks and broker/dealers, and independent money management firms (that is, firms not affiliated with an insurance company, bank, investment bank or broker dealer) also manage pension funds. Foreign entities are also permitted to participate in the management of pension funds. In fact, several foreign financial institutions acquired interests in U.S. money management firms in order to enter the pension fund money management business. Managers of pension fund money obtain their income from managing the assets by charging a fee.

In addition to money managers, advisors called plan sponsor consultants provide a number of services to pension plan sponsors, including the following:

- Develop plan investment policy and asset allocation among the major asset classes.
- Provide actuarial advice (liability modeling and forecasting).
- Design benchmarks against which the fund's money managers will be measured.
- Measure and monitor the performance of the fund's money managers.
- Search for and recommend money managers to pension plans.
- Provide specialized research.

◆ FOUNDATIONS

Foundations are another group of institutions with funds to invest in financial markets. These institutions were mainly set up by wealthy individuals and families for the benefit of universities, private schools, hospitals, religious institutions, museums, and other institutions. The initial bequest and the investment income thereon is used to gift funds to these beneficiaries. The investment income generated from the funds invested is also used for the operation of the foundation.

Most of the large foundations in the United States are independent of any firm or governmental group. Some foundations are company sponsored or linked to certain communities. Still others are termed *operating foundations* because they award most of their gifts to their own units rather than to organizations outside the foundations. The two largest foundations are The Ford Foundation and the Lily Endowment.

As with pension funds, qualified foundations are exempt from taxation. The board of trustees of the foundation, just like the plan sponsor for a pension fund, specifies the investment objectives and the acceptable investment alternatives. The endowment funds can either be managed in-house or by external money managers. The same organizations that manage money for pension funds also manage funds for foundations.

Typically, the managers of a foundation's funds invest in long-term assets with the primary goal of safeguarding the principal of the fund. For this reason, foundations tend to favor those equities that offer a steady dividend and comparatively little price volatility. Also, foundations often invest in government bonds and corporate bonds of high quality. The second goal, and an important one, is to generate a stream of earnings that allows the foundation to perform its functions of supporting certain operations or institutions.

Summary

In general, insurance companies bear risk from parties who wish to avert risk by transferring it to the insurance companies. The party seeking to transfer the risk pays an insurance premium to the insurance company. Insurance companies pay the insured if and/or when the insured event occurs. Because insurance companies collect premiums initially and pay the claims later, the initial revenues are invested in a portfolio, and portfolio returns become another important revenue for the insurance company. Consequently, insurance companies are financial intermediaries that function as risk bearers. The events insured can be death (insured by life insurance companies), health problems (health insurance companies), or housing or automobile damage (property and casualty insurance companies). In addition, different types of insurance cover different types of risks. Insurance companies are also active in providing retirement and investment products. These different types of insurance liabilities reflect different types of risks and, therefore, the investment portfolios of these types of insurance companies differ significantly.

Investment companies sell shares to the public and invest the proceeds in a diversified portfolio of securities, with each share representing a proportionate interest in the underlying portfolio of securities. The three types of investment companies are open-end or mutual funds, closed-end funds, and unit trusts. A wide range of funds with many different investment objectives is available. Securities law requires that a fund clearly set forth its investment objective in its prospectus, and the objective identifies the type or types of assets the fund will purchase and hold.

Mutual funds and closed-end funds provide two crucial economic functions associated with financial intermediaries—risk reduction via diversification and lower costs of contracting and information processing. Money market funds allow shareholders to write checks against their shares, thus providing a payments mechanism, another economic function of financial intermediaries.

Mutual funds are extensively regulated, with most of that regulation occurring at the federal level. The key legislation is the Investment Company Act of 1940. The most important feature regarding regulation is that the funds are exempt from taxation on their gains if the gains are distributed to investors within a relatively short period of time. Even allowing for that special tax-free status, it is necessary to recognize that regulations apply to many features of the funds' administration, including sales fees, asset management, degree of diversification, distributions, and advertising.

In recent years, consumer-investor acceptance of the concept of family (or group or complex) of funds enjoyed widespread growth. That is, an investment advisory company manages dozens of different funds that span the spectrum of potential investment objectives from aggressive growth to balanced income to international diversification. Competitors to mutual funds include variable annuities, exchange-traded funds (ETFs), segregated accounts, and Internet-executed folios.

A pension plan is a fund established by private employers, governments, or unions for the payment of retirement benefits. Favorable tax treatment helped pension plans grow rapidly. Qualified pension funds are exempt from federal income taxes, as are employer contributions. The two types of pension funds are defined benefit plans and defined contribution plans. A defined benefit plan sponsor agrees to make specified (or defined) payments to qualifying employees at retirement. In the defined contribution plan the sponsor is responsible only for making specified (or defined) contributions into the plan on behalf of qualifying employees, but does not guarantee any specific amount at retirement. Some hybrid plans blend features of both basic types of plans, the most prominent of which is the cash balance plan.

Federal regulation of pension funds is embodied in the Employee Retirement Income Security Act of 1974 (ERISA). ERISA sets minimum standards for employer contributions, establishes rules of prudent management, and requires vesting in a specified period of time. Also, ERISA provides for insurance of vested benefits.

Pension funds are managed by the plan sponsor and/or by management firms hired by the sponsor. Management fees may reflect the amount of money being managed or the performance of the managers in achieving suitable rates of return for the funds. In addition, consulting firms provide assistance in the planning, administration, and evaluation of the funds.

Key Terms ▪▪

- Active funds
- Annuity
- Back-end load
- Bankassurance
- Cash balance pension plan
- Closed-end fund
- Contingent deferred sales charge (CDSC)
- Defined benefit plan (DB)
- Defined contribution plan (DC)
- Demutualization
- Direct distribution
- Exchange-traded funds (ETFs)
- Expense ratio
- Family of funds
- Fiduciary standards
- Folios
- Front-end load
- Funding standards
- Funds of funds
- General account products
- Guaranteed Investment Contract (GIC)

- Hybrid pension plans
- Insurance premium
- Investment advisory fee
- Level load
- Life and health insurance company (L&H company)
- Load
- Management fee
- Mortality and expense fee
- Multiline insurance
- Mutual funds
- Mutual insurance companies
- Net asset value (NAV)
- No-load mutual funds
- Nonparticipating policies
- Open-end funds
- Operating expense
- Participating policy
- Passive (or indexed) funds
- Plan sponsors
- Property and casualty (P&C) insurance company

- Regulated investment company (RIC)
- Risk bearers
- Salesforce (wholesale) distribution
- Second-to-die insurance
- Separate account products
- Shareholder fee (or sales charge)
- Statutory surplus (or reserves)
- Stock insurance company
- Subadvisor
- Survivorship insurance
- Term insurance
- 12b-1 fee
- Unbundling
- Underwriting process
- Unit trusts
- Universal life
- Variable life insurance
- Vesting standards
- Whole life insurance

Questions ▪▪▪

1. a. What are the major sources of revenue for an insurance company?
   b. How are its profits determined?
2. Name the major types of insurance and investment-oriented products sold by insurance companies.
3. a. What is a GIC?
   b. Does a GIC carry a "guarantee" like a government obligation?
4. What are some key differences between a mutual fund and an annuity?
5. Why should a purchaser of life insurance be concerned about the credit rating of his or her insurance company?
6. What is the statutory surplus and why is it an important measure for an insurance company?
7. What is bankassurance?
8. a. What is meant by *demutualization*?
   b. What are the perceived advantages of demutualization?
9. a. What are term insurance, whole life insurance, variable life insurance, universal life insurance, and survivorship insurance?
   b. Why are all participating policies written in an insurance company's general account?
10. Whose liabilities are harder to predict, life and health insurers or property and casualty insurers? Explain why.
11. How does the Financial Modernization Act of 1999 affect the insurance industry?
12. An investment company has $1.05 million of assets, $50,000 of liabilities, and 10,000 shares outstanding.
    a. What is its NAV?
    b. Suppose the fund pays off its liabilities while at the same time the value of its assets double. How many shares will a deposit of $5,000 receive?

13. "The NAV of an open-end fund is determined continuously throughout the trading day." Explain why you agree or disagree with this statement.
14. What are closed-end funds?
15. Why might the price of a share of a closed-end fund diverge from its NAV?
16. What is the difference between a unit trust and a closed-end fund?
17. a. Describe the following: front-end load, back-end load, level load, 12b-1 fee, management fee.
    b. Why do mutual funds have different classes of shares?
18. What is a fund of funds?
19. What costs are incurred by a mutual fund?
20. Why might the investor in a mutual fund be faced with a potential tax liability arising from capital gains even though the investor did not benefit from such a gain?
21. Does an investment company provide any economic function that individual investors cannot provide for themselves on their own? Explain your answer.
22. a. How can a fund qualify as a regulated investment company?
    b. What is the benefit in gaining RIC status?
23. a. What is an exchange-traded fund?
    b. What are the advantages of an exchange-traded fund relative to open-end and closed-end investment companies?
24. Briefly describe the following:
    a. Wrap program
    b. Folios
    c. Segregated accounts
25. What is meant by a plan sponsor?
26. a. What is the difference between a defined contribution plan and a defined benefit plan?
    b. What is a hybrid pension plan?
27. a. What are the attractive features of a 401(k) plan?
    b. What role can a mutual fund play in this kind of plan?
28. What is meant by an insured pension plan?
29. What is the function of the Pension Benefit Guaranty Corporation?
30. a. What is the major legislation regulating pension funds?
    b. Does this legislation require that a corporation establish a pension fund?
31. What is the meaning of ERISA's "prudent man" rule?

CHAPTER 5

Investment Banking Firms

Learning Objectives

After reading this chapter you will understand:

◆ the nature of the investment banking business.

◆ the revenue-generating activities of investment banks.

◆ the activities of investment banking firms that require them to commit their own capital.

◆ the role investment bankers play in the underwriting of securities.

◆ the different types of underwriting arrangements.

◆ the difference between riskless arbitrage and risk arbitrage.

◆ the various roles investment bankers play in mergers and acquisitions.

◆ what is meant by merchant banking.

◆ why investment banking firms create and trade risk control instruments.

In this chapter, we look at investment banking firms and the key role that they play in capital markets. Investment banking firms perform two general functions. For corporations, U.S. government agencies, state and local governments, and foreign entities (sovereigns and corporations) that need funds, investment banking firms assist in obtaining those funds. For investors who wish to invest funds, investment banking firms act as brokers or dealers in the buying and selling of securities. Thus, investment banking firms perform a critical role in the primary market and the secondary market.

◆ INVESTMENT BANKING

Investment banking is performed by two groups: securities firms and commercial banks. **Securities firms** do not only distribute newly issued securities but are involved in the secondary market as makers and brokers. As discussed in Chapter 3, prior to 1999 the Glass-Steagall Act separated the activities of commercial banks, investment banks, and insurance companies and thereby restricted the types of securities that commercial banks in the United States could underwrite.[1] This act regulated the industry since the Great Depression. The Gramm-Leach-Bliley Financial Services Modernization Act of 1999 (GLB) supplanted the Glass-Steagall Act and eliminated the restrictions on the

---

[1] No restrictions were placed on the investment activities of commercial banks outside the United States.

activities conducted by companies in each financial sector. Now commercial banks as well as insurance companies can underwrite securities.

Table 5-1 shows a selective list of major national U.S. investment banks, major non-U.S. investment banks, and regional firms. The list shown in the table changes rapidly due to mergers and acquisitions.[2] In Japan, the major securities houses—popularly referred to as the Big Four—are Nomura, Daiwa, Yamaichi, and Nikko. These firms are actively involved in the underwriting of securities in the United States and Europe.

Investment banking firms are highly leveraged companies, that is, the amount of borrowed funds relative to the amount of equity is high. As we explain the activities in which investment banking firms are engaged, you will see why investment banks exhibit

TABLE 5-1 Selective List of Investment Banks

Major National U.S. Investment Banks

Merrill Lynch & Co.
Goldman Sachs & Co.
Morgan Stanley Dean Witter
Lehman Brothers
Salmon Smith Barney, Inc. (part of Citigroup)
Chase H&Q
   • J. P. Morgan & Co.
Bear, Stearns & Co. Inc.
Bank of America

Major Non-U.S. Investment Banks

UBS Warburg LLC
   • Dillion Read
   • Paine Webber
Credit Suisse First Boston Corporation
   • Donaldson, Lufkin & Jenrette
ABN AMRO Incorporated
CIBC World Markets
   • Oppenheimer Securities
Deutsche Bank
   • Banker's Trust
   • Alex Brown
Barclays Bank

Regional Firms

Jeffries & Company, Inc.
SG Cowen
U.S. Bankcorp Piper Jeffray
Robertson Stephens (subsidiary of Fleet Financial)

Note: As of June 20, 2001.

---

[2] At one time a popular classification of U.S. securities firms involved in the underwriting of securities included bulge-bracket firms, major bracket firms, submajor bracket firms, and regional firms. *Bulge-bracket firms* were viewed as the premier investment banking firms because of their size, reputation, presence in key markets, and customer base. Large investment banking firms without the same status as the bulge-bracket firms but nevertheless providing full-line services were called *major bracket firms. Submajor bracket firms* were frequently New York-based firms that catered to smaller issuing companies. Firms located outside New York that served regional issuers (corporate and local governments) were classified as *regional firms.*

such an appetite for capital. The increasing need for capital resulted in consolidation of firms in the industry and a change in many firms from the partnership structure to the corporate structure, which gives firms easier access to public funds. In addition to needing long-term sources of capital, investment banking firms borrow on a short-term basis to finance their inventory of securities. The primary means for borrowing on a short-term basis is the repurchase agreement, a form of collateralized borrowing. We will discuss repurchase agreements in Chapter 20.

Investment banking firms generate revenue from commissions, fee income, spread income, and principal activities. Specifically, these activities can be classified as follows:

- Public offering (underwriting) of securities
- Trading of securities
- Private placement of securities
- Securitization of assets
- Mergers and acquisitions
- Merchant banking
- Trading and creation of derivative instruments
- Money management

Not all investment banking firms are involved in each of these activities. In the 1980s, the philosophy in the industry was to throw people, money, and other resources at developing a market share in each of these activities, that is, to provide a full line of services. Investment banking firms today do not follow this philosophy as they reevaluate the economics of being in certain lines of business.

PUBLIC OFFERING (UNDERWRITING) OF SECURITIES

The traditional role associated with investment banking is the underwriting of securities. Entities that issue securities include agencies of the U.S. government, state and local governments, corporations, supranational entities, foreign governments, and foreign corporations.

The traditional process in the United States for issuing new securities involves investment bankers performing one or more of the following three functions:

1. Advising the issuer on the terms and the timing of the offering
2. Buying the securities from the issuer
3. Distributing the issue to the public

The advisor role may require investment bankers to design a security structure that is more palatable to investors than a particular traditional instrument. For example, the high interest rates in the United States in the late 1970s and early 1980s increased the cost of borrowing for issuers of even the highest quality rating. To reduce the cost of borrowing for their clients, investment bankers designed securities with characteristics that were more attractive to investors but not onerous to issuers. They also designed security structures for low-quality bond issues, so-called high-yield or junk bond structures. We will give several examples of these financial innovations in later chapters.

In the sale of new securities, investment bankers need not undertake the second function of buying the securities from the issuer. An investment banker may merely act as an advisor and/or distributor of the new security. The function of buying the securities from the issuer is called **underwriting**. When an investment banking firm buys the securities from the issuer and accepts the risk of selling the securities to investors at a lower price, it is referred to as an underwriter. When the investment banking firm agrees to buy the securities from the issuer at a set price, the underwriting arrangement is referred to as a **firm commitment**. The risk that the investment banking firm accepts in a firm commitment underwriting arrangement is that the price it pays to purchase the securities from the issuer will be less than the price it receives when it reoffers the securities to the public. In contrast, in a **best-efforts underwriting** arrangement, the investment banking firm agrees only to use its expertise to sell the securities, it does not buy the entire issue from the issuer.

The fee earned from underwriting a security is the difference between the price paid to the issuer and the price at which the investment bank reoffers the security to the public. This difference is called the **gross spread**, or the **underwriter discount**. Numerous factors affect the size of the gross spread.[3] Typical gross spreads for common stock offerings, **initial public offerings (IPOs)**, and fixed-income offerings are shown in Table 5-2. IPOs are typically common stock offerings issued by companies that had not previously issued common stock to the public. Because of the risk associated with pricing and then placing IPOs, the gross spread is higher.

The typical underwritten transaction involves so much risk of capital loss that for a single investment banking firm to undertake it alone would expose it to the danger of losing a significant portion of its capital. To share this risk, an investment banking firm puts together a group of firms to underwrite the issue. This group of firms is called an **underwriting syndicate**. The gross spread is then divided among the lead underwriter(s) and the other firms in the underwriting syndicate. The lead underwriter manages the deal ("runs the books" for the deal). In many cases more than one may act as lead underwriter, in which case they are said to "co-lead" or "co-manage" the deal. In a bond transaction, the lead underwriters customarily receive 20% of the gross spread as compensation for managing the deal.[4]

To realize the gross spread, the entire securities issue must be sold to the public at the planned reoffering price, which usually requires a great deal of marketing muscle. Investment banking firms attempt to sell the securities to their investor client base (retail and institutional). To increase the potential investor base, the lead underwriter puts together a **selling group**. This group includes the underwriting syndicate plus other firms not in the syndicate. Members of the selling group can buy the security at a **concession price** (i.e., a price less than the reoffering price). The gross spread is thereby divided among the lead underwriter, members of the underwriting syndicate, and members of the selling group.

The underwriting of securities is not limited to offerings in the United States. An issuer can select among many foreign securities markets to identify the one in which to offer securities to reduce its cost of funds. Indeed, some securities are offered simultaneously in several markets throughout the world.

Investment bankers also may assist in offering the securities of government-owned companies to private investors. This process is referred to as **privatization**. An example is the initial public offering of the U.S. government-owned railroad company Conrail in March 1987. More than 58 million shares were sold, raising a total of $1.65 billion. It was the largest IPO in the history of this country. Prior to the Conrail IPO, AT&T raised $1.5 billion in 1983. Non-U.S. examples include the United Kingdom's British Telecom, Chile's Pacifica, and France's Paribas. In the case of British Telecom (the

---

3   For a discussion of these factors, see G. Clyde Buck, "Spreads and Fees in Investment Banking." Chapter 5 in Robert Lawrence Kuhn (ed.), *The Library of Investment Banking, Volume II* (Homewood, IL: Dow Jones-Irwin, 1990).

4   Ernest Block, *Inside Investment Banking* (Homewood, IL: Dow Jones-Irwin, 1989), p. 323.

TABLE 5-2 Gross Spread by Offering Size During 1999: Stocks and Bonds

Initial Public Offerings of Stocks

Size of Individual Issue ($ Millions)	Total Principal Issued in the Range ($ Millions)	Issue Market Share	Number of Issues	Total Gross Spread over All Issues ($ Millions)	Gross Spread as a % of Principal
10–30	1,256.5	1.8%	64	83.2	6.62%
30–60	8,381.2	11.9%	186	564.8	6.74%
60–150	19,897.9	28.2%	222	1,326.3	6.67%
150+	40,999.4	58.1%	75	1,829.7	4.46%
Industry Total	70,534.9	100.0%	547	3,804.0	5.39%

Secondary Common Stock Offerings

Size of Individual Issue ($ Millions)	Total Principal Issued in the Range ($ Millions)	Issue Market Share	Number of Issues	Total Gross Spread over All Issues ($ Millions)	Gross Spread as a % of Principal
10–30	821.6	0.8%	39	46.4	5.65%
30–60	3,729.7	3.7%	81	199.0	5.34%
60–150	13,568.9	13.6%	136	662.2	4.88%
150+	81,908.1	81.9%	183	2,605.0	3.18%
Industry Total	100,028.3	100.0%	439	3,512.6	3.51%

Fixed Income Offerings*

Size of Individual Issue ($ Millions)	Total Principal Issued in the Range ($ Millions)	Issue Market Share	Number of Issues	Total Gross Spread over All Issues ($ Millions)	Gross Spread as a % of Principal
0–500	152,293.1	73.8%	1,221	763.4	0.50%
500–5,000	54,048.9	26.2%	65	286.2	0.53%
Industry Total	206,342.0	100.0%	1,286	1,049.6	0.51%

*Characteristics of included issues: underwritten, public, nonconvertible, U.S. corporate, bullet, issue size under $5 billion.

Source: Prepared for the authors by Thomson Financial Securities Data.

government-owned telephone company of the United Kingdom), the amount raised was $4.7 billion. This global offering was offered simultaneously in several countries.

In the 1990s, the role of investment bankers in placing the securities of government-owned companies into the hands of private investors increased. Eastern Europe, for example, followed a major program of privatization. In Chapter 6, we will describe the process of underwriting securities and the risks associated with this activity.

In the industry, investment banking firms that underwrite securities in the different areas are ranked by some measure of market share, referred to as the "league tables." Investment bankers view this rating as a key indicator of their importance in a market sector. Market share can be measured by one of the following: the number of deals done in a year, or the total dollar volume of all deals done in a year. However, it is not that simple. Recall that in an underwriting an investment banking firm may be the lead manager, co-manager, or just a member of the underwriting syndicate. Consequently, ranking by number of deals or total dollar volume of deals can be made by giving full credit only to the lead manager or some proportional credit to each manager. Some industry observers believe that measures such as the number of deals and the total dollar volume of deals are not completely adequate. One reason is that it is necessary to know how a transaction translates into profits. To draw an analogy to manufacturing, having the largest market share for a product does not necessarily mean the largest profit, particularly if the product is underpriced and/or the cost structure reflects operating inefficiencies. Returning to investment banking firms, the assembly of high-priced human capital coupled with a desire to buy market share by accepting lower gross spreads in the underwriting of some types of securities may cause some firms to be ranked number one in that area using the measures described. This underwriting revenue may not necessarily flow through to the bottom line, however.

TRADING OF SECURITIES

A successful underwriting of a security requires a strong salesforce. The salesforce provides feedback on advance interest in the deal, and the traders (or market makers) provide input in pricing the deal as well.

It would be a mistake to think that once the securities are all sold the investment banking firm's ties with the deal are ended. In the case of bonds, those who bought the securities will look to the investment banking firm to make a market in the issue. Therefore, the investment banking firm must be willing to take a principal position in secondary market transactions. Revenue from this activity is generated through (1) the difference between the price at which the investment banking firm sells the security and the price paid for the securities (called the bid-ask spread), and (2) appreciation of the price of the securities held in inventory. Obviously, if the securities depreciate in price, revenue will also be reduced.

To protect against a loss, investment banks engage in hedging strategies. Various strategies are employed by traders to generate revenue from positions in one or more securities: riskless arbitrage, risk arbitrage, and speculation.

Riskless Arbitrage   Of the two types of arbitrage transactions (riskless arbitrage and risk arbitrage), **riskless arbitrage** calls for a trader to find a security or package of securities trading at different prices. For example, some common stocks of companies trade in more than one location within the United States. Also, common stock of some multinational companies trades in both the United States and on an exchange in one or more foreign countries (see Chapter 13 for a discussion of common stock). If price discrepancies occur in the various markets, it may be possible to lock in a profit after transaction costs by selling the security in the market where it is priced higher and buying it in the market where it is priced lower. In the case of a security priced in a foreign currency, the price must be converted based on the exchange rate.

Traders do not expect such situations to occur because they are rare. Although they do exist periodically in financial markets, riskless arbitrage opportunities of the type described are short-lived. In some situations, however, packages of securities and derivative contracts, combined with borrowing, can produce a payoff identical to another security, yet the two are priced differently. The key point is that a riskless arbitrage transaction does not expose the investor to any adverse movement in the market price of the securities in the transaction.

We will give examples of this in later chapters because the concept of riskless arbitrage provides the underlying process by which assets are priced. For now, a simple example should suffice. Consider three securities A, B, and C that can be purchased today, and 1 year from now they can experience only two possible outcomes (State 1 and State 2):

Security	Price	Payoff in State 1	Payoff in State 2
A	$70	$50	$100
B	60	30	120
C	80	38	112

Let W_A and W_B be the quantity of security A and B, respectively, in the portfolio. Then the payoff (i.e., the terminal value of the portfolio) under the two states can be expressed mathematically as follows:

$$\text{if State 1 occurs: } \$50W_A + \$30W_B$$
$$\text{if State 2 occurs: } \$100W_A + \$120W_B$$

Can we create a portfolio consisting of A and B that will reproduce the payoff of C regardless of the state that occurs 1 year from now? That is, we want to select W_A and W_B such that:

$$\text{if State 1 occurs: } \$50W_A + \$30W_B = \$38$$
$$\text{if State 2 occurs: } \$100W_A + \$120W_B = \$112$$

The dollar payoff on the right-hand side of the two equations is the payoff of C in each state.

We can solve these two equations algebraically obtaining a value of 0.4 for W_A and 0.6 for W_B. Thus, a portfolio consisting of 0.4 of security A and 0.6 of security B will have the same payoff as security C. How much will it cost us to construct this portfolio? As the prices of A and B are $70 and $60, respectively, the cost is:

$$0.40(\$70) + 0.60(\$60) = \$64$$

Note that the price of C is $80. Thus, for only $64 an investor can obtain the same payoff as C. This riskless arbitrage opportunity can be exploited by buying A and B in the proportions given above and shorting (selling) C. (Short selling is discussed in Chapter 7). This action allows the investor to lock in a profit of $16 today regardless of what happens 1 year from now. By selling C, the investor must pay $38 if State 1 occurs and $112 if State 2 occurs. The investor will obtain the dollars necessary to make either payment from the payoff of A and B.

Risk Arbitrage Certain trading strategies are believed to carry a low level of risk. Because of the risk exposure, such trading strategies are unfortunately labeled as **risk arbitrage**. Of the two types of risk arbitrage, the first arises in the case of exchange offers for securities of corporations coming out of a bankruptcy proceeding. For example, suppose that company A is being reorganized, and one of its bonds is now selling in the market for $200. If the trader believes that the outcome of the bankruptcy proceedings will be the exchange of three securities with an estimated value of $280 for the existing bond worth $200, then the trader will buy the existing bond. The trader will realize a profit of $80 if in fact the final exchange offer is as anticipated, and the value of the package is worth $280.

The spread between the $280 potential package and the $200 price for the bond reflects two risks: the risk that the exchange will not take place on the terms that the trader believes, and the risk value of the package of three securities that will be received will be less than $200. The "risk" in this risk arbitrage transaction reflects these two risks.

The other type of risk arbitrage occurs when a merger or acquisition is announced. The merger or acquisition can involve only a cash exchange, an exchange of securities, or a combination of both. First consider a cash exchange: Suppose that company X announces that it plans to make an offer to buy company Y's common stock for $100 per share at a time when company Y's common stock is selling for $70. One would expect that the market price of Y's common stock would rise to around $100. The risk, however, is that company X will, for whatever reason, withdraw its planned purchase of the stock. The price of company Y's common stock consequently may rise to, say, $90 rather than $100. The $10 difference is the market's assessment of the likelihood of the planned purchase not being completed. An investor who buys the common stock of Y can lock in a profit of $10 if the purchase occurs at $100. The risk is that it will not occur and that the price will decline below $90.

The various attempts of UAL Corp. (the parent company of United Airlines) provide a classic example of the risk associated with this type of risk arbitrage. In September 1989, a group consisting of pilots and management made a $300 per share bid for UAL's stock. Even though the board of UAL approved the offer, the bidders could not obtain the necessary financing to complete the transaction. During this time, the stock reached a peak of $296 per share. In mid-October, when the bidding group acknowledged that the transaction would not take place, the stock fell in a matter of a few days by almost 50%. In January 1990, another bid for UAL Corp. for $201 per share was made by the union. Once again, the financing for the takeover could not be obtained, resulting in a plunge in the market price. Industry experts estimated these failed takeover attempts resulted in losses to risk arbitrageurs of more than $1 billion.

When the transaction involves the exchange of securities rather than cash, the announced terms of the exchange will not be reflected immediately in the price of the securities involved. For example, suppose that company B announces that it plans to acquire company T. Company B is called the bidding or acquiring firm and company T the target firm. Company B announces that it intends to offer one share of its stock in exchange for one share of company T stock. At the time of the announcement, suppose that the prices of the stock of B and T are $50 and $42, respectively. If the acquisition does take place as announced, a trader who acquires one share of company T for $42 can exchange it for stock worth $50, a spread of $8. This spread reflects three risks: (1) the acquisition may not be consummated for one reason or another and then T's stock may have to be sold, possibly at a loss; (2) the time delay means a cost is involved in financing the position in T's stock; and (3) the price of B's stock can decline in value so that when T's stock is exchanged for B's, less of a spread is realized.

The way to protect against this last risk is for the trader to buy shares of T and sell short an equal number of shares of B (recall the transaction is a one-for-one share exchange), in order to lock in a spread of $8 if the transaction is consummated. Let's look at what happens now if the price of B's stock changes at the time the transaction is consummated. At that time, the price of the stock of B and T will be the same.

Suppose the price of B's stock falls from $50 to $45. Then, when the trader exchanges one share of stock T for stock B, there will be a profit of $3 at the purchase price of $42 for stock T. The short sale of one share of stock B for $50 can now be covered by buying it back for $45, realizing a profit of $5. The trader's overall profit will be $8, the spread that the trader wanted to lock in.

Suppose instead that at the time the exchange is consummated one share of stock B is worth $60 per share. By exchanging stock T, which was purchased at $42, for one share of stock B, which is now worth $60, a profit of $18 is realized on this leg of the transaction. However, because stock B was sold short for $50 and must now be purchased for $60 to cover the short position, a loss of $10 is realized on the second leg of the transaction. Overall, a profit of $8 still is realized.

Thus, risk arbitrage to lock in a spread, *if the exchange is consummated on the announced terms,* involves buying the shares of the target company and shorting the shares of the acquiring or bidding company. The number of shares depends on the exchange terms. Our example assumes a one-for-one exchange, so one share of B was shorted for every share of T purchased. Had the exchange been one share of B for every two shares of T, then one share of B would be shorted for every two shares of T purchased.

The first risk remains: the risk that the deal will not be consummated. To reduce this risk, the trader or research department must carefully examine the likelihood of a successful takeover or merger.[5]

Speculation   **Speculative trading** or **speculation**, occurs when the trader positions the capital of the investment banking firm to take advantage of a specific anticipated movement of prices or a spread between two prices. The benefits of being right, particularly with a highly leveraged position, are rewarding. We read in the popular press that some investment banking firms have reaped millions of dollars from a certain speculative position; remember, however, that just as often we read about large trading losses from speculative strategies.

Execution of Trades for Clients   Commissions are generated by executing trades for investors, both retail and institutional investors. Two common institutional trades that investment bankers are called upon to execute are block trades and program (or basket) trades. These trades are discussed in Chapter 13.

Research and Trading   To encourage clients to use a firm to execute transactions so that commissions or the bid-ask spread income can be generated, investment banks provide research for clients. Typically, the research is provided free for clients that generate a certain amount of trades. For those that do not, the research is sold.

Some research is restricted to a firm's own traders. The purpose is to provide strategies or information that the firm's trader may be able to use to improve performance.

PRIVATE PLACEMENT OF SECURITIES

In addition to underwriting securities for distribution to the public, investment banking firms place securities with a limited number of institutional investors such as insurance companies, investment companies, and pension funds. Private placement is distinguished from the "public" offering of securities described so far and will be discussed further in the next chapter.

---

[5]   Of course, the Dennis Levin/Ivan Boesky risk-reduction approach to risk arbitrage is always available: through illegal means acquire material nonpublic information (called "inside information") about merger and acquisition transactions. It is, of course, not an approach we recommend.

Investment banking firms assist in the private placement of securities in several ways. They work with the issuer and potential investors on the design and pricing of the security. Investment bankers first design many of the new security structures in the private placement market. Field testing of innovative securities described in this book most often occurs in the private placement market.[6]

The investment bankers may be involved with lining up investors as well as designing the issue. Or, if the issuer already identified the investors, the investment banker may serve only in an advisory capacity. Work as an advisor generates fee income, as does arranging the placement with investors. An investment banker can also participate in the transaction on a best efforts underwriting arrangement.

The fees for arranging a private placement vary depending on the issuance amount and the complexity of the transaction. Moreover, in raising venture capital for clients, investment bankers are frequently offered the opportunity to share in the prosperity of the company. This opportunity typically comes in the form of an option to buy a specified number of shares at a price set at a time the funds are raised. An arrangement that allows the investment banking firm to benefit from the company's success is referred to as an "equity kicker."

SECURITIZATION OF ASSETS

As explained in Chapter 2, the securitization of assets refers to the issuance of securities using a pool of assets as collateral. The securitization of home mortgage loans to create mortgage-backed securities (which we discuss in Chapter 26) was the first example of this process. After 1985, investment bankers worked with corporations to either securitize a wide range of loans and receivables or buy loans and receivables in the market and issue securities backed by them. Securities backed by a pool of loans or receivables are called **asset-backed securities.**

When an investment banker works with a corporation to issue an asset-backed security it generates revenue from the bid-ask spread in the sale of the security. When an investment banker buys loans and receivables and then issues securities, it generates a profit on an asset-backed security transaction as follows: the differences between the price the security is sold for minus the price it paid to purchase the collateral (i.e., the cost of buying the loans and receivables) minus the interest cost of "warehousing" the collateral purchased until the securities are sold.

MERGERS AND ACQUISITIONS

Investment banking firms are active in mergers and acquisitions (M&A). Under M&A activity are also included leveraged buyouts (LBOs), restructuring and recapitalization of companies, and reorganization of bankrupt and troubled companies.

Investment bankers may participate in M&A activity in one of several ways: (1) finding M&A candidates, (2) advising acquiring companies or target companies with respect to price and nonprice terms of an exchange, or helping target companies fend off an unfriendly takeover attempt, and (3) assisting acquiring companies in obtaining the necessary funds to finance a purchase.

Fees charged by investment bankers in M&A work depend on the extent of their participation and the complexity of the activities they are asked to perform. An investment banker may simply receive an advisory fee or retainer. More likely, an investment

---

6   For example, zero coupon corporate bonds were first publicly issued by corporations in April 1981. (The first issue was by J. C. Penney.) Prior to that time a private offering was made by PepsiCo.

banker will receive a fee based on a percentage of the selling price. The fee structure in this case can be of one of three types: (1) the percentage can decline, the higher the selling price; (2) the percentage can be the same regardless of the selling price; or (3) the percentage can be fixed with addition of an incentive fee if the price is better than a specified amount. An example of the first fee structure is what is called the 5-4-3-2-1 "Lehman formula." In this fee structure that some firms have adopted, the fee would be 5% of the first $1 million, 4% of the second $1 million, 3% of the third $1 million, 2% of the fourth $1 million, and 1% for any excess amount. A typical flat percentage is 2% to 3% of the selling price.

Participating in an LBO can generate several fees. LBOs call for a firm to be acquired using mostly debt funds and taken private. The debt raised is from one of two sources—senior bank debt, and unsecured junior debt (called subordinated debt, or mezzanine financing). An investment banking firm can earn fees from (1) proposing the acquisition, (2) arranging the financing, (3) arranging bridge financing (that is, temporary funds loaned until permanent debt financing is completed), and (4) other advisory fees.

Under "other advisory fees" we would find fees charged by investment banking firms for providing a valuation of a firm that is the subject of a takeover or a merger, and for rendering a "fairness opinion." The question of fairness arises in such a transaction based on an issue of whether the purchasers of the company may have access to information that allows them to acquire the firm at a price less than its true market value. This situation is of increasing concern in LBOs, particularly management-led LBOs, that is, where the current management of the firm makes an offer to purchase the company. An investment banking firm is typically engaged by the board of directors of the company that is the subject of the takeover to render an independent and expert opinion as to the fairness of the price being offered for the shares. Fees for a fairness opinion range from $50,000 for a transaction involving a few million dollars to $1 million or more for large transactions

An investment banking firm may provide its own capital for bridge financing. This type of merchant banking is discussed in the next section.

MERCHANT BANKING

When an investment banking firm commits its own funds by either taking an equity interest or creditor position in companies, this activity is referred to as **merchant banking**. If an equity interest is taken, it usually creates a substantial upside potential. The interest rate charged on debt funding provided to a client, particularly for bridge financing, is high, reflecting the high risk associated with such lending activities.

First Boston Corporation's bridge loan of $450 million to Ohio Mattress Co. to finance an LBO illustrates the risk of bridge financing for an investment banking firm. After the LBO was completed and Ohio Mattress sought to acquire permanent debt financing to refinance the bridge loan, First Boston could not sell the securities. As a result, First Boston was stuck with the loan.[7]

Bridge financing is seen as important not only for its potential source of interest income, but also as a financing vehicle that can be used to attract clients considering an LBO.

---

[7] Eventually the parent company of First Boston, Credit Suisse First Boston provided assistance by buying the bridge loan from First Boston.

TRADING AND CREATION OF DERIVATIVE INSTRUMENTS

Futures, options, swaps, caps, and floors are examples of instruments that can be used to control the risk of an investor's portfolio, or, in the case of an issuer, the risk associated with the issuance of a security. These instruments are referred to as derivative instruments, and they allow an investment banking firm to realize revenue in several ways. Customers generate commissions from the exchange-traded instruments they buy and sell. This process is no different from the commissions generated by the brokerage service performed for customers when stocks are bought and sold.

Second, certain derivative instruments are created by an investment banking firm for its clients when it acts as a counterparty to the agreement. These products are called **over-the-counter** or **dealer-created derivative instruments**. An example is a swap, which we will describe in Chapter 12. The risk of loss of capital is present whenever an investment banking firm is a counterparty, because the investment banker becomes a principal to the transaction. To protect against capital loss, an investment banking firm will seek another party to take the other side of the transaction. When this occurs, spread income is generated.

Derivative instruments are also used to protect an investment bank's own position in transactions. Here are just two examples. Suppose an investment banking firm underwrites a bond issue. The risk that the firm is exposed to is a decline in the price of the bonds purchased from the issuer, which are to be reoffered to the public. (As we explain in Chapter 18, this event tends to occur if interest rates rise.) Using either interest rate futures or options (the subject of Chapter 18,) the investment banking firm can protect itself. As a second example, an investment banking firm has many trading desks with either long or short positions in a security. Derivative instruments can be used by the trading desks to protect the firm against an adverse price movement.

MONEY MANAGEMENT

Investment banking firms create subsidiaries that manage funds for either individual investors or institutional investors such as pension funds. Examples include Goldman Sachs Asset Management, a subsidiary of the investment banking firm of Goldman Sachs & Co.; and Bear Stearns Asset Management, a subsidiary of Bear Stearns, an investment banking firm. Money management activities generate fee income based on a percentage of the assets under management.

Summary

Investment banking activities are performed by securities firms and commercial banks. Securities firms distribute newly issued securities and are involved in the secondary market as market makers and brokers. Commercial banks were at one time restricted as to the types of activities that they could undertake but these restrictions were removed by the Gramm-Leach-Bliley Financial Services Modernization Act of 1999.

Investment bankers provide two general functions: raising funds for clients and assisting clients in the sale or purchase of securities. In this chapter we explained the various activities of investment banking and how these activities generate revenue. The activities include public offering of securities, public trading of securities, private placement of securities, securitization of assets, mergers and acquisitions, merchant banking, trading and creation of derivative instruments, and money management. Not all firms are active participants in each activity.

Key Terms ■

- Asset-backed securities
- Best-efforts underwriting
- Concession price
- Dealer-created derivative instruments
- Firm commitment
- Gross spread

- Initial public offerings (IPOs)
- Merchant banking
- Over-the-counter
- Privatization
- Risk arbitrage
- Riskless arbitrage
- Securities firms

- Selling group
- Speculation
- Speculative trading
- Underwriter discount
- Underwriting
- Underwriting syndicate

Questions ■

1. In what four ways can investment banking firms generate revenue?
2. In what three ways may an investment banking firm be involved in the issuance of a new security?
3. What is meant by the underwriting function?
4. What is the difference between a firm-commitment underwriting arrangement and a best-efforts arrangement?
5. Explain at least three circumstances in which investment banking firms must commit their own capital.
6. In a typical underwriting, why is it necessary to form an underwriting syndicate and a selling syndicate?
7. a. What is meant by the underwriting spread?
   b. How is the underwriting spread distributed between the lead manager, the members of the underwriting syndicate, and members of the selling syndicate?
8. What is meant by riskless arbitrage?
9. Suppose that 1 year from now the following two outcomes are possible for securities X, Y, and Z:

Security	Price	Payoff in State 1	Payoff in State 2
X	$35	$25	$40
Y	30	15	60
Z	40	19	66

   The prices of X, Y, and Z are respectively, $35, $30, and $40. Indicate whether a riskless arbitrage opportunity is possible?
10. Explain why an attempt to profit from a merger is not a riskless arbitrage.
11. What is meant by merchant banking?
12. What is meant by securitization of assets?
13. In its 10-K report filed with the Securities and Exchange Commission, the investment banking firm of Goldman Sachs & Co. made the following statements concerning factors that may affect its operations:
    a. "We generally maintain large trading and investment positions, including merchant banking investments, in the fixed income, currency, commodity and equity markets, and in real estate and other assets, and we may incur significant losses if market fluctuations or volatility adversely affect the value of these positions." Explain why market fluctuations can adversely affect the firm's operations.
    b. "Unfavorable financial or economic conditions would likely reduce the number and size of transactions in which we provide underwriting, mergers and acquisitions advisory, and other services, and could thereby adversely affect our results of operations." Explain why.

c. "Liquidity, i.e., ready access to funds, is essential to our businesses. Our liquidity could be impaired by an inability to access the long-term or short-term debt capital markets, an inability to access the repurchase and securities lending markets, or an impairment of our ability to sell assets." Explain why.

14. The following table shows the Global Capital Markets Net Revenues (in millions) reported by Goldman Sachs & Co. for 1999 as reported in its 10-K filing with the Securities and Exchange Commission:

Financial Advisory	$2,270
Underwriting	2,089
Investment Banking	4,359
Fixed Income, Currency and Commodities	2,862
Equities	1,961
Principal Investments	950
Trading and Principal Investments	5,773
Total	$10,132

Explain each of the sources of net revenue.

15. a. What two measures can be used to determine the market share of an investment banking firm?
    b. What are the drawbacks of these measures?

16. The *Economist* of September 22, 1990, provided this description of activities of investment bankers:

> *Ever since the Berlin Wall came down, the airlines, hotels and taxi ranks of Eastern Europe have been filled with business-suited Westerners hoping to make money in the wake of its collapse. In the first few months, many came, saw and left shaking their heads in disbelief at the mess. But fast on their heels came the professional advisers—accountants, management consultants, investment bankers—for whom the mess itself is money. Or may one day be.*

a. What types of functions can investment banks provide in restructuring the economies of Eastern Europe?
b. What kinds of investment banking skills will be required?
c. Can you think of potential problems that investment banks will face?

CHAPTER 6

The Primary Markets

Learning Objectives

After reading this chapter you will understand:

◆ how the SEC regulates the distribution of newly issued securities.

◆ what a registration statement is.

◆ what SEC rule 415 ("shelf registration") is.

◆ what a traditional private placement offering is.

◆ what Rule 144A is and its potential impact on the private placement market.

◆ what a bought deal underwriting for a bond issue is and why it is used.

◆ what a competitive bidding underwriting is and the different methods for determining the price of winning bidders.

◆ what a preemptive rights offering is and why a standby underwriting arrangement may be needed.

◆ what is meant by an integrated and segmented world capital market and the implications for fund raising.

◆ the motivation for firms to raise funds outside of their local capital market.

As we explained in Chapter 1, financial markets can be categorized as those dealing with newly issued financial claims, called the **primary market**; and those for exchanging financial claims previously issued, called the **secondary market**, or the market for seasoned securities. In this chapter we will focus on the primary market for securities. In the previous chapter we explained the role of investment bankers in the primary market. The next chapter will cover the secondary market.

◆ REGULATION OF THE ISSUANCE OF SECURITIES

Underwriting activities are regulated by the Securities and Exchange Commission. The Securities Act of 1933 governs the issuance of securities. The act requires that a **registration statement** be filed with the SEC by the issuer of a security. The type of information contained in the registration statement is the nature of the business of the issuer, key provisions or features about the security, the nature of the investment risks associated with the security, and the background of management.[1] Financial statements must be included in the registration statement and they must be certified by an independent public accountant.[2]

---

[1] SEC Regulations S-K and the Industry Guidelines (SEC Securities Act Release No. 6384, March 3, 1982) specify the information that must be included in the registration statement.

[2] SEC Regulation S-X specifies the financial statements that must be disclosed.

The registration is actually divided into two parts. Part I is the **prospectus**. This part is typically distributed to the public as an offering of the securities. Part II contains supplemental information, which is not distributed to the public as part of the offering but is available from the SEC upon request.

The act provides for penalties in the form of fines and/or imprisonment if the information provided is inaccurate or material information is omitted. Moreover, investors who purchased the security are entitled to sue the issuer to recover damages if they incurred a loss as a result of misleading information. The underwriter may also be sued if it can be demonstrated that the underwriter did not conduct a reasonable investigation of the information reported by the issuer.

One of the most important duties of an underwriter is to perform **due diligence**. The following quote is taken from a court decision that explains the obligation of an underwriter to perform due diligence:

> An underwriter by participating in an offering constructively represents that statements made in the registration materials are complete and accurate. The investing public properly relies upon the underwriter to check the accuracy of the statements and the soundness of the offer; when the underwriter does not speak out, the investor reasonably assumes that there are no undisclosed material deficiencies. The representation in the registration statement are those of the underwriter as much as they are those of the issuer.[3]

The filing of a registration statement with the SEC does not mean that the security can be offered to the public. The registration statement must be reviewed and approved by the SEC's Division of Corporate Finance before the security can be offered to the public. Typically, the staff of this division will find a problem with the registration statement. The staff then sends a "letter of comments" or "deficiency letter" to the issuer explaining the problem it encountered. The issuer must then remedy any problem by filing an amendment to the registration statement. If the SEC staff is then satisfied, they will issue an order declaring that the registration statement is "effective" and the underwriter can solicit sales. The approval of the SEC, however, does not mean that the securities have investment merit or are properly priced or that the information is accurate. It merely means that the appropriate information appears to have been disclosed.

The time interval between the initial filing of the registration statement and the time the registration statement becomes effective is referred to as the **waiting period**. During the waiting period, the SEC does allow the underwriters to distribute a preliminary prospectus. Because the prospectus is not effective, the cover page of the prospectus states this status in red ink and as a result, the preliminary prospectus is commonly referred to as a **red herring**. During the waiting period, the underwriter cannot sell the security nor may it accept written offers from investors to buy the security.

RULE 415: SHELF REGISTRATION RULE

In 1982 the SEC approved Rule 415, which permits certain issuers to file a single registration document indicating that it intends to sell a certain amount of a certain class of securities at one or more times within the next 2 years.[4] Rule 415 is popularly referred to as the

---

[3] *Chris-Craft Industries, Inc. v. Piper Aircraft Corp.,* 1973.
[4] The issuer qualifies for Rule 415 registration if the securities are investment-grade securities and/or are the securities of companies that have historically filed a registration statement and whose securities comply with minimum flotation requirements.

shelf registration rule because the securities can be viewed as sitting on a "shelf" and can be taken off that shelf and sold to the public without obtaining additional SEC approval.

In essence, the filing of a single registration document allows the issuer to come to market quickly because the sale of the security has been preapproved by the SEC. Prior to establishment of Rule 415, a lengthy period was required before a security could be sold to the public. As a result, in a fast-moving market, issuers could not come to market quickly with an offering to take advantage of what it perceived to be attractive financing opportunities. For example, if a corporation felt that interest rates were attractive and wanted to issue a bond, it had to file a registration statement and could not issue the bond until the registration statement became effective. The corporation then takes the chance that during the waiting period interest rates will rise, making the bond offering more costly.

CONTINUED REPORTING

Any company that publicly offers a security in the United States becomes a **reporting company** and, as such, is subject to the Securities Exchange Act of 1934. This act specifies that a reporting company file with the SEC annual and periodic financial reports. The financial reports must be prepared according to generally accepted accounting principles (GAAP).

Complying with the disclosure requirements can be quite costly for small companies. The disclosure requirements hold for non-U.S. companies publicly offering a security in the United States. Thus, non-U.S. companies must file financial statements not based on their home country's GAAP, but reconciled to U.S. GAAP. These disclosure requirements make the raising of funds in the United States by non-U.S. companies less attractive. However, as discussed later, the SEC eased access to the U.S. capital market for small companies and non-U.S. companies by amending the U.S. securities law.

Subject to certain exceptions, the reporting requirements also hold for companies whose securities are traded in the secondary market in the United States, despite the fact that the securities were not initially publicly offered in the United States. The significance of this exception (as we explain in Chapter 13) is that non-U.S. companies may list their common stock on United States stock exchanges. As such, companies that follow this practice would become reporting companies. Once again, the SEC amended the U.S. securities law so that if certain requirements are satisfied, a non-U.S. company need not comply with the full disclosure requirements.

PRIVATE PLACEMENT OF SECURITIES

Public and private offerings of securities differ in terms of the regulatory requirements that must be satisfied by the issuer. The Securities Act of 1933 and the Securities Exchange Act of 1934 require that all securities offered to the general public must be registered with the SEC, unless given a specific exemption. The securities acts allow three exemptions from federal registration. First, intrastate offerings—that is, securities sold only within a state—are exempt. Second, a small-offering exemption (Regulation A) specifically applies if the offering is for $1 million or less, then the securities need not be registered. Finally, Section 4(2) of the 1933 Act exempts from registration "transactions by an issuer not involving any public offering." However, the 1933 Act does not provide specific guidelines to identify what is a private offering or placement.

In 1982, the SEC adopted Regulation D, which sets forth the specific guidelines that must be satisfied to qualify for exemption from registration under Section 4(2). The guidelines require that, in general, the securities cannot be offered through any form of general advertising or general solicitation that would prevail for public offerings. Most importantly, the guidelines restrict the sale of securities to "sophisticated" investors. Such "accredited" investors are defined as those (1) with the capability to evaluate (or who can afford to employ an advisor to evaluate) the risk and return characteristics of the securities, and (2) with the resources to bear the economic risks.[5]

The exemption of an offering does not mean that the issuer need not disclose information to potential investors. The issuer must still furnish the same information deemed material by the SEC. This information is provided in a private placement memorandum, as opposed to a prospectus for a public offering. The distinction between the private placement memorandum and the prospectus is that the former does not include information deemed by the SEC as "non-material," whereas such information is required in a prospectus. Moreover, unlike a prospectus, the private placement memorandum is not subject to SEC review.

RULE 144A

In the United States, one restriction imposed on buyers of privately placed securities is that they may not be resold for 2 years after acquisition. Thus, the market contains no liquidity for that time period. Buyers of privately placed securities must be compensated for the lack of liquidity, which raises the cost to the issuer of the securities.

In April 1990, however, SEC Rule 144A became effective. This rule eliminates the 2-year holding period by permitting large institutions to trade securities acquired in a private placement among themselves without having to register these securities with the SEC. Under Rule 144A, a large institution is defined as one holding at least $100 million of the security.

Private placements are now classified as Rule 144A offerings or non-Rule 144A offerings. The latter are more commonly referred to as traditional private placements. Rule 144A offerings are underwritten by investment bankers.

Rule 144A will encourage non-U.S. corporations to issue securities in the U.S. private placement market for two reasons. First, it will attract new large institutional investors into the market who were unwilling previously to buy private placements because of the requirement to hold the securities for 2 years. Such an increase in the number of institutional investors may encourage non-U.S. entities to issue securities. Second, foreign entities have been unwilling to raise funds in the United States prior to the establishment of Rule 144A because they had to register their securities and furnish the necessary disclosure set forth by U.S. securities laws. Private placement requires less disclosure. Rule 144A also improves liquidity, reducing the cost of raising funds.

◆ **VARIATIONS IN THE UNDERWRITING OF SECURITIES**

In our discussion of the role of investment bankers in Chapter 5, we described the traditional syndication process; however, not all deals are underwritten using the traditional syndicate process. Variations include the "bought deal" for the underwriting of bonds, the auction process for both stocks and bonds, and a rights offering for common stock.

---

[5] Under the current law, an accredited investor is one who satisfies either a net worth test (at least $1 million excluding automobiles, home, and home furnishings) or an annual income test (at least $200,000 for a single individual, $300,000 for a couple for the last two years, with expectations of such income to continue for the current year).

BOUGHT DEAL

The **bought deal** was introduced in the Eurobond market in 1981 when Credit Suisse First Boston purchased from General Motors Acceptance Corporation a $100 million issue without lining up an underwriting syndicate prior to the purchase. Thus, Credit Suisse First Boston did not use the traditional syndication process to diversify the capital risk exposure associated with an underwriting that we described in chapter 5.

The mechanics of a bought deal—used solely for debt securities—are as follows. The lead manager, or a group of managers, offers a potential issuer of debt securities a firm bid to purchase a specified amount of the securities with a certain interest (coupon) rate and maturity. The issuer is given a day or so (it might even be a few hours) to accept or reject the bid. If the bid is accepted, the underwriting firm has "bought the deal." It can, in turn, sell the securities to other investment banking firms for distribution to their clients and/or distribute the securities to its own clients. Typically, the underwriting firm that buys the deal will have presold most of the issue to its institutional clients.

The bought deal appears to have found its way into the United States in mid-1985 when Merrill Lynch did a bond deal in which it was the only underwriter. The gross spread on the bond, a $50 million issue of Norwest Financial, was 0.268%. This is far less than the 0.7% gross spread that was typical of deals at that time. Merrill Lynch offered a portion of the securities to investors and the balance to other investment banking firms.

Some underwriting firms find the bought deal attractive for two reasons. First, prior to establishment of Rule 415, a lengthy period was required before a security could be sold to the public. Although Rule 415 gave certain issuers timing flexibility to take advantage of windows of opportunity in the global marketplace, it required that investment banking firms be prepared to respond on short notice to commit funds to a deal. This requirement meant the underwriting firm had little time to line up a syndicate, favoring the bought deal. However, as a consequence, underwriting firms needed to expand their capital in order to commit greater amounts of funds to such deals.

Second, the risk of capital loss in a bought deal may not be as great as it may first appear. Some deals are so straightforward that a large underwriting firm may have enough institutional investor interest to minimize the risks of distributing the issue at the reoffering price. Moreover, in the case of bonds, hedging strategies using the interest rate risk control tools, which we will discuss in Chapter 28, reduce the risk of realizing a loss of selling the bonds at a price below the reoffering price.

AUCTION PROCESS

Another variation for the issuance of securities is the auction process. In this method, the issuer announces the terms of the issue, and interested parties submit bids for the entire issue. The auction form is mandated for certain securities of regulated public utilities and many municipal debt obligations. It is commonly referred to as a **competitive bidding underwriting**. For example, suppose that a public utility wishes to issue $200 million of bonds. Various underwriters will form syndicates and bid on the issue. The syndicate that bids the lowest yield (i.e., the lowest cost to the issuer) wins the entire $200 million bond issue and then reoffers it to the public.

In a variant of the process, the bidders indicate the price they are willing to pay and the amount they are willing to buy. The security is then allocated to bidders on the basis of the highest bid price (lowest yield in the case of a bond) to lower bid prices (higher yield bids in the case of a bond) until the entire issue is allocated. For example, suppose that an issuer is offering $500 million of a bond issue, and nine bidders submitted the following yield bids:

Bidder	Amount ($ millions)	Bid
A	$150	5.1%
B	110	5.2
C	90	5.2
D	100	5.3
E	75	5.4
F	25	5.4
G	80	5.5
H	70	5.6
I	85	5.7

Bidders A, B, C, and D will be allocated the amount of the issue for which they bid because they submitted the lowest yield bid. In total, they will receive $450 million of the $500 million to be issued. That leaves $50 million to be allocated to the next lowest bidders. Both E and F submitted the next lowest yield bid, 5.4%. In total, they bid for $100 million. Because the total they bid for exceeds the $50 million remaining to be allocated, they will receive an amount proportionate to the amount for which they bid. Specifically, E will be allocated three quarters ($75 million divided by $100 million) of the $50 million, or $37.5 million; and F will be allocated one quarter ($25 million divided by $100 million) of the $50 million, or $12.5 million.

The next question is the yield that all of the six winning bidders will have to pay for the amount of the issue allocated to them. One way in which a competitive bidding can occur is all bidders pay the highest winning yield bid (or, equivalently, the lowest winning price). In our example, all bidders would buy the amount allocated to them at 5.4%. This type of auction is referred to as a **single-price auction** or a **Dutch auction**. Another way is for each bidder to pay whatever they bid. This type of auction is called a **multiple-price auction**. Although the U.S. Department of the Treasury currently issues securities using only a single-price auction, historically both the single-price auction and the multiple-price auction were used.

Using an auction allows corporate issuers to place newly issued debt obligations directly with institutional investors rather than follow the indirect path of using an investment banking firm to underwrite the securities. Internet auctions of municipal originations began during 1997. As will be explained in Chapter 24, one method of issuing municipal securities (i.e., securities issued by state and local governments and their authorities) is via a competitive bidding process. During November 1997, MuniAuction auctioned over the Internet $70 million City of Pittsburgh municipal bonds despite the opposition of some major Wall Street traditional, competitive bond underwriters. In 1999, the City of Pittsburgh used MuniAuction to offer bonds directly to institutional investors, allowing them to bypass traditional underwriters. By late 2000, MuniAuction reported it conducted more than 250 municipal auctions totaling $13.4 billion. As of late November 2000, 14% of all competitive municipal bond underwritings were conducted over the MuniAuction system. By contrast, with the exception of two corporate bonds sales (Dow Chemical and Deutsche Bank), the corporate bond market has avoided electronic bidding for new issues.

Investment bankers' response to the practice of direct purchase of publicly registered securities is that, as intermediaries, they add value by searching their institutional client base, which increases the likelihood that the issuer will incur the lowest cost, after adjusting for the underwriting fees. By dealing with just a few institutional investors, investment bankers argue, issuers cannot be sure of obtaining funds at the lowest cost. In addition, investment bankers say they often play another important role: They make a secondary market in the securities they issue. This market improves the perceived liquidity of the issue and, as a result, reduces the cost to issuers. Whether investment bankers can obtain lower-cost funding (after accounting for underwriting fees) for issuers, by comparison to the cost of funding from a direct offering, remains an interesting empirical question.

PREEMPTIVE RIGHTS OFFERING

A corporation can issue new common stock directly to existing shareholders via a **preemptive rights offering**. A preemptive right grants existing shareholders the right to buy some proportion of the new shares issued at a price below market value. The price at which new shares can be purchased is called the **subscription price**. A rights offering insures that current shareholders may maintain their proportionate equity interest in the corporation. In the United States, the practice of issuing common stock via a preemptive rights offering is uncommon. In other countries it is much more common; in some countries, it is the only means by which a new offering of common stock may be sold.

For the shares sold via preemptive rights offering, the underwriting services of an investment banker are not needed. However, the issuing corporation may use the services of an investment banker for the distribution of common stock that is not subscribed to. A **standby underwriting arrangement** will be used in such instances. This arrangement calls for the underwriter to buy the unsubscribed shares. The issuing corporation pays a **standby fee** to the investment banking firm.

◆ WORLD CAPITAL MARKETS INTEGRATION AND FUND-RAISING IMPLICATIONS

An entity may seek funds outside its local capital market with the expectation of doing so at a lower cost than if its funds are raised in its local capital market. Whether lower costs are possible depends on the degree of integration of capital markets. At the two extremes, the world capital markets can be classified as either completely segmented or completely integrated.

In the former case, investors in one country are not permitted to invest in the securities issued by an entity in another country. As a result, in a **completely segmented market**, the required return on securities of comparable risk traded in different capital markets throughout the world will be different even after adjusting for taxes and foreign exchange rates. An entity may be able to raise funds in the capital market of another country at a cost that is lower than doing so in its local capital market.

At the other extreme, a **completely integrated market** contains no restriction to prevent investors from investing in securities issued in any capital market throughout the world. In such an ideal world capital market, the required return on securities of comparable risk will be the same in all capital markets after adjusting for taxes and foreign exchange rates. This situation implies that the cost of funds will be the same regardless of where in the capital markets throughout the world a fund-seeking entity elects to raise funds.

Real-world capital markets are neither completely segmented nor completely integrated, but fall somewhere in between. A **mildly segment market** or **mildly integrated market** implies that world capital markets offer opportunities to raise funds at a lower cost outside the local capital market.

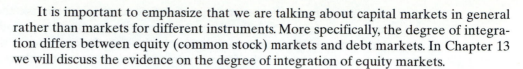

It is important to emphasize that we are talking about capital markets in general rather than markets for different instruments. More specifically, the degree of integration differs between equity (common stock) markets and debt markets. In Chapter 13 we will discuss the evidence on the degree of integration of equity markets.

◆ MOTIVATION FOR RAISING FUNDS OUTSIDE OF THE DOMESTIC MARKET

A corporation may seek to raise funds outside of its domestic market for four reasons. First, in some countries, large corporations seeking to raise a substantial amount of funds may have no other choice but to obtain financing in either the foreign market sector of another country or the Euromarket, because the fund-raising corporation's domestic market is not fully developed enough to be able to satisfy its demand for funds on globally competitive terms. Governments of developing countries use these markets in seeking funds for government-owned corporations in the process of privatizing.

The second reason is the opportunities for obtaining a reduced cost of funding (taking into consideration issuing costs) compared to that available in the domestic market. As explained in Chapter 17, in the case of debt the cost will reflect two factors: (1) the risk-free rate, which is accepted as the interest rate on a U.S. Treasury security with the same maturity or some other low-risk security (called the **base rate**); and (2) a **spread** to reflect the greater risks that investors perceive as being associated with the issue or issuer.

A corporate borrower who seeks reduced funding costs is seeking to reduce the spread. The integration of capital markets throughout the world diminishes such opportunities. Nevertheless, as discussed in the next chapter, imperfections in capital markets throughout the world prevent complete integration and thereby may permit a reduced cost of funds. These imperfections, or market frictions, occur because of differences in security regulations in various countries, tax structures, restrictions imposed on regulated institutional investors, and the credit risk perception of the issuer. In the case of common stock, a corporation seeks to gain a higher value for its stock and to reduce the market impact cost of floating a large offering.

The third reason to seek funds in foreign markets is a desire by corporate treasurers to diversify their source of funding in order to reduce reliance on domestic investors. In the case of equities, diversifying funding sources may encourage foreign investors who have different perspectives of the future performance of the corporation. Two additional advantages of raising foreign equity funds, from the perspective of U.S. corporations, include (1) some market observers believe that certain foreign investors are more loyal to corporations and look at long-term performance rather than short-term performance as do investors in the United States;[6] and (2) diversifying the investor base reduces the dominance of U.S. institutional holdings and its impact on corporate governance.

Finally, a corporation may issue a security denominated in a foreign currency as part of its overall foreign currency management. For example, consider a U.S. corporation that plans to build a factory in a foreign country where the construction costs will be denominated in the foreign currency. Also assume that the corporation plans to sell the output of the factory in the same foreign country. Therefore, the revenue will be denominated in the

---

[6] "U.S. Firms Woo Investors in Europe and Japan," *Euromoney Corporate Finance* (March 1985), p. 45; and Peter O'Brien. "Underwriting International Corporate Equities," Chapter 4 in Robert L. Kuhn (ed.), *Capital Raising and Financial Structure,* Vol. II in The Library of Investment Banking (Homewood, IL: Dow Jones-Irwin, 1990), p. 120.

foreign currency. The corporation then faces exchange rate risk: the construction costs are uncertain in U.S. dollars because during the construction period the U.S. dollar may depreciate relative to the foreign currency. Also, the projected revenue is uncertain in U.S. dollars because the foreign currency may depreciate relative to the U.S. dollar. Suppose that the corporation arranges debt financing for the plant in which it receives the proceeds in the foreign currency and the liabilities are denominated in the foreign currency. This financing arrangement can reduce exchange rate risk because the proceeds received will be in the foreign currency and will be used to pay the construction costs, and the projected revenue can be applied to service the debt obligation.

Corporate Financing Week asked the corporate treasurers of several multinational corporations why they used nondomestic markets to raise funds.[7] Their responses reflected one or more of the reasons just cited. For example, the director of corporate finance of General Motors said that the company uses the Eurobond market with the objective of "diversifying funding sources, attract new investors and achieve comparable, if not, cheaper financing." A managing director of Sears Roebuck stated that the company "has a long-standing policy of diversifying geographical [funding] sources and instruments to avoid reliance on any specific market, even if the cost is higher." He further stated that "Sears cultivates a presence in the international market by issuing every three years or so."

Summary ▪

The primary market involves the distribution to investors of newly issued securities. The SEC is responsible for regulating the issuance of newly issued securities, with the major provisions set forth in the Securities Act of 1933. The act requires that the issuer file a registration statement with the SEC and that the registration statement be approved by the SEC.

Rule 415, the shelf registration rule, permits certain issuers to file a single registration document indicating that it intends to sell a certain amount of a certain class of securities at one or more times within the next 2 years.

Variations in the underwriting process include the bought deal for the underwriting of bonds, the auction process for both stocks and bonds, and preemptive rights offering for underwriting common stock.

A private placement is different from the public offering of securities in terms of the regulatory requirements that must be satisfied by the issuer. If an issue qualifies as a private placement, it is exempt from the more complex registration requirements imposed on public offerings. Rule 144A will contribute to the growth of the private placement market by improving the liquidity of securities issued in this market.

World capital markets can be classified as either completely segmented or completely integrated. Real-world capital markets are neither completely segmented or completely integrated but are best described as mildly segmented or mildly integrated. In a world capital market that can be characterized in this way, opportunities exist to raise funds at a lower cost in some capital markets outside the local capital market.

A firm may seek to raise funds outside of its domestic capital market for one or more of the following reasons: (1) the amount sought cannot be accommodated by its local market; (2) outside markets provide an opportunity to raise funds at a lower cost; (3) the diversification of its funding sources is sought, and (4) as part of its overall currency management it needs funds denominated in another currency.

---

7 Victoria Keefe, "Companies Issue Overseas for Diverse Reasons," *Corporate Financing Week* (November 25, 1991, Special Supplement), pp. 1, 9.

Key Terms

- Base rate
- Bought deal
- Competitive bidding underwriting
- Completely integrated market
- Completely segmented market
- Due diligence
- Mildly integrated market
- Mildly segmented market
- Multiple-price auction
- Preemptive rights offering
- Primary market
- Prospectus
- Red herring
- Registration statement
- Reporting company
- Secondary market
- Shelf registration rule
- Single-price (Dutch) auction
- Spread
- Standby fee
- Standby underwriting arrangement
- Subscription price
- Waiting period

Questions

1. a. What is a registration statement?
    b. What is a prospectus?
    c. What is meant by the waiting period?
2. The Securities Act of 1933 and the Securities Exchange Act of 1934 require that all securities offered to the general public must be registered with the SEC, unless granted a specific exemption. The Securities Acts allow three exemptions from federal registration. What are the three exemptions?
3. What is meant by a bought deal?
4. Why do bought deals expose investment banking firms to greater capital risk than the traditional underwriting process?
5. How does Rule 415 encourage investment banking firms to underwrite issues using the bought deal rather than the traditional underwriting process?
6. An underwriter is responsible for performing due diligence before offering a security to investors. What does due diligence mean?
7. Suppose that a corporation is issuing a bond on a competitive basis. The corporation has indicated that it will issue $200 million of an issue. The following yield bids and the corresponding amounts were submitted.

Bidder	Amount ($ millions)	Bid
A	$20	7.4%
B	40	7.5
C	10	7.5
D	50	7.5
E	40	7.6
F	20	7.6
G	10	7.7
H	10	7.7
I	20	7.8
J	25	7.9
K	28	7.9
L	20	8.0
M	18	8.1

  a. Who are the winning bidders?
  b. How much of the security will be allocated to each winning bidder?
  c. If this auction is a single-price auction, at what yield will each winning bidder pay the amount they will be awarded?
  d. If this auction is a multiple-price auction, at what yield will each winning bidder pay the amount they will be awarded?

8. Indicate whether you agree or disagree with the following statement: "A preemptive rights offering always requires the issuer to use the services of an investment banker to underwrite the unsubscribed shares."

9. The following statements come from the December 24, 1990, issue of *Corporate Financing Week*:

   > *As in the public market, growth in the private placement market was slowed this year by a rise in interest rates that pushed many issuers to the sidelines, by the Mideast crisis and by a flight to quality by investors. . . . Foreign private placements saw a marked increase due to Rule 144A.*

   a. What are the key distinctions between a private placement and a public offering?
   b. Why would Rule 144A increase foreign private placements?

10. What is meant by a completely integrated world capital market?

11. How can the integration of world capital markets best be described and what are the implications for fund raising?

12. Why might a corporation seek to raise funds outside of its local capital market even if it results in a higher cost of funds?

CHAPTER

7

Secondary Markets

Learning Objectives

After reading this chapter you will understand:

◆ the definition of a secondary market.

◆ the need for secondary markets for financial assets.

◆ the various trading locations for securities.

◆ the difference between a continuous and a call market.

◆ the requirements of a perfect market.

◆ frictions that cause actual financial markets to differ from a perfect market.

◆ trading mechanisms such as the types of orders.

◆ why brokers are necessary.

◆ the role of a dealer as a market maker and the costs associated with market making.

◆ what is meant by the operational efficiency of a market.

◆ what is meant by the pricing efficiency of a market and the different forms of pricing efficiency.

◆ the implications of pricing efficiency for market participants.

◆ transaction costs, which include commissions, fees, executions costs, and opportunity costs.

Already-issued financial assets trade in the secondary market. The key distinction between a primary market and a secondary market is that in the secondary market the issuer of the asset does not receive funds from the buyer. Rather, the existing issue changes hands in the secondary market, and funds flow from the buyer of the asset to the seller. In this chapter, we explain the various features of secondary markets. These features are common to any type of financial instrument traded. We take a closer look at individual markets in later chapters.

◆ FUNCTION OF SECONDARY MARKETS

It is worthwhile to review once again the function of secondary markets. The secondary market provides to an issuer of securities, whether the issuer is a corporation or a governmental unit, regular information about the value of the security. The periodic trading of the asset reveals to the issuer the consensus price that the asset commands in an open market. Thus, firms can discover what value investors attach to their stocks, and firms and noncorporate issuers can observe the prices of their bonds and the implied interest rates investors expect and demand from them. Such information helps issuers assess how well they are using the funds acquired from earlier primary market activities, and it also indicates how receptive investors would be to new offerings.

The other service a secondary market offers issuers is that it provides the opportunity for the original buyers of the asset to reverse their investment by selling it for cash. Unless investors feel confident that they can shift from one financial asset to another as they may deem necessary, they would naturally be reluctant to buy any financial asset. Such reluctance would harm potential issuers in one of two ways: either issuers would be unable to sell new securities at all or they would have to pay a high rate of return, because investors would demand greater compensation for the expected illiquidity of the securities.

Investors in financial assets receive several benefits from a secondary market. Such a market obviously offers them liquidity for their assets as well as information about the assets' fair or consensus values. Further, secondary markets bring together many interested parties and so can reduce the costs of searching for likely buyers and sellers of assets. Moreover, by accommodating many trades, secondary markets keep the cost of transactions low. By keeping the costs of both searching and transacting low, secondary markets encourage investors to purchase financial assets.

◆ TRADING LOCATIONS

One indication of the usefulness of secondary markets is that they exist throughout the world. Here, we give just a few examples of these markets.

In the United States, secondary trading of common stock occurs in a number of trading locations. Many shares are traded on major national stock exchanges and regional stock exchanges, which are organized, and somewhat regulated markets in specific geographical locations. Additional significant trading in stocks takes place on the so-called over-the-counter (OTC) market, which is a geographically dispersed group of traders who are linked to one another via telecommunication systems. Some bonds are traded on exchanges; however, most trading in bonds in the United States and throughout the world occurs in the OTC market.

The London International Stock Exchange (ISE) is basically an over-the-counter market whose members are in various places but communicate directly with one another through sophisticated electronic and computer facilities. Assets traded on the ISE include stocks of domestic and international firms as well as a wide array of bonds and options. Germany has eight organized stock exchanges, the most important of which is the Frankfurt Stock Exchange, which handles more than half of the turnover on listed shares and also trades in bonds and currencies. The Paris Bourse, another organized exchange located in a specific place, is France's main secondary market for stocks, bonds, and some derivative securities. Japan has eight exchanges; the largest is the Tokyo Stock Exchange where trading in stocks, bonds, and futures takes place. The second largest is the Osaka Stock Exchange. The Stock Exchange of Hong Kong Limited (SEHK) is an organized secondary market for shares and bonds in that major Southeast Asian city.

◆ MARKET STRUCTURES

Many secondary markets are **continuous markets**, which means that prices are determined continuously throughout the trading day as buyers and sellers submit orders. For example, given the order flow at 10 A.M., the market clearing price of a stock on some organized stock exchange may be $70; at 11 A.M. of the same trading day, the market clearing price of the same stock, but with different order flows, may be $70.75. Thus, in a continuous market, prices may vary with the pattern of orders reaching the market and not because of any change in the basic situation of supply and demand. We return to this point later.

A contrasting market structure is the **call market**, in which orders are batched or grouped together for simultaneous execution at the same price. That is, at certain times in the trading day (or possibly more than once in a day), a market maker holds an auction for a stock. The auction may be oral or written. In either case, the auction will determine or "fix" the market clearing price at a particular time of the trading day. This use of the word *fix* is traditional and not pejorative or suggestive of illegal activity. For example, the *Financial Times* reports on the activities of the London gold bullion market, which is a call market, and records prices set at the "morning fix" and the "afternoon fix." These fixes take place at the two call auctions which are held daily. Until the mid 1980s, the Paris Bourse was a call market, with auctions for large stocks being oral and auctions for smaller issues being written. Since then, it operates as a continuous market and trading takes place "en continu."

Currently, some markets are mixed, using elements of the continuous and the call frameworks. For example, the New York Stock Exchange begins trading (at 9:30 A.M.) with a call auction. With opening prices set in that manner, trading proceeds in a continuous way until closing. The Tokyo Stock Exchange also begins trading in large stocks with an auction. Exchanges in Germany and Switzerland still use the call market system to a significant extent.

◆ PERFECT MARKETS

In order to explain the characteristics of secondary markets, we first describe a "perfect market" for a financial asset. Then we can show how common occurrences in real markets keep them from being theoretically perfect.

In general, a perfect market results when the number of buyers and sellers is sufficiently large, and all participants are small enough relative to the market so that no individual market agent can influence the commodity's price. Consequently, all buyers and sellers are price takers, and the market price is determined at the point that supply equals demand. This condition is more likely to be satisfied if the commodity traded is fairly homogeneous (for example, corn or wheat).

More is involved in a perfect market than market agents being price takers. No transaction costs or impediments must interfere with the supply and demand of the commodity. Economists refer to these various costs and impediments as "frictions." The costs associated with frictions generally result in buyers paying more than in the absence of frictions, and/or sellers receiving less.

In the case of financial markets, frictions would include the following:

- Commissions charged by brokers
- Bid-ask spreads charged by dealers
- Order handling and clearance charges
- Taxes (notably on capital gains) and government-imposed transfer fees
- Costs of acquiring information about the financial asset
- Trading restrictions, such as exchange-imposed restrictions on the size of a position in the financial asset that a buyer or seller may take
- Restrictions on market makers
- Halts to trading that may be imposed by regulators where the financial asset is traded

◆ SECONDARY MARKET TRADING MECHANICS

In this chapter we describe the key features involved in secondary market trading of securities. In Chapter 13, we will discuss trading arrangements that developed specifically for coping with the trading needs of institutional investors.

TYPES OF ORDERS

Investors must provide information to the broker about the conditions under which they will transact. The parameters that the investor must provide are the specific security, the number of shares in the case of common stock and the quantity in the case of bonds, and the type of order. We now describe seven types of orders that an investor can place.

Market Orders   When an investor wants to buy or sell a share of common stock, the price and conditions under which the order is to be executed must be communicated to a broker. The simplest type of order is the **market order**, an order executed at the best price available in the market. The best price is assured by requiring that when more than one buy order or sell order reaches the market at the same time, the order with the best price is given priority. Thus, buyers offering a higher price are given priority over those offering a lower price; sellers asking a lower price are given priority over those asking a higher price.

In the case of common stock traded on an exchange, another priority rule is needed to handle the receipt of more than one order at the same price. Most often, the priority in executing such orders is based on the time of arrival of the order—first orders in are the first orders executed—although another rule may give higher priority to certain types of market participants over others who are seeking to transact at the same price. For example, an exchange may classify orders as either "public orders" or orders of those member firms dealing for their own account. Exchange rules require that public orders be given priority over orders of member firms dealing for their own account.

Limit Orders   The danger of a market order is that an adverse move may take place between the time the investor places the order and the time the order is executed. For example, suppose Ms. Hieber wants to buy the stock of Walt Disney Corporation at $42, but not at $44. If she places a market order when the stock is trading at $42, Ms. Hieber faces the risk that the price will rise before her order is carried out, and she will have to pay an unacceptable price. Similarly, suppose Ms. Davis owns Ford Motors and wants to sell the stock at its current price of $65, but not at $63. If Ms. Davis places a market order to sell Ford at the same time Ford announces a major recall of one of its cars, the stock would be sold at the best available price, but the price might be unacceptable to Ms. Davis.

To avoid the danger of adverse unexpected price changes, an investor can place a **limit order** that designates a price threshold for the execution of the trade. The limit order is a conditional order—it is executed only if the limit price or a better price can be obtained. A **buy limit order** indicates that the security may be purchased only at the designated price or lower. A **sell limit order** indicates that the security may be sold at the designated price or higher. Using our earlier examples, Ms. Hieber, who wants to purchase Disney but will not want to pay more than $42, can place a buy limit order at $42; and Ms. Davis can place a sell limit order for $65.

The danger of a limit order is that it comes with no guarantee it will be executed at all. The designated price may simply not be obtainable. On an exchange, a limit order that is not executable at the time it reaches the market is recorded in a **limit order book**. The orders recorded in this book are treated equally with other orders in terms of priority.

Stop Orders   Another type of conditional order is the **stop order**, which specifies that the order is not to be executed until the market moves to a designated price, at which time it becomes a market order. A **stop order to buy** specifies that the order is not to be executed until the market rises to a designated price (i.e., trades or bids at or above the designated price). A **stop order to sell** specifies that the order is not to be executed until the market price falls below a designated price (i.e., trades or offers at or below the designated price). Once the designated price in the stop order is reached, the order becomes a market order.

A stop order is useful when an investor cannot watch the market constantly. Profits can be preserved or losses minimized on a security position by allowing market movements to trigger a trade. In a sell stop order, the designated price is less than the current market price of the security. By contrast, in a sell limit order the designated price is greater than the current market price of the security. In a buy stop order the designated price is greater than the current market price of the security. However, in a buy limit order the designated price is less than the current market price of the security. These relationships are depicted in Figure 7-1.

For example, suppose Ms. Hiber is uncertain about buying the stock of Disney at its current price of $42 but wants to be sure that if the price moves up she does not pay more than $45. If she places a stop order to buy at $45, the order becomes a market order when the price reaches $45. In the case of the sale of Ford by Ms. Davis, if she wants to assure that she will not sell at less than $60 a share, she can place a stop order to sell at $60.

Two dangers are associated with stop orders. Security prices sometimes exhibit abrupt price changes, so the direction of a change in a security's price may be quite temporary, resulting in premature trading of a security. Also, once the designated price is reached, the stop order becomes a market order and is subject to the uncertainty of the execution price noted earlier for market orders.

A **stop-limit order** is a hybrid of a stop order and a limit order, in that it is a stop order that designates a price limit. In contrast to the stop order, which becomes a market order if the stop is reached, the stop-limit order becomes a limit order if the stop is reached. The order can be used to cushion the market impact of a stop order. The investor may limit the possible execution price after the activation of the stop. As with a limit order, the limit price may never be reached after the order is activated, which therefore defeats one purpose of the stop order—to protect a profit or limit a loss.

Market-If-Touched Orders   An investor may also enter a **market-if-touched order**. This order becomes a market order if a designated price is reached. However, a market-if-touched order to buy becomes a market order if the market *falls* to a given

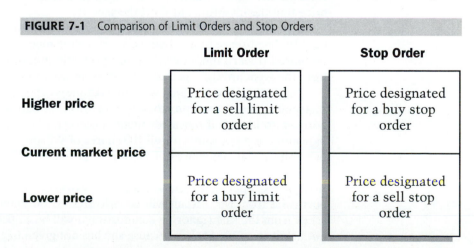

FIGURE 7-1   Comparison of Limit Orders and Stop Orders

	Limit Order	**Stop Order**
Higher price	Price designated for a sell limit order	Price designated for a buy stop order
Current market price		
Lower price	Price designated for a buy limit order	Price designated for a sell stop order

price, while a stop order to buy becomes a market order if the market *rises* to a given price. Similarly, a market-if-touched order to sell becomes a market order if the market rises to a specified price, while the stop order to sell becomes a market order if the market falls to a given price. We can think of the stop order as an order designed to get out of an existing position at an acceptable price (without specifying the exact price), and the market-if-touched order as an order designed to get into a position at an acceptable price (also without specifying the exact price).

Time-Specific Orders   Orders may be placed to buy or sell at the open or close of trading for the day—that is, time-specific orders. An opening order indicates a trade to be executed only in the opening range for the day, and a closing order indicates a trade to be executed only within the closing range for the day.

An investor may enter orders that contain order cancellation provisions. A **fill-or-kill order** must be executed as soon as it reaches the trading floor or it is immediately canceled. Orders may designate the time period for which the order is effective—a day, week, or month, or perhaps by a given time within the day. An **open order**, or **good-till-canceled order**, is good until the order is specifically canceled.

Size-Related Orders   For common stock, orders are also classified by their size. A **round lot** is typically 100 shares of a stock. An **odd lot** is defined as less than a round lot; for example, an order of 75 shares of Digital Equipment Corporation (DEC) is an odd lot order. An order of 350 shares of DEC includes an odd lot portion of 50 shares. A **block trade** is defined on the NYSE as an order of 10,000 shares of a given stock or a total market value of $200,000 or more.

SHORT SELLING

An investor who expects that the price of a security will increase can benefit from buying that security. However, suppose that an investor expects that the price of a security will decline and wants to benefit should the price actually decline. What can the investor do? The investor may be able to sell the security without owning it. Various institutional arrangements allow an investor to borrow securities so that the borrowed security can be delivered to satisfy the sale.

This practice of selling securities that are not owned at the time of sale is referred to as **selling short**. The security is purchased subsequently by the investor and returned to the party that lent it. When the security is returned, the investor is said to have "covered the short position." A profit will be realized if the purchase price is less than the price that the investor sold short the security.

The ability of investors to sell short is an important mechanism in financial markets. In the absence of an effective short-selling mechanism, security prices will tend to be biased toward the view of more optimistic investors, causing a market to depart from the standards of a perfect price-setting situation.

To illustrate short selling with an example, suppose Ms. Stokes believes that Wilson Pharmaceuticals common stock is overpriced at $20 per share and wants to be in a position to benefit if her assessment is correct. Ms. Stokes calls her broker, Mr. Yats, indicating that she wants to sell 100 shares of Wilson Pharmaceuticals. Mr. Yats will do two things: sell 100 shares of Wilson Pharmaceuticals on behalf of Ms. Stokes, and arrange to borrow 100 shares of that stock. Suppose that Mr. Yats is able to sell the stock for $20 per share and arrange to borrow the stock from Mr. Jordan. The shares borrowed from Mr. Jordan will be delivered to the buyer of the 100 shares. The proceeds from the sale (ignoring commissions) will be $2,000. However, the proceeds will not be given to Ms. Stokes because she has not given her broker the 100 shares.

Now, suppose that one week later the price of Wilson Pharmaceuticals stock declines to $15 per share. Ms. Stokes may instruct her broker to *buy* 100 shares of Wilson Pharmaceuticals. The cost of buying the shares (once again ignoring commissions) is $1,500. The shares purchased are then delivered to Mr. Jordan, who loaned the original 100 shares to Ms. Stokes. At this point, Ms. Stokes has sold 100 shares and bought 100 shares, so she no longer has any obligation to her broker or Mr. Jordan—she has covered her short position. She is entitled to the funds in her account that were generated by the selling and buying activity. She sold the stock for $2,000 and bought it for $1,500. Thus, she realizes a profit of $500 before commissions and fees. The broker's commission and a fee charged by the lender of the stock are then subtracted from the $500. Furthermore, if any dividends were paid by Wilson Pharmaceuticals while the stock was borrowed, Ms. Stokes must return them to Mr. Jordan, who still owned the stock at the time.

If instead of falling, suppose the price of Wilson Pharmaceuticals stock rises. Ms. Stokes will realize a loss when she is forced to cover her short position. For example, if the price rises $27, Ms. Stokes will lose $700, to which must be added commissions and the cost of borrowing the stock.

Exchange-imposed restrictions—the so-called **tick-test rules**—designate when a short sale may be executed in order to prevent investors from destabilizing the price of a stock when the market price is falling. A short sale can be made only when either (1) the sale price of the particular stock is higher than the last trade price (referred to as an **uptick trade**), or (2) there is no change in the last trade price of the particular stock, and the previous trade price must be higher than the trade price that preceded it (referred to as a **zero uptick**). For example, if Ms. Stokes wanted to "short" Wilson Pharmaceuticals at a price of $20, and the two previous trade prices were $20\frac{1}{8}$ and then $20, she could not sell short at that time because of the uptick trade rule. If the previous trade prices were $19\frac{7}{8}$, $19\frac{7}{8}$, and then $20, she could short the stock at $20 because of the uptick trade rule. Suppose that the sequence of the last three trades is: $19\frac{7}{8}$, $20, and $20. Ms. Stokes could short the stock at $20 because of the zero uptick rule.

MARGIN TRANSACTIONS

Investors can borrow cash to buy securities and use the securities themselves as collateral. For example, suppose Mr. Boxer has $10,000 to invest and is considering buying Wilson Pharmaceuticals, which is currently selling for $20 per share. With his $10,000, Mr. Boxer can buy 500 shares. Suppose his broker can arrange for him to borrow an additional $10,000 so that Mr. Boxer can buy an additional 500 shares. Thus, with a $10,000 investment, he can purchase a total of 1,000 shares. The 1,000 shares will be used as collateral for the $10,000 borrowed, and Mr. Boxer will have to pay interest on the amount borrowed.

A transaction in which an investor borrows to buy additional securities using the securities themselves as collateral is called **buying on margin**. By borrowing funds, an investor creates financial leverage. Note that Mr. Boxer, for a $10,000 investment, realizes the consequences associated with a price change of 1,000 shares rather than 500 shares. He will benefit if the price rises but be worse off if the price falls (compared to not borrowing funds).

To illustrate what happens if the price subsequently changes, suppose the price of Wilson Pharmaceuticals rises to $29 per share. Mr. Boxer will then realize a profit of $9 per share on 1,000 shares, or $9,000, ignoring commissions and the cost of borrowing. Had Mr. Boxer not borrowed $10,000 to buy the additional 500 shares, his profit would have been only $4,500. Suppose, instead, that the price of Wilson Pharmaceuticals stock declines to $13 per share. Then by borrowing so that he could buy 500 additional shares, he will lose $7,000 ($7 per share on 1,000 shares) instead of just $3,500 ($7 on 500 shares).

The funds borrowed to buy the additional stock will be provided by a broker, and the broker gets the money from a bank. The interest rate that banks charge brokers for these transactions is known as the **call money rate** (also called the **broker loan rate**). The broker charges the investor the call money rate plus a service charge.

MARGIN REQUIREMENTS

The broker is not free to lend as much as it wishes to the investor to buy securities. The Securities and Exchange Act of 1934 prohibits brokers from lending more than a specified percentage of the market value of the securities. The **initial margin requirement** is the proportion of the total market value of the securities that the investor must pay for in cash. The 1934 act gives the Board of Governors of the Federal Reserve the responsibility to set initial margin requirements, under Regulations T and U. The initial margin requirement varies for stocks and bonds and is currently 50%, though it has been below 40%. The Fed also establishes a **maintenance margin requirement**. It is the minimum amount of equity needed in the investor's margin account as compared to the total market value. If the investor's margin account falls below the minimum maintenance margin, the investor is required to put up additional cash. The investor receives a **margin call** from the broker specifying the additional cash to be put into the investor's margin account. If the investor fails to put up the additional cash, the securities are sold.

As we will explain in Chapter 10, investors who take positions in the futures market are also required to satisfy initial and maintenance margin requirements. Margin requirements for the purchase of securities are different in concept from those in futures markets. In a margin transaction involving securities, the initial margin requirement is equivalent to a down payment; the balance is borrowed funds for which interest is paid (the call rate plus a service charge). In the futures market, the initial margin requirement is effectively "good faith" money, indicating that the investor will satisfy the obligation of the futures contract. No money is borrowed by the investor.

◆ ROLE OF BROKERS AND DEALERS IN REAL MARKETS

Common occurrences in real markets keep them from being theoretically perfect. Because of these occurrences, brokers and dealers are necessary to the smooth functioning of a secondary market.

BROKERS

One way in which a real market might not meet all the exacting standards of a theoretically perfect market is that many investors may not be present at all times in the marketplace. Further, a typical investor may not be skilled in the art of the deal or completely informed about every facet of trading in the asset. Clearly, most investors in even smoothly functioning markets need professional assistance. Investors need someone to receive and keep track of their orders for buying or selling, to find other parties wishing to sell or buy, to negotiate for good prices, to serve as a focal point for trading, and to execute the orders. The broker performs all of these functions. Obviously, these functions are more important for the complicated trades, such as the small or large trades, than for simple transactions or those of typical size.

A **broker** is an entity that acts on behalf of an investor who wishes to execute orders. In economic and legal terms, a broker is said to be an "agent" of the investor. It is important to realize that the brokerage activity does not require the broker to buy and hold in inventory or sell from inventory the financial asset that is the subject of the trade. (Such activity is termed "taking a position" in the asset, and it is the role of the dealer.) Rather, the broker receives, transmits, and executes investors' orders with other investors. The broker receives an explicit commission for these services, and the commission is a transaction cost of the capital markets.

DEALERS AS MARKET MAKERS

A real market might also differ from the perfect market because of the possibly frequent event of a temporary imbalance in the number of buy and sell orders that investors may place for any security at any one time. Such unmatched or unbalanced flow causes two problems. First, the security's price may change abruptly even if there has been no shift in either supply or demand for the security. Second, buyers may have to pay higher than market-clearing prices (or sellers accept lower ones) if they want to make their trade immediately.

For example, suppose the consensus price for ABC security is $50, which was determined in several recent trades. Also suppose that a flow of buy orders from investors who suddenly have cash arrives in the market, but is not matched by an accompanying supply of sell orders. This temporary imbalance could be sufficient to push the price of ABC security to, say, $55. Thus, the price would change sharply even though no change in any fundamental financial aspect of the issuer occurred. Buyers who want to buy immediately must pay $55 rather than $50, and this difference can be viewed as the price of "immediacy." By immediacy, we mean that buyers and sellers do not want to wait for the arrival of sufficient orders on the other side of the trade, which would bring the price closer to the level of recent transactions.

The fact of imbalances explains the need for the dealer or market maker, who stands ready and willing to buy a financial asset for its own account (add to an inventory of the security) or sell from its own account (reduce the inventory of the security). At a given time, dealers are willing to buy a security at a price (the bid price) that is less than what they are willing to sell the same security for (the ask price).

In the 1960s, economists George Stigler[1] and Harold Demsetz[2] analyzed the role of dealers in securities markets. They viewed dealers as the suppliers of immediacy—the ability to trade promptly—to the market. The bid-ask spread can be viewed in turn as the price charged by dealers for supplying immediacy, together with short-run price stability (continuity or smoothness) in the presence of short-term order imbalances. Dealers play two other roles: They provide better price information to market participants, and in certain market structures they provide the services of an auctioneer in bringing order and fairness to a market.[3]

The price stabilization role relates to our earlier example of what may happen to the price of a particular transaction in the absence of any intervention in the case of a temporary imbalance of orders. By taking the opposite side of a trade when no other orders are available, the dealer prevents the price from materially diverging from the price at which a recent trade was consummated.

Investors are concerned with immediacy, and they also want to trade at reasonable prices, given prevailing conditions in the market. Although dealers cannot know with certainty the true price of a security, they do occupy a privileged position in some market

[1] George Stigler, "Public Regulation of Securities Markets," *Journal of Business* (April 1964), pp. 117–34.
[2] Harold Demsetz, "The Cost of Transacting," *Quarterly Journal of Economics* (October 1968), pp. 35–6.
[3] Robert A. Schwartz, *Equity Markets: Structure, Trading, and Performance* (New York: Harper & Row Publishers, 1988), pp. 389–97.

structures with respect to the flow of market orders. They also enjoy a privileged position regarding "limit" orders, the special orders that can be executed only if the market price of the security changes in a specified way. (See Chapter 13 for more information on limit orders).

Finally, the dealer acts as an auctioneer in some market structures, thereby providing order and fairness in the operations of the market. For example, as we will explain in Chapter 13, the market maker on organized stock exchanges in the United States performs this function by organizing trading to make sure that the exchange rules for the priority of trading are followed. The role of a market maker in a call market structure is that of an auctioneer. The market maker does not take a position in the traded security, as a dealer does in a continuous market.

What factors determine the price dealers should charge for the services they provide? Or equivalently, what factors determine the bid-ask spread? One of the most important is the order processing costs incurred by dealers, such as the costs of equipment necessary to do business and the administrative and operations staff. The lower these costs, the narrower is the bid-ask spread. With the reduced cost of computing and better-trained personnel, these costs have declined since the 1960s.

Dealers also have to be compensated for bearing risk. A **dealer's position** may involve carrying inventory of a security (a *long* position) or selling a security that is not in inventory (a *short* position). Three types of risks are associated with maintaining a long or short position in a given security. First, the uncertainty about the future price of the security presents a substantial risk. A dealer who takes a long position in the security is concerned that the price will decline in the future; a dealer who is in a short position is concerned that the price will rise.

The second type of risk concerns the expected time it will take the dealer to unwind a position and its uncertainty, which, in turn, depends primarily on the rate at which buy and sell orders for the security reach the market (i.e., the thickness of the market). Finally, although a dealer may be able to access better information about order flows than the general public, in some trades the dealer takes the risk of trading with someone in possession of better information.[4] This situation results in the better-informed trader obtaining a better price at the expense of the dealer. Consequently, in establishing the bid-ask spread for a trade, a dealer will assess whether the trader may hold better information.[5]

◆ MARKET EFFICIENCY

The term *efficient,* used in several contexts, describes the operating characteristics of a capital market. A distinction, however, can be made between an *operationally* (or *internally*) *efficient market* and a *pricing* (or *externally*) *efficient capital market.*[6]

OPERATIONAL EFFICIENCY

In an **operationally efficient market**, investors can obtain transaction services as cheaply as possible, given the costs associated with furnishing those services. For example, in national equity markets throughout the world the degree of operational effi-

---

[4] Walter Bagehot, "The Only Game in Town," *Financial Analysts Journal* (March/April 1971), pp. 12–14, 22.
[5] Some trades that we will discuss in Chapter 13 can be viewed as "informationless trades," meaning that the dealer knows or believes a trade is being requested to accomplish an investment objective not motivated by the potential future price movement of the security.
[6] Richard R. West, "Two Kinds of Market Efficiency," *Financial Analysts Journal* (November/December 1975), pp. 30–4.

ciency varies. At one time, brokerage commissions in the United States were fixed, and the brokerage industry charged high fees. That changed in May 1975, as the U. S. exchanges were forced to adopt a system of competitive and negotiated commissions. Non-U.S. markets continue to move toward more competitive brokerage fees. France, for example, adopted a system of negotiated commissions for large trades in 1985. In its "Big Bang" of 1986, the London Stock Exchange abolished fixed commissions.

Commissions are only part of the cost of transacting, as already noted. The other part is the dealer spread. Bid-ask spreads for bonds vary by type of bond. For example, the bid-ask spread on U.S. Treasury securities are much smaller than for other bonds. Even with the U.S. Treasury securities market, certain issues have a narrower bid-ask spread than other issues. Other components of transaction costs are discussed later in this chapter.

PRICING EFFICIENCY

Pricing efficiency refers to a market where prices at all times fully reflect all available information that is relevant to the valuation of securities. That is, relevant information about the security is quickly integrated into the price of securities.

In his seminal review article on pricing efficiency, Eugene Fama points out that in order to test whether a market is price efficient, two definitions are necessary. First, it is necessary to define what it means that prices "fully reflect" information. Second, the "relevant" set of information that is assumed to be "fully reflected" in prices must be defined.[7]

Fama, as well as others, defines "fully reflects" in terms of the expected return from holding a security. The expected return over some holding period is equal to expected cash distributions plus the expected price change, all divided by the initial price. The price formation process defined by Fama and others is that the expected return one period from now is a stochastic (i.e., random) variable that already takes into account the "relevant" information set.[8]

In defining the "relevant" information set that prices should reflect, Fama classified the pricing efficiency of a market into three forms: weak, semi-strong, and strong. The distinction between these forms lies in the relevant information that is hypothesized within the price of the security. **Weak efficiency** means that the price of the security reflects the past price and trading history of the security. **Semi-strong efficiency** means that the price of the security fully reflects all public information, which includes but is not limited to historical price and trading patterns. **Strong efficiency** exists in a market where the price of a security reflects all information, whether or not it is publicly available.

A price-efficient market carries certain implications for the investment strategy investors may wish to pursue. Throughout this book, we refer to various active strategies employed by investors. In an active strategy, investors seek to capitalize on what they perceive to be the mispricing of a security or securities. In a market that is price efficient, active strategies will not consistently generate a return after taking into consideration transaction costs and the risks associated with a strategy that is greater than simply buying and holding securities. In certain markets that empirical evidence suggests are price efficient, investors may pursue a strategy of **indexing**, which simply seeks to match the performance of some financial index. We will look at the pricing efficiency of the stock market in Chapter 13; the greatest amount of empirical evidence exists in this market.

---

[7] Eugene F. Fama, "Efficient Capital Markets: A Review of Theory and Empirical Work," *Journal of Finance* (May 1970), pp. 383–417.

[8] If it is assumed that investors will not invest in a security unless its expected return is greater than zero, then the price formation process is called a *submartingale process*.

◆ TRANSACTION COSTS[9]

In an investment era where one-half of one percentage point can make a difference when a money manager is compared against a performance benchmark, an important aspect of the investment process is the cost of implementing an investment strategy. Transaction costs are more than merely brokerage commissions—they consist of commissions, fees, execution costs, and opportunity costs.

Commissions are the fees paid to brokers to trade securities. In May 1975 commissions became fully negotiable and have declined dramatically since then. Included in the category of fees are custodial fees and transfer fees. Custodial fees are the fees charged by an institution that holds securities in safekeeping for an investor.

Execution costs represent the difference between the execution price of a security and the price that would have existed in the absence of the trade. Execution costs can be further decomposed into **market** (or **price**) **impact** and **market timing costs**. Market impact cost is the result of the bid-ask spread and a price concession extracted by dealers to mitigate their risk that an investor's demand for liquidity is information-motivated.[10] Market timing cost arises when an adverse price movement of the security during the time of the transaction can be attributed in part to other activity in the security and is not the result of a particular transaction. Execution costs, then, are related to both the demand for liquidity and the trading activity on the trade date.

A distinction can be made between **information-motivated trades** and **information-less trades**.[11] Information-motivated trading occurs when investors believe they possess pertinent information not currently reflected in the security's price. This style of trading tends to increase market impact because it emphasizes the speed of execution, or because the market maker believes a desired trade is driven by information and increases the bid-ask spread to provide some protection. It can involve the sale of one security in favor of another. Informationless trades result from either a reallocation of wealth or implementation of an investing strategy that utilizes only existing information. An example of the former is a pension fund's decision to invest cash in the stock market. Other examples of informationless trades include portfolio rebalances, investment of new money, or liquidations. In these circumstances, the demand for liquidity alone should not lead the market maker to demand the significant price concessions associated with new information.

The problem with measuring execution costs is that the true measure—which is the difference between the price of the security in the absence of the investor's trade and the execution price—is not observable. Furthermore, the execution prices depend on supply and demand conditions at the margin. Thus, the execution price may be influenced by competitive traders who demand immediate execution, or other investors with similar motives for trading. Then, the execution price realized by an investor is the consequence of the structure of the market mechanism, the demand for liquidity by the marginal investor, and the competitive forces of investors with similar motivations for trading.

The cost of not transacting represents an opportunity cost.[12] Opportunity costs may arise when a desired trade fails to be executed. This component of costs represents

---

[9] The discussion in this section draws from Bruce M. Collins and Frank J. Fabozzi, "A Methodology for Measuring Transactions Costs," *Financial Analysts Journal* (March/April 1991), pp. 27–36.

[10] By a price concession we mean the investor will have to pay a higher price when buying and a lower price when selling.

[11] L. Cuneo and W. Wagner, "Reducing the Cost of Stock Trading," *Financial Analysts Journal* (November/December 1975), pp. 835–43.

[12] For a discussion of opportunity cost, within the context of costs defined as the implementation shortfall of an investment strategy, see André F. Perold, "The Implementation Shortfall: Paper Versus Reality," *Journal of Portfolio Management* (Summer 1988), pp. 4–9.

the difference in performance between an investor's desired investment and the same investor's actual investment after adjusting for execution costs, commissions, and fees.

Opportunity costs are characterized as the hidden cost of trading. Some analysts suggest that the shortfall in performance of many actively managed portfolios is the consequence of failing to execute all desired trades.[13] Measurement of opportunity costs is subject to the same problems as measurement of execution costs. The true measure of opportunity costs depend on knowing the resulting performance of a security if all desired trades were executed at the desired time across an investment horizon. Because these desired trades were not executed, the benchmark is inherently unobservable. [14]

Summary

In a secondary market in financial assets, existing or outstanding assets are traded among investors. A secondary market serves several needs of the firm or governmental unit that issues securities in the primary market. The secondary market provides the issuer with regular information about the value of its outstanding stocks or bonds, and it encourages investors to buy securities from issuers because it offers them an ongoing opportunity for liquidating their investments in securities.

Investors also get services from the secondary market. The market supplies them with liquidity and prices for the assets they are holding or want to buy; and the market brings interested investors together, thereby reducing the costs of searching for other parties and of making trades.

Secondary markets for securities exist around the world. Such markets may be continuous, where trading and price determination go on throughout the day as orders to buy and sell reach the market. Some markets are call markets where prices are determined by executions of batched or grouped orders to buy and sell at a specific time (or times) within the trading day. Some secondary markets combine features of call and continuous trading.

Even the most developed and smoothly functioning secondary market falls short of being "perfect" in the economically theoretical meaning of the term. Actual markets tend to experience numerous "frictions" that affect prices and investor's behavior. Some key frictions are the various transaction costs.

Investors can place different types of orders with brokers, including market orders, limit orders, stop orders, stop-limit orders, market-if-touched orders, and time-specific orders. Size-related orders are also an option.

An investor who expects that the price of a security will decline can benefit by selling a security short. A mechanism to allow investors to sell short is critical in financial markets because in the absence of such a mechanism, security prices will tend to be biased toward the view of more optimistic investors. Exchange-imposed restrictions determine when a short sale can be executed.

When buying on margin, an investor borrows to buy additional securities, using the securities themselves as collateral. By borrowing funds to buy securities, an investor creates financial leverage. The funds borrowed to buy the additional securities will be provided by a broker. The call money rate is the interest rate that banks charge brokers for buying on margin. Margin requirements must be satisfied when buying on margin.

Because of imperfections in actual markets, investors need the services of two types of market participants: dealers and brokers. Brokers aid investors by collecting and

---

[13] See J. L. Treynor, "What Does It Take to Win the Trading Game?" *Financial Analysts Journal* (January/February 1981), pp. 55–60, for a discussion of the consequences of high opportunity costs.

[14] Methodologies have been proposed to estimate execution costs and opportunity costs. See, for example, Collins and Fabozzi, "A Methodology for Measuring Transactions Costs."

transmitting orders to the market, by bringing willing buyers and sellers together, by negotiating prices, and by executing orders. The fee for these services is the broker's commission.

Dealers perform three functions in markets: (1) they provide the opportunity for investors to trade immediately rather than waiting for the arrival of sufficient orders on the other side of the trade ("immediacy"), and dealers do this while maintaining short-run price stability ("continuity"); (2) dealers offer price information to market participants; and (3) in certain market structures, dealers serve as auctioneers in bringing order and fairness to a market. Dealers buy for their own accounts and maintain inventories of securities, and their profits come from selling assets at higher prices than they purchased them.

A market is operationally efficient if it offers investors reasonably priced services related to buying and selling. A market is price efficient if at all times prices fully reflect all available information that is relevant to the valuation of securities. Three forms of pricing efficiency are based on the relevant information set: weak form, semi-strong form, and strong form. In such a price-efficient market, pursuing active strategies will not consistently produce superior returns after adjusting for risk and transaction costs.

Transaction costs include commissions, fees, execution costs, and opportunity costs. Execution costs represent the difference between the execution price of a security and the price that would have existed in the absence of the trade, and arise out of the demand for immediate execution through both the demand for liquidity and the trading activity on the trade date. Opportunity costs arise when a desired trade fails to be executed.

Key Terms ▪▪

- Block trade
- Broker
- Buy limit order
- Buying on margin
- Call market
- Call money rate (broker loan rate)
- Continuous market
- Dealer's position
- Execution costs
- Fill-or-kill order
- Good-till-canceled order
- Indexing
- Informationless trades
- Information-motivated trades

- Initial margin requirements
- Limit order
- Limit order book
- Maintenance margin requirement
- Margin call
- Market-if-touched order
- Market order
- Market price impact
- Market timing costs
- Odd lot
- Open order
- Operationally efficient market
- Pricing efficiency
- Round lot

- Sell limit order
- Selling short
- Semi-strong efficiency
- Stop-limit order
- Stop order
- Stop order to buy
- Stop order to sell
- Strong efficiency
- Tick-test rules
- Uptick trade
- Weak efficiency
- Zero uptick

Questions ▪▪▪

1. How do secondary markets benefit investors?
2. What is an organized exchange?
3. What is meant by an over-the-counter market?
4. What are the basic features of the call method of trading?
5. What is meant by a continuous market?
6. The following quote is taken from "The Taxonomy of Trading Strategies," by Wayne H. Wagner, which appears in *Trading Strategies and Execution Costs* published by The Institute of Chartered Financial Analysts in 1988:

   When a trader decides how to bring an order to the market, he or she must deal with some very important issues; to me, the most important is: What kind of trade is this? It could be either an active or a passive trade. The

*type of trade will dictate whether speed of execution is more or less impor-
tant than cost of execution. In other words, do I want immediate trading (a
market order); or am I willing to forgo the immediate trade for the possibility of trading less expensively if I am willing to "give" on the timing of
the trade (a limit order)?*

   a. What is meant by a market order and why would one be placed when a trader
      wants immediate trading?
   b. What is meant by a limit order and why may it be less expensive than a market
      order?

7. Suppose that Mr. Mancuso has purchased the stock of Harley Bike Company for
   $45 and that he sets a maximum loss that he will accept on this stock of $6. What
   type of order can Mr. Mancuso place?

8. a. A market can be perfect, in a theoretical sense, only if it meets certain condi-
      tions. What are those conditions?
   b. What is meant by a market friction?

9. a. Why would an investor sell short a security?
   b. What happens if the price of a security that is sold short rises in price?
   c. What are the restrictions on shorting common stock?
   d. What is the role of the broker in a short sale?

10. a. What is meant by buying on margin?
    b. How does margin increase an investor's leverage?
    c. Who determines margin requirements for purchasing securities on margin?

11. What is the difference between a broker and a dealer?

12. How does a dealer make a profit when making a market?

13. What are the risks that a dealer accepts in making a market?

14. What is meant by the bid-ask spread?

15. How does the rate of order flow (or thickness) of a market affect a dealer's bid-
    ask spread?

16. What are the benefits that a market derives from the actions of dealers?

17. The residential real estate market boasts many brokers but very few dealers. What
    explains this situation?

18. What makes a market operationally or internally efficient?

19. What is the key characteristic of a market that has pricing or external efficiency?

20. What is meant by the semi-strong form of market efficiency?

21. Indicate why you agree or disagree with the following statement: "An investor who
    believes a market is price efficient should pursue an active investment strategy."

22. The following statements are taken from Greta E. Marshall's article "Execution
    Costs: The Plan Sponsor's View," which appears in *Trading Strategies* and *Execution
    Costs* published by The Institute of Chartered Financial Analysts in 1988.
    a. "There are three components of trading costs. First there are direct costs which
       may be measured—commissions. Second, there are indirect—or market
       impact—costs. Finally, there are the undefined costs of not trading." What are
       market impact costs, and what do you think the "undefined costs of not trad-
       ing" represent?
    b. "Market impact, unlike broker commissions, is difficult to identify and mea-
       sure." Why is market impact cost difficult to measure?

23. a. What is meant by an information-motivated trade?
    b. What is meant by an informationless trade?

CHAPTER 8

Risk and Return Theories: I

Learning Objectives

After reading this chapter you will understand:

◆ how to calculate the historical single-period investment return for a security or portfolio of securities.

◆ the different methods for calculating the return over several unit periods.

◆ what is meant by an efficient portfolio.

◆ how to calculate the expected return and risk of a single asset and a portfolio of assets.

◆ why the expected return of a portfolio of assets is a weighted average of the expected return of the assets included in the portfolio.

◆ how portfolio theory assumes that investors make investment decisions.

◆ the difference between systematic risk and unsystematic risk.

◆ the impact of diversification on total risk.

◆ the importance of the correlation between two assets in measuring a portfolio's risk.

◆ what is meant by a feasible portfolio and a set of feasible portfolios.

◆ what is meant by the Markowitz efficient frontier.

◆ what is meant by an optimal portfolio and how an optimal portfolio is selected from all the portfolios available on the Markowitz efficient frontier.

As we explained in Chapter 1, valuation is the process of determining the fair value of a financial asset. The value of any financial asset is the present value of the cash flow expected. The process requires two steps: estimating the cash flow and determining the appropriate interest rate that should be used to calculate the present value. The appropriate interest rate is the minimum interest rate plus a risk premium. The amount of the risk premium depends on the risk associated with realizing the cash flow. In this chapter and the next, theories about how to determine the appropriate risk premium are presented, through demonstrating the theoretical relationship between risk and expected return that should prevail in capital markets.

The development of the theoretical relationship between risk and expected return is built on two economic theories: portfolio theory and capital market theory. Portfolio theory deals with the selection of portfolios that maximize expected returns consistent with individually acceptable levels of risk. Capital market theory deals with the effects of investor decisions on security prices. More specifically, it shows the relationship that

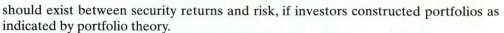

should exist between security returns and risk, if investors constructed portfolios as indicated by portfolio theory.

Together, portfolio and capital market theories provide a framework to specify and measure investment risk and to develop relationships between risk and expected return (and hence between risk and the required return on an investment). These theories have revolutionized the world of finance, by allowing portfolio managers to quantify the investment risk and expected return of a portfolio and allowing corporate treasurers to quantify the cost of capital and risk of a proposed capital investment.

In this chapter, we begin with the basic concepts of portfolio theory and then build upon these concepts in the next chapter to develop the theoretical relationship between the expected return of an asset and risk. Because the risk and return relationship indicates how much an asset's expected return should be given its relevant risks, it also tells us how an asset should be priced. Hence the risk and return relationship is also referred to as an **asset pricing model**. In the next chapter we present three asset pricing models that dominate financial thinking today.

Prior to the development of the theories we present, investors would often speak of risk and return, but the failure to quantify these important measures made the goal of constructing a portfolio of assets highly subjective and provided no insight as to the return investors should expect. Moreover, investors would focus on the risks of individual assets without understanding how combining them into a portfolio can affect the portfolio's risk. The theories we present here quantify the relationship between risk and expected return. In October 1990, as confirmation of the importance of these theories, the Alfred Nobel Memorial Prize in Economic Science was awarded to Professor Harry Markowitz,[1] the developer of portfolio theory, and to Professor William Sharpe who is one of the developers of capital market theory.[2]

◆ MEASURING INVESTMENT RETURN

Before proceeding with the theories, we explain how the actual investment return of a portfolio should be measured. The return on an investor's portfolio during a given interval is equal to the change in value of the portfolio plus any distributions received from the portfolio, expressed as a fraction of the initial portfolio value. It is important that any capital or income distributions made to the investor be included, or the measure of return will be deficient.

Another way to look at return is as the amount (expressed as a fraction of the initial portfolio value) that can be withdrawn at the end of the interval while maintaining the initial portfolio value intact. The return on the investor's portfolio, designated R_p, is given by:

$$R_P = \frac{V_1 - V_0 + D}{V_0} \qquad (8.1)$$

where V_1 = the portfolio market value at the end of the interval
V_0 = the portfolio market value at the beginning of the interval
D = the cash distributions to the investor during the interval

The calculation assumes that any interest or dividend income received on the portfolio of securities and not distributed to the investor is reinvested in the portfolio (and

---

[1]   Harry M. Markowitz, "Portfolio Selection," *Journal of Finance* (March 1952), pp. 77–91; and *Portfolio Selection*, Cowles Foundation Monograph 16 (New York: John Wiley & Sons, 1959).
[2]   William F. Sharpe, *Portfolio: Theory and Capital Markets* (New York: McGraw-Hill, 1970).

thus reflected in V_1). Further, the calculation assumes that any distributions occur at the end of the interval, or are held in the form of cash until the end of the interval. If the distributions were reinvested prior to the end of the interval, the calculation would have to be modified to consider the gains or losses on the amount reinvested. The formula also assumes no capital inflows during the interval. Otherwise, the calculation would have to be modified to reflect the increased investment base. Capital inflows at the end of the interval (or held in cash until the end), however, can be treated as just the reverse of distributions in the return calculation.

Thus, given the beginning and ending portfolio values, plus any contributions from or distributions to the investor (assumed to occur at the end of an interval), equation (8.1) lets us compute the investor's return. For example, if the XYZ pension fund contained a market value of $100 million at the end of June, benefit payments of $5 million made at the end of July, and an end-of-July market value of $103 million, the return for the month would be 8%.

$$R_P = \frac{103,000,000 - 100,000,000 + 5,000,000}{100,000,000} = 0.08$$

In principle, this sort of calculation of returns could be carried out for any interval of time, say, for 1 month or 10 years. Yet several problems arise with this approach. First, it is apparent that a calculation made over a long period of time, say, more than a few months, would not be reliable because of the underlying assumption that all cash payments and inflows are made and received at the end of the period. Clearly, if two investments have the same return as calculated by equation (8.1), but one investment makes cash payment early and the other late, the one with early payment will be understated. Second, we cannot rely on the preceding formula to compare return on a 1-month investment with that on a 10-year portfolio. For purposes of comparison the return must be expressed per unit of time—say, per year.

In practice, we handle these two problems by first computing the return over a reasonably short unit of time, perhaps a quarter of a year or less. The return over the relevant horizon, consisting of several unit periods, is computed by averaging the return over the unit intervals. Three generally used methods of averaging include (1) the arithmetic average return, (2) the time-weighted rate of return (also referred to as the geometric rate of return), and (3) the dollar-weighted return. The averaging produces a measure of return per unit of time period. The measures can be converted to an annual or other period return by standard procedures.

ARITHMETIC AVERAGE RATE OF RETURN

The **arithmetic average rate of return** is an unweighted average of the returns achieved during a series of such measurement intervals. The general formula is:

$$R_A = \frac{R_{P1} + R_{P2} + \cdots + R_{PN}}{N}$$

R_A = the arithmetic average return
R_{Pk} = the portfolio return in interval k as measured by equation (8.1),
   $k = 1, \ldots, N$
N = the number of intervals in the performance evaluation period

For example, if the portfolio returns were -10%, 20%, and 5% in July, August, and September, respectively, the arithmetic average monthly return is 5%.

The arithmetic average can be thought of as the mean value of the withdrawals (expressed as a fraction of the initial portfolio value) that can be made at the end of each interval while maintaining the initial portfolio value intact. In the preceding example, the investor must add 10% of the initial portfolio value at the end of the first interval and can withdraw 20% and 5% of the initial portfolio value per period.

TIME-WEIGHTED RATE OF RETURN

The **time-weighted rate of return** measures the compounded rate of growth of the initial portfolio during the performance evaluation period, assuming that all cash distributions are reinvested in the portfolio. It is also commonly referred to as the "geometric rate of return." It is computed by taking the geometric average of the portfolio returns computed from equation (8.1). The general formula is:

$$R_T = \left[\left(1 + R_{P1}\right)\left(1 + R_{P2}\right) \ldots \left(1 + R_{PN}\right) \right]^{1/N} - 1$$

where R_T is the time-weighted rate of return and R_{Pk} and N are as defined earlier.

For example, if the portfolio returns were −10%, 20%, and 5% in July, August, and September, as in the preceding example, then the time-weighted rate of return is:

$$R_T = \left[\left(1 + -0.10\right)\left(1 + 0.20\right)\left(1 + 0.05\right) \right]^{1/3} - 1$$

$$= \left[\left(0.90\right)\left(1.20\right)\left(1.05\right) \right]^{1/3} - 1 = 0.043$$

As the time-weighted rate of return is 4.3% per month, $1 invested in the portfolio at the end of June would have grown at a rate of 4.3% per month during the 3-month period.

In general, the arithmetic and time-weighted average returns do not provide the same answers, because computation of the arithmetic average assumes the initial amount invested to be maintained (through additions or withdrawals) at its initial portfolio value. The time-weighted return, on the other hand, is the return on a portfolio that varies in size because of the assumption that all proceeds are reinvested.

We can use an example to show how the two averages fail to coincide. Consider a portfolio with a $100 million market value at the of 1999, a $200 million value at the end of 2000, and a $100 million value at the end of 2001. The annual returns are 100% and −50%. The arithmetic return is 25%, while the time-weighted average return is 0%. The arithmetic average return consists of the average of the $100 million withdrawn at the end of 2000 and the $50 million replaced at the end of 2001. The rate of return is clearly zero, however, the 100% in 2000 being exactly offset by the 50% loss in 2001 on the larger investment base. In this example, the arithmetic average exceeds the time-weighted average return. This outcome always proves to be true, except in the special situation where the returns in each interval are the same, in which case the averages are identical.

DOLLAR-WEIGHTED RATE OF RETURN

The **dollar-weighted rate of return** (also called the **internal rate of return**) is computed by finding the interest rate that will make the present value of the cash flows from all the interval periods plus the terminal market value of the portfolio equal to the initial market value of the portfolio. The internal rate of return calculation, as explained in

Chapter 18, is calculated exactly the same way as the yield to maturity on a bond. The general formula for the dollar-weighted return is:

$$V_0 = \frac{C_1}{\left(1 + R_D\right)} + \frac{C_2}{\left(1 + R_D\right)^2} + \cdots + \frac{C_N + V_N}{\left(1 + R_D\right)^n}$$

where R_D = the dollar-weighted rate of return
V_0 = the initial market value of the portfolio
V_N = the terminal market value of the portfolio
C_k = the cash flow for the portfolio (cash inflows minus cash outflows) for interval k, $k = 1, \ldots, N$

For example, consider a portfolio with a market value of $100 million at the end of 1999, capital withdrawals of $5 million at the end of 2000, 2001, and 2002, and a market value at the end of 2002 of $110 million. Then V_0 = $100,000,000; $N = 3$; $C_1 = C_2 = C_3$ = $5,000,000; V_3 = $110,000,000; and R_D is the interest rate that satisfies the equation:

$$\$110,000,000 = \frac{\$5,000,000}{\left(1 + R_D\right)^1} + \frac{\$5,000,000}{\left(1 + R_D\right)^2} + \frac{\$5,000,000 + \$110,000,000}{\left(1 + R_D\right)^3}$$

It can be verified that the interest rate that satisfies this expression is 8.1%, which is the dollar-weighted return.

Under special conditions, both the dollar-weighted return and the time-weighted return produce the same result. This outcome will occur when no further additions or withdrawals occur, and all dividends are reinvested.

Throughout this chapter we generally use rate of return to refer to an appropriately standardized measure.

◆ PORTFOLIO THEORY

In constructing a portfolio of assets, investors seek to maximize the expected return from their investment given some level of risk they are willing to accept.[3] Portfolios that satisfy this requirement are called **efficient portfolios**. Portfolio theory tells us how to achieve efficient portfolios. Because Markowitz is the developer of portfolio theory, efficient portfolios are sometimes referred to as "Markowitz efficient portfolios."

To construct an efficient portfolio of risky assets, it is necessary to make some assumption about how investors behave in making investment decisions. A reasonable assumption is that investors are **risk averse**. A risk-averse investor, when faced with two investments with the same expected return but two different risks, will prefer the one with the lower risk. Given a choice of efficient portfolios from which an investor can select, an **optimal portfolio** is the one most preferred.

To construct an efficient portfolio, one needs to understand what is meant by *expected return* and *risk*. The latter concept, risk, could mean any one of many types of risk. We shall be more specific about its meaning as we proceed in this chapter.

◆ RISKY ASSETS VERSUS RISK-FREE ASSETS

It is important to distinguish between risky assets and risk-free assets. A **risky asset** is one for which the return that will be realized in the future is uncertain. For example, suppose an investor purchases the stock of General Motors today and plans to hold the

---

[3] Alternatively stated, investors seek to minimize the risk that they are exposed to given some target expected return.

stock for 1 year. At the time she purchased the stock, she does not know what return will be realized. The return will depend on the price of General Motors stock 1 year from now and the dividends that the company pays during the year. Thus, General Motors stock, and indeed the stock of all companies, are risky assets.

Even securities issued by the U.S. government are risky assets. For example, an investor who purchases a U.S. government bond that matures in 30 years does not know the return that will be realized if this bond is to be held for only 1 year. Because, as we explain in Chapter 18, a change in interest rates will affect the price of the bond 1 year from now, and therefore affects the return from investing in that bond for 1 year.

For certain assets, however, the return that will be realized in the future is known for sure today. Such assets are referred to as **risk-free** or **riskless assets**. The risk-free asset is commonly defined as short-term obligations of the U.S. government. For example, if an investor buys a U.S. government security that matures in 1 year and plans to hold that security for 1 year, then there is no uncertainty about the return that will be realized. The investor knows that in 1 year, on the maturity date of the security, the government will pay a specific amount to retire the debt. Notice how this situation differs for the U.S. government security that matures in 30 years. Although the 1-year and the 30-year securities are obligations of the U.S. government, the former matures in 1 year so that there is no uncertainty about the return that will be realized. In contrast, even though the investor knows what the government will pay at the end of 30 years for the 30-year bond, the investor does not know what the price of the bond will be 1 year from now.

◆ MEASURING PORTFOLIO RISK

The definition of investment risk leads us into less-explored territory. Not everyone agrees on how to define risk, let alone measure it. Nevertheless, some attributes of risk are reasonably well accepted.

An investor holding a portfolio of Treasury securities until the maturity date faces no uncertainty about monetary outcome. The value of the portfolio at maturity of the securities will be identical with the predicted value; the investor bears no price risk. In the case of a portfolio composed of common stocks, however, it will be impossible to predict the value of the portfolio at any future date. The best an investor can do is to make a best-guess or most-likely estimate, qualified by statements about the range and likelihood of other values. In this case, the investor does bear price risk.

Defining risk in terms of price risk, one measure of risk is the extent to which future portfolio values are likely to diverge from the expected or predicted value. More specifically, risk for most investors is related to the chance that future portfolio values will be less than expected. That is, if the investor's portfolio has a current value of $100,000, and an expected value of $110,000 at the end of the next year, what matters is the probability of values less than $110,000.

Before proceeding to the quantification of risk, it is convenient to shift our attention from the terminal value of the portfolio to the portfolio rate of return, R_p, because the increase in portfolio value is related directly to R_p.[4]

---

[4]   The transformation changes nothing of substance because:

$$\tilde{M}_T = \left(1 + \tilde{R}_p\right)M_0 = M_0 + M_0 R_p$$

where $\tilde{M}_T$ is the terminal portfolio value and $\tilde{R}_p$ is the portfolio return. [The tilde (~) above a variable indicates that it is a random variable.] Because $\tilde{M}_T$ is a linear function of $\tilde{R}_p$ any risk measures developed for the portfolio return will apply equally to the terminal market value.

EXPECTED PORTFOLIO RETURN

A particularly useful way to quantify the uncertainty about the portfolio return is to specify the probability associated with each of the possible future returns. Assume, for example, that an investor identifies five possible outcomes for the portfolio return during the next year. Associated with each return is a subjectively determined probability, or relative chance of occurrence. The five possible outcomes are shown in Table 8-1.

Note that the probabilities sum to 1 so that the actual portfolio return is confined to assume one of the five possible values. Given this probability distribution, we can measure the expected return and risk for the portfolio.

The expected return is simply the weighted average of possible outcomes, where the weights are the relative chances of occurrence. In general, the expected return on the portfolio, denoted $E(R_p)$, is given by:

$$E\left(R_p\right) = P_1 R_1 + P_2 R_2 + \cdots + R_n P_n \qquad \textbf{(8.2)}$$

$$E\left(R_p\right) = \sum_{j=1}^{n} P_j R_j$$

where each R_j is a possible return, each P_j an associated probability, and n the number of possible outcomes.

The expected return of the portfolio in our illustration is:

$$E\left(R_p\right) = 0.1\left(50\%\right) + 0.2\left(30\%\right) + 0.4\left(10\%\right) + 0.2\left(-10\%\right) + 0.1\left(-30\%\right)$$
$$= 10\%$$

VARIABILITY OF EXPECTED RETURN

If risk is defined as the chance of achieving returns less than expected, it would seem logical to measure risk by the dispersion of the possible returns below the expected value. Risk measures based on below-the-mean variability are difficult to work with, however, and moreover are unnecessary as long as the distribution of future return is reasonably symmetric about the expected value. Figure 8-1 shows three probability distributions: the first symmetric, the second skewed to the left, and the third skewed to the right. For a symmetrical distribution, the dispersion of returns on one side of the expected return is the same as the dispersion on the other side of the expected return.

Empirical studies of realized rates of return on diversified portfolios consisting of more than 20 stocks show that skewness is not a significant problem.[5] If future distribu-

TABLE 8-1	Five Possible Outcomes for Portfolio Return	
Outcome	*Possible Return*	*Probability*
1	50%	0.1
2	30	0.2
3	10	0.4
4	−10	0.2
5	−30	0.1

[5] For example, see Marshall E. Blume, "Portfolio Theory: A Step Toward Its Practical Application," *Journal of Business* (April 1970), pp. 152–73.

Symmetric probability distribution

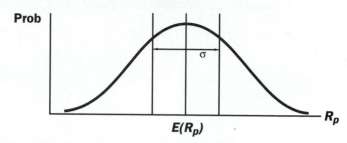

Probability distribution skewed to left

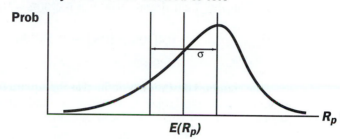

Probability distribution skewed to right

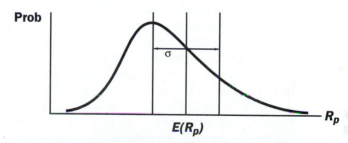

FIGURE 8-1 Possible Shapes for Probability Distributions

tions are shaped like historical distributions, it makes little difference whether we measure variability of returns on one or both sides of the expected return. If the probability distribution is symmetric, measures of the total variability of return will be twice as large as measures of the portfolio's variability below the expected return. Thus, if total variability is used as a risk surrogate, the risk ranking for a group of portfolios will be the same as when variability below the expected return is used. For this reason, total variability of returns is used widely as a surrogate for risk.

It now remains to choose a specific measure of total variability of returns. The most commonly used measures are the variance and standard deviation of returns.

The **variance of return** is a weighted sum of the squared deviations from the expected return. Squaring the deviations ensures that deviations above and below the expected value contribute equally to the measure of variability regardless of sign. The variance for the portfolio, designated var(R_p), is given by:

$$\text{var}\left(R_p\right) = P_1\left[R_1 - E\left(R_p\right)\right]^2 + P_2\left[R_2 - E\left(R_p\right)\right]^2 + \cdots + P_n\left[R_n - E\left(R_p\right)\right]^2 \quad \textbf{(8.3)}$$

or

$$\text{var}\left(R_p\right) = \sum_{j=1}^{n} P_j\left[R_j - E\left(R_p\right)\right]^2$$

In the previous example, the variance for the portfolio is

$$\text{var}\left(R_p\right) = 0.1\left(50\% - 10\%\right)^2 + 0.2\left(30\% - 10\%\right)^2$$
$$+ 0.4\left(10\% - 10\%\right)^2 + 0.2\left(-10\% - 10\%\right)^2 + 0.1\left(-30\% - 10\%\right)^2$$
$$= 480\%$$

The **standard deviation** is defined as the square root of the variance. It is equal to 22% in our example. The larger the variance or standard deviation, the greater the possible dispersion of future realized values around the expected value, and the larger the investor's uncertainty. As a rule of thumb for symmetric distributions, it is often suggested that roughly two-thirds of the possible returns will lie within one standard deviation either side of the expected value, and that 95% will be within two standard deviations.

Historical return distributions for a portfolio of a large number of securities show that the distribution is approximately, but not perfectly, symmetric. In contrast, the return distribution for individual securities is highly skewed. The most interesting aspect of observed historical return distributions, however, is the standard deviation of historical returns, which tend to be considerably higher for individual securities than for diversified portfolios. We discuss this result further in the following paragraphs.

Thus far we confined our discussion of portfolio risk to a single-period investment horizon such as the next year—that is, the portfolio is held unchanged and evaluated at the end of the year. An obvious question relates to the effect of holding the portfolio for several periods—say, for the next 20 years. Will the 1-year risks tend to cancel out over time? The answer depends on the random process that security prices follow. Specifically, it has been observed that security prices follow a **random walk**, which means that the expected value of future price changes is independent of past price changes. Given the random walk nature of security prices, the answer to this question is "no." If the risk level (standard deviation) is maintained during each year, the portfolio risk for longer horizons will increase with the horizon length. The standard deviation of possible terminal portfolio values after N years is equal to $\sqrt{N}$ times the standard deviation after 1 year.[6] Thus, the investor cannot rely on the "long run" to reduce the risk of loss.

---

[6] This result can be illustrated as follows. The portfolio market value after N years, M_N, is equal to

$$\tilde{M}_N = M_0\left[\left(1 + \tilde{R}_{p1}\right)\left(1 + \tilde{R}_{p2}\right)\cdots\left(1 + \tilde{R}_{pN}\right)\right]$$

where M_0 is the initial value, and $\tilde{R}_{pt}$ ($t = 1, \ldots, N$) is the return during a year t [as given by equation (8.1)]. For reasonably small values of the annual returns, the preceding expression can be approximated by

$$\tilde{M}_N = M_0\left[1 + \tilde{R}_{p1} + \tilde{R}_{p2} + \cdots + \tilde{R}_{pN}\right]$$

◆ DIVERSIFICATION

Often, one hears investors talking about diversifying their portfolio. By diversifying, an investor means constructing a portfolio in such as way as to reduce portfolio risk without sacrificing return. This goal is certainly one that investors should seek. However, the question is how one carries out this goal in practice.

When the distribution of historical returns over a long period of time for a portfolio of diversified common stock is compared to the distribution for individual stocks, a curious relationship is observed. Even though the standard deviation of returns for the stock alone can be significantly greater than that of the portfolio, the stock average return is less than the portfolio return! Is the capital market so imperfect that it rewards substantially higher risk with lower stock return?

Not so. The answer lies in the fact that not all of a security's risk is relevant. Much of the total risk (standard deviation of return) of an individual security is diversifiable. That is, if that investment were combined with other securities, a portion of the variation in its returns could be smoothed or canceled by complementary variation in other securities. The same portfolio diversification effect accounts for the low standard deviation of return for a diversified stock portfolio of 20 or more stocks. In fact, it would be found that the portfolio standard deviation is lower than that of the typical security in the portfolio. Much of the total risk of the component securities is eliminated by diversification. As long as much of the total risk can be eliminated simply by holding a stock in a portfolio, it presents no economic requirements for the return earned to be in line with the total risk. Instead, we should expect realized returns to be related to that portion of security risk that cannot be eliminated by portfolio combination—so-called **systematic risk**.

Diversification results from combining securities whose returns are less than perfectly correlated in order to reduce portfolio risk. As already noted, the portfolio return is simply a weighted average of the individual security returns, no matter the number of securities in the portfolio. Therefore, diversification will not systematically affect the portfolio return, but it will reduce the variability (standard deviation) of return. In general, the less the correlation among security returns, the greater is the impact of diversification on reducing variability. This result is true no matter how risky the securities of the portfolio are when considered in isolation.

Studies of common stock returns show that although some common stock risks can be eliminated through diversification, others cannot.[7] Thus we are led to distinguish between a security's "unsystematic" risk, which can be washed away by mixing the security with other securities in a diversified portfolio, and its "systematic" risk, which cannot be eliminated by diversification. This proposition is illustrated in Figure 8-2. It shows total portfolio risk declining as the number of holdings increases. Increasing diversification gradually tends to eliminate the unsystematic risk, leaving only systematic, or market-related risk. The remaining variability results from the fact that the

---

Now, if the annual returns, $\tilde{R}_{pt}$ are independently and identically distributed with variance σ^2, the variance of $\tilde{M}_N$ will equal $(M_0)^2 N\sigma^2$, or N times the variance after 1 year. Therefore, the standard deviation of the terminal value will equal $\sqrt{N}$ times the standard deviation after 1 year. The key assumption of independence of portfolio returns over time is realistic because security returns appear to follow a random walk through time.

A similar result could be obtained without the restriction on the size of the $\tilde{R}_{pt}$ if we dealt with continuously, as opposed to annually, compounded rates of return. However, the analysis would be more complicated.

[7] Wayne H. Wagner and Sheila Lau, "The Effect of Diversification on Risks," *Financial Analysts Journal* (November/December 1971), pp. 48–53.

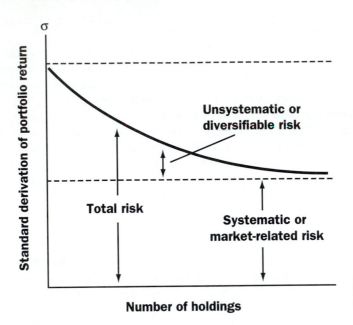

FIGURE 8-2 Systematic and Unsystematic Portfolio Risk

return on nearly every security depends to some degree on the overall performance of the market. Consequently, the return on a well-diversified portfolio is highly correlated with the market, and its variability or uncertainty is basically the uncertainty of the market as a whole. Investors are exposed to market uncertainty no matter how many stocks they hold.

The major findings of the studies on the impact of diversification on the risk of a portfolio of common stock are as follows:

1. The average return is unrelated to the number of issues in the portfolio, yet the standard deviation of return declines as the number of holdings increases.
2. At a portfolio size of about 20 randomly selected common stocks, the level of total portfolio risk is reduced such that what is left is systematic risk.
3. For individual stocks the average ratio of systematic risk to total risk is about 30%.
4. On the average, approximately 40% of the single-security risk is eliminated by forming randomly selected portfolios of 20 stocks. Additional diversification yields rapidly diminishing reduction in risk. The improvement is slight when the number of securities held is increased beyond, say, 10.
5. The return on a diversified portfolio follows the market closely with the ratio of systematic risk to total risk exceeding 90%.

◆ CHOOSING A PORTFOLIO OF RISKY ASSETS

Diversification in the manner suggested previously leads to the construction of portfolios with the highest expected return at a given level of risk, called **Markowitz efficient portfolios**. In order to construct Markowitz efficient portfolios, the theory requires some assumptions about asset selection behavior by investors. First, it assumes that only two parameters affect an investor's decision: the expected return and the risk. Second, it assumes that an investor is risk averse. Third, it assumes that an investor seeks to achieve the highest expected return at a given level of risk.

CALCULATING THE PORTFOLIO RISK USING HISTORICAL DATA

Equation (8.3) gives the variance of an *n*-asset portfolio based on a probability for the return of the individual asset's return. In practice, the variance of a portfolio's return—which we shall simply refer to as the portfolio variance—is calculated from historical data, generally monthly. It can be shown that the variance of a two-asset portfolio is:

$$\text{var}\left(R_p\right) = w_i^2 \, \text{var}\left(R_i\right) + w_j^2 \, \text{var}\left(R_j\right) \\ + 2 \, w_i w_j \, \text{std}\left(R_i\right) \text{std}\left(R_j\right) \text{cor}\left(R_i, R_j\right)$$

(8.4)

where var(R_p)=portfolio variance
w_i=percentage of the portfolio's funds invested in asset *i*
w_j=percentage of the portfolio's funds invested in asset *j*
var(R_i)=variance of asset *i*
var(R_j)=variance of asset *j*
std(R_i)=standard deviation of asset *i*
std(R_j)=standard deviation of asset *j*
cor(R_i,R_j)=correlation between the return for assets *i* and *j*

In words, equation (8.4) states that the portfolio variance is the sum of the weighted variances of the two assets plus the weighted correlation between the two assets. Given our earlier discussion, it should not be surprising that the correlation between the two assets affects the portfolio variance. Notice from equation (8.4) that the lower the correlation between the return on two assets, the lower the portfolio variance. The portfolio variance is the lowest if the two assets have a correlation of −1.

The equation for the portfolio variance when it contains more than two assets is more complicated. The extension to three assets—*i, j*, and *k*—is as follows:

$$\text{var}\left(R_p\right) = w_i^2 \, \text{var}\left(R_i\right) + w_j^2 \, \text{var}\left(R_j\right) + w_k^2 \, \text{var}\left(R_k\right) \\ + 2 \, w_i w_j \, \text{std}\left(R_i\right) \text{std}\left(R_j\right) \text{cor}\left(R_i, R_j\right) \\ + 2 \, w_i w_k \, \text{std}\left(R_i\right) \text{std}\left(R_k\right) \text{cor}\left(R_i, R_k\right) \\ + 2 \, w_j w_k \, \text{std}\left(R_j\right) \text{std}\left(R_k\right) \text{cor}\left(R_j, R_k\right)$$

(8.5)

where w_k=percentage of the portfolio's funds invested in asset *k*
std(R_k)=standard deviation of asset *k*
cor(R_i,R_k)=correlation between the return for assets *i* and *k*
cor(R_j,R_k)=correlation between the return for assets *j* and *k*

In words, equation (8.5) states that the portfolio variance is the sum of the weighted variances of the individual assets plus the sum of the weighted correlations of the assets. Hence, the portfolio variance is the weighted sum of the individual variances of the assets in the portfolio plus the weighted sum of the degree to which the assets vary together. The formula for the portfolio variance of any size will involve the variances and standard deviations of all the assets and each pair of correlations.[8]

---

[8]   In general, for a portfolio with *G* assets, the portfolio variance is

$$\text{var}\left(R_p\right) = \sum_{g=1}^{G} w_g^2 \, \text{var}\left(R_g\right) + \sum_{g=1}^{G}\sum_{h=1}^{G} w_g w_h \, \text{cov}\left(R_g, R_h\right)$$

for $h \neq g$

CONSTRUCTING MARKOWITZ EFFICIENT PORTFOLIOS

An investor who is constructing a portfolio will calculate the portfolio risk (as measured by the portfolio variance) and expected return. For all of the portfolios with the same level of risk, a large number of portfolios will each yield its own expected return. The investor will select the portfolio with the greatest expected return for a given portfolio risk. This portfolio is the Markowitz efficient portfolio for that level of risk.

In practice, the procedure for determining the maximum expected return for a given level of portfolio risk can be found by using a management science technique called quadratic programming. A discussion of this technique is beyond the scope of this chapter. However, it is possible to illustrate the general idea of the construction of Markowitz efficient portfolios graphically by using Figure 8-3.

Figure 8-3 shows all possible portfolios that can be created from the available assets. Any portfolio that can be created is called a **feasible portfolio**. The collection of all feasible portfolios is called the **feasible set of portfolios**. In Figure 8-3, the feasible set of portfolios is the shaded area, including the boundaries of the shaded area.

In contrast to a feasible portfolio, a Markowitz efficient portfolio is one that gives the highest expected return of all feasible portfolios with the same risk. A Markowitz efficient portfolio is also said to be a **mean-variance efficient portfolio**. Thus, each level of risk is associated with a Markowitz efficient portfolio. The collection of all efficient portfolios is called the **Markowitz efficient set of portfolios**.

In Figure 8-3, the Markowitz efficient set is the upper part of the boundary of the feasible set of portfolios, because every point on the upper part of the boundary of the feasible set of portfolios provides the greatest expected return for a given level of risk. The Markowitz efficient set of portfolios is sometimes called the **Markowitz efficient frontier**, because graphically all the Markowitz efficient portfolios lie on the boundary of the set of feasible portfolios with the maximum return for a given level of risk. Any portfolios above the Markowitz efficient frontier cannot be achieved. Any below the Markowitz efficient frontier are dominated by portfolios on the Markowitz efficient frontier.

CHOOSING A PORTFOLIO IN THE MARKOWITZ EFFICIENT SET

Now that we have constructed the Markowitz efficient set of portfolios, the next step is to determine the optimal portfolio. An investor will want to hold one of the portfolios on the Markowitz efficient frontier. Notice that the portfolios on the Markowitz efficient frontier represent trade-offs in terms of risk and return. Moving from left to right on the Markowitz efficient frontier, the expected risk increases, but so does the expected return. The question is, which is the best portfolio to hold? The best portfolio to hold of all those on the Markowitz efficient frontier is called the optimal portfolio.

Intuitively, the optimal portfolio should depend on the investor's preference or utility as to the trade-off between risk and expected return. A natural question is how to estimate an investor's utility function so that the optimal portfolio can be determined. Unfortunately, not much guidance exists as to how to construct one. In general, economists experience little success in measuring utility functions. However, the inability to measure utility functions does not mean that the theory is flawed. What it does mean is that once an investor constructs the Markowitz efficient frontier, an investor will subjectively determine which Markowitz efficient portfolio is appropriate given his or her tolerance to risk.

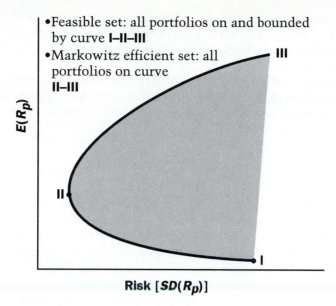

•Feasible set: all portfolios on and bounded by curve **I–II–III**
•Markowitz efficient set: all portfolios on curve **II–III**

FIGURE 8-3 Feasible and Efficient Sets of Portfolios

THE MARKOWITZ EFFICIENT FRONTIER AND ASSET CORRELATIONS

As we explained earlier, the lower the correlation between assets, the lower is the portfolio variance. Figure 8-4 shows the Markowitz efficient frontier for different correlations among assets. Notice that the lower the correlation, the higher the expected return for a given level of risk.

Studies attempting to support the diversification of investors into different types of assets use a figure such as Figure 8-4 to support their contention. For example, the

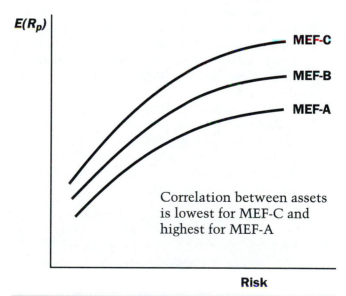

Correlation between assets is lowest for MEF-C and highest for MEF-A

FIGURE 8-4 Markowitz Efficient Frontier for Different Correlations Between Assets

correlation between the return on U.S. stocks and foreign stocks is less than 1. Thus, the Markowitz efficient frontier if an investor limits investments to only U.S. stocks is below that of the Markowitz efficient frontier if an investor expands those investments to foreign stocks.

In general, an investor realizes diversification benefits when expanding into different types of investments if the correlation with existing assets in which the investor already invests is less than one. The diversification benefits come in the form of shifting up the Markowitz efficient frontier.

Summary

In this chapter we introduced portfolio theory. Developed by Harry Markowitz, this theory explains how investors should construct efficient portfolios and select the best or optimal portfolio from among all efficient portfolios. The theory differs from previous approaches to portfolio selection in that Markowitz demonstrated how the key parameters should be measured. These parameters include the risk and the expected return for an individual asset and a portfolio of assets.

The goal of diversifying a portfolio is to reduce a portfolio's risk without sacrificing expected return. This goal can be cast in terms of these key parameters plus the correlation between assets. A portfolio's expected return is simply a weighted average of the expected return of each asset in the portfolio. The weight assigned to each asset is the market value of the asset in the portfolio relative to the total market value of the portfolio. The risk of an asset is measured by the variance or standard deviation of its return. Unlike the portfolio's expected return, a portfolio's risk is not a simple weighting of the standard deviation of the individual assets in the portfolio. Rather, the portfolio risk is affected by the correlation between the assets in the portfolio. The lower the correlation, the smaller is the portfolio risk.

Studies of common stock returns support the view that diversification can reduce portfolio variance, because the return of a portfolio can be divided into two types of risk: systematic and unsystematic risk. The former cannot be eliminated by diversification, while the latter can be. For common stock portfolios, studies found that at a portfolio size of about 20 randomly selected common stocks, the level of total portfolio risk is reduced such that all that is left is systematic risk. The average ratio of systematic risk to total risk is about 30% for individual stocks while for a diversified portfolio it exceeds 90%.

Markowitz set forth the theory for the construction of an efficient portfolio, called a Markowitz efficient portfolio. It is a portfolio with the highest expected return of all feasible portfolios with the same level of risk. The collection of all Markowitz efficient portfolios is called the Markowitz efficient set of portfolios or the Markowitz efficient frontier. The optimal portfolio is the one that maximizes an investor's preferences with respect to return and risk.

Key Terms

- Arithmetic average rate of return
- Asset pricing model
- Correlation of return
- Dollar-weighted rate of return
- Efficient portfolios

- Expected return
- Feasible portfolio
- Feasible set of portfolios
- Internal rate of return
- Markowitz efficient frontier
- Markowitz efficient portfolios

- Markowitz efficient set of portfolios
- Mean-variance efficient portfolio
- Optimal portfolio
- Random walk

- Risk averse
- Risk free or riskless asset
- Risky asset

- Standard deviation
- Systematic risk
- Time-weighted rate of return

- Variance of return

Questions ■

1. Calculate the historical rate of return for the months of January and February for the Minniefield Corporation.

Price on January 1:	$20
Cash dividends in January=	$ 0
Price on February 1:	$21
Cash dividends in February=	$ 2
Price on March 1:	$24

2. Suppose that the monthly return for two investors is as follows:

Month	Investor I	Investor II
1	9%	25%
2	13%	13%
3	22%	22%
4	−18%	−24%

    a. What is the arithmetic average monthly rate of return for the two investors?
    b. What is the time-weighted average monthly rate of return for the two investors?
    c. Why does the arithmetic average monthly rate of return diverge more from the time-weighted monthly rate of return for investor II than for investor I?

3. The Mabelle Company is a money management firm that manages the funds of pension plan sponsors. For one of its clients it manages $200 million. The cash flow for this particular client's portfolio for the past three months was $20 million, −$8 million, and $4 million. The market value of the portfolio at the end of 3 months was $208 million.

    a. What is the dollar-weighted rate of return for this client's portfolio over the 3-month period?
    b. Suppose that the $8 million cash outflow in the second month was a result of withdrawals by the plan sponsor and that the cash flow after adjusting for this withdrawal is therefore zero. What would the dollar-weighted rate of return then be for this client's portfolio?

4. Suppose the probability distribution for the one-period return of some asset is as follows:

Return	Probability
0.20	0.10
0.15	0.20
0.10	0.30
0.03	0.25
−0.06	0.15

    a. What is this asset's expected one-period return?
    b. What is this asset's variance and standard deviation for the one-period return?

5. What statistical measures are used in calculating the risk of an asset or a portfolio?

6. "A portfolio's expected return and variance of return are simply the weighted average of the individual asset expected returns and variances." Do you agree with this statement?

7. Professor Harry Markowitz, corecipient of the 1990 Nobel Prize in Economics, wrote the following:

   A portfolio with 60 different railway securities, for example, would not be as well diversified as the same size portfolio with some railroad, some public utility, mining, various sort of manufacturing, etc.

   Why is this true?

8. Two portfolio managers are discussing modern portfolio theory. Manager A states that the objective of Markowitz portfolio analysis is to construct a portfolio that maximizes expected return for a given level of risk. Manager B disagrees, believing that the objective is to construct a portfolio that minimizes risk for a given level of return. Which portfolio manager is correct?

9. Explain what is meant by a risk-averse investor.

10. What is meant by a Markowitz efficient frontier?

11. Explain why all feasible portfolios are not on the Markowitz efficient frontier.

12. What is meant by an optimal portfolio and how is it related to an efficient portfolio?

13. a. How does an investor select the optimal portfolio?
    b. Explain the role of an investor's preference in selecting an optimal portfolio.

14. Explain the critical role of the correlation between assets in determining the potential benefits from diversification.

15. "The maximum diversification benefits will be achieved if asset returns are perfectly correlated." Explain whether you agree or disagree with this statement.

16. Investment advisors who argue for investing in a portfolio consisting of both stocks and bonds point to the fact that the correlation of returns between these two asset classes is less than 1 and therefore provides benefits of diversification.
    a. What does the correlation of the returns between two asset classes measure?
    b. In what sense would a correlation of return of less than 1 between stocks and bonds suggest potential diversification benefits?

17. The following excerpt is from Warren Bailey and Rene M. Stulz, "Benefits of International Diversification: The Case of Pacific Basin Stock Markets," (*Journal of Portfolio Management*, Summer 1990).

    Recent international diversification literature uses monthly data from foreign stock markets to make the point that American investors should hold foreign stock to reduce the variance of a portfolio of domestic stocks without reducing its expected return.

    a. Why would you expect that the justification of diversifying into foreign stock markets would depend on empirical evidence regarding the ability to "reduce the variance of a portfolio of domestic stocks without reducing its expected return."
    b. Typically in research papers that seek to demonstrate the benefits of international diversification by investing in a foreign stock market, two efficient frontiers are compared. One is an efficient frontier constructed using only domestic stocks; the other is an efficient frontier constructed using both domestic and foreign stocks. If benefits can be realized by diversifying into foreign stocks, should the efficient frontier constructed using both domestic and foreign stocks lie above or below the efficient frontier constructed using only domestic stocks? Explain your answer.

18. The following excerpt is from John E. Hunter and T. Daniel Coggin, "An Analysis of the Diversification from International Equity Investment" (*Journal of Portfolio Management*, Fall 1990).

The extent to which investment risk can be diversified depends upon the degree to which national markets were completely dominated by a single world market factor (i.e., if all cross-national correlations were 1.00), then international diversification would have no benefit. If all national markets were completely independent (that is, if all cross-national correlations were zero), then international diversification over an infinite number of countries would completely eliminate the effect of variation in national markets.

a. Why are the "cross-national correlations" critical in justifying the benefits from international diversification?

b. Why do Hunter and Coggin argue that no benefit results from international diversification if these correlations are all 1.00?

19. Indicate why you agree or disagree with the following statement: "Because it is difficult to determine an investor's utility function, Markowitz portfolio theory cannot be employed in practice to construct a Markowitz efficient portfolio."

20. The following is an excerpt from Marshall E. Blume, "The Capital Asset Pricing Model and the CAPM Literature," in Diana R. Harrington and Robert A. Korajczyk (eds.), *The CAPM Controversy: Policy and Strategy Implications for Investment Management* (Charlottesville, VA: Association for Investment Management and Research, 1993), p. 5 (the first sentence was modified):

Implicit in Graham and Dodd's original theory (Security Analysis, 1934) was the idea that a stock has an intrinsic value. If an investor purchased an asset or stock at a price below its intrinsic value, the asset over time would move up to its intrinsic value without risk. Graham and Dodd recognized that people hold different expectations for the future, but they had little to say about diversification. The basic idea was that, if every stock bought was below its intrinsic value, the overall portfolio would be a good one and would make money as the values of the component stocks rose to their intrinsic values.

The legal profession translated this intellectual idea into the Prudent Man rule for investing personal trusts. According to this rule, a trust manager must invest in each asset on its own merit. If each asset is safe, then the total portfolio will be safe. For example, futures cannot be used under the Prudent Man rule because they are inherently risky—even though investment managers now know that when futures are combined with other assets, they can reduce portfolio risk.

Markowitz in 1959 then developed mathematics for the efficient set . . . This concept of looking at the entire portfolio changed the way investors think about investing.

Markowitz focused on the portfolio as a whole, not explicitly on the individual assets in the portfolio, which was clearly at odds with the Prudent Man rule for personal trusts. In fact, under the Employee Retirement Income Security Act passed in the mid-1970s, investing in derivatives to reduce the risk of a portfolio was, for the most part, legally imprudent.

Why is the Prudent Man rule for investing personal trusts in conflict with the way to construct a portfolio as suggested by Markowitz portfolio theory?

Risk and Return Theories: II

Learning Objectives

After reading this chapter you will understand:

◆ the assumptions underlying capital market theory.

◆ the capital market line and the role of a risk-free asset in its construction.

◆ why the capital market line dominates the Markowitz efficient frontier.

◆ what the security market line is.

◆ the difference between systematic and unsystematic risk.

◆ the capital asset pricing model, the relevant measure of risk in this model, and the limitations of the model.

◆ what the market model is.

◆ the findings of empirical tests of the capital asset pricing model and the difficulties of testing this model.

◆ the multifactor CAPM and the difficulties in applying it.

◆ the arbitrage pricing theory model.

◆ the different types of factor models used in practice: statistical, macroeconomic, and fundamental.

◆ some fundamental principles concerning risk and return that are valid regardless of the asset pricing model used.

In Chapter 8, we introduced the principles of portfolio theory. Here, we describe capital market theory and the implications of both that theory and portfolio theory for the pricing of financial assets. The discussion focuses on one well-known asset pricing model called the capital asset pricing model (CAPM). We also discuss other asset pricing models.

The asset pricing models we describe in this chapter are equilibrium models. Given assumptions about the behavior and expectations of investors, and assumptions about capital markets, these models predict the expected return an investor should require in order to acquire an asset. Thus, the models provide an answer to the question of what risk premium an investor should demand. Knowing the expected cash flow and the expected return, one can determine the theoretical value of an asset, therefore these models are referred to as asset pricing models.

◆ ECONOMIC ASSUMPTIONS

Economic theories are an abstraction of the real world and, as such, are based upon some simplifying assumptions. These assumptions simplify matters a great deal and some of them may even seem unrealistic. However, these assumptions make economic theories more tractable from a mathematical standpoint.

ASSUMPTIONS ABOUT INVESTOR BEHAVIOR

Capital market theory makes assumptions about the behavior of investors in constructing a portfolio of risky assets.

Behavioral Assumption 1 Capital market theory assumes that investors make investment decisions based on two parameters: the expected return and the variance of returns. Portfolio theory, described in the previous chapter, is sometimes referred to as a **two-parameter model**.

The two-parameter assumption tells us what investors use as inputs in making their investment decisions. Their specific behavior follows the assumption that in order to accept greater risk, they must be compensated by the opportunity of realizing a higher return. We refer to such investors as risk averse. This definition is oversimplified. A more rigorous definition of risk aversion is described by a mathematical specification of an investor's utility function. However, this complexity need not concern us here. What is important is that an investor who faces a choice between two portfolios with the same expected return will select the portfolio with the lower risk. Certainly, this assumption is reasonable.

Behavioral Assumption 2 Capital market theory assumes that the risk-averse investor will ascribe to the methodology of reducing portfolio risk by combining assets with counterbalancing correlations as explained in the previous chapter.

Behavioral Assumption 3 Capital market theory assumes all investors make investment decisions over some single-period investment horizon. The length of that period (6 months, 1 year, 2 years, etc.) is not specified. In reality, the investment decision process is more complex, with many investors looking at more than one investment horizon. Nonetheless, the assumption of a one-period investment horizon is necessary to simplify the mathematics of the theory.

Behavioral Assumption 4 Capital market theory assumes that investors have the same expectations with respect to the inputs that are used to derive the Markowitz efficient portfolios: asset returns, variances, and correlations. This is called the **homogeneous expectations assumption**.

ASSUMPTIONS ABOUT CAPITAL MARKETS

The previous assumptions dealt with the behavior of investors in making investment decisions. It is also necessary to make assumptions about the characteristics of the capital market in which investors transact. The three assumptions in this regard follow.

Capital Market Assumption 1 Capital market theory assumes that the capital market is perfectly competitive. In general, the number of buyers and sellers is sufficiently large, and all investors are small enough relative to the market, so that no individual investor can influence an asset's price. Consequently, all investors are price takers, and the market price is determined where supply equals demand.

Capital Market Assumption 2   Capital market theory assumes no transaction costs or impediments interfere with the supply and demand for an asset. Economists refer to these various costs and impediments as "frictions." The costs associated with frictions generally result in buyers paying more than in the absence of frictions and/or sellers receiving less. In the case of financial markets, frictions include commissions charged by brokers and bid-ask spreads charged by dealers. They also include taxes and government-imposed transfer fees.

Capital Market Assumption 3   Capital market theory assumes a risk-free asset exists in which investors can invest. Moreover, it assumes that investors can borrow funds at the same interest rate offered on that risk-free asset. That is, it is assumed that investors can lend and borrow at some risk-free rate.

◆ CAPITAL MARKET THEORY

In the previous chapter, we distinguished between a risky asset and a risk-free asset. We explained that an investor should create a portfolio with the highest expected return for a given level of risk, where risk is measured by the portfolio's variance. We did not consider the possibility of constructing efficient portfolios in the presence of a risk-free asset, that is, an asset where the return is known with certainty.

In the absence of a risk-free rate, portfolio theory tells us that Markowitz efficient portfolios can be constructed based on expected return and variance. Once a risk-free asset is introduced and assuming that investors can borrow and lend at the risk-free rate (Capital Market Assumption 3), the conclusion of portfolio theory can be qualified as illustrated in Figure 9-1. Every combination of the risk-free asset and the Markowitz efficient portfolio M is shown on the tangent line in the figure. This line is drawn from the vertical axis as the risk-free rate tangent to the Markowitz efficient

FIGURE 9-1   The Capital Market Line

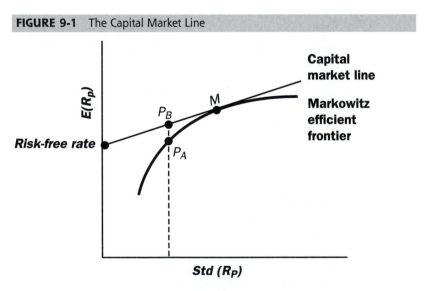

Portfolios to the right of M are leveraged portfolios (borrowing at a risk-free rate to buy a market portfolio).

Portfolios to the left of M are combinations of risk-free asset and market portfolio.

frontier. The point of tangency is denoted by *M*. All of the portfolios on the line are feasible for the investor to construct. Portfolios to the left of *M* represent combinations of risky assets and the risk-free asset. Portfolios to the right of *M* include purchases of risky assets made with funds borrowed at the risk-free rate.

Now compare a portfolio on the line to the portfolio on the Markowitz efficient frontier with the same risk. For example, compare portfolio P_A which is on the Markowitz efficient frontier with portfolio P_B which is on the line and therefore has some combination of the risk-free rate and the Markowitz efficient portfolio *M*. Notice that for the same risk the expected return is greater for P_B than for P_A. In fact, this dominance is true for all but one portfolio on the line: portfolio *M* which is on the Markowitz efficient frontier.

Recognizing this preference, we must modify the conclusion from portfolio theory that an investor will select a portfolio on the Markowitz efficient frontier, depending on the investor's level of risk aversion. With the introduction of the risk-free asset, we can now say that an investor will select a portfolio on the line representing a combination of borrowing or lending at the risk-free rate and purchases of the Markowitz efficient portfolio *M*. The particular efficient portfolio that the investor will select on the line will depend on the investor's risk preference.

It was William Sharpe,[1] John Lintner,[2] Jack Treynor,[3] and Jan Mossin[4] who demonstrated that the opportunity to borrow or lend at the risk-free rate implies a capital market where risk-averse investors will prefer to hold portfolios consisting of combinations of the risk-free asset and some portfolio *M* on the Markowitz efficient frontier. Sharpe called the line from the risk-free rate to portfolio *M* on the efficient frontier the **capital market line (CML)**, the name adopted in the industry.

One more key question remains: How does an investor construct portfolio *M*? Eugene Fama answered this question by demonstrating that *M* must consist of all assets available to investors, and each asset must be held in proportion to its market value relative to the total market value of all assets.[5] So, for example, if the total market value of some asset is $500 million and the total market value of all assets is X, then the percentage of the portfolio that should be allocated to that asset is $500 million divided by X. Because portfolio *M* consists of all assets, it is referred to as the **market portfolio**.

Now we can restate how a risk-averse investor who makes investment decisions as suggested by portfolio theory and who can borrow and lend at the risk-free rate should construct efficient portfolios. This process combines an investment in the risk-free asset with the market portfolio. The theoretical result that all investors will hold a combination of the risk-free asset and the market portfolio is known as the **two-fund separation theorem**[6]—one fund consists of the risk-free asset and the other is the market portfolio. Although all investors will select a portfolio on the capital market line, the optimal portfolio for a specific investor is the one that will maximize that investor's risk preference.

---
1   William F. Sharpe, "Capital Asset Prices," *Journal of Finance* (September 1964), pp. 425–42.
2   John Lintner, "The Valuation of Risk Assets and the Selection of Risky Investments in Stock Portfolio and Capital Budgets," *Review of Economics and Statistics* (February 1965), pp. 3–37.
3   Jack L. Treynor, "Toward a Theory of Market Value of Risky Assets," unpublished paper. Arthur D. Little, 1961.
4   Jan Mossin, "Equilibrium in a Capital Asset Market," *Econometrica* (October 1966), pp. 768–83.
5   Eugene F. Fama, "Efficient Capital Markets: A Review of Theory and Empirical Work," *Journal of Finance* (May 1970), pp. 383–417.
6   James Tobin, "Liquidity Preference as Behavior Toward Risks," *Review of Economic Studies* (February 1958), pp. 65–86.

DERIVING THE FORMULA FOR THE CAPITAL MARKET LINE

Figure 9-1 shows us graphically the capital market lines, but we can derive a formula for the capital market line algebraically as well. This formula will be key in our goal of showing how a risky asset should be priced.

To derive the formula for the capital market line, we combine the two-fund separation theorem with the assumption of homogeneous expectations (Behavioral Assumption 4). Suppose an investor creates a two-fund portfolio: a portfolio consisting of w_F invested in the risk-free asset and w_M in the market portfolio, where w represents the corresponding percentage (weight) of the portfolio allocated to each asset. Thus,

$$w_F + w_M = 1 \text{ or } w_F = 1 - w_M$$

What is the expected return and the risk of this portfolio? As we explained in the previous chapter, the expected return is equal to the weighted average of the two assets. Therefore, for our two-fund portfolio, the expected portfolio return, $E(R_p)$, is equal to:

$$E(R_p) = w_F R_F + w_M E(R_M)$$

Because we know that $w_F = 1 - w_M$, we can rewrite $E(R_p)$ as follows:

$$E(R_p) = (1 - w_M)R_F + w_M E(R_M)$$

which can be simplified to

$$E(R_p) = R_F + w_M \left[E(R_M) - R_F \right] \tag{9.1}$$

Now that we know the expected return of our hypothetical portfolio, we turn to the portfolio's risk as measured by the variance of the portfolio. We know from equation (8.4) of the previous chapter how to calculate the variance of a two-asset portfolio. We repeat equation (8.4) here:

$$\text{var}(R_p) = w_i^2 \, \text{var}(R_i) + w_j^2 \, \text{var}(R_j) + 2w_i w_j \, \text{std}(R_i) \, \text{std}(R_j) \, \text{cor}(R_i, R_j)$$

We can use this equation for our two-fund portfolio. Asset i in this case is the risk-free asset F and asset j is the market portfolio M. Then,

$$\text{var}(R_p) = w_F^2 \, \text{var}(R_F) + w_M^2 \, \text{var}(R_M) + 2w_F w_M \, \text{std}(R_F) \, \text{std}(R_M) \, \text{cor}(R_F, R_M)$$

We know that the variance of the risk-free asset, $\text{var}(R_F)$, is equal to zero, because no possible variation in the return results when the future return is known. The correlation between the risk-free asset and the market portfolio, $\text{cor}(R_F, R_M)$, is zero, because the risk-free asset has no variability and therefore does not move at all with the return on the market portfolio, which is a risky asset. Substituting these two values into the formula for the portfolio's variance provides

$$\text{var}(R_p) = w_M^2 \, \text{var}(R_M)$$

In other words, the variance of the two-fund portfolio is represented by the weighted variance of the market portfolio. We can solve for the weight of the market portfolio by substituting standard deviations for variances.

Since the standard deviation is the square root of the variance, we can write

$$\text{std}(R_p) = w_M \, \text{std}(R_M)$$

and therefore

$$w_M = \frac{\text{std}(R_p)}{\text{std}(R_M)}$$

Now let's return to equation (9.1) and substitute for w_M the result we just derived:

$$E(R_p) = R_F + \frac{\text{std}(R_p)}{\text{std}(R_M)}\left[E(R_M) - R_F\right]$$

Rearranging, we get

$$E(R_p) = R_F + \frac{E(R_M) - R_F}{\text{std}(R_M)}\,\text{std}(R_p) \qquad\qquad \textbf{(9.2)}$$

This equation yields the capital market line (CML).

INTERPRETING THE CML EQUATION

Capital market theory assumes that all investors hold the same expectations for the inputs into the model (Behavioral Assumption 4). With homogeneous expectations, $\text{std}(R_M)$ and $\text{std}(R_p)$ are the market's consensus for the expected return distributions for the market portfolio and portfolio p. The slope of the CML is

$$\frac{E(R_M) - R_F}{\text{std}(R_M)}$$

Let's examine the economic meaning of the slope. The numerator is the expected return of the market beyond the risk-free return. It provides a measure of the risk premium or the reward for holding the risky market portfolio rather than the risk-free asset. The denominator is the risk of the market portfolio. Thus, the slope measures the reward per unit of market risk. Because the CML represents the return offered to compensate for a perceived level of risk, each point on the line is a balanced market condition, or equilibrium. The slope of the line determines the additional return needed to compensate for a unit change in risk. For this reason, the slope of the CML is also referred to as the **market price of risk**.

The CML says that the expected return on a portfolio is equal to the risk-free rate plus a risk premium. As we noted in Chapter 1 and Chapter 8, we seek a measure of the risk premium. According to capital market theory, the risk premium is equal to the market price of risk times the quantity of risk for the portfolio (as measured by the standard deviation of the portfolio). That is,

$$E(R_p) = R_F + \text{Market price of risk} \times \text{Amount of portfolio risk}$$

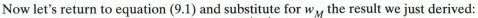
◆ THE CAPITAL ASSET PRICING MODEL

Up to this point, we know how a risk-averse investor who makes decisions based on two parameters (risk and expected return) should construct an efficient portfolio—by using a combination of the market portfolio and the risk-free rate. Based on this result, we can derive a model that shows how a risky asset should be priced. In the process of doing so, we can refine our thinking about the risk associated with an asset. Specifically, we can show that the appropriate risk that investors should be compensated for accepting is not the variance of an asset's return but some other quantity. To illustrate, we need to take a closer look at portfolio risk.

SYSTEMATIC AND UNSYSTEMATIC RISK

In our discussion of portfolio theory in Chapter 8, we initially defined the variance of return as the appropriate measure of risk. We suggested, however, that this risk measure can be decomposed into two general types of risk: systematic risk and unsystematic risk.

Systematic risk is the portion of an asset's return variability that can be attributed to a common factor. It is also called **undiversifiable risk** or **market risk**. Systematic risk is the minimum level of risk that can be obtained for a portfolio by means of diversification across a large number of randomly chosen assets. As such, systematic risk results from general market and economic conditions that cannot be diversified away.

The portion of an asset's return variability that can be diversified away is referred to as **unsystematic risk**. It is also sometimes called **diversifiable risk**, **residual risk**, or **company-specific risk**. This is the risk that is unique to a company such as a strike, the outcome of unfavorable litigation, or a natural catastrophe. As examples of this type of risk, one need only recall the case of product tampering involving Tylenol capsules (manufactured by Johnson & Johnson, Inc.) in October 1982, or the chemical accident at the Union Carbide plant in Bhopal, India, in December 1984. Both of these unforecastable and hence unexpected tragedies negatively affected the stock prices of the two companies involved.

How diversification reduces unsystematic risk for portfolios was illustrated in Figure 8-2. As we indicated, at a portfolio size of about 20 randomly selected securities, the level of unsystematic risk is almost completely diversified away. Essentially, all that is left is systematic or market risk.

Therefore the total risk of an asset can be measured by its variance. However, the total risk can be decomposed into its systematic and unsystematic risk components. Next we will show how this process can quantify both components.

QUANTIFYING SYSTEMATIC RISK

Quantification of systematic risk can be accomplished by dividing security return into two parts: one perfectly correlated with and proportionate to the market return, and a second independent from (uncorrelated with) the market. The first component of return is usually referred to as systematic, the second as unsystematic or diversifiable return. Thus we have

$$\text{Security return} = \text{Systematic return} + \text{Unsystematic return} \qquad \textbf{(9.3)}$$

As the systematic return is proportional to the market return, it can be expressed as the symbol beta (β) times the market return, R_M. The proportionality factor beta is a **market sensitivity index**, indicating how sensitive the security return is to changes in the market level. (How to estimate beta for a security or portfolio will be discussed later.) The unsystematic return, which is independent of market returns, is usually represented by the symbol epsilon (ε'). Thus, the security return, R, may be expressed as

$$R = \beta R_M + \varepsilon' \qquad \textbf{(9.4)}$$

For example, if a security has a β of 2.0, then a 10% market return will generate a 20% systematic return for the stock. The security return for the period would be the 20% plus the unsystematic component. The unsystematic component depends on factors unique to the company, such as labor difficulties, higher-than-expected sales, and so on.

The security returns model given by equation (9.4) is usually written in such a way that the average value of the residual term, ε', is zero, by adding a factor, alpha (α), to the model to represent the average value of the unsystematic returns over time. That is we set $\varepsilon' = \alpha + \varepsilon$ so that

$$R = \alpha + \beta R_M + \varepsilon \qquad \textbf{(9.5)}$$

where the average ε over time should tend to zero.

The model for security returns given by equation (9.5) is usually referred to as the **market model**. Graphically, the model can be depicted as a line fitted to a plot of security returns against rates of return on the market index as shown for a hypothetical security in Figure 9-2.

The beta factor can be thought of as the slope of the line. It gives the expected increase in security return for a 1% increase in market return. In Figure 9-2, if a security has a beta of 1.0, a 10% market return will result, *on the average*, in a 10% security return.

The alpha factor is represented by the intercept of the line on the vertical security return axis. It is equal to the average value over time of the unsystematic returns (ε') on the stock. For most stocks, the alpha factor tends to be small and unstable.

Using the definition of security return given by the market model, the specification of systematic and unsystematic risk is straightforward—they are simply the standard deviations of the two return components.[7]

The systematic risk of a security is equal to β times the standard deviation of the market return.

$$\text{Systematic risk} = \beta \, \text{std}\left(R_M\right) \qquad \textbf{(9.6)}$$

The unsystematic risk equals the standard deviation of the residual return factor ε:

$$\text{Unsystematic risk} = \text{std}\left(\varepsilon\right) \qquad \textbf{(9.7)}$$

FIGURE 9-2   Graphical Depiction of the Market Model

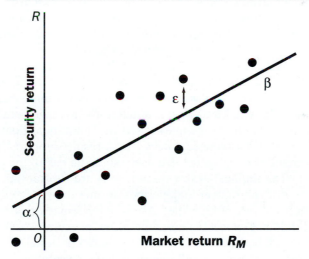

Beta (β), the market sensitivity index, is the slope of the line.
Alpha (α), the average of the residual returns, is the intercept of the line on the security axis.
Epsilon (ε), the residual returns, are the perpendicular distances of the points from the line.

---

[7]   The relationship between the risk components is given by

$$\text{var}\left(R_p\right) = \beta^2 \, \text{var}\left(R_M\right) + \text{var}\left(\varepsilon'\right)$$

This follows directly from equation (9.5) and the assumption of statistical independence of R_M and ε'. The R^2 term previously discussed is a ratio of systematic to total risk (both measured in terms of variance):

$$R^2 = \frac{\beta^2 \, \text{var}\left(R_M\right)}{\text{var}\left(\varepsilon'\right)}$$

Given measures of individual security systematic risk, we can now compute the systematic risk of the portfolio. It is equal to the beta factor for the portfolio, β_p, times the risk of the market index, $\text{std}(R_M)$:

$$\text{Portfolio systematic risk} = \beta_p \, \text{std}\left(R_M\right) \qquad (9.8)$$

The portfolio beta factor in turn can be shown to be simply an average of the individual security betas, weighted by the proportion of each security in the portfolio:

$$\beta_p = w_1\beta_1 + w_2\beta_2 + \ldots + w_n\beta_n$$

Or more concisely as

$$\beta_p = \sum_{i=1}^{n} w_i\beta_i \qquad (9.9)$$

where

w_i = the proportion of portfolio market value represented by security i
n = the number of securities

Thus, the systematic risk of a portfolio is simply the market value-weighted average of the systematic risk of the individual securities. It follows that the β for a portfolio consisting of all securities is 1. If a stock's β exceeds 1, it is above the average. If the portfolio is composed of an equal dollar investment in each security, the β_p is simply an unweighted average of the component security betas.

The unsystematic risk of the portfolio is also a function of the unsystematic security risks, but the form is more complex.[8] The important point is that with increasing diversification this risk approaches zero.

With these results for portfolio risk, it is useful to return to the studies of the impact of diversification on risk. One study compared the standard deviation for 20-stock portfolios with the predicted lower limits based on average security systematic risks. The lower limit is equal to the average beta for the portfolio times the standard deviation of the market return. The standard deviations in all cases studied were close to the predicted values. These results support the contention that portfolio systematic risk equals the average systematic risk of the component securities.

The implications of these results are substantial. First, we would expect realized rates of return over long periods of time to be related to the systematic as opposed to the total risk of securities. As the unsystematic risk is relatively easily eliminated, we should not expect the market to offer investors a "risk premium" for bearing such risk. Second, because security systematic risk is equal to the security beta times $\text{std}(R_M)$, which is common to all securities, beta is useful as a *relative* risk measure. The β gives the systematic risk of a security (or portfolio) relative to the risk of the market index. Thus, it is often convenient to speak of systematic risk in relative terms, that is, in terms of beta rather than beta times $\text{std}(R_M)$.

---

[8] Assuming the unsystematic returns (ε'_i) of securities to be uncorrelated (reasonably true in practice), the unsystematic portfolio risk is given by

$$\text{var}\left(\varepsilon'_p\right) = \sum_{i=1}^{n} w_i^2 \, \text{var}\left(\varepsilon'_i\right)$$

where $\text{var}(\varepsilon'_i)$ is the unsystematic risk for stock i. Assume the portfolio is made up of an equal percentage invested in each security and $\text{var}(\varepsilon')$ is the average value of the $\text{var}(\varepsilon'_i)$. Then, $w_i = 1/n$ and

$$\text{var}\left(\varepsilon'_p\right) = \frac{1}{n} \, \text{var}\left(\varepsilon'\right)$$

which—assuming $\text{var}(\varepsilon')$ is finite—obviously approaches zero as the number of issues in the portfolio increases.

ESTIMATING BETA

The beta of a security or portfolio can be estimated using statistical analysis. More specifically, we use regression analysis on historical data to estimate the market model given by equation (9.5). The estimated slope for the market model is the estimate of beta. A series of returns is computed according to equation (8.1), given in Chapter 8, over some time interval for some broad market index (such as the S&P 500 stock market index) and for the stock (or portfolio).[9] For example, monthly returns can be calculated for the past 5 years, providing 60 return observations for both the market index and the stock or portfolio. Or, weekly returns can be calculated for the past year. Nothing in portfolio theory indicates whether weekly, monthly, or even daily returns should be used. Nor does theory indicate any specific number of observations, except that statistical methodology requires that more observations give a more reliable measure of beta.[10]

Table 9-1 gives estimates of beta using historical data plus systematic and unsystematic risk for five stocks estimated from 60 months of return data from January 1996 to December 2000. For the values reported in Table 9-1 the Standard & Poor's 500, which is a broad market index, was used as a surrogate for the return on the market portfolio.

Another product of the statistical technique used to estimate beta is the percentage of systematic risk to total risk. In statistical terms, it is measured by the coefficient of determination from the regression, which indicates the percentage of the variation in the return of the asset explained by the market portfolio return. The value of the coefficient ranges from 0 to 1. For example, a coefficient of determination of 0.3 for an asset means that 30% of the variation in the return of that asset is explained by the return of the market portfolio. Unsystematic or unique risk is then the amount not explained by the market portfolio's return. That is, it is one minus the coefficient of determination.

Studies show that for the average NYSE common stock, systematic risk is about 30%, while unsystematic risk is about 70% of return variance. In contrast, the coefficient of determination for a well-diversified portfolio of stocks will typically exceed 90%, indicating that unsystematic risk is less than 10% of total portfolio return variance.

Our purpose here is not to provide an explanation of the mechanics of calculating beta but to point out the practical problems in obtaining beta. (Other econometric issues are involved, but we do not focus on these.)

TABLE 9-1 Historical Betas for Five Stocks*

	General Electric	*McGraw Hill*	*IBM*	*General Motors*	*Xerox*
Beta	1.24	0.86	1.22	1.11	1.27
Systematic Risk	0.62	0.28	0.33	0.28	0.19
Unsystematic risk	0.38	0.72	0.67	0.72	0.81

*S&P500 is used as the market index. Monthly returns from January 1996 to December 2000 are used.

[9] We discuss several broad market indexes in Chapter 13.
[10] This assumes that the economic determinants that affect the beta of a stock do not change over the measurement period.

The difference in the calculated beta will depend on the following factors:

1. The length of time over which a return is calculated (e.g., daily, weekly, monthly)
2. The number of observations used (e.g., 3 years of monthly returns or 5 years of monthly returns)
3. The specific time period used (e.g., January 1, 1998, to December 31, 2002, or January 1, 1996, to December 31, 2000)
4. The market index selected (e.g., the S&P 500 stock market index or an index consisting of all stocks traded on exchanges weighted by their relative market value)

Moreover, the question of the stability of beta arises over different time intervals—that is, does the beta of a stock or portfolio remain relatively unchanged over time, or does it change?[11]

The interesting question concerns the economic determinants of the beta of a stock. The risk characteristics of a company should be reflected in its beta. Several empirical studies have attempted to identify these macroeconomic and microeconomic factors.[12]

THE SECURITY MARKET LINE

The capital market line represents an equilibrium condition in which the expected return on a *portfolio* of assets is a linear function of the expected return on the market portfolio. A directly analogous relationship holds for *individual security* expected returns:

$$E(R_i) = R_F + \frac{E(R_M) - R_F}{\text{std}(R_M)} \text{std}(R_i) \qquad (9.10)$$

Equation (9.10) simply uses risk and return variables for an individual security in place of the portfolio values in the equation for the CML given by equation (9.2). This version of the risk-return relationship for individual securities is called the **security market line (SML)**. As in the case of the CML, the expected return for an asset is equal to the risk-free rate plus the product of the market price of risk and the quantity of risk in the security.

Another more common version of the SML relationship uses the beta of a security. To see how this relationship is developed, look back at equation (9.3). In a well-diversified portfolio (i.e., Markowitz diversified), the unique or unsystematic risk is eliminated. Consequently, it can be demonstrated that

$$\text{var}(R_i) = \beta_i^2 \text{var}(R_M)$$

and the standard deviation is

$$\text{std}(R_i) = \beta_i \text{std}(R_M)$$

Therefore,

$$\beta_i = \frac{\text{std}(R_i)}{\text{std}(R_M)}$$

---

[11] See Frank J. Fabozzi and Jack C. Francis, "Stability Tests for Alphas and Betas over Bull and Bear Markets," *Journal of Finance* (September 1977), pp. 1093–99; and "Beta as a Random Coefficient," *Journal of Financial and Quantitive Analysis* (March 1978), pp. 101–16.

[12] See, for example, Frank J. Fabozzi and Jack C. Francis, "Industry Effects and the Determinants of Beta," *Quarterly Review of Economics and Business* (Autumn 1979), pp. 61–74; Frank J. Fabozzi, Teresa Garlicki, Arabinda Ghosh, and Peter Kislowski, "Market Power as a Determinant of Systematic Risk: Empirical Evidence," *Review of Business and Economic Research* (Spring 1986), pp. 6–70; and Frank Fabozzi and Jack C. Francis, "The Effects of Changing Macroeconomic Conditions on the Parameters of the Single-Index Market Model," *Journal of Financial and Quantitative Analysis* (June 1979), pp. 351–56.

If β_i is substituted into equation (9.10), we have the beta version of the SML as shown in equation (9.11), popularly referred to as the **capital asset pricing model (CAPM)**:[13]

$$E(R_i) = R_F + \beta_i\left[E(R_M) - R_F\right] \tag{9.11}$$

This equation states that, given the assumptions of capital market theory described earlier, the expected (or required) return on an individual asset is a positive linear function of its index of systematic risk as measured by beta. The higher the beta, the higher the expected return. Notice that it is only an asset's beta that determines its expected return.

Let's look at the prediction of the CAPM for several values of beta. The beta of a risk-free asset is zero, because the variability of the return of a risk-free asset is zero and therefore it does not covary with the market portfolio. So, if we want to know the expected return for a risk-free asset, we would substitute zero for β_1 in equation (9.11):

$$E(R_i) = R_F + 0\left[E(R_M) - R_F\right] = R_F$$

Thus, the return on a risk-free asset is simply the risk-free return, as expected.

The beta of the market portfolio is 1. If asset i has the same beta as the market portfolio, then substituting 1 into equation (9.11) gives

$$E(R_i) = R_F + 1\left[E(R_M) - R_F\right] = E(R_M)$$

In this case, the expected return for the asset is the same as the expected return for the market portfolio. If an asset has a beta greater than the market portfolio (i.e., greater than 1), then the expected return will be higher than for the market portfolio. The reverse is true if an asset has a beta less than the market portfolio. A graph of the SML is presented in Figure 9-3.

THE SML, CML, AND MARKET MODEL

In equilibrium, the expected return of individual securities will lie on the SML and not on the CML because of the high degree of unsystematic risk that remains in individual securities that can be diversified out of portfolios of securities. It follows that the only risk investors will pay a premium to avoid is market risk. Hence, two assets with the same amount of systematic risk will have the same expected return. In equilibrium, only efficient portfolios will lie on both the CML and the SML, which underscores the fact that the systematic risk measure, beta, is most correctly considered as an *index* of the contribution of an individual security to the systematic risk of a well-diversified portfolio of securities.

It is important to point out the difference between the market model, and the CML and SML. The CML and the SML represent a predictive model for expected

---

[13] The model is sometimes stated in risk premium form. Risk premiums, or excess returns, are obtained by subtracting the risk-free rate from the rate of return. The expected security and market risk premiums—designated $E(r_i)$ and $E(r_M)$, respectively—are given by:

$$E(r_i) = E(R_i) - R_F$$
$$E(r_M) = E(R_M) - R_F$$

Substituting these risk premiums into equation (9.11), we obtain:

$$E(r_i) = \beta_i\left[E(r_M)\right]$$

In this form, the CAPM states that the expected risk premium for the investor's portfolio is equal to its beta value times the expected market risk premium. Or, equivalently stated, the expected risk premium should be equal to the quantity of risk (as measured by beta) and the market price of risk (as measured by the expected market risk premium).

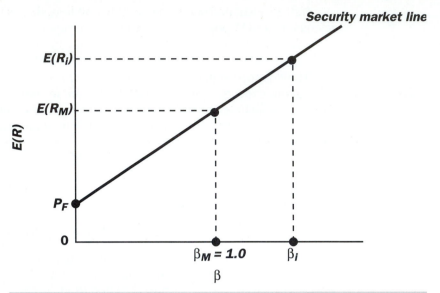

FIGURE 9-3 The Security Market Line

returns. The market model is a descriptive model used to describe historical data. Hence, the market model makes no prediction of what expected returns should be.

TESTS OF THE CAPITAL ASSET PRICING MODEL

The CAPM is indeed a simple and elegant model, but these qualities do not in and of themselves guarantee that it will be useful in explaining observed risk/return patterns. Here we briefly review the empirical literature on attempts to verify the model.

The major difficulty in testing the CAPM is that the model is stated in terms of investor's expectations and not in terms of realized returns. To test the CAPM, it is necessary to convert the theoretical CAPM given by equation (9.11) into a form that can be tested empirically. We will not go through this exercise here, but will simply provide the model that is typically tested.[14] Nor will we delve into the econometric problems associated with testing the CAPM, although we will discuss later an important theoretical issue that raises serious questions about the testability of the CAPM and therefore the empirical findings of researchers.

The empirical analogue of equation (9.11) asserts that over the period of time analyzed, (1) a linear relationship exists between the average risk premium return on the market and the average risk premium return on a stock or portfolio, and its slope is β_i; and (2) the linear relationship should pass through the origin. Moreover, according to the CAPM, beta is a complete measure of a stock's risk. Consequently, alternative risk measures that might be proposed, the most common being the standard deviation of return, should not be significant contributors to the explanation of a stock's return. Recall that the standard deviation measures a stock's total risk, which includes both systematic and unsystematic components.

The CAPM holds for both individual securities and portfolios. Therefore, the empirical tests can be based on either. Tests based on individual securities, however,

---

[14] The interested reader can find the procedure for developing the empirical model tested in Franco Modigliani and Gerald A. Pogue, "Introduction to Risk and Return: Concepts and Evidence: Part II," *Financial Analysts Journal* (May/June 1974), pp. 69–86.

are not the most efficient method of obtaining estimates of the magnitude of the risk/return trade-off for two reasons.

The first problem is called the "errors in variables bias"; it results from the fact that the beta of a stock typically is measured by correlating the stock's return over some sample of historical data. The slope of the resulting line (the regression coefficient) is the estimate of beta. It is subject to errors from various sources. These errors are random in their effect, that is, some stocks' betas are overestimated and some are underestimated. Nevertheless, when these estimated beta values are used in the test, the measurement errors tend to attenuate the relationship between average return and risk. By carefully grouping the securities into portfolios of securities with similar betas, much of this measurement error problem can be eliminated. The errors in individual stocks' betas cancel out so that the portfolio beta can be measured with much greater precision. In turn, tests based on portfolio returns will be more efficient than tests based on security returns.

The second problem relates to the obscuring effect of residual variation. Realized security returns include a large random component, which typically accounts for about 70% of the variation of return (the diversifiable or unsystematic risk of the stock). By grouping securities into portfolios, we can eliminate much of this "noise" and thereby get a much clearer view of the relationship between return and systematic risk.

It should be noted that grouping does not distort the underlying risk/return relationship. The relationship that exists for individual securities is exactly the same for portfolios of securities.

The major results of the empirical tests conducted in the early 1970s are summarized as follows:[15]

1. The evidence shows a significant positive relationship between realized returns and systematic risk as measured by beta. The average market risk premium estimated is usually less than predicted by the CAPM, however.
2. The relationship between risk and return appears to be linear. The studies give no evidence of significant curvature in the risk/return relationship.
3. Tests that attempt to discriminate between the effects of systematic and unsystematic risk do not yield definitive results. Both kinds of risk appear to be positively related to security returns, but substantial evidence supports the proposition that the relationship between return and unsystematic risk is at least partly spurious—that is, partly a reflection of statistical problems rather than the true nature of capital markets.

Obviously, we cannot claim that the CAPM is absolutely right. On the other hand, the early empirical tests do support the view that beta is a useful risk measure and that high-beta stocks tend to be priced so as to yield correspondingly high rates of return.

In 1977, however, Richard Roll wrote a paper criticizing the previously published tests of the CAPM.[16] Roll argued that while the CAPM is testable in principle, no correct test of the theory had yet been presented. He also argued for the practical impossibility that a correct test would ever be accomplished in the future.

---

[15] Some of the earlier studies include Nancy Jacob, "The Measurement of Systematic Risk for Securities and Portfolios: Some Empirical Results," *Journal of Financial and Quantitative Analysis* (March 1971), pp. 815–34; Merton H. Miller and Myron S. Scholes, "Rates of Returns in Relation to Risk: A Reexamination of Recent Findings," and Fischer Black, Michael C. Jensen, and Myron S. Scholes, "The Capital Asset Pricing Model: Some Empirical Evidence," in Michael C. Jensen (ed.), *Studies in the Theory of Capital Markets* (New York: Praeger Books, 1972); Marshall E. Blume and Irwin Friend, "A New Look at the Capital Asset Pricing Model," *Journal of Finance* (March 1973), pp. 19–33; and Eugene F. Fama and James D. MacBeth, "Risk, Return and Equilibrium: Empirical Tests," Working Paper No. 7237, University of Chicago, Graduate School of Business, August 1972.

[16] Richard Roll, "A Critique of the Asset Pricing Theory: Part I. On the Past and Potential Testability of the Theory," *Journal of Financial Economics* (March 1977), pp. 129–76.

The reasoning behind Roll's assertions revolves around his contribution that only one potentially testable hypothesis is associated with the CAPM, namely, that the true market portfolio lies on the Markowitz efficient frontier (i.e., it is mean-variance efficient). Furthermore, because the true market portfolio must contain all worldwide assets, the value of most of which cannot be observed (e.g., human capital), the hypothesis is in all probability untestable.[17]

Since 1977 a number of studies purport either to support or reject the CAPM. These tests attempt to examine implications of the CAPM other than the linearity of the risk/return relation as the basis of their methodology. Unfortunately, none provides a definitive test, and most are subject to substantial criticism, suffering from the same problem of identifying the "true" market portfolio.

◆ THE MULTIFACTOR CAPM

The CAPM just described assumes that the only risk that an investor is concerned with is uncertainty about the future price of a security. Investors, however, usually are concerned with other risks that will affect their ability to consume goods and services in the future. Three examples would be the risks associated with future labor income, the future relative prices of consumer goods, and future investment opportunities.

Recognizing these other risks that investors face, Robert Merton extended the CAPM based on consumers deriving their optimal lifetime consumption when they face these "extra-market" sources of risk.[18] These extra-market sources of risk are also referred to as "factors," hence the model derived by Merton is called a **multifactor CAPM** and is as follows:

$$E(R_p) = R_F + \beta_{p,M}\left[E(R_M) - R_F\right] + \beta_{p,F1}\left[E(R_{F1}) - R_F\right]$$
$$+ \beta_{p,F2}\left[E(R_{F2}) - R_F\right] + \ldots + \beta_{p,FK}\left[E(R_{FK}) - R_F\right] \tag{9.12}$$

where

$$R_F = \text{the risk-free return}$$
$$F1, F2, \ldots, FK = \text{factors or extra-market sources of risk, 1 to } K$$
$$K = \text{number of factors or extra-market sources of risk}$$
$$\beta_{p,Fk} = \text{the sensitivity of the portfolio to the } k\text{th factor}$$
$$E(R_{Fk}) = \text{the expected return of factor } k$$

The total extra-market sources of risk is equal to:

$$\beta_{p,F1}\left[E(R_{F1}) - R_F\right] + \beta_{p,F2}\left[E(R_{F2}) - R\right] + \ldots + \beta_{p,FK}\left[E(R_{FK}) - R_{FK}\right] \tag{9.13}$$

---

[17] The hypothesis tested in the traditional tests of the CAPM cited earlier—namely, that a linear relationship exists between average security returns and beta values—sheds no light on the question whatsoever. This result follows because an approximately linear relation between risk and return would be achieved in tests involving large, well-diversified common stock portfolios, irrespective of whether securities were priced according to the CAPM or some totally different model. The result is tautological. The fact that a positive relationship between realized returns and betas is typically found simply indicates that the returns on the proxy indexes used for the true market portfolio were larger than the average return to the global minimum-variance portfolio.

[18] Robert C. Merton, "An Intertemporal Capital Asset Pricing Model," *Econometrica* (September 1973), pp. 867–88. A less technical version is published in "A Reexamination of the CAPM," in Irwin Friend and James Bicksler (eds.), *Risk and Return in Finance* (Cambridge, MA: Ballinger Publishing, 1976). Other papers on multifactor CAPMs include John C. Cox, Jonathan E. Ingersoll, and Stephen A. Ross, "An Intertemporal Asset Pricing Model with Rational Expectations," *Econometrica* (1985), pp. 363–84, and Douglas Breeden, "An Intertemporal Asset Pricing Model with Stochastic Consumption and Investment Opportunities," *Journal of Financial Economics* (1979), pp. 265–96.

This expression says that investors want to be compensated for the risk associated with each source of extra-market risk, in addition to market risk. Note that if no extra-market sources of risk are present, then equation (9.12) reduces to the expected return for the portfolio as predicted by the CAPM:

$$E\left(R_p\right) = R_F + \beta_p\left[E\left(R_M\right) - R_F\right]$$

In the case of the CAPM, investors hedge the uncertainty associated with future security prices by diversification by holding the market portfolio, which can be thought of as a mutual fund that invests in all securities based on their relative capitalizations. In the multifactor CAPM, in addition to investing in the market portfolio, investors will also allocate funds to something equivalent to a mutual fund that hedges a particular extra-market risk. Although not all investors are concerned with the same sources of extra-market risk, those that are concerned with a specific extra-market risk will basically hedge them in the same way.

We just described the multifactor model for a portfolio. How can this model be used to obtain the expected return for an individual security? Since individual securities are nothing more than portfolios consisting of only one security, equation (9.13) must hold for each security, *i*. That is,

$$
\begin{aligned}
E\left(R_i\right) = R_F &+ \beta_{i,M}\left[E\left(R_M\right) - R_F\right] + \beta_{i,F1}\left[E\left(R_{F1}\right) - R_F\right] \\
&+ \beta_{i,F2}\left[E\left(R_{F2}\right) - R_F\right] + \ldots + \beta_{i,FK}\left[E\left(R_{FK}\right) - R_F\right]
\end{aligned}
\tag{9.14}
$$

The multifactor CAPM is an attractive model because it recognizes nonmarket risks. The pricing of an asset by the marketplace, then, must reflect risk premiums to compensate for these extra-market risks. Unfortunately, it may be difficult to identify all the extra-market risks and to value each of these risks empirically. Furthermore, when these risks are taken together, the multifactor CAPM begins to resemble the arbitrage pricing theory model described next.

◆ ARBITRAGE PRICING THEORY MODEL

An alternative model to the CAPM and the multifactor CAPM was developed by Stephen Ross in 1976.[19] This model is based purely on arbitrage arguments, and hence is called the **arbitrage pricing theory (APT)** model.

ASSUMPTIONS OF THE ARBITRAGE PRICING THEORY

The APT model postulates that a security's expected return is influenced by a variety of factors, as opposed to just the single market index of the CAPM. Specifically, look back at equation (9.5), which states that the return on a security is dependent on its market sensitivity index and an unsystematic return. The APT in contrast states that the return on a security is linearly related to *H* "factors." The APT does not specify what these factors are, but it is assumed that the relationship between security returns and the factors is linear.

---

[19]   Stephen A. Ross, "The Arbitrage Theory of Capital Asset Pricing," *Journal of Economic Theory* (December 1976), pp. 343–62, and "Return, Risk and Arbitrage," in Friend and Bicksler (eds.). *Risk and Return in Finance.* Since the publication by Ross, several studies refined the theory. See, for example, Gur Huberman, "A Simple Approach to Arbitrage Pricing Theory," *Journal of Economic Theory* (October 1982), pp. 183–91, and Jonathan E. Ingersoll, "Some Results in the Theory of Arbitrage Pricing," *Journal of Finance* (September 1984), pp. 1021–39.

To illustrate the APT model, assume a simple world with a portfolio consisting of three securities with two factors (otherwise more complicated mathematical notation must be introduced). The following notation will be used:

$\tilde{R}_i$ = the random rate of return on security i (i = 1,2,3)

$E(R_i)$ = the expected return on security i (i = 1,2,3)

F_h = the hth factor that is common to the returns of all three assets (h = 1,2)

$\beta_{i,h}$ = the sensitivity of the ith security to the hth factor

$\tilde{e}_i$ = the unsystematic return for security i (i = 1,2,3)

The APT model asserts that the random rate of return on security i is given by the following relationship:

$$\tilde{R}_i = E(R_i) + \beta_{i,1}F_1 + \beta_{i,2}F_2 + \tilde{e}_i \tag{9.15}$$

DERIVATION OF THE APT MODEL

For equilibrium to exist among these three assets, the following arbitrage condition must be satisfied: Using no additional funds (wealth) and without increasing risk, it should not be possible, on average, to create a portfolio to increase return. In essence, this condition states that no "money machine" is available in the market.

To see how this principle works, let V_i equal the *change* in the dollar amount invested in the ith security as a percentage of the investor's wealth. For example, suppose that the market value of the investor's portfolio is initially $100,000, comprised of $20,000 in security 1, $30,000 in security 2, and $50,000 in security 3. Suppose an investor changes the initial portfolio to $35,000 in security 1, $25,000 in security 2, and $40,000 in security 3; then the percentage changes would be as follows:

$$V_1 = \frac{\$35,000 - \$20,000}{\$100,000} = 0.15$$

$$V_2 = \frac{\$25,000 - \$30,000}{\$100,000} = -0.05$$

$$V_3 = \frac{\$40,000 - \$50,000}{\$100,000} = -0.10$$

Note that the sum of the percentage changes equals zero because no additional funds were invested. That is, rebalancing of the portfolio does not change the market value of the initial portfolio. Rebalancing does accomplish two things. First, it changes the future return of the portfolio. Second, it changes the total risk of the portfolio, both the systematic risk associated with the two factors and the unsystematic risk.

Consider the first consequence. Mathematically, the *change* in the portfolio's future return ($\Delta\tilde{R}_P$) can be shown to be as follows:

$$\begin{aligned}
\Delta\tilde{R}_P = &\left[V_1 E(R_1) + V_2 E(R_2) + V_3 E(R_3)\right] \\
&+ \left[V_1\beta_{1,1} + V_2\beta_{2,1} + V_3\beta_{3,1}\right]F_1 \\
&+ \left[V_1\beta_{1,2} + V_2\beta_{2,2} + V_3\beta_{3,2}\right]F_2 + \left[V_1\tilde{e}_1 + V_2\tilde{e}_2 + V_3\tilde{e}_3\right]
\end{aligned} \tag{9.16}$$

Equation (9.16) indicates that the change in the portfolio return includes a component that depends on systematic risk as well as unsystematic risk. Even though in our example we included only three securities, when a portfolio contains a large number of securities, the unsystematic risk can be eliminated by diversification as explained in Chapter 8. Thus, equation (9.16) would reduce to:

$$\Delta \tilde{R}_p = \left[V_1 E(R_1) + V_2 E(R_2) + V_3 E(R_3) \right]$$
$$+ \left[V_1 \beta_{1,1} + V_2 \beta_{2,1} + V_3 \beta_{3,1} \right] F_1 + \left[V_1 \beta_{1,2} + V_2 \beta_{2,2} + V_3 \beta_{3,2} \right] F_2 \quad \textbf{(9.17)}$$

Now look at the systematic risk with respect to each factor. The *change* in the portfolio risk with respect to factor 1 is just the betas of each security multiplied by their respective V_i. Consequently, the change in the portfolio's sensitivity to systematic risk from factor 1 is:

$$V_1 \beta_{1,1} + V_2 \beta_{2,1} + V_3 \beta_{3,1} \quad \textbf{(9.18)}$$

For factor 2, it is

$$V_1 \beta_{1,2} + V_2 \beta_{2,2} + V_3 \beta_{3,2} \quad \textbf{(9.19)}$$

One of the conditions imposed for no arbitrage is that the change in systematic risk with respect to each factor will be zero. That is, equations (9.18) and (9.19) should satisfy the following:

$$V_1 \beta_{11} + V_2 \beta_{21} + V_3 \beta_{31} = 0 \quad \textbf{(9.20)}$$

$$V_1 \beta_{12} + V_2 \beta_{22} + V_3 \beta_{32} = 0 \quad \textbf{(9.21)}$$

If equations (9.20) and (9.21) are satisfied, then equation (9.17) reduces to

$$\Delta E(\tilde{R}_p) = V_1 E(R_1) + V_2 E(R_2) + V_3 E(R_3) \quad \textbf{(9.22)}$$

Now we can put all the conditions for no arbitrage together in terms of the preceding equations. As stated earlier, using no additional funds (wealth) and without increasing risk, it should not be possible, on average, to create a portfolio to increase return. No additional funds (wealth) means the following condition $V_1 + V_2 + V_3 = 0$.

The condition of no change in the portfolio's sensitivity to each systematic risk is set forth in equations (9.20) and (9.21). Finally, the expected additional portfolio return from reshuffling the portfolio must be zero, expressed by setting equation (9.22) equal to zero:

$$V_1 E(R_1) + V_2 E(R_2) + V_3 E(R_3) = 0$$

Taken together, these equations, as well as the condition that a sufficiently large number of securities be included so that unsystematic risk can be eliminated, describe mathematically the conditions for equilibrium pricing. These conditions can be solved mathematically, because the number of securities is greater than the number of factors, to determine the equilibrium value for the portfolio as well as the equilibrium value for each of the three securities. Ross showed the following risk and return relationship results for each security i:

$$E(R_i) = R_F + \beta_{i,F1} \left[E(R_{F1}) - R_F \right] + \beta_{i,F2} \left[E(R_{F2}) - R_F \right] \quad \textbf{(9.23)}$$

where

$$\beta_{i,Fj} = \text{the sensitivity of security } i \text{ to the } j\text{th factor}$$
$$E(R_{Fj}) - R_F = \text{the excess return of the } j\text{th systematic factor over the risk-free rate, and can be thought of as the price (or risk premium) for the } j\text{th systematic risk}$$

Equation (9.23) can be generalized to the case that includes H factors as follows:

$$E\left(R_i\right) = R_F + \beta_{i,F1}\left[E\left(R_{F1}\right) - R_F\right] + \beta_{i,F2}\left[E\left(R_{F2}\right) - R_F\right]$$
$$+ \ldots + \beta_{i,FH}\left[E\left(R_{FH}\right) - R_F\right] \qquad \textbf{(9.24)}$$

Equation (9.24) is the APT model. It states that investors want to be compensated for all the factors that *systematically* affect the return of a security. The compensation is the sum of the products of each factor's systematic risk ($\beta_{i,Fh}$), and the risk premium assigned to it by the market $[E(R_{Fh}) - R_F]$. As in the case of the two other risk and return models described earlier, an investor is not compensated for accepting unsystematic risk.

COMPARISON OF APT MODEL AND CAPM

Examining the equations, we can see that the CAPM equation (9.11) and the multifactor CAPM equation (9.14) are actually special cases of the APT model equation (9.24).

$$\text{CAPM: } E\left(R_i\right) = R_F + \beta_i\left[E\left(R_M\right) - R_F\right]$$

$$\text{Multifactor CAPM: } = E\left(R_i\right) = R_F + \beta_{i,M}\left[E\left(R_M\right) - R_F\right] + \beta_{i,F1}\left[E\left(R_{F1}\right) - R_F\right]$$
$$+ \beta_{i,F2}\left[E\left(R_{F2}\right) - R_F\right] + \ldots + \beta_{i,FH}\left[E\left(R_{FH}\right) - R_F\right]$$

$$\text{APT: } E\left(R_i\right) = R_F + \beta_{i,F1}\left[E\left(R_{F1}\right) - R_F\right] + \beta_{i,F2}\left[E\left(R_{F2}\right) - R_F\right]$$
$$+ \ldots + \beta_{i,FK}\left[E\left(R_{FK}\right) - R_F\right]$$

If the only factor is market risk, the APT model reduces to the CAPM. Contrast the APT with the multifactor CAPM. They look similar. Both say that investors are compensated for accepting all systematic risk and no unsystematic risk. The multifactor CAPM states that one of these systematic risks is market risk, while the APT model does not specify the systematic risks.

ADVANTAGES OF APT

Supporters of the APT model argue that it offers several major advantages over the CAPM or multifactor CAPM. First, it makes less-restrictive assumptions about investor preferences toward risk and return. As explained earlier, the CAPM theory assumes investors trade off between risk and return solely on the basis of the expected returns and standard deviations of prospective investments. The APT, on the other hand, simply requires some rather unobtrusive bounds be placed on potential investor utility functions.

Second, no assumptions are made about the distribution of security returns. Finally, because the APT does not rely on the identification of the true market portfolio, the theory is potentially testable.

FACTOR MODELS IN PRACTICE

Thus far we presented the arbitrage pricing theory that tells us how a security should be priced based on its exposure to various types of risk referred to as risk factors or simply factors. In practice, three types of factor models are used in evaluating common stock: statistical factor models, macroeconomic factor models, and fundamental factor models.[20]

---

[20] Gregory Connor, "The Three Types of Factor Models: A Comparison of Their Explanatory Power," *Financial Analysts Journal* (May/June 1995), pp. 42–57.

Statistical Factor Models   As we just explained, identifying the factors presents certain difficulties. In a **statistical factor model**, historical and cross-sectional data on stock returns are tossed into a statistical model. The statistical model used is *principal components analysis,* which is a special case of a statistical technique called *factor analysis.* The goal of the statistical model is to best explain the observed stock returns with "factors" that are linear return combinations and uncorrelated with each other.

For example, suppose that monthly returns for 1,500 companies for 10 years are computed. The goal of principal components analysis is to produce factors that best explain the observed stock returns. Let's suppose that six factors provide explanations. These factors are statistical artifacts. The objective in a statistical factor model then becomes to determine the economic meaning of each of these statistically derived factors.

Because of the problem of interpretation, it is difficult to use the factors from a statistical factor model to obtain expected returns. Instead, practitioners prefer two other models, which allow them to prespecify meaningful factors, and thus produce a more intuitive model.

Macroeconomic Factor Models   In a **macroeconomic factor model**, the inputs to the model are historical stock returns and observable macroeconomic variables called *raw descriptors.* The goal is to determine which macroeconomic variables are pervasive in explaining historical stock returns. Those variables that are pervasive in explaining the returns are then the factors included in the model. The responsiveness of a stock to these factors is estimated using historical time series data. The sensitivity of the factors are estimated so that they are statistically independent. This means that there will be no double counting.

Two examples of proprietary macroeconomic factor models are the Burmeister, Ibbotson, Roll, and Ross (BIRR) model[21] and the Salomon Smith Barney (SSB) model.[22] SSB refers to its model as the Risk Attribute Model, or RAM. A RAM is built for the United States and other countries.

In the BIRR model, there are five macroeconomic factors that reflect unanticipated changes in the following macroeconomic variables:

1. Investor confidence (confidence risk)
2. Interest rates (time horizon risk)
3. Inflation (inflation risk)
4. Real business activity (business cycle risk)
5. Market index (market timing risk)

In the U.S. version of the Salomon Brothers RAM model, the following six macroeconomic factors have been found to best describe the financial environment and are therefore the factors used:

1. Change in expected long-run economic growth
2. Short-run business cycle risk
3. Long-term bond yield changes
4. Short-term Treasury bill changes
5. Inflation shock
6. Dollar changes versus trading partner currencies

---

[21] Edwin Burmeister, Roger Ibbotson, Richard Roll, and Stephen A. Ross, "Using Macroeconomic Factors to Control Portfolio Risk," unpublished paper. The information used in this chapter regarding the BIRR model is obtained from various pages of the BIRR Web site, available at www.birr.com.
[22] This model is described in Eric H. Sorenson, Joseph J. Mezrich, and Chee Thum, "The Salomon Brothers U.S. Risk Attribute Model, Salomon Brothers," *Quantitative Strategy* (October 1989); and Joseph J. Mezrich, Mark O'Donnell, and Vele Samak, *U.S. RAM Model: Model Update,* Salomon Brothers, Equity Portfolio Analysis (April 8, 1997).

Fundamental Factor Models Fundamental factor models use company and industry attributes and market data as raw descriptors. Examples include price/earnings ratios, book/price ratios, estimated economic growth, and trading activity. The inputs into a fundamental factor model are stock returns and the raw descriptors about a company. Those fundamental variables about a company that are pervasive in explaining stock returns are then the raw descriptors retained in the model. Using cross-sectional analysis the sensitivity of a stock's return to a raw descriptor is estimated.

The most commonly used fundamental factor available commercially is the one developed by the consulting firm BARRA. The BARRA E3 model begins with raw descriptors. It then combines raw descriptors to obtain risk indices to capture related company attributes. For example, raw descriptors such as debt-to-asset ratio, debt-to-equity ratio, and fixed-rate coverage are measures that capture a company's financial leverage. These measures would be combined to obtain a risk index for financial leverage. The BARRA E3 fundamental factor model uses 13 risk indices and 55 industry groups.

◆ SOME PRINCIPLES TO TAKE AWAY

In this chapter and in Chapter 8, we covered the heart of what is popularly called modern portfolio theory and asset pricing theory. We pointed out the assumptions and their critical role in the development of these theories and explained the empirical findings. Even though you may understand the topics covered, you may still be uncomfortable as to where we progressed given the lack of theoretical and empirical support for the CAPM or the difficulty of identifying the factors in the multifactor CAPM and APT model. You are not alone—a good number of practitioners and academics feel uncomfortable with these models, particularly the CAPM.

Nevertheless, comfort comes from several general principles about risk and return derived from these theories that few would question.

1. Investing has two dimensions, risk and return. Therefore, focusing only on the actual return that an investor achieved without looking at the risk that was accepted to achieve that return is inappropriate.
2. It is inappropriate to look at the risk of an individual asset when deciding whether it should be included in a portfolio. What is important is how the inclusion of an asset in a portfolio will affect the risk of the portfolio.
3. Whether investors consider one risk or 1,000 risks, risk can be divided into two general categories: systematic risks that cannot be eliminated by diversification, and unsystematic risk, which can be diversified.
4. Investors should only be compensated for accepting systematic risks. Thus, it is critical in formulating an investment strategy to identify the systematic risks.

Summary

This chapter explains the implications of portfolio theory, a theory that deals with the construction of efficient portfolios by rational risk-averse investors. Once a risk-free asset is introduced, the new efficient frontier is the capital market line, which represents a combination of a risk-free asset and the market portfolio.

The capital asset pricing model is an economic theory that describes the relationship between risk and expected return; or, equivalently, it is a model for the pricing of risky securities. The CAPM asserts that the only risk priced by rational investors is systematic risk, because that risk cannot be eliminated by diversification. Essentially, the

CAPM says that the expected return of a security or a portfolio is equal to the rate on a risk-free security plus a risk premium. The risk premium in the CAPM is the product of the quantity of risk times the market price of risk.

The beta of a security or portfolio is an index of the systematic risk of the asset and is estimated statistically. Beta is calculated from historical data on both the asset's return and the market portfolio's return.

Numerous empirical tests of the CAPM, in general, fail to fully support the theory. Richard Roll criticized these studies because of the difficulty of identifying the true market portfolio. Furthermore, Roll asserts that such tests are not likely to appear soon, if at all.

The CAPM assumes that investors are concerned with only one source of risk: the risk having to do with the future price of a security. However, other risks include the capacity of investors to consume goods and services in the future. The multifactor CAPM assumes that investors face such extra-market sources of risk called *factors*. The expected return in the multifactor CAPM is the market risk (as in the case of the basic CAPM) plus a package of risk premiums. Each risk premium is the product of the beta of the security or portfolio with respect to the particular factor, times the difference between the expected return for the factor less the risk-free rate.

The arbitrage pricing theory is developed purely from arbitrage arguments. It postulates that the expected return on a security or a portfolio is influenced by several factors. Proponents of the APT model cite its less-restrictive assumptions as a feature that makes it more appealing than the CAPM or multifactor CAPM. Moreover, testing the APT model does not require identification of the "true" market portfolio. It does, however, require empirical determination of the factors because they are not specified by the theory. Consequently, the APT model replaces the problem of identifying the market portfolio in the CAPM with the problem of choosing and measuring the underlying factors.

Despite the fact that the theories presented are controversial or difficult to implement in practice, several principles are not controversial and can be used in understanding how to price financial assets.

Key Terms

- Arbitrage pricing theory (APT) model
- Capital asset pricing model (CAPM)
- Capital market line (CML)
- Company-specific risk
- Diversifiable risk
- Efficient portfolio
- Homogeneous expectation assumption
- Macroeconomic factor model
- Market model
- Market portfolio
- Market price of risk
- Market risk
- Market sensitivity index
- Multifactor CAPM
- Residual risk
- Security Market Line (SML)
- Statistical factor model
- Systematic risk
- Two-fund separation theorem
- Two-parameter model
- Undiversifiable risk
- Unsystematic risk

Questions

1. a. Explain how the capital market line is constructed on a graph.
   b. Explain why the capital market line assumes a risk-free asset and that investors can borrow or lend at the risk-free rate.
   c. Using a graph, demonstrate why the capital market line dominates the Markowitz efficient frontier.
2. How should an investor construct an efficient portfolio in the presence of a risk-free asset?

3. a. What is meant by two-fund separation?
   b. What do the two funds consist of?
4. Indicate why you agree or disagree with the following statement: "As a percent of the total risk, the unsystematic risk of a diversified portfolio is greater than that of an individual asset."
5. In the CAPM, why is systematic risk also called market risk?
6. Indicate why you agree or disagree with the following statement: "An investor should be compensated for accepting unsystematic risk."
7. a. Suppose that a stock has a beta of 1.15. How do you interpret that value?
   b. Suppose that a stock has a beta of 1.00. Can one mimic the performance of the stock market by buying shares in only that stock?
8. a. What is the market model?
   b. What input into the CAPM is estimated from the market model?
9. Assume the following: expected market return equals 15%; risk-free rate equals 7%. If a security's beta is 1.3, what is its expected return according to the CAPM?
10. Following is an excerpt from an article, "Risk and Reward," in *The Economist* of October 20, 1990:

    > [I]s the CAPM supported by the facts? That is controversial, to put it mildly. It is a tribute to Mr. Sharpe (cowinner of the 1990 Nobel Prize in Economics) that his work, which dates from the early 1960s, is still argued over so heatedly. Attention has lately turned away from beta to more complicated ways of carving up risk. But the significance of CAPM for financial economics would be hard to exaggerate.

    a. What are the general conclusions of studies that empirically investigated the CAPM?
    b. Summarize Roll's argument on the problems inherent in empirically verifying the CAPM.
11. What was the motivation for the development of the multifactor CAPM?
12. a. What is meant by the extra-market sources of risk in the multifactor CAPM?
    b. If no extra-market sources of risk exist, explain why the multifactor CAPM reduces to the pure CAPM.
13. What are the fundamental principles underlying the APT model?
14. What are the advantages of the APT model relative to the CAPM?
15. What are the difficulties in practice of applying the arbitrage pricing theory model?
16. Does Richard Roll's criticism also apply to the arbitrage pricing theory model?
17. "In the CAPM, investors should be compensated for accepting systematic risk; for the APT model, investors are rewarded for accepting both systematic risk and unsystematic risk." Explain why you agree or disagree with this statement.
18. What are the difficulties of using a statistical factor model?
19. How does a macroeconomic factor model differ from a fundamental factor model?
20. Indicate why you agree or disagree with the following statements.
    a. "There is considerable controversy concerning the theories about how assets are priced. Therefore, the distinction between systematic risks and unsystematic risk is meaningless."
    b. "The theories of the pricing of capital assets are highly questionable. Basically, there is only one type of risk and investors should seek to avoid it when they purchase individual securities."

CHAPTER

10

Introduction to Financial Futures Markets

Learning Objectives

After reading this chapter you will understand:

◆ what a futures contract is.

◆ the basic economic function of a futures contract.

◆ the difference between futures and forward contracts.

◆ the role of the clearinghouse.

◆ the mark-to-market and margin requirements of a futures contract.

◆ the risk/return relationship of futures positions.

◆ how a futures contract is priced.

◆ why the actual futures price may differ from the theoretical futures price.

◆ the principles of hedging and the risks associated with hedging.

◆ the role of futures markets in the economy.

A **futures contract** is an agreement that requires a party to the agreement either to buy or sell something at a designated future date at a predetermined price. The basic economic function of futures markets is to provide an opportunity for market participants to hedge against the risk of adverse price movements.

Futures contracts are categorized as either commodity futures or financial futures. **Commodity futures** involve traditional agricultural commodities (such as grain and livestock), imported foodstuffs (such as coffee, cocoa, and sugar), and industrial commodities. Futures contracts based on a financial instrument or a financial index are known as **financial futures**. Financial futures can be classified as (1) stock index futures, (2) interest rate futures, and (3) currency futures. Because the value of a futures contract is derived from the value of the underlying instrument, they are commonly called **derivative instruments**. Other derivative instruments include options (discussed in Chapter 11) and swaps (discussed in Chapter 12).

In Chapters 16, 28, and 30, we shall take a closer look at stock index futures, interest rate futures, and currency futures, respectively. Our purpose in this chapter is to provide an introduction to financial futures contracts, how they are priced, and how they can be used for hedging. More detailed strategies employing futures contracts will be discussed in later chapters.

◆ MECHANICS OF FUTURES TRADING

A futures contract is a firm legal agreement between a buyer (seller) and an established exchange or its clearinghouse in which the buyer (seller) agrees to take (make) delivery of something at a specified price at the end of a designated period of time. The price at which the parties agree to transact in the future is called the **futures price**. The designated date at which the parties must transact is called the **settlement** or **delivery date**.

To illustrate, suppose a futures contract is traded on an exchange where the something to be bought or sold is Asset XYZ, and the settlement is 3 months from now. Assume further that Bob buys this futures contract, and Sally sells this futures contract, and the price at which they agree to transact in the future is $100. Then $100 is the futures price. At the settlement date, Sally will deliver Asset XYZ to Bob; Bob will give Sally $100, the futures price.

LIQUIDATING A POSITION

Most financial futures contracts have settlement dates in the months of March, June, September, or December, which means that at a predetermined time in the contract settlement month the contract stops trading, and a price is determined by the exchange for settlement of the contract. The contract with the closest settlement date is called the **nearby futures contract**. The next futures contract is the one that settles just after the nearby contract. The contract farthest away in time from the settlement is called the **most distant futures contract**.

A party to a futures contract has two choices on liquidation of the position. First, the position can be liquidated prior to the settlement date. For this purpose, the party must take an offsetting position in the same contract. For the buyer of a futures contract, it means selling the same number of identical futures contracts; for the seller of a futures contract, it means buying the same number of identical futures contracts.

The alternative is to wait until the settlement date. At that time the party purchasing a futures contract accepts delivery of the underlying element (financial instrument, currency, or commodity) at the agreed-upon price; the party that sells a futures contract liquidates the position by delivering the underlying element at the agreed-upon price. For some futures contracts that we shall describe in later chapters in the book, settlement is made in cash only. Such contracts are referred to as **cash settlement contracts**.

THE ROLE OF THE CLEARINGHOUSE

Associated with every futures exchange is a clearinghouse, which performs several functions. One of these functions is guaranteeing that the two parties to the transaction will perform. To see the importance of this function, consider potential problems in the futures transaction described earlier from the perspective of the two parties—Bob the buyer and Sally the seller. Each must be concerned with the other's ability to fulfill the obligation at the settlement date. Suppose that at the settlement date the price of Asset XYZ in the cash market is $70. Sally can buy Asset XYZ for $70 and deliver it to Bob who, in turn, must pay her $100. If Bob does not have the capacity to pay $100 or refuses to pay, however, Sally has lost the opportunity to realize a profit of $30. Suppose, instead, that the price of Asset XYZ in the cash market is $150 at the settlement date. In this case, Bob is ready and willing to accept delivery of Asset XYZ and

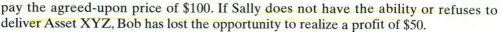

pay the agreed-upon price of $100. If Sally does not have the ability or refuses to deliver Asset XYZ, Bob has lost the opportunity to realize a profit of $50.

The clearinghouse exists to meet this problem. When an investor takes a position in the futures market, the clearinghouse takes the opposite position and agrees to satisfy the terms set forth in the contract. Because of the clearinghouse, the investor need not worry about the financial strength and integrity of the party taking the opposite side of the contract. After initial execution of an order, the relationship between the two parties ends. The clearinghouse interposes itself as the buyer for every sale and the seller for every purchase. Thus investors are free to liquidate their positions without involving the other party in the original contract, and without worry that the other party may default. For this reason, we define a futures contract as an agreement between a party and a clearinghouse associated with an exchange.

Besides its guarantee function, the clearinghouse makes it simple for parties to a futures contract to unwind their positions prior to the settlement date. Suppose that Bob wants to get out of his futures position. He will not have to seek out Sally and work out an agreement with her to terminate the original agreement. Instead, Bob can unwind his position by selling an identical futures contract. As far as the clearinghouse is concerned, its records will show that Bob has bought and sold an identical futures contract. At the settlement date, Sally will not deliver Asset XYZ to Bob but will be instructed by the clearinghouse to deliver to someone who bought and still has an open futures position. In the same way, if Sally wants to unwind her position prior to the settlement date, she can buy an identical futures contract.

MARGIN REQUIREMENTS

When a position is first taken in a futures contract, the investor must deposit a minimum dollar amount per contract as specified by the exchange. This amount is called the **initial margin** and is required as deposit for the contract.[1] The initial margin may be in the form of an interest-bearing security such as a Treasury bill. As the price of the futures contract fluctuates, the value of the investor's equity in the position changes. At the end of each trading day, the exchange determines the settlement price for the futures contract. This price is used to mark to market the investor's position, so that any gain or loss from the position is reflected in the investor's equity account.

Maintenance margin is the minimum level (specified by the exchange) by which an investor's equity position may fall as a result of an unfavorable price movement before the investor is required to deposit additional margin. The additional margin deposited is called **variation margin**, and it is an amount necessary to bring the equity in the account back to its initial margin level. Unlike initial margin, variation margin must be in cash, not interest-bearing instruments. Any excess margin in the account may be withdrawn by the investor. If a party to a futures contract who is required to deposit variation margin fails to do so within 24 hours, the futures position is closed out.

Although initial and maintenance margin requirements for buying securities on margin were explained in Chapter 7, the concept of margin differs for securities and futures. When securities are acquired on margin, the difference between the price of the security and the initial margin is borrowed from the broker. The security purchased serves as collateral for the loan, and the investor pays interest. For futures contracts, the initial margin, in effect, serves as "good faith" money, an indication that the investor will satisfy the obligation of the contract. Normally no money is borrowed by the investor.

---

[1]   Individual brokerage firms are free to set margin requirements above the minimum established by the exchange.

We illustrate futures margin requirements and the mark-to-market procedure more fully in Chapter 16 where we discuss stock index futures.

MARKET STRUCTURE

All futures exchanges in the United States trade more than one futures contract. On the exchange floor, each futures contract is traded at a designated location in a polygonal or circular platform called a pit. The price of a futures contract is determined by open outcry of bids and offers in an auction market. Because of the large number of traders attempting to communicate to other traders the price and quantity that they wish to transact at, pit traders are often forced to communicate using a system of hand signals. No designated market maker operates in the futures market as in an exchange where common stock is traded.

Trading on the floor of the exchange is restricted to members of the exchange. A membership is said to be a seat on the exchange. The price of a seat is determined by supply and demand. Nonexchange members can lease a seat, which conveys to them the right to trade on an exchange. Floor traders include two types: locals and floor brokers. **Locals** buy and sell futures contracts for their own account, thereby risking their own capital. They are professional risk takers. Their presence in the futures market adds liquidity to the market and brings bid and offer prices closer together. Consequently, collectively they play the same effective role as a market maker. Most locals do not maintain an open position overnight. The number of locals and the amount of capital that they can commit to the market far exceeds that of the floor brokers.

Floor brokers, also called **pit brokers**, just like locals, buy and sell for their own account. They execute customer orders as well. These orders come through an authorized futures broker, called a **futures commissions merchant**, or in the form of orders requested by other floor traders. For trades that they execute on behalf of others, floor brokers receive a commission. Although floor brokers can both execute orders for customers and trade for their own account, most of their trades involve the former. When floor brokers do trade for their own account, such trades must not conflict with the interests of customers for whom they are executing trades.

This system of trading in futures markets is not very different from what it was in the 1800s. Monitoring of this sort of system is difficult, which leads to allegations that floor traders profit at the expense of customers whose orders are to be executed.

Several approaches for improving the system of trading futures via electronic trading are at the experimental stage. One approach is a computerized automated system for executing routine trades. Another approach is to automate the entire competitive trading system that now takes place in the pit. The Chicago Mercantile Exchange in conjunction with Reuters Holdings developed such a system (called the Globex system) for trading of futures contracts globally when a futures exchange is closed. Outside the United States, various forms of electronic trading of futures contracts have already been introduced.

DAILY PRICE LIMITS

The exchange may exercise the right to impose a limit on the daily price movement of a futures contract from the previous day's closing price. A daily price limit sets the minimum and maximum price at which the futures contract may trade that day. When a daily price limit is reached, trading does not stop but rather continues at a price that does not violate the minimum or maximum price.

The rationale offered for the imposition of daily price limits is that they provide stability to the market at times when new information may cause the futures price to exhibit extreme fluctuations. Those who support daily price limits argue that giving market participants time to digest or reassess such information when trading ceases at the point that price limits would be violated gives them greater confidence in the market. Not all economists agree with this rationale. The question of the role of daily price limits and whether they are necessary remains the subject of extensive debate.

◆ FUTURES VERSUS FORWARD CONTRACTS

A **forward contract**, just like a futures contract, is an agreement for the future delivery of something at a specified price at the end of a designated period of time. Futures contracts are standardized agreements as to the delivery date (or month) and quality of the deliverable, and are traded on organized exchanges. A forward contract differs in that it is usually nonstandardized (that is, the terms of each contract are negotiated individually between buyer and seller), no clearinghouse coordinates forward contract trading, and secondary markets are often nonexistent or extremely thin. Unlike a futures contract, which is an exchange-traded product, a forward contract is an over-the-counter instrument.

Although both futures and forward contracts set forth terms of delivery, futures contracts are not intended to be settled by delivery. In fact, generally fewer than 2% of outstanding contracts are settled by delivery. Forward contracts, in contrast, are intended for delivery.

Futures contracts are marked to market at the end of each trading day. Consequently, futures contracts are subject to interim cash flows as additional margin may be required in the case of adverse price movements, or as cash is withdrawn in the case of favorable price movements. A forward contract may or may not be marked to market, depending on the wishes of the two parties. A forward contract that is not marked to market does not experience interim cash flow effects because no additional margin is required.

Finally, the parties in a forward contract are exposed to credit risk because either party may default on the obligation. Credit risk is minimal in the case of futures contracts because the clearinghouse associated with the exchange guarantees the other side of the transaction.

Other than these differences, most of what we say about futures contracts applies equally to forward contracts.

◆ RISK AND RETURN CHARACTERISTICS OF FUTURES CONTRACTS

When an investor takes a position in the market by buying a futures contract, the investor is said to be in a **long position** or to be **long futures**. If, instead, the investor's opening position is the sale of a futures contract, the investor is said to be in a **short position** or **short futures**.

The buyer of a futures contract will realize a profit if the futures price increases; the seller of a futures contract will realize a profit if the futures price decreases. For example, suppose 1 month after Bob and Sally take their positions in the futures contract, the futures price of Asset XYZ increases to $120. Bob, the buyer of the futures contract, could then sell the futures contract and realize a profit of $20. Effectively, at the settlement date he agreed to buy Asset XYZ for $100 and agreed to sell Asset XYZ for $120. Sally, the seller of the futures contract, will realize a loss of $20.

If the futures price falls to $40 and Sally buys the contract, she realizes a profit of $60 because she agreed to sell Asset XYZ for $100 and now can buy it for $40. Bob would realize a loss of $60. Thus, if the futures price decreases, the buyer of the futures contract realizes a loss while the seller of a futures contract realizes a profit.

LEVERAGING ASPECT OF FUTURES

When a position is taken in a futures contract, the party need not put up the entire amount of the investment. Instead, only initial margin must be put up. Consequently, suppose Bob has $100 to invest in Asset XYZ because he believes its price will appreciate. If Asset XYZ is selling for $100, he can buy one unit of the asset. His payoff will then be based on the price action of one unit of Asset XYZ.

Suppose instead that the exchange where the futures contract for Asset XYZ is traded requires initial margin of $5. Then Bob can purchase 20 contracts with his $100 investment. (This example ignores the fact that Bob may need funds for variation margin.) His payoff will then depend on the price action of 20 units of Asset XYZ. Thus he can leverage the use of his funds. Although the degree of leverage available in the futures market varies from contract to contract, the leverage attainable is considerably greater than in the cash market by buying on margin.

At first, the leverage available in the futures market may suggest that the market benefits only those who want to speculate on price movements. This assumption is not true. As we shall see later in this chapter, futures markets can be used to reduce price risk. Without the leverage possible in futures transactions, the cost of reducing price risk using futures would be too high for many market participants.

◆ PRICING OF FUTURES CONTRACTS

To understand what determines the futures price, consider once again the futures contract where the underlying instrument is Asset XYZ. The following assumptions will be made:

1. In the cash market Asset XYZ is selling for $100.
2. Asset XYZ pays the holder (with certainty) $12 per year in four quarterly payments of $3, and the next quarterly payment is exactly 3 months from now.
3. The futures contract requires delivery 3 months from now.
4. The current 3-month interest rate at which funds can be loaned or borrowed is 8% per year.

What should the price of this futures contract be? That is, what should the futures price be? Suppose the price of the futures contract is $107. Consider this strategy:

- Sell the futures contract at $107.
- Purchase Asset XYZ in the cash market for $100.
- Borrow $100 for 3 months at 8% per year.

The borrowed funds are used to purchase Asset XYZ, resulting in no initial cash outlay for this strategy. At the end of 3 months, $3 will be received from holding Asset XYZ. Three months from now, Asset XYZ must be delivered to settle the futures contract, and the loan must be repaid. This strategy produces an outcome as follows:

1. From Settlement of the Futures Contract

Proceeds from sale of Asset XYZ to settle the futures contract	=	$107
Payment received from investing in Asset XYZ for 3 months	=	3
Total proceeds		$110

2. From the Loan

Repayment of principal of loan	=	$100
Interest on loan (2% for 3 months)		2
Total outlay	=	$102
Profit		$ 8

Notice that this strategy guarantees a profit of $8. Moreover, this profit is generated with no investment outlay because the proceeds obtained to purchase Asset XYZ were borrowed. The profit will be realized regardless of what the futures price at the settlement date is. The profit is a riskless arbitrage profit. Obviously, in a well-functioning market, arbitrageurs would sell the futures and buy Asset XYZ, forcing the futures price down and bidding up Asset XYZ's price so as to eliminate this profit. This strategy that results in the capturing of the arbitrage profit is referred to as a **cash and carry trade**. The reason for this name is that it involves borrowing cash to purchase a security and "carrying" that security to the futures settlement date.

Suppose instead that the futures price is $92 and not $107. Consider the following strategy:

- Buy the futures contract at $92.
- Sell (short) Asset XYZ for $100.
- Invest (lend) $100 for 3 months at 8% per year.[2]

Once again, no initial cash outlay is made using the strategy. Three months from now, Asset XYZ must be purchased to settle the long position in the futures contract. Asset XYZ accepted for delivery will then be used to cover the short position (i.e., to cover the short sale of Asset XYZ in the cash market). By shorting Asset XYZ, the short seller must pay the lender of Asset XYZ the proceeds that the lender would have earned for the quarter. Therefore, $3 must be paid to the lender of Asset XYZ. The outcome in 3 months would be as follows:

1. From Settlement of the Futures Contract

Price paid for purchase of Asset XYZ to settle the futures contract	=	$ 92
Proceeds to lender of Asset XYZ in order to borrow the asset	=	3
Total outlay	=	$ 95

2. From the Loan

Proceeds received from maturing of investment	=	$100
Interest earned from the 3-month loan investment (2% for 3 months)	=	2
Total proceeds	=	$102
Profit	=	$ 7

The $7 profit from this strategy is also a riskless arbitrage profit. It requires no initial cash outlay, and again a profit will be realized regardless of what the futures price is at the settlement date. This strategy that results in the capturing of the arbitrage profit is referred to as a **reverse cash and carry trade**. That is, with this strategy a security is sold short and the proceeds received from the short sale are invested.

Will a specific futures price eliminate the riskless arbitrage profit? Yes, no arbitrage profit can be realized if the futures price is $99. Look at what would happen if the two previous strategies (cash and carry trade and reverse cash and carry trade) are followed, assuming a futures price of $99. First, consider this strategy:

- Sell the futures contract at $99.
- Purchase Asset XYZ for $100.
- Borrow $100 for 3 months at 8% per year.

---

[2]   Technically, a short seller may not be entitled to the full use of the proceeds resulting from the sale. We shall discuss this later in this section.

In 3 months the outcome will be as follows:

1. From Settlement of the Futures Contract

Proceeds from sale of Asset XYZ to settle the futures contract	=	$ 99
Payment received from investing in Asset XYZ for 3 months	=	3
Total proceeds		$102

2. From the Loan

Repayment of the principal of loan	=	$100
Interest (2% for 3 months)	=	2
Total outlay	=	$102
Profit	=	0

No arbitrage profit results from this strategy.

Next consider this strategy:

- Buy the futures contract at $99.
- Sell (short) XYZ for $100.
- Invest (lend) $100 for 3 months at 8% per year.

The outcome in 3 months would be as follows:

1. From Settlement of the Futures Contract

Price paid for purchase of Asset XYZ to settle futures contract	=	$ 99
Proceeds to lender of Asset XYZ in order to borrow the asset	=	3
Total outlay	=	$102

2. From the Loan

Proceeds received from maturing of investment	=	$100
Interest earned from the 3-month loan investment (2% for 3 months)	=	2
Total proceeds	=	$102
Profit	=	$ 2

Thus, neither strategy results in an arbitrage profit. Hence, a futures price of $99 is the equilibrium price because any higher or lower futures price will permit riskless arbitrage profits. This equilibrium price is also called the **theoretical futures price**.

◆ THEORETICAL FUTURES PRICE BASED ON ARBITRAGE MODEL

According to the arbitrage arguments just presented, we see that the theoretical futures price can be determined based on the following information:

1. The price of the asset in the cash market.
2. The cash yield earned on the asset until the settlement date. In our example, the cash yield on Asset XYZ is $3 on a $100 investment or 3% quarterly (12% annual cash yield).
3. The interest rate for borrowing and lending until the settlement date. The borrowing and lending rate is referred to as the **financing cost**. In our example, the financing cost is 2% for the 3 months.

We will assign the following:

r = financing cost
y = cash yield
P = cash market price ($)
F = futures price ($)

Now consider the strategy:

- Sell the futures contract at F.
- Purchase Asset XYZ for P.
- Borrow P until the settlement date at r.

The outcome at the settlement date then is:

1. *From Settlement of the Futures Contract*

Proceeds from sale of Asset XYZ to settle the futures contract	=	F
Payment received from investing in Asset XYZ for 3 months	=	yP
Total proceeds	=	$F + yP$

2. *From the Loan*

Repayment of the principal of loan	=	P
Interest on loan	=	rP
Total outlay	=	$P + rP$

The profit will equal:

Profit = Total proceeds − Total outlay

Profit = $F + yP - (P + rP)$

The theoretical futures price is where the profit from this strategy is zero. Thus, to have equilibrium, the following must hold:

$$0 = F + yP - \left(P + rP\right)$$

Solving for the theoretical futures price, we have:

$$F = P + P\left(r - y\right) \tag{10.1}$$

Alternatively, consider the strategy:

- Buy the futures contract at F.
- Sell (short) Asset XYZ for P.
- Invest (lend) P at r until the settlement date.

The outcome at the settlement date would be:

1. *From Settlement of Futures Contract*

Price paid for purchase of Asset XYZ to settle futures contract	=	F
Payment to lender of Asset XYZ in order to borrow the asset	=	yP
Total outlay	=	$F + yP$

2. *From the Loan*

Proceeds received from maturing of the loan investments	=	P
Interest earned	=	rP
Total proceeds	=	$P + rP$

The profit will equal:

Profit = Total proceeds − Total outlay

Profit = $P + rP - (F + yP)$

Setting the profit equal to zero so that no arbitrage profit results and solving for the futures price, we would obtain the same equation for the futures price as given by equation (10.1).

We shall apply this equation to our previous example to determine the theoretical futures price. Here:

$r = 0.02$
$y = 0.03$
$P = \$100$

Then, from equation (10.1) the theoretical futures price is

$$F = \$100 + \$100\big(0.03 - 0.02\big)$$
$$= \$100 + \$1 = \$99$$

This result agrees with the theoretical futures price as we demonstrated earlier.

The theoretical futures price may be at a premium to the cash market price (higher than the cash market price) or at a discount from the cash market price (lower than the cash market price) depending on $P(r - y)$. The term $r - y$, which reflects the difference between the cost of financing and the asset's cash yield, is called the **net financing cost**. The net financing cost is more commonly called the **cost of carry** or, simply, carry. Positive carry means that the yield earned is greater than the financing cost; negative carry means that the financing cost exceeds the yield earned. Then the relationships shown in Table 10-1 hold.

PRICE CONVERGENCE AT THE DELIVERY DATE

At the delivery date, the futures price must be equal to the cash market price. Thus, as the delivery date approaches, the futures price converges to the cash market price. This convergence can be seen by looking at equation (10.1) for the theoretical futures price. As the delivery date approaches, the financing cost approaches zero, and the yield that can be earned by holding the investment approaches zero. Hence the cost of carry approaches zero, and the futures price will approach the cash market price.

A CLOSER LOOK AT THE THEORETICAL FUTURES PRICE

To derive the theoretical futures price as given by equation (10.1) using the arbitrage argument, we made several assumptions. When the assumptions are violated, a divergence occurs between the actual futures price and the theoretical futures price as given by equation (10.1); that is, the difference between the two prices will differ from carry. The implications for pricing will be discussed in more detail when we focus on stock index futures in Chapter 16 and interest rate futures in Chapter 28. For the time being we shall look at reasons for the deviation of the actual futures price from the theoretical futures price that are common to all financial futures contracts.

Interim Cash Flow   No interim cash flows due to variation margin are assumed. In addition, any dividends or coupon interest payments are assumed to be paid at the delivery date rather than at an interim date. However, we know that interim cash flows can occur for both of these reasons. Because we assume no variation margin, the theoretical price for the contract is technically the theoretical price for a forward contract that is not marked to market, not the theoretical price for a futures contract. Unlike a futures contract, a forward contract that is not marked to market at the end of each trading day does not require additional margin.

TABLE 10-1   Relationship Between Carry and Futures Price

Carry	Futures Price
Positive ($y > r$)	will sell at a discount to cash price ($F < P$)
Negative ($y < r$)	will sell at a premium to cash price ($F > P$)
Zero ($r = y$)	will be equal to the cash price ($F = P$)

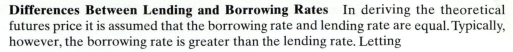

Differences Between Lending and Borrowing Rates   In deriving the theoretical futures price it is assumed that the borrowing rate and lending rate are equal. Typically, however, the borrowing rate is greater than the lending rate. Letting

r_B = borrowing rate
r_L = lending rate

and using the strategy

- Sell the futures contract at F.
- Purchase the asset for P.
- Borrow P until the settlement date at r_B.

the futures price that would produce no arbitrage profit is

$$F = P + P\left(r_B - y\right)$$ **(10.2)**

For the strategy:

- Buy the futures contract at F.
- Sell (short) the asset for P.
- Invest (lend) P at r_L until the settlement date.

the futures price that would produce no profit is

$$F = P + P\left(r_L - y\right)$$ **(10.3)**

Equations (10.2) and (10.3) together provide boundaries between which the futures price will be in equilibrium. Equation (10.2) establishes the upper boundary, and equation (10.3) the lower boundary. For example, assume that the borrowing rate is 8% per year, or 2% for 3 months, while the lending rate is 6% per year, or 1.5% for 3 months. According to equation (10.2), the upper boundary for the theoretical futures price is

$$F\left(\text{upper boundary}\right) = \$100 + \$100\left(0.02 - 0.03\right) = \$99$$

The lower boundary for the theoretical futures price according to equation (10.3) is

$$F\left(\text{lower boudary}\right) = \$100 + \$100\left(0.015 - 0.03\right) = \$98.50$$

Thus the theoretical futures price must satisfy the condition: $98.50 < F < 99$.

Transaction Costs   In determining the theoretical futures price, we so far ignored transaction costs involved in establishing the positions. In actuality, transaction costs include entering into and closing the cash position as well as round-trip transaction costs for the futures contract that do affect the theoretical futures price. Transaction costs widen the boundaries for the theoretical futures price.

Proceeds from Short Selling   In the strategy involving short-selling of Asset XYZ, it is assumed that the proceeds from the short sale are received and reinvested. In practice, for individual investors, the proceeds are not received, and, in fact, the individual investor is required to put up margin (securities margin not futures margin) to short-sell. For institutional investors, the asset may be borrowed, but the borrowing comes at a cost. This cost of borrowing can be incorporated into the model by reducing the yield on the asset.

Deliverable Asset and Settlement Date Known   Our example assumes that only one asset is deliverable, and that the settlement date occurs 3 months from now. In Chapter 21, where we discuss Treasury bond futures contracts, we will see that several Treasury bond issues can be delivered to satisfy the futures contract. The choice of which Treasury bond issue to deliver is given to the short. Thus, the buyer of this futures contract does not know what the deliverable asset will be. Also, for the same futures contract, the short is also given the choice of when in the settlement month to deliver the Treasury bond issue. As a result, the buyer does not know the specific settlement date. These factors influence the futures price.

Deliverable Is a Basket of Securities   The underlying instrument for some futures contracts is not a single asset but a basket of assets, or an index. Stock index futures, discussed in Chapter 16, and the municipal bond index futures contract, explained in Chapter 28, are examples. The problem in arbitraging these two futures contracts is that it is too expensive to buy or sell every asset included in the index. Instead, a portfolio containing a smaller number of assets may be constructed to "track" the index. The arbitrage, however, is no longer risk-free because of the risk that the portfolio will not track the index exactly. All of which leads to higher transaction costs and uncertainty about the outcome of the arbitrage.

◆ GENERAL PRINCIPLES OF HEDGING WITH FUTURES

The major function of futures markets is to transfer price risk from hedgers to speculators. That is, risk is transferred from those willing to pay to avoid risk to those wanting to assume the risk in the hope of gain. **Hedging** in this case is the employment of a futures transaction as a temporary substitute for a transaction to be made in the cash market. The hedge position locks in a value for the cash position. As long as cash and futures prices move together, any loss realized on one position (whether cash or futures) will be offset by a profit on the other position. When the profit and loss are equal, the hedge is called a **perfect hedge**. In a market where the futures contract is correctly priced, a perfect hedge should provide a return equal to the risk-free rate.

RISKS ASSOCIATED WITH HEDGING

In practice, hedging is not that simple. The amount of the loss or profit on a hedge will be determined by the relationship between the cash price and the futures price when a hedge is placed and when it is lifted. The difference between the cash price and the futures price is called the **basis**. That is, basis = cash price − futures price.

As we explained earlier, if a futures contract is priced according to its theoretical value, the difference between the cash price and the futures price should be equal to the cost of carry. The risk that the hedger takes is that the basis will change, called **basis risk**. Therefore, hedging involves the substitution of basis risk for price risk, that is, the substitution of the risk that the basis will change for the risk that the cash price will change.

When a futures contract is used to hedge a position where either the portfolio or the individual financial instrument is not identical to the instrument underlying the futures, it is called cross-hedging. **Cross-hedging** is common in asset/liability and portfolio management because no futures contracts are available on specific common stock shares and bonds. Cross-hedging introduces another risk—the risk that the price movement of the underlying instrument of the futures contract may not accurately track the price movement of the portfolio or financial instrument to be hedged. It

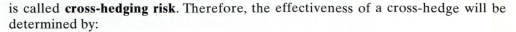

is called **cross-hedging risk**. Therefore, the effectiveness of a cross-hedge will be determined by:

1. The relationship between the cash price of the underlying instrument and its futures price when a hedge is placed and when it is lifted.
2. The relationship between the market (cash) value of the portfolio and the cash price of the instrument underlying the futures contract when the hedge is placed and when it is lifted.

SHORT HEDGE AND LONG HEDGE

A **short hedge** is used to protect against a decline in the future cash price of a financial instrument or portfolio. To execute a short hedge, the hedger sells a futures contract (agrees to make delivery). Consequently, a short hedge is also known as a **sell hedge**. By establishing a short hedge, the hedger has fixed the future cash price and transferred the price risk of ownership to the buyer of the futures contract.

A **long hedge** is undertaken to protect against an increase in the price of a financial instrument or portfolio to be purchased in the cash market at some future time. In a long hedge, the hedger buys a futures contract (agrees to accept delivery). A long hedge is also known as a **buy hedge**.

HEDGING ILLUSTRATIONS

To illustrate hedging, we shall present several numerical examples from the traditional commodities markets. It is better to start with the traditional commodities because they are simpler than most financial futures contracts. The principles we illustrate still are equally applicable to financial futures contracts but it is easier to grasp the sense of the commodities product example without involving financial contract nuances. In Chapter 16, we will illustrate hedging for a stock portfolio.

Assume that a gold mining company expects to sell 1,000 ounces of gold 1 week from now and that the management of a jewelry company plans to purchase 1,000 ounces of gold 1 week from now. The managers of both the gold mining company and the jewelry company want to lock in today's price—that is, they both want to eliminate the price risk associated with gold 1 week from now. The cash price for gold is currently $352.40 per ounce. The cash price is also called the **spot price**. The futures price for gold is currently $397.80 per ounce. Each futures contract is for 100 ounces of gold.

Because the gold mining company seeks protection against a decline in the price of gold, the company will place a short hedge. That is, the company will promise to make delivery of gold at the current futures price. The gold mining company will sell 10 futures contracts.

The management of the jewelry company seeks protection against an increase in the price of gold. Consequently, it will place a long hedge. That is, it will agree to accept delivery of gold at the futures price. Because it is seeking protection against a price increase for 1,000 ounces of gold, it will buy 10 contracts.

Let's look at what happens under various scenarios for the cash price and futures price of gold 1 week from now, when the hedge is lifted.

Perfect Hedge   Suppose that at the time the hedge is lifted the cash price has declined to $304.20 and the futures price has declined to $349.60. Notice what has happened to the basis under this scenario. At the time the hedge is placed, the basis is −$45.40 ($352.40 − $397.80). When the hedge is lifted, the basis is still −$45.40 ($304.20 − $349.60).

The gold mining company wanted to lock in a price of $352.40 per ounce of gold, or $352,400 for 1,000 ounces. The company sold 10 futures contracts at a price of $397.80 per ounce or $397,800 for 1,000 ounces. When the hedge is lifted, the value of 1,000 ounces of gold is $304,200 ($304.20 × 1,000). The gold mining company realizes a decline in the cash market in the value of its gold of $48,200. However, the futures price has declined to $349.60, or $349,600 for 1,000 ounces. The mining company thus realizes a $48,200 gain in the futures market. The net result is that the gain in the futures market matches the loss in the cash market. Consequently, the gold mining company does not realize an overall gain or loss. This example of a perfect hedge is summarized in Table 10-2.

The outcome for the jewelry company of its long hedge is also summarized in Table 10-2. Because of the decline in the cash price, the jewelry company gains in the cash market by $48,200 but realizes a loss of the same amount in the futures market. Therefore the long hedge is also a perfect hedge.

This scenario illustrates two important points. First, both participants incur no overall gain or loss. The reason is that the basis did not change when the hedge was

TABLE 10-2   A Hedge That Locks in the Current Price of Gold: Cash Price Decreases

Assumptions

Cash price at time hedge is placed	$352.40 per oz
Futures price at time hedge is placed	397.80 per oz
Cash price at time hedge is lifted	304.20 per oz
Futures price at time hedge is lifted	349.60 per oz
Number of ounces to be hedged	1,000
Number of ounces per futures contract	100
Number of futures contracts used in hedge	10

Short (Sell) Hedge by Gold Mining Company

Cash Market	Futures Market	Basis
At time hedge is placed		
Value of 1,000 oz:	Sell 10 contracts:	−$45.40 per oz
1,000 × $352.40 = $352,400	10 × 100 × $397.80 = $397,800	
At time hedge is lifted		
Value of 1,000 oz:	Buy 10 contracts:	−$45.40 per oz
1,000 × $304.20 = $304,200	10 × 100 × $349.60 = $349,600	
Loss in cash market = $48,200	Gain in futures market = $48,200	
	Overall gain or loss = $0	

Long (Buy) Hedge by Jewelry Company

Cash Market	Futures Market	Basis
At time hedge is placed		
Value of 1,000 oz:	Buy 10 contracts:	−$45.40 per oz
1,000 × $352.40 = $352,400	10 × 100 × $397.80 = $397,800	
At time hedge is lifted		
Value of 1,000 oz:	Sell 10 contracts:	−$45.40 per oz
1,000 × $304.20 = $304,200	10 × 100 × $349.60 = $349,600	
Gain in cash market = $48,200	Loss in futures market = $48,200	
	Overall gain or loss = $0	

lifted. Consequently, if the basis does not change, the effective purchase or sale price ends up being the cash price on the day the hedge is set. Second, note that the management of the jewelry company would have been better off if it had not hedged. The cost of the gold would have been $48,200 less. This result, however, should not be interpreted as a sign of a bad decision. Managers are usually not in the business of speculating on the price of gold and hedging is the standard practice used to protect against an increase in the cost of doing business in the future. The "price" of obtaining this protection is the potential windfall that one gives up.

Suppose that when the hedge is lifted the cash price of gold has increased to $392.50 and that the futures price has increased to $437.90. Notice that the basis is unchanged at −$45.40. Because the basis is unchanged, the effective purchase and sale price will equal the price of gold at the time the hedge is placed.

The gold mining company will gain in the cash market because the value of 1,000 ounces of gold is $392,500 ($392.50 × 1,000) and represents a $40,100 gain compared to the cash value at the time the hedge was placed. However, the gold mining company must liquidate its position in the futures market by buying 10 futures contracts at a total price of $437,900, which is $40,100 more than the price when the contracts were sold. The loss in the futures market offsets the gain in the cash market. The results of this hedge are summarized in Table 10-3.

The jewelry company realizes a $40,100 gain in the futures market but will have to pay $40,100 more in the cash market to acquire 1,000 ounces of gold. The results of this hedge are also summarized in Table 10-3.

Notice that in this scenario the management of the jewelry company saved $40,100 by employing a hedge. The gold mining company, on the other hand, would have been better off if it had not hedged and had simply sold its product on the market 1 week later. However, it must be emphasized that the management of the gold mining company, just like the management of the jewelry company, employed a hedge to protect against unforeseen adverse price changes in the cash market, and the price of this protection is that one forgoes the favorable price changes enjoyed by those who do not hedge.

Basis Risk   In the two previous scenarios we assumed that the basis does not change. In the real world, however, the basis frequently changes between the time a hedge is placed and the time it is lifted.

Assume that the cash price of gold decreases to $304.20, just as in the first scenario; however, assume further that the futures price decreases to $385.80 rather than $349.60. The basis has now declined from −$45.40 to −$81.60 ($304.20 − $385.80). The results are summarized in Table 10-4. For the short hedge, the $48,200 loss in the cash market is only partially offset by the $12,000 gain realized in the futures market. Consequently, the hedge resulted in an overall loss of $36,200.

Several points are pertinent here. First, if the gold mining company did not hedge, the loss would have been $48,200, because the value of its 1,000 ounces of gold is $304,200 compared to the $352,400 just 1 week earlier. Although the hedge is not perfect, the loss of $36,200 is less than the loss of $48,200 that would have occurred without the hedge, which is what we meant earlier by stating that hedging substitutes basis risk for price risk. Second, the management of the jewelry company faces the same problem from an opposite perspective. An unexpected gain for one participant results in an unexpected loss of equal dollar value for the other. That is, the participants face a zero-sum game because they hold identically opposite cash and futures positions. Consequently, the jewelry company would realize an overall gain of $36,200 from its long (buy) hedge. This gain represents a gain in the cash market of $48,200 and a realized loss in the futures market of $12,000.

TABLE 10-3   A Hedge That Locks in the Current Price of Gold: Cash Price Increases

Assumptions

Cash price at time hedge is placed	$352.40 per oz
Futures price at time hedge is placed	397.80 per oz
Cash price at time hedge is lifted	392.50 per oz
Futures price at time hedge is lifted	437.90 per oz
Number of ounces to be hedged	1,000
Number of ounces per futures contract	100
Number of futures contracts used in hedge	10

Short (Sell) Hedge by Gold Mining Company

Cash Market	Futures Market	Basis
At time hedge is placed		
Value of 1,000 oz:	Sell 10 contracts:	−$45.40 per oz
1,000 × $352.40 = $352,400	10 × 100 × $397.80 = $397,800	
At time hedge is lifted		
Value of 1,000 oz:	Buy 10 contracts:	−$45.40 per oz
1,000 × $392.50 = $352,500	10 × 100 × $437.90 = $437,900	
Gain in cash market = $40,100	Loss in futures market = $40,100	
	Overall gain or loss = $0	

Long (Buy) Hedge by Gold Mining Company

Cash Market	Futures Market	Basis
At time hedge is placed		
Value of 1,000 oz:	Buy 10 contracts:	−$45.40 per oz
1,000 × $352.40 = $352,400	10 × 100 × $397.80 = $397,800	
At time hedge is lifted		
Value of 1,000 oz:	Sell 10 contracts:	−$45.40 per oz
1,000 × $392.50 = $392,500	10 × 100 × $437.90 = $437,900	
Loss in cash market = $40,100	Gain in futures market = $40,100	
	Overall gain or loss = $0	

Suppose that the cash price increases to $392.50 per ounce, just as in the second scenario, but that the basis widens to −$81.60. That is, at the time the hedge is lifted the futures price has increased to $474.10. The results of this hedge are summarized in Table 10-5.

As a result of the long hedge, the jewelry company realizes a gain of $76,300 in the futures market but only a $40,100 loss in the cash market for an overall gain of $36,200. For the gold mining company, the overall loss is $36,200.

In the two previous scenarios it was assumed that the basis widened. It can be demonstrated that if the basis narrowed, the outcome will not be a perfect hedge.

Cross-Hedging   Suppose that a mining company on a far-away planet plans to sell 2,500 ounces of kryptonite 1 week from now and that a jewelry company plans to purchase the same amount of kryptonite in 1 week. Both parties want to hedge against price risk.[3] However, kryptonite futures contracts are not currently traded. Both

---

[3]   We will ignore interplanetary exchange rate risk in our illustrations.

TABLE 10-4   Hedge: Cash Price Decreases and Basis Widens

Assumptions

Cash price at time hedge is placed	$352.40 per oz
Futures price at time hedge is placed	397.80 per oz
Cash price at time hedge is lifted	304.20 per oz
Futures price at time hedge is lifted	385.80 per oz
Number of ounces to be hedged	1,000
Number of ounces per futures contract	100
Number of futures contracts used in hedge	10

Short (Sell) Hedge by Gold Mining Company

Cash Market	Futures Market	Basis
At time hedge is placed		
Value of 1,000 oz:	Sell 10 contracts:	−$45.40 per oz
1,000 × $352.40 = $352,400	10 × 100 × $397.80 = $397,800	
At time hedge is lifted		
Value of 1,000 oz:	Buy 10 contracts:	−$81.60 per oz
1,000 × $304.20 = $304,200	10 × 100 × $385.80 = $385,800	
Loss in cash market = $48,200	Gain in futures market = $12,000	
	Overall loss = $36,200	

Long (Buy) Hedge by Jewelry Company

Cash Market	Futures Market	Basis
At time hedge is placed		
Value of 1,000 oz:	Buy 10 contracts:	−$45.40 per oz
1,000 × $352.40 = $352,400	10 × 100 × $397.80 = $397,800	
At time hedge is lifted		
Value of 1,000 oz:	Sell 10 contracts:	−$81.60 per oz
1,000 × $304.20 = $304,200	10 × 100 × $385.80 = $385,800	
Gain in cash market = $48,200	Loss in futures market = $12,200	
	Overall gain $36,200	

parties believe a close relationship exists between the price of kryptonite and the price of gold. Specifically, both parties believe that the cash price of kryptonite will remain at 40% of the cash price of gold. The cash price of kryptonite is currently $140.96 per ounce, and the cash price of gold is currently $352.40 per ounce. The futures price of gold is currently $397.80 per ounce.

We shall examine various scenarios to see how effective the cross-hedge will be. In each scenario, the gold basis is held constant at −$45.40. We make this assumption so that we can focus on the importance of the relationship between the two cash prices at the two points in time.

Before proceeding, we must first determine how many gold futures contracts should be used in the cross-hedge. The value of 2,500 ounces of kryptonite at the cash price of $140.96 per ounce is $352,400. To protect the value of the kryptonite using gold futures, the cash value of 1,000 ounces of gold ($352,400/$352.40) must be hedged. Because each gold futures contract covers 100 ounces, 10 gold futures contracts will be used.

TABLE 10-5 Hedge: Cash Price Increases and Basis Widens

Assumptions

Cash price at time hedge is placed	$352.40 per oz
Futures price at time hedge is placed	397.80 per oz
Cash price at time hedge is lifted	392.50 per oz
Futures price at time hedge is lifted	474.10 per oz
Number of ounces to be hedged	1,000
Number of ounces per futures contract	100
Number of futures contracts used in hedge	10

Short (Sell) Hedge by Gold Mining Company

Cash Market	Futures Market	Basis
At time hedge is placed		
Value of 1,000 oz:	Sell 10 contracts:	−$45.40 per oz
1,000 × $352.40 = $352,400	10 × 100 × $397.80 = $397,800	
At time hedge is lifted		
Value of 1,000 oz:	Buy 10 contracts:	−$81.60 per oz
1,000 × $392.50 = $392,500	10 × 100 × $474.10 = $474,100	
Gain in cash market = $40,100	Loss in futures market = $76,300	
	Overall loss = $36,200	

Long (Buy) Hedge by Jewelry Company

Cash Market	Futures Market	Basis
At time hedge is placed		
Value of 1,000 oz:	Buy 10 contracts:	−$45.40 per oz
1,000 × $352.40 = $352,400	10 × 100 × $397.80 = $397,800	
At time hedge is lifted		
Value of 1,000 oz:	Sell 10 contracts:	−$81.60 per oz
1,000 × $392.50 = $392,500	10 × 100 × $474.10 = $474,100	
Loss in cash market = $40,100	Gain in futures market = $76,300	
	Overall gain = $36,200	

Suppose that the cash prices of kryptonite and gold decrease to $121.68 and $304.20 per ounce, respectively, and that the futures price of gold decreases to $349.60 per ounce. The relationship between the cash price of kryptonite and the cash price of gold when the cross-hedge was placed holds when the cross-hedge is lifted. That is, the cash price of kryptonite is 40% of the cash price of gold. The gold basis stays constant at −$45.40. The outcome for the short and long cross-hedge is summarized in Table 10-6.

The short cross-hedge produces a gain of $48,200 in the futures market and an exactly offsetting loss in the cash market. The opposite occurs for the long cross-hedge. Neither an overall gain nor a loss from the cross-hedge accrues for either hedger in this scenario. The same would occur if the cash prices of both commodities increase by the same percentage and the basis does not change.

Suppose that the cash price of both commodities decreases but the cash price of kryptonite falls by a greater percentage than the cash price of gold. For example, suppose that the cash price of kryptonite falls to $112.00 per ounce, while the cash price of gold falls to $304.20 per ounce. The futures price of gold falls to $349.60 so that the

TABLE 10-6   Cross Hedge: Cash Price of Kryptonite to Be Hedged and Price of Futures Used Decreased by Same Percentage

Assumptions

Price of kryptonite	
Cash price at time hedge is placed	$140.96 per oz
Cash price at time hedge is lifted	121.68 per oz
Price of gold	
Cash price at time hedge is placed	$352.40 per oz
Futures price at time hedge is placed	397.80 per oz
Cash price at time hedge is lifted	$304.20 per oz
Futures price at time hedge is lifted	349.60 per oz
Number of ounces of kryptonite to be hedged	2,500
Number of ounces of gold to be hedged	
assuming ratio of cash price of kryptonite to gold is 0.4	1,000
Number of ounces per futures contract for gold	100
Number of gold futures contracts used in hedge	10

Short (Sell) Cross-Hedge by Kryptonite Mining Company

Cash Market	Futures Market	Gold Basis
At time hedge is placed		
Value of 2,500 oz:	Sell 10 contracts:	−$45.40 per oz
2,500 × $140.96 = $352,400	10 × 100 × $397.80 = $397,800	
At time hedge is lifted		
Value of 2,500 oz:	Buy 10 contracts:	−$45.40 per oz
2,500 × $121.68 = $304,200	10 × 100 × $349.60 = $349,600	
Loss in cash market = $48,200	Gain in futures market = $48,200	
	Overall gain or loss = $0	

Long (Buy) Cross-Hedge by Jewelry Company

Cash Market	Futures Market	Gold Basis
At time hedge is placed		
Value of 2,500 oz:	Buy 10 contracts:	−$45.40 per oz
2,500 × $140.96 = $352,400	10 × 100 × $397.80 = $397,800	
At time hedge is lifted		
Value of 2,500 oz:	Sell 10 contracts:	−$45.40 per oz
2,500 × $121.68 = $304,200	10 × 100 × $349.60 = $349,600	
Gain in cash market = $48,200	Loss in futures market = $48,200	
	Overall gain or loss = $0	

basis is not changed. The cash price of kryptonite at the time the cross-hedge is lifted is 37% of the cash price of gold, rather than the 40% when the cross-hedge was constructed. The outcome for the long and short cross-hedge is shown in Table 10-7.

For the short cross-hedge, the loss in the cash market exceeds the realized gain in the futures market by $24,200. For the long cross-hedge, the opposite is true. An overall gain of $24,200 results from the cross-hedge.

If the cash price of kryptonite had fallen by a smaller percentage amount than the cash price of gold, the short cross-hedge would have produced an overall gain, while the long cross-hedge would have generated an overall loss.

TABLE 10-7 Cross-Hedge: Cash Price of Kryptonite to Be Hedged Falls by a Greater Percentage Than the Futures Used for the Hedge

Assumptions

Price of kryptonite	
Cash price at time hedge is placed	$140.96 per oz
Cash price at time hedge is lifted	112.00 per oz
Price of Gold	
Cash price at time hedge is placed	$352.40 per oz
Futures price at time hedge is placed	397.80 per oz
Cash price at time hedge is lifted	304.20 per oz
Futures price at time hedge is lifted	349.60 per oz
Number of ounces of kryptonite to be hedged	2,500
Number of ounces of gold to be hedged	
assuming ratio of cash price of kryptonite to gold is 0.4	1,000
Number of ounces per futures contract for gold	100
Number of gold futures contracts used in hedge	10

Short (Sell) Cross-Hedge by Kryptonite Mining Company

Cash Market	Futures Market	Basis
At time hedge is placed		
Value of 2,500 oz:	Sell 10 contracts:	−$45.40 per oz
2,500 × $140.96 = $352,400	10 × 100 × $397.80 = $397,800	
At time hedge is lifted		
Value of 2,500 oz:	Buy 10 contracts:	−$45.40 per oz
2,500 × $112.00 = $280,000	10 × 100 × $349.60 = $349,600	
Loss in cash market = $72,400	Gain in futures market = $48,200	
	Overall loss = $24,200	

Long (Buy) Cross-Hedge by Jewelry Company

Cash Market	Futures Market	Basis
At time hedge is placed		
Value of 2,500 oz:	Buy 10 contracts:	−$45.40 per oz
2,500 × $140.96 = $352,400	10 × 100 × $397.80 = $397,800	
At time hedge is lifted		
Value of 2,500 oz:	Sell 10 contracts:	−$45.40 per oz
2,500 × $112.00 = $280,000	10 × 100 × $349.60 = $349,600	
Gain in cash market = $72,400	Loss in futures market = $48,200	
	Overall gain = $24,200	

Suppose that the cash price of kryptonite falls to $121.68 per ounce, while the cash and futures price of gold rise to $392.50 and $437.90, respectively. The results of the cross-hedge are shown in Table 10-8.

The short cross-hedge results in a loss in both the cash market and the futures market. The overall loss is $88,300. Had the kryptonite mining company not used the cross-hedge, its loss would have been limited to the decline in the cash price—$48,200 in this instance. The long hedger, on the other hand, realizes a gain in both the cash and futures market, and therefore an overall gain.

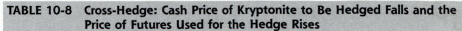

TABLE 10-8 Cross-Hedge: Cash Price of Kryptonite to Be Hedged Falls and the Price of Futures Used for the Hedge Rises

Assumptions

Price of kryptonite	
Cash price at time hedge is placed	$140.68 per oz
Cash price at time hedge is lifted	121.68 per oz
Price of gold	
Cash price at time hedge is placed	$352.40 per oz
Futures price at time hedge is placed	397.80 per oz
Cash price at time hedge is lifted	392.50 per oz
Futures price at time hedge is lifted	437.90 per oz
Number of ounces of kryptonite to be hedged	2,500
Number of ounces of gold to be hedged	
assuming ratio of cash price of kryptonite to gold is 0.4	1,000
Number of ounces per futures contract for gold	100
Number of gold futures contracts used in hedge	10

Short (Sell) Cross-Hedge by Kryptonite Mining Company

Cash Market	Futures Market	Gold Basis
At time hedge is placed		
Value of 2,500 oz:	Sell 10 contracts:	
2,500 × $140.96 = $352,400	10 × 100 × $397.80 = $397,800	−$45.40 per oz
At time hedge is lifted		
Value of 2,500 oz:	Buy 10 contracts:	
2,500 × $121.68 = $304,200	10 × 100 × $437.90 = $437,900	−45.40 per oz
Loss in cash market = $48,200	Loss in futures market = $40,100	
	Overall loss = $88,300	

Long (Buy) Cross-Hedge by Jewelry Company

Cash Market	Futures Market	Gold Basis
At time hedge is placed		
Value of 2,500 oz:	Buy 10 contracts:	
2,500 × $140.96 = $352,400	10 × 100 × $397.80 = $397,800	−$45.40 per oz
At time hedge is lifted		
Value of 2,500 oz:	Sell 10 contracts:	
2,500 × $121.68 = $304,200	10 × 100 × $437.90 = $437,900	−$45.40 per oz
Gain in cash market = $48,200	Gain in futures market = $40,100	
	Overall gain = $88,300	

If, instead, the cash price of kryptonite increases to $189.10 per ounce, while the cash and futures price of gold decline to $304.20 and $349.60, respectively, it can be demonstrated that the long cross-hedge results in a loss in both the cash and futures markets. The total loss is $168,550. The loss would have been only $120,350, the loss in the cash market, had the management of the jewelry company not cross-hedged with gold.

These illustrations demonstrate the risks associated with cross-hedging.

◆ THE ROLE OF FUTURES IN FINANCIAL MARKETS

Without financial futures, investors would have only one trading location to alter portfolio positions when they get new information that is expected to influence the value of assets—the cash market. If economic news that is expected to impact the value of an asset adversely is received, investors can reduce their price risk exposure to that asset. The opposite is true if the new information is expected to impact the value of that asset favorably: an investor would increase price-risk exposure to that asset. Of course, transaction costs are associated with altering exposure to an asset—explicit costs (commissions), and hidden or execution costs (bid-ask spreads and market impact costs).[4]

Futures provide another market that investors can use to alter their risk exposure to an asset when new information is acquired. But which market—cash or futures—should the investor employ to alter a position quickly on the receipt of new information? The answer is simple: the one that is the more efficient to use in order to achieve the objective. The factors to consider are liquidity, transaction costs, taxes, and leverage advantages of the futures contract.

The market that investors feel is the one that is more efficient to use to achieve their investment objective should be the one where prices will be established that reflect the new economic information. That is, it will be the market where price discovery takes place. Price information is then transmitted to the other market. In many of the markets that we discuss in this book, it is in the futures market that it is easier and less costly to alter a portfolio position. We give evidence for this proposition when we discuss the specific contracts in later chapters. Therefore, it is the futures market that will be the market of choice and will serve as the price discovery market. It is in the futures market that investors send a collective message about how any new information is expected to impact the cash market.

How is this message sent to the cash market? Recall our discussion on determination of the theoretical futures price, where we showed that the futures price and the cash market price are tied together by the cost of carry. If the futures price deviates from the cash market price by more than the cost of carry, arbitrageurs (in attempting to obtain arbitrage profits) would pursue a strategy to bring them back into line. Arbitrage brings the cash market price into line with the futures price. This mechanism assures that the cash market price will reflect the information collected in the futures market.

EFFECT OF FUTURES ON VOLATILITY OF UNDERLYING ASSET

Some investors and the popular press consider that the introduction of a futures market for an asset will increase the price volatility of the asset in the cash market. This criticism of futures contracts is referred to as the "destabilization hypothesis."[5]

Two variants of the destabilization hypothesis are the liquidity variant and the populist variant. According to the liquidity variant, large transactions that are too difficult to accommodate in the cash market will be executed first in the futures markets because of better liquidity. The increased volatility that may occur in the futures contracts market is only temporary because volatility will return to its normal level once

---

[4]   These costs are discussed in Chapters 7 and 13.
[5]   Lawrence Harris, "S&P 500 Futures and Cash Stock Price Volatility," University of Southern California, unpublished paper, 1987.

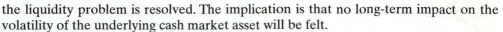

the liquidity problem is resolved. The implication is that no long-term impact on the volatility of the underlying cash market asset will be felt.

The populist variant, in contrast, asserts that as a result of speculative trading in derivative contracts, the cash market instrument does not reflect fundamental economic value. The implication here is that the asset price would better reflect economic value in the absence of a futures market.

Whether the introduction of futures markets destabilizes prices is an empirical question. We will look at the evidence for the stock market in Chapter 16, but for now, it is worth noting that the analysis of one researcher concludes that in general it would take a substantial number of "irrational" speculators to destabilize cash markets.[6]

IS INCREASED ASSET PRICE VOLATILITY BAD?

Whether or not the introduction of futures contracts increases cash market price volatility, we might ask whether greater volatility inflicts negative effects on markets. At first glance, it might seem that volatility adversely affects allocative efficiency and market participation.

Actually, some analysts point out that this inference may not be justified if, say, the introduction of new markets lets prices respond more promptly to changes in fundamentals, and if the fundamentals themselves are subject to large shocks.[7] Thus the greater volatility resulting from an innovation may simply more faithfully reflect the actual variability of fundamental values. In this case, "more" asset volatility need not be bad but rather may be a manifestation of a well-functioning market. Of course, to say that more volatility need not be bad does not mean that it is good. Clearly, price volatility greater than what can be justified by relevant new information or fundamentals (or by standard asset pricing models) is undesirable. By definition, it makes prices inefficient and is referred to as "excess volatility."[8]

No one has been able to test whether recent financial innovations actually increased or decreased excess volatility. Moreover, as Franklin Edwards points out, "Too little volatility is equally bad, although this concept does not seem to have generated enough interest to have been given the label of 'deficient volatility.'"[9]

In any event, as Edwards notes in the case of stock index futures:

Investors are concerned about the present and future value of their investments (and wealth). Greater volatility leads to a perception of greater risk, which threatens investors' assets and wealth. When the stock market takes a sharp nose-dive, investors see the value of their assets rapidly dissipating. They are not consoled by being told that there is no social cost associated with this price change, only a redistribution of wealth. Even more fundamental, when asset prices exhibit significant volatility over very short periods of time (such as a day), investors "lose confidence in the market." They begin to see financial markets as the province of the speculator and the insider, not the rational.[10]

---

[6] Jerome L. Stein, "Real Effects of Futures Speculation: Rational Expectations and Diverse Opinions," working paper no. 88. Center for the Study of Futures Markets, Columbia University, 1984.

[7] Eugene F. Fama, "Perspectives on October 1987 or What Did We Learn from the Crash?" in Robert J. Barro et al. (eds.) *Black Monday and the Future of Financial Markets* (Homewood, IL: Dow Jones-Irwin, 1989), p. 72.

[8] Franklin R. Edwards, "Futures Trading and Cash Market Volatility: Stock Index and Interest Rate Futures," *Journal of Futures Markets* 8, no. 4 (1988), p. 423.

[9] Ibid.

[10] Franklin R. Edwards, "Does Futures Trading Increase Stock Price Volatility?" *Financial Analysts Journal* (January/February 1988), p. 64.

Summary ▪

This chapter explains the basic features of financial futures markets. The traditional purpose of futures markets is to provide an important opportunity to hedge against the risk of adverse future price movements. Futures contracts are creations of exchanges, which require initial margin from parties. Each day positions are marked to market. Additional (variation) margin is required if the equity in the position falls below the maintenance margin. The clearinghouse guarantees that the parties to the futures contract will satisfy their obligations.

A forward contract differs in several important ways from a futures contract. In contrast to a futures contract, the parties to a forward contract are exposed to the risk that the other party to the contract will fail to perform. The positions of the parties are not necessarily marked to market, so no interim cash flows are associated with a forward contract. Finally, unwinding a position in a forward contract may be difficult.

A buyer (seller) of a futures contract realizes a profit if the futures price increases (decreases). The buyer (seller) of a futures contract realizes a loss if the futures price decreases (increases). Because only initial margin is required when an investor takes a futures position, futures markets provide investors with substantial leverage for the money invested.

Using simple arbitrage arguments, the theoretical or equilibrium futures price can be determined. Specifically, to capture the arbitrage profit for an overpriced futures contract, a cash and carry trade can be implemented, and to capture the arbitrage profit for an underpriced futures contract a reverse cash and carry trade. The ability of market participants to implement these two trades (or arbitrage strategies) results in the theoretical futures price being equal to the cash price plus the cost of carry.

At the delivery date, the futures price converges to the cash market price. The actual futures price will depart from the theoretical futures price. In practice, not one theoretical futures price exists but rather a band above and below it. The actual futures price tends to remain within the band through the operation of arbitrageurs.

The basis is the difference between the cash price and the futures price. The basis should equal the cost of carry. Basis risk occurs when the basis changes between the time a hedge is placed and the time it is lifted. Hedging eliminates price risk but substitutes basis risk. Cross-hedging occurs when the underlying instrument of the futures contract is different from the financial instrument or portfolio to be hedged, and most hedging in financial markets involves cross-hedging. The risk associated with cross-hedging is that the financial instrument or portfolio to be hedged will not be tracked exactly by the instrument underlying the futures contract.

Investors can use the futures market or the cash market to react to economic news that is expected to change the value of an asset. Futures markets are often the market of choice for altering asset positions and therefore represent the price discovery market, because of the lower transactions costs involved and the greater speed with which orders can be executed. The actions of arbitrageurs assure that price discovery in the futures markets will be transmitted to the cash market.

Critics of futures markets believe that they are the source of greater price volatility in the cash market for the underlying asset. Although this empirical question cannot be fully discussed here, even if price volatility in the cash market were greater because of the introduction of futures markets, it does not necessarily follow that greater volatility is bad for the economy.

Key Terms ■

- Basis
- Basis risk
- Buy hedge
- Cash and carry trade
- Cash settlement contracts
- Commodity futures
- Cost of carry
- Cross-hedging
- Cross-hedging risk
- Delivery date
- Derivative instruments
- Financial futures
- Financing cost

- Floor brokers
- Forward contract
- Futures commissions merchant
- Futures contract
- Futures price
- Hedging
- Initial margin
- Locals
- Long futures
- Long hedge
- Long position
- Maintenance margin
- Most distant futures contract

- Nearby futures contract
- Net financing cost
- Perfect hedge
- Pit brokers
- Reverse cash and carry trade
- Sell hedge
- Settlement date
- Short futures
- Short hedge
- Short position
- Spot price
- Theoretical futures
- Variation margin

Questions ■

1. The chief financial officer of the corporation you work for recently told you he has a strong preference to use forward contracts rather than futures contracts to hedge: "You can get contracts tailor-made to suit your needs." Comment on the CFO's statement. What other factors influence the decision to use futures or forward contracts?

2. You work for a conservative investment firm. You recently asked the firm's managing director for permission to open up a futures account so that you could trade financial futures as well as cash instruments. She replied, "Are you crazy? I might as well write you a check, wish you good luck, and put you on a bus to Atlantic City. The futures markets are nothing more than a respectable game of craps. Don't you think you're taking enough risk trading cash instruments?" How would you try to persuade the managing director to let you use futures?

3. Explain why you agree or disagree with the following statement: "Of course the futures are more expensive than the cash price—there's positive carry."

4. Suppose a financial asset, ABC, is the underlying asset for a futures contract with settlement 6 months from now. You know the following about this financial asset and futures contract: in the cash market ABC is selling for $80; ABC pays $8 per year in two semiannual payments of $4, and the next semiannual payment is due exactly 6 months from now; and the current 6-month interest rate at which funds can be loaned or borrowed is 6%.
   a. What is the theoretical (or equilibrium) futures price?
   b. What action would you take if the futures price is $83?
   c. What action would you take if the futures price is $76?
   d. Suppose that ABC pays interest quarterly instead of semiannually. If you know that you can reinvest any funds you receive 3 months from now at 1% for 3 months, what would the theoretical futures price for 6-month settlement be?
   e. Suppose that the borrowing rate and lending rate are not equal. Instead, suppose that the current 6-month borrowing rate is 8% and the 6-month lending rate is 6%. What is the boundary for the theoretical futures price?

5. You are a major producer of goat cheese. Concerned that the price of goat cheese might plummet, you consider some kind of hedging strategy. Unfortunately, you discover that no exchange-traded futures are available for goat cheese. A business

associate suggests a cross-hedge with orange juice futures. Specifically, your business associate suggests a short hedge using orange juice futures.
a. Before you commit to this hedging strategy, what other kinds of information would you like to know?
b. Why is it likely that this hedge will not turn out to be a perfect hedge?

6. Explain why you agree or disagree with the following statement: "Hedging with futures involves substituting basis risk for price risk."

7. Suppose that a corn farmer expects to sell 30,000 bushels of corn 3 months from now. Assume further that the management of a food-processing company plans to purchase 30,000 bushels of corn 3 months from now. Both the corn farmer and the management of the food-processing company want to lock in a price today. That is, each wants to eliminate the price risk associated with corn 3 months from now. The cash or spot price for corn is currently $2.75 per bushel.

A corn futures contract is available with the following terms: the settlement date for the contract is 5 months from now, and 5,000 bushels of corn must be delivered. Notice that the settlement date is 2 months after the parties expect to lift their hedge. Because each contract is for 5,000 bushels of corn, six corn futures contracts cover 30,000 bushels. The futures price for this futures contract is currently $3.20 per bushel.
a. If the corn farmer seeks to lock in the price of corn to eliminate the risk of a decline in the price 3 months from now, will he place a long hedge or a short hedge?
b. If the management of the food-processing company seeks to lock in the cost of corn to eliminate the risk of an increase in the price of corn 3 months from now, will it place a short hedge or long hedge?
c. What is the basis at the time of the hedge?
d. Suppose that when the hedge is lifted, the cash price declines to $2.00 and the futures contract price declines to $2.45. What has happened to the basis? What is the outcome for the corn farmer and the food-processing company?
e. Suppose that the cash price of corn when the hedge is lifted increases to $3.55, and that the futures price increases to $4.00. What has happened to the basis? What is the outcome for the corn farmer and the food-processing company?
f. Suppose that the cash price of corn decreases to $2.00 and that the futures price decreases to $2.70. What has happened to the basis? What is the outcome for the corn farmer and the food-processing company?

8. Suppose that a zucchini farmer plans to sell 37,500 bushels of zucchini 3 months from now and that a food-processing company plans to purchase the same amount of zucchini 3 months from now. Each party wants to hedge against price risk, but zucchini futures contracts are not traded. Both parties believe a close price relationship exists between zucchini and corn. Specifically, both parties believe that the cash price of zucchini will be 80% of the cash price of corn. The cash price of zucchini is currently $2.20 per bushel, and the cash price of corn is currently $2.75 per bushel. Information about the futures contract is given in the previous question. The futures price of corn is currently $3.20 per bushel.

The parties must determine how many corn futures contracts must be used in the cross-hedge. The cash value of 37,500 bushels of zucchini at the cash price of $2.20 per bushel is $82,500. To protect a value of $82,500 using corn futures with a current cash price of $2.75, the price of 30,000 bushels of corn ($82,500/$2.75) must be hedged. Each corn futures contract involves 5,000 bushels, so six corn futures contracts are used.
a. Why is this transaction a cross-hedge?
b. Suppose at the time the cross-hedge is lifted that the cash prices of zucchini and corn decrease to $1.60 and $2.00 per bushel, respectively, and the futures

price of corn decreases to $2.45 per bushel; and that the relationship between the cash price for zucchini and corn assumed when the cross-hedge was placed holds at the time the cross-hedge is lifted. That is, the cash price of zucchini is 80% of the cash price of corn. What has happened to the basis between cash corn and futures corn? What is the outcome for the zucchini farmer and the food-processing company?

c. Suppose at the time the hedge is lifted that the cash price of zucchini falls to $1.30 per bushel while the cash price of corn falls to $2.00 per bushel; and that the futures price of corn falls to $2.45. What has happened to the basis between cash corn and futures corn? What is the outcome for the zuccini farmer and the food-processing company?

9. Explain why you agree or disagree with the following statement: "The futures market is where price discovery takes place."

10. Explain why you agree or disagree with the following statement: "The introduction of futures contracts creates greater price volatility for the underlying commodity or asset."

11. What is the destabilization hypothesis, and what are the two variants of this hypothesis?

CHAPTER 11

Introduction to Options Markets

Learning Objectives

After reading this chapter you will understand:

◆ what an option contract is.

◆ the difference between a futures contract and an option contract.

◆ the risk/return characteristics of an option.

◆ the basic components of the option price.

◆ the factors that influence the option price.

◆ the fundamentals of option pricing models.

◆ the principles of the binomial option pricing model and how it is derived.

◆ the role of options in financial markets.

◆ two types of exotic options known as alternative options and outperformance options.

In Chapter 10 we introduced our first derivative instrument, a futures contract. In this chapter we introduce a second derivative contract, an options contract. Here, we look not at specific options contracts, but instead focus on the general characteristics of the contract. We discuss options on common stocks in Chapter 15, options on stock indexes in Chapter 16, options on bonds in Chapter 28, and options on currencies in Chapter 30.

In this chapter we discuss the differences between options and futures contracts and show how to determine the price of an option based on arbitrage arguments. In later chapters we will illustrate how investors can use options to create payoffs that better satisfy their investment objectives.

◆ OPTION CONTRACT DEFINED

An **option** is a contract in which the writer of the option grants the buyer of the option the right, but not the obligation, to purchase from or sell to the writer something at a specified price within a specified period of time (or at a specified date). The **writer**, also referred to as the **seller**, grants this right to the buyer in exchange for a certain sum of money, which is called the **option price** or **option premium**. The price at which the asset may be bought or sold is called the **exercise** or **strike price**. The date after which an option is void is called the **expiration date**. Our focus in this book is on options where the "something" underlying the option is a financial instrument, financial index, or financial futures contract. Our discussion of options on futures contracts (called futures options) is in Chapter 28.

When an option grants the buyer the right to purchase the designated instrument from the writer (seller), it is referred to as a **call option**, or **call**. When the option buyer has the right to sell the designated instrument to the writer, the option is called a **put option**, or **put**.

An option is also categorized according to when the option buyer may exercise the option. Some options may be exercised at any time up to and including the expiration date. Such an option is referred to as an **American option**. Other options may be exercised only at the expiration date. An option with this feature is called a **European option**.

To demonstrate the fundamental option contract, suppose that Jack buys a call option for $3 (the option price) with the following terms:

1. The underlying asset is one unit of Asset XYZ.
2. The strike price is $100.
3. The expiration date is 3 months from now, and the option can be exercised any time up to and including the expiration date (that is, it is an American option).

At any time up to and including the expiration date, Jack can decide to buy from the writer of this option one unit of Asset XYZ, for which he will pay a price of $100. If it is not beneficial for Jack to exercise the option, he will not, and we explain shortly how he decides when it will be beneficial. Whether Jack exercises the option or not, the $3 he paid for the option will be kept by the option writer. If Jack buys a put option rather than a call option, then he would be able to sell Asset XYZ to the option writer for a price of $100.

The maximum amount that an option buyer can lose is the option price. The maximum profit that the option writer can realize is the option price. The option buyer has substantial upside return potential, while the option writer has substantial downside risk. The risk/reward relationship for option positions will be discussed later in this chapter.

MARGIN REQUIREMENTS

The buyer of an option is not subject to margin requirements after the option price is paid in full. Because the option price is the maximum amount the investor can lose, no matter how adverse the price movement of the underlying asset, margin is not necessary. Because the writer of an option agreed to accept all of the risk (and none of the reward) of the position in the underlying asset, the writer is generally required to put up the option price received as margin. In addition, as price changes occur that adversely affect the writer's position, the writer is required to deposit additional margin (with some exceptions) as the position is marked to market.

EXCHANGE-TRADED VERSUS OTC OPTIONS

Options, like other financial instruments, may be traded either on an organized exchange or in the over-the-counter market. An exchange that wants to create an options contract must obtain approval from either the Commodities Futures Trading Commission (CFTC) or the Securities and Exchange Commission (SEC).[1] Exchange-traded

---

[1] By an agreement between the CFTC and the SEC and pursuant to an act of Congress, options on futures are regulated by the former.

options offer three advantages. First, the exercise price and expiration date of the contract are standardized. Second, as in the case of futures contracts, the direct link between buyer and seller is severed after order execution because of the interchangeability of exchange-traded options. The clearinghouse associated with the exchange where the option trades performs the same function in the options market that it does in the futures market. Finally, the transactions costs are lower for exchange-traded options than for OTC options.

The higher cost of an OTC option reflects the cost of customizing the option for the many situations where an institutional investor needs a tailor-made option because the standardized exchange-traded option does not satisfy its investment objectives. As we explained in Chapters 3 and 5, some commercial and investment banking firms act as principals as well as brokers in the OTC options market. OTC options are sometimes referred to as **dealer options**. Even though an OTC option is less liquid than an exchange-traded option, its liquidity is typically not of concern to an institutional investor—most institutional investors who use OTC options as part of an asset/liability strategy intend to hold them to expiration.

◆ DIFFERENCES BETWEEN OPTIONS AND FUTURES CONTRACTS

Notice that, unlike in a futures contract, one party to an option contract is not obligated to transact—specifically, the option buyer has the right but not the obligation to transact. The option writer does have the obligation to perform. In the case of a futures contract, both buyer and seller are obligated to perform. Of course, a futures buyer does not pay the seller to accept the obligation, while an option buyer pays the seller an option price.

Consequently, the risk/reward characteristics of the two contracts are also different. In the case of a futures contract, the buyer of the contract realizes a dollar-for-dollar gain when the price of the futures contract increases and suffers a dollar-for-dollar loss when the price of the futures contract drops. The opposite occurs for the seller of a futures contract. Options do not provide this symmetric risk/reward relationship. The most that the buyer of an option can lose is the option price. The buyer of an option retains all the potential benefits, but the gain is always reduced by the amount of the option price. The maximum profit that the writer may realize is the option price; this potential is offset against substantial downside risk. This difference is extremely important because, as we shall see in subsequent chapters, investors can use futures to protect against symmetric risk and options to protect against asymmetric risk.

We return to the difference between options and futures for hedging at the end of the chapter.

◆ RISK AND RETURN CHARACTERISTICS OF OPTIONS

Here we illustrate the risk and return characteristics of the four basic option positions: buying a call option, selling a call option, buying a put option, and selling a put option. The illustrations *assume that each option position is held to the expiration date and not exercised early.* Also, to simplify the illustrations, we ignore transactions costs.

BUYING CALL OPTIONS

The purchase of a call option creates a financial position referred to as a **long call position**. To illustrate this position, assume that a call option on Asset XYZ expires in 1 month and states a strike price of $100. The option price is $3. Suppose that the current price of Asset XYZ is $100. What is the profit or loss for the investor who purchases this call option and holds it to the expiration date?

The profit and loss from the strategy will depend on the price of Asset XYZ at the expiration date. A number of outcomes are possible.

1. If the price of Asset XYZ at the expiration date is less than $100, then the investor will not exercise the option. It would be foolish to pay the option writer $100 when Asset XYZ can be purchased in the market at a lower price. In this case, the option buyer loses the entire option price of $3. Notice, however, that it is the maximum loss that the option buyer will realize regardless of how low Asset XYZ's price declines.

2. If Asset XYZ's price is equal to $100 at the expiration date, the option buyer would again find no economic value in exercising the option. As in the case where the price is less than $100, the buyer of the call option loses the entire option price, $3.

3. If Asset XYZ's price is more than $100 but less than $103 at the expiration date, the option buyer exercises the option. By exercising, the option buyer can purchase Asset XYZ for $100 (the strike price) and sell it in the market for the higher price. Suppose, for example, that Asset XYZ's price is $102 at the expiration date. The buyer of the call option will realize a $2 gain by exercising the option. Of course, the cost of purchasing the call option was $3, so $1 is lost on this position. By failing to exercise the option, the investor loses $3 instead of only $1.

4. If Asset XYZ's price at the expiration date is equal to $103, the investor will exercise the option. In this case, the investor breaks even, realizing a gain of $3 that offsets the cost of the option, $3.

5. If Asset XYZ's price at the expiration date is more than $103, the investor exercises the option and realizes a profit. For example, if the price is $113, exercising the option generates a profit on Asset XYZ of $13. Reducing this gain by the cost of the option ($3), the investor realizes a net profit from this position of $10.

Table 11-1 shows the profit and loss in tabular form for the buyer of the hypothetical call option, while Figure 11-1 graphically portrays the result. Even though the breakeven point and the loss depend on the option price and the strike price, the profile shown in Figure 11-1 holds for all buyers of call options. The shape indicates that the maximum loss is the option price and is subject to substantial upside potential.

It is worthwhile to compare the profit and loss profile of the call option buyer to taking a long position in one unit of Asset XYZ. The payoff from the position depends on Asset XYZ's price at the expiration date. Consider again the five price outcomes as given:

1. If Asset XYZ's price at the expiration date is less than $100, then the investor loses the entire option price of $3. In contrast, a long position in Asset XYZ ends in one of three possible outcomes:

   a. If Asset XYZ's price is less than $100 but greater than $97, the loss on the long position in Asset XYZ is less than $3.

   b. If Asset XYZ's price is $97, the loss on the long position in Asset XYZ is $3.

   c. If Asset XYZ's price is less than $97, the loss on the long position in Asset XYZ is greater than $3. For example, if the price at the expiration date is $80, the long position in Asset XYZ results in a loss of $20.

2. If Asset XYZ's price is equal to $100, the buyer of the call option realizes a loss of $3 (option price), resulting in no gain or loss on the long position in Asset XYZ.

3. If Asset XYZ's price is more than $100 but less than $103, the option buyer realizes a loss of less than $3, while the long position in Asset XYZ realizes a profit.

TABLE 11-1	Profit/Loss Profile for a Long Call Position

Assumptions:

Option price = $3
Strike price = $100
Time to expiration = 1 month

Price of Asset XYZ at Expiration Date	Net Profit/Loss*
$150	$47
140	37
130	27
120	17
115	12
114	11
113	10
112	9
111	8
110	7
109	6
108	5
107	4
106	3
105	2
104	1
103	0
102	−1
101	−2
100	−3
99	−3
98	−3
97	−3
96	−3
95	−3
94	−3
93	−3
92	−3
91	−3
90	−3
89	−3
88	−3
87	−3
86	−3
85	−3
80	−3
70	−3
60	−3

*Price at expiration − $100 − $3
Maximum loss = $3

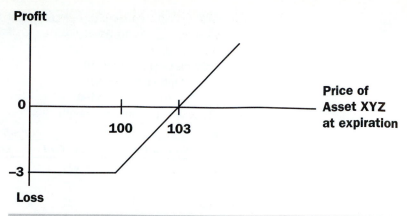

FIGURE 11-1 Profit/Loss Profile for a Long Call Position

4. If the price of Asset XYZ at the expiration date is equal to $103, no loss or gain is realized from buying the call option. The long position in Asset XYZ, however, produces a gain of $3.
5. If Asset XYZ's price at the expiration date is greater than $103, both the call option buyer and the long position in Asset XYZ post a profit, but the profit for the buyer of the call option is $3 less than that for the long position. If Asset XYZ's price is $113, for example, the profit from the call position is $10, while the profit from the long position in Asset XYZ is $13.

Table 11-2 compares the long call strategy and the long position in Asset XYZ. This comparison clearly demonstrates the way in which an option can change the risk/return profile for investors. An investor who takes a long position in Asset XYZ realizes a profit of $1 for every $1 increase in Asset XYZ's price. As Asset XYZ's price falls, however, the investor loses dollar-for-dollar. If the price drops by more than $3, the long position in Asset XYZ results in a loss of more than $3. The long call strategy, in contrast, limits the loss to only the option price of $3 but retains the upside potential, which is $3 less than for the long position in Asset XYZ.

Which alternative is better, buying the call option or buying the asset? The answer depends on what the investor is attempting to achieve. The answer to this question becomes clearer in later chapters as we explain various strategies using either option positions or cash market positions.

We can also use this hypothetical call option to demonstrate the speculative appeal of options. Suppose an investor has strong expectations that Asset XYZ's price will rise in 1 month. At an option price of $3, the speculator can purchase 33.33 call options for each $100 invested. If Asset XYZ's price rises, the investor realizes the price appreciation associated with 33.33 units of Asset XYZ; while with the same $100, the investor could buy only one unit of Asset XYZ selling at $100, realizing the appreciation associated with one unit if Asset XYZ's price increases. Now, suppose that in 1 month the price of Asset XYZ rises to $120. The long call position results in a profit of $566.50 [($20 × 33.33) − $100)] or a return of 566.5% on the $100 investment in the call option. The long position in Asset XYZ results in a profit of $20, for only a 20% return on $100.

This greater leverage attracts investors to options when they wish to speculate on price movements. Leverage encounters some drawbacks, however. Suppose that Asset XYZ's price is unchanged at $100 at the expiration date. The long call position results in this case in a loss of the entire investment of $100, while the long position in Asset XYZ produces neither a gain nor a loss.

TABLE 11-2 Comparison of Long Call Position and Long Asset Position

Assumptions:

Price of Asset XYZ = $100
Option price = $3
Strike price = $100
Time to expiration = 1 month

Price of Asset XYZ at Expiration Date	Net Profit/Loss	
	Long Call	*Long Asset XYZ*
$150	$47	$50
140	37	40
130	27	30
120	17	20
115	12	15
114	11	14
113	10	13
112	9	12
111	8	11
110	7	10
109	6	9
108	5	8
107	4	7
106	3	6
105	2	5
104	1	4
103	0	3
102	−1	2
101	−2	1
100	−3	0
99	−3	−1
98	−3	−2
97	−3	−3
96	−3	−4
95	−3	−5
94	−3	−6
93	−3	−7
92	−3	−8
91	−3	−9
90	−3	−10
89	−3	−11
88	−3	−12
87	−3	−13
86	−3	−14
85	−3	−15
80	−3	−20
70	−3	−30
60	−3	−40

WRITING (SELLING) CALL OPTIONS

The writer of a call option is said to be in a **short call position**. To illustrate the option seller's (writer's) position, we use the same call option we used to illustrate buying a call option. The profit and loss profile of the short call position (that is, the position of the call option writer) is the mirror image of the profit and loss profile of the long call position (the position of the call option buyer.) That is, the profit of the short call position for any given price for Asset XYZ at the expiration date is the same as the loss of the long call position. Consequently, the maximum profit that the short call position can produce is the option price. The maximum loss is not limited because it is the highest price reached by Asset XYZ on or before the expiration date, less the option price; this price can be indefinitely high. Figure 11-2 shows the profit/loss profile for a short call position.

BUYING PUT OPTIONS

The buying of a put option creates a financial position referred to as a **long put position**. To illustrate this position, we assume a hypothetical put option on one unit of Asset XYZ with 1 month to maturity and a strike price of $100. Assume the put option is selling for $2. The current price of Asset XYZ is $100. The profit or loss for this position at the expiration date depends on the market price of Asset XYZ. The possible outcomes are as follow:

1. If Asset XYZ's price is greater than $100, the buyer of the put option chooses not to exercise it because exercising would mean selling Asset XYZ to the writer for a price that is less than the market price. A loss of $2 (the option price) results in this case from buying the put option. Once again, the option price represents the maximum loss to which the buyer of the put option is exposed.
2. If the price of Asset XYZ at expiration is equal to $100, the put is not exercised, leaving the put buyer with a loss equal to the option price of $2.
3. Any price for Asset XYZ that is less than $100 but greater than $98 results in a loss; exercising the put option, however, limits the loss to less than the option price of $2. For example, suppose that the price is $99 at the expiration date. By exercising the option, the option buyer realizes a loss of $1, because the buyer of the put option can sell Asset XYZ, purchased in the market for $99, to the writer for $100, realizing a gain of $1. Deducting the $2 cost of the option results in a loss of $1.

FIGURE 11-2 Profit/Loss Profile for a Short Call Position

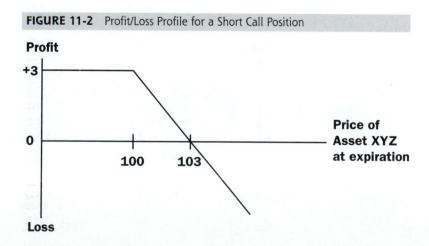

4. At a $98 price for Asset XYZ at the expiration date, the put buyer breaks even. The investor realizes a gain of $2 by selling Asset XYZ to the writer of the option for $100, offsetting the cost of the option ($2).
5. If Asset XYZ's price is below $98 at the expiration date, the long put position (the put buyer) realizes a profit. For example, suppose the price falls at expiration to $80. The long put position produces a profit of $18: a gain of $20 for exercising the put option less the $2 option price.

The profit and loss profile for the long put position is shown in tabular form in the second column of Table 11-3 and in graphical form in Figure 11-3. As with all long positions, the loss is limited to the option price. The profit potential, however, is substantial: the theoretical maximum profit is generated if Asset XYZ's price falls to zero. Contrast this profit potential with that of the buyer of a call option. The theoretical maximum profit for a call buyer cannot be determined beforehand because it depends on the highest price that can be reached by Asset XYZ before or at the option expiration date.

To see how an option alters the risk/return profile for an investor, we again compare it to a position in Asset XYZ. The long put position is compared to taking a short position in Asset XYZ because this position would realize a profit if the price of the asset falls. Suppose an investor sells Asset XYZ short for $100. The short position in Asset XYZ produces the profit or loss compared with the long put position.

1. If Asset XYZ's price rises above $100, the long put option results in a loss of $2, but the short position in Asset XYZ realizes one of the following:
   a. If the price of Asset XYZ is less than $102, a loss of less than $2 results.
   b. If the price of Asset XYZ is equal to $102, the loss is $2, the same as the long put position.
   c. If the price of Asset XYZ is greater than $102, the loss is greater than $2. For example, if the price is $125, the short position realizes a loss of $25, because the short-seller must now pay $125 for Asset XYZ sold short at $100.
2. If Asset XYZ's price at expiration is equal to $100, the long put position realizes a $2 loss, and no profit or loss is realized on the short position in Asset XYZ.
3. Any price for Asset XYZ less than $100 but greater than $98 results in a loss of less than $2 for the long put position but a profit for the short position in Asset XYZ.

FIGURE 11-3 Profit/Loss for a Long Put Position

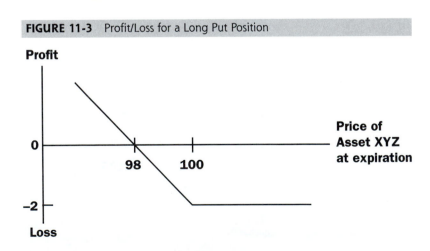

TABLE 11-3 Profit/Loss Profile for a Long Put Position and Comparison with a Short Asset Position

Assumptions:
Price of Asset XYZ = $100
Option price = $2
Strike price = $100
Time to expiration = 1 month

Price of Asset XYZ at Expiration Date	Net Profit /Loss for Long Put*	Net Profit /Loss for Short Asset XYZ**
$150	−$2	−$50
140	−2	−40
130	−2	−30
120	−2	−20
115	−2	−15
110	−2	−10
105	−2	−5
100	−2	0
99	−1	1
98	0	2
97	1	3
96	2	4
95	3	5
94	4	6
93	5	7
92	6	8
91	7	9
90	8	10
89	9	11
88	10	12
87	11	13
86	12	14
85	13	15
84	14	16
83	15	17
82	16	18
81	17	19
80	18	20
75	23	25
70	28	30
65	33	35
60	38	40

*$100 − Price at expiration − $2
Maximum loss = $2
**$100 − Price of Asset XYZ

For example, a price of $99 at the expiration date results in a loss of $1 for the long put position but a profit of $1 for the short position.

4. At a $98 price for Asset XYZ at the expiration date, the long put position breaks even, but the short position in Asset XYZ generates a $2 profit.
5. At a price below $98, both positions generate a profit; however, the profit is always $2 less for the long put position.

Table 11-3 gives this comparison of the profit and loss profile for the long put position and short position in Asset XYZ. Even though the investor who takes a short position in Asset XYZ faces all the downside risk as well as the upside potential, the long put position limits the downside risk to the option price while still maintaining upside potential (reduced only by an amount equal to the option price).

WRITING (SELLING) PUT OPTIONS

Writing a put option creates a financial position referred to as a **short put position**. The profit and loss profile for a short put option is the mirror image of the long put option. The maximum profit from this position is the option price. The theoretical maximum loss can be substantial should the price of the underlying asset fall; at the outside, if the price fell all the way to zero, the loss would be as large as the strike price less the option price. Figure 11-4 graphically depicts this profit and loss profile.

To summarize, buying calls or selling puts allows the investor to gain if the price of the underlying asset rises. Selling calls and buying puts allows the investor to gain if the price of the underlying asset falls.

CONSIDERING THE TIME VALUE OF MONEY

Our illustration of the four option positions do not address the time value of money. Specifically, the buyer of an option must pay the seller the option price at the time the option is purchased. Thus, the buyer must finance the purchase price of the option or, assuming the purchase price does not have to be borrowed, the buyer loses the income that can be earned by investing the amount of the option price until the option is sold or exercised. In contrast, assuming that the seller does not have to use the option price amount as margin for the short position or can use an interest-earning asset as security, the seller has the opportunity to earn income from the proceeds of the option sale.

The time value of money changes the profit/loss profile of the option position as just discussed. The breakeven price for the buyer and the seller of an option changes

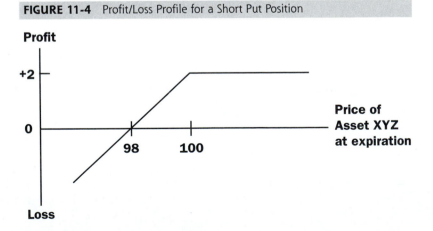

FIGURE 11-4 Profit/Loss Profile for a Short Put Position

from our illustrations. The breakeven price for the underlying asset at the expiration date is higher (lower) for the buyer (seller) of a call option. The reverse is true for a put option.

Our comparisons of the option position with positions in the underlying instrument also ignore the time value of money. We did not consider the fact that the underlying asset may generate interim cash flows (dividends in the case of common stock, interest in the case of bonds). The buyer of a call option is not entitled to any interim cash flows generated by the underlying asset. The buyer of the underlying asset, however, would receive any interim cash flows and would have the opportunity to reinvest them. A complete comparison of the position of the long call option position and the long position in the underlying asset must take into account the additional dollars from reinvesting any interim cash flows. Moreover, any effect on the price of the underlying asset as a result of the distribution of cash must be considered. This occurs, for example, when the underlying asset is common stock and, as a result of a dividend payment, the stock declines in price. For simplicity, however, we continue to ignore the time value of money in the discussion to follow.

◆ PRICING OF OPTIONS

So far, in our illustrations we simply picked an option price as a given. The next question we ask is: How is the price of an option determined in the market?

BASIC COMPONENTS OF THE OPTION PRICE

The option price reflects the option's intrinsic value and any additional amount over its intrinsic value. The premium over intrinsic value is often referred to as the **time value** or **time premium**. The former term is more common; however, we use the term *time premium* to avoid confusion between the time value of money and the time value of the option.

Intrinsic Value   The **intrinsic value** of an option is the economic value of the option if it is exercised immediately. If no positive economic value will result from exercising immediately then the intrinsic value is zero.

The intrinsic value of a call option is the difference between the current price of the underlying asset and the strike price if positive; it is otherwise zero. For example, if the strike price for a call option is $100 and the current asset price is $105, the intrinsic value is $5. That is, an option buyer exercising the option and simultaneously selling the underlying asset would realize $105 from the sale of the asset, which would be covered by acquiring the asset from the option writer for $100, thereby netting a $5 gain.

When an option holds intrinsic value, it is said to be "in the money." When the strike price of a call option exceeds the current asset price, the call option is said to be "out of the money"; it has no intrinsic value. An option for which the strike price is equal to the current asset price is said to be "at the money." The intrinsic value of both at-the-money and out-of-the-money options is zero because it is not profitable to exercise the option. Our call option with a strike price of $100 would be (1) in the money when the current asset price is greater than $100, (2) out of the money when the current asset price is less than $100, or (3) at the money when the current asset price is equal to $100.

For a put option, the intrinsic value equals the amount by which the current asset price is below the strike price. For example, if the strike price of a put option is $100 and the current asset price is $92, the intrinsic value is $8. That is, the buyer of the put option who exercises the put option and simultaneously sells the underlying asset nets $8 by exercising. The asset is sold to the writer for $100 and purchased in the market for $92. For our put option with a strike price of $100, the option would be (1) in the money when the asset price is less than $100, (2) out of the money when the current asset price exceeds the strike price, or (3) at the money when the strike price is equal to the asset's price.

Time Premium   The time premium of an option is the amount by which the option price exceeds its intrinsic value. The option buyer hopes that, at some time prior to expiration, changes in the market price of the underlying asset will increase the value of the rights conveyed by the option. For this prospect, the option buyer is willing to pay a premium above the intrinsic value. For example, if the price of a call option with a strike price of $100 is $9 when the current asset price is $105, the time premium of this option is $4 ($9 minus its intrinsic value of $5). A current asset price of $90 instead of $105 means that the time premium of this option would be the entire $9 because the option has no intrinsic value. Clearly, other things being equal, the time premium of an option increases with the amount of time remaining to expiration.

An option buyer may realize the value of a position taken in the option in one of two ways. The first is to exercise the option. The second is by selling the call option for $9. In the first example, selling the call is preferable because the exercise of an option realizes a gain of only $5—it causes the immediate loss of any time premium. Under certain circumstances an option may be exercised prior to the expiration date, depending on whether the total proceeds at the expiration date would be greater by holding the option or exercising and reinvesting any cash proceeds received until the expiration date.

PUT-CALL PARITY RELATIONSHIP

Now we look at the relationship between the price of a call option and the price of a put option on the same underlying instrument, with the same strike price and the same expiration date. To illustrate this relationship, commonly referred to as the **put-call parity relationship**, we use the following example.

In previous illustrations we used a put and call option on the same underlying asset (Asset XYZ), with 1 month to expiration, and a strike price of $100. The price of the underlying asset was assumed to be $100. The call price and put price were assumed to be $3 and $2, respectively. Consider this strategy:

- Buy Asset XYZ at a price of $100.
- Sell a call option at a price of $3.
- Buy a put option at a price of $2.

This strategy involves:

- Long Asset XYZ
- Short the call option
- Long the put option

Table 11-4 shows the profit and loss profile at the expiration date for this strategy. Notice that, no matter what Asset XYZ's price is at the expiration date, the strategy produces a profit of $1.

The net cost of creating this position is the cost of purchasing Asset XYZ ($100) plus the cost of buying the put ($2) less the cost from selling the call ($3), which is $101. Suppose that the net cost of creating the position for 1 month is less than $1. Then, by

TABLE 11-4 Profit/Loss Profile for a Strategy Involving a Long Position in Asset XYZ, Short Call Option Position, and Long Put Option Position

Assumptions:

Price of Asset XYZ = $100

Call option price = $3

Put option price = $2

Strike price = $100

Time to expiration = 1 month

Price of Asset XYZ at Expiration Date	Price from Asset XYZ*	Price Received for Call	Price Paid for Put	Overall Profit
$150	0	3	−2	1
140	0	3	−2	1
130	0	3	−2	1
120	0	3	−2	1
115	0	3	−2	1
110	0	3	−2	1
105	0	3	−2	1
100	0	3	−2	1
95	0	3	−2	1
90	0	3	−2	1
85	0	3	−2	1
80	0	3	−2	1
75	0	3	−2	1
70	0	3	−2	1
65	0	3	−2	1
60	0	3	−2	1

*No profit can be realized because at a price above $100, Asset XYZ will be called from the investor at a price of $100; and at a price below $100, Asset XYZ will be put by the investor at a price of $100.

borrowing $101 to create the position so that no investment outlay is made by the investor, this strategy produces a net profit of $1 (as shown in the last column of Table 11-4) less the cost of borrowing $101, which is assumed to be less than $1. This situation cannot exist in an efficient market. In implementing the strategy to capture the $1 profit, the actions of market participants result in one or more of the following consequences that eliminate the $1 profit: (1) the price of Asset XYZ increases, (2) the call option price drops, and/or (3) the put option price rises.

In our example, assuming Asset XYZ's price does not change, the call price and the put price must tend toward equality. This outcome is true only when we ignore the time value of money (financing cost, opportunity cost, cash payments, and reinvestment income). Also, our illustration does not consider the possibility of early exercise of the options. Thus, we consider a put-call parity relationship for only European options.

It can be shown that the put-call parity relationship for an option where the underlying asset makes cash distributions is

Put option price − Call option price =
Present value of strike price + Present value of cash distribution
− Price of underlying asset

This relationship is actually the put-call parity relationship for European options though it is approximately true for American options. If this relationship does not hold, arbitrage opportunities exist. That is, portfolios that consist of long and short positions in the asset and related options will provide an extra return with (practical) certainty.

FACTORS THAT INFLUENCE THE OPTION PRICE

Six factors influence option prices:

1. Current price of the underlying asset
2. Strike price
3. Time to expiration of the option
4. Expected price volatility of the underlying asset over the life of the option
5. Short-term risk-free interest rate over the life of the option
6. Anticipated cash payments on the underlying asset over the life of the option

The impact of each of these factors may depend on whether the option is a call or a put, and whether the option is an American option or a European option. Table 11-5 presents a summary of the effect of each factor on put and call option prices.

Current Price of the Underlying Asset   The option price changes as the price of the underlying asset changes. For a call option, as the price of the underlying asset increases (all other factors being constant, and the strike price in particular), the option price increases. The opposite holds for a put option. As the price of the underlying asset increases, the price of a put option decreases.

Strike Price   The strike price is fixed for the life of the option. All other factors being equal, the lower the strike price, the higher the price of a call option. For put options, the higher the strike price, the higher the price of a put option.

Time to Expiration of the Option   An option is a "wasting asset." That is, after the expiration date the option has no value. All other factors being equal, the longer the time to expiration of the option, the greater the option price, because as the time to expiration decreases, less time remains for the underlying asset's price to rise (for a call buyer) or fall (for a put buyer)—that is, to compensate the option buyer for any time premium paid—and therefore the probability of a favorable price movement decreases. Consequently, for American options, as the time remaining until expiration decreases, the option price approaches its intrinsic value.

Expected Price Volatility of the Underlying Asset over the Life of the Option   All other factors being equal, the greater the expected volatility (as measured by the standard deviation or variance) of the price of the underlying asset, the more an

TABLE 11-5   Summary of Factors That Affect the Price of an Option

Factor	Effect of an Increase of Factor on	
	Call Price	*Put Price*
Current price of underlying asset	increase	decrease
Strike price	decrease	increase
Time to expiration of option	increase	increase
Expected price volatility	increase	increase
Short-term interest rate	increase	decrease
Anticipated cash payments	decrease	increase

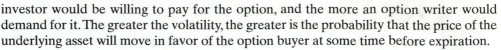

investor would be willing to pay for the option, and the more an option writer would demand for it. The greater the volatility, the greater is the probability that the price of the underlying asset will move in favor of the option buyer at some time before expiration.

Notice that the standard deviation or variance, rather than the systematic risk as measured by beta,[2] provides the relevant factor in the pricing of options.

Short-Term Risk-Free Interest Rate over the Life of the Option   Buying the underlying asset ties up one's money. Buying an option on the same quantity of the underlying asset makes the difference between the asset price and the option price available for investment at (at least) the risk-free rate. Consequently, all other factors being constant, the higher the short-term risk-free interest rate, the greater the cost of buying the underlying asset and carrying it to the expiration date of the call option. Hence, the higher the short-term risk-free interest rate, the more attractive the call option will be relative to the direct purchase of the underlying asset. As a result, the higher the short-term risk-free interest rate, the greater is the price of a call option.

Anticipated Cash Payments on the Underlying Asset over the Life of the Option   Cash payments on the underlying asset tend to decrease the price of a call option because the cash payments make it more attractive to hold the underlying asset than to hold the option. For put options, cash payments on the underlying asset tend to increase their price.

OPTION PRICING MODELS

In Chapter 10, we illustrated how the theoretical price of a futures contract can be determined on the basis of arbitrage arguments. Theoretical boundary conditions for the price of an option also can be derived through arbitrage arguments. For example, using arbitrage arguments it can be shown that the minimum price for an American call option is its intrinsic value, that is

$$\text{Call option price} \geq \text{Max } (0, \text{Price of asset} - \text{Strike price})$$

This expression says that the call option price will be greater than or equal to the difference between the price of the underlying asset and the strike price (intrinsic value), or zero, whichever is higher.

The boundary conditions can be "tightened" by using arbitrage arguments coupled with certain assumptions about the cash distribution of the asset.[3] The extreme case is an option pricing model that uses a set of assumptions to derive a single theoretical price, rather than a range. As we shall see, deriving a theoretical option price is much more complicated than deriving a theoretical futures price, because the option price depends on the expected price volatility of the underlying asset over the life of the option.

Several models determine the theoretical value of an option and include the most popular one that Fischer Black and Myron Scholes developed in 1973 for valuing European call options.[4] Several modifications to their model followed later. We discuss the Black-Scholes model and its assumptions in Chapter 15. For now, we use another

[2]   Beta is explained in Chapter 9.
[3]   See John C. Cox and Mark Rubenstein. *Option Markets* (Upper Saddle River, NJ: Prentice Hall, 1985), Chapter 4.
[4]   Fischer Black and Myron Scholes, "The Pricing of Corporate Liabilities," *Journal of Political Economy* (May/June 1973), pp. 637–59.

pricing model called the binomial option pricing model to see how arbitrage arguments can be used to determine a fair value for a call option.

Basically, the idea behind the arbitrage argument is that if the payoff from owning a call option can be replicated by purchasing the asset underlying the call option and borrowing funds, the price of the option is then (at most) the cost of creating the replicating strategy.

DERIVING THE BINOMIAL OPTION PRICING MODEL

To derive a one-period binomial option pricing model for a call option, we begin by constructing a portfolio consisting of (1) a long position in a certain amount of the asset, and (2) a short call position in the underlying asset. The amount of the underlying asset purchased is such that the position will be hedged against any change in the price of the asset at the expiration date of the option. That is, the portfolio consisting of the long position in the asset and the short position in the call option will produce the risk-free interest rate. A portfolio constructed in this way is called a hedged portfolio.

To illustrate, assume that an asset has a current market price of $80 and only two possible future values 1 year from now:

State	Price
1	$100
2	70

Assume further that a call option on this asset with a strike price of $80 (the same as the current market price) expires in 1 year. Suppose an investor forms a hedged portfolio by acquiring two-thirds of a unit of the asset and selling one call option. The two-thirds of a unit of the asset is the so-called hedge ratio (how we derive the hedge ratio will be explained later). Let us consider the outcomes for this hedged portfolio corresponding to the two possible outcomes for the asset.

If the price of the asset 1 year from now is $100, the buyer of the call option will exercise it. Then the investor must deliver one unit of the asset in exchange for the strike price, $80. Because the investor has only two-thirds of a unit of the asset, she must buy one-third at a cost of $33\frac{1}{3}$ (the market price of $100 times $\frac{1}{3}$). Consequently, the outcome will equal the strike price of $80 received, minus the $33\frac{1}{3}$ cost to acquire the one-third unit of the asset to deliver, plus whatever price the investor initially sold the call option for. That is, the outcome will be

$$\$80 - 33\tfrac{1}{3} + \text{Call option price} = \$46\tfrac{1}{3} + \text{Call option price}$$

If, instead, the price of the asset 1 year from now is $70, the buyer of the call option will not exercise it. Consequently, the investor will own two-thirds of a unit of the asset. At the price of $70, the value of two-thirds of a unit is $46\frac{2}{3}$. The outcome in this case is then the value of the asset plus whatever price the investor received when she initially sold the call option. That is, the outcome also will be $46\frac{2}{3}$ plus the call option price.

It is apparent that, given the possible asset prices, the portfolio consisting of a short position in the call option and two-thirds of a unit of the asset will generate an outcome that hedges changes in the price of the asset; hence, the hedged portfolio is riskless. Furthermore, this strategy holds regardless of the price of the call, which affects only the magnitude of the outcome.

Deriving the Hedge Ratio   To show how the hedge ratio can be calculated, we will use the following notation:

S = current asset price

u = 1 plus the percentage change in the asset's price if the price goes up in the next period.

d = 1 plus the percentage change in the asset's price if the price goes down in the next period.

r = a risk-free one-period interest rate (the risk-free rate until the expiration date)

C = current price of a call option

C_u = intrinsic value of the call option if the asset price goes up

C_d = intrinsic value of the call option if the asset price goes down

E = strike price of the call option

H = hedge ratio, that is, the amount of the asset purchased per call sold

In the first illustration we started with, u, d, and H:

u = 1.250 ($100/$80)
d = 0.875 ($70/$80)
$H = \frac{2}{3}$

State 1 in our illustration means that the asset's price goes up; State 2 means that the asset's price goes down.

The investment made in the hedged portfolio is equal to the cost of buying H amount of the asset minus the price received from selling the call option. Therefore, because the amount invested in the asset equals HS, then the cost of the hedged portfolio = $HS - C$.

The payoff of the hedged portfolio at the end of one period is equal to the value of the H amount of the asset purchased minus the call option price. The payoffs of the hedged portfolio for the two possible states are:

If the asset's price goes up:

$$uHs - C_u$$

If the asset's price goes down:

$$dHs - C_d$$

From our illustration:

If the asset's price goes up:

$$1.250H\$80 - C_u$$

or

$$\$100H - C_u$$

If the asset's price goes down:

$$0.875H\$80 - C_d$$

or

$$\$70H - C_d$$

Regardless of the state that occurs, we want the payoff of the hedged portfolio to be the same. That is, we want:

$$uHS - C_u = dHS - C_d \qquad \textbf{(11.1)}$$

Solving equation (11.1) for H we have

$$H = \frac{C_u - C_d}{(u - d)S} \qquad \textbf{(11.2)}$$

To determine the hedge ratio, H, we must know C_u and C_d. These two values equal the difference between the price of the asset and the strike price. Of course, the minimum value of the call option is zero. Mathematically, this calculation can be expressed as follows:

If the asset's price goes up:

$$C_u = \text{Max}\,[0, (uS - E)]$$

If the asset's price goes down:

$$C_d = \text{Max}\,[0, (dS - E)]$$

As the strike price in our illustration is $80, uS is $100, and dS is $70. Then:
If the asset's price goes up:

$$C_u = \text{Max}\,[0, (\$100 - \$80)] = \$20$$

If the asset's price goes down:

$$C_d = \text{Max}\,[0, (\$70 - \$80)] = \$0$$

For our illustration, we substitute the values of u, d, s, C_u, and C_d into equation (11.2) to obtain the hedge ratio:

$$H = \frac{\$20 - \$0}{(1.25 - 0.875)\,\$80} = \frac{2}{3}$$

The value for H agrees with the amount of the asset purchased in our earlier illustration.

Now we can derive a formula for the call option price. Figure 11-5 diagrams the situation. The top left half of the figure shows the current price of the asset for the current period and at the expiration date. The lower left-hand portion of the figure does the same thing using the preceding notation. The upper right-hand side of the figure gives the current price of the call option and the value of the call option at the expiration date; the lower right-hand side does the same thing using our notation. Figure 11-6 uses the values in our illustration to construct the outcomes for the asset and the call option.

Deriving the Price of a Call Option   To derive the price of a call option we can rely on the basic principle that the hedged portfolio, being riskless, must have a return equal to the riskless rate. Given that the amount invested in the hedged portfolio is $HS - C$, the amount that should be generated one period from now is

$$(1 + r)\,(HS - C) \qquad \textbf{(11.3)}$$

We also know what the payoff will be for the hedged portfolio if the asset's price goes up or goes down. Because the payoff of the hedged portfolio will be the same whether the asset's price goes up or down, we can use the payoff if it goes up, which is $uHS - C_u$. The payoff of the hedged portfolio as given should be the same as the

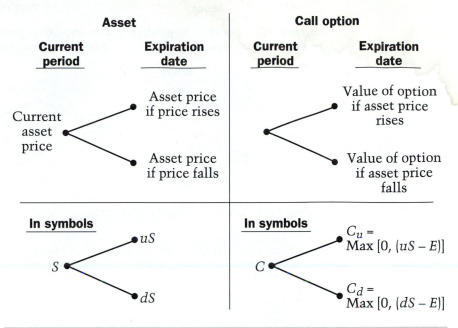

FIGURE 11-5 One-Period Option Pricing Model

amount to be generated by investing the initial cost of the portfolio given by equation (11.3). Equating the two, we have

$$(1 + r)(HS - C) = uHS - C_u \tag{11.4}$$

Substituting equation (11.2) for H in equation (11.4), and solving for the call option price, C, we find:

$$C = \left(\frac{1+r-d}{u-d} \right) \frac{C_u}{(1+r)} + \left(\frac{u-1-r}{u-d} \right) \frac{C_d}{(1+r)} \tag{11.5}$$

Equation (11.5) is the formula for the one-period binomial option pricing model. We would derive the same formula by using the payoff if the asset's price goes down.

FIGURE 11-6 One-Period Option Pricing Model Illustration

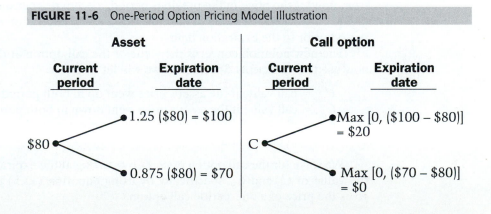

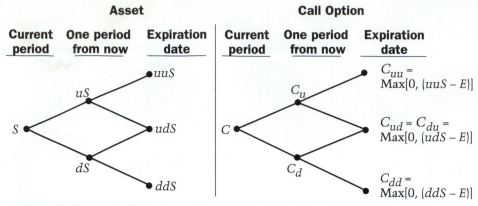

FIGURE 11-7 Two-Period Option Pricing Model

Applying equation (11.5) to our illustration where:

$u = 1.250$
$d = 0.875$
$r = 0.10$
$C_u = \$20$
$C_d = \$0$

we get:

$$C = \left(\frac{1 - 0.10 - 0.875}{1.25 - 0.875}\right)\frac{\$20}{1 + 0.10} + \left(\frac{1.25 - 1 - 0.10}{1.25 - 0.875}\right)\frac{\$0}{1 + 0.10}$$

$$= \$10.90$$

This value agrees with our first finding for the call option price.

This approach to pricing options may seem oversimplified, given that we assume only two possible future states for the underlying asset. In fact, we can extend the procedure by making the periods smaller and smaller, so we can calculate a fair value for the option. To illustrate these basic principles we extend the original illustration to a two-period model.

Extension to Two-Period Model The extension to two periods requires that we introduce more notation. To help understand the notation, look at Figure 11-7. The left panel of the figure shows for the asset, the initial price, the price one period from now if the price goes up or goes down, and the price at the expiration date (two periods from now) if the price in the previous period goes up or goes down. The right panel of Figure 11-7 shows the value of the call option at the expiration date and the value one period prior to the expiration date.

The new notation concerns the value of the call option at the expiration date. We now use two subscripts. Specifically, we will let

C_{uu} = call value if the asset's price went up in both periods
C_{dd} = call value if the asset's price went down in both periods.
$C_{ud} = C_{du}$ = call value if the asset's price went down in one period and up in one period

We solve for the call option price, C, by starting at the expiration date to determine the value of C_u and C_d, specifically by using equation (11.5) because that equation gives the price of a one-period call option.

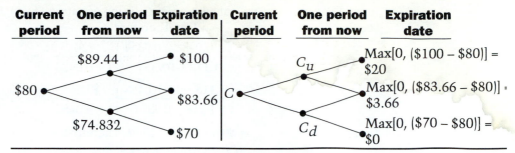

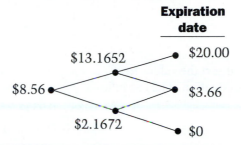

Option price one period from now

FIGURE 11-8   Two-Period Option Pricing Model Illustration

$$C_u = \left(\frac{1+r-d}{u-d}\right)\frac{C_{uu}}{(1+r)} + \left(\frac{u-1-r}{u-d}\right)\frac{C_{ud}}{(1+r)} \qquad \textbf{(11.6)}$$

$$C_d = \left(\frac{1+r-d}{u-d}\right)\frac{C_{du}}{(1+r)} + \left(\frac{u-1-r}{u-d}\right)\frac{C_{dd}}{(1+r)} \qquad \textbf{(11.7)}$$

Once C_u and C_d are known, we can solve for C using equation (11.5).

To make this concept more concrete, substitute numbers. We assume that the asset's price can go up by 11.8% per period or down by 6.46% per period, that is, $u = 1.118$ and $d = 0.9354$. Then, as shown in the top left panel of Figure 11-8, the asset can have three possible prices at the end of two periods:

Price goes up both periods: $uuS = (1.118)\,(1.118)\,\$80 = \$100$
Price goes down both periods: $ddS = (0.9354)\,(0.9354)\,\$80 = \$70$
Price goes up one period and down the other: $udS = (1.118)\,(0.9354)\,\$80$
$= duS = (0.9354)\,(1.118)\,\$80 = \$83.66$

Notice that the first two prices are the same as in the one-period illustration. By extending the length of time until expiration to two periods rather than one, and adjusting the change in the asset price accordingly, we now have three possible outcomes. If we increase the number of periods, the number of possible outcomes that the asset price may take on at the expiration date will increase. Consequently, what seemed like an unrealistic assumption about two possible outcomes for each period becomes more realistic with respect to the number of possible outcomes that the asset price may take at the expiration date.

Now we can use the values in the top right panel of Figure 11-8 to calculate C. The riskless interest rate for one period is now 4.88% because when compounded this rate produces an interest rate of 10% from now to the expiration date (two periods from now). First, consider the calculation of C_u using equation (11.6). From Figure 11-8 we see that $C_{uu} = \$20$ and $C_{ud} = \$3.66$. Therefore

$$C_u = \left(\frac{1 + 0.0488 - 0.9354}{1.118 - 0.9354}\right)\frac{\$20}{1 + 0.0488}$$

$$+ \left(\frac{1.118 - 1 - 0.0488}{1.118 - 0.9354}\right)\frac{\$3.66}{1 + 0.0488} = \$13.1652$$

From Figure 11-8, $C_{dd} = \$0$ and $C_{du} = \$3.66$. Therefore

$$C_d = \left(\frac{1 + 0.0488 - 0.9354}{1.118 - 0.9354}\right)\frac{\$3.66}{1 + 0.0488}$$

$$+ \left(\frac{1.118 - 1 - 0.0488}{1.118 - 0.9354}\right)\frac{\$0}{1 + 0.0488} = \$2.1672$$

We insert the values for C_u and C_d in the bottom panel of Figure 11-8 and calculate C using equation (11.5) as follows:

$$C = \left(\frac{1 + 0.0488 - 0.9354}{1.118 - 0.9354}\right)\frac{\$13.1652}{1 + 0.0488}$$

$$+ \left(\frac{1.118 - 1 - 0.0488}{1.118 - 0.9354}\right)\frac{\$2.1672}{1 + 0.0488} = \$8.58$$

◆ ECONOMIC ROLE OF THE OPTION MARKETS

In the previous chapter, we explained the important role that futures play in our financial markets because they allow investors to hedge the risks associated with adverse price movements. Hedging with futures lets a market participant lock in a price, and thereby eliminates price risk. In the process, however, the investor gives up the opportunity to benefit from a favorable price movement. In other words, hedging with futures involves trading off the benefits of a favorable price movement for protection against an adverse price movement.

Hedging with options offers a variety of potential benefits, which we discuss in later chapters. For now, we provide an overview of how options can be used for hedging, and how the outcomes of hedging with options differ from those of hedging with futures. To see this difference, let us return to the initial illustration in this chapter where the underlying instrument for the option is Asset XYZ.

First, consider an investor who owns Asset XYZ, which is currently selling for $100. The investor expects to sell it 1 month from now but is concerned that Asset XYZ's price may decline below $100 in that month. One alternative available to this investor is to sell Asset XYZ now. Suppose, however, the investor does not want to sell this asset now because either she expects that the price will rise in 1 month or some restriction prevents the sale of Asset XYZ now. Suppose also that an insurance company is aware of the situation faced by this investor and offers to sell her an insurance policy providing that, if at the end of 1 month Asset XYZ's price is less than $100, the insurance company makes up the difference between $100 and the market price. That is, if 1 month from now Asset XYZ's price is $80, the insurance company will pay the investor $20.

The insurance company naturally charges the investor a premium to write this policy. Let us suppose that the premium is $2. Holding aside the cost of the insurance policy, the payoff that this investor then faces is as follows. The minimum price for Asset XYZ that the investor is assured is $100 because if the price is less, the insurance company will make up the difference. If Asset XYZ's price is greater than $100, however, the investor will receive the higher price. Once we consider the premium of $2 to purchase this insurance premium, the investor is effectively assured a minimum price of $98 ($100 minus $2), but if the price is above $100 the investor realizes the benefits of a higher price (reduced always by the $2 for the insurance policy). By buying this insurance policy, the investor purchases protection against an adverse price movement, while maintaining the opportunity to benefit from a favorable price movement reduced by the cost of the insurance policy.

Insurance companies do not offer such policies, but we have described a contract in this chapter that provides the same protection as this hypothetical insurance policy. Consider the put option on Asset XYZ with 1 month to expiration, a strike price of $100, and an option price of $2 that we used in our illustrations earlier in this chapter. The payoff is identical to the hypothetical insurance policy. The option price resembles the hypothetical insurance premium; for this reason the option price is referred to as the option premium. A put option can be used to hedge against a decline in the price of the underlying instrument.

It offers quite a different payoff from a futures contract. Suppose that a futures contract with Asset XYZ as the underlying instrument is available with a futures price equal to $100 and a settlement date 1 month from now. By selling this futures contract, the investor would be agreeing to sell Asset XYZ for $100 in 1 month. If Asset XYZ's price falls below $100, the investor is protected because she receives $100 upon delivery of the asset to satisfy the futures contract. If Asset XYZ's price rises above $100, however, the investor cannot realize the price appreciation because she must deliver the asset for an agreed-upon amount of $100. By selling the futures contract, the investor locks in a price of $100, and fails to realize a gain if the price rises but avoids a loss if the price declines.

Call options, too, can be used to hedge. A call option can be used to protect against a rise in the price of the underlying instrument while maintaining the opportunity to benefit from a decline in the price of the underlying instrument. Suppose, for example, that an investor expects to receive $100 1 month from now, and plans to use that money to purchase Asset XYZ, which is currently selling for $100. The risk that the investor faces is that Asset XYZ's price will rise above $100 in 1 month. By purchasing the call option with a strike price of $100 and with an option price of $3 that we used earlier in this chapter, the investor hedges the risk of a rise in the price of Asset XYZ.

The hedge outcome is as follows. If the price rises above $100 in 1 month, the investor exercises the call option and realizes the difference between the market price of Asset XYZ and $100. Thus, holding aside the cost of the option, the investor assures that the maximum price she will pay for Asset XYZ is $100. Should the asset's price fall below $100, the call option expires worthless, but the investor benefits by being able to purchase Asset XYZ at a price less than $100. Once the $3 cost of the option is considered, the payoff is as follows. The maximum price that the investor will have to pay for Asset XYZ is $103 (the strike price plus the option price), but if the price of the asset declines below $100 the investor will benefit by the amount of the price decline less $3.

Compare this situation to a futures contract where Asset XYZ is the underlying instrument, settlement is in 1 month, and the futures price is $100. Suppose that the investor buys this futures contract. If 1 month from now the price of Asset XYZ rises above $100, the investor has contracted to buy the asset for $100, thereby eliminating the risk of a price rise; if the price falls below $100, however, the investor cannot benefit because of the contract to pay $100 for the asset.

It should be clear by now how hedging with options differs from hedging with futures. This difference cannot be overemphasized. Options and futures are not interchangeable instruments.

Is it possible to create the same hedging payoff that an option provides against an adverse price movement in a world without option contracts? Our illustrations explain how to price an option in order to accomplish the same payoff synthetically with an appropriate position in the cash market instrument and by borrowing funds. So why do we need option contracts? The reason is that an option contract is a more *efficient* vehicle to create the hedged positions.

Although our focus has been on hedging price risk, options also allow investors an efficient way to expand the range of return characteristics available. Investors can use options to "mold" a return distribution for a portfolio to fit particular investment objectives.[5]

◆ EXOTIC OPTIONS

As we explained earlier in this chapter, OTC options can be customized in any manner sought by an institutional investor. Basically, if a dealer can reasonably hedge the risk associated with the opposite side of the option sought, it creates the option desired by a customer. OTC options are not limited to European or American types. An option can be created in which the option can be exercised at several specified dates as well as the expiration date of the option. Such options are referred to as **limited exercise options**, **Bermuda options**, and **Atlantic options**.

More complex options are called **exotic options**, several of which are discussed throughout this book. Here we examine two types: alternative options and outperformance options. An **alternative option**, also called an **either-or option**, provides a payoff that is the best independent payoff of two distinct assets. For example, suppose that Donna buys an alternative call option with the following terms:

1. The underlying asset is one unit of Asset M or one unit of Asset N.
2. The strike price for Asset M is $80.
3. The strike price for Asset N is $110.
4. The expiration date is 3 months from now.
5. The option can only be exercised 3 months from now (that is, it is a European option).

At the expiration date, Donna can decide to buy from the writer of this option *either* one unit of Asset M at $80 *or* Asset N at $110. Donna will buy the asset with the larger payoff. So, for example, if Asset M and Asset N at the expiration date are $84 and $140, respectively, then the payoff would be $4 if Donna elects to exercise to buy Asset M but $30 if she elects to exercise to buy Asset N. Thus, she will exercise to buy Asset N. If the price for either asset at the expiration date is below its strike price, Donna will let the option expire worthless.

An **outperformance option** is an option whose payoff is based on the relative payoff of two assets at the expiration date. For example, consider the following outperformance call option purchased by Karl.

1. Portfolio A consists of the stock of 50 public utility companies with a market value of $1 million.
2. Portfolio B consists of the stock of 50 financial services companies with a market value of $1 million.
3. The expiration date is 6 months from now and is a European option.
4. The strike is equal to the market value of Portfolio B less the market value of Portfolio A.

---

5   See Stephen A. Ross, "Options and Efficiency." *Quarterly Journal of Economics* (February 1976), pp. 75–89; and Fred Arditti and Kose John, "Spanning the State Space with Options," *Journal of Financial and Quantitative Analysis* (March 1980), pp. 1–9.

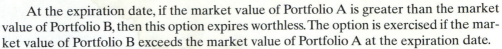

At the expiration date, if the market value of Portfolio A is greater than the market value of Portfolio B, then this option expires worthless. The option is exercised if the market value of Portfolio B exceeds the market value of Portfolio A at the expiration date.

The motivation for the use of exotic options such as alternative options and outperformance options will become evident when we discuss various investment and financing strategies in later chapters.

Summary

In this chapter we reviewed the fundamentals of options. An option grants the buyer of the option the right either to buy (in the case of a call option) or to sell (in the case of a put option) the underlying asset to the seller (writer) of the option at a stated price called the strike (exercise) price by a stated date called the expiration date. The price that the option buyer pays to the writer of the option is called the option price or option premium. An American option allows the option buyer to exercise the option at any time up to and including the expiration date; a European option may be exercised only at the expiration date.

The buyer of an option cannot realize a loss greater than the option price, and has all the upside potential. By contrast, the maximum gain that the writer (seller) of an option can realize is the option price; the writer is exposed to all the downside risk.

The option price consists of two components: the intrinsic value and the time premium. The intrinsic value is the economic value of the option if it is exercised immediately (except if no positive economic value results from exercising immediately, then the intrinsic value is zero). The time premium is the amount by which the option price exceeds the intrinsic value. Six factors influence the option price: (1) the current price of the underlying asset, (2) the strike price of the option, (3) the time remaining to the expiration of the option,(4) the expected price volatility of the underlying asset, (5) the short-term risk-free interest rate over the life of the option, and (6) anticipated cash payments on the underlying asset.

Arbitrage arguments can be used to place a lower boundary on the option price. The relationship between the call option price, the put option price, and the price of the underlying asset is known as the put-call parity relationship. The theoretical option price can be calculated using the binomial option pricing model, also based on arbitrage arguments.

Dealer-created or OTC options can be customized to satisfy the desires of institutional investors. More complex OTC options are called exotic options, which include alternative and outperformance options.

Key Terms

- Alternative option
- American option
- Atlantic option
- Bermuda option
- Call
- Call option
- Dealer options
- Either-or option
- European option
- Exercise price
- Exotic options
- Expiration date
- Intrinsic value
- Limited exercise option
- Long call position
- Long put position
- Option
- Option premium
- Option price
- Outperformance option
- Put
- Put option
- Put-call parity relationship
- Seller
- Short call position
- Short put position
- Strike price
- Time premium
- Time value
- Writer

Questions ▪▪

1. What is the difference between a put option and a call option?
2. What is the difference between an American option and a European option?
3. Why does an option writer need to post margin?
4. Identify two important ways in which an exchange-traded option differs from a typical over-the-counter option.
5. "There's no real difference between options and futures. Both are hedging tools, and both are derivative products. It's just that with options you have to pay an option premium, while futures require no upfront payment except for a 'good faith' margin. I can't understand why anyone would use options." Do you agree with this statement?
6. Explain how this statement can be true: "A long call position offers potentially unlimited gains if the underlying asset's price rises, but a fixed, maximum loss if the underlying asset's price drops to zero."
7. Suppose a call option on a stock has a strike price of $70 and a cost of $2, and suppose you buy the call. Identify the profit to your investment, at the call's expiration, for each of these values of the underlying stock: $25, $70, $100, $400.
8. Consider the situation in the previous question once more. Suppose you had sold the call option. What would your profit be at expiration for each of those stock prices?
9. Explain why you agree or disagree with this statement: "Buying a put is just like short-selling the underlying asset. You gain the same thing from either position if the underlying asset's price falls. If the price goes up, you have the same loss."
10. You just opened up the morning newspaper to check the prices of call options on Asset ABC. It is now December, with the near contract maturing in 1 month's time. Asset ABC is currently trading at $50.

Strike	Jan.	March	June
$40	$11	$12	$11.50
50	6	7	8.50
60	7	8	9.00

Glancing at the figures, you note that two of these quotes seem to violate some of the rules you learned regarding option pricing.
   a. What are these discrepancies?
   b. How could you take advantage of the discrepancies? What is the minimum profit you would realize by arbitraging based on these discrepancies?
   c. Suppose the price of the January $40 call were $9 rather than $11. The option would thus be selling for less than its intrinsic value. Why might it not be the case that an arbitrage profit is instantly available?
11. The payoff from a long position in a forward contract on the settlement date is the difference between the spot price of the underlying asset at the maturity of the forward contract and the forward price. For example, if you are long a forward contract to purchase an asset at $100, your payoff at the settlement date would be as follows:

Spot Price	Forward Price	Payoff
$80	$100	$20
90	100	−10
100	100	0
110	100	10
120	100	20

A forward contract is equivalent to being long a call option and short a put option, with the strike price such that the price of the call is equal to the price of the put.

    a. For the five spot prices listed, demonstrate that being long a forward is equivalent to being long a call and short a put.

    b. Why do you think that the strike price must be set such that the price of the call is equal to the price of the put?

12. Indicate whether you agree or disagree with the following statements.

    a. "To determine the theoretical value of an option, we need some measure of the volatility of the underlying asset. Because financial theorists tell us that the appropriate measure of risk is beta (i.e., systematic risk), then we should use this value."

    b. "It does not make sense that the price of a call option should rise in value if the price of the underlying asset falls."

13. For an asset that does not make cash distributions over the life of an option, it does not pay to exercise a call option prior to the expiration date. Why?

14. Consider the following two strategies. *Strategy 1:* Purchase one unit of Asset M currently selling for $103. A distribution of $10 is expected 1 year from now. *Strategy 2:* Purchase a call option on Asset M with an expiration date 1 year from now and a strike price of $100; and place funds in a 10% interest-bearing bank account sufficient to exercise the option at expiration ($100) and to pay the cash distribution that would be paid by Asset M ($10).

    a. What is the investment required under Strategy 2?

    b. What are the payoffs of Strategy 1 and Strategy 2, assuming that the price of Asset M 1 year from now is $120; $103; $100; $80?

    c. For the four prices of Asset M 1 year from now, demonstrate that the following relationship holds:

          Call option price > Max [0, (Price of underlying asset − Present value of strike price − Present value of cash distribution)]

15. The current price of Asset W is $25. No cash distributions are expected for this asset for the next year. The 1-year interest rate is 10%. The asset's price will be either $35 or $15 1 year from now. What is the price of a European call option on Asset W with a strike price of zero that expires in 1 year's time?

16. a. Calculate the option value for a two-period European call option with the following terms:

       • Current price of the underlying asset equals $100.
       • Strike price equals $10.
       • One-period risk-free rate is 5%.
       • The stock price can either go up or down by 10% at the end of one period.

    b. Recalculate the value for the option when the stock price can move either up or down by 50% at the end of one period. Compare your answer with the calculated value in part (a). Why is the answer different from what you might expect?

17. Suppose that you buy an alternative call option with the following terms:

       • The underlying asset is one unit of Asset G or one unit of Asset H.
       • The strike price for Asset G is $100.
       • The strike price for Asset H is $115.
       • The expiration date is 4 months from now.
       • The option can only be exercised at the expiration date.

    a. What is the payoff from this option if at the expiration date the price of Asset G is $125 and price of Asset H is $135?

b. What is the payoff from this option if at the expiration date the price of Asset G is $90 and price of Asset H is $125?

c. What is the payoff from this option if at the expiration date the price of Asset G is $90 and price of Asset H is $105?

18. Suppose that you buy an outperformance call option with the following terms:

- Portfolio X consists of bonds with a market value of $5 million.
- Portfolio Y consists of stocks with a market value of $5 million.
- The expiration date is 9 months from now and is a European option.
- The strike is equal to the market value of Portfolio X minus the market value of Portfolio Y.

What is the payoff of this option if at the expiration date the market value of Portfolio X is $10 million and the market value of Portfolio Y is $12 million?

12 Introduction to Swaps, Caps, and Floors Markets

Learning Objectives

After reading this chapter you will understand:

◆ what a swap is.

◆ what is meant by the notional amount.

◆ the various types of swaps, including interest rate swap, interest rate-equity swap, equity swap, and currency swap.

◆ the relationship between a swap and a forward contract.

◆ how swaps can be used for asset/liability management.

◆ how swaps can be used to create securities.

◆ what a cap and a floor are.

◆ the relationship between a cap and a floor and an option.

◆ how a cap can be used by a depository institution.

Swaps, caps, and floors are derivative instruments that can be used to control risks faced by borrowers and investors. Moreover, particularly in the case of swaps, these instruments give investment bankers the ability to create a wide range of securities to meet the objectives of investors. These derivative contracts are traded in the over-the-counter market.

In this chapter, we provide an overview of these contracts and some basic applications. In Chapters 16, 28, and 30, we shall take a closer look at these contracts and their mechanics. Our motivation for introducing them at this early stage is to emphasize the key role they play in the development of a global financial market and the development of new financial instruments and strategies.

◆ SWAPS

A **swap** is an agreement whereby two parties (called **counterparties**) agree to exchange periodic payments. The dollar amount of the payments exchanged is based on some predetermined dollar principal, called the **notional amount** or **notional principal**. The dollar amount each counterparty pays to the other is the agreed-upon periodic rate times the notional amount. The only dollars exchanged between the parties are the agreed-upon payments, not the notional amount.

To illustrate a swap and give you a flavor for the wide range of swaps, consider the following four swap agreements in which the payments are exchanged once a year for the next 5 years.

1. The counterparties to the swap are the First Renwick Bank and the General Manufacturing Corporation. The notional amount of this swap is $100 million. Every year for the next 5 years, First Renwick Bank agrees to pay General Manufacturing 8% per year, while General Manufacturing agrees to pay First Renwick the rate on a 1-year Treasury security. Therefore, every year First Renwick will pay $8 million (8% times $100 million) to General Manufacturing. The amount that General Manufacturing pays the bank depends on the rate on a 1-year Treasury security. For example, if this rate is 5%, General Manufacturing pays the bank $5 million (5% times $100 million).

2. The counterparties to this swap agreement are the Brotherhood of Basket Weavers (a pension sponsor) and the Reliable Investment Management Corporation (a money management firm). The notional amount is $50 million. Every year for the next 5 years the Brotherhood agrees to pay Reliable the return realized on the Standard & Poor's 500 stock index for the year minus 200 basis points. (This index will be described in Chapter 13.) In turn, Reliable agrees to pay the pension sponsor 10%. So, for example, if over the past year the return on the S&P 500 stock index is 14%, then the pension sponsor pays Reliable 12% (14% minus 2%) of $50 million, or $6 million, and the money management firm agrees to pay the pension sponsor $5 million (10% times $50 million).

3. The counterparties to this swap agreement are the Beneficial Pension Fund (a pension fund sponsor) and Investment Management Associates (a German money management firm). The notional amount is $80 million. Every year for the next 5 years Beneficial Pension agrees to pay Investment Management the return realized on the S&P 500 stock index for the year. In turn, Investment Management agrees to pay the pension fund sponsor the return realized on the German stock index (called the DAX index) for the year. So, for example, if over the past year the return on the S&P 500 stock index and the German stock index are 14% and 10%, respectively, then the pension fund sponsor pays Investment Management $11.2 million (14% times $80 million), and the German money management firm agrees to pay Beneficial Pension $8 million (10% times $80 million).

4. The two counterparties to this swap agreement are the Regency Electronics Corporation (a U.S. manufacturing firm) and the All-Swiss Watches Corporation (a Swiss manufacturing firm). The notional amount is $100 million and its Swiss franc equivalent at the time the contract was entered into was SF 127 million. Every year for the next 5 years the U.S. manufacturing firm agrees to pay All-Swiss Watches Swiss francs equal to 5% of the Swiss franc notional amount, or SF 6.35 million. In turn, the Swiss manufacturing firm agrees to pay Regency Electronics 7% of the U.S. notional amount of $100 million, or $7 million.

TYPES OF SWAPS

Swaps are classified based on the characteristics of the swap payments. The four types of swaps are interest rate swaps, interest rate-equity swaps, equity swaps, and currency swaps.

In an **interest rate swap**, the counterparties swap payments in the same currency based on an interest rate. For example, one of the counterparties can pay a fixed interest rate and the other party a floating interest rate. The floating interest rate is commonly referred to as the **reference rate**. The swap between First Renwick Bank and General Manufacturing Corporation described in the first swap agreement is an example of an interest rate swap. The payments made by both parties can be based on different reference rates. For example, one of the counterparties can pay an interest rate based on the 1-year Treasury security rate and the other party can pay an interest rate based on the federal funds rate.

In an **interest rate-equity swap**, one party is exchanging a payment based on an interest rate and the other party based on the return of some equity index. The payments are made in the same currency. Our second swap agreement is an interest rate-equity swap. In this agreement one of the counterparties paid a fixed interest rate, but other interest rate-equity swaps include agreements whereby one of the parties pays a floating interest rate.

In an **equity swap**, both parties exchange payments in the same currency based on some equity index. The third swap agreement provides an example of an equity swap.

Finally, in a **currency swap**, two parties agree to swap payments based on different currencies as in the fourth swap agreement.

INTERPRETATION OF A SWAP

If we look carefully at a swap, we can see that it is not a new derivative instrument. Rather, it can be decomposed into a package of derivative instruments that we have already discussed. Consider our first illustrative swap. Every year for the next 5 years Renwick Bank agrees to pay General Manufacturing Corp. 8% per year, while General Manufacturing agrees to pay First Renwick the rate on a 1-year Treasury security. Because the notional amount is $100 million, General Manufacturing agrees to pay $8 million. Alternatively, we can rephrase this transaction as follows: Every year for the next 5 years, General Manufacturing agrees to deliver to First Renwick something (the rate on a 1-year Treasury security) and to accept payment of $8 million. Look at it in this way: The two parties enter into multiple forward contracts. One party agrees to deliver something at some time in the future, and the other party agrees to accept delivery. The reason for saying that there are multiple forward contracts is because the agreement calls for making the exchange each year for the next 5 years.

Even though a swap may be nothing more than a package of forward contracts, it is not a redundant contract for several reasons. First, in many markets with forward and futures contracts, the longest maturity does not extend out as far as that of a typical swap. Second, a swap is a more transactionally efficient instrument, which means that in one transaction an entity can effectively establish a payoff equivalent to a package of forward contracts. The forward contracts would each have to be negotiated separately. Third, the liquidity of the swap market continues to grow since its beginning in 1981; it is now more liquid than many forward contracts, particularly long-dated (i.e., long-term) forward contracts.

APPLICATIONS

Now that you know what a swap is and how it can be viewed as a package of forward contracts, the next question is how can a market participant use a swap to accomplish a financial objective? We provide more detailed applications in later chapters, but for our purposes here, we provide two simple ones. The first application demonstrates how a swap, more specifically an interest rate swap, can be used by a depository institution for asset/liability management. In our second application, we show how we can create a new financial instrument by using an interest rate-equity swap.

Application to Asset/Liability Management   Suppose that the Buckingham Bank raises $100 million for 3 years at a fixed interest rate of 8% and then lends that money to All American Airlines for 3 years. The loan calls for an interest rate that changes every year. The interest rate that the airline company agrees to pay is the London interbank offered rate (LIBOR) plus 250 basis points. Suppose LIBOR is 7.5% when the loan is initiated. Therefore, in the first year the airline company will pay 10% (LIBOR of 7.5% plus 2.5%). The bank locks in a spread of 2% for the first year.

The interest rate risk exposure for this bank occurs if LIBOR declines. Should LIBOR fall below 5.5%, the interest rate for the loan for that 1-year period would be less than Buckingham Bank must pay on the money it borrowed at 8%. Thus, the bank would realize a negative spread for that period.

Suppose that Buckingham Bank could find another party, say Deutsche Bank, that would be willing to enter into an interest rate swap on the following terms: (1) the term of the swap is 5 years with a notional amount of $100 million; (2) every year Deutsche Bank pays Buckingham Bank 7.5% of $100 million; and (3) at the same time Buckingham Bank pays Deutsche Bank LIBOR plus 100 basis points of $100 million. Each year the outcome of this interest rate swap, coupled with the fixed interest rate that Buckingham Bank must pay on the money it borrowed, and the interest income it receives on the loan it made to the airline company, is as follows.

1. It earns LIBOR plus 250 basis points on the $100 million loan.
2. It pays 8% on the $100 million it borrowed.
3. As part of the swap, it receives 7.5% of $100 million from Deutsche Bank.
4. As part of the swap, it pays LIBOR plus 100 basis points of $100 million to Deutsche Bank.

Buckingham Bank therefore earns LIBOR plus 250 basis points (from the loan) and pays LIBOR plus 100 basis points (as per the swap), resulting in a net inflow of 150 basis points. In addition, it pays 8% (to borrow funds) and receives 7.5% (as per the swap), resulting in a net outflow of 50 basis points. As the net result, then, it locked in a spread of 1% (150 basis points minus 50 basis points) on the $100 million, regardless of how LIBOR changes.

This simple illustration demonstrates how an interest rate swap can be employed for asset/liability management. You might wonder: Who would be willing to take the other side of the swap (i.e., who would be the counterparty)? How does one find a counterparty? How are the terms of the swap determined? Why couldn't this depository institution just issue a floating-rate note rather than issue a fixed-rate note? These questions are addressed in Chapter 29 when we discuss interest rate swaps more fully.

Application to Creation of a Security   Swaps can be used by investment bankers to create a security. To see how, suppose the following scenario: The Universal Information Technology Company (UIT) seeks to raise $100 million for the next 5 years on a fixed-rate basis. UIT's investment banker, the Credit Suisse First Boston CSFB, indicates that if bonds with a maturity of 5 years are issued, the interest rate on the issue would have to be 8%. At the same time, institutional investors are seeking to purchase bonds but are interested in making a play on the stock market. These investors are willing to purchase a bond whose annual interest rate is based on the actual performance of the S&P 500 stock market index.

CSFB recommends to UIT's management that it consider issuing a 5-year bond whose annual interest rate is based on the actual performance of the S&P 500. The risk with issuing such a bond is that UIT's annual interest cost is uncertain because it depends on the performance of the S&P 500. However, suppose that the following two transactions are entered:

1. On January 1, UIT agrees to issue, using CSFB as the underwriter, a $100 million 5-year bond issue whose annual interest rate is the actual performance of the S&P 500 that year minus 300 basis points. The minimum interest rate, however, is set at zero. The annual interest payments are made on December 31.
2. UIT enters into a 5-year, $100 million notional amount interest rate-equity swap with CSFB in which each year for the next 5 years UIT agrees to pay 7.9% to CSFB, and CSFB agrees to pay the actual performance of the S&P 500 that year minus 300 basis points. The terms of the swap call for the payments to be made on December 31 of each year. Thus, the swap payments coincide with the payments that must be made on the bond issue. Also as part of the swap agreement, if the S&P 500 minus 300 basis points results in a negative value, CSFB pays nothing to UIT.

Consider the accomplishment of these two transactions from the perspective of UIT. Specifically, focus on the payments that must be made by UIT on the bond issue and the swap and the payments it will receive from the swap. These results are summarized here:

Interest payments on bond issue:	S&P 500 return − 300 basis points
Swap payment from CSFB:	S&P 500 return − 300 basis points
Swap payment to CSFB:	7.9%
Net interest cost:	7.9%

Thus, the net interest cost is a fixed rate despite the bond issue paying an interest rate tied to the S&P 500, which was accomplished with the interest rate-equity swap.

Several questions in this scenario need to be addressed. First, what was the advantage to UIT in entering into this transaction? Recall that if UIT issued a bond, CSFB estimated that UIT would have to pay 8% annually. Thus, UIT saved 10 basis points (8% minus 7.9%) per year. Second, why would investors purchase this bond issue? As explained in earlier chapters, regulations impose certain restrictions on institutional investors as to types of investment. For example, a U.S. depository institution is not entitled to purchase common stock, however it may be permitted to purchase a bond of an issuer such as UIT despite the fact that the interest rate is tied to the performance of common stocks. Third, is CSFB exposed to the risk of the performance of the S&P 500? Although is it difficult to demonstrate at this point, CSFB can protect itself in a number of different ways.

This example may seem like a far-fetched application, but it is not. In fact, it is quite common and one of the reasons for discussing swaps so early in this book. Debt instruments created by using swaps are commonly referred to as *structured notes* (discussed in Section VI of this book).

COUNTERPARTY RISKS

In a swap, two parties exchange payments. Consequently, each faces the risk that the other party will fail to meet its obligation to make payments (default). This risk is referred to as **counterparty risk**.

◆ CAP AND FLOOR AGREEMENTS

Agreements are available in the financial market in which one party, for a fee (premium), agrees to compensate the other if a designated reference is different from a predetermined level. The party that receives payment if the designated reference differs from a predetermined level and pays a premium to enter into the agreement is called the buyer. The party that agrees to make the payment if the designated reference differs from a predetermined level is called the seller.

When the seller agrees to pay the buyer if the designated reference exceeds a predetermined level, the agreement is referred to as a **cap**. The agreement is referred to as a **floor** when the seller agrees to pay the buyer if a designated reference falls below a predetermined level.

The designated reference could be a specific interest rate such as LIBOR or the prime rate, the rate of return on some domestic or foreign stock market index such as the S&P 500 or the DAX, or an exchange rate such as the exchange rate between the U.S. dollar and the Japanese yen. The predetermined level is called the **strike**. As with a swap, a cap and a floor are based on a notional amount.

In general, the payment made by the seller of the cap to the buyer on a specific date is determined by the relationship between the designated reference and the strike. If the former is greater than the latter, then the seller pays the buyer the following:

$$\text{Notional amount} \times (\text{Actual value of designated reference} - \text{Strike})$$

If the designated reference is less than or equal to the strike, then the seller pays the buyer nothing.

For a floor, the payment made by the seller to the buyer on a specific date is also determined by the relationship between the strike and the designated reference. If the designated reference is less than the strike, then the seller pays the buyer the following:

$$\text{Notional principal amount} \times (\text{Strike} - \text{Actual value of designed reference})$$

If the designated reference is greater than or equal to the strike, then the seller pays the buyer nothing.

The following two examples show how these agreements work.

Example 1. The Peterson Shipping Company enters into a 5-year cap agreement with Citibank with a notional amount of $50 million. The terms of the cap specify that if LIBOR exceeds 8% on December 31 each year for the next 5 years, Citibank (the seller of the cap) will pay Peterson Shipping Company the difference between 8% (the strike) and LIBOR (the designated reference). The fee or premium Peterson Shipping agrees to pay Citibank each year is $200,000.

The payment made by Citibank to Peterson Shipping on December 31 for the next 5 years based on LIBOR on that date will be as follows. If LIBOR > 8%, then Citibank pays $50 million × (Actual value of LIBOR − 8%). If LIBOR ≤ 8%, then Citibank pays nothing.

So, for example, if LIBOR on December 31 of the first year of the cap is 10%, Citibank pays Peterson Shipping Company $1 million.

$$\$50 \text{ million} \times (10\% - 8\%) = \$1 \text{ million}$$

Example 2. The R&R Company, a money management firm, enters into a 3-year floor agreement with Merrill Lynch with a notional amount of $100 million. The terms of the floor specify that if the S&P 500 is less than 3% on December 31 each year for the next 3 years, Merrill Lynch (the seller of the floor) pays R&R Company the difference between 3% (the strike) and the return realized on the S&P 500 (the designated reference). The premium R&R Company agrees to pay Merrill Lynch each year is $600,000.

The payment made by Merrill Lynch to R&R Company on December 31 for the next 3 years based on the performance of the S&P 500 for that year will be as follows. If the actual return on S&P 500 < 3%, then Merrill Lynch pays: $100 million × 3% − (Actual return on S&P 500). If the actual return on S&P 500 ≥ 3%, then Merrill Lynch pays nothing.

For example, if the actual return on the S&P 500 in the first year of the floor is 1%, Merrill Lynch pays R&R Company $2 million.

$$\$100 \text{ million} \times (3\% - 1\%) = \$2 \text{ million}$$

INTERPRETATION OF A CAP AND FLOOR

In a cap or floor, the buyer pays a fee that represents the maximum amount the buyer can lose and the maximum amount the seller of the agreement can gain. The only party required to perform is the seller. The buyer of a cap benefits if the designated reference rises above the strike because the seller must compensate the buyer. The buyer of a floor benefits if the designated reference falls below the strike because the seller must compensate the buyer.

In essence the payoff of these contracts is the same as in an option. A call option buyer pays a fee and benefits if the value of the option's underlying asset (or equivalently, designated reference) is higher than the strike price at the expiration date. A cap has a similar payoff. A put option buyer pays a fee and benefits if the value of the option's underlying asset (or equivalently, designated reference) is less than the strike price at the expiration date. A floor has a similar payoff. An option seller is only entitled to the option price. The seller of a cap or floor is only entitled to the fee.

Thus, a cap and a floor can be viewed as simply a package of options. As with a swap, a complex contract consists of basic contracts (forward contracts in the case of swaps and options in the case of caps and floors) packaged together.

APPLICATION TO ASSET/LIABILITY MANAGEMENT

To see how a cap can be used for asset/liability management, consider the problem faced by Buckingham Bank in our earlier illustration. Recall that as its objective the bank wishes to lock in an interest rate spread over its cost of funds. Yet because it borrows short term, its cost of funds is uncertain. The Buckingham Bank may be able to purchase a cap such that the cap rate plus the cost of purchasing the cap is less than the rate it earns on its fixed-rate commercial loans. If short-term rates decline, Buckingham Bank does not benefit from the cap, but its costs of funds declines. The cap therefore allows the bank to impose a ceiling on its cost of funds while retaining the opportunity to benefit from a decline in rates.

Summary

In this chapter we covered three types of derivative contracts: swaps, caps, and floors. In a swap the counterparties agree to exchange periodic payments. The dollar amount of the payments exchanged is based on the notional amount. The four types of swaps are interest rate swaps, interest rate-equity swaps, equity swaps, and currency swaps. A swap offers the risk/return profile of a package of forward contracts. Swaps can be used for asset/liability management and the creation of securities.

A cap is an agreement whereby the seller agrees to pay the buyer when a designated reference exceeds a predetermined level (the strike). A floor is an agreement whereby the seller agrees to pay the buyer when a designated reference is less than a predetermined level (the strike). The designated reference could be a specific interest rate, the rate of return on some stock market index, or an exchange rate. A cap and a floor are equivalent to a package of options.

Key Terms ▪

- Cap
- Counterparties
- Counterparty risk
- Currency swap
- Equity swap

- Floor
- Interest rate swap
- Interest rate-equity swap
- Notional amount
- Notional principal

- Reference rate
- Strike
- Swap

Questions ▪

1. The Window Wipers Union (a pension sponsor) and the All-Purpose Asset Management Corp. (a money management firm) enter into a 4-year swap with a notional amount of $150 million with the following terms: Every year for the next 4 years the Window Wipers Union agrees to pay All-Purpose Asset Management the return realized on the S&P 500 stock index for the year minus 400 basis points and receive from All-Purpose Asset Management 9%.
   a. What type of swap is it?
   b. In the first year payments are to be exchanged, suppose that the return on the S&P 500 is 7%. What is the amount of the payment that the two parties must make to each other?

2. Burlingame Bank and the ABC Manufacturing Corp. enter into the following 7-year swap with a notional amount of $75 million and the following terms: Every year for the next 7 years. Burlingame Bank agrees to pay ABC Manufacturing 7% per year and receive from ABC Manufacturing LIBOR.
   a. What type of swap is it?
   b. In the first year payments are to be exchanged, suppose that LIBOR is 4%. What is the amount of the payment that the two parties must make to each other?
   c. Suppose that the swap agreement called for ABC Manufacturing to pay the rate on a 1-year Treasury security. What type of swap would it be?

3. The American Dishwashers Union (a pension sponsor) and the Nippon Investment Management Company (a Japanese money management firm) enter into the following 3-year swap with a notional amount of $40 million: Every year for the next 3 years American Dishwashers Union agrees to pay Nippon the return realized on the S&P 500 stock index for the year minus 200 basis points and receive from Nippon the return realized on a Japanese stock index for the year.
   a. What type of swap is it?
   b. In the first year payments are to be exchanged, suppose that the return realized on the S&P 500 and the Japanese stock index are 18% and 23%, respectively. What is the amount of the payment that the two parties must make to each other?
   c. Explain why this swap allows the American Dishwashers Union to participate in the performance of the Japanese stock market without actually investing in any Japanese stocks.

4. Explain why a swap is similar to a futures (or forward) contract.
5. The Ringwood Bank raised $30 million for 4 years at a fixed interest rate of 7% and then loaned the funds to Micro-Technology Inc. The loan calls for an interest rate that changes every year. The interest rate that Micro-Technology agreed to pay is LIBOR plus 400 basis points. At the same time, Ringwood Bank entered into a 4-year interest rate swap with an investment banking firm, Goldman Sachs, with a notional amount of $30 million. The swap terms are as follows: Every year Goldman Sachs pays Ringwood Bank 7.3%; and every year Ringwood Bank pays Goldman Sachs LIBOR plus 150 basis points.
   a. What is the risk that Ringwood bank faces if it does not enter into the interest rate swap?
   b. Suppose that LIBOR at a payment date is 3%, what is the interest rate spread that Ringwood Bank would realize?
   c. What did Ringwood Bank accomplish by entering into this interest rate swap?
6. Several depository institutions offer certificates of deposit where the interest rate paid is based on the performance of the S&P 500 stock index.
   a. What is the risk a depository institution encounters by offering such certificates of deposit?
   b. How do you think that a depository institution can protect itself against the risk you identified in part (a) of this question?
7. The Acme Insurance Company purchased a 5-year bond whose interest rate floats with LIBOR. Specifically, the interest rate in a given year is equal to LIBOR plus 200 basis points. At the same time the insurance company purchases this bond, it enters into a floor agreement with Bear Stearns in which the notional principal amount is $35 million with a strike of 6%. The premium Acme Insurance Company agrees to pay Bear Stearns each year is $300,000.
   a. Suppose at the time that it is necessary to determine whether a payment must be made by Bear Stearns, LIBOR is 9%. How much must Bear Stearns pay Acme Insurance Company?
   b. Suppose at the time that it is necessary to determine whether a payment must be made by Bear Stearns, LIBOR is 3%. How much must Bear Stearns pay Acme Insurance Company?
   c. What is the minimum interest rate that Acme Insurance Company locked in each year for the next 5 years by entering into this floor agreement and buying the 5-year bond, ignoring the premium that Acme Insurance Company must make each year?
8. Rogers Asset Management, a money management firm, entered into a 4-year agreement with Merrill Lynch. The terms of the agreement specify that if the annual return realized by the German stock index, the DAX, is greater than 15% for the year ending December 31, Rogers Asset Management agrees to pay Merrill Lynch the excess over 15%. Merrill Lynch agrees to pay Rogers Asset Management $300,000 each year. The notional amount for this agreement is $90 million.
   a. What type of agreement is it?
   b. Who is the buyer of this agreement
   c. Who is the seller of this agreement?
   d. What is the strike?
   e. If the actual return on the DAX in the first year of this agreement is 24%, how much will Rogers Asset Management pay Merrill Lynch?
9. What is the relationship between a cap and an option?
10. What is meant by counterparty risk?

CHAPTER 13

Common Stock Market: I*

Learning Objectives

After reading this chapter you will understand:

◆ where stocks are traded.

◆ the practical categorization of markets in terms of exchange-listed stocks (national and regional exchanges), Nasdaq-listed over-the-counter stocks, and non-Nasdaq over-the-counter stocks.

◆ the four types of markets where stocks are traded: first market, second market, third market, and fourth market.

◆ the structure of the New York Stock Exchange and the Nasdaq.

◆ alternative trading systems, including electronic communications networks and crossing networks.

◆ the role and regulation of dealers in exchange and over-the-counter markets in the United States.

◆ the basic characteristics of the exchanges of the United Kingdom, Germany, Japan, and China.

◆ the reasons why issuers raise equity funds outside their domestic stock market.

◆ how prices are determined on most exchanges, whether set continuously during the day as buy and sell orders reach the market or through a call auction procedure.

◆ what global depositary receipts and American depositary receipts are and how they make international equity investing easier.

Equity securities represent an ownership interest in a corporation. Holders of equity securities are entitled to the earnings of the corporation when those earnings are distributed in the form of dividends. They are also entitled to a pro-rata share of the remaining equity in case of liquidation. The two types of equity securities are common stock and preferred stock. The key distinction between these two forms of equity securities lies in the degree to which they may participate in any distribution of earnings and capital and the priority given to each in the distribution of earnings. Typically, preferred stockholders are entitled to a fixed dividend that they receive

---

* This chapter is coauthored with Frank J. Jones and is based on material developed by Frank J. Fabozzi, Frank J. Jones, and Robert Johnson, Jr., "Common Stock," published in Frank J. Fabozzi (ed.), *The Handbook of Financial Instruments* (New York: John Wiley & Son, 2002).

before common stockholders may receive dividends. We refer therefore to preferred stock as a senior corporate security. We postpone an explanation of preferred stock to Chapter 22 where we discuss the market for senior corporate securities.

In the secondary market for common stock the opinions of investors about the economic prospect of a company are expressed through the trades they execute. These trades together give the market consensus opinion about the price of the stock. In turn, the company's cost of common stock is determined. Three interacting factors contributed to significant changes experienced by this market since the 1960s: (1) the institutionalization of the stock market as a result of a shift away from traditional small investors to large institutional investors, (2) changes in government regulation of the market, and (3) innovation due largely to advances in computer technology. The institutionalization of this market imposes important implications for the design of trading systems, because the demands made by institutional investors differ from those made by traditional small investors.

In this chapter we describe the common stock markets in the United States, as well as briefly review the stock markets in the United Kingdom, Germany, Japan, and China. In the next chapter we describe trading arrangements in the secondary market for common stocks—particularly those that evolved to accommodate institutional investors—and review the efficiency with which common stocks are priced and the implications of this efficiency for investment strategies.

◆ OVERVIEW OF TRADING LOCATIONS IN THE UNITED STATES

In the United States, secondary market trading in common stocks occurs in two different ways. The first is on organized **exchanges**, which are specific geographical locations called **trading floors**, where buyers and sellers physically meet. The trading mechanism on exchanges is the **auction system**, which results from the presence of many competing buyers and sellers assembled in one place.

The second type is via **over-the-counter (OTC) trading**, which results from geographically dispersed traders or market makers linked to one another via telecommunication systems, which requires no trading floor. This trading mechanism is a **negotiated system** whereby individual buyers negotiate with individual sellers.

Exchange markets are called **central auction specialist systems,** and OTC markets are called **multiple market maker systems**. A more recently developed method of trading common stocks via independently owned and operated **electronic communications networks (ECNs)** continues to experience rapid growth.

In the United States, the two national stock exchanges are the New York Stock Exchange (NYSE), commonly called the "Big Board," and the American Stock Exchange (AMEX or ASE), also called the "Curb." National stock exchanges trade stocks of foreign as well as U.S. corporations. In addition to the national exchanges, regional stock exchanges include Boston, Chicago (called the Midwest Exchange), Cincinnati, San Francisco (called the Pacific Coast Exchange), and Philadelphia, primarily trade stocks from corporations based within their region.

The major OTC market in the United States is Nasdaq (the National Association of Securities Dealers Automated Quotation System), which is owned and operated by the NASD (the National Association of Securities Dealers). The NASD is a securities industry self-regulatory organization (SRO) that operates subject to the oversight of the SEC. Nasdaq is a national market. During 1998, Nasdaq and AMEX merged to form the Nasdaq-AMEX Market Group, Inc.

TABLE 13-1	Exchange Data	
Exchange	*Number of Listed Companies*	*Market Capitalization*
NYSE	2,807	$11,531.8 billion
Nasdaq	4,152	$2,878.9 billion
AMEX	690	$100.4 billion

Source: www.marketdata.nasdaq.com (November 30, 2001).

Table 13-1 provides the number of listed companies and the market capitalizations of the three largest U.S. stock markets as of November 30, 2001. The NYSE is the largest exchange in the United States with approximately 2,000 companies' shares listed. The AMEX is the second largest national stock exchange in the United States with nearly 700 companies listed for trading. Nasdaq boasts an even greater number of listed stocks but with much less market capitalization than the NYSE.

The Securities Act of 1934 defines two categories of traded stocks. The first is exchange-traded stocks, also called "listed" stocks. The second is OTC stocks, or nonexchange-traded stocks and thus, by inference, "nonlisted." However, as we describe later in this chapter, certain Nasdaq stocks are subject to specific listing requirements (the Nasdaq National Market and the Nasdaq Small Capitalization Market). Thus, a more useful and practical categorization of traded stocks is as follows:

1. Exchange-listed stocks (national and regional exchanges)
2. Nasdaq-listed OTC stocks
3. Non-Nasdaq OTC stocks

We focus on each of these markets later in this section.

The four major types of markets on which stocks are traded are referred to as follows:

- *First Market:* trading on exchanges of listed stocks
- *Second Market:* trading in the OTC market of stocks not listed on an exchange
- *Third Market:* trading in the OTC market of listed stocks
- *Fourth Market:* private transactions between institutional investors who deal directly with each other without utilizing the services of a broker/dealer intermediary

◆ STOCK EXCHANGES

Stock exchanges are formal organizations, approved and regulated by the Securities and Exchange Commission (SEC). These exchanges are physical locations and are made up of "members" that use the exchange facilities and systems to exchange or trade listed stocks. Stocks traded on an exchange are said to be **listed stocks**. To be listed, a company must apply and satisfy requirements established by the exchange for minimum capitalization, shareholder equity, average closing share price, and other criteria. Even after being listed, exchanges may delist a company's stock if it no longer meets the exchange requirements.[1]

The right to trade securities or make markets on an exchange floor is granted to a firm or individual who becomes a **member** of the exchange by buying a **seat** on the

---

[1] Stocks may also be delisted after a merger with another company or by the choice of the company. For example, a corporation may choose to list its stock on a different exchange or on Nasdaq. After 1976, regulations permitted the listing of a common stock on more than one exchange, for example on a national and regional exchange.

exchange. The number of seats is fixed by the exchange, and the cost of a seat is determined by supply and demand. In early 2001, 1,366 seats on the NYSE could be purchased for $2 million each.

Two kinds of stocks are listed on the five regional stock exchanges: (1) stocks of companies that either could not qualify for listing on one of the major national exchanges or could qualify for listing but chose not to list; and (2) stocks, known as **dually listed stocks**, that are also listed on one of the major national exchanges. A company may be motivated to dual list if a local brokerage firm that purchases a membership on a regional exchange can trade the company's listed stocks without having to purchase a considerably more expensive membership on the national stock exchange where the stock is also listed. Alternatively, a local brokerage firm could use the services of a member of a major national stock exchange to execute an order, but in this case it gives up part of its commission.

The regional stock exchanges compete with the NYSE for the execution of smaller trades. In recent years, major national brokerage firms route such orders to regional exchanges because of the lower cost they charge for executing orders or better prices.

NEW YORK STOCK EXCHANGE

The NYSE was formed in 1792. Members trade stocks listed on the NYSE in a centralized continuous auction market at a designated location on the trading floor, called a *post,* with brokers representing their customers' buy and sell orders. A single **specialist** is the market maker for each stock. A member firm may be designated as a specialist for the common stock of more than one company, that is, several stocks can trade at the same post. But only one specialist is designated for the common stock of each listed company.

A specialist for each stock stands at a trading position around one of the 17 NYSE posts. Each post is essentially an auction site where orders, bids, and offers arrive. Most orders arrive from floor brokers and via SuperDot. SuperDot is an electronic order routing and reporting system that links member firms electronically worldwide directly to the specialist's post on the trading floor of the NYSE. The majority of NYSE orders are processed electronically through SuperDot.

In addition to the single specialist market maker on an exchange, member firms of an exchange can trade for themselves or on behalf of their customers. NYSE member firms, which are broker/dealer organizations that serve the investing public, employ brokers on the trading floor who serve as fiduciaries in the execution of customer orders.

The largest membership category on the NYSE is that of the **commission broker**. A commission broker is an employee of one of the nearly 500 securities houses, known as stockbrokers or wirehouses, devoted to handling business on the exchange. Commission brokers execute orders for their firm on behalf of their customers at agreed-upon commission rates. These houses may deal for their own account as well as on behalf of their clients.[2]

Other transactors in addition to commission brokers and specialists work on the exchange floor. **Independent floor brokers** execute orders for other exchange members who have more orders than they can handle alone or who require assistance in carrying out large orders. Floor brokers take a share in the commission received by the firm they assist. **Registered traders** are individual members who buy and sell for their

---

[2]   Banks, however, are not allowed to act as principals and may only deal on their customers' behalf.

own account. Alternatively, they may be trustees who maintain membership for the convenience of dealing and to save fees.

NYSE Specialist   As explained earlier, specialists are dealers or market makers assigned by the NYSE to conduct the auction process and maintain an orderly market in one or more designated stocks. Specialists may act as both a broker (agent) and a dealer (principal). In their role as a broker or agent, specialists transact customer orders in their assigned stocks, which arrive at their post electronically or are entrusted to them by a floor broker to be executed if and when a stock reaches a price specified by a customer (limit or stop order). As a dealer or principal, specialists buy and sell shares in their assigned stocks for their own account as necessary to maintain an orderly market. Specialists must always give precedence to public orders over trading for their own account.

In general, public orders for stocks traded on the NYSE, if not sent to the specialist's post via SuperDot, are sent from the member firm's office to its representative on the exchange floor, who attempts to execute the order in the trading crowd. (Later in this chapter we discuss the various types of orders that an investor can ask a broker to execute.) Certain types of orders not immediately executed on the trading floor are known as limit orders and stop orders. If the order is a limit or stop order, the member firm's floor broker can wait in the trading crowd or give the order to the specialist in the stock, who enters the order in that specialist's **limit order book** (or simply, **book**) for later execution based on the relationship between the market price and the price specified in the limit or stop order. The book lists the limit and stop orders, arranged by size and nearness to the current market price. The book used to be an actual physical paper book but is now maintained electronically. Before January 23, 2002, only the specialist could see the orders in the book. This exclusivity with respect to the limit order book gave an advantage to the specialist, which somewhat offsets the obligation to make fair and orderly markets. On January 23, 2002, the NYSE announced the NYSE OpenBook that allows traders to see the total limit-order volume at every bid and offer price and is available electronically from several market vendors. This NYSE OpenBook provides greater market transparency.

The diversity of its participants represents a significant advantage for the NYSE market. At the exchange, public orders meet each other often with minimal dealer intervention, which contributes to an efficient mechanism for achieving fair securities prices. The liquidity provided in the NYSE market stems from the active involvement of the following principal groups: the individual investor; the institutional investor; the member firm acting as both agent and dealer; the member-firm broker on the trading floor acting as agent, representing the firm's customer orders; the independent broker on the trading floor, acting as agent and handling customer orders on behalf of other member firms; and the specialist, with assigned responsibility in individual securities on the trading floor. Together these groups provide a beneficial depth and diversity to the market.

NYSE-assigned specialists have four major roles:

1. As dealers, they trade for their own accounts in any temporary absence of public buyers or sellers, and only after executing all public orders in their possession at a specified price.
2. As agents, they execute market orders entrusted to them by brokers, as well as orders awaiting a specific market price.
3. As catalysts, they help to bring buyers and sellers together.
4. As auctioneers, they quote current bid-ask prices that reflect total supply and demand for each of the stocks assigned to them.

In carrying out their duties, specialists may act as either an agent or a principal. When acting as an **agent**, the specialist simply fills customer market orders or limit or stop orders (either new orders or from the limit order book) by opposite orders (buy or sell). When acting as a **principal**, the specialist assumes the responsibility of maintaining a fair and orderly market. Regulations prohibit specialists from engaging in transactions in securities unless such transactions are necessary to maintain a fair and orderly market. Specialists profit only from those trades in which they are involved; that is, they realize no revenue for trades in which they act as agent.

The term *fair and orderly market* means a market is characterized by price continuity and reasonable depth. Thus, specialists are required to maintain a reasonable spread between bids and offers and small changes in price between transactions. Specialists are expected to bid and offer for their own account if necessary to promote such a fair and orderly market. They cannot put their own interests ahead of public orders and are obliged to trade on their own accounts against the market trend to help maintain liquidity and continuity as the price of a stock goes up or down. They may purchase stock for their investment account only if such purchases are necessary to create a fair and orderly market.

Specialists balance buy and sell orders at the opening of the trading day in order to arrange an equitable opening price for the stock. They participate in the opening of the market only to the extent necessary to balance supply and demand. Although trading throughout the day is via a continuous auction-based system, the opening is conducted via a single-priced call auction system, as determined by the specialists.

If an *imbalance* between buy and sell orders either at the opening or during the trading day results in the inability to maintain a fair and orderly market, a specialist may, under restricted conditions, close the market in that stock (that is, discontinue trading) until the specialist is able to determine a price that reestablishes a balance of buy and sell orders. Such closes of trading can occur either during the trading day or at the opening, which is more common, and can last for minutes or days. Closings of a day or more may occur when, for example, one firm acquires another or when a corporation makes an extreme announcement. (For this reason, many announcements are made after the close of trading.)

NYSE trading officials oversee the activities of the specialist and trading-floor brokers. Approval from these officials must be sought for a delay in trading at the opening or to halt trading during the trading day when unusual trading situations or price disparities develop.

Because of their critical public role, and the necessity of capital in performing their function as a market maker, specialists are subject to capital requirements imposed by the exchanges. Specialists must be able to assume a position of at least 150 round lots in each common stock in which they are registered.[3] The 10 specialist firms, at the NYSE, along with the number of stocks for which they act as specialists, are shown in Table 13-2. Traditionally, NYSE specialist firms were small, privately owned businesses. As of this writing, the three biggest specialist firms include Fleet Boston Financial's specialist unit (which bought M. J. Meehan during 2000), Spear, Leads & Kellogg (owned by Goldman Sachs), and Labranche & Co. (a public company).

Increases in capital requirements for specialists contribute to a consolidation of the specialist firms. These specialists continue to face increasing competition such as

---

3 In addition, effective October 30, 2000, if a specialist holds a market share of greater than 5% by any of various concentration measures, they are subject to certain "net liquid asset" requirements for each specialist security.

TABLE 13-2   NYSE Specialist Firms

Specialist Firm	Number of Common Stocks
1. LaBranche & Co. LLC	591
2. Spear Leeds & Kellogg Specialists	501
3. Fleet Meehan Specialist, Inc.	427
4. Wagner Stott Bear Specialists, LLC	347
5. Van Der Moolen Specialists USA	311
6. Performance Specialist Group, LLC	133
7. Susquehanna Specialists, Inc.	118
8. Lynden Dolan Nick & Co. LLC	81
9. Walter N. Frank & Co. LLC	73
Total	2,582

10. Bear Hunter Structured Products Trading LLC is the specialist solely in two exchange-traded funds.

Source: www.nyse.com (December 3, 2001).

ECNs. Nevertheless, the specialist business remains profitable, with a return on capital exceeding that of most brokerage firms.[4]

Commissions   Before 1975, regulations allowed stock exchanges to set minimum commissions on transactions. The fixed commission structure did not allow the commission rate to decline as the number of shares in the order increased. For example, brokers incur lower total costs in executing an order of 10,000 shares of one stock for one investor than in executing 100 orders for the same stock from 100 investors. Consequently, fixed commissions did not reflect economies of scale in executing transactions.

Pressure from institutional investors, who transacted large trades, led the SEC to eliminate fixed commission rates during May 1975, at which time commissions became fully negotiable between investors and their brokers. May 1, 1975, called "Black Thursday," ushered in a period of severe price competition among brokers. Many firms failed, and numerous consolidations occurred within the brokerage industry.

The introduction of negotiated commissions provided the opportunity for the development of **discount brokers**. These brokers charge commissions at rates much less than those charged by other brokers, but offer little or no advice or any other service apart from the execution of the transaction. Discount brokers have been particularly effective in inducing retail investors to participate in the market for individual stocks.

◆ THE OTC MARKET

The OTC market is called the market for unlisted stocks. Technically, both the exchanges, as well as the Nasdaq National and Small Capitalization OTC markets maintain "listing requirements." Nevertheless, exchange-traded stocks are called *listed,* and stocks traded in the OTC markets are called *unlisted.*

4   See Jeff D. Opdyke, "Goldman Boosts Clout in Trading," *The Wall Street Journal* (January 30, 2001), pp. C1, C18; Charles Gasparino, "Bear Stearns to Acquire Specialist," *The Wall Street Journal* (February 15, 2001), p. C1, C16; Patrick McGeehan, "A Bear Stearns Partnership Expands Its Stock Trading Role," *New York Times* (February 16, 2001), p. C1.

The OTC market consists of three parts: two under the aegis of NASD (the Nasdaq markets) and a third market for truly unlisted stocks, the non-Nasdaq OTC markets.

NASDAQ STOCK MARKET

Established in 1971, the Nasdaq stock market developed as a wholly owned subsidiary of the NASD. The NASD, subject to oversight by the SEC, is a private organization that represents and regulates the dealers in the OTC market. Nasdaq is the flagship market of the NASD.

Nasdaq is essentially a telecommunications network that links thousands of geographically dispersed market-making participants. Its electronic quotation system provides price quotations to market participants on Nasdaq-listed stocks. Although it maintains no central trading floor, Nasdaq functions as an electronic "virtual trading floor." As shown in Table 13-3, more than 4,100 common stocks trade in the Nasdaq system with a total market value greater than $2.8 trillion. Some 535 dealers, known as market makers, representing some of the world's largest securities firms, provide competing bids to buy and offers to sell Nasdaq stocks to investors.

Nasdaq Market Tiers   The Nasdaq stock market has two broad tiers of securities: (1) the *Nasdaq National Market* (NNM) and the *Small Capitalization Market*. Newspapers devote separate sections to these two tiers of stocks (labeled the "Nasdaq National Market" and the "Nasdaq Small Capitalization Market"). The Nasdaq NMS is the dominant OTC market in the United States.

As of November 2001, approximately 3,600 stocks traded on the Nasdaq NNM system and 848 on the Small Cap Market. Some features of the two tiers of Nasdaq are shown in Table 13-3.

Securities are actually listed on both tiers of Nasdaq and must meet fairly stringent listing requirements for size, issuer profitability, trading volume, governance, public disclosure, and other factors including specified minimum standards for both initial listing and continued listing. The financial criteria for listing in the Small Cap Market are not as stringent as in the NNM system, although the corporate governance standards for the two are the same. Small Cap companies often grow and move up to the NNM market. The NNM issues are more widely known, with greater trading volumes and more market makers.

One difference in the listing requirements for the NYSE and Nasdaq (NNM) is that profitability is required for companies listed on NYSE but not on Nasdaq. The requirement for market capitalization also differs: Nasdaq requires $6 million of net tangible assets for an initial listing, while NYSE requires a market capitalization of

TABLE 13-3   Nasdaq and Its National Market and Small Cap Market

Year 2000	*Nasdaq* (NMS)	Components of Nasdaq	
		National Market (NNM)	*Small Cap Market*
Share volume (billions)	435.1	429.9	5.2
Dollar volume ($ billions)	$10,211.1	$10,191.9	$19.0
Market value ($ billions)	$2,879.0	$2,810.6	$68.4
Companies	4,152	3,387	765
Issues	4,410	3,562	848

Source: www.marketdata.nasdaq.com (November 2001).

$6.5 million over 3 years. The lower listing standards for Nasdaq permit smaller and newer companies to list.

Many stocks that qualify for listing on the NYSE remain on Nasdaq, including Microsoft and Intel at the end of 2001. Occasionally companies switch from Nasdaq to the NYSE.

Nasdaq market makers face an increased level of affirmative obligation. The main responsibility of a Nasdaq NNM market maker is to post continuous two-sided quotes (bid and ask), which consist of a price and a size. Between 9:30 A.M. and 4:00 P.M. Eastern time, these quotes must be firm, which means that if any NASD member presents an order to a market maker, the market maker is obligated to trade at terms no worse than its quotes. Failure to do so constitutes "backing away," which may be subject to regulatory sanction.

More specifically, Nasdaq NNM market makers must (1) continuously post these firm two-sided quotes good for 1,000 shares (for most stocks), (2) report trades promptly, (3) be subject to automatic execution against their quotes via Small Order Execution System (SOES), (4) integrate customer limit orders into their proprietary quotes, and (5) give precedence to customer limit orders and not place a quote on any system different from their Nasdaq quote unless that system is linked backed into Nasdaq. Market makers must report price and volume in NMS issues to the NASD through their Nasdaq terminals within 90 seconds of the trade.

On Nasdaq, many trades are "internalized," which means that a broker/dealer firm acts as market maker in executing on a principal basis the trade of one of its customers. Internalization is not permitted on the exchanges.

Some large wirehouses have acquired major Nasdaq trading firms that were independent. For example, as of August 2000, Herzog Heine Geduld and Spear, and Leads & Kellogg were the third and fourth largest traders on Nasdaq. By the end of 2000, these two firms had been acquired by Merrill Lynch and Goldman Sachs, respectively. A major reason for these acquisitions is that Nasdaq trading is becoming increasingly retail, and the large investment banks wanted to maintain and increase their retail business.

OTHER OTC MARKETS

Even though the Nasdaq stock markets are the major parts of the U.S. OTC markets, the vast majority of the OTC issues (about 8,000) do not trade on either of the two Nasdaq systems. The securities traded on these markets are not listed, that is have no listing requirements. Thus, these two OTC markets are not "issuer services." Rather, they are "subscriber services," that is, subscribers can make bids and offers for any stock not listed on exchanges or Nasdaq.

The first of these two non-Nasdaq OTC markets is the **OTC Bulletin Board (OTCBB)**, sometimes called simply the Bulletin Board. OTCBB is owned and operated by Nasdaq and regulated by NASD. The OTCBB displays real-time quotes, last-sale prices, and volume information for approximately 5,500 securities. It includes stocks not traded on the NYSE, AMEX, or Nasdaq.

The second non-Nasdaq OTC market is the "Pink Sheets," which is owned and operated by the National Quotation Bureau. Prior to the creation of Nasdaq in 1971, dealer quotations were disseminated by paper copy only. These copies were printed on pink paper, which is why OTC securities became known as "pink sheet stocks." The Pink Sheets are still published weekly. In addition, an electronic version of the Pink Sheets is updated daily and disseminated over market data vendor terminals. In order to provide greater visibility to these issues, many of which are low priced and thinly traded, transactions in pink sheet issues are subject to price and volume reporting under NASD Schedule D. Pink sheet securities are often pejoratively called "penny stocks."

These two markets are subscriber markets only; any subscriber can enter quotes for securities on the systems. However, the trades on these markets are executed not on these systems but via telephone. If the trades are conducted by NASD members, which is usually the case, they are reported to NASD and disseminated by ACT (the Nasdaq trade reporting system).

Of the two markets, the OTCBB tends to trade the more active stocks than does the Pink Sheets. OTCBB trades approximately the most active 4,000 stocks.

◆ THE THIRD MARKET

A stock may be both listed on an exchange and also traded in the OTC market, called the **third market**. Dealers in this market could not be members of the NYSE until NYSE Rule 390 was repealed in 1999. Consequently, these non-NYSE member dealers were not restricted by the fixed minimum commissions set prior to 1975. The third market grew as institutional investors used it in the early 1960s to avoid these fixed minimum commissions. Even after 1975, however, only a handful of dealers actively participated in the third market, primarily because of NYSE Rule 390. After the repeal of Rule 390 during late 2000, however, third market activity for NYSE-listed stocks showed significant growth potential.

Like Nasdaq, the third market is a network of broker/dealers that aggregates quotation information and provides interparticipant order routing tools, but leaves order execution to market participants. Dealers that make markets in the third market operate under the regulatory jurisdiction of the NASD. Although the third market is not owned by the NASD, market makers in the third market use some of the facilities provided by Nasdaq. When the NASD created Nasdaq in 1971, it included substantially similar functionality for third market-listed trading, including the CQS (Consolidated Quotations Service) for third market quotes, and CTS for third market trades.

◆ THE FOURTH MARKET: ALTERNATIVE TRADING SYSTEMS

It is not necessary for two parties to a transaction to use an intermediary; that is, the services of a broker or a dealer are not required to execute a trade. The direct trading of stocks between two customers without the use of a broker is called the **fourth market**. This market grew for the same reasons as the third market; the excessively high minimum commissions established by the exchanges prior to 1975.

A number of proprietary **alternative trading systems (ATSs)**, which comprise the fourth market, are operated by the NASD members or member affiliates. These fourth market ATSs are for-profit "broker's brokers" that match investor orders and report trading activity to the marketplace via Nasdaq or the third market. In a sense, ATSs are similar to exchanges because they are designed to allow two participants to meet directly on the system and are maintained by a third party who also serves a limited regulatory function by imposing requirements on each subscriber.

Broadly, an ATS takes one of two forms: electronic communications networks or crossing networks.

ELECTRONIC COMMUNICATIONS NETWORKS

Electronic communications networks (ECNs) are privately owned broker/dealers that operate as market participants within the Nasdaq system. They display quotes that reflect actual orders and provide institutions and Nasdaq market makers with an anonymous way to enter orders. Essentially, an ECN is a limit order book that is widely disseminated and open for continuous trading to subscribers who may enter and access orders displayed on the ECN. ECNs offer transparency, anonymity, automated service, and reduced costs, and are therefore effective for handling small orders. ECNs are used to disseminate firm commitments to trade (firm bids or offers) to participants, or subscribers, which have typically either purchased or leased hardware for the operation of the ECN or have built a custom connection to the ECN. ECNs may also be linked into the Nasdaq marketplace via a quotation representing the ECN's best buy-and-sell quote. In general, ECNs use the Internet to link buyers and sellers, bypassing brokers and trading floors.

As part of the Nasdaq execution, ECN volume is counted as part of the Nasdaq volume. ECNs account for more than 30% of Nasdaq trading in exchange trading. However, even after the repeal of NYSE Rule 390, ECNs amount to less than 5% of executed volume on the NYSE.

Instinet, the first ECN, began operating in 1969, and continues to be a large ECN in terms of activity. Instinet was acquired by Reuters Holdings in 1987. Instinet is an NASD member broker/dealer and trades both Nasdaq and exchange-listed stocks. It was originally intended as a system through which institutional investors could cross trades, that is a crossing network; however, market makers are now significant participants in Instinet. Instinet usage for Nasdaq securities, that is usage as an ECN, began to grow in the mid-1980s when market makers were allowed to subscribe.

Since 1969, nine additional ECNs include Island, Archipelago, REDI Book, Bloomberg Tradebook, BRASS Utility, Strike, Attain, NexTrade, and Market XT. Two of the ECNs, Archipelago and Island, applied to the SEC to become exchanges.

CROSSING NETWORKS

Systems developed to allow institutional investors to "cross" trades, matching buyers and sellers directly, typically via computer. **Crossing networks** are batch processes that aggregate orders for execution at specified times. Crossing networks provide anonymity and reduced cost, and are specifically designed to minimize a trading cost that we will describe later (market impact cost). They vary considerably in their approach to market structure, including the type of order information that can be entered by the subscriber and the amount of pretrade transparency that is available to participants.

At present, the three major crossing networks include ITG Posit, the Arizona Stock Exchange (AZX), and Optimark. Instinet, the original crossing network, operates a fourth crossing network in addition to its current ECN offering.

Instinet provides an interactive **hit-and-take system**, which means that participants search for buyers or sellers electronically, negotiate, and execute trades. It is a computerized execution service (Institutional Networks Corporation), registered with the SEC. The service permits subscribers to search for the opposite side of a trade without the cost of brokerage during Instinet's evening crossing network. Many mutual funds and other institutional investors use Instinet.

ITG Posit is more than a simple order-matching system. Rather, it matches the purchase and sale of portfolios in a way that optimizes the liquidity of the system. ITG's hourly Posit operates only during the trading day.

The AZX in Phoenix, which commenced trading in March 1992, operates as an after-hours electronic marketplace where anonymous participants trade stocks via personal computers. This exchange provides a call auction market, which accumulates bids and offers for a security and, at designated times, derives a single price that maximizes the number of shares to be traded. It now conducts call auctions at 9:30 and 10:30 A.M., and 12:30, 2:30, and 4:30 P.M.[5]

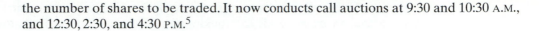

◆ OTHER TYPES OF COMMON STOCK TRADING

Other types of common stock trading vehicles and security types are available to investors.

OFFSHORE TRADING

Broker/dealers may trade exchange-listed and Nasdaq equities offshore via foreign exchanges (e.g., the Bermuda Stock Exchange) or OTC via foreign trading desks (e.g., a broker/dealer's London office). In general, such transactions must be reported to a U.S. marketplace (typically the third market) during the next trading day.

RULE 144A SECURITIES

Rule 144A, adopted by the SEC in April 1990, is designed to facilitate secondary market trading in nonfungible unregistered securities among qualified institutional buyers (QIBs) by providing a "safe harbor" from the registration requirements of the Securities Act of 1933. QIBs are institutions with $100 million invested in securities of issuers not affiliated with the qualified buyer. Basically Rule 144A permits the issue of nonregistered securities and their purchase by qualified institutions.

AMERICAN DEPOSITORY RECEIPTS

American depository receipts (ADRs) are negotiable certificates in registered form, issued in the United States by a U.S. bank, which certify that a specific number of foreign shares have been deposited with an overseas branch of the bank (or another financial institution) that acts as a custodian in the country of origin.

ADRs provide an opportunity for investors who want to invest in the shares of a foreign corporation to buy, hold, and sell their interests in these foreign securities without having to take physical possession of the securities, and while receiving dividends and exercising voting rights conveniently. A holder of an ADR can, at any time, request the underlying shares. Conversely, ADRs enable foreign corporations with shares that have not been admitted to a U.S. stock exchange to obtain access to the U.S. public capital market. Usually, only shares traded on a recognized foreign stock exchange are represented by ADRs. ADRs are discussed in greater detail later in this chapter.

◆ THE ROLE AND REGULATION OF DEALERS IN EXCHANGE AND OTC MARKETS

In Chapter 7 we explained the role of dealers in secondary markets. An important structural difference between exchanges and the OTC market affects the activities of dealers. The main difference is that exchanges use a single market maker, whereas OTC markets allow multiple market makers. On exchanges, the one market maker or dealer per stock is the specialist.

---

[5] For a discussion of the concepts underlying the Arizona Stock Exchange, see the AZX Web site, available at www.azx.com.

With only one specialist for a given stock, no other market makers on the exchange are available to provide competition. Does it mean that the specialist enjoys a monopolistic position? Not necessarily. Specialists face competition from several sources. Brokers in the crowd may have public market or limit orders that compete with specialists. In the case of multiple listed stocks, competition comes from specialists on other exchanges where the stock is listed. Since the repeal of Rule 390 during late 1999, competition can come from dealers in the OTC market. Finally, as discussed later in this chapter, when a block trade is involved, specialists compete with the upstairs market.

In the OTC market, the number of dealers depends on the volume of trading in a stock. For example, at the time of this writing, there were nearly 82 dealers on Nasdaq for Microsoft. If a stock is not actively traded, it may have only one or two dealers. As trading activity increases in a stock, no barriers prevent more entities from becoming dealers in that stock, other than satisfaction of capital requirements. Competition from more dealers—or the threat of new dealers—forces bid-ask spreads to more competitive levels. Moreover, the capital-providing capacity of more than one dealer may benefit the markets more than a single specialist performing the role of a market maker.

Those who think the OTC market is superior to an organized exchange often cite the greater competition from numerous dealers and the greater amount of capital they bring to the trading in a security. The exchanges, however, insist that the commitment of the dealers to provide a market for shares in the OTC market is not the same obligation as that of the specialist on the exchange. On the NYSE we described the specialist as obligated to maintain fair and orderly markets. Failure to fulfill this obligation results in a loss of specialist status. A dealer in the OTC market is under no such obligation to continue its market-making activity during volatile and uncertain market conditions.

Overall, NYSE specialists are under an obligation to make fair and orderly markets. And Nasdaq NNM market makers answer to an affirmative obligation to continuously post firm two-sided quotes good for 1,000 shares (for most stocks). However, both types of market maker have escape valves for extenuating circumstances. If the NYSE specialists are unable to maintain a balanced market, then, with the approval of the exchange authorities, they can close the market until they are able to restore the balance. Similarly, Nasdaq market makers are relieved of their obligation to make markets if companies make news announcements or in cases of unusual trading when an issuer's executives cannot be reached. Nasdaq is also considering a request to the SEC that would give it greater latitude in halting and canceling aberrant trades in stocks.

On the NYSE, 8 out of 10 trades happen directly between a buyer and a seller; that is, no intermediate market maker collects a spread. Thus, the two parties simply pay only their own broker for the service. The exchange levies a fee only on orders larger than 2,100 shares. On the other hand, most Nasdaq trades take place through a market maker who benefits from the bid-ask spread.

The age-old securities debate continues: Are investors better off in a central market distilling highly accurate prices from a huge pool of liquidity, as at the NYSE, at the risk of sanctioning a lethargic monopoly? Or are they better off in a sea of competing market makers, as Nasdaq offers? The results of an SEC study on the costs of trading in these two markets addresses this question and will be discussed later.

BACKGROUND OF REGULATORY ISSUES

In the 1960s and early 1970s, the U.S. secondary markets for stocks became increasingly fragmented. In a **fragmented market**, some orders for a given stock are handled differently from other orders. An example of fragmentation is a stock that can be bought on several exchanges as well as in the OTC market. An order to buy IBM stock, thus, could be executed on one of the exchanges where IBM is listed via the specialist system. Alternatively, it could be executed in the third market using the multiple-dealer system. Thus, the treatment of the order differs, depending upon where it is ultimately executed. A differential treatment of orders may also arise if those orders vary in size, even if they pertain to the same stock and are executed on the same exchange.

Some public policymakers were concerned that investors did not uniformly receive the best execution, that is, transactions were not necessarily being executed by a broker on behalf of a customer at the most favorable price available. Another concern with the increased fragmentation of the secondary market for stocks centered around the growing number of completed transactions in listed stocks not reported to the public. This lapse in reporting happened because transactions in the third market and on the regional exchanges were not immediately disclosed on the major national exchange ticker tapes where the stock was listed.

As a result of these concerns, Congress enacted the Securities Act of 1975. The most important and relevant provision of this legislation is Section 11A(a)(2), which amended the Securities and Exchange Act of 1934 and directed the SEC to "facilitate the establishment of a national market system for securities." The SEC, in its efforts to implement a national market system (NMS), targeted six elements, described as follows by Posner:[6]

1. A system for public reporting of completed transactions on a consolidated basis (consolidated tape)
2. A composite system for the collection and display of bid and asked quotations (composite quotation system)
3. Systems for transmitting from one market to another both orders to buy and sell securities and reports of completed transactions (market linkage systems)
4. Elimination of restrictions on the ability of exchange members to effect over-the-counter transactions in listed securities (off-board trading rules)
5. Nationwide protection of limit price orders against inferior execution in another market
6. Rules defining the securities that are qualified to be traded in the NMS

These six elements required changes in technology, legislative initiative, or both. For example, a consolidated tape, a composite quotation system, a market linkage system, and a system for nationwide protection of limit price orders required changes in technology. The elimination of off-board trading rules and specification of securities to be included in a national market system required legislative initiative. In fact, changes of both types occurred.

Overall, the general issue that the SEC faced was how to design the national market system. Should it be structured as an electronic linkage of existing exchange floors? Or should it be an electronic trading system that was not tied to any existing exchange? After experimentation with several pilot programs, the SEC developed a set of arrangements for listed stocks. These arrangements included the two following systems. The **Intermarket Trading System (ITS)**, whose operations began in April 1978, is an electronic system that displays the quotes posted on all the exchanges where a stock is listed, as well as in the OTC market, and provides for intermarket executions. The **Consolidated Quotation System** is a display system providing data on trades of listed

---

[6] N. S. Posner, "Restructuring the Stock Markets: A Critical Look at the SEC's National Market System," *New York University Law Review* (November/December 1981), p. 916.

stocks in different market centers. The implementation of these systems improved the intermarket trading and reduced fragmentation.

Even though addressing these Posner elements resulted in considerable progress, the initiatives, both technological and legislative, remain a work in progress.

Nasdaq Pricing Controversy   In 1994, economists William Christie and Paul Schultz raised a new issue about the behavior of dealers on the Nasdaq. They published research revealing that the quoted bid-ask spreads on a number of important Nasdaq stocks were frequently even-eighths, such as two-eighths, which equals $0.25 per share.[7] According to Christie and Schultz, the lack of odd-eighths quotes suggested the possibility that the dealers at least "implicitly" colluded to ensure high spreads and high profits for themselves. This research prompted a large class action lawsuit against many Nasdaq dealers, although numerous economists publicly expressed doubt that almost 500 dealers could secretly maintain a long-running, collusive arrangement.[8]

Influenced by the Christie-Schultz research, during 1994 the SEC and the Department of Justice (DOJ) alleged that several major dealers on the Nasdaq market conspired in a form of price-fixing that cost ordinary investors billions of dollars on their stock trades. These investigations discovered widespread abuse by the dealers (or market makers) that effectively kept the bid-offer spreads artificially wide.

One outcome of the SEC allegations was that during January 1997, the U.S. equity markets implemented two new order handling rules (OHR), which were intended to fundamentally change the way Nasdaq operated. The first OHR, known as the "Limit Order Display Rule," required that market makers display investors' limit orders in their quotes when they are priced better than the market maker quote. It meant that the best-priced limit orders are displayed to all market participants. The second rule, called the "Quote Rule," required market makers to publicly display their most competitive quotes to the public. Previously, market makers placed orders on proprietary systems that may have been more favorable than their public quotes. These proprietary system prices were available only to professionals. In addition to creating a more level playing field for individual investors, these order handling rules improved prices and narrowed spreads and further improved market liquidity and depth.

The final resolution of the SEC allegation was announced by the SEC on January 11, 1999, when the SEC fined 28 Wall Street firms a total of $26 million for the alleged Nasdaq price-rigging. In addition to the $26 million in civil fines, the firms also agreed to pay back alleged illegal profits of $792,000. The firms did not admit or deny wrongdoing. In addition, in its own settlement with the SEC in 1996, the NASD agreed to, among other things, spend $100 million over 5 years to improve market surveillance.

Other outcomes resulted from the Christie-Schultz controversy. The DOJ began an antitrust investigation of Nasdaq market makers, and the SEC began an investigation of the NASD. The DOJ investigation ended in a settlement with the market maker defendants. The SEC investigation of the NASD also ended in a settlement. According to the SEC settlement, the NASD, while neither admitting nor denying guilt, agreed to censure by the SEC and to strengthen its regulatory activity.

The work of Christie and Schultz may have also influenced an inquiry, led by former Senator Warren Rudman (New Hampshire), into restructuring the NASD. The Rudman Commission released its report in the fall of 1995. It concluded that self-regulation was indeed feasible. It also deemed, however, that in the case of the NASD,

[7]   William G. Christie and Paul Schultz, "Why Do Nasdaq Market Makers Avoid Odd-Eighths Quotes?" *Journal of Finance* (December 1994), pp. 1813–40.
[8]   William Powell, "Economists Group Says It's 'Skeptical' About Allegations of Nasdaq Collusion," *The Wall Street Journal* (September 19, 1995), p. A8.

more separation was needed between the regulatory arm of the NASD and the arm that operates and markets Nasdaq. It recommended that the NASD be divided into two primary subsidiaries, each with its own chief executive and with its own Board of Governors. The boards were to be composed of a membership of which at least 50% was drawn from outside the securities industry. The Rudman Commission recommendations were accepted and implemented by the NASD. In February 1996, a new subsidiary called NASD Regulation, Inc. (NASDR) began operation. In October 1996 the Nasdaq Stock Market, Inc. commenced.

SEC Cost Study   Nasdaq steadily improved its public image after the dealers' price-fixing scandal of the mid-1990s faded. On January 8, 2001, however, the SEC released a study indicating that for many types of orders, investors get worse prices when they trade on the Nasdaq than on the NYSE. The study was based on the cost of trading comparable stocks on the NYSE and Nasdaq during the week of June 5, 2000.

The SEC study found that for orders of 100 to 499 shares, the spread was between 5.7¢ and 10.9¢ per share wider for Nasdaq stocks for all but the largest stocks. Offsetting this negative finding for Nasdaq, the study found that on small orders of 100–499 shares, orders are executed 10–19 seconds faster on Nasdaq; on 500–1,999 share orders little difference was noted; and, on 2,000–4,999 share orders, the NYSE was faster by 29–47 seconds. The study also found that limit orders are filled more often on the NYSE than on Nasdaq.[9]

The study identified, however, structural differences between the NYSE and Nasdaq that could explain the cost differences. As discussed earlier in this chapter, the NYSE is a central agency auction market where more than 80% of the volume in its stocks is executed on the floor. This process maximizes the chances that a buyer will transact directly with a seller. In contrast, Nasdaq is decentralized or "fragmented," with no market maker or ECN responsible for a majority of the volume. Thus, dealers fill a much greater portion of the orders on Nasdaq (where they are called market makers) than on the NYSE (the specialist). As a result, for a Nasdaq stock the investor is less likely to do better than the quoted bid or ask (that is, receive "price improvement"), because the market maker captures the spread as profit. On the NYSE, however, buyers and sellers are typically matched at the bid, the ask, or in between. That means either the buyer, the seller, or both do better than the quoted spread.

Overall, dealers attempt to profit at the price at which they trade with customers, and their greater involvement on Nasdaq may lead to higher customer transaction costs. Thus, the disparity in trading costs may be due simply to differences between a "dealer" stock market such as Nasdaq and an "auction" market such as the NYSE.

Nasdaq proponents also point out that Nasdaq stocks are smaller (on average) and technology related, and such stocks are more volatile. It is argued that this characteristic accounts for the difference in trading costs.

DECIMALIZATION

On June 5, 1997, the NYSE voted to adopt a system of trading in decimals, that is with the minimum change being $0.01 (1 cent). At that time, the trading practice was using eighths. Although decimal trading was originally planned to be phased in beginning in 2000, the NYSE began trading in sixteenths (a spread of a 16th is equivalent to $6\frac{1}{4}$ cents), the so-called "teenies," on June 24, 1997.

---

9   Greg Ip and Michael Schroeder, "SEC Price Study Deals Blow to Nasdaq," *The Wall Street Journal* (January 9, 2001), pp. C1, C4; and Gretchen Morgenson, "A Friendlier Nasdaq: Work in Progress," *New York Times* (January 9, 2001), p. 1, 12.

In the eyes of some analysts, decimalization compares to the end of fixed commissions on May Day 1975. As a result of the May Day change, as already discussed, firms for the first time could compete on the basis of commissions, and price competition intensified. Although the outcome of decimalization is unlikely to be as severe as the outcome of the end of fixed commissions, undoubtedly spreads will decline. An additional benefit of decimalization provides a global uniformity of pricing; that is, U.S. securities will be denominated in the same decimal units as the rest of the world.

The NYSE and the AMEX began trading all their stocks in decimals on January 29, 2001, referred to as "Decimal Monday."[10] Nasdaq began trading all its shares in "pennies" on April 9, 2001.

One effect of decimalization may be that because of the increased number of prices at which a stock can trade, large orders will be transacted in many partial transactions rather than one large transaction. For example, if a 10,000 share (buy) trade was previously conducted via 7,000 shares at $30\frac{1}{4}$ and 3,000 at $30\frac{5}{16}$ the decimal system trade might instead be conducted in six separate transactions at six different decimal prices. This outcome may reduce the market depth at any single price (i.e., a decimal price) and cause brokerage houses to settle more trades (even for the same total trading volume).[11]

Although the actual market spread may not decrease up to 1 cent, it may decline significantly from $\frac{1}{16}$ (6.25¢). Of course, a decrease in the spread benefits both retail and institutional investors and is a negative for brokers, dealers, and market makers.

The introduction of decimal trading proved to be controversial, with the outcome yet to be seen. Some assert the NYSE specialists benefit unduly from decimalization by being able to step in front of large institutional orders in 1-cent increments.

REGULATION FD (FULL DISCLOSURE)

During 2000, the SEC approved a rule, over the objection of most Wall Street firms, that bars selective disclosure of material corporate information and makes it more readily available to individual investors. The rule went into effect on October 23, 2000. **Regulation FD (Fair Disclosure)**, a new selective disclosure rule, requires that information such as earnings and revenue estimates, which was typically distributed initially and selectively to equity analysts and institutional money managers, be made available to all investors at the same time.

In recent years, the Internet completely changed the way investors receive stock prices, quotes, and volume information. Whereas investors formerly obtained stock prices and quotes on a delayed basis in newspapers and other periodicals, investors can now access these data in "real time," just as the exchange and financial professionals do. Regulation FD requires that other company-specific information also be made available by the company to all investors at the same time, as are the prices and quotes in the markets. As a result, company-sponsored conference calls become much more important for professional analysts, because such conference calls, rather than private meetings with the company, may be their only venue for obtaining company data. Institutional investors, who previously received company information early via informal and nonpublic methods, claim that companies now withhold information until the formal release, and that the universal dissemination of the complete information at the same time tends to destabilize the markets. The outcome remains to be assessed.

---

[10] Michael A. Goldstein and Kenneth A. Kavajecz, "Eighths, Sixteenths, and Market Depth: Changes in Tick Size and Liquidity Provision on the NYSE," *Journal of Financial Economics* (April 2000), pp. 125–49.

[11] Jeff D. Opdyke, "NYSE Adds Decimals, Subtracts Fractions," *The Wall Street Journal* (January 29, 2001), pp. C1, C2.

SUPERMONTAGE

The SEC approved in January 2001 the Nasdaq's plan to centralize the display of its best stock quotes via a SuperMontage system. This plan was initially filed on October 1, 1999, and approved over considerable opposition from the ECNs and others who could lose business to Nasdaq.

SuperMontage makes the three best customer orders visible to investors on Nasdaq, thus increasing transparency. Prior to this plan, Nasdaq screens displayed only the single best buy-and-sell orders. Investors wanting the next-best quotes had to search the ECNs. The Nasdaq plan is designed to link the scattered markets created by the nine ECN screen-based networks and dozens of dealers fulfilling orders from their own inventories. ECNs and dealers can enter quotes on SuperMontage.[12]

Through SuperMontage, Nasdaq responded to changes resulting from the order-handling rules implemented by the SEC in 1997, which were intended to give investors access to the best quoted prices. The SuperMontage System makes Nasdaq more of a conventional stock exchange and less of a network of market makers by centralizing display of the market's stock quotes. By integrating better execution with deeper quote display, the new system also makes it harder for market makers to back away from their quotes.

◆ MAJOR INTERNATIONAL STOCK EXCHANGES

In this section we review the main characteristics of selected major international stock markets. Specifically, we look at stock exchanges in the United Kingdom, Germany, and Japan. We also provide a quick review of the stock exchange in China. Before discussing these exchanges, we address three related topics: the multiple listing on national markets, global depository receipts, and Euroequity issues.

MULTIPLE LISTINGS ON NATIONAL MARKETS

It is important to understand that stocks of corporations can be listed for trading on stock exchanges in other countries as well as an exchange in their own country. Stocks of some large corporations are listed on stock exchanges in several countries. As an example, the number of stocks of firms from other countries that were listed on the German national exchange (Deutsche Borse) as of year end 1999 was 7,682. German domestic companies only numbered 933. As another example, in the United Kingdom, the stocks of 1,945 domestic companies and 499 foreign companies were listed on the London Stock Exchange as of year end 1999.[13] Multiple listing of stocks is clearly an increasingly common phenomenon.

The readiness of an exchange to list and trade the shares of a foreign company varies by country and exchange according to its international orientation. Foreign firms that seek listing for their shares on U.S. exchanges may face additional costs in terms of disclosure standards. In other countries, however, regulations on the listing and trading of the stock of a foreign company are not as stringent.

A firm may want to list its shares on the exchanges of other countries for several reasons. Firms seek to diversify their sources of capital across national boundaries and

---

[12] Michael Schroeder and Greg Ip, "Plan to Upgrade Nasdaq Trading Passes the SEC," *The Wall Street Journal* (January 11, 2001), pp. C1, C20.

[13] This information was obtained from *The Salomon Smith Barney Guide to World Equity Markets, 2000* (Euromoney Books, 2000).

to tap various funds available globally for investment in new issues. In addition, firms may believe that an internationally varied ownership diminishes the prospect of takeover by other domestic concerns. Finally, firms may expect foreign listings to boost their name awareness and, as a result, the sales of their products.[14] Research tends to support these views of multiple listing. Firms whose shares are listed on exchanges in different countries tend to be quite large and to have a relatively substantial amount of foreign sales revenue.[15]

An important question is whether a share traded in different markets is subject to different prices in those markets. The answer is "no" because investors can buy or sell the shares in any of the markets, and they would arbitrage any meaningful differences in prices. If the price of a stock were significantly lower in country X than in country Y, investors would buy as many shares as they could in country X and sell shares in country Y. Investors would continue this strategy until the pressure they put on prices in both markets would drive the prices together. A decreasing gap in prices reduces the arbitrage profits. Investors stop arbitraging when profits due to the price differences equal the costs of the transactions. Therefore, when the various costs of the transactions, including commissions and taxes and costs of exchanging currencies, are fully acknowledged, the price of any share tends to be the same across the different markets where the stock is traded.

GLOBAL DEPOSITARY RECEIPTS

When a corporation's equities are traded in a foreign market, whether they were issued in the foreign market or not, they are typically in the form of a **global depositary receipt (GDR)**. GDRs are issued by banks as evidence of ownership of the underlying stock of a foreign corporation that the bank holds in trust. Each GDR may represent ownership of one or more shares of common stock of a corporation. The advantage of the GDR structure to the corporation is that the corporation does not have to comply with all the regulatory issuing requirements of the foreign country where the stock is to be traded. GDRs are typically, but not always, sponsored by the issuing corporation. That is, the issuing corporation works with a bank to offer its common stock in a foreign country via the sale of GDRs.

As an example, consider the U.S. version of the GDR, the American depositary receipt (ADR), discussed earlier in this chapter. The combination of GDRs and ADRs for a given company is called simply a DR (depositary receipt). The initial success of the ADR structure in the United States resulted in the rise of GDRs throughout the world. ADRs are denominated in U.S. dollars and pay dividends in U.S. dollars. Although ADRs are priced in U.S. dollars and their dividends are paid in U.S. dollars, the basis for these payments is the local currency of the underlying stock. Thus, a change in the exchange rate between the local currency of the underlying corporation and the U.S. dollar will affect the ADR's U.S. dollar price and dividend.

ADRs can be created in one of two ways. First, one or more banks or brokerage firms can assemble a large block of the shares of a foreign corporation and issue ADRs without the participation of the foreign corporation, which are called **nonsponsored ADRs**. The Bank of New York is the leading U.S. depositary bank for ADRs. More typically, however, with **sponsored ADRs**, the foreign corporation seeks to have its stock traded in the United States. In these instances, only one depositary bank issues the

---

[14] Bruno Solnik, *International Investments*, 2nd ed. (Reading, MA: Addison Wesley, 1991), pp. 112–13.

[15] Shahrokh M. Saudagran, "An Empirical Study of Selected Factors Influencing the Decision to List on Foreign Stock Exchanges," *Journal of International Business Studies* (Spring 1988), pp. 101–127.

ADRs. Periodic financial reports are provided by the issuing corporation in English to the holders of an ADR.

By construction, ADRs are not a direct holding in the company but a derivative created by a financial institution that holds the underlying securities. The holder of an ADR typically does not have voting or preemptive rights. The decision to treat ADR holders differently from direct stockholders, however, is at the discretion of the company. This distinction may sometimes not be applied.[16]

ADRs can either be traded on one of the two major organized stock exchanges (NYSE or AMEX) or traded in the over-the-counter market. The nonsponsored ADR is typically traded on the over-the-counter market. Because ADRs can be continuously created to meet investor demand, they provide the same trading liquidity as the home market securities they represent.

A U.S. investor who buys an ADR of an international company rather than hold the international stock directly can realize several advantages. First, the investor can trade the stock on a U.S. market (exchange or OTC) during U.S. hours and according to U.S. trading practices. Second, the investor makes and receives payments in U.S. dollars rather than foreign currency, although as already mentioned, the investor is subject to foreign exchange risk. Finally, the U.S. investor can use a U.S., rather than a global, custodian which can be easier and save costs and, in some cases, can avoid some country-specific taxes.

As U.S. investors, both institutional and individual, become more open to international investing, the popularity of U.S. ADRs increases significantly. The share volume of listed depository receipt programs (DRPs), a total of ADRs and GDRs, increased by 71% (from 16.8 billion shares to 28.7 billion shares) from 1999 to 2000 and the U.S. dollar volume by 78% (from $667 billion to $1,185 billion). The number of sponsored DR programs grew from 352 representing 24 countries in 1990 to more than 1,800 from 78 countries in 2001.[17]

EUROEQUITY

Corporations may issue equities outside their home market to finance subsidiaries in other countries or to reduce the cost of raising equity capital. In fact, new equity issues may be offered in more than one country simultaneously. The term **Euroequity** applies to a stock issue offered simultaneously in several countries by an international syndicate. In addition, U.S. corporations engage in equity offerings that, in addition to the primary U.S. component, include a portion of the issuance reserved for sale in the Euromarkets. This portion of a newly issued stock is referred to as a **Euroequity tranche**. Similarly, European firms offer equity securities with a U.S. tranche. The innovation of the Euroequity markets was not a matter of new equity securities or structures. Rather, the innovation consisted of an efficient international system for selling and distributing equity offerings to various markets in different countries at the same time.

UNITED KINGDOM

The London Stock Exchange (LSE) plays a vital role in maintaining London's position as one of the world's leading financial centers. One of the three major exchanges globally, it is also the world's leading international equity market, with more international companies listed and more international equities traded than on any other exchange.

---

16 Craig Karmin, "ADR Holders Find They Have Unequal Rights," *The Wall Street Journal* (March 1, 2001), pp. C1, C15.
17 The Bank of New York Web site, available at www.adrbny.com.

In 1973, all seven exchanges in the British Isles amalgamated to form the Stock Exchange of Great Britain and Ireland, with trading floors in London, Birmingham, Manchester, Liverpool, Glasgow, and Dublin. Regional trading floors in the United Kingdom ceased operations in the late 1980s, however, and all trading, even in regional stocks, was routed through the central market in London. In December 1995, the Dublin Stock Exchange separated from the United Kingdom exchange, which then became formally known as the London Stock Exchange.

Financial reform occurred in England in 1986. This reform was called the "Big Bang" after the astronomical theory that the universe originated from a gigantic explosion. The reforms centered on the LSE and were a response to the following factors:

1. The decline of the status of the British securities market (the LSE's volume was only a small fraction of that of New York and Tokyo)
2. The delayed response of the British securities markets to internationalization while foreign, mainly U.S., traders supplanted British firms in their own markets
3. Technological developments and the expansion of transactions occurring outside the exchange

As a result, several reforms were adopted during October 1986. One of the reforms was the liberalization of commissions, specifically abolishing minimum commissions. Another outcome of the reform was that during 1987 the LSE's trading floor system was closed and replaced by "screen" trading, that is, a dealer over-the-counter market. In October 1997, the introduction of the new order book transformed the way that the FTSE 100 shares, the major U.K. stock index (international stock indexes are discussed in the next chapter) are traded. Under the new system (called the Stock Exchange Trading Service, or SETS), when bid and ask prices match, orders are automatically executed against one another on the screen. Shares outside the FTSE 100 are traded using the quote-driven trading structure introduced during the Big Bang of 1986. This system is based on the competing market-maker system. Throughout the trading day, registered market makers are obliged to display to the market their bid and offer prices and the corresponding maximum sizes. These quotes are displayed on the exchange's SEAQ (Stock Exchange Automated Quotations) bulletin board.

GERMANY

Since 1991, the FSE has been operated by Frankfurt Wertpapierborsen AG (FWB). Although the exchange is denoted by FWB, it is commonly referred to as the FSE. In late 1992, the FWB was renamed the Deutsche Borse (DB) AG.

Technically, eight independent stock exchanges operate in Germany: Frankfurt, Dusseldorf, Munich, Hamburg, Berlin, Stuttgart, Hanover, and Bermen. However, they actually cooperate closely. Recently the stock exchanges of Frankfurt, Dusseldorf, and Munich extended their cooperation in order to establish uniform pricing mechanisms for the DAX 100 securities. (The DAX is an index described in the next chapter). Although these several regional exchanges exist, equity trading is highly concentrated in Frankfurt, where floor trading and electronic trading coexist for cash transactions. Each exchange operates three market segments: the official market, the regulated market, and the Neuer Market for smaller growth companies.

Owners or prospective buyers of securities can bring orders to the FSE only through a bank represented on the FSE because, according to the Banking Act, "the purchase and sale of securities for the accounts of others" is a banking transaction. Germany maintains minimum fees for brokered exchange transactions.

In November 1997, the exchange introduced a new electronic trading system, Xetra (Exchange Electronic Trading). Xetra is a modern, cost-efficient, order-driven trading system with automatic matching, which brings together wholesale and retail trading in a central order book. Limit and market orders (discussed in the next chapter) can be entered with various validity constraints, trading limits, and conditions for execution, and can be kept in the order book for up to one year. The order book, which is basically transparent, is designed to give all market participants the opportunity to react quickly to changes in the market while preserving their anonymity. In the event of sharp price swings, the system reacts with volatility interruptions to support price continuity.

JAPAN

The Japanese stock market's 120+ years of history began with the establishment of the Tokyo Stock Exchange (TSE) in 1878. During the 1980s, the Japanese securities market changed substantially with rapid deregulation and globalization. More recently, during November 1999, the TSE launched a new market, Mothers, for stocks of emerging companies with high growth potential in order to foster new companies and to provide investors with a wider range of investment products. This market adds to the shares listed on the TSE first and second sections (discussed below) and thereby offers investors a wider range of investment products.

Since March 2000, when the Hiroshima and Niigata exchanges were merged with the TSE, six stock exchanges operate in Japan. They are located in Tokyo, Osaka, Nagoya, Kyoto, Fukuoka, and Sapporo. Shares listed on the TSE are generally classified into either the *first section* or the *second section* depending principally upon size, turnover, and share ownership. At the end of 1999, more than 1,800 domestic companies were listed on the TSE, of which 1,364 were listed on the first section.

The TSE market is a continuous auction market where buy and sell orders directly interact with one another. The trading of shares is carried out under the "zaraba method," which is similar to an open outcry system. Prices are first established at the beginning of the trading session based on orders placed by regular members before the start of trading. The central book is kept by "Saitori members" who function solely as intermediaries between the regular members. They are not allowed to trade any listed stock for their own account, nor to accept orders from the investing public. After the opening price is established, Saitori members match orders in accordance with price priority and time precedence.

All securities must be traded through an authorized securities dealer who is a member of the Japan Securities Dealer's Association. The three main dealers are Nomura, Nikko, and Daiwa. Collectively these three firms handle the major portion of all transactions in shares by domestic securities companies. Transactions of all shares take place under the Computer-Assisted Order-Routing and Execution System (CORES). (The TSE closed its trading floor in April 1999.)

Until the late 1970s, Japan's financial markets were highly regulated. During November 1996, the Japanese Prime Minister proposed the Japanese version of the "Big Bang" to institute significant financial market reform and revitalize the Japanese financial market in order to make Tokyo competitive with New York and London by 2001. The Japanese Big Bang was known locally as "Kinyu biggo ban," literally "financial big bang."

In general, the goals of the Big Bang for the Japanese financial markets were to be "fair, free, and global." More specifically, the Big Bang reform included development of the following four general goals:

1. Free market that employs market principles
2. Fair and transparent market
3. Global market
4. A market less susceptible to domestic political pressures

More pragmatically, the Big Bang intended to lower the barriers separating banks, securities companies, and insurance companies, and to ease the regulation of the products financial companies offered and the fees that they could charge. The first step in the Big Bang deregulated the foreign exchange markets on April 6, 1998. This change enabled Japanese investors to invest more easily in other countries.

CHINA

China is the most populous country in the world, and even though its stock market is currently rudimentary, given the recent actual growth and the potential growth of the Chinese economy, China's stock market will inevitably be an important world stock market. Prior to February 2001, the Chinese stock market was divided into two types, A shares, which were restricted to Chinese investors, and B shares, which were reserved for foreign (non-Chinese) investors. The A share market was denominated in Chinese yuan (which are nonconvertible) and was much larger than the B share market. Although large, the A share market was primarily limited to state-owned companies; private companies' access to the larger A share market was limited.

The B share market was started in 1991 to give private companies and entrepreneurs access to foreign capital (although it is subject to government listing requirements) and to give foreigners with hard currency the opportunity to invest in Chinese companies. Shanghai B-shares are quoted in U.S. dollars and Shenzen B-shares are quoted in Hong Kong dollars, even though these two currencies are linked. The B share market, however, never developed and grew as the Chinese government intended. It listed only 114 shares as of the beginning of 2001. In fact, B share trading was not dominated by foreigners but by Chinese using various ploys. Another indication of the lack of success of the B share market was that the prices of the few companies listed on both the A and B share markets were considerably higher on the A share market.

In addition, Chinese disclosure and accounting standards, which foreign investors have deemed inadequate, led to offerings of Chinese shares in Hong Kong (called "H shares"). Finally, "red chips"—that is, Hong Kong companies with strong Chinese ties—were traded in Hong Kong.

As a result of these failings in the B share market and China's increasing participation in the global markets of all types, during February 2001 the Chinese government legalized Chinese ownership of B shares and Chinese investors were allowed to transfer foreign currencies into a trading account under new rules by the China Securities Regulator Commissions (CSRC) to fund these purchases. In addition, all Chinese companies, private and state-owned, were permitted to sell either A or B shares. Thus, Chinese investors were given more access to the Class B market and companies more access to the Class A market. In fact, these changes could cause an amalgamation of the Class A, B, and H markets.[18] The initial trading in B shares after the implementation of these policies on February 28, 2001, was quite volatile. At the time of this writing, however, the success of these new regulations could not be evaluated.[19]

---

[18] Leslie P. Norton, "China Moves Toward Reducing Stock-Trading Complexity," *Barron's* (February 26, 2001), p. MW 17; and Craig S. Smith, "Chinese Investors May Get Access to Wider Market," *New York Times* (February 21, 2001), p. C1.

[19] Craig S. Smith, "Hot Trading in B Shares Chills Rapidly for Chinese," *New York Times* (March 8, 2001), p. W1.

◆ DEALERS IN MAJOR MARKETS[20]

A continuous stock market can actually take two forms, according to how the dealer's function is carried out. In one form adopted by the organized U.S. stock exchanges such as the NYSE and AMEX, the exchange designates a specialist for specific shares who is the sole market maker or dealer for those shares. The second form is the competitive dealer system like the one found in the U.S. over-the-counter or Nasdaq market. Here, several dealers may be market makers for any stock, and the dealers do not have a special authorization from the exchange to play this role.

Outside the United States, the specialist system appears only in the Montreal Exchange. The Amsterdam Stock Exchange gives certain firms specialist status and duties; a firm of this type is called a *hoekman*. The hoekman is responsible for acting as market maker only for trades of small to moderate size, and large trades are managed by the transacting parties themselves. Market makers on the Toronto Stock Exchange are similar to specialists. Limited in number and selected by the exchange, these registered traders trade for their own accounts and try to create orderly price changes in stocks that the exchange assigns to them. Also, these traders are obligated to post bid and ask prices all through the day and to keep their bid-ask spreads rather small.

Aside from these exceptions, all continuous markets in the world employ some version of the competitive dealer mechanism. The London Stock Exchange is a good example of a full-scale commitment to this approach. On the LSE, any well-capitalized firm that abides by certain regulations can enter the competition as a dealer on any security. Market makers publish firm bid-ask quotes for their stocks in standardized lots. More than 10 dealers represent the majority of the large and actively traded shares.

The Tokyo Stock Exchange employs a variation of the competitive dealer system. A broker, called a *saitori,* functions as an intermediary between the dealers and the brokers who are members of the exchange. The saitoris cannot buy or sell for their own accounts but rather arrange transactions among dealers. Saitoris also conduct the auctions during the trading day and match buy and sell orders submitted by the brokers on behalf of their own accounts or those of their clients.

Dealers in London tend to take larger positions—they commit more of their capital than do American dealers.[21] Also, the London SEAQ system does not quote the full size of an offered block trade, thus protecting block traders from a disclosure of their needs to potential parties on the other side of the trades. For these reasons, while block trading in London also uses negotiation among institutions, the trades go through the computerized trading system in the normal manner. Because the CATS system of Toronto and Paris provides more information about bids than does London's SEAQ, it discloses more about block trades (discussed in the next chapter) than those initiating the trades generally want to disclose. Thus, block traders do not find Paris and Toronto well suited to block trades, and large institutional trades flow toward New York and London. In response, the Paris Bourse is experimenting with more off-exchange trading of large orders.

---

[20]   Robert A. Schwartz, *Reshaping the Equity Markets: A Guide for the 1990's* (New York: Harper Business, 1991) contains more information on large markets around the world.

[21]   Roger D. Huang and Hans R. Stoll, *Major World Equity Markets* (New York: New York University Salomon Center Monograph in Finance and Economics, 1991), p. 49.

Summary

Common stock represents an ownership interest in a corporation. In the United States, secondary trading of common stock occurs in one or more of the following trading locations: two major national stock exchanges (the NYSE and AMEX), five regional stock exchanges, and the OTC market (Nasdaq system). More recent alternative trading systems, which include electronic communication networks and cross-trading networks, permit a new type of stock trading.

An important structural difference between exchanges and the OTC market is that exchanges use only one market maker, or dealer, per stock, the specialist, however, no restrictions are imposed on the number of dealers per stock in the OTC market. The markets mandate obligations by both types of market makers, although these obligations differ substantially.

Issuers of common stock issue their shares internationally to reduce financing costs, broaden their ownership, and improve their brand internationally. Listing their shares in other countries via GDRs and ADRs helps accomplish these objectives. Methods of trading vary considerably throughout the world. Electronically assisted market-maker trading has become prevalent throughout the world. The NYSE and the other U.S. exchanges are among the few markets to have a trading floor and trade via the auction method with specialists. Thus, the market-maker system has become more common and the specialist system less common. Exchanges in Europe and throughout the world model their exchanges after Nasdaq, thus permitting the trading of the shares of newer and smaller companies.

Key Terms

- Agent
- Alternative trading systems (ATSs)
- American depository receipts (ADRs)
- Auction system
- Book
- Central auction specialist system
- Commission broker
- Consolidated quotation system
- Crossing networks
- Discount broker
- Dually listed stock
- Electronic communications networks (ECNs)
- Euroequity
- Euroequity tranche
- Exchanges
- Fourth market
- Fragmented market
- Global depository receipt (GDR)
- Hit-and-take system
- Imbalance
- Independent floor broker
- Intermarket Trading System (ITS)
- Limit order book
- Listed Stocks
- Member
- Multiple market maker system
- Negotiated system
- Nonsponsored ADRs
- OTC bulletin board (OTCBB)
- Over-the-counter (OTC) trading
- Principal
- Registered traders
- Regulation FD (fair disclosure)
- Seat
- Specialist
- Sponsored ADRs
- Third market
- Trading floors

Questions

1. "Stocks traded on the Nasdaq are nonlisted stocks." Explain why you agree or disagree with this statement.
2. When the NYSE refers to a "fair and orderly market," what does it mean?
3. What is meant by the "pink sheets" and the "bulletin board"?
4. a. What is an ECN?
   b. Give three examples of ECNs.
5. This quotation is from a 1990 interview appearing in The *New York Times* with William Donaldson, then chairman of the New York Stock Exchange:

   There's a need to understand the advantages of an auction market versus a dealer market. The auction market allows a buyer and a seller to get together and agree on a price and the dealer is not involved at all. That's opposed to a dealer market where the house is on both sides of the trade and the dealer makes the spread rather than having the spread shared by the buyer and the seller. One of the things we're coming to the forefront on now is the whole idea of what makes a good market. I think the best market is where you have the maximum number of people coming together in a single location and bidding against each other. . . . That is far superior to what we are getting now, which is a fractionalization of the market: traders on machines, trades in the closet, trades in many areas where buyers and sellers don't have the opportunity to meet.

Discuss Donaldson's opinion. In your answer be sure to address the pros and cons of the different trading locations and practices addressed in the chapter.

6. a. What do crossing networks seek to do?
   b. Give two examples of crossing networks.
7. What is Rule 144A?
8. What factors led to the development of the third market?
9. a. What is a Euroequity issue and a Euroequity tranche?
   b. What is the most important innovation that Euroequities have achieved?
10. Some stocks are listed on several exchanges around the world. Give two reasons why a firm might want its stock to be listed on an exchange in the firm's home country as well as on exchanges in other countries.
11. a. Identify the types of trades for which many markets use the call auction method.
    b. Why do markets tend to favor continuous methods for the pricing of actively traded stocks?
    c. Can you name and distinguish the two methods of auction used by the Tokyo Stock Exchange?
12. a. What does the term *first section* mean on the Tokyo Stock Exchange?
    b. What are "Mothers"?
13. a. What is a GDR?
    b. How does a GDR facilitate issuance of a domestic firm's securities in a foreign country?
14. What are the differences between a sponsored and an unsponsored GDR?

CHAPTER 14

Common Stock Market: II*

Learning Objectives

After reading this chapter you will understand:

◆ the reasons for significant structural changes in the stock market.

◆ trading mechanisms such as the types of orders, short selling, and margin transactions.

◆ the different types of transaction costs.

◆ trading arrangements to accommodate institutional traders such as block trades and program trades.

◆ what the upstairs market is and its role in institutional trading.

◆ price limits and collars imposed by exchanges.

◆ the role played by stock market indicators and how those indicators are constructed.

◆ various stock market indicators of interest to market participants.

◆ evidence on the pricing efficiency of the stock market.

◆ the implications of pricing efficiency for a common stock strategy.

◆ the correlation of the price movements of world equity markets and the implications for international investing.

In the previous chapter we looked at the major trading locations for common stock in both the United States and selected countries outside of the United States. In this chapter we focus on trading mechanics, transaction costs, stock market indexes, evidence on pricing efficiency, and the implications of pricing efficiency for the development of investment strategies.

◆ TRADING MECHANICS

Trading mechanics involve the types of orders placed by investors. We begin with the types of orders, trading priority rules, and transaction costs. We then discuss trading arrangements for retail trading and those for institutional investors (block trades and program trades) for coping with the trading needs of institutional investors.

---

* This chapter is coauthored with Frank J. Jones and is based on material developed by Frank J. Fabozzi, Frank J. Jones, and Robert Johnson, Jr. "Common Stock" in Frank J. Fabozzi (ed.), *The Handbook of Financial Instruments* (New York: John Wiley & Son, 2002).

TYPES OF ORDERS AND TRADING PRIORITY RULES

When an investor wants to buy or sell a share of common stock, the price and conditions under which the order is to be executed must be communicated to a broker. The simplest type of order is the **market order**, an order to be executed at the best price available in the market. If the stock is listed and traded on an organized exchange, the best price is assured by the exchange rule that when more than one order on the same side of the buy/sell transaction reaches the market at the same time, the order with the best price is given priority. Thus, buyers bidding a higher price are given priority over those bidding a lower price; sellers offering a lower price are given priority over those offering a higher price.

Another priority rule of exchange trading is needed to handle receipt of more than one order at the same price. Most often, the priority in executing such orders is based on the time of arrival of the order—first orders in are the first orders executed—although higher priority is given to certain types of market participants over other types of market participants seeking to transact at the same price. For example, on exchanges, orders can be classified as either public orders or orders of those member firms dealing for their own account (both nonspecialists and specialists). Exchange rules require that public orders be given priority over orders of member firms dealing for their own account.

The danger of a market order is that an adverse price movement may take place between the time the investor places the order and the time the order is executed. To avoid this danger, the investor can place a **limit order** that designates a price threshold for the execution of the trade. A **buy limit order** indicates that the stock may be purchased only at the designated price or lower. A **sell limit order** indicates that the stock may be sold at the designated price or higher. The key disadvantage of a limit order is it offers no guarantee it will be executed at all; the designated price may simply not be obtainable. A limit order that is not executable at the time it reaches the market is recorded in a **limit order book**, mentioned in the previous chapter.

The limit order is a **conditional order**: It is executed only if the limit price or a better price can be obtained. Another type of conditional order is the **stop order**, which specifies that the order is not to be executed until the market moves to a designated price, at which time it becomes a market order. A **buy stop order** specifies that the order is not to be executed until the market rises to a designated price, that is, until it trades at or above, or is bid at or above, the designated price. A **sell stop order** specifies that the order is not to be executed until the market price falls below a designated price, that is, until it trades at or below, or is offered at or below, the designated price. A stop order is useful when an investor cannot watch the market constantly. Profits can be preserved or losses minimized on a stock position by allowing market movements to trigger a trade. In a sell (buy) stop order, the designated price is lower (higher) than the current market price of the stock. In a sell (buy) limit order, the designated price is higher (lower) than the current market price of the stock. The relationship between the two types of conditional orders, and the market movements that trigger them, appear in Table 14-1.

Two dangers are associated with stop orders. Stock prices sometimes exhibit abrupt price changes, so the direction of a change in a stock price may be quite temporary, resulting in the premature trading of a stock. Also, once the designated price is reached, the stop order becomes a market order and is subject to the uncertainty of the execution price noted earlier for market orders.

A **stop-limit order**, a hybrid of a stop order and a limit order, is a stop order that designates a price limit. In contrast to the stop order, which becomes a market order if the stop is reached, the stop-limit order becomes a limit order if the stop is reached.

TABLE 14-1 Conditional Orders and the Direction of Triggering Security Price Movements

Price of Security	Limit Order	Market-if-Touched Order	Stop-Limit Order	Stop Order
Higher price	Price specified for a sell limit order	Price specified for a sell market if touched order	Price specified for a limit buy stop order	Price specified for a buy stop order
Current Price				
Lower Price	Price specified for a buy limit order	Price specified for a buy market if touched order	Price specified for a sell stop-limit order	Price specified for a sell stop order
Comment	Can be filled only at price or better; does not become a market order until price is reached	Becomes market order when price is reached	Does not become a market order when price is reached; can be executed only at price or better	Becomes market order when price is reached

The stop-limit order can be used to cushion the market impact of a stop order. The investor may limit the possible execution price after the activation of the stop. As with a limit order, the limit price may never be reached after the order is activated, which therefore defeats one purpose of the stop order—to protect a profit or limit a loss.

An investor may also enter a **market-if-touched order**. This order becomes a market order if a designated price is reached. A market-if-touched order to buy becomes a market order if the market falls to a given price, while a stop order to buy becomes a market order if the market price rises to a given price. Similarly, a market-if-touched order to sell becomes a market order if the market rises to a specified price, while the stop order to sell becomes a market order if the market falls to a given price. We can think of the stop order as an order designed to get out of an existing position at an acceptable price (without specifying the exact price), and the market-if-touched order as an order designed to get into a position at an acceptable price (also without specifying the exact price).

Orders may be placed to buy or sell at the open or the close of trading for the day. An **opening order** indicates a trade to be executed only in the opening range for the day, and a **closing order** indicates a trade is to be executed only within the closing range for the day.

An investor may enter orders that contain order cancellation provisions. A **fill-or-kill order** must be executed as soon as it reaches the trading floor or it is immediately canceled. Orders may designate the time period for which the order is effective—a day, week, or month, or perhaps by a given time within the day. An **open order**, or **good until canceled order**, is good until the investor specifically terminates the order.

Orders are also classified by their size. One **round lot** is typically 100 shares of a stock. An **odd lot** is defined as less than a round lot. For example, an order of 75 shares of Digital Equipment Corporation (DEC) is an odd lot order. An order of 350 shares of DEC includes an odd lot portion of 50 shares. A **block trade** is defined on the NYSE as an order of 10,000 shares of a given stock or a total market value of $200,000 or more.

Both the major national stock exchanges and the regional stock exchanges have systems for routing orders of a specified size (submitted by brokers) through a computer directly to the specialists' posts where the orders can be executed. On the NYSE, this system is the SuperDot (Super Designated Order Turnaround) system. The

AMEX's Post Execution Reporting system allows orders up to 2,000 shares to be routed directly to specialists. The regional stock exchanges have computerized systems for routing small orders to specialists. The Small Order Execution system of the Nasdaq routes and executes orders up to 1,000 shares of a given stock.

SHORT SELLING

Short selling involves the sale of a security not owned by the investor at the time of sale. The investor can arrange to have her broker borrow the stock from someone else, and the borrowed stock is delivered to implement the sale. To cover her short position, the investor must subsequently purchase the stock and return it to the party that loaned the stock.

Let us look at an example of how short selling is done in the stock market. Suppose Ms. Stokes believes that Wilson Steel common stock is overpriced at $20 per share and wants to be in a position to benefit if her assessment is correct. Ms. Stokes calls her broker, Mr. Yats, indicating that she wants to sell 100 shares of Wilson Steel. Mr. Yats will do two things: (1) sell 100 shares of Wilson Steel on behalf of Ms. Stokes and (2) arrange to borrow 100 shares of that stock to deliver to the buyer. Suppose that Mr. Yats is able to sell the stock for $20 per share and borrows the stock from Mr. Jordan. The shares borrowed from Mr. Jordan will be delivered to the buyer of the 100 shares. The proceeds from the sale (ignoring commissions) will be $2,000. However, the proceeds do not go to Ms. Stokes because she has not given her broker the 100 shares. Thus, Ms. Stokes is said to be "short 100 shares."

Now, suppose 1 week later the price of Wilson Steel stock declines to $15 per share. Ms Stokes may instruct her broker to buy 100 shares of Wilson Steel. The cost of buying the shares (once again ignoring commissions) is $1,500. The shares purchased are then delivered to Mr. Jordan, who loaned 100 shares to Ms. Stokes. At this point, Ms. Stokes sold 100 shares and bought 100 shares, so she no longer has any obligation to her broker or to Mr. Jordan—she covered her short position. She is entitled to the funds in her account that were generated by the selling and buying activity. She sold the stock for $2,000 and bought it for $1,500. Thus, she realizes a profit before commissions of $500. From this amount, commissions are subtracted.

Two more costs reduce the profit further. First, a fee is charged by the lender of the stock. Second, for any dividends paid by Wilson Steel while the stock is borrowed, Ms. Stokes must compensate Mr. Jordan for the dividends to which he was entitled as actual owner of the stock.

If, instead of falling, the price of Wilson Steel stock rises, Ms. Stokes realizes a loss when she is forced to cover her short position. For example, if the price rises to $27, Ms. Stokes loses $700, to which must be added commissions and the cost of borrowing the stock (and possibly dividends).

Exchanges impose restrictions as to when a short sale may be executed; these so-called **tick-test rules** are intended to prevent investors from destabilizing the price of a stock when the market price is falling. A short sale can be made only when either (1) the sale price of the particular stock is higher than the last trade price (referred to as an uptick trade), or (2) if there is no change in the last trade price of the particular stock (referred to as a zero uptick), the previous trade price must be higher than the trade price that preceded it. For example, if Ms. Stokes wanted to short Wilson Steel at a price of $20, and the two previous trade prices were $20\frac{1}{8}$, and then $20, she could not do so at this time because of the uptick trade rule. If the previous trade prices were $19\frac{7}{8}$, $19\frac{7}{8}$ and then $20, she could short the stock at $20 because of the uptick trade rule. Suppose that the sequence of the last three trades is: $19\frac{7}{8}$, $20, and $20. Ms. Stokes could short the stock at $20 because of the zero uptick rule.

MARGIN TRANSACTIONS

Investors can borrow cash to buy securities and use the securities themselves as collateral. For example, suppose Mr. Boxer wants to invest $10,000 and is considering buying Wilson Steel, which is currently selling for $20 per share. With his $10,000 Mr. Boxer can buy 500 shares. Suppose his broker can arrange for him to borrow an additional $10,000 so that Mr. Boxer can buy an additional 500 shares. Thus, with a $20,000 investment, he can purchase a total of 1,000 shares. The 1,000 shares will be used as collateral for the $10,000 borrowed, and Mr. Boxer will have to pay interest on the amount borrowed.

A transaction in which an investor borrows to buy shares using the shares themselves as collateral is called *buying on margin.* By borrowing funds, an investor creates financial leverage. Note that Mr. Boxer, for a $10,000 investment, realizes the consequences associated with a price change of 1,000 shares rather than 500 shares. He benefits if the price rises but is worse off if the price falls (compared to borrowing no funds).

To illustrate, we now look at what happens if the price subsequently changes. If the price of Wilson Steel rises to $29 per share, ignoring commissions and the cost of borrowing, Mr. Boxer realizes a profit of $9 per share on 1,000 shares, or $9,000. Had Mr. Boxer not borrowed $10,000 to buy the additional 500 shares, his profit would be only $4,500. Suppose, instead, the price of Wilson Steel stock decreases to $13 per share. Then, by borrowing to buy 500 additional shares, he lost $7 per share on 1,000 shares instead of $7 per share on just 500 shares.

The funds borrowed to buy the additional stock will be provided by the broker, and the broker gets the money from a bank. The interest rate that banks charge brokers for funds for this purpose is named the **call money rate** (also labeled the broker loan rate). The broker charges the borrowing investor the call money rate plus a service charge.

Setting Initial Margin Requirements   The broker is not free to lend as much as it wishes to the investor to buy securities. The Securities Exchange Act of 1934 prohibits brokers from lending more than a specified percentage of the market value of the securities. The initial margin requirement is the proportion of the total market value of the securities that the investor must pay as an equity share, and the remainder is borrowed from the broker. The 1934 act gives the Board of Governors of the Federal Reserve (the Fed) the responsibility to set initial margin requirements, which it does under Regulations T and U. The Fed changes margin requirements as an instrument of economic policy. The initial margin requirement was previously below 40%; it is 50% as of this writing. Initial margin requirements vary for stocks and bonds.

Maintenance Margin   The Fed also establishes a maintenance margin requirement, which is the minimum proportion of the equity in the investor's margin account to the total market value. If the investor's margin account falls below the minimum maintenance margin (which would happen if the share's price fell), the investor is required to put up additional cash. The investor receives a margin call from the broker specifying the additional cash to be put into the investor's margin account. If the investor fails to put up the additional cash, the broker has the authority to sell the securities for the investor's account.

Let us illustrate maintenance. Assume an investor buys 100 shares of stock at $60 per share for $6,000 of stock on 50% margin and the maintenance margin is 25%. By purchasing $6,000 of stock on 50% margin, the investor must put up $3,000 of cash (or other equity) and, thus, borrows $3,000 (referred to as the debit balance). The investor, however, must maintain 25% of margin. To what level must the stock price decline to hit the maintenance margin level? The price is $40. At this price, the stock position has a value of $4,000 ($40 × 100 shares). With a loan of $3,000, the equity in the account is

TABLE 14-2   Margin Summary Position

Margin	Long	Short
Initial	50%	50%
Maintenance	25%	30%
Multiple of debit (long) or credit (short) balance to require maintenance	4/3	10/13

$1,000 ($4,000 − $3,000), or 25% of the account value ($1,000/$4,000 = 25%). If the price of the stock decreases below $40, the investor must deposit more equity to bring the equity level up to 25%. In general, the account level has to decrease to $\frac{4}{3}$ (1.333) times the amount borrowed (the debit balance) to hit the minimum maintenance margin level.

Margin practices also apply in short selling. Consider a similar margin example for a short position. An investor shorts (borrows and sells) 100 shares of stock at $60 for total stock value of $6,000. With an initial margin of 50%, the investor must deposit $3,000 (in addition to leaving the $6,000 from the sale in the account). This leaves the investor with a credit balance of $9,000 (which does not change with the stock price since it is in cash). However, the investor owes 100 shares of the stock at the current market price. To what level must the stock price increase to hit the maintenance margin level, assumed to be 30% (which is the equity in the account as a percentage of the market value of the stock)? The answer is $69.23, for a total stock value of $6,923. If the stock is worth $6,923, the account contains $2,077 of equity ($9,000 − $6,923), which represents 30% of the market value of the stock ($2,077/$6,923 = 30%). The value of the stock that triggered the maintenance level is calculated by multiplying the credit balance by $\frac{10}{13}$ ($\frac{10}{13}$ × $9,000 = $6,923).

A summary of the long (i.e., stock purchased) and short margin requirements is provided in Table 14-2.

TRANSACTION COSTS

Investment managers must meet performance standards, which are typically based on the total rate of return of their portfolios. The returns on their portfolios are net of transaction (or trading) costs. One-half of one percentage point in return can substantially affect a manager's record. Therefore, an important aspect of an investment strategy is controlling the transaction costs necessary to implement the strategy. The measurement of trading costs, although important, is difficult.[1]

We begin by defining trading costs. Trading costs can be decomposed into two major components: explicit costs and implicit costs. **Explicit trading costs** are the direct costs of trading, such as broker commissions, fees, and taxes. **Implicit trading costs** represent such indirect costs as the price impact of the trade and the opportunity costs of failing to execute in a timely manner or at all. Whereas explicit costs are associated with identifiable accounting charges, no such reporting of implicit costs occurs.

EXPLICIT COSTS

The main explicit cost is the commission paid to the broker for execution. Commission costs are fully negotiable and vary systematically by broker type and

[1]   For more on this point, see Bruce M. Collins and Frank J. Fabozzi, "A Methodology for Measuring Transactions Costs," *Financial Analysts Journal* (March/April 1991), pp. 27–36.

market mechanism. The commission may depend on both the price per share and the number of shares in the transaction. In addition to commissions, other explicit costs include custodial fees (the fees charged by an institution that holds securities in safe-keeping for an investor) and transfer fees (the fees associated with transferring an asset from one owner to another).

In general, commissions began a downward trend in 1975, which continued through 1996, when it reached 4.5¢ per share. Based on a study by the Plexus Group, after increasing during 1997, commissions reached 4.5¢ per share again in the first quarter of 1999. Only small, easily traded orders continued to become cheaper, not the larger and more difficult trades. Commissions for larger trades (10,000 shares or more) remained relatively stable at about 4.8¢ per share. Commissions for trades under 10,000 shares, on the other hand, declined to 2.8¢ per share.[2]

The Plexus Group study also found that the commission on capital-committing trades—trades that require a commitment of the dealer's own capital to accomplish the trade rather than simply executing the trade by matching two customer orders on an agency basis—experienced no decline. Investors should expect to pay for the use of the dealer's capital and the associated risk. Similarly, soft dollar trades, discussed next, require high and stable commissions. Consequently, investors may be penalized for not being able to "shop around" for lower commissions. Overall, it was the commissions on the agency trades (trades on which the dealer need not commit capital) and nonsoft dollar trades (for which the customer can shop around) that declined the most and remain the lowest.

Two other issues relate to transaction costs: soft dollars and payment for order flow.

Soft Dollars   Investors often choose their broker/dealer based on who will give them the best execution at the lowest transaction cost on a specific transaction, and also based on who will provide complementary services (such as research) over a period of time. Order flow can also be "purchased" by a broker/dealer from an investor with "soft dollars." In this case, the broker/dealer provides the investor, without charge, services such as research or electronic services, typically from a third party, for which the investor would otherwise pay "hard dollars" to the third party, in exchange for the investor's order flow. Of course, the investor pays the broker/dealer for the execution service.

According to such a relationship, the investor preferentially routes orders to the broker/dealer specified in their soft dollar relationship and does not pay "hard dollars," or real money, for the research or other services. This practice is called paying soft dollars (i.e., directing their order flow) for the ancillary research. For example, client A preferentially directs its order flow to broker/dealer B (often a specified amount of order flow over a specified period, such as a month or year) and pays the broker/dealer for these execution services. In turn, broker/dealer B pays for some research services provided to client A. Very often the research provider is a separate firm, say, firm C. Thus, soft dollars refer to money paid by an investor to a broker/dealer or a third party through commission revenue rather than by direct payments.

The disadvantage to the broker/dealer is that they pay hard dollars (to the research provider) for the client's order flow. The client is disadvantaged by not being free to "shop around" for the best bid or best offer, net of commissions, for all their

---

2   Plexus Group, "Withering Commissions, Winning Brokers: Who Will Survive?"

transactions, when the client commits to an agreed amount of volume of transactions with the specific broker/dealer. In addition, the research provider may give a preferential price to the broker/dealer. Thus, each of these participants in the soft dollar relationship experiences some advantage, but also an offsetting disadvantage.

The SEC imposes formal and informal limitations on the type and amount of soft dollar business institutional investors can conduct. For example, even though an institutional investor can accept research in a soft dollar relationship, they cannot accept furniture or vacations. SEC disclosure rules, passed in 1995, require investment advisors to disclose, among other things, the details on any product or services received through soft dollars.

Payment for Order Flow   In payment for order flow arrangements, an OTC market maker may offer a cash payment to other brokerage firms with customer order flow in exchange for the right to execute the broker's order flow, thus providing a reason for the broker preferencing trades to certain market makers for each stock. Such payment for order flow occurs mainly on Nasdaq, where several market makers cover each stock. Rebates are typically on a per-share basis, historically about 2¢ a share.

The reasons for payment for order flow remain controversial. One possible reason is that the traditional minimum quote increment, $\frac{1}{8}$, was too large and that payment for order flow permits, in effect, smaller quote increments. If so, the advent of decimalization should reduce payment for order flow.

A second potential reason for payment for order flow is that it is a device for price discrimination based on the information content of the order. Specifically, market makers may pay for orders placed by "uninformed traders," and hence are more profitable to execute; but may not pay for orders placed by "informed traders," which are less profitable. In general, retail order flow is considered to be uninformed, and institutional and professional order flow to be informed. In fact, most payment for order flow arrangements are with retail brokerage houses and the average size of purchased orders is significantly below the overall average trade size. Obviously small retail trades are preferred by the market makers who pay for order flow. The data appear consistent with the uninformed/informed trader hypothesis.

Intermarket market-maker competition and interexchange competition via payment for order flow remain controversial.[3] The relevant policy question is whether the retail broker/dealers are diverted from sending their retail orders to the best markets, thereby disadvantaging the customers, or whether a portion of the payment accrues to the customer, thereby benefiting the customer. Overall, both soft dollars and payment for order flow continue to spark debate.

IMPLICIT COSTS

Implicit trading costs include impact costs, timing costs, and opportunity costs.

Impact Costs   The impact cost of a transaction is the change in market price due to supply/demand imbalances caused by the presence of the trade. Bid-ask spread estimates, although informative, fail to capture the fact that large trades—those that exceed the number of shares the market maker is willing to trade at the quoted bid and ask prices—may move prices in the direction of the trade. That is, large trades may increase the price for buy orders and decrease the price for sell orders. The resulting

---

[3]   Floyd Norris, "Wall St. Said to Gain Most in Policy Shift," *New York Times* (December 20, 2000), pp. C1,C6.

market impact or price impact of the transaction can be thought of as the deviation of the transaction price from the "unperturbed price" that would prevail if the trade did not occur. Crossing networks discussed in the previous chapter are designed to minimize impact costs.

Timing Cost   The timing cost is measured as the price change between the time the parties to the implementation process assume responsibility for the trade and the time they complete the responsibility. Timing costs occur when orders sit on the trading desk of a buy side firm (e.g., an investment management firm), but are not yet released to the broker because the trader fears that the trade may swamp the market.

Opportunity Costs   The opportunity cost is the "cost" of securities not traded. This cost results from missed or only partially completed trades. These costs are the natural consequence of the release delays. For example, if the price moves too much before the trade can be completed, the manager will not make the trade. In practice, this cost is measured on shares not traded based on the difference between the market price at the time of decision and the closing price 30 days later.

Although commissions and impact costs are actual and visible out-of-pocket costs, opportunity costs and timing costs are the costs of forgone opportunities and are invisible. Opportunity costs can arise for two reasons. First, some orders are executed with a delay, during which the price moves against the investor. Second, some orders incur an opportunity cost because they are only partially filled or are not executed at all.

CLASSIFICATION OF TRADING COSTS

We thus far classified four main trading costs—commissions, impact costs, timing costs, and opportunity costs—as explicit and implicit trading costs. This categorization is based on whether the costs are identifiable accounting costs. Another categorization of these costs is execution costs versus opportunity costs, based on whether the trades are completed. A schematic diagram of trading costs using this categorization is shown in Figure 14-1.

FIGURE 14-1   Diagram of Types of Trading Costs

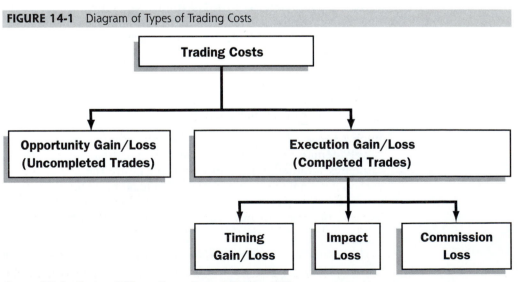

Source: "Alpha Capture," *Plexus Group,* Second Quarter, 1999.

The categorization of the four costs according to the two criteria is as follows:

Explicit vs. Implicit	Execution vs. Opportunity
Explicit	*Visible*
Commission	Commission
	Impact
Implicit	*Invisible*
Impact	Timing
Timing	Opportunity
Opportunity	

RESEARCH ON TRANSACTION COSTS

Overall, while the trading commission is the most obvious, measurable, and discussed trading cost, it is only one of the four types of trading costs and, in fact, may be the smallest. The implicit trading costs, however, are much more difficult to measure.

Recent studies in transaction costs allow several conclusions. They are:

1. Although considerable debate still surrounds how to measure trading costs, the consensus is that implicit trading costs are economically significant relative to explicit costs (and also relative to realized portfolio returns).
2. Equity trading costs vary systematically with trade difficulty and order-placement strategy.
3. Differences in market design, investment style, trading ability, and reputation are important determinants of trading costs.
4. Even after researchers control for trade complexity and trade venue, trading costs vary considerably among managers.
5. Accurate prediction of trading costs requires more detailed data on the entire order submission process than are available, especially information on pretrade decision variables.

The recent literature on equity trading costs offers important lessons for policy-makers and investors. For example, it suggests that the concept of "best execution" for institutional traders is difficult to measure and to enforce.[4]

◆ TRADING ARRANGEMENTS FOR RETAIL AND INSTITUTIONAL INVESTORS

Individuals, called **retail investors**, and institutions exhibit several distinct differences in the way they trade. The first is size: institutions typically transact much larger orders than individuals. The second is commissions: consistent with their larger size, institutions typically pay lower commissions than individuals. Even though institutional commissions declined after 1975, some retail commissions also declined significantly recently as a result of discount brokers.

The third difference is the method of order execution. Both an individual and an institution may trade through a broker/dealer, but the ways in which their orders are entered and executed may differ considerably, even if the trades are through the same broker/dealer. An individual trading through a broker/dealer typically goes through a

---

[4]   Donald B. Keim and Ananth Madhavan, "The Cost of Institutional Equity Trades," *Financial Analysts Journal* (July/August 1998, pp. 50–59).

stockbroker (although stockbrokers now operate under a variety of different names, such as financial consultant, or FC). These orders go to a retail exchange execution desk and from there to the NYSE (usually through SuperDot) or to the OTC execution desk, which transacts it with another market maker on Nasdaq (perhaps through SOES) or possibly internalizes the order. Retail investors receive a "confirm" (confirmation) of the trade, typically in the mail.

Institutional investors typically give their orders directly to the institutional broker/dealer execution desk, for both exchange and OTC orders. Exchange orders may be sent to the broker/dealer's floor broker, and OTC orders may be transacted with another broker/dealer or internalized at a competitive bid-ask rate. Competing bids or offers are typically obtained in all cases.

Because of these differences in the execution of stock trades by individuals and institutions, the trends in common stock holdings is of consequence. During the past 50 years, common stock holdings in the United States became increasingly institutionalized. For example, during 1950, institutional ownership of common stock in the United States was 9.8%, while in 1988 it was 58.9%. The major institutional holders include pension funds (private, usually corporate; state and local government; and labor union), investment companies (mutual funds and closed-end funds), life insurance companies, bank trusts, endowments, and foundations.

Historically, the direct household ownership of common stocks showed a decline. This decline does not necessarily lead to the conclusion that households decreased their common stock holdings. Rather, it means that households hold more of their common stock through intermediaries such as mutual funds rather than directly in the form of common stock. Thus, households "intermediated" their stock holdings. Even though households hold more total common stock than before, they hold less common stock directly, and, thus, increasingly the stock executions are done by institutions, such as mutual funds, rather than by individuals.

RETAIL STOCK TRADING

For individuals the benefit of owning stocks through mutual funds rather than directly is transaction costs; that is, institutions can transact stocks more cheaply than individuals. Although this advantage for institutions remains, transaction costs also declined significantly for individuals during the past decade.

Since May Day 1975, stock trading commissions declined both for institutions and individuals. However, prior to approximately 1990, individuals traded stocks mainly through so-called "full service brokers." Their commissions reflected not only the stock trade execution, but also the counsel of a stockbroker and perhaps research. The largest full-service broker/dealers are also known as "wirehouses." These firms typically do institutional trading and investment banking as well as retail business. The commissions for these full-service brokers have declined since 1975.

However, in addition, a "discount broker" industry developed in which the stockbroker provided no advice and no research. Individuals entered their orders via a telephone. More recently, individuals could enter their orders via their computer through online or Web-based brokerage firms. Consistent with the lower provision of service by discount brokers and online brokers, stock trading commissions decreased significantly. Thus, individuals could trade and own stocks more efficiently.

To remain competitive to a wide range of clients in this environment, the traditional full-service brokerage firms responded by offering their customers alternative means of transacting common stock. For example, many full-service brokerage firms offer the traditional services of a stockbroker and research at a high commission, and, in addition, offer direct order entry at a lower commission. On the other hand, some discount brokers offer more service at a higher commission.

Thus, the balance between more service and low commissions in the retail trading of common stock continues to ebb and flow. Both online brokers, who offer no service and low commissions, and managers of segregated accounts, who offer enhanced service for a large fee, are growing along with full-service stock brokerages and mutual funds.

Despite paying higher commissions than institutions, individual investors may have some advantages over institutions. Because individuals usually transact smaller orders, they incur smaller impact costs. In addition, if individual investors transact online, they may have shorter time lags. For these reasons and others, "packaged products" of individual stocks, such as folios as discussed in Chapter 8, become more attractive.

Due to the increased amount of institutional stock trading relative to individual trading and the more varied type of trading, the remainder of this section deals with institutional stock trading.

INSTITUTIONAL TRADING

With the increase in trading by institutional investors, trading arrangements more suitable to these investors developed. Institutional investor needs include trading in large size and trading groups of stocks, both at a low commission and with low market impact. These requirements resulted in the evolution of special arrangements for the execution of certain types of orders commonly sought by institutional investors: (1) orders requiring the execution of a trade of a large number of shares of a given stock, and (2) orders requiring the execution of trades in a large number of different stocks as simultaneously as possible. The former types of trades are called *block trades*; the latter are called *program trades*. An example of a block trade would be a mutual fund that seeks to buy 15,000 shares of IBM stock. An example of a program trade would be a pension fund that wants to buy shares of 200 companies at the end of a trading day.

The institutional arrangement that accommodates these two types of institutional trades is a network of trading desks of the major securities firms and other institutional investors that communicate with each other by means of electronic display systems and telephones. This network is referred to as the **upstairs market**. Participants in the upstairs market play a key role (1) by providing liquidity to the market so that such institutional trades can be executed, and (2) through arbitrage activities that help to integrate the fragmented stock market.

Block Trades   On the NYSE, block trades are defined as either trades of at least 10,000 shares of a given stock, or trades of shares with a market value of at least $200,000, whichever is less. In 1961, about nine block trades occurred per day, which accounted for about 3% of the trading volume of the NYSE. By contrast, in 1999 the market saw 16,600 block trades per day, accounting for 50.2% of the reported trading volume. On the Nasdaq National Market (NNM), block trades were 24.6% of the total NNM trading volume during 1999.

Because the execution of large numbers of block orders places strains on the specialist system, the NYSE implemented special procedures to handle them. Typically, an institutional customer contacts its salesperson at a brokerage firm, indicating that it wishes to place a block order. The salesperson then gives the order to the brokerage firm's block execution department. Notice that the salesperson does not submit the order to be executed to the exchange where the stock might be traded or, in the case of an unlisted stock, try to execute the order on the Nasdaq system. The sales traders in the block execution department then contact other institutions to attempt to find one or more institutions that would be willing to take the other side of the order. That is, they use the upstairs market in their search to fill the block trade order.

If the sales traders cannot find enough institutions to take the entire block (for example, if the block trade order is for 40,000 shares of IBM, but only 25,000 can be "crossed" with other institutions), then the balance of the block trade order is given to the firm's market maker. The market maker must then make a decision as to how to handle the balance of the block trade order. First, the brokerage firm can take a position in the stock and buy the shares for its own account. Second, the unfilled order can be executed by using the services of competing market makers. In the former case, the brokerage firm is committing its own capital.

NYSE Rule 127 states that if a member firm receives an order for a large block of stock that might not be readily absorbed by the market, the member firm should nevertheless explore the market on the floor, including, where appropriate, consulting with the specialist as to the specialist's interest in the security. If a member firm intends to cross a large block of stock for a public account at a price that is outside of the current quote, it should inform the specialist of its intention.

One study found that approximately 27% of the NYSE block volume is facilitated by upstairs traders.[5] Many people incorrectly believe that 100% of block trades are facilitated by upstairs trading desks and then brought to the floor to be printed. This misconception is caused by confusion about the difference between upstairs-facilitated trades and block trades.

A block trade is defined by its size, not the method of execution. Although negotiation in the informal upstairs market provides better execution than the downstairs market (i.e., the NYSE floor) for large trades, these differences are economically small. The study found that traders who can credibly signal that their trades are liquidity motivated use upstairs markets. Thus, upstairs markets allow trades that may not otherwise occur. The study concluded that the NYSE floor market is a significant source of liquidity.

Secondary distributions are one source of block trades. **Secondary distributions** are an offering by a member firm of a block of listed stock off the floor at a price not exceeding the last sale price at the time of the sale. Rule 393 of the NYSE states that member firms may engage in secondary distributions of a listed stock with the prior approval of the exchange. Approval will be granted if the exchange determines that the auction market cannot absorb the block of stock within a reasonable time and at a reasonable price.

Program Trades **Program trades** involve the buying and/or selling of a large number of names simultaneously. Such trades are also called **basket trades** because effectively a "basket" of stock is being traded. The NYSE defines a program trade as any trade involving the purchase or sale of a basket of at least 15 stocks with a total value of $1 million or more.

The two major applications of program trades are asset allocation and index arbitrage. With respect to asset allocation trades, some examples of why an institutional investor may want to use a program trade are deployment of new cash into the stock market; implementation of a decision to move funds invested in the bond market to the stock market, or vice versa; and rebalancing the composition of a stock portfolio because of a change in investment strategy. A mutual fund money manager can, for example, move funds quickly into or out of the stock market for an entire portfolio of stocks through a single program trade. All these strategies relate to asset allocation.

5 *NYSE 1999 Fact Book*; and Minder Cheng and Ananth Madhavan. "In Search of Liquidity: Block Trades in the Upstairs and Downstairs Markets," *The Review of Financial Studies* (Spring 1997), pp. 175–203.

The growth of mutual fund sales and massive equity investments by pension funds and insurance companies during the 1990s provides an impetus to such methods for trading baskets or bundles of stocks efficiently. Other reasons why an institutional investor may want to execute a program trade should be apparent later when we discuss an investment strategy called indexing.

Program trading is also used for a strategy called **index arbitrage**. In Chapter 16 we will discuss futures contracts traded on stock indexes, called stock index futures. In Chapter 10 we discussed how the price of a stock index futures contract derives from the underlying cash product, namely the stocks included in the stock index. Specifically, a mathematical relationship exists between the price of the stock index and the value of the stocks included in the index taking into account transaction costs and the cost of borrowing funds. This relationship establishes bounds for the price of the stock index futures contract. When the price of the stock index futures contract deviates from these bounds, an opportunity arises for a riskless profit by trading the two. For example, suppose that the price of the S&P 500 futures contract (which we discuss in Chapter 16) is higher than the upper bound established by the cash market price of the basket of 500 stocks and transaction costs and borrowing costs. Then, it would be profitable to sell the index in the futures market and buy the basket in the cash market. To the NYSE specialists, this strategy would show up as a large simultaneous purchase of all stocks in the S&P 500 index. Index fund managers sometimes use program trades to choose between taking a position in the stock market by buying or selling stock or by buying or selling stock index futures contracts.

Unfortunately, the popular press often uses the terms *program trading* and *index arbitrage* interchangeably, which is incorrect. One is an investment strategy (index arbitrage), and the other is an institutional trading arrangement (program trading), even though a program trade is necessarily employed to implement an index arbitrage. Another confusion is worth noting. Because computers are used to execute a program trade, the popular press often wrongly characterizes program trading as computerized trading. Program trading does not have to be, and generally is not, computer-initiated. Sometimes computer algorithms facilitate the decision process, and almost always computers help route the trade to each individual stock in the program, but traders make the decisions and implement them.

Index arbitrage trades are subject to NYSE Rule 80A, which we discuss later. This rule provides that derivative-related program strategies be executed only in a stabilizing manner after the Dow Jones Industrial Average moves 210 points or more (as of this writing) from the previous day's close. Some suggest that this rule inhibits liquidity by discouraging arbitrage just when market liquidity is most important.

Several commission arrangements are available to an institution for a program trade, and each arrangement offers numerous variants. Considerations in selecting one (in addition to commission costs) are the risk of failing to realize the best execution price, and the risk that the brokerage firms to be solicited about executing the program trade will use their knowledge of the program trade to benefit from the anticipated price movement that might result—in other words, that they will **front-run** the transaction, for example buying a stock for their own account before filling the customer buy order.

From a dealer's perspective, program trades can be conducted in two ways, namely on an agency basis and on a principal basis. An intermediate type of program trade, the agency incentive arrangement, is also an alternative. A program trade executed on an **agency basis** involves the selection by the investor of a brokerage firm solely on the basis of commission bids (cents per share) submitted by various brokerage firms. The brokerage firm selected uses its best efforts as an agent of the institution to obtain the best price. Such trades entail low explicit commissions. To the investor, the disadvantage of the agency program trade is that, although commissions may be the lowest, the execution price may not be the best because of impact costs and the potential front-running by the brokerage firms that were solicited to submit a commission bid. The investor knows in advance the commission paid, but does not know the price at which its trades will be executed. Another disadvantage is an increased risk of adverse selection of the counterparty in the execution process.

Related to the agency basis is an **agency incentive arrangement**, in which a benchmark portfolio value is established for the group of stocks in the program trade. The price for each "name" (i.e., specific stock) in the program trade is determined as either the price at the end of the previous day or the average price of the previous day. If the brokerage firm can execute the trade on the next trading day such that a better-than-benchmark portfolio value results—a higher value in the case of a program trade involving selling, or a lower value in the case of a program trade involving buying—then the brokerage firm receives the specified commission plus some predetermined additional compensation. In this case the investor does not know in advance the commission or the execution price precisely, but has a reasonable expectation that the price will be better than a threshold level.

If the brokerage firm does not achieve the benchmark portfolio value, a number of variations come into play. One arrangement may call for the brokerage firm to receive only a previously agreed-upon commission. Other arrangements may involve sharing the risk of not realizing the benchmark portfolio value with the brokerage firm. That is, if the brokerage firm falls short of the benchmark portfolio value, it must absorb a portion of the shortfall. In these risk-sharing arrangements, the brokerage firm risks its own capital. As the level of risk sharing the brokerage firm must accept increases, so does the commission it will charge.

The brokerage firm can also choose to execute the trade on a **principal basis**. In this case, the dealer commits its own capital to buy or sell the portfolio and complete the investor's transaction immediately. Because the dealer incurs market risk, it also charges higher commissions. The key factors in pricing principal trades are liquidity characteristics, absolute dollar value, nature of trade, customer profile, and market volatility. In this case, the investor knows the trade execution price in advance, but pays a higher commission.

To minimize front-running, institutions often use other types of program trade arrangements. They call for brokerage firms to receive, not specific names and quantities of stocks, but only aggregate statistical information about key portfolio parameters. Several brokerage firms then bid on a cents-per-share basis on the entire portfolio (also called blind baskets), guaranteeing execution at either closing price (termed *market-at-close*) or a particular intraday price to the customer. Note that this trade is a principal trade. If mutual fund net asset values are calculated using closing prices, a mutual fund that follows an indexing strategy (i.e., an index fund), for instance, would want guaranteed market-at-close execution to minimize its risk of not performing as well as the stock index. The selected bidder receives the details of the portfolio. Even though the commission in this type of transaction is higher, this procedure increases the risk to the brokerage firm of successfully executing the program trade. However, the brokerage firm can use stock index futures (described in Chapter 16) to protect itself from market-wide movements if the characteristics of the portfolio in the program trade are similar to the index underlying the stock index futures contract.

Brokerage firms can also execute the trade in the upstairs market or send orders electronically to exchange floors or the Nasdaq system through the automated order-routing systems such as the SuperDot System on the NYSE.

To a specialist on an exchange, the counterparties in program trades are uninformed traders; that is, the specialist knows that the trade is being made for index-wide or portfolio-wide reasons and not stock-specific reasons. Such trades are called "informationless trades." Indeed, by observing the relative price movements in the stock index futures markets and cash stock markets on their screens, the specialist can anticipate the arrival of index arbitrage trades. Thus, to the specialist, program trades, in small doses, represent profitable order flow with very little risk.

NYSE releases weekly statistics on the extent of program trading by its member firms.[6] For example, during the week ended January 19, 2001, program trading in all markets averaged 598.8 million shares a day. About 61.3% of these took place on the NYSE, 18.6% in non-U.S. markets, and 20.1% in other domestic exchanges, including Nasdaq, the American Stock Exchange, and regional markets. In aggregate, program trade volume executed on the NYSE by firms as agents for nonmember cus-tomers amounted to 63.7%, and 31.9% when executed as principal for their own accounts. Another 4.4% was designated as customer facilitation, in which a member firm established or liquidated a principal position to facilitate a program order initiated by a customer.[7] In addition, 9.8% of the program volume executed by NYSE member firms during this period related to index arbitrage; another 0.5% involved derivative product-related strategies. All other types of portfolio trading strategies combined accounted for 89.7% of their volume. Although these figures only pertain to a particular week, they are indicative of the current levels of program trading in general. Program trading volume accounted for 20.2% of the total NYSE volume in 2000.

◆ PRICE LIMITS AND COLLARS

The largest single-day decline in the history of the U.S. stock market (and in most of the world's other stock markets) occurred on Monday, October 19, 1987, popularly referred to as "Black Monday." This event is often referred to simply as "the crash." On that day, a popular market index, the Dow Jones Industrial Average (DJIA), declined by 23%, and other market indexes declined by roughly the same amount.

Afterward, the U.S. government and some exchanges commissioned several studies to assess the causes of the crash and to offer possible remedial measures to prevent any recurrence. Several government-sponsored studies and exchange-sponsored studies were conducted, including a study by a presidential task force that became known as the Brady Report.[8] These studies explained the crash as the result of (1) deficiencies in institutional arrangements in stock trading, (2) an overvaluation of stock prices, and (3) various forms of overreaction to economic news.

While several potential reasons for the crash were identified, no unambiguous conclusions resulted. One clear dynamic for the price decline, however, did exist. This dynamic was that selling caused price declines, which caused further selling, and so on. (The opposite dynamic of "buying on dips," occurs when price declines cause buying rather than selling, which became more common after the crash.) Two potential reasons explain why price declines cause further selling. One is emotional; that is, price

---

[6] Available at www.nyse.com, using the Market Information tab and the Program Trading section.
[7] The high level of principal program trading by member firms may be a consequence of their negligible transaction costs, which shrinks the bounds on prices for profitable arbitrage trades.
[8] Brady Report, *Presidential Task Force on Market Mechanisms*, 1988.

declines cause fear, which causes further selling. The second is a trading strategy, used by some institutional investors, that exacerbates any plunge in the market.[9]

A stock market policy called **trading limits** or **price limits** resulted from Black Monday. Trading or price limits specify a minimum price limit, below which the market price index level may not decline due to an institutionally mandated termination of trading, at least at prices below the specified price (the price limit), for a specified period of time. For example, if the DJIA was trading at 11,000 and its price limit was 500 points below that, then no trades could occur below 10,500. This pause in trading is intended to "give the market a breather" to at least calm emotions. Previously, trading limits were used in the futures markets but not in the stock market.

Soon after the crash, the NYSE implemented these price limits, which they modified several times, bringing limits to their present design. Two different types of price limits are discussed in the following sections.

RULE 80B OR "CIRCUIT BREAKERS"

On April 15, 1998, the NYSE, following approval by the SEC, implemented new regulations to increase and widen thresholds at which trading is halted for single-day declines in the DJIA. The point levels are set quarterly at 10%, 20%, and 30% of the DJIA by using the DJIA average closing value of the previous month, rounded to the nearest 50 points. Point levels are adjusted on January 1, April 1, July 1, and October 1. Trigger levels might be set as follows:

- A 1,050-point drop in the DJIA halts trading for 1 hour if the decline occurs before 14:00; for 30 minutes if before 14:30; and has no effect between 14:30 and 16:00.
- A 2,150-point drop halts trading for 2 hours if the decline occurs before 13:00; for 1 hour if before 14:00; and for the rest of the day if after 14:00.
- A 3,200-point drop halts trading for the remainder of the day regardless of when the decline occurs.

RULE 80A OR "TRADING COLLAR"

Another type of trading restriction applies to index arbitrage trading whereby, for example, a basket of S&P 500 stocks is bought (sold) against the sale (purchase) of an S&P 500 futures contract. On February 16, 1999, following approval by the SEC, the NYSE implemented revisions to Rule 80A, which restrict index arbitrage trading. Specifically, the set 50-point collar was eliminated and the trigger level was allowed to track the DJIA. The revised collar is calculated quarterly as 2% of the average closing value of the DJIA for the last month of the previous quarter, rounded down to the nearest 10 points, and currently implemented as follows:[10]

- A decline in the DJIA of 210 points or more requires all index arbitrage sell orders of the S&P 500 stocks to be stabilizing, or "sell plus," for the remainder of the day, unless on the same trading day, the DJIA advances to a value of 100 points or less below its previous close.
- An advance in the DJIA of 210 points requires all index arbitrage buy orders of the S&P 500 stocks to be stabilizing, or "buy minus," for the remainder of the day, unless the DJIA retreats to 100 points or less above its previous close.
- The restrictions will be reimposed each time the DJIA advances or declines the predetermined amount.

---

[9] The strategy was called "portfolio insurance" or dynamic asset allocation.
[10] Market-on-close orders to liquidate previously established stock positions against expiring derivative products on expiration Fridays are exempt from the index-arbitrage tick restrictions of Rule 80A.

◆ STOCK MARKET INDICATORS

Stock market indicators perform a variety of functions, from serving as benchmarks for evaluating the performance of professional money managers to answering the question "How did the market do today?" Thus, stock market indicators (indexes or averages) are a part of everyday life. Even though many of the stock market indicators are used interchangeably, it is important to realize that each indicator applies to, and measures, a different facet of the stock market.

The most commonly quoted stock market indicator is the Dow Jones Industrial Average (DJIA). Other stock market indicators cited in the financial press are the Standard & Poor's 500 Composite (S&P 500), the New York Stock Exchange Composite Index (NYSE Composite), the Nasdaq Composite Index, and the Value Line Composite Average (VLCA). A myriad of other stock market indicators, such as the Wilshire stock indexes and the Russell stock indexes, are followed primarily by institutional money managers.

In general, market indexes rise and fall in fairly similar patterns. Table 14-3 shows the correlation coefficients, which measure the degree of similarity in changes in value, for eight prominent market indexes. Although the coefficients are high, the indexes do not move in exactly the same ways at all times. The differences in movement reflect the different ways in which the indexes are constructed. Three factors enter into that construction: the universe of stocks represented by the sample underlying the index, the relative weights assigned to the stocks included in the index, and the method of averaging across all the stocks.

Some indexes represent only stocks listed on an exchange. Examples are the DJIA and the NYSE Composite, which represent only stocks listed on the Big Board. By contrast, the Nasdaq includes only stocks traded over the counter. A favorite of professionals is the S&P 500 because it contains both NYSE-listed and OTC-traded shares. Each index relies on a sample of stocks from its universe, and that sample may be small or quite large. The DJIA uses only 30 of the largest corporations, while the NYSE Composite includes every one of the NYSE-listed shares. The Nasdaq also includes all shares in its universe, while the S&P 500 has a sample that contains only 500 of the more than 8,000 shares in the universe it represents.

The stocks included in a stock market index must be combined in certain proportions, and each stock must be given a weight. The three main approaches to weighting are (1) weighting by the market capitalization of the stock's company, which is the

TABLE 14-3 Correlation Coefficients for Selected U.S. Stock Indexes, Based on Monthly Returns (January 1987 to March 2000)

	Dow Jones 30	*Nasdaq Composite*	*NYSE Composite*	*Russell 1000*	*Russell 2000*	*S&P 500*	*Value Line Composite*	*Wilshire 5000*
Dow Jones 30	1.00							
Nasdaq Composite	0.74	1.00						
NYSE Composite	0.95	0.80	1.00					
Russell 1000	0.93	0.85	0.98	1.00				
Russell 2000	0.70	0.88	0.76	0.79	1.00			
S&P 500	0.95	0.83	0.98	0.99	0.75	1.00		
Value Line Composite	0.87	0.84	0.92	0.91	0.90	0.89	1.00	
Wilshire 5000	0.92	0.89	0.97	0.99	0.85	0.98	0.93	1.00

Source: Investment Technologies, Inc.

value of the number of shares times price per share; (2) weighting by the price of the stock; and (3) equal weighting for each stock, regardless of its price or its firm's market value. With the exception of the Dow Jones averages (such as the DJIA) and the VLCA, all the most widely used indexes are market-value weighted. The DJIA is a price-weighted average, and the VLCA is an equally weighted index.

Stock market indicators can be classified into three groups: (1) those produced by stock exchanges based on all stocks traded on the exchanges; (2) those produced by organizations that subjectively select the stocks to be included in indexes; and (3) those where stock selection is based on an objective measure, such as the market capitalization of the company. The first group includes the New York Stock Exchange Composite Index, which reflects the market value of all stocks traded on the exchange. Although it is not an exchange, the Nasdaq Composite Index falls into this category because the index represents all stocks tracked by the Nasdaq system.

The three most popular stock market indicators in the second group are the Dow Jones Industrial Average, the Standard & Poor's 500, and the Value Line Composite Average. The DJIA is constructed from 30 of the largest blue-chip industrial companies. The companies included in the average are those selected by Dow Jones & Company, publisher of the *Wall Street Journal*. The S&P 500 represents stocks chosen from the two major national stock exchanges and the over-the-counter market. The stocks in the index at any given time are determined by a committee of Standard & Poor's Corporation, which may occasionally add or delete individual stocks or the stocks of entire industry groups. The aim of the committee is to capture present overall stock market conditions as reflected in a broad range of economic indicators. The VLCA, produced by Value Line Inc., covers a broad range of widely held and actively traded NYSE, AMEX, and OTC issues selected by Value Line.

In the third group we have the Wilshire indexes produced by Wilshire Associates (Santa Monica, California) and Russell indexes produced by the Frank Russell Company (Tacoma, Washington), a consultant to pension funds and other institutional investors. The criterion for inclusion in each of these indexes is solely a firm's market capitalization. The most comprehensive index is the Wilshire 5000, which actually includes more than 6,700 stocks now, up from 5,000 at its inception. The Wilshire 4500 includes all stocks in the Wilshire 5000 except for those in the S&P 500. Thus, the shares in the Wilshire 4500 have smaller capitalization than those in the Wilshire 5000. The Russell 3000 encompasses the 3,000 largest companies in terms of their market capitalization. The Russell 1000 is limited to the largest 1,000 of those, and the Russell 2000 has the remaining smaller firms.

Two methods of averaging may be used. The first and most common is the arithmetic average. An arithmetic mean is just a simple average of the stocks, calculated by summing them (after weighting, if appropriate) and dividing by the sum of the weights. The second method is the geometric mean, which involves multiplication of the components, after which the product is raised to the power of (1/number of stocks).

MAJOR INTERNATIONAL STOCK MARKET INDEXES

Many indexes of stock prices chart and measure the performance of foreign stock markets. In every country where stock trading takes place, at least one index measures general share price movements. If a country has more than one stock exchange, each exchange usually has its own index. Also, news organizations and financial advisory services create indexes. In the United States, examples of the exchange indexes are the NYSE Composite Index and the AMEX Composite Index, while examples of the indexes constructed by nonexchange firms include Standard & Poor's 500 Common Stock Index and the Dow Jones Industrial Average.

In Japan, there are two major indexes. The Tokyo Stock Exchange produces the Tokyo Stock Price Index, or TOPIX. This composite index is based on all the shares in the Tokyo market's First Section, a designation reserved for the established and large companies whose shares are the most actively traded and widely held. (The TOPIX is computed based on the included firms' market value, not just their prices.) A financial information firm, Nihon Keizai Shimbun, Inc., calculates and publishes the Nikkei 225 Stock Average. This average (computed in the same way as the Dow Jones 30) is based on 225 of the largest companies in the First Section.

The United Kingdom's London Stock Exchange is covered by several widely followed indexes. The *Financial Times* Industrial Ordinary Index is based on the prices of shares of 30 leading companies and is known as the FT 30. A broader index is the *Financial Times*—Stock Exchange 100, which is a market-value index and is commonly referred to as the FTSE 100 (pronounced "Footsie 100"). This index is based on the shares of the largest 100 U.K. firms, whose market value makes up a majority of the market value of all U.K. equities.[11] Indexes for different sectors, and a composite index across sectors, are produced by the *Financial Times* and the Institute for Actuaries. These FT-A indexes are broadly based, with the composite including more than 700 shares.

The primary German stock index is the DAX, which stands for the Deutscher Aktienindex, produced by the Frankfurt Stock Exchange. (The German name for this exchange is the Frankfurter Wertpapierbörse. Some financial services regularly refer to the exchange by its initials, FWB.) The DAX is based on the 30 most actively traded shares listed on the Frankfurt exchange. The FAZ Index is another popular German index. Compiled by the *Frankfurter Allgemeine Zeitung*, which is a daily newspaper, the FAZ index is computed from the share prices of the 100 largest companies listed on the Frankfurt exchange.

In France, a national association of stockbrokers and the Paris Bourse produce an index based on the shares of 40 large and prominent firms traded on the exchange. The index is known as the CAC 40 Index, after the name of the Bourse's electronic trading system. Given the increasing economic integration of Europe, the CAC 40, like the FTSE 100 and possibly the DAX, may well be a reliable indicator of the overall performance of European stocks and markets.

Other widely followed national stock indexes include the Hang Seng Index produced by the Stock Exchange of Hong Kong, the TSE 300 Composite of the Toronto Stock Exchange, and the Swiss Performance Index or SPI, which applies to almost 400 firms and is published by the stock exchanges in that country.

To meet the increased interest in global equity investing, financial institutions crafted several respected international equity indexes. The international equity index followed most by U.S. pension funds is the Morgan Stanley Capital International Europe, Australasia, and the Far East Index, or EAFE Index. This index, started by Capital International in 1968 and acquired by Morgan Stanley in 1986, covers more than 2,000 companies in 21 countries. Relatively new international equity indexes include the *Financial Times* World Index (a joint product of the Institute of Actuaries in the United Kingdom, Goldman Sachs & Co., and Wood MacKenzie & Co.), the Salomon Smith Barney–Russell Global Equity Index (a joint product of Salomon Smith Barney and Frank Russell, Inc.), and the Global Index (a joint product of Credit Suisse First Boston Corporation and London-based *Euromoney* magazine).

---

[11] Euromoney, *The Guide to World Equity Markets 1995* (London: Euromoney Publications PLC, 1995), p. 348.

As explained in Chapter 7, a price-efficient market is one in which security prices at all times fully reflect all available information relevant to their valuation. When a market is price efficient, investment strategies pursued to outperform a broad-based stock market index will not consistently produce superior returns after adjusting for risk and transaction costs.

Numerous studies examined the pricing efficiency of the stock market. Although it is not our intent in this chapter to provide a comprehensive review of these studies, we can summarize their basic findings and their implications for investment strategies.

FORMS OF EFFICIENCY

The three different forms of pricing efficiency include (1) weak form, (2) semi-strong form, and (3) strong form. The distinctions among these forms lie in the relevant information assumed to be taken into consideration in the price of the security at all times. *Weak efficiency* means that the price of the security reflects the past price and trading history of the security. *Semi-strong efficiency* means that the price of the security fully reflects all public information, which includes but is not limited to historical price and trading patterns. *Strong efficiency* exists in a market where the price of a security reflects all information, whether it is publicly available or known only to insiders such as the firm's managers or directors.

The preponderance of empirical evidence supports the claims that the common stock market is efficient in the weak form. The evidence emerges from sophisticated tests that explore whether historical price movements can be used to project future prices in such a way as to produce returns above what one would expect from market movements and the risk class of the security. Such returns are known as **positive abnormal returns**. The implications are that investors who follow a strategy of selecting stocks solely on the basis of price patterns or trading volume—such investors are referred to as **technical analysts** or **chartists**—should not expect to do better than the market. In fact, they may fare worse because of higher transaction costs associated with frequent buying and selling of stocks.

Evidence on whether the stock market is price efficient in the semi-strong form is mixed. Some studies support the proposition of efficiency when they suggest that investors who select stocks on the basis of **fundamental security analysis**—which consists of analyzing financial statements, the quality of management, and the economic environment of a company—will not outperform the market. This result is certainly reasonable: So many analysts use the same approach, with the same publicly available data, that the price of the stock remains in line with all the relevant factors that determine value. On the other hand, a sizable number of other studies produced evidence indicating instances and patterns of pricing inefficiency in the stock market over long periods of time. Economists and financial analysts often label these examples of inefficient pricing as **anomalies in the market**, that is, phenomena that cannot be easily explained.

Empirical tests of strong form pricing efficiency fall into two groups: (1) studies of the performance of professional money managers, and (2) studies of the activities of insiders (individuals who are either company directors, major officers, or major stockholders). Studies of the performance of professional money managers to test the strong form of pricing efficiency are based on the belief that professional managers have access to better information than the general public. Whether this point is true is moot because the empirical evidence suggests professional managers do not outperform the market consistently. In contrast, evidence based on the activities of insiders generally reveals that this group often achieves higher returns than the stock market. Of course, insiders could not get those high abnormal returns if the stock prices fully reflected all relevant information about the values of the firms. Thus, the empirical evidence on insider trading argues against the notion that the market is efficient in the strong-form sense.

IMPLICATIONS FOR INVESTING IN COMMON STOCK

Common stock investment strategies can be classified into two general categories: active strategies and passive strategies. **Active investment strategies** attempt to outperform the market by one or more of the following: timing the selection of transactions, such as in the case of technical analysis; identifying undervalued or overvalued stocks using fundamental security analysis; or selecting stocks according to market anomalies. Obviously, the decision to pursue an active strategy must be based on the belief that some type of gain can be made from such costly efforts, but gains are possible only if pricing inefficiencies exist. The particular strategy chosen depends on what pricing inefficiencies the investor believes are occurring.

Investors who believe that the market prices stocks efficiently should accept the implication that attempts to outperform the market cannot be systematically successful, except by luck. This implication does not mean that investors should shun the stock market, but rather that they should pursue a **passive investment strategy**, which is one that does not attempt to outperform the market. Is there an optimal investment strategy for someone who holds this belief in the pricing efficiency of the stock market? There is. Its theoretical basis is in modern portfolio theory and capital market theory that we discussed in Chapter 8. According to modern portfolio theory, the market portfolio offers the highest level of return per unit of risk in a market that is price efficient. A portfolio of financial assets with characteristics similar to those of a portfolio consisting of the entire market—the market portfolio—will capture the pricing efficiency of the market.

But how can such a passive strategy be implemented? More specifically, what is meant by a market portfolio, and how should that portfolio be constructed? In theory, the **market portfolio** consists of all financial assets, not just common stock. The reason is that investors compare all investment opportunities, not just stock, when committing their capital. Thus, our principles of investing must be based on capital market theory, not just stock market theory. When the theory is applied to the stock market, the market portfolio consists of a large universe of common stocks. But how much of each common stock should be purchased when constructing the market portfolio? Theory states that the chosen portfolio should be an appropriate fraction of the market portfolio; hence, the weighting of each stock in the market portfolio should be based on its relative market capitalization. Thus, if the aggregate market capitalization of all stocks included in the market portfolio is $\$T$ and the market capitalization of one of these stocks is $\$A$, then the fraction of this stock that should be held in the market portfolio is $\$A/\$T$.

The passive strategy just described is called **indexing**. Pension fund sponsors increasingly found in the 1990s that money managers are unable to outperform the stock market. Subsequently, the amount of funds managed using an indexing strategy grew substantially. Index funds, however, still account for a relatively small fraction of institutional stock investments.

We conclude this chapter with a discussion of the benefits of international stock diversification. Numerous studies document the potential portfolio diversification benefits of global investing. Specifically, the inclusion of securities from other countries can increase a portfolio's expected return without increasing its risk or its variability in returns (as discussed in Chapter 8). Similarly, including securities from other countries in a portfolio may reduce the portfolio's risk with no decrease in its expected return. The basis of these benefits from diversification is that international capital markets are less than perfectly correlated; that is, their returns do not increase and decrease in unison. Correlation is a statistical measurement of the similarity in the movement of two variables, such as rates of return on groups of stocks from two different countries. Stock markets that are not highly correlated move in ways different from one another.

This dissimilarity in changes in market returns is not surprising. Different countries tend to have different experiences in such important areas as taxation, monetary management, banking policies, political goals and stability, population growth, and so on. Because the largest influences on prices for many stocks are domestic or local events and policies, the prices of groups of stocks from different areas tend to move up or down at somewhat different times and to somewhat different degrees. This pattern of dissimilar security price changes allows investors to diversify away a certain amount of risk in individual countries and creates the benefits of international or global investing.

Tables 14-4 and 14-5 provide evidence regarding the degree of dissimilarity in the movement of stock prices on selected national stock exchanges. Table 14-4 presents the correlation coefficients for the monthly returns for the stock market indexes of eight developed countries. Table 14-5 does the same for the stock market indexes of 16 emerging market countries. The correlations are based on the general level of share prices on the exchanges in those countries for the period 1970 to 2000.

To interpret the table, it is necessary to keep in mind a few properties of the correlation coefficient. The correlation coefficient has a maximum value of 1.00, which occurs if two variables always move in the same way; and a minimum value of −1.00, which occurs if two variables always move in the exact opposite way. Thus, any variable has a correlation of 1.00 with itself, which simply means that it moves in exactly the same way that it does. For example, Australia's index moves just as Australia's index does, and so the correlation of Australia's index with itself is 1.00, as indicated in

TABLE 14-4 Correlation Coefficients of Selected Developed Stock Market Indexes

Country	United States	France	United Kingdom	Japan	Germany	Switzerland	Canada	Australia
United States	1.00	0.44	0.51	0.29	0.38	0.49	0.71	0.47
France		1.00	0.54	0.39	0.61	0.60	0.44	0.37
United Kingdom			1.00	0.36	0.43	0.56	0.50	0.47
Japan				1.00	0.36	0.41	0.30	0.30
Germany					1.00	0.67	0.34	0.30
Switzerland						1.00	0.44	0.39
Canada							1.00	0.59
Australia								1.00

Note: Correlations are based on monthly returns for the period January 1970 to December 2000.

Source: Correlations were calculated from gross monthly index level data available on www.msci.com.

TABLE 14-5   Correlation Coefficients of Selected Emerging Stock Market Indexes

Country	Chile	China	Columbia	India	Indonesia	Israel	Korea	Malaysia	Mexico	Pakistan	Philippines	Poland	S. Africa	Turkey
Chile	1.00													
China	0.41	1.00												
Columbia	0.34	0.04	1.00											
India	0.40	0.18	0.09	1.00										
Indonesia	0.50	0.36	0.25	0.21	1.00									
Israel	0.32	0.14	0.06	0.30	0.20	1.00								
Korea	0.26	0.15	0.12	0.12	0.36	0.04	1.00							
Malaysia	0.42	0.46	0.23	0.24	0.56	0.17	0.26	1.00						
Mexico	0.45	0.38	0.10	0.28	0.30	0.43	0.18	0.26	1.00					
Pakistan	0.32	0.17	0.39	0.39	0.18	0.20	0.06	0.24	0.24	1.00				
Philippines	0.50	0.51	0.14	0.13	0.59	0.12	0.30	0.60	0.35	0.15	1.00			
Poland	0.24	0.20	0.09	0.24	0.26	0.20	0.21	0.30	0.34	0.12	0.26	1.00		
South Africa	0.48	0.45	0.01	0.13	0.34	0.26	0.36	0.39	0.44	0.18	0.60	0.28	1.00	
Turkey	0.24	0.09	0.21	0.13	0.18	0.31	0.02	0.19	0.28	0.25	0.11	0.16	0.22	1.00

Note: All the above are MSCI US$ indexes. "China" is the Chine Free index. "Malaysia" is the Malaysia Emerging Market index. Correlations are based on monthly returns for the period of January 1993 to December 2000.

Source: Investment Technologies, Inc.

Table 14-4. A positive correlation that is less than 1.00 but greater than 0 means that the two variables move generally in the same direction. For example, in Table 14-4 it can be seen that Germany's stock market has a correlation coefficient of 0.61 with France's market, which implies that these two markets do not move identically to each other but move in the same way much of the time. Finally, the correlation of Germany's market with France's is the same as the correlation of France's market with Germany's. So Table 14-4 reports that coefficient only once in the row for France. As a result, the table of coefficients is diagonal and only half-filled.

Table 14-4 reveals some interesting points. First, these international stock markets behave quite differently from one another; that is the correlations of their returns tend to be substantially less than unity. Although the highest coefficient is 0.71 between the United States and Canada, many values are below 0.50. Thus, investors can diversify their holdings by spreading their portfolio across these various markets.

The second notable point is that geography and political alliances do influence the correlations. Thus, stock prices in Germany and Japan move less similarly (correlation equals 0.36) than do the prices in Germany and France (correlation of 0.61) or the prices in the United States and Canada (correlation of 0.71). Consequently, investors seeking diversification must choose carefully from among the various markets.

Finally, it is interesting that all the correlations are positive and well above zero. This implies the absence of complete dissimilarity in the movement of stock prices. The positive values mean that the world's stock prices are, like their economies, somewhat integrated. Thus, the benefit of international diversification has limits. In other words, the markets of the world are members of a somewhat loosely connected system of economies, and allocating funds among the various economies provides some, but not complete, reduction of variability in returns on securities.

Two factors, however, generally increased the correlation among the various countries' stock markets during the 1990s; that is, these factors reduced the advantages of diversification among the world's equity markets. One factor is behavioral and the other is due to the structure of the economies and their stock markets. The first relates to the behavior of investors during times of financial crisis, the times when investors would find diversification potentially the most beneficial. At such times, the reasoning goes, investors become especially risk averse and flee to safety and liquidity. So if a crisis starts in one country for a legitimate fundamental reason, investors will sell stocks (and perhaps bonds) not just in that country or region alone, but in many or all other countries as well. This "flight to quality" results in unusually high temporary demand for low-risk, high-liquidity assets (most likely U.S. Treasuries), and a simultaneous decrease in the demand for and price of all risky assets. Such a crisis mentality increases the correlation among all or most risky assets and does so at a time when diversification is needed most.

The second factor that may increase international correlation relates to the structure of national economies and their stock markets. A country's economy can be postulated to be made up of two sectors, a global sector and a country sector. The **global sector** provides goods and services to the global economy through international trade. Thus, the companies in a country's global sector respond more to global forces than to national forces according to this reasoning. Microchip manufacturing, automobile manufacturing, and telecommunications are examples of global sectors. A microchip manufacturer in one country is affected by economic forces much more like a microchip manufacturer in other countries than like nonglobal companies in the same country.

In contrast, the **country sector** produces goods and services mainly for the local economy. Companies in this sector are affected by economic forces more like the other local economy companies in the same country than like the global companies in that country. Railroads, retailing, and construction are examples of country sectors.

The conclusion is that companies in global sectors tend to follow the global market for their goods and services rather than their local economy and consequently are not highly diversifying. For example, the stocks of telecommunications companies all over the world declined significantly during 2000. Companies in the country sector, in contrast, follow the indigenous economy and their stocks, and therefore would be diversifying in a global portfolio.

An example of this concept is that a U.S. stock investor would not buy the Finland stock index to pursue international stock diversification since Nokia, which manufactures telecommunications equipment, represents 67% of the Finland stock index.

The evidence indicates that the share of global sectors is increasing relative to country sectors in most developed countries during the last several years. As a result, globally diversified portfolios currently provide less market diversification than they did previously.[12]

Overall, however, diversification continues to provide a benefit to an investment portfolio, although the diversification exercise may need to be done more carefully by considering both the country effects and the sector effects.

Summary

Different types of orders may be submitted to the stock markets. The most common type is a market order, which means that the order must be filled immediately at the best price. Other types of orders, such as stop and limit orders, are filled only if the market price reaches a price specified in the order.

The brokerage commission is the most obvious type of trading cost and object of competition among broker/dealers for both institutional and retail investors. However, other types of trading costs, such as impact costs and opportunity costs, may be larger than commissions.

To accommodate the trading needs of institutional investors who tend to place orders of larger sizes and with a large number of names, special arrangements evolved in the markets. Block trades are trades of 10,000 shares or more of a given stock or trades with a market value of $200,000 or more. Program trades, or basket trades, involve the buying and/or selling of a large number of names simultaneously. The institutional arrangement developed to accommodate these needs is the upstairs market, which is a network of trading desks of the major securities firms and institutional investors that communicate with each other by means of electronic display systems and telephones.

As a result of the stock market crash in October 1987, exchanges imposed various forms of price limits or caps.

Stock market indicators can be classified into three groups: (1) those produced by stock exchanges and that include all stocks to be traded on the exchange (such as the Nasdaq Composite Index and the NYSE Composite Index); (2) those in which a committee subjectively selects the stocks to be included in the index (such as the S&P 500 Index); and (3) those in which the stocks selected are based solely on stocks' market capitalizations (such as the Russell 3000, 1000, and 2000 Indexes). Every market in the world has an index that measures the general movement in the prices of shares on the market. Some indexes are produced by exchanges and some by financial news services

---

[12] See Stefano Cavaglia, Christopher Brightman, and Michael Akid, "The Increasing Importance of Industry Factors," *Financial Analysts Journal* (September/October 2000), pp. 41–54, and Sean P. Baca, Brian L. Garbe, and Richard Weiss, "The Rise of Sector Effects in Major Equity Markets," *Financial Analysts Journal* (September/October 2000), pp. 34–40.

or other nonexchange organizations. The large markets have well-known and widely followed indexes: the TOPIX and the Nikkei 225 in Japan; the FTSE 100 in the United Kingdom; the DAX and FAZ indexes in Germany; and the CAC 40 in France.

Three forms of pricing efficiency follow according to what is hypothesized to be the relevant information embodied in the price of a stock at all times: (1) weak form, (2) semi-strong form, and (3) strong form. Most of the empirical evidence appears to suggest that markets are efficient in the weak form. The evidence on the semi-strong form is mixed because of observed pockets of inefficiency. Empirical tests of strong-form pricing efficiency also produce conflicting results.

Active investment strategies, consisting of efforts to time purchases and select stocks, are pursued by investors who believe that securities are mispriced enough that it is possible to capitalize on strategies designed to exploit the perceived inefficiency. The optimal strategy to pursue when the stock market is perceived to be price efficient is indexing because it allows the investor to capture the efficiency of the market.

The prices of stocks on markets around the world do not move together in an exact way because the economic systems in which those markets are located are characterized by dissimilar environments in terms of taxation, industrial growth, political stability, monetary policy, and other factors. Low levels of co-movement of stock prices offer investors a benefit from diversifying their holdings across the markets of countries. That is, investors who allocate some of their portfolio to shares from other countries can increase the portfolio's expected return with no increase in risk. This benefit of international diversification has led many investors to allocate some of their wealth to foreign markets and shares of foreign firms.

Key Terms

- Active investment strategies
- Agency basis
- Agency incentive arrangement
- Anomalies in the market
- Basket trades
- Block trade
- Buy limit order
- Buy stop order
- Call money rate
- Chartist
- Closing order
- Conditional order
- Country sector
- Debit balance
- Explicit trading costs
- Fill-or-kill order

- Front-run
- Fundamental security analysis
- Global sector
- Good until canceled order
- Implicit trading costs
- Index arbitrage
- Indexing
- Limit order
- Limit order book
- Market-if-touched order
- Market order
- Market portfolio
- Odd lot
- Open order
- Opening order
- Passive investment strategy

- Positive abnormal return
- Price limits
- Principal basis
- Program trades
- Retail investors
- Round lot
- Secondary distribution
- Sell limit order
- Sell stop order
- Short selling
- Stop-limit order
- Stop order
- Technical analyst
- Tick-test rules
- Trading limits
- Upstairs market

Questions

1. The following quote is taken from Wayne H. Wagner, "The Taxonomy of Trading Strategies," in Katrina F. Sherrerd (ed.), *Trading Strategies and Execution Costs* (Charlottesville, VA: The Institute of Chartered Financial Analysts, 1988).

When a trader decides how to bring an order to the market, he or she must deal with some very important issues; to me, the most important is: What kind of trade is this? It could be either an active or a passive trade. The type of trade will dictate whether speed of execution is more or less important than cost of execution. In other words, do I want immediate trading (a market order); or am I willing to forgo the immediate trade for the possibility of trading less expensively if I am willing to "give" on the timing of the trade (a limit order)?

   a. What is meant by a market order?
   b. Why would a market order be placed when an investor wants immediate trading?
   c. What is meant by a limit order?
   d. What are the risks associated with a limit order?

2. Suppose that Mr. Mancuso has purchased the stock of AOL for $23 and that he sets a maximum loss that he will accept on this stock at $20. What type of order can Mr. Mancuso place?

3. a. What is a program trade?
   b. What are the various types of commission arrangements for executing a program trade and the advantages and disadvantages of each?

4. What types of restriction on stock price movements are imposed by the New York Stock Exchange?

5. Explain these terms:
   a. Good till canceled order
   b. Public order
   c. Stop loss order
   d. Block trade
   e. Closing order

6. a. Explain the mechanics and some key rules of a short sale.
   b. What restrictions are imposed on short selling activities?
   c. What role does the broker loan rate play in a margin purchase?

7. a. What is meant by maintenance margin when stocks are purchased on margin?
   b. What is meant by debit balance?
   c. What is meant by credit balance?

8. a. What are soft dollars?
   b. What is payment for flow?

9. What is meant by decimialization?

10. The following statements are taken from Greta E. Marshall's article "Execution Costs: The Plan Sponsor's View," which appears in *Trading Strategies and Execution Costs*, published by The Institute of Chartered Financial Analysts in 1988. (The publication is the product of a conference held in New York City on December 3, 1987.)
   a. "There are three components of trading costs. First there are direct costs which may be measured—commissions. Second, there are indirect—or market impact—costs. Finally, there are the undefined costs of not trading." What are market impact costs, and what do you think the "undefined costs of not trading" represent?
   b. "Market impact, unlike broker commissions, is difficult to identify and measure." Why is market impact cost difficult to measure?

11. What is the difference between a market-value-weighted index and an equally weighted index?

12. a. What are the main features of the S&P 500 common stock index?
   b. "The stocks selected for the S&P 500 are the largest 500 companies in the United States." Indicate whether you agree or disagree with this statement.

13. Some participants and analysts in the stock market are called chartists or technical analysts. What does the theory that the market is weak-form efficient say about these investors' chances of beating the market?

14. Why should an investor who believes that the market is efficient pursue an indexing strategy?

15. Provide a general explanation of why stocks of Dutch companies in the Netherlands might sustain a significant decline over the same time period that brings about a sharp increase in the value of shares of a typical Australian company, which are traded in Australia.

16. a. What is the correlation coefficient and how does a low value (say, +0.30) of correlation between stocks in two countries offer investors an interesting investment opportunity?
    b. Why, if the correlation coefficient were + 0.95, would the same kind of opportunity not exist?
    c. Claudia Barelli and Roberto Moro-Visconti, in their working paper titled, "The Link Between Volatility and Correlation in International Stock Markets," report that share price volatility, especially sharp falls as in times of market "crashes," actually encourages investors to increase the international diversification of their holdings because they want to protect themselves against severe market declines. Comment on whether you find this analysis intuitively appealing.

17. What two factors tended to increase the correlation among the various countries' stock markets during the 1990s?

18. A country's economy can be postulated to be made up of two sectors: a global sector and a country sector. What are these two sectors?

19. Often, a news report will survey the day's trading with a statement like this: "The Footsie 100 rose 1.5% today, while the DAX dropped 0.25% and the CAC 40 finished unchanged." What are the formal names of the indexes referred to, and to which country do they apply?

CHAPTER 15

Stock Options Market

Learning Objectives

After reading this chapter you will understand:

◆ the basic features of stock options.

◆ how stock options can change the risk/return profile of a stock portfolio.

◆ the different stock options strategies that institutional investors use.

◆ the empirical evidence on whether a given stock option strategy consistently beats other strategies.

◆ the institution behind the Black-Scholes option pricing model and its limitations.

◆ evidence on the pricing efficiency of the stock options market.

◆ what a warrant is.

Chapter 11 provided an introduction to options contracts. In this chapter, we look at options on individual common stocks (or, simply, stock options). We will discuss strategies that institutional investors use, and we introduce a popular model used to determine the theoretical price of a stock option, the Black-Scholes option pricing model. We also discuss another stock option product, a warrant.

Although the most important use of options is to alter return distributions to satisfy particular investment objectives, investors also try to use the options market to generate abnormal returns.[1] We review the evidence on stock option strategies, focusing on two critical empirical questions. First, is there (as often suggested in promotional literature) an option strategy that outperforms other option and stock strategies? Second, is the market for stock options efficient?

◆ HISTORY OF EXCHANGE-TRADED OPTIONS

Options were traded only in the over-the-counter market until 1973, when the Securities and Exchange Commission authorized the establishment of a "pilot" program for the trading of options on organized exchanges. On February 1, 1973, the Chicago Board Options Exchange (CBOE) was granted permission by the SEC to register as a national securities exchange so that the CBOE could be used to "test the market" for the trading of listed options on common stock. CBOE began trading on

---

[1] Abnormal returns are defined in Chapter 13.

call options on common stock in April 1973. Since then the SEC has granted permission to other exchanges to trade options: the American Stock Exchange in 1974, the Philadelphia Stock Exchange in 1975, the Pacific and the Midwest Stock Exchanges in 1976, and the New York Stock Exchange in 1982. SEC permission to trade put options on common stocks on organized exchanges was not granted until March 1977.

The SEC did not grant permission to trade options without extensive investigation. Public hearings were held in February of 1974 to address several questions concerning options: did they serve a useful economic role, are they in the public interest, and what impact would listed options have on the trading habits of the investing public. The evidence presented at the hearings supported the view that listed option trading would benefit the financial markets and the economy.

The SEC was concerned about the listing of options on the same common stock on more than one exchange, so it recommended that options terms and conditions be standardized, that a common clearing system be established, and that a common tape for recording transactions in listed options be developed. The SEC approved the creation of a national clearing system for options, the Options Clearing Corporation (OCC), established jointly at the time by the CBOE and the American Stock Exchange. Since its establishment in 1974, the OCC issues, guarantees, registers, clears, and settles all transactions involving listed options on all exchanges.

As the listed options market grew, evidence of manipulative practices and fraudulent and deceptive selling practices emerged. In July 1977 the SEC imposed a moratorium on the listing of additional options until it could study the matter further. The *Options Study* began in October 1977 to "determine whether standardized options trading is occurring in a manner and in an environment which is consistent with fair and orderly markets, the public interest, the protection of investors, and other objectives of the Act."[2] The study addresses what, if any steps the SEC should take to protect investors from abusive practices. Among its key recommendations were procedures to improve market surveillance in order to detect manipulative practices and policies that the exchanges and brokerage firms should implement to improve the caliber of brokers selling options and prevent abusive selling practices. The SEC worked with several groups to implement its recommendations.

In March 1980, the SEC was satisfied that the major regulatory deficiency it cited in the *Options Study* had been adequately addressed, and it lifted the moratorium on expansion of the listed options markets and granted permission to list options on the other financial products discussed in Chapters 16, 28, and 30. Even though ending the moratorium did allow the four exchanges that were approved for trading options to list options on more companies, the SEC did not allow the multiple listing of options. That is, the SEC did not allow the listing of an option on the same underlying common stock on more than one exchange. Instead, the SEC worked out a mechanism for allocating options on stocks among the four exchanges. These rules on multiple listing were subsequently changed. Effective January 1990, any exchange could list any new stock and 10 stocks from other exchanges. Effective January 1991, any exchange can list options on any stock eligible for option trading.

◆ FEATURES OF EXCHANGE-TRADED STOCK OPTIONS

Exchange-traded stock options are for 100 shares of the designated common stock. All exchange-traded stock options in the United States may be exercised any time before the expiration date; that is, they are American options. Options are designated by the

---

[2] Securities Exchange Act Release No. 14056 (October 17, 1977).

name of the underlying common stock, the expiration month, the strike price, and the type of option (put or call). Thus, an IBM call option with a strike price of 90 and expiring in November is referred to as the "IBM November 90 call."

The expiration dates are standardized. Each stock is assigned an option cycle—the three option cycles being January, February, and March. The expiration months for each option cycle are as follows:

Option cycle	Expiration months
January	January, April, July, October
February	February, May, August, November
March	March, June, September, December

In addition, the practice is to trade options with an expiration date of the current calendar month, the next calendar month, and the next two expiration months in the cycle. For example, suppose a stock is assigned the January option cycle. In February, options with the following expiration months would be traded: February (the current calendar month), March (the next calendar month), April (next first-expiration month in January option cycle), and July (next second-option cycle month in January option cycle). In May the following expiration months would be traded for a stock assigned to the January option cycle: May (the current calendar month), June (the next calendar month), July (next first-expiration month in January option cycle), and October (next second-expiration month in January option cycle).

Given that only the next two expiration months are traded, the longest time for an option on a stock is 6 months. Exceptions would include some stocks that have an expiration date up to 3 years in the future. These options are called **long-term equity anticipation securities**, commonly referred to as **LEAPS**.

◆ STOCK OPTION PRICING MODELS

In the Chapter 11 introduction to option pricing, we explained the factors that influence the price of an option and that a lower boundary for the option price can be determined based only on arbitrage arguments. We also set forth the basic principle behind an option pricing model. Here we provide more detailed discussion of option pricing models.

BLACK-SCHOLES OPTION PRICING MODEL

Arbitrage conditions provide boundaries for option prices, but to identify investment opportunities and construct portfolios to satisfy their investment objectives, investors want an exact price for an option. By imposing certain assumptions (to be discussed later) and using arbitrage arguments, Black and Scholes developed the following formula to compute the fair (or theoretical) price of a European call option on a nondividend-paying stock.[3]

$$C = S\,N\!\left(d_1\right) - Xe^{-rt}N\!\left(d_2\right)$$

where

$$d_1 = \frac{ln\!\left(S \,/\, X\right) + \left(r + 0.5s^2\right)t}{s\sqrt{t}}$$

$$d_2 = d_1 - s\sqrt{t}$$

---

[3]   Fischer Black and Myron Scholes, "The Pricing of Options and Corporate Liabilities," *Journal of Political Economy* (May 1973) pp. 637–54.

C = call option price
S = current stock price
X = strike price
r = short-term risk-free interest rate over the life of the option
t = time remaining to the expiration date (measured as a fraction of 1 year)
s = standard deviation of the stock price
$N(.)$ = the cumulative probability density [the value for $N(.)$ is obtained from a normal distribution function that is tabulated in most statistics textbooks]

Notice that five of the factors that we said in Chapter 11 influence the price of an option are included in the formula. (The sixth factor, anticipated cash dividends, is not included because the model is for a nondividend-paying stock.) In the Black-Scholes model, the direction of the influence of each of these factors is the same as stated in Chapter 11. Four of the factors—strike price, stock price, time to expiration, and short-term risk-free interest rate—are easily observed. The standard deviation of the stock price must be estimated.

The option price from the Black-Scholes option pricing model is "fair" in the sense that if any other price existed, it would be possible to earn riskless arbitrage profits by taking an offsetting position in the underlying stock. That is, if the price of the call option in the market is higher than that derived from the Black-Scholes option pricing model, an investor could sell the call option and buy a certain number of shares in the underlying stock.[4] If the reverse is true, that is, the market price of the call option is less than the "fair" price derived from the model, the investor could buy the call option and sell short a certain number of shares in the underlying stock. This process of hedging by taking a position in the underlying stock allows the investor to lock in the riskless arbitrage profit. The number of shares necessary to hedge the position changes as the factors that affect the option price change, so the hedged position must be changed constantly.

Figures 15-1 and 15-2 provide illustrations to demonstrate calculation of the fair value of a call option using the Black-Scholes option pricing model. The two illustrations differ only in the assumption made about the volatility (variance) of the price of the underlying stock. Notice that with the higher assumed volatility, the price of the call option is greater. The higher the expected price volatility of the underlying stock price, the higher the price of a call option.

Table 15-1 shows the option value as calculated from the Black-Scholes option pricing model for different assumptions concerning (1) the standard deviation, (2) the risk-free rate, and (3) the time remaining to expiration. Notice that (1) the lower (higher) the volatility, the lower (higher) the option price; (2) the lower (higher) the risk-free rate, the lower (higher) the option price; and (3) the shorter (longer) the time remaining to expiration, the lower (higher) the option price. All of these findings agree with what we stated in Chapter 11 as to the effect of a change in one of the factors on the price of a call option.

We have been focusing our attention on call options. How do we value put options? Recall from Chapter 11 that the put-call parity relationship indicates the relationships among the price of the common stock, the call option price, and the put option price. If we can calculate the fair value of a call option, the fair value of a put with the same strike price and expiration on the same stock can be calculated from the put-call parity relationship.

---

[4] The number of shares will not necessarily be equal to the number of shares underlying the call option. The reason is that the change in the value of the call price generally will be less than the change in the stock price. In the Black-Scholes model, the number of shares is given by the function $N(d_1)$.

Call option:

Strike price = $45

Time remaining to expiration = 183 days

Current stock price = $47

Expected price volatility = standard deviation = 25%

Short-term risk-free rate = 10%

Therefore:

$S = 47$

$X = 45$

$t = 0.5$ (183 days/365, rounded)

$s = 0.25$

$r = 0.10$

The call option price *(C)* is found as follows:

$$C = SN(d_1) - Xe^{-rt}N(d_2)$$

$$d_1 = \frac{ln(S/X) + (r + 0.5s^2)t}{s\sqrt{t}}$$

Substituting:

$$d_1 = \frac{ln(47/45) + \left[.10 + .5(.25)^2\right].5}{.25\sqrt{.5}} = 0.61722$$

$$d_2 = d_1 - s\sqrt{t}$$

Substituting:

$$d_2 = .61722 - .25\sqrt{.5} = .440443$$

From a normal distribution table:

$$N(.6172) = .7315 \text{ and } N(.4404) = .6702$$

Then:

$$C = 47(.7315) - 45\left(e^{-(.10)(.5)}\right)(.6702) = \$5.69$$

FIGURE 15-1 First Illustration of Black-Scholes Option Pricing Model

ASSUMPTIONS UNDERLYING THE BLACK-SCHOLES MODEL AND EXTENSIONS

The Black-Scholes model is based on several restrictive assumptions. These assumptions were necessary to develop the hedge to realize riskless arbitrage profits if the market price of the call option deviates from the price obtained from the model. We shall look at these assumptions, along with extensions of the basic model.

A European Option   The Black-Scholes model assumes that the call option is a European call option. Because the Black-Scholes model is based on a nondividend-paying stock,

Call option:
Strike price = $45
Time remaining to expiration = 183 days
Current stock price = $47
Expected price volatility = standard deviation = 40%
Short-term risk-free rate = 10%

Therefore:
$S = 47$
$X = 45$
$t = 0.5$ (183 days/365, rounded)
$s = 0.40$
$r = 0.10$

The call option price *(C)* is found as follows:

$$C = SN\left(d_1\right) - Xe^{-rt}N\left(d_2\right)$$

$$d_1 = \frac{ln\left(S/X\right) + \left(r + 0.5s^2\right)t}{s\sqrt{t}}$$

Substituting:

$$d_1 = \frac{ln\left(47/45\right) + \left[.10 + .5\left(.40\right)^2\right]0.5}{.40\sqrt{.5}} = 0.471941$$

$$d_2 = d_1 - s\sqrt{t}$$

Substituting:

$$d_2 = .471941 - .40\sqrt{.5} = .189098$$

From a normal distribution table:

$$N\left(.4719\right) = .6815 \text{ and } N\left(.1891\right) = .5750$$

Then:

$$C = 47\left(.6815\right) - 45\left(e^{-\left(.10\right)\left(.5\right)}\right)\left(.5750\right) = \$7.42$$

FIGURE 15-2   Second Illustration of Black-Scholes Option Pricing Model

early exercise of an option will not be economic because by selling rather than exercising the call option, the option holder can recoup the option's time premium. The binomial option pricing model, also known as the Cox-Rubenstein-Ross model, can easily handle American call options.[5] (See Chapter 11 for the basic principle of this model.) The fair value of the option in the case of a binomial option pricing model cannot be given by a formula but requires an iterative process.

---

[5]   John C. Cox, Stephen A. Ross and Mark Rubenstein. "Option Pricing: A Simplified Approach," *Journal of Financial Economics* 7(1979), pp. 229–63.

TABLE 15-1	Comparison of Black-Scholes Call Option Price Varying One Factor at a Time

Base Case

Call Option:

Strike price = $45
Time remaining to expiration = 183 days
Current stock price = $47
Expected price volatility = standard deviation = 25%
Short-term risk-free rate = 10%

Holding All Factors Constant
Except Expected Price Volatility

Expected Price Volatility	Call Option Price
15%	4.69
20	5.17
25 (base case)	5.69
30	6.26
35	6.84
40	7.42

Holding All Factors Constant
Except the Short-Term Risk-Free Rate

Risk-Free Interest Rate	Call Option Price
7%	5.27
8	5.41
9	5.50
10 (base case)	5.69
11	5.84
12	5.99
13	6.13

Holding All Factors Constant
Except Time Remaining to Expiration

Time Remaining to Expiration	Call Option Price
30 days	2.85
60	3.52
91	4.15
183 (base case)	5.69
273	6.99

Variance of the Stock Price The Black-Scholes model assumes two aspects regarding the variance of the stock price: that it is constant over the life of the option, and that it is known with certainty. If the first aspect does not hold, an option pricing model can be developed that allows the variance to change. Violation of the second aspect is more serious. As the Black-Scholes model depends on the riskless hedge argument, and, in turn, the variance must be known to construct the proper hedge, then if the variance is not known, the hedge will not be riskless.

Stochastic Process Generating Stock Prices To derive an option pricing model, an assumption is needed about the way stock prices move. The Black-Scholes model is based on the assumption that stock prices are generated by one kind of stochastic (random) process called a **diffusion process.** In a diffusion process, the stock price can take on any positive value, but when it moves from one price to another, it must take on all values in between; that is, the stock price does not jump from one stock price to another, skipping over interim prices. An alternative assumption is that stock prices follow a **jump process**; that is, prices are not continuous and smooth but do jump from one price across intervening values to the next. Merton[6] and Cox and Ross[7] developed option pricing models assuming a jump process, which is more realistic.

Short-Term Risk-Free Interest Rate In deriving the Black-Scholes model, its developers made two assumptions about the short-term risk-free interest rate. First, they assumed that the interest rates for borrowing and lending were the same. Second, they assumed that the interest rate was constant and known over the life of the option. The first assumption is unlikely to hold because borrowing rates are higher than lending rates. The effect on the Black-Scholes model is that the option price will be bounded between the call price derived from the model using the two interest rates. The model can handle the second assumption by replacing the risk-free rate over the life of the option by the geometric average of the period returns expected over the life of the option.[8]

Dividends The original Black-Scholes model is for a nondividend-paying stock. In the case of a dividend-paying stock, it may be advantageous for the holder of the call option to exercise the option early. To understand why, suppose that a stock pays a dividend such that, if the call option is exercised, dividends would be received prior to the option's expiration date. If the dividends plus the accrued interest earned from investing the dividends from the time they are received until the expiration date are greater than the time premium of the option, then it would be optimal to exercise the option.[9] In the case where dividends are not known with certainty, it will not be possible to develop a model using the riskless arbitrage argument.

In the case of known dividends, a shortcut to adjust the Black-Scholes model is to reduce the stock price by the present value of the dividends. Black suggested an approximation technique to value a call option for a dividend-paying stock.[10] A more accurate model for pricing call options in the case of known dividends was developed by Roll,[11] Geske,[12] and Whaley.[13]

---

[6] Robert Merton, "The Theory of Rational Option Pricing," *Bell Journal of Economics and Management Science* 4 (Spring 1973), pp. 141–83.

[7] John C. Cox and Stephen A. Ross, "The Valuation of Options for Alternative Stochastic Processes," *Journal of Financial Economics* 3 (March 1976), pp. 145–66.

[8] Returns on short-term Treasury bills cannot be known with certainty over the *long* term; only the *expected* return is known, along with a variance associated with it. The effects of variable interest rates are considered in Merton. "The Theory of Rational Option Pricing."

[9] Recall from Chapter 11 that the time premium is the excess of the option price over its intrinsic value.

[10] See Fischer Black, "Fact and Fantasy in the Use of Options," *Financial Analysts Journal* (July/August 1975), pp. 36–41, 61–72. The approach requires that the investor at the time of purchase of the call option and for every subsequent period specify the exact date the option will be exercised.

[11] Richard Roll, "An Analytic Formula for Unprotected American Call Options on Stocks with Known Dividends," *Journal of Financial Economics* (November 1977), pp. 251–8.

[12] Robert Geske, "A Note on an Analytical Formula for Unprotected American Call Options with Known Dividends," *Journal of Financial Economics* (December 1979), pp. 375–80; and Robert Geske, "Comment on Whaley's Note," *Journal of Financial Economics* (June 1981), pp. 213–5.

[13] Robert Whaley, "On the Valuation of American Call Options on Stocks with Known Dividends," *Journal of Financial Economics* (June 1981), pp. 207–11.

Taxes and Transaction Costs   The Black-Scholes model ignores taxes and transaction costs. The model can be modified to account for taxes, but a problem arises because no single unique tax rate applies in all situations. Transaction costs include both commissions and the bid-ask spreads for the stock and the option, as well as other costs associated with trading options.

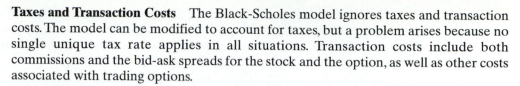

◆ OPTION STRATEGIES

Numerous strategies involve options as employed by investors. Here we discuss two types: naked strategies and covered (hedge) strategies. We then present evidence as to whether a superior option strategy exists.

NAKED STRATEGIES

Four basic option strategies include (1) long call strategy (buying call options), (2) short call strategy (selling or writing call options), (3) long put strategy (buying put options), and (4) short put strategy (selling or writing put options). We illustrated the risk/reward characteristics of these four strategies in Chapter 11; they are usually referred to as "positions." By themselves these positions are called **naked strategies** because they do not involve an offsetting or risk-reducing position in either another option or the underlying common stock.

The profit and loss from each strategy depends on the price of the underlying asset, in our case common stock, at the expiration date (on the assumption that the option is not exercised or sold earlier). The most that the option buyer can lose with each strategy is the option price. At the same time, the option buyer preserves the benefits of a favorable price movement of the underlying asset (a price increase for a call option and a price decline for a put option) reduced by the option price. By contrast, the maximum profit that the option writer can realize is the option price, while remaining exposed to all the risks associated with an unfavorable price movement.

The long call strategy (buying call options) is the most straightforward option strategy for taking advantage of an anticipated increase in the stock price, while at the same time limiting the maximum loss to the option price. The speculative appeal of call options is that they provide an investor with the opportunity to capture the price action of more shares of common stock for a given number of dollars available for investment. An investor who believes that the price of some common stock will decrease or change little can, if the expectation is correct, realize income by writing (selling) a call option (following a short call strategy). The profit and loss of the option writer is the mirror image of the option buyer's.

The most straightforward option strategy for benefiting from an expected decrease in the price of some common stock, while avoiding the unfavorable consequences should the price rise, is to follow a long put strategy (buying put options). The short put strategy (selling put options) is employed if the investor expects that the price of a stock will increase or stay the same. The maximum profit from this strategy is the option price. The maximum loss for the short put strategy occurs if the price of the stock declines to zero at or before the expiration date.

Individual investors and institutional investors use at least two other naked option strategies: (1) the long call/paper buying strategy, and (2) the cash-secured put writing strategy.

Long Call/Paper Buying Strategy   This naked strategy involves allocating a portion of a portfolio's funds to purchase a call option and investing the balance of the funds in a risk-free or low-risk money market instrument[14] such as Treasury bills or commercial

---

[14] Money market instruments are the subject of Chapter 20.

paper.[15] This strategy is less risky than allocating all the portfolio's funds to stocks. The long call option allows the investor to participate in any stock price increase. The funds invested in the risk-free or low-risk money market instrument provide a cushion against any stock price decline.

Cash-Secured Put Writing Strategy   If an investor wants to purchase a stock at a price less than the prevailing market price, one way is to place a limit buy order—of course, the result may be that the order never gets placed.[16] Alternatively, the investor can use the options market to accomplish effectively the same thing: write a put option with a strike price near the desired price. Sufficient funds are then placed in escrow to satisfy the investor's obligation if the buyer of the put option exercises the option.

COVERED (HEDGE) STRATEGIES

In contrast to naked option strategies, **covered** or **hedge strategies** involve a position in an option and a position in the underlying stock. The aim is for one position to help offset any unfavorable price movement in the other position. The two popular covered or hedge strategies that we discuss, and for which we give empirical evidence later in this chapter, are (1) the covered call writing strategy, and (2) the protective put buying strategy.

Covered Call Writing Strategy   A covered call writing strategy involves writing a call option on stocks in the portfolio. That is, the investor takes a short position in a call option and a long position in the underlying stock. If the price of the stock declines, a loss results on the long stock position. However, the income generated from the sale of the call option will either (1) fully offset, (2) partially offset, or (3) more than offset the loss in the long stock position so as to generate a profit.

To illustrate, suppose that a money manager holds 100 shares of XYZ corporation and that the current price of a share is $100. The total value of the portfolio is $10,000. Also suppose that a call option on 100 shares of XYZ with a $100 strike price that expires in 3 months can be sold for $700. (The option is at the money because the strike price is equal to the current price of the stock.) If the money manager decides to hold the 100 shares and write one call option (each call option is for 100 shares of the underlying stock), the profit or loss for this strategy depends on the price of XYZ stock at the expiration date. One of the following five outcomes will occur.

1. If the price of XYZ stock is greater than $100, the call option buyer will exercise the option and pay the option writer $100 per share. The 100 shares in the portfolio are exchanged for $10,000. The value of the portfolio at the expiration date is then $10,700 ($10,000 received from the option buyer exercising the option plus $700 received from writing the call option). In fact, more than $10,700 will be in the portfolio if the $700 is invested when it is received. At a minimum, though, the profit from this strategy if the price of XYZ stock is greater than $100 is $700, the option price. If the price of XYZ stock rises above $107, however, the investor incurs an opportunity loss equal to the excess of the value of the stock over $10,700.

2. If the price of XYZ stock is equal to $100 at the expiration date, the call option buyer will not exercise the option. The value of the portfolio will still be at least

---

[15] Although this strategy involves investing in some risk-free or low-risk money market instrument, it does not involve a long or short position in the stock. For this reason, it is still classified as a naked option strategy.

[16] Limit buy orders are explained in Chapter 4.

$10,700: 100 shares of XYZ with a market value of $100 per share and the proceeds of $700 received from writing the call option.

3. If the price of XYZ stock is less than $100 but greater than $93, there will be a profit but it will be less than $700. For example, suppose that the price of the stock is $96; the long position will have a value of $9,600 while the short call position will have a value of $700. The portfolio value is therefore $10,300, resulting in a profit of $300.

4. At a price of $93, the long stock premium will have a value of $9,300 and the short call position will have a value of $700, resulting in no profit or loss, because the portfolio value is $10,000.

5. Should the price of XYZ stock be less than $93 at expiration, the portfolio will realize a loss. For example, suppose that the price of the stock at expiration is $88. The portfolio value will be $9,500: the long stock position will be worth $8,800 and the short call position will have produced $700. Hence, there is a loss of $500. The worst case is if the price of XYZ stock declines to zero, which results in a portfolio value of $700 and a loss of $9,300.

The profit and loss profile for this covered call writing strategy is graphically portrayed in Figure 15-3. Two important points merit mention in this illustration. First, this strategy allows the investor to reduce the downside risk for the portfolio. In this example, for the at-the-money call option, the risk is reduced by an amount equal to the option price. In exchange for this reduction of downside risk, the investor agrees to cap the potential profit. For the at-the-money option used in our illustration, the maximum profit is the option price.

The second point can be seen by comparing Figure 11-4 with Figure 15-3. Notice that the shape of the two profit-and-loss profiles is the same. That is, the covered call writing strategy results in the same profit-and-loss profile as a naked short put strategy. Indeed, in our example, the covered call writing strategy results in the same profit and loss outcome as writing a put on 100 shares of XYZ stock with a strike price of $100 and 3 months to expiration (provided the price of the call and put options are the

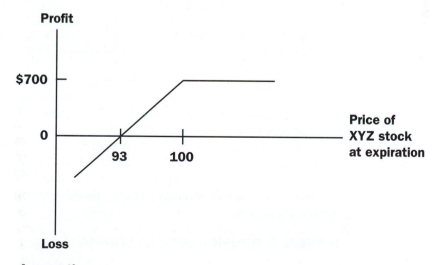

Assumptions
    Initial portfolio = 100 shares @ $100 = $10,000
    Proceeds from sale of call option = $700

FIGURE 15-3 Profit/Loss Profile for a Covered Call Writing Strategy

same). This outcome is not an accident. As we explained in Chapter 11, portfolios with equivalent payoffs can be constructed with different positions in options and the underlying instrument. A covered call writing position is equivalent to a long position in the stock and a short call position, and a long position in a stock and a short position in a call provide a similar payoff to a short put position.

Protective Put Buying Strategy   An investor may want to protect the value of a stock held in the portfolio against the risk of a decline in market value. A way to accomplish this goal with options is to buy a put option on that stock. By doing so, the investor is guaranteed the strike price of the put option less the cost of the option. Should the stock price rise rather than decline, the investor is able to participate in the price increase, with the profit reduced by the cost of the option. This strategy is called a protective put buying strategy; it involves a long put position (buying a put option) and a long position in the underlying stock that is held in the portfolio.

As an illustration, suppose that a money manager has 100 shares of XYZ stock in a portfolio and that the current market value of the stock is $100 per share (a portfolio value of $10,000). Assume further that a 2-month put option selling for $500 can be purchased on 100 shares of XYZ stock with a strike price of $100. Two months from now at the expiration date the profit or loss can be summarized as follows:

1. If the price of XYZ stock is greater than $105, the investor will realize a profit from this strategy. For example, if the price is $112, the long stock position will have a value of $11,200. The cost of purchasing the put option was $500, so the value of the portfolio is $10,700, for a profit of $700.
2. If the price of XYZ stock is equal to $105, no profit or loss will be realized from this strategy.
3. A loss occurs if the price of XYZ stock is less than $105 but at least $100. For example, a price of $102 results in a loss for this strategy of $300: a gain in the long stock position of $200 but a loss of $500 to acquire the long put position.
4. In none of the previous outcomes will the investor exercise the put option, but if the price of XYZ stock is below $100 per share, the option will be exercised. At any price below $100 per share, the investor is assured of receiving $100 per share for the 100 shares of stock. In this case, the value of the portfolio is $10,000 minus the cost of the option ($500), resulting in a loss of $500.

The graphical presentation of the profit-and-loss profile for this protective put buying strategy is shown in Figure 15-4. By implementing this strategy, the money manager effectively assures a price of $95 per share. She maintains all the upside potential, reduced only by the cost of the put option.

A wide variety of other strategies combine two or more options on the same underlying stock. These include spread strategies (vertical spreads, horizontal spreads, diagonal spreads, and butterfly spreads) and combination strategies (the most popular of which is the straddle strategy). These strategies are discussed elsewhere in books on options strategies.

IS THERE A SUPERIOR OPTIONS STRATEGY?

The development of the options market brought with it a number of myths about strategies allegedly able to generate consistently superior returns over purchasing stocks. For example, the popular literature and advertising by the options industry recommends that individual and institutional investors follow a covered call strategy that could be expected to generate "extra return" from the income received by selling

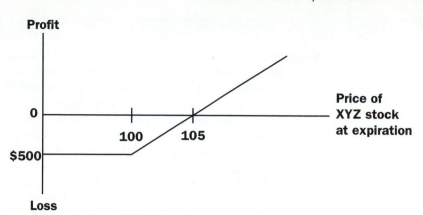

Assumptions:

    Initial portfolio = 100 shares @ $100 = $10,000
    Cost of call option = $500

FIGURE 15-4 Profit/Loss Profile for a Protective Put Buying Strategy

(writing) a call option on stocks held in their portfolio. The proliferation of this popular literature and misleading advertisements led Fischer Black to write: "For every fact about options, there is a fantasy—a reason given for trading or not trading in options that doesn't make sense when examined carefully."[17]

Does any options strategy consistently outperform the simple strategy of buying common stocks? Several studies published in highly respected academic and practitioner journals examined this issue.

Even though all the studies suffer from shortcomings due to the complexity of testing various strategies, the preponderance of evidence—particularly those studies conducted after the equity options market fully developed—indicate that no one option strategy is superior. The empirical evidence suggests that option strategy investment characteristics are consistent with the familiar trade-off between risk and return: the higher the expected return, the more the expected risk as measured by return volatility. The relative risk characteristics of the strategies described by the simulations are consistent with those expected from the risk/return characteristics of the portfolio. This view is best summarized by the authors of one study:

> *The specific levels of the returns generated, however, are strongly dependent on the actual experience of the underlying stocks during the simulation period. To avoid the creation of new myths about option strategies, the reader is warned not to infer from our findings that any one of the strategies is superior to the others for all investors. Indeed if options and their underlying stocks are correctly priced, then there is no single best strategy for investors.*[18]

The last sentence is particularly noteworthy. In a market that prices options fairly, no options strategy can be superior. We turn next to the question of whether options are fairly priced.

---

[17] Black, "Fact and Fantasy in the Use of Options." p. 36.

[18] Robert C. Merton, Myron S. Scholes, and Matthew L. Gladstein, "The Return and Risk of Alternative Call Option Portfolio Investment Strategies," *Journal of Business* 51, no. 2 (1978), p. 184.

◆ PRICING EFFICIENCY OF THE STOCK OPTIONS MARKET

A market is said to be efficient if investors cannot earn abnormal returns after accounting for risk and transactions costs. A problem encountered by researchers in the stock option market is that tests require information on the price of two instruments at the exact same time—the stock price and the option price. When prices are available on both assets at the same time, the data are said to be synchronous. In empirical tests, prices used may be nonsynchronous because of data availability limitations. That is, the stock price used in a study may be the closing price for the day, while the option price may be the price at the begining of the same trading day. An empirical study that finds abnormal trading profits using nonsynchronous data does not necessarily indicate that the options market is inefficient.

Beyond the problem of nonsynchronous data, the problem of determining the fair price of an option to be used in the empirical tests arises. Thus, researchers must rely on some option pricing model, which makes the findings only as good as the option pricing model employed.

Tests of market efficiency fall into two categories. The first category is tests using no option pricing model. Instead, violations of boundary conditions or violations of put-call parity are examined to determine whether abnormal trading profits are possible after transaction costs. Studies find that although opportunities for abnormal profits may arise before transaction costs, these opportunities disappear after these costs are considered.[19]

Tests in the second category employ various option-pricing models to assess whether mispriced options can be identified and exploited. The earlier studies in the 1970s reported mixed results concerning market efficiency.[20] Criticisms of these studies included a failure to take transaction costs into consideration. In the options market, transaction costs include (1) floor trading and clearing costs, (2) any state transfer tax that might be imposed. (3) SEC transaction fees, (4) margin requirements, (5) net capital charges, and (6) bid-ask spreads. The magnitude of these costs needs to be considered in empirical studies that investigate market efficiency. These costs vary for market makers, arbitrageurs, and individuals in the options markets, so the market may be efficient for one type of market participant but not another. Studies that took one or more of these costs into account found that the abnormally high returns reported in earlier studies were eliminated.[21] Thus, in the stock options market, the hypothesis that the options market is efficient is supported.

---

[19] See Mihtu Bhattacharya, "Transactions Data Tests of Efficiency of the Chicago Board Options Exchange," *Journal of Financial Economics* 12 (August 1983), pp. 161–65; Robert C. Klemkosky and Bruce G. Resnick, "Put-Call Parity and Market Efficiency," *Journal of Finance* (December 1979), pp. 1141–55; and Robert C. Klemkosky and Bruce G. Resnick, "An Ex Ante analysis of Put-Call Parity," *Journal of Financial Economics* 8 (1980), pp. 363–78.

[20] See, for example, Fischer Black and Myron Scholes, "The Valuation of Option Contracts and a Test of Market Efficiency," *Journal of Finance* (May 1972), pp. 399–417; Dan Galai "Tests of Market Efficiency and the Chicago Board Options Exchange," *Journal of Business* 50 (1970), pp. 167–97; Dan Galai, "Empirical Tests of Boundary Conditions for CBOE Options," *Journal of Financial Economics* 6 (1978), pp. 187–211; Robert Trippi, "A Test Option Market Efficiency Using a Random-Walk Valuation Model," *Journal of Economics and Business* 29 (1977), pp. 93–8; Donald Chiras and Steven Manaster, "The Information Content of Option Prices and a Test of Market Efficiency," *Journal of Financial Economics* 6 (1978), pp. 213–34.

[21] See Susan M. Phillips and Clifford W. Smith, "Trading Costs for Listed Options: Implications for Market Efficiency," *Journal of Financial Economics* 8 (1980), pp. 179–201; and Edward C. Blomeyer and Robert C. Klemkosky, "Tests of Market Efficiency for American Call Options," in Menachem Brenner (ed.), *Option Pricing* (Lexington, MA: Heath, 1983), pp. 101–21.

◆   **WARRANTS**

A **warrant** is a contract that gives the holder of the warrant the right but not the obligation to buy a designated number of shares of a stock at a specified price before a set date. Consequently, a warrant is nothing more than a call option. As a warrant can be exercised at any time up to and including the expiration date of the warrant, it is an American call option.

Several differences distinguish the exchange-traded call options on common stocks that we have described in this chapter from warrants, however. First, the expiration date for an exchange-traded call option is much shorter than that for a warrant at the time of issuance. Some warrants, for example, have no expiration date; these are called perpetual warrants. Second, and most important, the issuer of a warrant is the company itself. Unlike exchange-traded options, which allow entities other than the issuer of the common stock to write a call option, the option writer in the case of a warrant is the company itself. Consequently, when a warrant is exercised, the number of shares of stock outstanding will increase accordingly, which tends to dilute earnings. The fact that the exercise of a warrant dilutes earnings means that a model used to price warrants must take any dilution into account. Several warrant pricing models do just that.[22]

When initially issued, a warrant is part of another type of security. Warrants are typically attached to a bond or preferred stock. Usually warrants may be detached from the host security that they were attached to and then be traded separately. Warrants trade in all the trading locations described in the previous chapter: the major national exchanges, regional exchanges, and the over-the-counter market.

Summary ■

Stock options permit investors to mold the shape of return distribution to meet investment objectives better. Among the strategies that institutional investors use to control portfolio risk are basic naked option strategies, covered call writing, and protective put buying. The empirical evidence reviewed in this chapter suggests that no options strategy dominates any other.

In 1973, Black and Scholes introduced a model that could be used to price a European call option on a nondividend-paying stock. Subsequent researchers modified and extended the Black-Scholes model.

The empirical evidence on the pricing efficiency of the stock options market suggest that, after considering transactions costs, the market appears to be efficient. An investor who wishes to use this market should do so for its original purpose: to shape return distributions so that they are more consistent with investment objectives. It does seem, however, that astute investors can earn abnormal returns in an efficient market if they can predict volatility better than the market can.

Warrants are effectively long-term call options where the writer of the option is the company itself. The pricing of a warrant must take into consideration the potential dilution effect on earnings.

---

[22] See George M. Constantides, "Warrant Exercise and Bond Conversion," *Journal of Financial Economics* (September 1984), pp. 371–98; David C. Emanuel, "Warrant Valuation and Exercise Strategy," *Journal of Financial Economics* (August 1983), pp. 211–35; Dan Galai and Meir Schneller, "The Pricing of Warrants and the Value of the Firm," *Journal of Finance* (December 1978), pp. 1333–42; and Eduardo S. Schwartz, "The Valuation of Warrants: Implementing a New Approach," *Journal of Financial Economics* (January 1977), pp. 79–93.

Key Terms ■

- Covered strategy
- Diffusion process
- Hedge strategy

- Jump process
- Long-term equity anticipation securities (LEAPS)

- Naked strategies
- Warrant

Questions ■

1. How many shares does an exchange-traded option involve?
2. What does the "IBM February 100 put" mean?
3. What is a LEAP?
4. "The option price depends on the volatility of the underlying stock. If capital market theory asserts that the appropriate measure of volatility is a stock's beta, then the option price should depend on the stock's beta." Explain why you agree or disagree with this statement.
5. a. Assuming the following values for a European call option, calculate the theoretical option price using the Black-Scholes model:
   Strike price = $100
   Current stock price = $100
   Dividend = $0
   Short-term risk-free rate = 8%
   Expected price volatility = 20%
   Time to expiration = 91 days
   b. What is the intrinsic value and time premium for this call option?
6. For the call option in the previous question, what would be the theoretical option price, intrinsic value, and time premium if:
   a. The current stock price is $55 instead of $100?
   b. The current stock price is $150 instead of $100?
7. a. Explain why it would not be economical for the buyer of an American call option on a nondividend-paying stock to exercise the option prior to the expiration date.
   b. Is this reasoning true for an American call option on a dividend-paying stock? Under what circumstances (if any) would early exercise be economical?
   c. Would it be economical for the buyer of an American put option to exercise the option early? (Hint: Think about what happens if the price of the stock falls to zero before the expiration date.)
8. What is the difference between a naked strategy and a covered strategy?
9. What naked strategy or strategies would an investor pursue if she thought a stock's price was going to rise?
10. What is the general conclusion of empirical studies that investigated whether a superior option strategy exists?
11. Comment on the following statement: "Investors should pay closer attention to the options markets because option strategies offer risk and reward opportunities that are clearly superior to investing directly in common stock."
12. Suppose an investor wants to follow a protective put buying strategy for a stock he owns that has a market price of $60. He is told that three 180-day put options are available on that stock with strike prices of $56, $58, and $60.
    a. Which put option will give him the greatest price protection?
    b. Which put option will be the most expensive?
    c. Which put option should be selected?

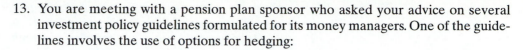

13. You are meeting with a pension plan sponsor who asked your advice on several investment policy guidelines formulated for its money managers. One of the guidelines involves the use of options for hedging:

> *Protective put buying and covered call writing strategies are recognized by the investment community as means for hedging a stock position. The former will not be permitted by any of our fund managers because it involves a cost that may not be recouped if the put option is not exercised. We will permit covered call writing because there is no cost generated to protect the portfolio.*

What advice would you give the plan sponsor concerning this investment policy guideline?

14. The quote following is from the June 22, 1992, issue of *Derivatives Week*, p. 4:

> *Aetna Investment Management, the London-based fund management arm of U.S. insurer Aetna Life & Casualty, expects to start using derivatives within weeks in more than £200 million of U.K. equity holdings, according to Tom Chellew, director. The firm has not used derivatives before in its total of £700 million under management in the U.K.*
>
> *Aetna is talking to trustees over the next two weeks and expects to get approval to start dealing thereafter, he said. Initially, it will only use derivatives in its more than £200 million of U.K. holdings in its £250 million of unit trusts under management.*
>
> *Chellew said initial strategies are likely to include writing covered calls and writing puts on stock Aetna doesn't mind buying. The firm will likely be interested in both U.K. index and individual stock options.*
>
> *Subsequently, Aetna expects to expand use into other holdings—specifically, equity and later possibly fixed income—and into pension and life insurance money under management, he said. Aetna will use derivatives to enhance yields and for risk reduction, and will trade futures for asset allocation.*

What does Mr. Chellew mean by "writing puts on stock Aetna doesn't mind buying"?

15. The following was overheard at a party:

> *You have to be foolish not to sell a call option on stock you own. You don't really lose anything because if the stock is called, you own it and just have to give it up. In return, you receive fee income that you get to keep no matter what the buyer of the call option does. It is a no-lose proposition in my opinion.*

a. What type of strategy is this person suggesting?
b. Is this view of call options correct?

16. The following is from an article entitled "Analytic Uses Options to Protect Tenneco Position," that appeared in the November 16, 1992, issue of *Derivatives Week*, p. 7:

> *Analytic Investment Management in Irvine, CA., last Monday sold 70 Nov. 40 puts and bought 70 Feb. 35 puts on Tenneco for its Analytic Optioned Equity Fund—a derivatives-driven mutual fund, according to Chuck Dobson, the fund's executive v.p. By selling and buying an equal number of exchange-traded puts, the firm maintained a fully-hedged position while*

using profits on its options to counterbalance paper losses on the 7,000 Tenneco shares it owns for a net gain of $1\frac{7}{8}$ per option, Dobson said.

Though Dobson could not give the price at which the stock was bought, he noted that since Tenneco was trading around $35 last Monday, the 7,000 shares were worth roughly $245,000, or about 0.27% of the total $91 million portfolio. Dobson explained that the firm takes a nondirectional approach to picking stock, relying instead on the stock's volatility, option premium and dividends.

Dobson explained that the fund, which contains 130–140 mostly high capitalization stocks, is governed by four basic derivatives-linked strategies: 1) buy a stock and sell a call on the stock; 2) buy a stock and a put on the stock; 3) sell a put and place the exercise price in a cash reserve fund; and 4) buy a call and place the exercise price in a money market fund.

    a. Explain the option strategy cited in the first paragraph of this excerpt. Be sure to explain what Mr. Dobson meant by the "firm maintained a fully-hedged position."

    b. Explain the first two strategies listed in the third paragraph.

17. What is the difference between a stock option and a stock warrant?

18. Explain why you agree or disagree with the following statement: "As a warrant is nothing more than a European call option, the Black-Scholes option pricing model can be used to value it."

19. Two option-type products that were issued in the market are "Primes" and "Scores." Primes and Scores separate the cash flow components of certain stocks into two components: dividend income and capital appreciation. Specifically, a Prime entitles the holder of the security to receive (1) the dividends of the underlying stock, and (2) the market value of the stock at a specified future date up to a preset amount, called the "termination value." The term *Prime* stands for "prescribed right to income." A Score entitles the instrument holder to all the appreciation above the termination value. Usually, the termination value is 20% to 25% above the current stock price. The term *Score* stands for "special claim on residual income."

    Twenty-five trusts were issued and all matured some time in 1992.

    Primes and Scores on individual stocks are not issued originally as securities. Instead, a trust is created in which the stock of a specific company is placed. The trust then issues a Prime and a Score for each share of stock placed in the trust. The trust has a maturity of 5 years, with its size restricted to no more than 5% of the total number of shares of the outstanding stock of the company. At the end of 5 years, the trust is terminated, and the Prime and Score holders receive the agreed-upon amount. Before the termination date, the Prime and Score created are traded separately on the American Stock Exchange. At any time during a trading day, a combination of one unit of a Prime and one unit of a Score may be redeemed from the trust for one share of the underlying stock. No charge is required for the redemption.

    Even though probably no new Primes and Scores will be created in the future because of adverse tax circumstances, it is still interesting to examine these instruments in order to understand that some instruments have option features even though they are not labeled options.

    a. Explain why the Score has the payoff profile of a call option.

    b. Explain why the Prime has the payoff of a covered call option.

    c. In an efficient market, a package of a Prime and a Score should sell for the same price as the underlying stock after adjusting for transaction costs. However, in a study on the pricing of Primes and Scores, one study found that they were mispriced relative to the underlying stock. [Robert A. Jarrow and Maureen O'Hara, "Primes and Scores: An Essay on Market Imperfections," *Journal of Finance* (December 1989), pp. 1263–87]. More specifically, they found that a package of Primes and Scores often exceeded the price of the underlying stock by a considerable amount. They explain the discrepancy as arising from market imperfections with respect to short-selling and transactions costs. Explain why these two factors could cause the discrepancy.

CHAPTER 16

Stock Index Derivative Markets

Learning Objectives

After reading this chapter you will understand:

◆ the investment features of stock index options and futures.

◆ institutional strategies that employ stock index options and futures.

◆ why stock index futures prices may diverge from their theoretical price based on a simple cost-of-carry model.

◆ the empirical evidence on the pricing efficiency of the stock index options and futures market.

◆ the role of stock index options and futures in the financial market.

◆ what an equity swap is and its potential applications.

◆ the role, if any, that these contracts played in the stock market crash of October 19, 1987.

In Chapter 15 we covered options on individual stocks. In this chapter we discuss equity index derivatives. These include stock index options, stock index futures, and equity swaps. The underlying instrument for these contracts is a stock index.

For each contract, we discuss its basic characteristics, how it can be employed by institutional investors, and empirical evidence on market efficiency. Because we reviewed the pricing of futures and options in previous chapters, our focus here is on the pricing nuances associated with index derivative products. We also look at the empirical evidence on the role of stock index futures and options in the U.S. financial market and the role these contracts played in the October 19, 1987, stock market crash.

◆ STOCK INDEX OPTIONS

In March 1983, a revolution in stock options and investments in general occurred. At that time, trading in an option whose underlying instrument was a stock index, the S&P 100 (originally called the CBOE 100), began on the Chicago Board Options Exchange. Shortly afterward, the American Stock Exchange initiated trading in an option based on what the exchange called the Major Market Index (MMI).[1] These index options proved useful and popular with many kinds of investors. As in the case of options on individual stocks, stock index options are regulated by the Securities and Exchange Commission.

---

[1] The index includes 20 stocks and was constructed to be similar to the Dow Jones Industrial Average.

Table 16-1 presents a list of stock index option contracts trading on exchanges in the United States. The most liquid index options are the S&P 100 index (OEX) and the S&P 500 index. Both trade on the CBOE. Index options can be listed as American or European. Both index option contracts have specific standardized features and contract terms. Moreover, both have short expiration cycles. Table 16-1 also shows selected industry options, sector options, and style options.

The level of trading volume for each contract differs. A useful statistic measuring the liquidity of a contract is the number of contracts that are entered into but not yet liquidated. This figure is called the contract's **open interest**. An open interest figure is reported for all listed contracts.

If a stock option is exercised, a stock must be delivered. It would be complicated, to say the least, to settle a stock index option by delivering all the stocks that make up the index. Instead, stock index options are cash-settlement contracts, which means that if the option is exercised, the exchange-assigned option writer pays cash to the option buyer. No delivery of any stock occurs.

The dollar value of the stock index underlying an index option is equal to the current cash index value multiplied by the contract's multiple. That is,

Dollar value of the underlying index = Cash index value × Contract multiple

Each stock index option has a contract multiple. The contract multiple for the S&P 100 is $100. So, for example, if the cash index value for the S&P 100 is 720, then the dollar value of the S&P 100 contract is 720 × $100 = $72,000.

For a stock option, the price at which the buyer of the option can buy or sell the stock is the strike price. For an index option, the **strike index** is the index value at which the buyer of the option can buy or sell the underlying stock index. The strike index is converted into a dollar value by multiplying the strike index by the multiple for the contract. For example, if the strike index is 700 for an S&P 100 index option, the dollar value is $70,000 (700 × $100). If an investor purchases a call option on the S&P 100 with a strike index of 700, and exercises the option when the index value is 720, then the investor has the right to purchase the index for $70,000 when the dollar value of the index is $72,000. The buyer of the call option would then receive $2,000 from the option writer.

As shown in Table 16-1, exercise provisions for stock index options come in both the American and European variety. The S&P 100 index options are American options. The S&P 500, the Major Market, and the Institutional Index options are European options, which means that they cannot be exercised until expiration. (Later we will explain what "FLEX" means.) Institutional investors find writing European options attractive because they need not fear that the option they write in order to accomplish an investment objective will be exercised early.

Options available on stock index futures are not as widely used as options on stock indexes. Options on futures contracts are the contracts of choice in the interest rate options market. We will postpone our discussion of options on futures until Chapter 28.

PRICING EFFICIENCY OF THE STOCK INDEX OPTIONS MARKETS

Empirical tests of the pricing of index options are subject to the same problems as stock options discussed in Chapter 15. Moreover, investors face the added problem of estimating the amount and timing of dividends for the stocks in the index.

TABLE 16-1 U.S.-Listed Equity Index Option Contracts

Contract	Index Description	Exchange*	Exercise Provisions
Large Cap Contracts			
Major Market Index	20 stocks, price weighted	AMEX	European, FLEX
Dow Jones Industrial Average	30 stocks, price weighted	CBOE	European, FLEX
NASDAQ 100	100 stocks, cap weighted	CBOE	European, FLEX
Standard & Poor's 100	100 stocks, cap weighted	CBOE	American, FLEX
Standard & Poor's 500	500 stocks, cap weighted	CBOE	European, FLEX
NYSE Composite Index	2,600+ stocks, cap weighted	CBOE	European, FLEX
Institutional Index	75 stocks, cap weighted	AMEX	European, FLEX
Small Cap Contracts			
Russell 2000 Index	2,000 stocks, cap weighted	CBOE	European
Standard & Poor's Small Cap 600	600 stocks, cap weighted	CBOE	European
PSE Wilshire Small Cap 250	250 stocks, cap weighted	PSE	European
Style or Nonindustry Sector Options			
Standard & Poor's BARRA Growth	100+ stocks, cap weighted	CBOE	European
Standard & Poor's BARRA Value	300+ stocks, cap weighted	CBOE	European
AMEX MS Consumer Index	30 stocks, equal weighted	AMEX	European
AMEX MS Cyclical Index	30 stocks, equal weighted	AMEX	European
AMEX MS Gold Bugs Index	13 stocks, equal weighted	AMEX	European
AMEX MS Commodity Related	21 stocks, equal weighted	AMEX	European
CBOE Lipper Analytical Salomon Brothers Growth Fund	30 stocks, equal weighted	CBOE	European
CBOE Lipper Analytical Salomon Brothers Growth & Income Fund	30 stocks, equal weighted	CBOE	European
CBOE Morgan Stanley Multinational Company Index	40+ stocks, cap weighted	CBOE	European
Dow Jones Trans. Average	20 stocks, price weighted	CBOE	European
Dow Jones Utility Average	15 stocks, price weighted	CBOE	European
PSE Morgan Stanley Emerging Growth Index	50 stocks, cap weighted	PSE	European
Sector Options			
Chicago Board Options Exchange	10 CBOE Sector Indexes	CBOE	European
	6 Goldman Sachs Technology Indexes		
	6 S&P Industry Sectors		
American Stock Exchange	15+ AMEX Sector Indexes	AMEX	European
	5+ MS Sector Indexes		
Philadelphia Stock Exchange	12 PSE Sector Indexes	PSE	European

*AMEX = American Stock Exchange; CBOE = Chicago Board Options Exchange; PSE = Philadelphia Stock Exchange.

Source: Bruce M. Collins and Frank J. Fabozzi, *Derivatives and Equity Portfolio Management* (New Hope, PA: Frank J. Fabozzi Associates, 1999), Exhibit 4, pp. 20–1.

Two studies examined the pricing efficiency of the stock index options market. Evnine and Rudd looked at the S&P 100 and Major Market Index (MMI) options.[2] Their database consisted of prices from a real-time pricing service for the period between June 26 and August 30, 1984. For each trading day prices for every hour were included, for a total of 1,798 observations. For every hour, the information in the database contained essentially the same information that would be displayed on screens on the exchange floor. A problem remained because the last option trade recorded for the hour was not synchronized with the last value recorded for the index. The index option prices included bid-ask prices, so part of the cost of transacting was considered in the analysis.

Don Chance investigated the S&P 100 index options for the period January 3 through April 27, 1984, using a database supplied by a regional brokerage and investment banking firm.[3] The final daily bid and ask quotes and their update times were included in his database. The prices were market makers' quotes as the market closed and the final index level. Because the prices are quotes rather than the closing transaction price, the problem of nonsynchronicity of the option and the index is not present. Although problems in updating both the option quotes and the index continued to be an issue, Chance argues that all quotes reflected transactions that could have been executed.

As we explained in Chapter 11, arbitrage arguments can be used to put a lower boundary on the price of a call option. Evnine and Rudd tested for violations of the lower boundary, that is, instances where the ask price of the call was below the difference between the value of the cash index and the strike price. They found 30 instances when the lower boundary for the call option on the S&P 100 was violated, 11 instances for the MMI. Evnine and Rudd report occasions when the size of the violation became so large that even "upstairs traders" would have been capable of taking advantage of these violations.[4]

A possible explanation for the large size of these violations, as Evnine and Rudd note, is that during the week when these violations were observed (August 1 to August 6), the market rose dramatically. Consequently, the value of the cash index was being updated faster than the bid-ask prices, possibly causing the observed violations.

Both Evnine and Rudd and Chance tested for violations of the put-call parity relationship. The Evnine and Rudd results suggest that if stock index options are treated as European, significant profit opportunities are possible. The violations suggest that the S&P 100 index call options were underpriced, which means that the puts were overpriced. The reverse is true for the MMI options. Even if the options are considered American options, these results suggest profit opportunity. When Chance tested the put-call parity relationship, he found a significant number of violations in the 1,690 portfolios examined.

Why do we observe these violations? The reason is more than likely attributable to the difficulty of arbitraging between the index option market and the cash market. Two problems in arbitraging are the difficulty and expense of creating a portfolio to replicate the performance of the cash market index, and estimating dividends for the stocks in the index. We elaborate on these issues when we discuss stock index futures later in this chapter.

---

[2] Jeremy Evnine and Andrew Rudd, "Index Options: The Early Evidence," *Journal of Finance* (July 1985), pp. 743–56.

[3] Don M. Chance, "Parity Tests of Index Options," *Advances in Futures and Options Research 2* (1987), pp. 47–64.

[4] As explained in Chapter 14, block trades (trades of 10,000 shares or more) typically are negotiated between traders and institutional investors using a network that links them together, referred to as the upstairs market.

PORTFOLIO STRATEGIES WITH STOCK INDEX OPTIONS

In Chapter 15, we explained how stock options can be used to take advantage of the anticipated price movement of individual stocks. Alternatively, they can be used to protect current or anticipated positions in individual stocks. For example, an investor can protect against a decline in the price of a stock held in her portfolio by buying a put option on that stock. By doing so, the investor is guaranteed a minimum price equal to the strike price minus the option price. Also, if an investor anticipates buying a stock in the future but fears that the stock price will rise making it more expensive to buy the stock, she can buy a call option on the stock. By pursuing this strategy, the investor guarantees that the maximum price that will be paid in the future is the strike price plus the option price.

Consider an institutional investor that holds a portfolio consisting of a large number of stock issues. To protect against an adverse price movement, the institutional investor must buy a put option on every stock issue in the portfolio, which would be quite costly. By taking an appropriate position in a suitable stock index option, an institutional investor with a diversified portfolio can protect against adverse price movements.[5] For example, suppose that an institutional investor holding a diversified portfolio of common stock that is highly correlated with the S&P 100 is concerned that the stock market will decline in value over the next 3 months. Suppose that a 3-month put option on the S&P 100 is available. Because the put option buyer gains when the price of the underlying stock index declines, if an institutional investor purchases this put option (i.e., follows a protective put buying strategy) rather than liquidating the portfolio, adverse movements in the value of the portfolio due to a decline in the stock market will be offset (in whole or in part) by the gain in the put option.

When stock options or stock index options are used to protect an existing or anticipated position, the investor need not exercise the option if a favorable price movement occurs. This important characteristic of options compares favorably to futures in attempting to protect a position. An institutional investor can obtain downside protection using options at a cost equal to the option price, but preserve upside potential (reduced by the option price).

FLEX OPTIONS[6]

A **FLEX option** is an option contract with some customized terms. It is traded on an options exchange and cleared and guaranteed by the associated clearinghouse for the exchange. The need for customization of certain terms arises because of the wide range of portfolio strategy needs of institutional investors that cannot be satisfied by standard exchange-traded options.

A FLEX option can be created for individual stocks and stock indexes. The value of FLEX options comes from the ability to customize the terms of the contract along four dimensions: underlying, strike price, expiration date, and settlement style (i.e., American versus European). Moreover, the exchange provides a secondary market to offset or alter positions and an independent daily marking of prices.

The development of the FLEX option is a response to the growing over-the-counter market. The exchanges seek to make the FLEX option attractive by providing price discovery through a competitive auction market, an active secondary market,

---

5   The appropriate number of stock index options to buy depends on the beta of the portfolio with respect to the underlying stock. The procedure for calculating the appropriate position in a stock index option is beyond the scope of this chapter.

6   For a more detailed description of FLEX options, see James J. Angel, Gary L. Gastineau, and Clifford J. Weber, *Equity FLEX Options* (New Hope, PA: Frank J. Fabozzi Associates, 1999).

daily price valuations, and the virtual elimination of counterparty risk. The FLEX option represents a link between listed options and OTC products.

EXOTIC OPTIONS

In Chapter 11 we discussed exotic options. These are complex options created by dealer firms for their clients. The two options described in Chapter 11 were alternative options and outperformance options.

INDEX WARRANTS

In Chapter 15 we described warrants on common stock. Warrants on stock indexes are called **index warrants**. As with a stock index option, the buyer of an index warrant can purchase the underlying stock index. Index warrants are issued by either corporate or sovereign entities as part of a security offering, and they are guaranteed by an option clearing corporation.

OPTIONS MARKETS OUTSIDE THE UNITED STATES

Options markets have developed in many countries. In the United Kingdom, the London Traded Options Market is part of the International Stock Exchange and hosts trading in options on stocks and on indexes. In Canada, numerous options are traded on both the Toronto Stock Exchange and the Montreal Exchange. The European Options Exchange is in Amsterdam, and it sponsors trading in a wide variety of European equity options and index options.

Table 16-2 shows selected international stock index options. Among the latest arrivals of international options are options traded on the Dow Jones STOXX 50 and the Dow Jones EURO 50 stock indexes. The indexes are comprised of 50 industrial, commercial, and financial European blue-chip companies.

TABLE 16-2 International-Listed Stock Index Option Contracts			
Contract	*Index Description*	*Exchange**	*Exercise Provisions*
Dow Jones STOXX 50	50 stocks, cap weighted	DBT	European
Dow Jones EURO STOXX 50	50 stocks, cap weighted	DBT	European
Eurotop 100	225 stocks, price weighted	AMSE	European
Nikkei 225 Average (Japan)	100 stocks, price weighted	OSE	American
TOPIX (Japan)	1,300+ stocks, cap weighted	TSE	American
FTSE 100 Index (U.K.)	100 stocks, cap weighted	LIFFE	American, FLEX
DAX 30 Index (Germany)	30 stocks, cap weighted	DBT	American
CAC 40 Index (France)	40 stocks, cap weighted	MONEP	American
Hang Seng Index (Hong Kong)	600+ stocks, cap weighted	HKFE	European
Australian All Ordinaries	300+ stocks, cap weighted	ASE	American

*Symbols Directory:

OSE	Osaka Stock Exchange
TSE	Tokyo Stock Exchange
LIFFE	London International Financial Futures and Options Exchange
DBT	Deutsche Terminborse
MONEP	Marche des Options Negociables de Paris
HKFE	Hong Kong Futures Exchange
ASE	Australian Stock Exchange
AMSE	Amsterdam Stock Exchange

Source: Bruce M. Collins and Frank J. Fabozzi, *Derivatives and Equity Portfolio Management* (New Hope, PA: Frank J. Fabozzi Associates, 1999), Exhibit 4, pp. 20–1.

Chapter 10 covers the fundamental characteristics of futures contracts. A futures contract is a firm legal agreement between a buyer and an established exchange or its clearinghouse in which the buyer agrees to take delivery of something at a specified price at a designated time (called the settlement date). On the other side of the contract is a seller who agrees to deliver the "something." A stock index futures contract is a futures contract where the underlying "something" is a stock index.

In 1982, three futures contracts on broad-based common stock indexes made their debut: the S&P 500 futures contract traded on the International Monetary Market of the Chicago Mercantile Exchange, the NYSE Composite futures contract traded on the New York Futures Exchange, and the Value Line Average traded on the Kansas City Board of Trade. Since then, broad-based and specialized stocks index futures contracts have been introduced.

Table 16-3 lists the stock index futures contracts traded in the United States. The most actively traded contract is the S&P 500 futures contract. Table 16-4 lists stock index futures contracts traded on non-U.S. exchanges.

As of January 2002, single stock futures are in the process of being listed on U.S. exchanges. A single stock futures contract is an agreement between two parties to buy or sell shares of individual companies (as opposed to a stock index in the case of a stock index futures contract) at some time in the future with the terms agreed upon today. Single stock futures currently trade on numerous exchanges around the world including those in Australia, Denmark, Finland, Hong Kong, Hungary, Portugal, South Africa, Sweden, and, most recently, Canada and the United Kingdom.

Stock index futures contracts are regulated by the Commodity Futures Trading Commission (CFTC), although recent proposals suggest shifting regulatory authority to the SEC or to combine the SEC and CFTC.

The dollar value of a stock index futures contract is the product of the futures price and the contract's multiple, that is,

Dollar value of a stock index futures contract = Futures price × Multiple

TABLE 16-3   Stock Index Futures Contracts Traded on Exchanges in the United States

Index Futures Contract	*Index Description*	*Exchange**	*Contract Size/Multiple*
Standard & Poor's 500	500 stocks, cap weighted	CME	Index × $250
Standard & Poor's Midcap	400 stocks, cap weighted	CME	Index × $500
Russell 2000 Index	2,000 stocks, cap weighted	CME	Index × $500
Nikkei 225 Index	225 stocks, price weighted	CME	Index × $5
Major Market Index	20 stocks, price weighted	CME	Index × $500
S&P 500/BARRA Growth Index	100+ stocks, cap weighted	CME	Index × $250
Standard & Poor's BARRA Value	300+ stocks, cap weighted	CME	Index × $250
Nasdaq 100 Index	100 stocks, cap weighted	CME	Index × $100
IPC Stock Index	35 stocks, cap weighted	CME	Futures × $25
NYSE Composite Index	2,600+ stocks, cap weighted	NYFE	Index × $500

*CME = Chicago Mercantile Exchange; NYFE = New York Futures Exchange.

Source: Bruce M. Collins and Frank J. Fabozzi, *Derivatives and Equity Portfolio Management* (New Hope, PA: Frank J. Fabozzi Associates, 1999), Exhibit 12, p. 33.

TABLE 16-4   Selected Non-U.S. Stock Index Futures Contracts

Index Futures Contract	Index Description	Exchange*	Contract Size/Multiple
JSE Actuaries Top 40 All Shares Index (South Africa)	40, cap weighted	SAFEX	Index × R10
Australian All Ordinaries	300+ stocks, cap weighted	SFE	Index × $25
Hang Seng Index (Hong Kong)	600+ stocks, cap weighted	HKFE	Index × $50
Nikkei 225 Average (Japan)	225 stocks, price weighted	OSE	Index × ¥1,000
Nikkei 300 Average (Japan)	300 stocks, cap weighted	OSE	Index × ¥10,000
SIMEX MSCI Singapore Stock Index	35 stocks, cap weighted	SIMEX	Index × S$200
Nikkei 225 Average (Japan)	225 stocks, price weighted	SIMEX	Index × ¥500
Nikkei 300 Average (Japan)	300 stocks, cap weighted	SIMEX	Index × ¥10,000
Kuala Lumpur Composite Index (Malaysia)	50 stocks, cap weighted	KLOFFE	Index × RM100
NZSE10 Index (New Zealand)	10 stocks, cap weighted	NZFOE	Index × NZ$25
FTSE 100 Index (U.K.)	100 stocks, cap weighted	LIFFE	Index × £10
FTSE 250 Index (U.K.)	250 stocks, cap weighted	LIFFE	Index × £10
Eurotop 100 (European Stocks)	100 stocks, cap weighted	LIFFE	Index × ECU20
Dow Jones STOXX 50**	50 stocks, cap weighted	EUREX	Index × ECU10
Dow Jones EURO STOXX 50**	50 stocks, cap weighted	MATIF	Index × ECU10
DAX 30 Index (Germany)	30 stocks, cap weighted	DBT	Index × DM100
CAC 40 Index (France)	40 stocks, cap weighted	MATIF	Index × FF200
IBEX 35 Stock Index (Spain)	35 stocks, cap weighted	RV	Index × ESP1,000
Milan Stock Exchange MIB 30 (Italy)	30 stocks, cap weighted	IDEM	Index × ITL10,000
TSE 35 Index (Canada)	35 stocks, cap weighted	TFE	Index × C$500
Bovespa Index (Brazil)	51 stocks, cap weighted	BM&F	Index × BRL3

Symbols Directory

SAFEX	South African Futures Exchange
SFE	Sydney Futures Exchange
OSE	Osaka Stock Exchange
SIMEX	Singapore International Monetary Exchange
LIFFE	London International Financial Futures and Options Exchange
KLOFFE	Kuala Lumpur Options and Futures Exchange
TSE	Toronto Stock Exchange
TFE	Toronto Futures Exchange
HKFE	Hong Kong Futures Exchange
DBT	Deutsche Terminborse
NZFOE	New Zealand Futures and Options Exchange
MATIF	Marche à Terme International de France
RV	Meff Renta Variable
IDEM	Italian Derivatives Market; Italian Stock Exchange
BM&F	Bolsa de Mercadorias & Futuros
EUREX	Swiss-German Futures and Options Exchange

**Dow Jones STOXX 50 and Dow Jones EURO STOXX 50 futures contracts trade on both the EUREX and the MATIF. Options on the futures trade on the DBT.

Source: Bruce M. Collins and Frank J. Fabozzi, *Derivatives and Equity Portfolio Management* (New Hope, PA: Frank J. Fabozzi Associates, 1999), Exhibit 12, p. 33.

The multiples for the key contracts are indicated in the last column of Table 16-4. For example, if the futures price for the S&P 500 is 1300 and the multiple is $250, the dollar value of a stock index futures contract is

$$1300 \times \$250 = \$325,000$$

If an investor buys (takes a long position in) an S&P 500 futures contract at 1300 and sells it at 1315, the investor realizes a profit of 15 times $250, or $3,750. If the futures contract is sold instead for 1280, the investor will realize a loss of 20 times $250, or $5,000.

Stock index futures contracts are cash-settlement contracts. Therefore, at the settlement date, cash will be exchanged to settle the contract. For example, if an investor buys an S&P 500 futures contract at 1300 and the settlement index is 1350, settlement would be as follows. The investor has agreed to buy the S&P 500 for 1300 times $250, or $325,000. The S&P 500 value at the settlement date is 1350 times $250, or $337,500. The seller of this futures contract must pay the investor $12,500 ($337,500 − $325,000). Had the index at the settlement date been 1280 instead of 1350, the value of the S&P 500 would be $320,000 (1280 × $250). The investor must pay the seller of the contract $5,000 ($325,000 − $320,000).

MARGIN REQUIREMENTS

As we explained in Chapter 10, futures contracts come with margin requirements (initial, maintenance, and variation). Margin requirements are revised periodically. The exchanges classify users of contracts as hedgers or speculators, with the margin for the former being less than that for the latter.[7]

Futures positions are marked to market at the end of each trading day. The following illustration demonstrates the mechanics of margin requirements and the mark-to-market procedure. First we give the particulars of the illustration. We use a hypothetical stock index futures contract, which we refer to as SIF.

1. An investor buys 193 SIF contracts on Day 1. The actual closing settlement price for the contract on that day was 259.
2. The closing settlement prices for the nine trading days following Day 1, are shown in the second column of Table 16-5.
3. The initial and maintenance margin requirements are $10,000 per contract.

The dollar value of each SIF contract when the settlement index was 259 was $129,500 (= the multiple of 500 times 259).

Because the investor purchased 193 contracts, the total dollar value of the contracts was $24,993,500. The third column of Table 16-5 shows the dollar value for each of the nine trading days following Day 1. The initial margin requirement is $1,930,000 for the 193 contracts; maintenance margin is $1,930,000 for the 193 contracts. The last column in Table 16-5 shows the variation margin for the nine trading days following Day 1. A negative number (i.e., a number in parentheses) means a margin call is made; a positive number means that funds can be withdrawn.

On Day 1, the investor must put up initial margin of $1,930,000, which may be in the form of a Treasury bill. Once the equity in the account falls below the maintenance margin (which in the case of an investor is the same as the initial margin of $1,930,000), additional margin (variation margin) will be required. Margin calls must be met in cash (Treasury bills are not acceptable to satisfy variation margin) and must be supplied in 24 hours.

---

[7]   As explained later in this chapter, investors commonly use stock index futures to hedge a position. The clearinghouse requires less margin for investors who are using contracts for this purpose.

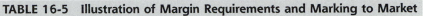

TABLE 16-5 Illustration of Margin Requirements and Marking to Market

Initial margin per contract = $10,000*
Initial margin for 193 contracts = $1,930,000 (193 × $10,000)
Maintenance margin per contract = $10,000*
Maintenance margin for 193 contracts = $1,930,000

Day	Settlement Price	Value for 193 Contracts	Equity in Account	Variation Margin
1	259.00	$24,993,500	$1,930,000	—
2	258.60	24,954,900	1,891,400	$(38,600)
3	259.25	25,017,625	1,992,725	62,725
4	257.30	24,829,450	1,804,550	(188,175)
5	257.90	24,887,350	1,987,900	57,900
6	256.20	24,723,300	1,823,850	(164,050)
7	261.85	25,268,525	2,475,225	545,225
8	263.85	25,461,525	2,668,225	193,000
9	264.80	24,553,200	2,759,900	91,675
10	264.00	25,476,000	2,682,700	(77,200)

*Margin requirements at the time.

On Day 2 of our illustration, the settlement price falls to 258.60, reducing the value of the 193 contracts to $24,954,900. The decrease in the contract value is subtracted from the equity in the account, and the account is marked to market. The equity therefore declines to $1,891,400. Because the equity on Day 2 falls below the maintenance margin of $1,930,000, a margin call for $38,600 ($1,930,000 − $1,891,400) goes out.

When the equity in the account exceeds the maintenance margin, the investor can withdraw the excess. On Day 3, for example, the settlement price for the index was 259.25, increasing the value of the contracts to $25,017,625. The resulting equity in the account was $1,992,725, which is $62,725 greater than the maintenance margin requirement. The investor can withdraw the $62,725. This example surely shows that anyone using the stock index futures market to pursue some strategy must have sufficient funds to satisfy margin calls.

PRICING OF STOCK INDEX FUTURES

In Chapter 10 we demonstrated that arbitrage arguments can be used to determine the theoretical futures price. In the case of stock index futures, we need the following information:

1. The value of the cash (spot) market index
2. The dividend yield on the stocks in the index that would be earned until the settlement date
3. The interest rate for borrowing and lending until the settlement date (referred to as the financing cost)

The theoretical futures price that will prevent arbitrage profits can be shown to be equal to:

Futures price = Cash market price
+ Cash market price (Financing cost − Dividend yield)

where "Financing cost" is the cost of financing a position until the settlement date of the futures contract, and "Dividend yield" is the dividends over the same period.

Moreover, it is assumed that dividends are received only at the settlement date. The difference between the financing cost and the dividend yield is called the **net financing cost** because it adjusts the financing cost for the yield earned. The net financing cost is more commonly called the cost of carry, or simply, carry. *Positive* carry means that the yield earned is greater than the financing cost; *negative* carry means that the financing cost exceeds the yield earned.

This equation for the theoretical futures price indicates that it may sell at a premium to the cash market price (higher than the cash market price) or at a discount from the cash market price (lower than the cash market price), depending on the financing cost and the dividend yield.

Recall from Chapter 10 that to derive the theoretical futures price using the arbitrage argument, also called the cost of carry model, several assumptions must be made. When these assumptions do not hold, a divergence occurs between the actual futures price and the theoretical futures price. We discussed several of these assumptions for futures contracts in general in Chapter 10. Here we highlight the six assumptions unique to stock index futures.

1. No interim cash flows from dividend payments are assumed in the futures pricing model. We know that interim cash flows do occur, and incorporating interim dividend payments into the futures pricing model is not difficult. The problem is that the value of the dividend payments at the settlement date will depend on the interest rate at which the dividend payments can be reinvested. The lower the dividend and the closer the dividend payments to the settlement date of the futures contract, the less important the reinvestment income is in determining the futures price.

2. In determining the cost of carry, both the financing cost and the dividend yield must be known. Although the financing cost may be known, the dividend rate and the pattern of dividend payments are not known with certainty. They must be projected from the historical dividend payments of firms in the index.

3. For the arbitrage to work when the futures price is below its theoretical value, the investor must be able to use the proceeds from selling the cash index short. In practice, for individual investors, the proceeds are not received, and, in fact, the individual investor is required to put up margin (securities margin, not futures margin) to short-sell. For institutional investors, the securities may be borrowed, but borrowing entails a cost.

4. In the case of a short sale of the stocks in the index, all stocks must be sold simultaneously. The stock exchange rule for the short-selling of stock may prevent the arbitrage strategy from bringing the actual futures price in line with the theoretical futures price. The short-selling rule for stocks specifies that a short sale can be made only at a price that is higher than the previous trade (referred to as an up-tick), or at a price that is equal to the previous trade but higher than the last trade at a different price (referred to as a zero-tick). If the arbitrage requires selling the stocks in the index simultaneously, and the last transaction for some of the stocks is not an up-tick, the stocks cannot be shorted simultaneously.

5. Another difficulty in arbitraging the cash and futures market is that it is too expensive to buy or sell every stock included in the index. Instead, a portfolio containing a smaller number of stocks may be constructed to "track" the index. The arbitrage, however, is no longer risk-free because we have introduced the risk that the portfolio will not track the index exactly, referred to as **tracking-error risk**.

6. The basic arbitrage model ignores not only taxes but also the differences between the tax treatment of cash market transactions and futures transactions.

Violation of the assumptions made in developing the cost-of-carry pricing model results in discrepancies between the actual price and the theoretical futures price from a simple cost-of-carry model. Basically, boundaries around the futures trading price will not permit arbitrage profits. Researchers derived upper and lower bounds for the theoretical futures prices that take into consideration several of these factors.[8]

PRICING EFFICIENCY OF THE STOCK INDEX FUTURES MARKET

Using theoretical futures prices and their bounds, several studies examined the pricing efficiency of the stock index futures market. The first study to examine this issue empirically was by Cornell and French.[9] In this study they compared actual futures prices to theoretical futures prices for the S&P 500 futures contract and the NYSE futures contract on the first days of trading of June, July, August, and September 1982. In all but two of the cases they examined, the theoretical (predicted) futures price was higher than the actual futures price. They attributed the discrepancy they found to the difference in the tax treatment of futures and cash market transactions.

After deriving upper and lower bounds for the theoretical futures price, Modest and Sundaresan examined the June 1982 S&P futures contract from April 21 to June 16, 1982, and the December 1982 S&P 500 futures contracts from April 21 to September 15, 1982, to determine whether the actual futures prices were outside the bounds.[10] Recall from our discussion of the theoretical futures price that the futures pricing model assumes that short-sellers have the use of the proceeds from selling the cash index short. In tests of three sets of theoretical bounds, Modest and Sundaresan assumed the following: (1) no use of the proceeds by short-sellers, (2) use of half the proceeds by short-sellers, and (3) use of all the proceeds by short-sellers. Recall also that the theoretical futures price depends on the expected dividend yield. Modest and Sundaresan constructed theoretical bounds with and without adjustment for dividends. Thus, six theoretical bounds were constructed for the two S&P 500 futures contracts investigated: theoretical bounds constructed with and without dividend adjustments for each of the three assumptions about how much of the proceeds short-sellers of the cash index would have available to use.

Modest and Sundaresan found that the actual futures prices for both futures contracts were within the theoretical bounds constructed when the investor had no use of the proceeds from short-selling the cash index when dividends were considered. Thus, under these conditions, no arbitrage profits were possible during the time frame studied, even though, in sporadic instances, the theoretical bounds were violated, under realistic assumptions. Modest and Sundaresan found few opportunities to generate arbitrage profits (i.e., few violations of the theoretical bounds) even at the inception of stock index futures trading.

Although the Cornell and French, and Modest and Sundaresan studies examined pricing efficiency when the contracts started trading, Ed Peters looked at whether the stock index futures market became more efficient over time.[11] He examined market efficiency for the S&P 500 futures contract and the NYSE futures contract from the

8 David M. Modest and Mahadevan Sundaresan, "The Relationship Between Spot and Futures Prices in Stock Index Futures: Some Preliminary Evidence," *Journal of Futures Markets* (Spring 1983), pp. 15–42.

9 Bradford Cornell and Kenneth R. French, "Taxes and the Pricing of Stock Index Futures," *Journal of Finance* (June 1983), pp. 675–94.

10 Modest and Sundaresan, "The Relationship Between Spot and Futures Prices in Stock Index Futures: Some Preliminary Evidence."

11 Ed Peters, "The Growing Efficiency of Index-Futures Markets," *Journal of Portfolio Management* (Summer 1985), pp. 52–6.

September 1982 contract to the December 1983 contract to determine whether the actual prices moved closer to the theoretical prices. Results showed that the market became more efficient in pricing futures, a finding that he attributed to better estimation of the dividend stream for each index contract.

Bruce Collins tested the pricing efficiency of the futures market by examining whether an investment strategy of buying the cash market index and selling the futures could generate an abnormal return.[12] In an efficient market, the return on this strategy should approximately equal the return on a Treasury security with a maturity equal to the maturity of the futures contract. An abnormal return occurs if the return realized from this strategy exceeds the yield on a comparable-maturity Treasury security. Selected S&P 500 futures contracts were examined beginning with the December 1982 contract and extending to the September 1985 contract. Transactions costs were considered. His results suggested that, despite instances of pricing inefficiency, the market became increasingly efficient. Other statistical tests performed by Collins led to the same conclusion.

PORTFOLIO STRATEGIES WITH STOCK INDEX FUTURES

We now examine seven investment strategies for which institutional investors can use stock index futures:

1. Speculating on the movement of the stock market
2. Controlling the risk of a stock portfolio (altering beta)
3. Hedging against adverse stock price movements
4. Constructing indexed portfolios
5. Index arbitrage
6. Creating portfolio insurance
7. Asset allocation

Speculating on the Movement of the Stock Market   Prior to development of stock index futures, an investor who wanted to speculate on the future course of stock prices had to buy or short individual stocks. Now, the stock index can be bought or sold in the futures market. But making speculation easier for investors is not the main function of stock index futures contracts. The other strategies discussed will show how institutional investors can effectively use stock index futures to meet investment objectives.

Controlling the Risk of a Stock Portfolio   An institution that wishes to alter its exposure to the market can do so by revising the portfolio's beta through a rebalancing of the portfolio with stocks that will produce the target beta. However, transaction costs are associated with rebalancing a portfolio. Because of the leverage embedded in futures, institutions can use stock index futures to achieve a target beta at a considerably lower cost. Buying stock index futures increases a portfolio's beta, and selling reduces it.

Hedging Against Adverse Stock Price Movement   Hedging is a special case of controlling a stock portfolio's exposure to adverse price changes. In a hedge, the objective is to alter a current or anticipated stock portfolio position so that its beta is zero. A portfolio with a beta of zero should generate a risk-free interest rate, which is consistent with the capital asset pricing model discussed in Chapter 9, and also consistent with our discussion of futures contracts in Chapter 10.

---

[12] Bruce M. Collins, "An Empirical Analysis of Stock Index Futures Prices," unpublished doctoral dissertation, Fordham University, 1987.

Remember that using stock index futures to hedge locks in a price, although the hedger cannot then benefit from a favorable movement in the portfolio's value. With stock index options, the hedger locks in downside protection but retains the upside potential reduced by the cost of the option.

An illustration shows how stock index futures can be used to hedge the risk of a portfolio against an adverse price movement.[13] Suppose that a portfolio manager owns all the stocks in the Dow Jones Industrial Average on July 1, 1986, and the market value of the portfolio held is $1 million. Also assume that the portfolio manager wants to hedge the position against a decline in stock prices from July 1 to August 31, 1986, using the September 1986 S&P 500 futures contract. As the S&P 500 futures September contract is used here to hedge a portfolio of Dow Jones Industrials to August 31, it is a cross-hedge, as explained in Chapter 10.

The first step in the hedge is to determine whether to buy or sell the futures contract. Because the portfolio manager wants to protect against a decline in the portfolio's value, he will sell stock index futures contracts. The second step is to determine the appropriate number of contracts to sell. Although computation is beyond the scope of this chapter, it can be demonstrated that for our illustration six is the appropriate number of contracts to sell to obtain the same market risk exposure with the futures as with the portfolio of Dow Jones Industrial stocks.

Table 16-6 summarizes the actual outcome of this hedge, assuming that it is lifted on August 31, 1986. The hedge results in a loss of $11,100. And assuming commissions of $20 per contract, commissions for six futures contracts would be $120, for an overall loss of $11,220. The reason for the loss is the adverse change in the basis (which is the difference between the cash price and futures price), as shown in the last column of the lower panel of Table 16-6. Had the hedge not been employed, however, the loss would have been $72,500—the loss in the cash market. As we explained in Chapter 10, hedging substitutes basis risk for price risk.

This hedge is called a short or sell hedge. A long or buy hedge can be used in anticipation of the purchase of stocks at some future date. In this case, stock index futures contracts are purchased. For example, shortly after stock index futures began trading, Westinghouse Electric Corporation's pension fund bought 400 stock index contracts between July 29 and August 11, 1982. The reason cited by a company source for purchasing these contracts, which were worth more than $20 million, was that the company was not "ready to buy individual stocks in such a short period of time." A company source stated that stock index futures gave the pension fund "a quick way of putting money into the market," and one "much cheaper" than if the fund had purchased stock in the cash market.[14] This Westinghouse hedging strategy can be viewed as a long hedge.

Two examples of how investment banking firms can use stock index futures to hedge their activities were reported shortly after stock index futures began trading. In the first example in June 1982, International Harvester traded its stock portfolio to Goldman Sachs in exchange for a bond portfolio.[15] As recipient of the stock portfolio, Goldman Sachs was exposed to market risk. To protect itself against a decline in the value of the stock portfolio, Goldman Sachs placed a short hedge on a "significant"

[13] This illustration is adapted from Frank J. Fabozzi and Edgar E. Peters, "Hedging with Stock Index Futures," Chapter 13 in Frank J. Fabozzi, (ed.), *The Handbook of Stock Index Futures and Options* (Homewood, IL: Dow Jones Irwin, 1989).

[14] "Stock Futures Used in Rally," *Pension & Investment Age* (October 25, 1982), pp. 1, 52.

[15] Kimberly Blanton, "Index Futures Contracts Hedge Big Block Trades," *Pension & Investments Age* (July 19, 1982), pp. 1, 38.

TABLE 16-6 Hedging a $1 Million Dow Jones Industrial Index Fund Using S&P 500 Futures

Own $1 million worth of Dow Jones Industrial stocks on 7/1/86.
Need to hedge against an adverse market move.
Hedge is lifted 8/31/86.

Facts		
	July 1, 1986	*August 31, 1986*
Value of portfolio	$1,000,000	$927,500
Cash price of S&P 500	252.04	234.91
Price of Sept. 1986 S&P futures	253.95	233.15

	Outcome	
Cash Market	*Futures Market*	*Basis*
Time hedge is placed		
Own $1,000,000 portfolio	Sell six Sept. 1986 S&P 500 futures contracts at 253.95	−1.91
Time hedge is lifted		
Own $927,500 portfolio	Buy six Sept. 1986 S&P 500 futures contracts at 233.15	+1.76
Loss in cash market = $72,500	Gain in futures market = $61,400	
	Overall loss = $11,100	

portion of the stock portfolio, using all three stock index futures trading at the time to implement the hedge.

In the second example, Salomon Brothers used stock index futures to protect itself against a decline in stock prices in a transaction involving $400 million of stock. In that transaction, the New York City Pension Fund switched $400 million of funds that were being managed by Alliance Capital to Bankers Trust so that the latter could manage the funds using an indexing approach. Salomon Brothers guaranteed prices at which the city and Bankers Trust could purchase or sell the stocks in the portfolio being transferred by using options on individual stocks to protect certain stock prices, but also used stock index futures to protect itself against broad market movements that would decrease the value of the stocks in the portfolio.

Constructing Indexed Portfolios   As we explained in Chapter 14, an increasing number of institutional equity funds are indexed to some broad-based stock market index. Management fees and transaction costs are associated with creating a portfolio to replicate a stock index targeted to be matched. The higher these costs, the greater the divergence between the performance of the indexed portfolio and the target index. Moreover, because a fund manager creating an indexed portfolio will not purchase all the stocks that comprise the index, the indexed portfolio is exposed to tracking-error risk. Instead of using the cash market to construct an indexed portfolio, the manager can use stock index futures. In fact, one trade publication, *Pensions and Investments,* reports that of the 60 or so largest pension funds that are indexed, about one-third use stock index futures in managing the fund.

We now illustrate how and under what circumstances stock index funds can be used to create an indexed portfolio. If stock index futures are priced according to their theoretical value, a portfolio consisting of a long position in stock index futures and

Treasury bills produces the same portfolio as that of the underlying cash index. For example, suppose that an index fund manager wishes to index a $9 million portfolio using the S&P 500 as the target index. Also assume the following:

1. The S&P 500 is currently 300.
2. The S&P 500 futures index with 6 months to settlement is currently selling for 303.
3. The expected dividend yield for the S&P 500 for the next 6 months is 2%.
4. Six-month Treasury bills are currently yielding 3%.
5. The theoretical futures price is 303.[16]

Consider two strategies that the index fund manager may choose to pursue:

Strategy 1: Purchase $9 million of stocks in such a way as to replicate the performance of the S&P 500.

Strategy 2: Buy 60 S&P 500 futures contracts with settlement 6 months from now at 303, and invest $9 million in 6-month Treasury bills.[17]

How will the two strategies perform under various scenarios for the S&P 500 value when the contract settles 6 months from now? We shall investigate three scenarios in which the S&P 500 increases to 330, remains at 300, and declines to 270. At settlement, the futures price converges to the value of the index. Table 16-7 shows the value of the portfolio for both strategies for each of the three scenarios. For a given scenario, the performances of the two strategies end up identical.

This result should not be surprising because a futures contract can be replicated by selling the instrument underlying the futures contract and buying Treasury bills. In the case of indexing, we replicate the underlying instrument by buying the futures contract and investing in Treasury bills. Therefore, if stock index futures contracts are properly priced, index fund managers can use stock index futures to create an index fund.

Several points should be noted. First, in Strategy 1 the ability of the portfolio to replicate the S&P 500 depends on how well the portfolio is constructed to track the index. On the other hand, assuming that the expected dividends are realized and that the futures contract is fairly priced, the futures/Treasury bill portfolio (Strategy 2) will mirror the performance of the S&P 500 exactly. Thus, tracking error is reduced. Second, the cost of transacting is less for Strategy 2. For example, if the cost of one S&P 500 futures is $15, then the transactions cost for Strategy 2 would be only $900 for a $9 million fund. This cost would be considerably less than the transaction costs associated with the acquisition and maintenance of a broadly diversified stock portfolio designed to replicate the S&P 500. In addition, for a large fund that wishes to index, the market impact cost is less by using stock index futures rather than using the cash market to create an index. The third point is that custodial costs are obviously less for an index fund created using stock index futures. The fourth point is that the performance of the synthetically created index fund will depend on variation margin. Finally, in the analysis of the performance of each strategy, the dollar value of the portfolio at the end of the 6-month period is the amount in the absence of taxes. For Strategy 1, no taxes will be paid if the securities are not sold, though taxes will be paid on dividends. For Strategy 2, taxes must be paid on the interest from the Treasury bills and on any gain from the liquidation of the futures contract.

---

[16] The theoretical futures price is found using the formula presented earlier:

$$\text{Cash market price} + \text{Cash market price (Financing cost} - \text{Dividend yield)}$$

The financing cost is 3% and the dividend yield is 2%. Therefore, $300 + 300 (0.03 - 0.02) = 303$.

[17] This illustration ignores margin requirements; the Treasury bills can be used for initial margin. Also, 60 contracts are selected in this strategy because with the current market index at 300 and a multiple of $500, the cash value of 60 contracts is $9 million.

TABLE 16-7 Comparison of Portfolio Value from Purchasing Stocks to Replicate an Index and a Futures/Treasury Bill Strategy When the Futures Contract Is Fairly Priced

Assumptions:

Amount to be invested = $9 million
Current value of S&P 500 = 300
Current value of S&P futures contract = 303
Expected dividend yield = 2%
Yield on Treasury bills = 3%
Number of S&P 500 contracts to be purchased = 60

Strategy 1: Direct Purchase of Stocks

	Index Value at Settlement*		
	330	*300*	*270*
Change in index value	10%	0%	− 10%
Market value of portfolio that mirrors the index	$ 9,900,000	$9,000,000	$8,100,000
Dividends 0.02 × $9,000,000	$ 180,000	$ 180,000	$ 180,000
Value of portfolio	$10,080,000	$9,180,000	$8,280,000
Dollar return	$ 1,080,000	$ 180,000	$ (720,000)

Strategy 2: Futures/T-bill Portfolio

	Index Value at Settlement*		
	330	*300*	*270*
Gain for 60 contracts 60 × $500 × gain per contract	$ 810,000	$ (90,000)	$ (999,000)
Value of Treasury bills $9,000,000 × 1.03	$ 9,270,000	$9,270,000	$9,270,000
Value of portfolio	$10,080,000	$9,180,000	$8,280,000
Dollar return	$ 1,080,000	$ 180,000	$ (720,000)

*Because of convergence of cash and futures price, the S&P 500 cash index and stock index futures price will be the same.

Therefore, if stock index futures contracts are properly priced, index fund managers can use stock index futures to create an index fund. Suppose instead that the futures price is less than the theoretical futures price (i.e., the futures contracts are cheap). If that situation occurs, the index fund manager can enhance the indexed portfolio's return by buying the futures and buying Treasury bills. That is, the return on the futures/Treasury bill portfolio will be greater than that on the underlying index when the position is held to the settlement date.

To see this result, suppose that in our previous illustration the current futures price is 301 instead of 303, so that the futures contract is cheap (undervalued). For all three scenarios shown in Table 16-7 the value of the portfolio would be $60,000 greater by buying the futures contract and Treasury bills rather than buying the stocks directly.

Alternatively, if the futures contract is expensive based on its theoretical price, an index fund manager who owns stock index futures and Treasury bills will swap that portfolio for the stocks in the index. An index manager who swaps between the futures/Treasury bills portfolio and a stock portfolio based on the value of the futures contract relative to the cash market index is attempting to enhance the portfolio's return. This strategy, referred to as a stock replacement strategy, is one of several strategies used to attempt to enhance the return of an indexed portfolio.[18]

Index Arbitrage Opportunities to enhance returns as a result of the mispricing of the futures contract are not restricted to index fund management. Money managers and arbitrageurs monitor the cash and futures market to see when the differences between the theoretical futures price and actual futures price are sufficient so that an arbitrage profit can be attained: selling the futures index if it is expensive and buying stocks, or buying the futures index if it is cheap and selling the stocks. Program trading is used to execute the buy and sell orders.[19]

Creating Portfolio Insurance In Chapter 11, we explained how a put option can protect the value of an asset. At the expiration date of the put option, the minimum value for the asset will be the strike price minus the cost of the put option. Put options on stock indexes can do the same for a diversified portfolio of stocks.

Alternatively, an institutional investor can create a put option synthetically by using either (1) stock index futures, or (2) stocks and a riskless asset. Allocation of the portfolio's funds to stock index futures or between stocks and a riskless asset is adjusted as market conditions change.[20] A strategy that seeks to insure the value of a portfolio using a synthetic put option is called **dynamic hedging.**

Given that put options on stock indexes are available to portfolio managers, why should they bother with dynamic hedging? A portfolio manager might do so for one of four reasons. First, the size of the market for options on stock indexes is not as large as that for stock index futures and therefore may not easily accommodate a large portfolio insurance program without moving the price of the option substantially. Second, exchanges impose position limits on the amount of contracts in which an investor can have a position.[21] In the case of institutions that want to protect large equity portfolios, position limits may effectively prevent them from using exchange-traded index options to protect their portfolio.

Third, existing exchange-traded index options contracts are of shorter maturity than the period over which some investors seek protection. Finally, the cost of a put option may be higher than the transaction costs associated with dynamic hedging. Yet while the cost of a put option is known (and is determined by expected price volatility), the cost of creating portfolio insurance by using stock index futures or stocks will be determined by actual price volatility in the market. The greater the actual price volatility in the market, the more rebalancing of the portfolio is necessary, and the higher the cost of creating portfolio insurance.

How does dynamic hedging work using stocks and a riskless asset? Recall that the buyer of a put option establishes a floor for the value of an asset but retains the opportunity to benefit if the asset's price rises. A dynamic hedging strategy seeks to reproduce the payoff of a long put option position by changing the allocation of the portfolio's funds between the risky asset and a riskless asset. In this case, the risky asset is the equity portfolio, and the riskless asset may be a money market instrument such as Treasury bills. When stock prices decline, the investor must reduce the exposure to the

---

[18] For a further discussion of this strategy, see Bruce M. Collins, "Index Fund Investment Management," Chapter 10 in Frank J. Fabozzi (ed.), *Portfolio and Investment Management* (Chicago: Probus Publishing, 1989).

[19] Program trading is discussed in Chapter 14.

[20] For a more detailed explanation of this strategy, see Mark Rubinstein and Hayne Leland, "Replicating Options with Positions in Stock and Cash." *Financial Analysts Journal* (July-August 1981), pp. 63–72, or Hayne Leland. "Portfolio Insurance," Chapter 12 in *The Handbook of Stock Index Futures and Options*.

[21] Regulators will grant approval for contract trading only if the exchange imposes a position limit because it is believed such a limit will stabilize the option price.

stock market and increase the holding of the riskless asset. Placing more funds in the riskless asset will help to insure the floor value for the portfolio. Thus, when stock prices decline, a commensurate amount of stocks are sold and the proceeds are invested in a riskless asset such as Treasury bills. When stock prices rise, a commensurate amount of stocks are purchased with the proceeds obtained from selling a portion of the riskless asset. This action increases the exposure of the portfolio to the equity market so that the investor can capture the benefits of a rising market. Fewer funds need to be placed in the riskless asset, because the likelihood of achieving the floor value for the portfolio declines in a rising equity market. To execute the orders to buy or sell stocks, program trading is used.

Instead of implementing dynamic hedging by changing the allocation of the portfolio between stocks and a riskless asset, stock index futures can be used. When stock prices decline, stock index futures are sold. This transaction is equivalent to selling stocks and investing the funds in a riskless asset. When stock prices rise, stock index futures are purchased, which is equivalent to buying stocks and reducing the portfolio's allocation to a riskless asset.[22]

Asset Allocation   The decision on how to divide funds across the major asset classes (for example, equities, bonds, foreign securities, real estate) is referred to as the **asset allocation decision**. Futures and options can be used to implement an asset allocation decision more effectively than transacting in the cash markets.

For example, suppose that a pension fund sponsor with assets of $1 billion allocates $300 million to the bond market and $700 million to the stock market. Suppose further that the sponsor decides to alter that bond/stock mix to $600 million in bonds and $400 million in stock. Liquidation of $300 million in stock involves significant transaction costs—both commissions and execution (market impact) costs.[23] Moreover, the external money managers who are managing the stock portfolios face disruption as funds are withdrawn by the sponsor. Rather than liquidating the stock portfolio immediately, the sponsor can sell an appropriate number of stock index futures contracts. This effectively decreases the exposure of the pension fund to the stock market. To increase the fund's exposure to the bond market, the sponsor can buy interest rate futures contracts.[24]

◆ EQUITY SWAPS

In Chapter 12 we introduced swaps. In recent years, the concept of swapping cash flows has been applied to the equity area. In an **equity swap**, the cash flows that are swapped are based on the total return on some stock market index and an interest rate (either a fixed rate or a floating rate). Moreover, the stock market index can be a non-U.S. stock market index and the payments could be nondollar-denominated. For example, a money manager can enter into a 2-year quarterly reset equity swap based on the German DAX market index versus some money market index in which the money manager receives the market index in deutchemarks and pays the floating rate in deutchemarks.

The notional amount of the contract is not exchanged by the counterparties, but both parties are exposed to counterparty risk. An important difference between an

---

[22] Determination of the amount of stock to buy or sell is based on an option pricing model.
[23] These costs are described in Chapter 7.
[24] These contracts are explained in Chapter 28.

equity swap and an interest rate swap (discussed in Chapter 29) is that it is possible for one of the parties in an equity swap—specifically, the party receiving the stock market index—to realize a negative total return. In such a case, that party must pay to the counterparty the amount of the negative total return plus the payment on the reference interest rate.

APPLICATIONS

As explained in Chapter 12, a swap is nothing more than a package of forward contracts. The advantage of the swap is that it is more transactionally efficient for accomplishing many investment objectives.

One of two uses suggested for equity swaps creates a portfolio that replicates an index. An indexed portfolio can be created by buying all or some of the stocks that comprise the index. Alternatively, this strategy can be accomplished more efficiently—in terms of cost and speed of execution—by buying stock index futures contracts and investing funds in Treasury bills. The stock index futures position must then be rolled over before the settlement date into a new futures position. Equity swaps provide a third alternative that offers three advantages: (1) there are quarterly cash flows; (2) the money manager can specify the maturity of the contract so that frequent rolling of a futures position is unnecessary; and (3) there is no concern with the mispricing of the futures contract. Another distinct advantage of an equity swap is that because they are customized, a money manager can use a swap to index a non-U.S. stock market index. We saw this feature used in our earlier illustration of swapping the DAX market index for DM LIBOR. Moreover, an equity swap can be used to hedge the currency risk. For example, an equity swap can be structured in which the money manager receives in U.S. dollars the DAX market index total return and pays in U.S. dollars LIBOR. Two disadvantages of using an equity swap rather than stock index futures include (1) counterparty risk, and (2) less liquidity in swaps compared to the very liquid stock index futures contract.

The second way in which equity swaps can be used is to enhance return.[25] For example, suppose a pension plan sponsor allocates a small portion of the portfolio to a specialty equity manager who exhibited on a fairly consistent basis superior investment performance relative to some stock market benchmark; yet diversification and other constraints may prevent more funds from being allocated to this manager. Also suppose that the plan sponsor establishes an asset-allocation policy fixing the amount in 3-year Treasury securities. Using an equity swap, the pension plan sponsor can enter into a swap in which it receives over the next 3 years a fixed coupon rate based on 3-year Treasuries and agrees to pay the total return on the stock market benchmark that the specialty equity manager outperforms. The amount then allocated to this manager can be increased. Then, if the manager outperforms the benchmark, the excess return over the benchmark is retained by the pension plan sponsor. The total return for the pension plan would then be the 3-year Treasury fixed coupon rate plus the excess return over the benchmark. The risk, of course, is that the specialty equity manager underperforms the index. The plan's return is then reduced by the amount of underperformance. Depending on the actual performance of the specialty equity manager, it is possible for the fund's return to be negative.

---

[25] Gary Gastineau, "Swaps and the Division of Labor," SBC Research, Swiss Bank Corporation Investment Banking Inc. (January 1993), p. 2.

A great deal of debate continues to surround stock index options and futures. In this section, we discuss the arguments at issue and review the empirical evidence. The first question is whether stock index futures and options trading—and strategies employing these contracts—add value to our financial markets, or whether index futures and options merely provide a form of legalized gambling for market participants. The second controversy is whether stock price volatility increased as a result of futures and options trading. Finally we focus on the extent to which the existence of these contracts contributed to the October 1987 market crash, popularly known as Black Monday.

ARE DERIVATIVE INDEX MARKETS BENEFICIAL TO THE FINANCIAL MARKETS?

In the absence of stock index futures and options markets, investors would be able to alter portfolio positions in only one place when new information is received—the cash market. If investors receive economic news that they expect might impact the cash flow of all stocks adversely, they can reduce their equity exposure by selling stocks. The opposite is true if investors expect the new information to increase the cash flow of all stocks: in that case, an investor would increase the equity exposure of the portfolio. Of course, transaction costs are associated with altering equity risk exposure—explicit costs (commissions), and hidden or execution costs (bid-ask spreads and market impact costs).

Stock index futures provide another market that institutional investors can use to alter equity risk exposure when new information is acquired. But which market—cash or futures—should the investor employ to alter a position *quickly* upon receipt of new information? As we explained in Chapter 10, it will be the one that is the more efficient to use to achieve the objective. The factors to consider are commissions, bid-ask spreads, market impact costs (hence the importance of market liquidity), and the leverage offered.

The market that investors feel is more efficient to use to achieve their investment objective will be where price discovery takes place. Price information is then transmitted to the other market. So, for example, if the futures market is the market of choice, it will serve as the price discovery market. That is, it will be the market where investors send their collective message about how any new information is expected to affect the cash market. Then, a mechanism is necessary for transmitting that message to the cash market. That mechanism is index arbitrage.

A comparison of transaction costs indicates that they are substantially lower in the stock index futures market. Typically, transaction costs in this market are between 5% to 10% of transaction costs in the cash market.

The speed at which orders can be executed also gives the advantage to the futures market. Estimated time to sell a block of stock at a reasonable price is only about 2 to 3 minutes, while a futures transaction can be accomplished in 30 seconds or less.[26] The advantage is also on the side of the futures market when it comes to the amount of money that must be put up in a transaction (i.e., leverage). As we explained earlier, margin requirements for transactions in the stock market are considerably higher than in the stock index futures market. Thus, a study by the SEC's Division of Market Regulation concludes:

> *[Institutions can] sell portions of their equity positions in a faster, less expensive manner by using index futures than by selling directly on stock exchanges. . . .*

---

[26] Thomas Byrne, "Program Trading—A Trader's Perspective," *Commodities Law Letter* VI, nos. 9 and 10, p. 9.

Futures are used instead of stocks because of the increased speed and reduced transaction costs entailed in trading a single product in the futures market. . . . As a result of the futures market's liquidity, investors can execute large transactions with much smaller market effects than is possible in the separate stocks.

Which market do investors select to alter their risk exposure? John Merrick found that prior to 1985 the cash market dominated the price discovery process, relative to the stock index futures market.[27] Since 1985, however, the S&P 500 futures market plays the dominant price discovery role. This reversal of the dominant market was not an accident. It followed the pattern of trading volume. When trading volume in the futures market surpassed that on the cash market, the futures market dominated.

How does the existence of competing markets with the attributes described previously affect the stock market? In her testimony before Congress on July 23, 1987, Susan Phillips, then the chairperson of the Commodity Futures Trading Commission, stated: "The depth and liquidity of the futures markets facilitate the absorption of new fundamental information quickly, thus improving the efficiency of the stock markets."[28]

Is it possible for the futures market to take on a life of its own, so that the futures price does not reflect the economic value of the underlying instrument? It could be, if no mechanism were available to bring futures prices and cash market prices in line. This mechanism is index arbitrage, which we described earlier.

Critics of stock index futures point to program trading, index arbitrage, and dynamic hedging (portfolio insurance) when substantial decline in the cash market and/or increased stock price volatility occurs. As we explained in Chapter 14, program trading is a technique for trading lists of stocks as close in time as possible. It is not, as is often stated in the popular press, a trading strategy. Program trades typically are implemented electronically using the automated order-execution facilities of the exchanges (e.g., the SuperDOT of the NYSE) that allows orders to be transmitted simultaneously to the appropriate specialist post.

Why is it important for an institution to execute a list of orders as close in time as possible? Several investment strategies depend on the timing of trades: indexing, index arbitrage, and portfolio insurance. The question is whether any of these strategies that rely on program trading and stock index futures are disruptive to the stock market.

Indexing   Indexing, as we explained in Chapter 14, is not a strategy that attempts to trade on information. Indexing is a strategy that theory tells us investors should employ in an efficient market in order to capture the efficiency embodied in the market. Yet the theory tells us nothing about how to implement the strategy. To manage an indexed portfolio, a money manager first constructs an initial portfolio to replicate the performance of the market. The money manager must rebalance the portfolio, however, as new monies are added to or withdrawn from an indexed portfolio. Program trading is used so that all stocks in the portfolio can be sold or purchased by simultaneous order at the closing prices, so that the performance of the indexed portfolio will do a good job tracking the index. Therefore, indexing should not be a disruptive market force.

---

[27]   John J. Merrick, Jr., "Price Discovery in the Stock Market," Federal Reserve Bank of Philadelphia Working Paper No. 87-4, March 1987.

[28]   Testimony before the Subcommittee on Telecommunications and Finance, Committee on Energy and Commerce, U.S. House of Representatives, July 23, 1987, p. 1.

Index Arbitrage   As we just explained, a mechanism is required to transmit the message about investor expectations from the price discovery market to the other market. Only if the cost of carry is zero will the futures price and the cash price be the same. Otherwise, the futures price will differ from the cash price by an amount equal to the cost of carry. Because of transaction costs and other factors, boundaries around the theoretical futures price limit generation of arbitrage profits if the futures price trades within the bounds. In an attempt to capture arbitrage profits, those who follow an index arbitrage are simply tying the futures and cash markets together. This link prevents futures contracts from taking on a life of their own, and thereby allows hedgers to use stock index futures to carry out strategies to protect portfolio values at a fair price.

What happens if the futures price is outside the boundaries? An investor can generate arbitrage profits by selling the more expensive instrument and buying the cheaper instrument, driving the price of the expensive one down and driving the price of the cheaper one up until the futures price is within the theoretical boundaries. Suppose that the cash market is cheap relative to the futures market. An investor borrows funds and buys the stocks while simultaneously selling the futures contract. At the expiration of the contract, the stocks are sold in order to provide cash to cover the loan. The investor liquidates the stock position by submitting market-on-close sell orders at the expiration of the futures contract.[29] If, in contrast, the futures price is cheap relative to the stocks, the investor buys the futures and sells the stocks. At the settlement date, the investor must cover the short sale of the stock and therefore must buy the stocks. The short position would be covered by submitting market-on-close orders to buy the stocks.

What might happen on the settlement date when the stock portfolio in an index arbitrage must be liquidated in the case of a long stock position and stocks purchased in the case of a short position? An increase in orders is certain, but the effect on stock prices is not. It depends on the composition of the orders. If they are balanced between arbitrageurs who have created long positions and short positions, then no significant price movement would be expected. If orders are not balanced, the action should result in a significant change in prices. Thus, it is possible that stock price volatility will increase at settlement dates. We look at the empirical evidence later.

Critics of index arbitrage argue that arbitrageurs consider only the relationship between cash and futures and the cost of transacting rather than making decisions based on the economic value of the underlying market. The response to these critics is that movement is necessary in at least one of the markets for arbitrage trading to be profitable. As long as nonarbitrageurs are pricing in at least one of the markets according to economic information, price changes capture assessments of this information. Arbitrage then irons out the inconsistency between the markets.

We can also see the importance of program trading in this strategy. An index arbitrage strategy requires program trading to implement the buy or sell orders so that trades occur as close in time as possible. Without program trading, the theoretical bounds for the futures price increases.

Dynamic Hedging   Recall that dynamic hedging (portfolio insurance) involves buying stocks or futures when the market is rising and selling when the market is falling. The concern with this strategy, expressed by the SEC Division of Market Regulation and other critics, is that it may lead to a "cascade" effect when stock prices decline. To understand this argument, consider what would happen if stock prices decline and dynamic hedging is employed using stocks and a riskless asset. The strategy

---

[29] A market-on-close order is a market order executed on the day it was entered at the official closing of the market.

requires that stocks be sold. But if many institutional investors are following a dynamic strategy, a substantial number of stocks will be sold, causing further decline in stock prices. In turn, more stocks must be sold, leading to a further decline in stock prices.

The same would happen if stock index futures are used to implement a dynamic hedging program. Their sales in the futures market would depress futures. What would arbitrageurs do? They would take offsetting positions in futures (by buying futures) and in stocks (by selling stocks). This action, it is argued, would lower cash prices further, and cause portfolio insurers to sell futures, resulting in a spiraling effect.

Proponents of dynamic hedging argue that the cascade effect is unlikely. At some point, value-oriented investors would step in when stocks are priced below their value based on economic fundamentals. However, Sanford Grossman (in a paper published several months before Black Monday) presented theoretical arguments suggesting that the imbalance of buyers and sellers of portfolio insurance could change stock market volatility. Specifically, if the demand for portfolio insurance exceeds the amount that market participants are willing to supply of portfolio insurance (that is, the amount of put options that market participants are willing to sell), volatility will increase; it would decrease if supply exceeded demand.[30]

SEC Study of the September 11–12, 1986 Market Decline   Some evidence is available in regard to index-related strategies during periods of sharp market declines. The Dow Jones Industrial Average dropped 86.61 points (a 4.61% decline) on September 11, 1986. The next day it dropped by another 34.17 points (1.91%). The Division of Market Regulation of the SEC investigated this two-day decline in stock prices to determine what, if any, role index-related strategies played.[31] It concluded: "The magnitude of the September decline was a result of changes in investors' perception of fundamental economic conditions, rather than artificial forces arising from index-related strategies." The SEC study further states: "Index-related futures trading was instrumental in the rapid transmission of these changed investor perceptions to individual stock prices, and may have condensed the time period in which the decline occurred."

The SEC study also looked at (1) the "cascade" effect resulting from the implementation of portfolio insurance strategies, and (2) potential manipulative uses employing stock index futures. The SEC did not find either present on September 11 and 12. Moreover, with respect to the "cascade effect," the SEC study concludes economic forces were sufficient to counteract it. As for potential manipulation, the SEC study notes that manipulation would be too costly and more risky than other potential manipulation targets.

The SEC study concludes, "Analysis of this particular market decline does not provide an independent basis to conclude that radical regulatory or structural changes are necessary at this time. . . . However, close monitoring should be maintained." The SEC study therefore exonerates index-related strategies.

WHAT HAS BEEN THE EFFECT ON STOCK PRICE VOLATILITY?

The view held by some investors and the popular press is that stock index futures and options, program trading, and index-related strategies (index arbitrage and dynamic hedging) result in an increase in the volatility of stock prices. This criticism of futures

---

[30] Sanford J. Grossman, "An Analysis of the Implications for Stock and Futures Price Volatility of Program Trading and Dynamic Hedging Strategies," presented at the Conference on the Impact of Stock Index Futures Trading at the Center for the Study of Futures Markets, Columbia University, June 8, 1987. The paper was subsequently published in the July 1988 issue of the *Journal of Business.* A less technical version of this paper is "Insurance Seen and Unseen: The Impact of Markets," *Journal of Portfolio Management* (Summer 1988), pp. 5–8.

[31] Securities and Exchange Commission, Division of Market Regulation, "The Role of Index-Related Trading in the Market Decline on September 11 and 12, 1986" (March 1987).

contracts is not confined to stock index futures, but as we explained in Chapter 10, is leveled at all futures contracts. In Chapter 10 we also questioned whether greater price volatility for a market was necessarily bad.

Several studies empirically investigated the effect of the introduction of futures trading and the effect of index-related strategies on stock price volatility. The difficulty in carrying out the empirical tests is determining what the volatility of the cash market price would be in the absence of futures trading. A simple comparison of price volatility before and after the introduction of futures trading, while informative, is not sufficient. The pitfall of this approach is that other factors influence volatility—the variability of economic information that affects stock price volatility. Thus, an increase in price volatility may be due to an increase in the variability of economic information that affects stock market prices. Or, failure to observe an increase in price volatility may be due to a decrease in the variability of economic information, masking any increase in price volatility. Thus, studies must control for the other factors that affect stock price volatility.

Studies examined *inter*day (i.e., day-to-day) price volatility[32] and *intra*day price volatility[33] using a wide range of measures. A fair conclusion of all these studies is that the introduction of stock index options and futures and index-related strategies did not increase stock price volatility except, possibly, during periods when stock index futures and options expire.

DID STOCK INDEX CONTRACTS CAUSE BLACK MONDAY?

On Monday, October 19, 1987 ("Black Monday"), the DJIA declined by 23%, the largest single-day decline in its history. The decline was not unique to the United States—every major stock market in the world suffered a decline in local currency units. In response to the crash, six studies were commissioned in the United States to assess the cause of the crash and make recommendations on reducing the likelihood of another crash. Studies were commissioned by President Reagan (Presidential Task Force on Market Mechanisms, popularly known as the Brady Report), the General Accounting Office, the Securities and Exchange Commission, the New York Stock Exchange, the Chicago Mercantile Exchange, and the Commodity Futures Exchange.

According to the popular press and many market observers, no study was needed; the culprits were well known to be the market participants who employed index-related strategies. For example, the day following the crash the *Wall Street Journal* reported: "In a nightmarish fulfillment of some traders' and academicians' worst fears, the five-year-old index futures for the first time plunged into a panicky, unlimited free-fall, fostering a sense of crisis throughout United States capital markets."[34] The evidence accumulated since, however, does not confirm that index-related trading was the culprit. We review the evidence here.

[32] Studies that address the impact of the introduction of stock price volatility include Carolyn D. Davis and Alice P. White, "Stock Market Volatility," Staff Study, Board of Governors of the Federal Reserve System (August 1987); John J. Merrick, Jr., "Volume Determination in Stock and Stock Index Futures Markets: An Analysis of Volume and Volatility Effects," *The Journal of Futures Markets* (October 1987), pp. 483–96; Lawrence Harris, "S&P 500 Cash Stock Price Volatilities," *Journal of Finance* (December 1989), pp. 1155–76; and Franklin R. Edwards, "Does Futures Trading Increase Stock Price Volatility?" *Financial Analysts Journal* (January/February 1988), pp. 63–9.
[33] Studies of intraday price volatility include Laszlo Birinyi, Jr., and H. Nicholas Hanson, "Market Volatility: An Updated Study" (Salomon Brothers, July 1986); and Hans R. Stoll and Robert E. Whaley, "Expiration Day Effects of Index Options and Futures," *Financial Analysts Journal* (March/April 1987), pp. 16–28.
[34] Scott McMurray and Robert L. Rose, "Chicago's Shadow Markets Led Free-Fall in a Plunge that Began Right at Opening," *The Wall Street Journal* (October 20, 1987), p. 28.

Index-Related Trading and the Crash   Program trading was severely limited on October 19 and the morning of October 20 because the unavailability of the NYSE Designated Order Turnaround (DOT) system made it difficult to execute trades. Suspension of the DOT system, however, gave the impression that program trading caused the chaotic market. The actual motivation for suspension was the fear that the specialist system could not execute all the program trades.

Index arbitrage traders could not operate in the chaotic market environment even before suspension of the DOT system. At the outset on October 19, index arbitrageurs could not transact in the cash market because many of the major issues in the S&P 500 did not open for trading until 11 A.M. or later. It was difficult to execute the program trades necessary to implement an index arbitrage strategy in the futures market, with prices too volatile and bid-ask spreads too wide. Later in the day, the execution of an index arbitrage strategy became even more difficult. Delays in reporting trades in the cash market made it impossible to identify profitable arbitrage opportunities between the cash and futures markets. Delays in executing orders in the cash market, particularly after suspension of the DOT system, meant that even if a profitable arbitrage could be identified, an investor could not be sure that one could execute at the prices used to identify the arbitrage opportunity. Thus, index arbitrage was not the culprit. It may be argued, on the contrary, that the impediments to index arbitraging made matters worse because they reduced demand in the stock index futures market.

Dynamic Hedging (Portfolio Insurance) and the Crash   Recall that Grossman argued that an imbalance between the demand for portfolio insurance and the supply of portfolio insurance alters the volatility of the market. When demand exceeds supply, volatility increases, causing a dramatic decline in prices when the market is declining. It is interesting to note that on the morning of October 19, 1987, several options exchanges did begin trading in long-term index options that were designed to satisfy the needs of the portfolio insurance market.[35] A supply of long-term put index options—that is, actual exchange-traded put options—it is argued, could have satisfied the demand from portfolio insurers. Two things probably prevented it from happening. First, the new exchange-traded contracts did not have sufficient time to develop so that market participants could be comfortable with using them. Second, even if market participants did want to use these new contracts, as we explained earlier in this chapter, position limits imposed on investors by the exchange may have prevented them from doing so. In discussing Black Monday, SEC Commissioner Joseph Grundfest, in an article published in mid-1989, wrote:

> *Had all investors involved in portfolio insurance found it possible, and desirable, to satisfy their demand for "insurance" by buying puts instead of relying on dynamic hedges, the market would have had more information about the intensity of investor concern about a downside move. Under those circumstances, there's reason to believe that prices might not have fallen as low on the downside had the market simply been better informed of investors' own concerns. Thus, to the extent position limits on index options forced investors away from the options market and into secret dynamic hedging strategies, the government's position limit restrictions may have unwittingly exacerbated the market's decline.*[36]

---

[35] Gary L. Gastineau, "Eliminating Option Position Limits: A Key Structural Reform" (New York: Salomon Brothers Inc., August 30, 1988), p. 3.

[36] Joseph A. Grundfest, "Perestroika on Wall Street: The Future of Securities Trading," *Financing Executive* (May/June 1989), p. 25.

Thus, the culprit might not be dynamic hedging/portfolio insurance but, instead (1) the inability to develop a long-term exchange-traded index option market, and (2) government imposition of the regulatory position limits that impeded the use of the exchange-traded market. Whether or not one is willing to accept this hypothesis, it should be understood that it is entirely untested and therefore has no empirical underpinning.

Index Trading Volume and the Crash   By looking at trading volume statistics, Joanne Hill provided some additional evidence on the size of the role that the stock index futures market played on October 19 and 20.[37] On that Monday, S&P 500 futures trading volume was 162,022 contracts, approximately 1.5 times the average daily number of contracts traded in the previous week. In contrast, trading volume on the NYSE was 2.7 times greater than the average daily number of shares traded in the previous week (604 million versus 224 million shares). Based on normal levels of S&P 500 futures trading to NYSE stock trading, approximately 250,000 to 300,000 contracts would have been traded. Thus, actual futures trading was considerably below normal trading according to the number of shares traded. This low level of futures trading continued on Tuesday, with NYSE trading remaining at 600 million shares, and futures trading volume down to 126,462 contracts.

Summary

Stock index options and futures were introduced in the early 1980s. The underlying stock market index may be a broad-based index or a narrow-based index. The dollar value of a contract is determined by the product of the index value and the contract's multiple. Unlike options on individual common stock, stock index products are cash settlement contracts. That is, the contracts are settled in cash at the expiration or settlement date. There are also complex OTC options, or exotic options, in which the underlying asset is a stock index.

Stock index options can be used to bet on the movement of stock prices (speculating) or to protect a portfolio position against an adverse price movement (hedging). In addition, the following index-related strategies can be employed by institutional investors: controlling market risk exposure, constructing an index fund, enhancing returns via index arbitrage, dynamic hedging, and implementing an asset allocation decision. Dynamic hedging is related to replicating a put option with stocks or stock index futures.

Studies of the efficiency of the stock index options market suggest that mispricing was present when these contracts began trading. The reason may stem from the difficulty of arbitraging an option where the underlying instrument is an index. More recent studies suggest that although stock index futures were occasionally mispriced when trading commenced in 1983, they are now fairly priced.

In equity swaps, the counterparties agree to exchange the return on some stock index for an interest rate (fixed or floating). Equity swaps can be used to create an indexed portfolio to match some U.S. or non-U.S. stock index.

Critics of stock index options and futures contracts believe that index-related trading increases stock price volatility and was responsible for Black Monday. A closer examination suggests that the stock index futures market provides a less expensive and more speedy transaction market for investors to alter their exposure to economic infor-

---

[37] Joanne M. Hill, "Program Trading, Portfolio Insurance, and the Stock Market Crash" (Kidder, Peabody, January 1988), pp. 27–8.

mation expected to affect stock prices. The stock index futures market acts as a price discovery market. The evidence cited in this chapter suggests that index-related trading does not increase stock market price volatility, nor was it responsible for Black Monday.

Key Terms

- Asset allocation decision
- Dynamic hedging
- Equity swap

- FLEX option
- Index warrants
- Net financing cost

- Open interest
- Strike index
- Tracking-error risk

Questions

1. Suppose you bought an index call option for $5.50 with a strike index of 1000 and that, at expiration, you exercised it. Also suppose that at the time you exercised the call option, the index had a value of $1,040.
   a. If the index option has a multiple of $100, how much money does the writer of this option pay you?
   b. What profit did you realize from buying this call option?
2. The following excerpt is from an article entitled "Scudder Writes Covered Calls on S&P 500," in the July 13, 1992, issue of *Derivatives Week,* p. 7:

   Scudder, Stevens & Clark writes covered calls on the S&P 500 Index to enhance the return of some of its equity portfolios, according to Harry Hitch, principal at Scudder. Hitch, who advises Scudder's equity portfolio managers on derivatives use, said that the S&P 500 has been in a trading range since the beginning of the year, making it a good candidate for covered call writing. Half of the index is made up of growth stocks, a group that Scudder sees as over-bought, whereas the other half is probably increasing in price. The combination of one half appreciating with the other half depreciating creates the range, rather than a decided one-way movement.

   The goal is to write calls at the top of the trading range, take the premium and wait for the options to expire worthless. . . . Typically, Scudder takes 1,000 contract positions, worth around $42 million.

   Explain the risks and rewards of the strategy discussed in this excerpt.
3. Suppose that an alternative call option is based on the performance of the S&P 500 and the return on a particular U.S. Treasury bond. The terms are as follows: the option expires in 1 year; the notional amount is $20 million; the strike for the S&P 500 is 1000; and the strike for the Treasury bond is 100.
   a. Suppose at the expiration date the return on the S&P 500 is 9% and the return on the Treasury bond is 11%. What is the payoff of this option?
   b. Suppose at the expiration date the return on S&P 500 is −4% and the return on the Treasury bond is −2%. What is the payoff of this option?
4. Explain how a money manager would use an alternative call option.
5. Explain how a money manager would use an outperformance call option.
6. The following statement comes from the September 1989 issue of *Institutional Investor:* "Two years ago Osaka became the first Japanese exchange to come out with a financial future—a stock index future known as the Osaka 50. It was only a modest success, mainly because it had to be delivered in shares rather than cash."
   Explain why cash settlement is preferred for stock index futures.
7. On February 16, 1995, open interest for the S&P 500 March 1995 futures contract was 199,447. Open interest for the December 1995 contract was 1,956. What is open

interest, and why would the open interest figures for the March and December contracts be of concern to a portfolio manager considering using stock index futures?

8. What is the dollar value of the S&P 500 if the futures price is $1,010?

9. Suppose you know the following facts: the S&P 500 Index is 1140; the dividend yield for the stocks comprising the index is 4%; the interest rate for 12 months is 12%; and the S&P 500 futures contract for settlement in 12 months' time is currently selling at $1,236.

   a. Is there an arbitrage opportunity? If so, how would you take advantage of it?
   b. What considerations would you want to address before executing this trade?

10. Donald Singleton is an investment banker for a regional firm. One of his clients, Dolby Manufacturing, Inc., is a private company that will be making an initial public offering of 20 million shares of common stock. Mr. Singleton's firm will buy the issue at $10 per share. He suggested to the managing director of the firm, John Wilson, that the firm should hedge the position using stock index futures contracts. What should Mr. Wilson's response be?

11. This quotation is from the June 8, 1987, issue of *Business Week*:

    The idea sounds almost un-American. Instead of using your smarts to pick stocks that will reach the sky, you put money in a fund that merely tracks a broad market index. But that is precisely what institutional investors are doing. . . . Indexing is a new force in the stock market. . . . But the impact of index-funds reaches far beyond stock price.

    Discuss how indexing contributed to the growth of the stock index derivatives markets.

12. This quotation is from the December 1988 issue of *Euromoney:*

    The proliferation of futures and options markets has created new opportunities for international investors. It is now possible to change investment exposure from one country to another through the use of derivative instruments, augmented by a limited number of individual securities. Asset allocation in most major markets is now feasible using futures and options.

    Discuss the reasons for using derivative rather than cash instruments to facilitate asset-allocation decisions.

13. The following statement from an article entitled "Program Trading Spreads from Just Wall Street Firms" appeared in the August 18, 1989, issue of the *Wall Street Journal*: "Brokerage firms in the business, which tiptoed back into program trading after the post-crash furor died down, argue that such strategies as stock-index arbitrage—rapid trading between stock index futures and stocks to capture fleeting price differences—link two related markets and thus benefit both." A second quotation in the article is from a senior vice president at Twenty First Securities Corp.: "Program trading is a product that is here, links markets, and it is not going to disappear. It is a function of the computerization of Wall Street."

    Explain why you agree or disagree with these statements.

14. The following excerpt appeared in the December 7, 1992, issue of *Derivatives Week* entitled "Prudential Reduces FT-SE Futures Exposure in Favour of CAC-40":

    Prudential Portfolio Managers in London, which manages over £10 billion in pension fund assets, recently used futures to reduce an over-weight position in U.K. equities while increasing its exposure to French equities, according to Martin Bookes, assistant director. Last June, Prudential used LIFFE-traded FT-SE futures to over-weight U.K. equities by 2–3% compared to benchmark indices which have a 60% exposure.

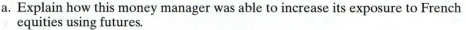

    a. Explain how this money manager was able to increase its exposure to French equities using futures.

    b. Explain how this money manager was able to decrease its exposure to U.K. equities using futures.

15. The following excerpt is from the article "Salomon Downplays Japan Stock Index Arbitrage" that appeared June 22, 1992, in *Derivatives Week,* p. 2:

> *Salomon Brothers Asia is deemphasizing Japanese equity index arbitrage, according to a spokesman for the firm. The increasing efficiency of the Tokyo market made index arbitrage less attractive, he explained. "It's a brokerage's work to find a market's inefficiency and earn profit, but [stock index arbitrage offers] less now," the Salomon spokesman said. The past two years, during which foreign firms dominated the business, were unusual, he added.*

    a. What is stock index arbitrage?

    b. Based on the comments in the excerpt, why is the experience with stock index arbitrage in Japan the same as in the United States?

16. Explain how equity swaps can be used by a money manager to create an index fund.

17. Explain why it is possible that in an equity swap the party receiving the stock index may have to pay the counterparty more than the reference interest rate.

18. Consider the following testimony given by Alan Greenspan, chairman of the Board of Governors of the Federal Reserve, before a subcommittee in the U.S. Senate:

> *In a more fundamental sense, we believe it is counterproductive to lay blame on one sector, in this case the market for stock index derivatives, for increasing occurrence of wide and rapid price swings in equity markets. . . . Rather, the volatility we observe reflects more basic changes in economic and financial processes prompted by technological advances and the increasing concentration of assets in institutional portfolios.*

    a. Do you agree with Greenspan's view?

    b. Do you think that stock index derivatives were responsible for increased volatility and the October 1987 crash?

The Theory and Structure of Interest Rates

Learning Objectives

After reading this chapter you will understand:

◆ the role of individual preference in choosing current and future consumption in the determination of interest rates.

◆ what is meant by the marginal rate of time preference.

◆ the role of the loan market in the determination of interest rates.

◆ the role of production opportunities in the determination of interest rates.

◆ what is meant by the real rate of interest.

◆ the factors that determine the real rate of interest in an economy.

◆ how the market equilibrium interest rate is determined.

◆ what is meant by Pareto optimality.

◆ the relationship between the real rate of interest and the nominal rate of interest and inflation (Fisher's Law).

◆ why historically the yields on securities issued by the U.S. Treasury have been used as the benchmark interest rates throughout the world.

◆ the reason for the decreasing popularity of U.S. Treasury securities yields as benchmark interest rates and what alternative benchmarks are being considered by market participants.

◆ what is meant by a risk premium.

◆ what factors affect the yield spread between two bonds.

Interest rates are a measure of the price paid by a "borrower" (or "debtor") to a "lender" (or "creditor") for the use of resources during some time interval. The sum transferred from the lender to the borrower is referred to as the **principal** and the price paid for the use is usually expressed as a percentage of the principal per unit of time (mostly per year).

The transfer from savers to investors occurs through a variety of financial instruments, and the price paid may differ between instruments. Indeed, at any one time a bewildering array of rates is offered on different instruments. The spread between the lowest and the highest rate in the market might run as high as 1500 basis points (15 percentage points).[1]

In this chapter we develop the theory of interest rates. In doing so, we focus on the one interest rate that can be said to provide the anchor for other rates—the short-term, riskless, real rate. By the **real rate** we mean the rate that would prevail in the economy if price levels remain constant, and are expected to be constant indefinitely. We then look at how all other rates differ from it by looking at the structure of interest rates. The yield offered on a particular bond depends on a myriad of factors related to the type of issuer, the characteristics of the bond issue, and the state of the economy. We look at the factors that affect the yield offered in the bond market.

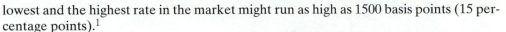

◆ THE THEORY OF INTEREST RATES

To understand what determines the basic rate we must inquire why some people might decide not to consume all their current resources (i.e., to save), and why some others would want to invest. It should be noted that those desirous to borrow might want to use the proceeds either to make further loans (i.e., acquire financial assets) or to invest (i.e., acquire income-yielding physical assets such as plant, equipment, and residential structures). In this chapter we abstract from financial intermediaries and assume that all loans, directly or indirectly, end up being transferred to an investor.

Saving reflects primarily the choice between current consumption and future consumption. To understand that choice (and all consumer choices) we need to consider two fundamental concepts: preference and opportunity.

DESCRIPTION OF PREFERENCES BETWEEN CURRENT AND FUTURE CONSUMPTION

Consider first the representation of preferences. Suppose that our consumer is to choose among a variety of "baskets" (or "bundles"), where each basket consists of a certain quantity of current consumption and a certain quantity of future consumption.

Preferences (or tastes) can then be described fully by a complete preference ranking of all the relevant baskets. Given that the amount of current and future consumption can vary by any small dose, some choices among the possible baskets will be ranked equally; that is, the consumer will be indifferent as to certain choices among baskets.

This consideration makes it possible to obtain an effective representation of preference, as shown in Figure 17-1. The figure measures current consumption (C_1), along the horizontal axis, and future consumption (C_2), along the vertical. Hence any point in the diagram represents a commodity basket, such as H. Some other point, H^*, represents an indifferent choice to H; more generally, a curve from H to H^* and beyond, consists of baskets indifferent to both H and H^*. Such a curve is called an **indifference curve**. We labeled the indifference curve in Figure 17-1 as u.

Note that an indifference curve goes through every point in the diagram, although they cannot intersect because that would imply that a given basket is ranked both higher and lower than another—a clear inconsistency. The indifference curve u here falls from left to right because both consumption now and later can be taken to be

---

[1]   It is common in the bond market to refer to differences or changes in interest rates in terms of basis points. A basis point is equal to 0.0001, or 0.01%, and 100 basis points represent 1%. So, for example, the difference between 10% and 11% is said to be 100 basis points. If the interest rate increases from 10% to 10.35%, it is said to have increased by 35 basis points.

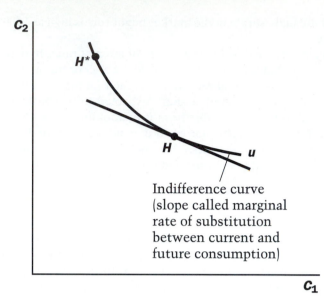

Indifference curve
(slope called marginal
rate of substitution
between current and
future consumption)

FIGURE 17-1 Indifference Curve Between Current and Future Consumption

desirable. As basket H in Figure 17-1 includes more current consumption than basket H^*, in order for it to be indifferent from basket H^*, basket H must have less future consumption, C_2. The reason the curve is drawn convex to the origin is the assumption that, as the consumer gives up successive equal amounts of current consumption, it will take growing quantities of future consumption to make up for the loss of an additional unit. This assumption appears reasonable, although complete justification of it is beyond the scope of this chapter.

At any point on an indifference curve, we can draw a tangent to the curve. Irving Fisher, the father of the theory of interest rates, calls the slope of this tangent the **marginal rate of time preference**.[2] It measures how much additional consumption next period is needed to compensate the consumer for the loss of a unit of consumption now. That is, the slope of the tangent measures the marginal rate of substitution between current and future consumption. We might conjecture that a particular person would be impatient to consume now rather than later, and therefore it would take more than one unit tomorrow to induce that person to give up the enjoyment of one unit today. In other words, the marginal rate of time preference, or the slope of the indifference curve, would be larger than 1. For this reason, Fisher proposed labeling the excess of the slope over unity a "measure of impatience."

It turns out, however, that this conjecture about the slope is wrong. It is easy to verify that the slope of the indifference curve changes as we move along it, and therefore that it is most unlikely to be everywhere more than unity. On the left side of the diagram where today's endowment is small, the slope can be counted on to be larger than unity. However, as we move to the right, and the current endowment grows larger relative to the future one, the slope must become smaller than 1, meaning that the consumer may be willing to give up a unit of today's abundant supply for less than one unit to add to tomorrow's scarce supply. This insight is important in understanding why interest rates can in principle be negative.

---

[2] Irving Fisher, *The Theory of Interest Rates* (New York: Macmillan, 1930).

OPPORTUNITY IN THE LOAN MARKET

To understand saving behavior, we need to look at how preferences interact with opportunities. Let us consider first a case where the opportunities or baskets among which the person can choose are defined by (1) an initial endowment of the commodity now and later, and (2) a loan market where individuals are free to exchange this initial or current endowment for a different one by lending or borrowing at a fixed exchange rate of $R = 1 + r$ units of the commodity in the next period (i.e., the future in our illustration) per unit of the commodity loaned in the current period. R is the gross return (principal plus interest) and r the net return, or interest rate. For example, if a unit of current consumption is loaned at 5%, then r is 0.05 and R is 1.05.

We represent this opportunity locus in Figure 17-2 by means of the negatively sloped straight line *mm* going through the endowment basket at point B (with current endowment as Y_1 and future endowment as Y_2). We refer to the opportunity locus in the loan market as the "market line." It slopes downward, because to get more C_1 you must reduce C_2. It is a straight line because, at any point on it, by giving up one unit of the current consumption we can get the same additional amount, R, of future consumption. And it goes through B, because if no lending made current consumption equal to the current endowment of Y_1, then future consumption would equal the future endowment of Y_2. Thus, the opportunity locus must include point B.

Now let us add to the diagram a family of indifference curves, as shown in Figure 17-3. One curve in the diagram is tangent to the market line, such as curve u_4 at point D. The consumption basket corresponding to point D can be shown to be the preferred one among all those available, given the market line; hence it will be the chosen basket.

Following this logic, suppose the consumer started by considering point H on indifference curve u_2, where current consumption is greater than at D. Suppose next he considered giving up some current consumption in favor of more future consumption along his market opportunity line. He would first reach point F and would find it a preferable choice, being on a higher indifference curve, u_3. Continuing, he would reach point D on u_4, offering yet higher utility. But beyond D he immediately starts reaching lower and lower utility curves, such as curves u_2 and u_3. We see that the point of tangency of the market line with an indifference curve provides the best of all feasible choices.

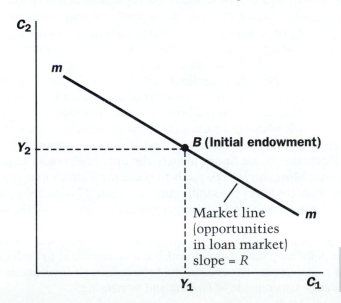

FIGURE 17-2   Representation of Opportunity Locus in the Loan Market (the Market Line)

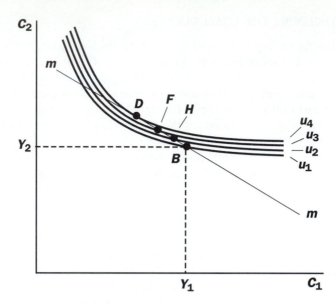

FIGURE 17-3 Family of Indifference Curves and the Market Line

Recalling that the slope of an indifference curve at any point measures the marginal rate of substitution between current and future consumption, we see that at the chosen point the marginal rate of substitution is equal to the market rate R (or the marginal rate of impatience equal to r). It is an important property of a perfect market that, because everybody is confronted with the same market rate r, everybody at the chosen point must exhibit the same degree of impatience. In particular, if r is positive, as it generally is in our type of economy, everybody will be "impatient"; that is, they will be willing to give up a unit of current consumption to lend more only if they can get $1 + r$ units later, with $r > 0$, because that opportunity is offered by the market.

ECONOMIC FORCES AFFECTING THE MARKET RATE

So far we presented the market rate r as a given. But what does in fact determine r in this simple economy? The answer, of course, is demand and supply. For any given R, each person will decide how much to consume now and how much to save or dissave (the difference between the current endowment and consumption). In this simple economy, saving or dissaving is the same as lending or borrowing. By summing up the net lending of each participant, for each R, we obtain a supply curve for loans, such as is graphed in Figure 17-4. We draw it as initially rising from left to right, on the commonly held assumption that net lending will rise as R rises. For sufficiently low R, net lending is negative because borrowing would exceed lending. Suppose zero investment at the outset. Then market equilibrium requires that net lending be zero. It therefore occurs at point E where the curve cuts the horizontal axis. (Note that we draw the net lending curve as declining in the rightmost section. We discuss the reason for this later.)

R reflects two major forces, namely, the time preferences of participants and their endowments. More impatience tends to make for a smaller supply of loans (saving) at any given R and to lower the supply curve in Figure 17-4, thereby shifting E to the right. A large endowment of the current commodity relative to the future makes people more eager to lend, raise the curve, and thus reduce R. If this situation is sufficiently prevailing, E may be pushed to the left until it is less than unity and therefore r is negative! This point may seem paradoxical, but it is important to understand that no opportunity of transferring resources to the future through investment (or money, which is disregarded) exists outside of lending and borrowing.

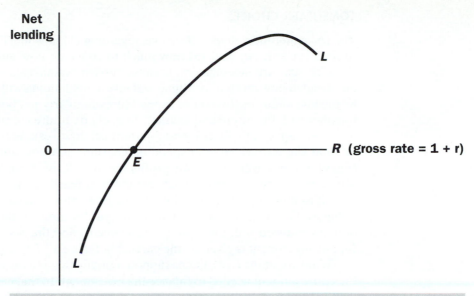

Net lending

0

E

L

L

R **(gross rate = 1 + r)**

FIGURE 17-4   Supply Curve for Loans

CARRYOVER THROUGH INVESTMENT

We now enlarge the model to allow for the possibilities of investments—a productive process through which, by using current resources as an input, we obtain an output of future commodities. An investment opportunity locus might look something like the curve *tt* of Figure 17-5, which is referred to as the **transformation curve** or the **production function**. It rises from left to right on the assumption that as more is invested, more future output will result. It is convex from below on the customary assumption of decreasing returns to scale (although increasing returns are possible in some regions without changing the argument). The slope of the transformation curve measures the **marginal productivity of capital**.

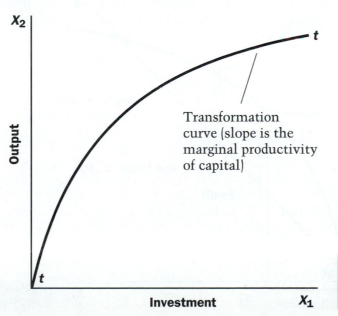

X_2

Output

t

t

Transformation curve (slope is the marginal productivity of capital)

Investment X_1

FIGURE 17-5   Representation of Opportunity Locus from Investment (Transformation Curve or Production Function)

CONSUMER CHOICES

The consumer faces several decisions regarding (1) how much to invest, (2) how much to lend (or borrow), and (3) how much to consume now and later. But only two of these choices are independent: because current resources are given, once the person has decided how much to consume and invest, net lending will be determined uniquely by income minus the two other expenditures. Similarly, net borrowing and investment, together with the future endowment, uniquely fix future consumption.

Consider first the decision as to how much to invest. As the consumer's "income," or what she has available to spend on consumption now and later, is limited by the sum of her endowment and any profits she may derive from her production opportunity, a necessary condition to achieve the best feasible consumption is to ensure for herself as large a profit as possible. To see how this result can be achieved, look again at Figure 17-5. Recall that profit at any output (or input) is the difference between the output produced with the input (or investment) and the cost of the input. The output for any investment is given by the curve *tt* in Figure 17-5.

What about the cost? Let us suppose initially that the owner of a firm must borrow the entire amount needed to finance the investment. In that case clearly the cost of any given investment will be what is to be repaid next period, namely, the amount borrowed times the gross market rate *R*. This cost can be represented in Figure 17-5 by a straight line going through the origin with a slope *R*, and as shown in Figure 17-6 by the line *MM*. Profit for any output, then, is the difference between the curve *tt* and the line *MM*, which is illustrated in Figure 17-6 for an assumed investment of X_1^*. We refer to the line *MM* in the figure as the "cost line." Because it represents the cost of borrowing, however, it has the same slope as the market line in Figure 17-2.

As the consumer increases investment from an investment of zero (at the origin), we can see from the graph that profits initially rise (provided there are profits at all). The additional profit attributable to increased investment gets smaller and smaller, though, until it reaches a point in the figure of no more incremental profit. This point is

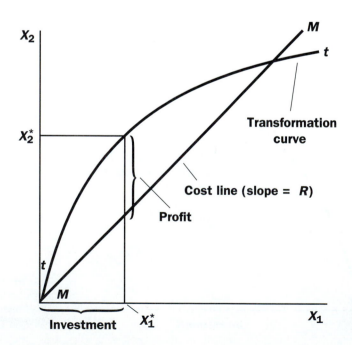

FIGURE 17-6 Measuring the Profit from Investing

shown as A in Figure 17-7. If the consumer continues to expand investment still further, the profit (as measured by the vertical distance between the cost line MM and the transformation curve tt) becomes smaller and smaller. Point A's one distinguishing characteristic is that it is where the curve tt has precisely the same slope R as the cost curve MM as shown in Figure 17-8. We draw through A a line mm with the same slope as R (and hence parallel to MM). This line is tangent to tt at A.

Because the slope of tt represents the marginal productivity of capital, we can conclude that the optimum rate of investment for the firm is where the marginal productivity of capital equals the market gross rate R or, equivalently, where the additional output that can be obtained from an additional unit of input is just equal to the cost of borrowing that additional unit of input (and the amount obtained by further increases in investment is less than the cost of borrowing).

We can now proceed to examine the consumption decision and its interaction with the investment decision. To this end, we first show in Figure 17-9 how the transformation curve, curve tt in Figure 17-5, would be represented if graphed on the earlier Figures 17-1 through 17-3. We obtain the transformation curve (production function), curve tt, in Figure 17-9 by rotating the curve tt in Figure 17-5 180 degrees and shifting the origin to point B, which represents the initial endowment as in Figure 17-2. The resulting curve is the locus of all achievable baskets of the current and future commodity available to the person through a combination of the initial endowment with the transformation opportunity.

The amount invested is shown in Figure 17-9 along the horizontal axis by the difference between the current endowment Y_1 and the point on the horizontal axis corresponding to any point on the transformation curve, which is illustrated in Figure 17-10. At point W, the corresponding value on the horizontal axis is I^W and the amount of the investment is the difference between Y_1 and I^W. Future consumption corresponding to the point W on the transformation curve is C_2^W, which consists of the future endowment Y_2 plus the profit from the investment as measured by the difference between C_2^W and Y_2.

Suppose for a moment that no market permitted an exchange of C_1 with C_2. Then the curve tt in Figure 17-10 would represent the household opportunity locus. The person's

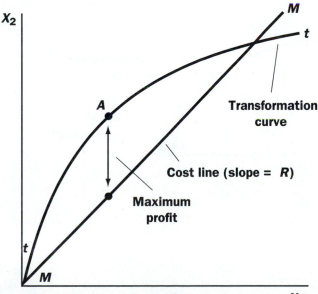

FIGURE 17-7   Profit Maximization Point

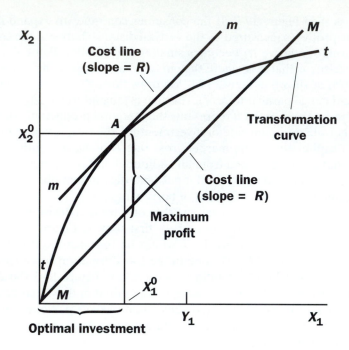

FIGURE 17-8 Profit Maximization and the Cost Line

best choice, the basket (C_1, C_2), would then be found at a point of tangency of that curve with an indifference curve. But in a market economy the budget constraint does not come from the initial endowment B in Figure 17-2, or from the initial endowment enlarged by the transformation function as in Figure 17-9, but instead from the endowment plus the profit that can be earned through the production and sale of C_2. It follows that to maximize satisfaction the agent should, to begin with, maximize the profits obtained from the transformation activity. This maximization will yield a new budget equation that includes the best choice of basket (C_1, C_2).

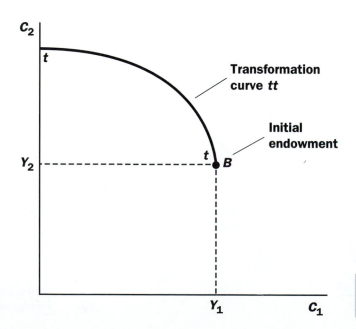

FIGURE 17-9 Transformation Curve Imposed on Current and Future Consumption Graph

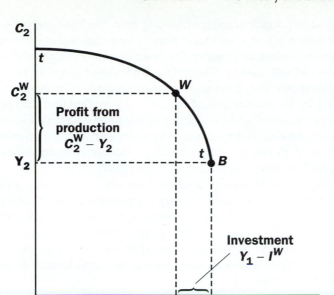

FIGURE 17-10   Measuring Investment and Profit from Investment

This optimal decision can be shown graphically in Figure 17-11. Here point A on the transformation function curve *tt* is such that the slope is equal to the slope of the market line *mm*. We know that this point, which corresponds to point A in Figure 17-8, represents the amount of investment $(Y_1 - X_1^0)$ and output (X_2^0) that will maximize profits. Through point A a new budget line *mm* (again tangent to *tt* at A) represents the outcome of adding maximum profits to the endowment. The utility-maximizing basket will then be at a point of tangency of this profit-augmented budget line with an indifference curve, such as point C^0.

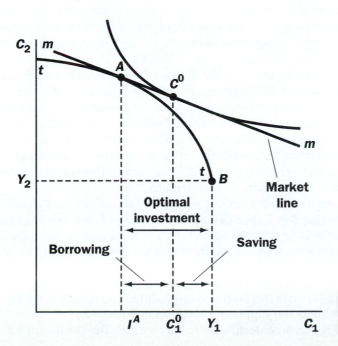

FIGURE 17-11   Optimal Investment and Borrowing Decisions

A most important property resulting from the existence of a perfect loan market, together with a transformation, is that it separates the current consumption decision from current income by opening the possibility to saving and dissaving through transformation and net lending. Similarly, it frees the investment from the saving decision, as the person can bridge the gap between saving and investment through lending and borrowing. In the specific case of Figure 17-11, we find that the chosen consumption C_1^0 is less than the initial endowment Y_1, so the person saves an amount shown in the figure. But that amount is not sufficient to finance an optimal investment equal to the distance between Y_1 and I_A of the chosen production. Hence, the difference $(C_1^0 - I_A)$ is made up by borrowing, as indicated in the figure.

This figure illustrates how a rational person can both save and borrow. Many other combinations can work out by varying the position of the chosen points A and C^0 relative to each other and to the endowment basket B as well. For example, if A falls between C^0 and B, the person ends up saving more than she needs for her investment, and thus she will save, invest, and lend. If on the other hand, C^0 falls to the right of B, the person will dissave, but she can invest at the same time by borrowing the sum of her investment and dissaving.

Incidentally, it should be apparent by now that we can drop our initial assumption that the investment is financed entirely by borrowing, for should it be financed by the owner's own saving, the cost to the investor of the funds would still be R per unit, which is the amount of interest that would have to be forgone in order to shift funds from making loans in the market to financing the investment (the opportunity cost).

MARKET EQUILIBRIUM

So far, we discussed how a person responds in terms of saving, investing, and borrowing to a given market R. But what determines R itself? The answer, once again, is demand and supply; that is, the price must be such as to clear the market. The situation we described needs to clear two markets. The first market for loans R must be such that gross lending equals gross borrowing; or, equivalently, that net borrowing is zero. The second market is the market for the current commodity. The two sources of demand for it are consumption and investment, and R must be such that aggregate consumption (C) plus aggregate investment (I) equals the given endowment (Y). Thus, $C + I = Y$, or equivalently, $I = Y - C = S$.

So, R must be such that the demand for investment equals the economy's net saving, denoted by S. But how can R clear two markets at the same time? One variable cannot satisfy two equations at the same time, *unless* one is redundant in the sense that the two provide identical solutions. Indeed it happens that the two market-clearing conditions here are redundant. To see how, recall that the decisions of each individual must satisfy a "budget constraint"; that is, a person's net lending must equal the excess of her saving over her investment. If we sum up this constraint over the entire market we get: $L = S - I$, where L is net lending.

It is apparent from this equation that if an interest rate clears the commodity market by making $S = I$, then that same rate makes $L = 0$, or clears the loan market. Thus we can conclude that the equilibrium R must equate the supply of saving and the demand for investment or, equivalently, the demand for and supply of loanable funds. If we want to graph the mechanism determining R, it will be more enlightening to use the commodity market (i.e., saving equals investment).

Equilibrium in this market is represented graphically in Figure 17-12, where the rising curve plots the supply of saving, analogous to LL in Figure 17-4. The investment function is drawn to decline uniformly with R. The justification for this choice can be

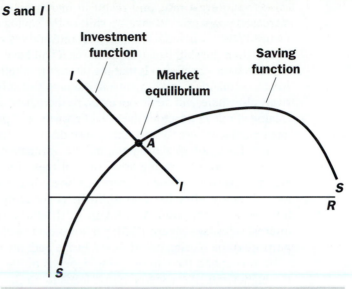

FIGURE 17-12   Market Equilibrium

found in Figure 17-8: we have shown that the investment chosen is at the point where the transformation curve has slope R. If R rises to R_1, the investment must shift to a point where the slope is R_1; because R_1 is larger than R, the transformation curve at R_1 must be steeper. But given the convexity of the transformation curve, it can occur only if investment is to the left of the initial level, that is, smaller. The market-clearing interest rate is then at the intersection of the saving and investment functions, where the two are equal.

It is also apparent from Figure 17-12 that as long as the intersection occurs in a region where the saving rises with R, the market-clearing interest rate will be higher, the higher the investment function. As can be seen in Figure 17-13, a shift of the investment function up and to the right (meaning more demand for investment at any given R) will

FIGURE 17-13   Change in *L*, *S*, and *R* If Investment Function Increases

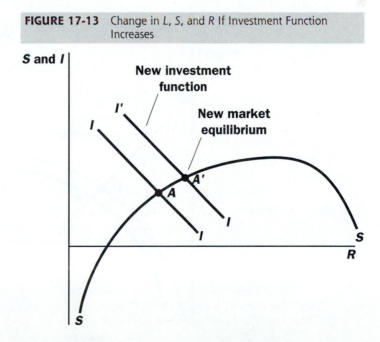

raise the interest rate, and result in increased saving and investment. Similarly, an increased propensity to save—a shift of the saving curve up and to the left as shown in Figure 17-14—will reduce the interest rate and result in saving and investment, although by less than the shift because the lower R will have a depressing effect on saving.

The basic conclusion is that the interest rate reflects a complex set of forces that control the demand for investment and the supply of saving. These forces are discussed extensively elsewhere, and we do not examine them here except for setting out a representative catalog of relevant factors: the rate of growth of population and productivity; fiscal policy, including incentives to save and invest; demographic variables; the role of bequests; the nature of technological progress; and the openness of international capital markets.

By way of illustrating how some of these forces work out, we discuss briefly the effect of fiscal investment incentives on saving, investment, and interest rates. If such incentives are effective, they shift the curve II upward and to the right. If the initial intersection is at point A in Figure 17-12, the effect will certainly be that of raising interest rates (see Figure 17-3); but how nearly will it succeed in achieving the intended purpose of increasing investment? In the end, investment can rise only if and as far as savings rise; and the rise in saving depends on the extent to which saving responds to the higher rate. A strong response leads to a relatively large rise in saving and investment, while the rise in interest rates is contained. But in the opposite case, the incentives mostly increase interest rates and have little effect on investment.

To complete the picture, we consider the case in which the two curves intersect at a point like G' in Figure 17-15, where saving decreases in response to higher interest rates. Is such a response conceivable? If people get paid more for saving, could they possibly respond by saving less? The answer is yes. Indeed, according to one school of thought, it is highly likely. The reason is simple. Suppose that initially you own a portfolio of loans. An increasing R influences your response in two ways. First, future consumption is cheaper in terms of current consumption, which should encourage you to consume more later and save more now. A second effect, as long as you are a creditor, of a higher interest rate makes you richer and pushes you toward consuming more now and later. It is entirely possible that the second effect may predominate. In this case the

FIGURE 17-14 Change in *I*, *S*, and *R* If Saving Function Increases

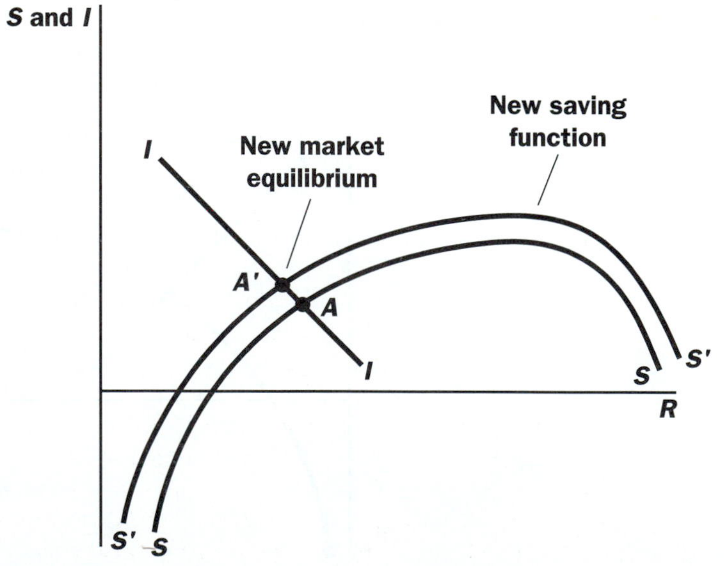

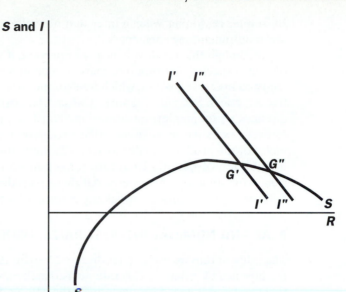

FIGURE 17-15 Possibility of Saving Decreasing in Response to Higher Interest Rate

supply of saving will decline with higher R, as shown by the terminal portion of the SS curve in Figure 17-15. If the intersection is in that region, the result of incentives can be quite perverse, as we can see if we shift the curve II up to the right from $I'I'$ to $I''I''$ and the equilibrium point from G' to G''. The effect is again to increase R, but now that increase will reduce saving and hence investment.

In other words, the fiscal incentive brings about the opposite effect from the intended one. The situation worsens if the incentives are financed not by new taxes but by increased deficit, which reduces investment further by cutting net national saving directly and through a higher interest rate. Some think that these considerations may help explain the catastrophic decline of saving during the years of Reaganomics. To be sure, net investment did not decline much, but it did not because of the huge borrowing from non-U.S. savers made attractive by the high domestic interest rates, which effectively made the country permanently poorer.

EFFICIENCY PROPERTIES OF MARKETS

The equilibrium achieved with the intermediation of the loan markets contributes an important property from the point of view of the efficiency of the economy in producing and allocating resources—a property that economists refer to as **Pareto optimality**. Instinctively we think of economic efficiency as implying the absence, or minimization, of waste. Pareto optimality makes that notion precise and conceptually operational: An allocation is Pareto optimal if it is not possible to reallocate the goods (inputs and outputs) in such a way that some will be better off while nobody will lose.

Clearly, if an allocation is not Pareto optimal, some slack or waste is present; conversely, if slack is present, the allocation cannot be Pareto optimal. Pareto optimality in our simplified economy is assured by profit maximization, plus the fact that, at market equilibrium, both the marginal productivity of capital and the marginal rate of time preference equals R for every firm and for every consumer. It means that it is impossible to increase output by reshuffling inputs among firms; the additional output by those who would gain inputs is offset precisely by the output lost by those losing inputs.

By similar reasoning, we can infer that no welfare gain can come from reshuffling the given output among consumers.

Although this result is logically important, it turns out we cannot make too much of it in respect to existing free market economies. First, the result presupposes a perfectly competitive market, which free competition may fail to assure because of restrictive practices. Second, it ignores transaction costs, information costs, and the consequences of incomplete information. Third, it presents an issue of externalities or effects—negative or positive—that production may have on people other than the buyer of the product. Finally, society may value things other than efficiency, such as the distribution of welfare. Therefore some non-Pareto optimal solution may trade efficiency for some other property. All these considerations are incentives to make markets more perfect and allow valuing externalities through the price mechanism.

REAL AND NOMINAL INTEREST RATES: FISHER'S LAW

The interest rate we used in our discussion so far is the real rate, which would prevail in the absence of inflation. This rate measures the amount of the commodity next period that can be exchanged for one unit of the commodity now. It generally differs from the nominal rate, which measures the amount of money to be repaid next period per unit borrowed now. The two rates are connected by a simple relation that is known as **Fisher's Law**. It rests on the principle that an exchange of money now for money later must imply the same rate of exchange between the commodity now and later, as implied by the real rate.

Suppose the real rate is $1 + r$; then by delivering one unit of the commodity now, we can obtain $(1 + r)$ units next period. But we could, alternatively, sell the commodity now at the spot price, p_1, and invest the proceeds in a loan at the nominal rate $(1 + i)$, obtaining $p_1 (1 + i)$ units of money next period.

How many units of the next-period commodity does that equation represent? To find the answer we must divide by the second-period price of the commodity, p_2. Thus the second-period quantity is $p_1 (1 + i)/(p_2)$. This quantity must equal the real rate $(1 + r)$. Thus:

$$\left(1+r\right) = \frac{1+i}{1+\dot{p}} \tag{17.1}$$

Where the denominator in equation (17.1) follows from

$$\frac{p_1}{p_2} = \frac{1}{p_2 / p_1} = \frac{1}{1 + \left[\left(p_2 - p_1\right)/p_1\right]}$$

and $(p_2 - p_1)/p_1) = \dot{p} =$ the percentage rise in the price level over the period of the loan.

Equation (17.1) can be restated in the form

$$\left(1+i\right) = \left(1+r\right)\left(1+\dot{p}\right)$$

Therefore, the nominal gross rate is the product of the gross real rate and 1 plus the rate of inflation. The equation, in turn, implies that, $i = r + \dot{p} + r\dot{p}$. For the more common values of r and $\dot{p}$, the product of r and $\dot{p}$ is small enough to be neglected, and the equation can be written as

$$i \approx r + \dot{p}$$

or

$$r \approx i - \dot{p} \tag{17.2}$$

Equation (17.2) is the formula commonly used to compute the ex post real rate of interest, which cannot be observed directly in the market. It is equally common to measure the anticipated or ex ante real rate of interest by replacing $\dot{p}$ by anticipated inflation. The ex ante rate differs from the ex post rate as a result of errors of expectation. It should be clear that the real rate so computed is not necessarily the same as the rate that would clear markets in the economy without inflation, because as a result of market imperfections, including taxation and possibly inflation illusion, inflation can alter the real rate. For instance, in the early phase of unanticipated inflation, the real rate typically falls. In other words, besides reflecting fundamental forces such as saving and productivity, the real rate may also be affected by other forces such as inflation, especially in the short run.

◆ THE STRUCTURE OF INTEREST RATES

Thus far we explained how the short-term, riskless interest rate is determined in a simple economy. However, no economy has just one interest rate, but rather a structure of interest rates. The interest rate that a borrower must pay depends on a myriad of factors, which we describe in this section. We begin with a discussion of the base interest rate, which is the interest rate on U.S. government securities. Next we explain the factors that affect the yield spread or risk premium for non-Treasury securities. Throughout this section we refer to the yield on a security, which is the interest rate offered on a security. The procedure for computing a security's yield is described in Chapter 18.

THE BASE INTEREST RATE

The securities issued by the U.S. Treasury, popularly referred to **Treasury securities** or simply **Treasuries**, are backed by the full faith and credit of the U.S. government. Consequently, market participants throughout the world view them as having no credit risk. As a result, historically the interest rates on Treasury securities served as the benchmark interest rates throughout the U.S. economy, as well as in international capital markets.

The U.S. Treasury is the largest single issuer of debt in the world, and the large size of any single issue contributes to making the Treasury market the most active and, hence, the most liquid market in the world. However, in recent years, the U.S. Treasury reduced its issuance of Treasury securities, particularly long-term securities, as well as buying back long-term Treasury securities in the market. This policy decreased the supply of these securities and, as a result, some market participants feel that the yields on Treasury securities are no longer a suitable benchmark for interest rates throughout the world. As of this writing, a search ensues for other benchmarks that can be used as the benchmark interest rates.[3] Moreover, outside of the United States, other countries are developing benchmark interest rates. In Europe, the yields on German government bonds are used as the benchmark.

Despite the potential decline of U.S. Treasury securities as a benchmark, in this book we continue to use them for benchmark interest rates. Any other benchmark that may be selected by market participants in the future must recognize the additional risks associated with the benchmark, as will be explained as we proceed.

The two categories of U.S. Treasury securities are discount and coupon securities. The fundamental difference between the two types results from the form of the stream

---

[3]   For a further discussion, see Michael J. Fleming, "The Benchmark U.S. Treasury Market: Recent Performance and Possible Alternatives," *FRBNY Economic Policy Review* (April 2000).

of payments that the holder receives, which, in turn, reflects the prices at which the securities are issued. Coupon securities pay interest every 6 months, plus principal at maturity. Discount securities pay only a contractually fixed amount at maturity. Treasury securities are typically issued on an auction basis according to regular cycles for securities of specific maturities. Current treasury practice is to issue all securities with maturities of 1 year or less as discount securities, called *Treasury bills.* All securities with maturities of 2 years or longer are issued as *Treasury coupon securities.*

The most recently auctioned Treasury issues for each maturity are referred to as **on-the-run** or **current coupon issues.** Table 17-1 shows the on-the-run U.S. Treasury yields as of the close of business on September 15, 2000. Issues auctioned prior to the current coupon issues are typically referred to as **off-the-run issues**; they are not as liquid as on-the-run issues, and, therefore, offer a higher yield than the corresponding on-the-run Treasury issue.

The minimum interest rate or **base interest rate** that investors demand for investing in a non-Treasury security is the yield offered on a comparable maturity for an on-the-run Treasury security. So, for example, if an investor wanted to purchase a 10-year bond on September 15, 2000, the minimum yield the investor would seek is 5.84%, the on-the-run Treasury yield reported in Table 17-1. The base interest rate is also referred to as the **benchmark interest rate**.

THE RISK PREMIUM

Market participants talk of interest rates on non-Treasury securities as "trading at a spread" to a particular on-the-run Treasury security (or a spread to any particular benchmark interest rate selected). For example, if the yield on a 10-year non-Treasury security is 7% and the yield on a 10-year Treasury security is 6%, the spread is 100 basis points. This spread reflects the additional risks the investor faces by acquiring a security that is not issued by the U.S. government and, therefore, can be called a **risk premium**. Thus, we can express the interest rate offered on a non-Treasury security as

Base interest rate + Spread

or equivalently,

Base interest rate + Risk premium

We already discussed the factors that affect the base interest rate. One of the factors is the expected rate of inflation. That is, the base interest rate can be expressed as

Base interest rate = Real rate of interest + Expected rate of inflation

TABLE 17-1 Yields for On-the-Run Treasuries on September 15, 2000

Maturity	Yield (%)
3-month	6.14
6-month	6.21
1-year	6.11
2-year	6.06
5-year	5.91
10-year	5.84
30-year	5.90

Source: Lehman Brothers, *Relative Value Report* Fixed Income Research (September 18, 2000), p. 3. © 2000 Lehman Brothers, Inc. All rights reserved.

How can the real rate of inflation required by market participants be estimated? As of 1997, the U.S. Treasury issues securities indexed to the Consumer Price Index. These securities are called *Treasury Inflation Protection Securities* (TIPS), and we discuss these securities in Chapter 21. What is important for us to understand here is that the yield on these securities can be used as an estimate of the real rate of interest. For example, the yield on a 10-year TIPS issue is an estimate of the real interest rate for a 10-year bond. On September 15, 2000, for example, the yield on the on-the-run 10-year TIPS issue was 4.02%. How do we get the expected rate of inflation? It is found by subtracting the real rate of interest (from the TIPS issue) from the base interest rate (i.e., the yield for the on-the-run non-TIPS issue). For example, as can be seen in Table 17-1, the base interest rate (i.e., the yield for the on-the-run 10-year issue) on September 15, 2000, was 5.84%. The yield on the 10-year TIPS issue on the same day was 4.02%. Therefore, the expected rate of inflation was 1.82% (5.84% minus 4.02%).

Turning to the spread, the factors that affect it include (1) the type of issuer, (2) the issuer's perceived creditworthiness, (3) the term or maturity of the instrument, (4) provisions that grant either the issuer or the investor the option to do something, (5) the taxability of the interest received by investors, and (6) the expected liquidity of the issue. It is important to note that yield spreads must be interpreted relative to the benchmark interest rate used, particularly in relation to the second and last factors that affect the spread when the benchmark interest rate is other than the yield on U.S. Treasury securities.

Types of Issuers   A key feature of a debt obligation is the nature of the issuer. In addition to the U.S. government, agencies of the U.S. government, municipal governments, corporations (domestic and foreign), and foreign governments issue bonds.

The bond market is classified by the type of issuer, and groups of securities of the various kinds of issuers are referred to as **market sectors**. The spread between the interest rates offered in two sectors of the bond market on obligations with the same maturity is referred to as an **intermarket sector spread**.

Excluding the Treasury market sector, the other market sectors include a wide range of issuers, each with different abilities to satisfy their contractual obligations. For example, within the corporate market sector, issuers are classified as follows: (1) utilities, (2) industrials, (3) finance, and (4) banks. The spread between two issues within a market sector is called an **intramarket sector spread**.

Perceived Creditworthiness of Issuer   *Default risk* or *credit risk* refers to the risk that the issuer of a bond may be unable to make timely principal or interest payments. Most market participants rely primarily on commercial rating companies to assess the default risk of an issuer. These companies perform credit analyses and express their conclusions by a system of ratings. The three commercial rating companies in the United States are Moody's Investors Service, Standard & Poor's Corporation, and Fitch.

In all systems the term **high grade** means low credit risk, or conversely, high probability of future payments. The highest-grade bonds are designated by Moody's by the symbol Aaa, and by S&P and Fitch by the symbol AAA. The next highest grade is denoted by the symbol Aa (Moody's) or AA (S&P and Fitch): for the third grade all rating systems use A. The next three grades are Baa or BBB, Ba or BB, and B, respectively. There are also C grades. Moody's uses 1, 2, or 3 to provide a narrower credit quality breakdown within each class, and S&P and Fitch use plus and minus signs for the same purpose.

Bonds rated triple A (AAA or Aaa) are said to be *prime,* double A (AA or Aa) are of *high quality;* single A issues are called *upper medium grade,* and triple B are *medium grade.* Lower-rated bonds are said to have speculative elements or be distinctly speculative.

Bond issues assigned a rating in the top four categories are referred to as **investment-grade bonds**. Issues that carry a rating below the top four categories are referred to as **noninvestment-grade bonds**, or more popularly as **high-yield bonds** or **junk bonds**. Thus the bond market can be divided into two sectors: the investment-grade and non-investment-grade markets.

The spread between Treasury securities and non-Treasury securities that are identical in all respects except for quality is referred to as a **quality spread**, or **credit spread**. For example, for the week of September 15, 2000, the yield on single-A, 10-year industrial bonds was 7.13% and the corresponding yield for the 10-year on-the-run Treasury (see Table 17-1) was 5.84%. Therefore, the quality spread was 129 basis points (7.13% minus 5.84%).

Let us return to the interpretation if the yield spread on a non-U.S. Treasury security is used as the benchmark interest rate. Because the U.S. Treasury securities are viewed by market participants as free of credit risk, the yield spread to U.S. Treasury securities reflects credit risk, as well as the other risks to be discussed. In the search for a new benchmark interest rate, it is desirable to use a benchmark with minimal credit risk. Three possible candidates for the benchmark include the yield on securities offered by government-sponsored enterprises. These entities are discussed in Chapter 21. They are viewed as having a triple A rating (AAA or Aaa) and therefore have minimal credit risk. The second alternative is corporate bond issuers that have triple A ratings. As we will see in our discussion of liquidity, corporate bond issuers may not be a viable candidate to replace Treasury securities as the benchmark. The third candidate comes from a market that we discuss in Chapter 28 of this book, the interest rate swap market. A measure that comes out of the swap market is called the *swap spread,* which many market participants, particularly in Europe, use as a benchmark.

Even though these are the alternatives being considered to replace Treasuries as the benchmark, there is a benchmark that is well established as a benchmark for floating-rate securities. The coupon interest rate for these securities is based on some reference interest rate. The benchmark used for these securities is the London interbank offer rate (LIBOR).

TERM TO MATURITY

As we explained in the previous chapter, the price of a financial asset fluctuates over its life as yields in the market change. As we demonstrated, the volatility of a bond's price depends on its maturity. More specifically, with all other factors constant the longer the maturity of a bond the greater is its price volatility resulting from a change in market yields. The spread between any two maturity sectors of the market is called a **maturity spread**, or **yield curve spread**. Table 17-2 shows various maturity spreads on September 15, 2000.

The relationship between the yields on comparable securities but different maturities is called the **term structure of interest rates**. The term-to-maturity topic is of such importance that we devote Chapter 18 to it.

INCLUSION OF OPTIONS

It is not uncommon for a bond issue to include a provision that gives either the bondholder or the issuer an option to take some action against the other party. An option that is included in a bond issue is referred to as an **embedded option**.

The most common type of option in a bond issue is a **call provision**. This provision grants the issuer the right to retire the debt, fully or partially, before the scheduled

TABLE 17-2	Various Maturity Spreads on September 15, 2000
Maturities	*Maturity Spread (in Basis Points)*
5-year to 2-year	−15
10-year to 5-year	−8
30-year to 2-year	−16
30-year to 10-year	6

Source: Lehman Brothers, *Relative Value Report*, Fixed Income Research (September 15, 2000), p. T-3. © 2000 Lehman Brothers, Inc. All Rights Reserved.

maturity date. The inclusion of a call feature benefits issuers by allowing them to replace an old bond issue with a lower interest cost issue should interest rates in the market decline. Effectively, a call provision allows the issuer to alter the maturity of a bond. A call provision is detrimental to the bondholder because the bondholder will be uncertain about maturity and might have to reinvest the proceeds received at a lower interest rate if the bond is called and the bondholder wants to keep his or her funds in issues of similar risk of default.

An issue may also include a provision that allows the bondholder to change the maturity of a bond. An issue with a **put provision** grants the bondholder the right to sell the issue back to the issuer at par value on designated dates. Here, the advantage to the investor is that, if interest rates rise after the issue date and result in a price that is less than the par value, the investor can force the issuer to redeem the bond at par value.

A **convertible bond** is an issue giving the bondholder the right to exchange the bond for a specified number of shares of common stock. This feature allows the bondholder to take advantage of favorable movements in the price of the issuer's common stock.

The presence of these embedded options affects the spread of an issue relative to a Treasury security and the spread relative to otherwise comparable issues that do not have an embedded option. In general, market participants require a larger spread over a comparable Treasury security for an issue with an embedded option that is favorable to the issuer (e.g., a call option) than for an issue without such an option. In contrast, market participants require a smaller spread over a comparable Treasury security for an issue with an embedded option that is favorable to the investor (for example, put option and conversion option). In fact, for a bond with an option that is favorable to an investor, the interest rate on an issue may be less than that on a comparable Treasury security!

To illustrate the impact of an embedded option on the spread, Table 17-3 shows the yield spread on government-sponsored enterprise securities—issuers that are discussed in Chapter 21—for issues with 5-year and 10-year maturities without a call provision (referred to as "noncallable" in the table) and with a call provision (identified as "noncallable for" a specified number of years) on September 15, 2000. So the issues that are callable (i.e., have an embedded option) are those identified in the table as "noncallable for." The restriction is simply that the issuer cannot call the issue for a specified number of years. The yield spread shown in the last column of the table is based on the yield spread between the issue and the on-the-run Treasury issue. Notice that for both the 5-year and 10-year issues, the yield spread relative to the on-the-run Treasury is larger for the callable issues than for the noncallable issue.

Also note that the 5-year and 10-year issues offer more than one callable issue. The callable issues differ with respect to when the issuer may call the bond issue. For example, consider the 5-year issue listed as "noncallable for 1 year." Although we explain the

TABLE 17-3 Yield Spread on Government-Sponsored Enterprise Issues: Noncallable and Callable Issues on September 15, 2000

Maturity	*Call Provision*	*Yield Spread (in basis points)*
5-year	Noncallable	80
5-year	Noncallable for 1 year	144
5-year	Noncallable for 2 years	120
5-year	Noncallable for 3 years	107
10-year	Noncallable	116
10-year	Noncallable for 3 years	167
10-year	Noncallable for 5 years	140

Source: Abstracted from Lehman Brothers, *Relative Value Report*, Fixed Income Research (September 15, 2000), p. T-3. Copyright © 2000 Lehman Brothers, Inc. All rights reserved.

details in Chapter 21, it simply means that the issuer may call the bond but the issuer cannot call the bond issue for 1 year. Similarly, 5-year issues identified as "noncallable for 2 years" and as "noncallable for 3 years" affect the spread. What is important to note from the table is that the longer the time before the issuer is permitted to call the bond, the lower the spread for a given maturity.

A major part of the bond market is the mortgage market. A wide range of mortgage-backed securities are discussed in Chapter 26. But these securities expose an investor to a form of call risk called "prepayment risk." Consequently, a yield spread between a mortgage-backed security and a comparable on-the-run Treasury security reflects this call risk. To see how, consider a basic mortgage-backed security called a Ginnie Mae pass-through security. This security is backed by the full faith and credit of the U.S. government. Consequently, the yield spread between a Ginnie Mae pass-through security and a comparable Treasury security is not due to credit risk. Rather, it is primarily due to call risk.

TAXABILITY OF INTEREST

Unless exempted under the federal income tax code, interest income is taxable at the federal level. In addition to federal income taxes, state and local taxes may apply to interest income.

The federal tax code specifically exempts the interest income from qualified municipal bond issues from taxation at the federal level. **Municipal bonds** are securities issued by state and local governments and by their creations, such as "authorities" and special districts. The large majority of outstanding municipal bonds are tax-exempt securities. Because of the tax-exempt feature of municipal bonds, the yield on municipal bonds is less than that on Treasuries with the same maturity. The difference in yield between tax-exempt securities and Treasury securities is typically measured not in basis points but in percentage terms. More specifically, it is measured as the percentage of the yield on a tax-exempt security relative to a comparable Treasury security.

The yield on a taxable bond issue after federal income taxes are paid is equal to

$$\text{After-tax yield} = \text{Pretax yield} \times (1 - \text{Marginal tax rate})$$

For example, suppose a taxable bond issue offers a yield of 9% and is acquired by an investor facing a marginal tax rate of 39.6%. The after-tax yield would then be

$$\text{After-tax yield} = 0.09 \times (1 - 0.396) = 0.0544 = 5.44\%$$

Alternatively, we can determine the yield that must be offered on a taxable bond issue to give the same after-tax yield as a tax-exempt issue. This yield is called the **equivalent taxable yield** and is determined as follows:

$$\text{Equivalent taxable yield} = \frac{\text{Tax-exempt yield}}{\left(1 - \text{Marginal tax rate}\right)}$$

For example, consider an investor facing a 39.6% marginal tax rate who purchases a tax-exempt issue with a yield of 5.44%. The equivalent taxable yield is then:

$$\text{Equivalent taxable yield} = \frac{0.0544}{\left(1 - 0.396\right)} = 0.09 = 9\%$$

Notice that the lower the marginal tax rate, the lower the equivalent taxable yield. Thus, in our previous example, if the marginal tax rate is 25% rather than 39.6%, the equivalent taxable yield would be 7.25% rather than 9%, as shown here:

$$\text{Equivalent taxable yield} = \frac{0.0544}{\left(1 - 0.25\right)} = 0.0725 = 7.25\%$$

State and local governments may tax interest income on bond issues that are exempt from federal income taxes. Some municipalities exempt interest income paid on all municipal issues from taxation; others do not. Some states exempt interest income from bonds issued by municipalities within the state but tax the interest income from bonds issued by municipalities outside of the state. The implication is that two municipal securities of the same quality rating and the same maturity may trade at some spread because of different tax policies and, hence, the relative demand for bonds of municipalities in different states. For example, in a high income tax state such as New York, the demand for bonds of municipalities in that state drive down their yield relative to municipalities in a low income tax state such as Florida.

Municipalities are not permitted to tax the interest income from securities issued by the U.S. Treasury. Thus, part of the spread between Treasury securities and taxable non-Treasury securities of the same maturity reflects the value of the exemption from state and local taxes.

Expected Liquidity of an Issue   Bonds trade with different degrees of liquidity. The greater the expected liquidity with which an issue trades, the lower the yield that investors require. As noted earlier, Treasury securities are the most liquid securities in the world. The lower yield offered on Treasury securities relative to non-Treasury securities reflects, to a significant extent, the difference in liquidity. Even within the Treasury market, some differences in liquidity occur, because on-the-run issues have greater liquidity than off-the-run issues.

An important factor that affects the liquidity of an issue is the size of the issue. One of the reasons that U.S. Treasury securities are highly liquid is the large size of each individual issue. As we will explain in Chapter 21, government-sponsored enterprises in recent years dramatically increased their issuance size. They do so in their attempt to have the yield on their securities become the benchmark interest rates in the U.S. economy. As we noted earlier, the triple A **credit rating** of government-sponsored enterprises makes the yield on their securities an attractive candidate to replace the yields on Treasury securities as the benchmark interest rates. The large size and therefore liquidity of the securities issued by government-sponsored enterprises increase their attractiveness as an alternative benchmark. We also noted earlier that the yields on corporate bond issues rated triple A may make them a potential alternative benchmark.

However, the size of each issue for the various triple A corporate bond issuers is considerably smaller than that of the securities issued by government-sponsored enterprises. For this reason, triple A corporate bond issuers may not be received by market participants as a benchmark alternative.

Summary

In this chapter we presented the theory of interest rates. We showed how consumers' choices between current and future consumption affect saving, relying on two fundamental concepts: preference and opportunity (in the loan market and production market).

An important property that results from the existence of a perfect loan market, together with production opportunities, is that it separates the current consumption decision from current income by creating the possibility to save or dissave through production and net lending. Our conclusion is that the equilibrium interest rate reflects a complex set of forces that control the demand for investment and the supply of savings.

The market equilibrium achieved with the intermediation of the loan market contributes an important property with respect to the efficiency of the economy in producing and allocating resources. It will not be possible to reallocate resources in such a way that some will be better off while nobody will be worse off. Economists refer to this property as Pareto optimality.

The real rate of interest is the interest rate that would prevail in the absence of inflation. It can be shown that the nominal rate of interest is approximately equal to the real rate of interest plus anticipated inflation, a relationship referred to as Fisher's Law.

Every economy operates with not just one interest rate but rather with a structure of interest rates. The difference between the yield on any two bonds is called the yield spread. Historically, the interest rate or yield on U.S. Treasury securities has served as the benchmark interest rates throughout the world. Today, because of the substantial reduction in issuance of U.S. Treasury securities, market participants believe that another benchmark will eventually be selected. The candidates suggested include the yield on securities issued by government-sponsored enterprises, the yield on securities issued by triple A-rated corporate bond issues, and the swap spread in the interest rate swap market. Moreover, as bond markets outside the United States develop, some countries are developing their own benchmark interest rates.

As of this writing, the base interest rate in the United States is the yield on a Treasury security. The base interest rate is equal to the real rate of interest plus the expected rate of inflation. The risk premium is the yield spread between a non-Treasury security and a comparable on-the-run Treasury security. The factors that affect the spread include (1) the type of issuer (agency, corporation, municipality), (2) the issuer's perceived creditworthiness as measured by the rating system of commercial rating companies, (3) the term or maturity of the instrument, (4) the embedded options in a bond issue (e.g., call, put, or conversion provisions), (5) the taxability of interest income at the federal and municipal levels, and (6) the expected liquidity of the issue.

Key Terms

- Base interest rate
- Benchmark interest rate
- Call provision
- Convertible bond
- Credit rating
- Credit spread
- Current coupon issues
- Embedded option
- Equivalent taxable yield
- Fisher's Law
- High grade
- High-yield bonds
- Indifference curve
- Intermarket sector spread
- Intramarket sector spread

- Investment-grade bonds
- Junk bonds
- Marginal productivity of capital
- Marginal rate of time preference
- Market sectors
- Maturity spread
- Municipal bonds
- Noninvestment-grade bonds

- Off-the-run issues
- On-the-run issues
- Pareto optimality
- Principal
- Production function
- Put provision
- Quality spread
- Real rate

- Risk premium
- Term structure of interest rates
- Transformation curve
- Treasuries
- Treasury securities
- Yield curve spread

Questions

1. Why is the indifference curve between current and future consumption convex to the origin?
2. What is meant by the marginal rate of time preference?
3. a. What is the market line?
   b. Explain why the market line slopes downward.
4. What determines the market rate in a simple economy?
5. What is the transformation curve?
6. What is meant by the marginal productivity of capital?
7. How is the equilibrium market rate determined?
8. What is meant by the real rate of interest?
9. What is meant by the nominal rate of interest?
10. According to Fisher's Law, what is the relationship between the real rate and the nominal rate?
11. What is the difficulty of measuring an economy's real rate of interest?
12. In the May 29, 1992, *Weekly Market Update*, published by Goldman Sachs & Co., the following information was reported in various exhibits for the Treasury market as of the close of business Thursday, May 28, 1992:

On-the-Run Treasuries	
Maturity	*Yield*
3-month	3.77%
6-month	3.95
1-year	4.25
2-year	5.23
3-year	5.78
5-year	6.67
7-year	7.02
10-year	7.37
20-year	7.65
30-year	7.88

Key Off-the-Run Treasuries	
Issue	*Yield*
Old 10-year	7.42%
Old 30-year	7.90

a. What is the credit risk associated with a Treasury security?
b. Why is the Treasury yield considered the base interest rate?
c. What is meant by *on-the-run Treasuries*?
d. What is meant by *off-the-run Treasuries*?

  e. What are the yield spreads between (i) the off-the-run 10-year Treasury issue and the on-the-run 10-year Treasury issue, and (ii) the off-the-run 30-year Treasury issue and the on-the-run 30-year Treasury issue?

  f. What does the yield spread between the off-the-run Treasury issue and the on-the-run Treasury issue reflect?

13. In the May 29, 1992, *Weekly Market Update,* published by Goldman Sachs, the following information was reported in various exhibits for certain corporate bonds as of the close of business Thursday, May 28, 1992:

Issuer	Rating	Yield	Spread	Treasury Benchmark
General Electric Capital Co.	Triple A	7.87%	50	10
Mobil Corp.	Double A	7.77	40	10
Southern Bell Tel & Teleg	Triple A	8.60	72	30
Bell Tel Co Pa	Double A	8.66	78	30
AMR Corp	Triple B	9.43	155	30

  a. What is meant by *rating*?

  b. Which of the five bonds has the greatest credit risk?

  c. What is meant by *spread*?

  d. What is meant by *Treasury benchmark*?

  e. Using the information for the Treasury market reported for May 29, 1992, in question 12, explain how each of the spreads reported was determined.

  f. Why does each spread reported reflect a risk premium?

14. For the corporate bond issues reported in the previous question, answer the following questions:

  a. Should a triple A-rated bond issue offer a higher or lower yield than a double A-rated bond issue of the same maturity?

  b. What is the spread between the General Electric Capital Company issue and the Mobil Corporation issue?

  c. Is the spread reported in part (b) consistent with your answer to part (a)?

  d. The yield spread between these two bond issues reflects more than just credit risk. What other factors would the spread reflect?

  e. The Mobil Corporation issue is not callable. However, the General Electric Capital Company issue is callable. How does this information help you in understanding the spread between these two issues?

15. For the corporate bond issues reported in question 13, answer the following questions:

  a. What is the yield spread between the Southern Bell Telephone and Telegraph bond issue and the Bell Telephone Company (Pennsylvania) bond issue?

  b. The Southern Bell Telephone and Telegraph bond issue is not callable but the Bell Telephone Company (Pennsylvania) bond issue is callable. What does the yield spread in part (a) reflect?

  c. AMR Corporation is the parent company of American Airlines and is therefore classified in the transportation industry. The bond issue cited is not callable. What is the yield spread between AMR Corporation and Southern Bell Telephone and Telegraph bond issue, and what does this spread reflect?

16. Historically speaking, why are the yields on U.S. Treasury securities used as the benchmark interest rates throughout the world?

17. Two possible candidates to replace the yields of U.S. Treasury securities as the benchmark interest rates are the yields on securities issued by government-sponsored enterprises and the yields on triple A-rated corporate issuers. Which of the two alternatives is likely to be better? Explain why.

18. In the May 29, 1992, *Weekly Market Update*, published by Goldman Sachs, the following information was reported in an exhibit for high-grade, tax-exempt securities as of the close of business Thursday, May 28, 1992:

Maturity	Yield	Yield as a % of Treasury Yield
1-year	3.20%	76.5%
3-year	4.65	80.4
5-year	5.10	76.4
10-year	5.80	78.7
30-year	6.50	82.5

a. What is meant by a *tax-exempt security*?
b. What is meant by a *high-grade* issue?
c. Why is the yield on a tax-exempt security less than the yield on a Treasury security of the same maturity?
d. What is meant by the *equivalent taxable yield*?
e. Also reported in the same issue of the Goldman Sachs report is information on "Intramarket Yield Spreads." What is an intramarket yield spread?

19. a. What is meant by an *embedded option* in a bond?
b. Give three examples of an embedded option that might be included in a bond issue.
c. Does an embedded option increase or decrease the risk premium relative to the base interest rate?

Valuation of Debt Contracts and Their Price Volatility Characteristics

18

Learning Objectives

After reading this chapter you will understand:

◆ the cash flow characteristics of a bond.

◆ how the price of a bond is determined.

◆ why the yield to maturity is used as a measure of a bond's return.

◆ the importance of the reinvestment rate in realizing the yield to maturity.

◆ why the price of a bond changes.

◆ that the price/yield curve of an option-free bond is convex.

◆ that the two characteristics of a bond that affect its price volatility are its coupon and its maturity.

◆ what duration is and how it is calculated.

◆ the limitations of duration as a measure of price volatility of a bond when interest rates change.

◆ what the convexity of a bond is and how it is related to bond price volatility.

In Chapter 17 we focused on determinants of the one-period rate on debt instruments and the structure of interest rates in any economy. Our concern in this chapter is the valuation of debt contracts. We will concentrate on one special case, namely, debt contracts that (1) are free of risk of default by the issuer, (2) enjoy no advantage from taxes, and (3) contain no embedded options (i.e., are not callable, putable, or convertible). Federal government debt, the subject of Chapter 21, is an example of this kind of obligation.[1] The rate earned on federal government debt instruments is usually characterized as "riskless," meaning that the risk that the U.S. government will default on its obligation to pay interest and repay principal is not a concern. After describing how debt obligations are valued, we look at the factors that affect the price volatility of a debt obligation and how to measure the price volatility of a debt obligation when interest rates change.

---

[1] Federal government bond returns actually do have a minor tax advantage because they are exempt from state and local taxes.

◆ FEATURES OF DEBT CONTRACTS

In later chapters we will describe the various features of debt contracts. Here we provide enough information about debt contracts to understand the basic principles for valuing them.

The term to maturity or maturity of a debt contract is the number of years during which the borrower promises to meet the conditions of the debt. The amount to be repaid by the borrower is called the principal. The entire principal can be repaid at the maturity date, in which case the debt contract is said to have a **bullet maturity**. Or, various amounts of the principal can be paid over the life of the debt contract in which case the remaining principal repaid at the maturity date is called a **balloon payment**. A special type of debt contract is a bond, and the amount paid at maturity is called **par value**, **maturity value**, or **face value**.

A debt contract's **coupon** is the periodic interest payment made to owners during the life of the contract. The coupon is in fact the **coupon rate** or rate of interest that, when multiplied by the unpaid outstanding principal provides the dollar amount of the coupon payment. Typically, but not universally, for bonds issued in the United States the coupon payments are made every 6 months.

For some debt contractors, no periodic coupon interest is paid over the life of the contract. Instead both the principal and the interest are paid at the maturity date. Such debt contracts are called **zero-coupon instruments**.

The price of most debt contracts are quoted as percentages of par value. To convert the price quote into a dollar figure, one simply multiplies the price by the par value. The following table will illustrate the matter:

Par Value	Price Quote	Price as Percentage of Par	Price in Dollars
$ 1,000	$91\frac{3}{4}$	91.75%	$ 917.50
5,000	$102\frac{1}{2}$	102.50	5,125.00
10,000	$87\frac{1}{4}$	87.25	8,725.00
25,000	$100\frac{7}{8}$	100.875	25,218.75
100,000	$71\frac{9}{32}$	71.28125	71,281.25

◆ BASIC VALUATION PRINCIPLES

A useful way of understanding the valuation of longer-term debt contracts and how their valuation relates to interest rates is to use the principle that, in perfect markets, all riskless instruments have the same short-term return, and it must coincide with the riskless short-term rate for that period. This condition may be expected to be enforced through arbitrage. The one-period rate of return from, say, an instrument with maturity n and a cash flow denoted by $(a_1, \ldots, a_n)$, consists of the cash payment, a_1, plus the capital gain, or the difference between the next-period price and the current price of the security, expressed as a percentage of initial value.

Let us denote by $_nP_j$ the price j periods $(j < n)$ from the present of an instrument maturing n periods later; the capital gain for the current period is: $_{n-1}P_1 - {_nP_0}$. Hence the condition that the one-period return from holding the instrument must be equal to the short-term rate for the forthcoming period, denoted by r_1, can be written as:

$$\frac{a_1 + \left(_{n-1}P_1 - {_nP_0} \right)}{_nP_0} = r_1 \tag{18.1}$$

Solving for $_nP_0$,

$$_nP_0 = \frac{a_1 + _{n-1}P_1}{1 + r_1} \tag{18.2}$$

The reason why the right-hand side of equation (18.2) must be the equilibrium price of the *n*-period asset is that, as can be verified, if the current price, $_nP_0$, were larger than the right-hand side of equation (18.2), then the one-period return of the instrument, given by equation (18.1), would be smaller than the return r_1 obtainable by investing in the one-period instrument. As a result, no one would want to hold it, causing its price to drop. Similarly, if $_nP_0$ is smaller than the right-hand side of equation (18.2), this yield for the instrument would be larger than r_1, and everyone would want to hold it.

Next we observe that $_{n-1}P_1$ must satisfy an equation like equation (18.2), or

$$_{n-1}P_1 = \frac{a_2 + _{n-2}P_2}{1 + r_2}$$

Substituting this equation into equation (18.2), we get

$$_nP_0 = \frac{a_1}{\left(1 + r_1\right)} + \frac{a_2 + _{n-2}P_2}{\left(1 + r_1\right)\left(1 + r_2\right)}$$

Repeating the same substitution recursively, up to the maturity of the instrument, we find

$$_nP_0 = \frac{a_1}{\left(1 + r_1\right)} + \frac{a_2}{\left(1 + r_1\right)\left(1 + r_2\right)}$$

$$+ \frac{a_{3n}}{\left(1 + r_1\right)\left(1 + r_2\right)\left(1 + r_3\right)} + \cdots \tag{18.3}$$

$$+ \frac{a_n}{\left(1 + r_1\right)\left(1 + r_2\right)\left(1 + r_3\right) \cdots \left(1 + r_n\right)}$$

Each term on the right-hand side of the preceding equation is the present value of the cash flow at each successive time. Thus the price of a debt instrument must equal the sum of the present value of the payments that the debtor is required to make until maturity.

Let us illustrate the principles to this point. Assume that the length of a period is 1 year. Suppose that an investor purchases a 4-year debt instrument with the following payments promised by the borrower.

Year	Interest Payment	Principal Repayment	Cash Flow
1	$100	0	$ 100
2	120	0	120
3	140	0	140
4	150	$1,000	1,150

In terms of our notation, $a_1 = \$100; a_2 = \$120; a_3 = \$140; a_4 = \$1,150$. Assume that the 1-year rates for the next 4 years are $r_1 = .07; r_2 = .08; r_3 = .09; r_4 = .10$. The current value or price of this debt instrument today, denoted $_4P_0$, using equation (18.3) is then

$$_4P_0 = \frac{100}{\left(1.07\right)} + \frac{120}{\left(1.07\right)\left(1.08\right)} + \frac{140}{\left(1.07\right)\left(1.08\right)\left(1.09\right)}$$

$$+ \frac{1,150}{\left(1.07\right)\left(1.08\right)\left(1.09\right)\left(1.10\right)}$$

$$= \$1,138.43$$

Next we must consider how to construct a measure that permits us to compare the rate of return of instruments having different cash flows and different maturities. For one-period instruments, the measure is clear; it is provided by the left-hand side of equation (18.1). But that approach cannot be generalized readily to long-term debt instruments. For instance, for an instrument with a cash flow (a_1, a_2), the measure $(a_1 + a_2)/P_0$ would not be a useful measure of yield. In the first place, if we seek a measure that can be used to compare instruments of different maturities, it must measure return per unit of time. And second, the proposed measure ignores the timing of receipts, thus failing to reflect the time value of money.

The widely accepted solution to this problem is provided by a measure known as the **yield to maturity**. It is defined as the interest rate that makes the present value of the cash flow equal to the market value (price) of the instrument. Thus for the debt instrument in equation (18.3), the yield to maturity is the interest rate y that satisfies equation (18.4), which must generally be found by trial and error.

$$_nP_0 = \frac{a_1}{(1+y)} + \frac{a_2}{(1+y)^2} + \frac{a_3}{(1+y)^3} + \ldots + \frac{a_n}{(1+y)^n} \qquad \textbf{(18.4)}$$

If the debt instrument is a bond, the cash flow $(a_1, \ldots, a_n)$ can be written as $(C, C, \ldots, C + M)$, where C is the coupon payment and M the maturity value. Equation (18.4) can be rewritten as

$$P = \frac{C}{(1+y)} + \frac{C}{(1+y)^2} + \frac{C}{(1+y)^3} + \ldots + \frac{C+M}{(1+y)^n} \qquad \textbf{(18.5)}$$

After dividing both sides of equation (18.5) by M, to obtain the price per dollar of maturity value, and factoring C, we obtain

$$\frac{P}{M} = \frac{C}{M} \sum_{t=1}^{n} \frac{1}{(1+y)^t} + \frac{1}{(1+y)^n} \qquad \textbf{(18.6)}$$

Recognizing that the summation on the right-hand side of equation (18.6) is the sum of a geometric progression,[2] we can rewrite the equation as

$$\frac{P}{M} = \frac{C}{M} \left[\frac{1-(1+y)^{-n}}{y} \right] + \frac{1}{(1+y)^n} \qquad \textbf{(18.7)}$$

The yield to maturity is the solution to equation (18.7) for y, the yield of an n-period bond. In equation (18.7) P/M is the so-called **par value relation**, usually expressed as a percentage. If it is equal to 1, the bond sells "at par"; if it is larger than 1, it sells at a "premium"; and if it is less than 1, it sells at a "discount." C/M is the coupon rate expressed as a ratio.

---

2   The sum of a geometric progression is

$$\sum_{t=1}^{n} \frac{1}{(1+k)^t} = \frac{1-(1+k)^{-n}}{k}$$

◆ PRICE OF AN OPTION-FREE BOND

So far we did not specify the unit of time for measuring the frequencies with which interest is computed and the coupons are paid. Interest rates (and maturity) customarily are quoted per year (e.g., 7% per year), and we shall follow this convention, which means that in equation (18.7) it is implicitly assumed that the coupon rate is C per year and paid once a year. In fact, in the United States almost all bonds pay interest twice a year. Each coupon payment therefore amounts to $C/2$, which must be discounted twice a year at half the annual yield or $y/2$. As a result, equation (18.7) is changed to:

$$\frac{P}{M} = \frac{C}{2M}\left[\frac{1-\left(1+y/2\right)^{-2n}}{y/2}\right] + \frac{1}{\left(1+y/2\right)^{2n}} \qquad \textbf{(18.8)}$$

To illustrate calculation of the yield to maturity of a bond with semiannual coupon payments, consider a 7%, 20-year bond with a maturity or par value of $100, and selling for 74.26%, or 74.26 cents per $1 of par value. The cash flow for this bond per dollar of par value is: forty 6-month payments of $0.035, and $1 received in forty 6-month periods from now. The present value at various semiannual interest rates ($y/2$) is:

Interest Rate ($y/2$)	3.5%	4.0%	4.5%	5.0%	5.5%	6.0%	6.5%
Present value (P/M):	1.0000	0.9010	0.8160	0.7426	0.6791	0.6238	0.5756

When a 5.0% semiannual interest rate is used, the present value of the cash flow is equal to 0.7426 per $1 of par value, which is the price of the bond. Hence, 5.0% is the semiannual yield to maturity.

The annual yield to maturity should, strictly speaking, be found by compounding 5.0% for 1 year. That is, it should be 10.25.[3] But the accepted convention in the market is to double $y/2$, the semiannual yield to maturity. Thus, the yield to maturity for the preceding bond is 10% (two times 5.0%). The yield to maturity computed using this convention—doubling the semiannual yield—is called the **bond equivalent yield**.

◆ REASONS FOR CHANGES IN BOND PRICE

One can infer from equation (18.7) or equation (18.8) that the value of a bond depends on three things: its coupon, its maturity, and interest rates. Hence the price of a bond can change over time for any one of the following reasons.

1. *A change in the level of interest rates in the economy.* For example, if interest rates in the economy increase because of Fed policy, the price of a bond will decrease; if interest rates fall, the price of a bond will rise.
2. *A change in the price of a bond selling at a price other than par as it moves toward maturity without any change in the required yield.* Over time the price of a discount bond rises if interest rates do not change; the price of a premium bond declines over time if interest rates do not change.
3. *For a non-Treasury security, a change in the required yield because of a change in the yield between non-Treasury and Treasury securities.* If the Treasury rate does

---

[3] The return at the end of the year is

$$(1.050)^2 - 1 = 1.1025\ -1 = 0.1025$$

not change, but the yield spread between Treasury and non-Treasury securities changes (narrows or widens), the price of non-Treasury securities will change.

   4. *A change in the perceived credit quality of the issuer.* Assuming interest rates in the economy and yield spreads between non-Treasury and Treasury securities do not change, the price of non-Treasury securities increases if the issuer's perceived credit quality improves; the price drops if perceived credit quality deteriorates.

◆ WHAT DETERMINES THE PREMIUM-PAR YIELD

In general, equation (18.7) and equation (18.8) cannot be solved explicitly for y (for $n > 2$); these equations must be solved by trial and error—with one important exception. It is apparent from equation (18.7) that the par value, P/M, increases as the coupon rate, C/M, increases. Now consider a bond whose coupon rate is such that the corresponding value of P/M is one—that is, the bond sells at par. Then equation (18.7) becomes

$$1 = \frac{C}{M}\left[\frac{1-\left(1+y\right)^{-n}}{y}\right] + \frac{1}{\left(1+y\right)^{n}} \qquad \textbf{(18.9)}$$

Equation (18.9) can be solved explicitly for y; the solution is $y = C/M$. In other words, if a bond sells at par, its yield to maturity is the same as its coupon rate; for example, if a 7.75%, 20-year bond sells at par, its yield to maturity is 7.75%. Therefore, for a bond to be issued at par, the coupon rate offered must be the same as the market-required yield for that maturity. The coupon rate of an n-period bond selling at par may be labeled the n-period par yield.

   It can also be verified from equation (18.9) that if the coupon rate on a bond is less than the required yield to maturity, or par yield, the bond will sell at a discount; the converse is true for a bond with a coupon above par yield. The explanation for this relation is self-evident: If the cash payment per period—namely, the coupon—is below the required yield per period, the difference must be made up by an increase in price, or capital gain, over the life of the instrument. The price of the bond must be lower than its maturity value. In the United States, debt contracts (other than zero-coupon issues) customarily are issued with a yield to maturity that will insure that the issue sells at close to par.[4]

◆ REINVESTMENT OF CASH FLOW AND YIELD

The yield to maturity takes into account the coupon income and any capital gain or loss that the investor will realize by holding the bond to maturity. The measure has its shortcomings, however. We might think that if we acquire for P a bond of maturity n and yield y, then at maturity we can count on obtaining a terminal value equal to $P(1 + y)^n$. This inference is not justified. By multiplying both sides of equation (18.5) by $(1 + y)^n$, we obtain

$$P\left(1+y\right)^{n} = C\left(1+y\right)^{n-1} + C\left(1+y\right)^{n-2} + C\left(1+y\right)^{n-3} + C + M$$

---

[4] This custom is reinforced by tax laws discouraging tax arbitrage by the substitution of low coupon payments for capital gains from a low issue price, because interest income is taxed as ordinary income at the full tax rate, while capital gains are taxed at a preferential (lower) tax rate. The provisions in the tax code that discourage this arbitrage are the "original issue discount" (OID) rules.

For the terminal value to be $P(1 + y)^n$, each of the coupon payments must be reinvested until maturity at an interest rate equal to the yield to maturity. If the coupon payment is semiannual, then each semiannual payment must be reinvested at the yield y.

An illustration demonstrates this point. Consider a 7%, 20-year bond that makes semiannual coupon payments of $3.50, and sells for $74.26 per $100 par value. As we demonstrated earlier, the yield to maturity for this bond is equal to 10%. If an investor can invest $74.26 in a certificate of deposit that pays 5% every 6 months for 20 years, or 10% per year (on a bond equivalent basis), at the end of 20 years (forty 6-month periods), the $74.26 investment will have grown to $522.79, that is, $74.26(1.05)^{40} = $522.79. The terminal value represents a return of the amount invested of $74.26 with interest earned over the 40 years of $448.53 ($522.79 minus $74.26).

Now we shall see what the investor receives by investing in the bond. Forty semiannual interest payments of $3.50 total $140. When the bond matures, the investor will receive $100. Thus, the total amount that the investor receives is $240 if the bond is held to maturity. This amount is $282.79 less than the terminal value of $522.79 necessary to produce a yield of 10% on a bond equivalent basis ($522.79 minus $240). How is this deficiency to be made up? If the investor reinvests the coupon payments at a semiannual interest rate of 5% (or a 10% annual rate on a bond equivalent basis), then the interest earned on the coupon payments will be $282.79. Consequently, of the return on an investment of $448.53 needed to generate a dollar return that gives a yield of 10%, about 63% ($282.79 divided by $448.53) must be generated by reinvesting the coupon payments.

Clearly, as the equation and the example demonstrate, the investor realizes the yield to maturity that is calculated at the time of purchase only if (1) all the coupon payments can be reinvested at the yield to maturity , and (2) the bond is held to maturity. With respect to the first assumption, the risk that an investor faces is that future interest rates at which the coupon can be reinvested will be less than the yield to maturity at the time the bond is purchased. This risk is referred to as **reinvestment risk**. And if the bond is not held to maturity, it may have to be sold for less than its purchase price, resulting in a return that is less than the yield to maturity. The risk that a bond will have to be sold at a loss is referred to as **interest rate risk**, or **price risk**.

We focused in this section on coupon-bearing bonds. In the special case of a debt instrument that produces only one cash flow, the maturity value, the yield to maturity does measure the rate at which the initial investment rises. We can see it if we substitute zero for the coupon payments in the last equation. Bonds that do not make coupon payments are called zero-coupon bonds. The advantage of these bonds is that they do not expose the investor to reinvestment risk. At the same time, they deprive the investor of the opportunity to reinvest the coupon at a rate higher than y.

◆ BOND PRICE VOLATILITY

The return from holding a bond over some time period less than the maturity of the bond is uncertain because of the uncertainty about the future price of a bond, due to the stochastic nature of future interest rates. When interest rates rise, the price of a bond will fall. Maturity is one of the characteristics of a bond that we said will determine the responsiveness of a bond's price to a change in yields. In this section, we demonstrate this price responsiveness with hypothetical bonds. We also show other characteristics that influence a bond's price volatility, and how to measure a bond's price volatility.

REVIEW OF PRICE/YIELD RELATIONSHIP

As explained earlier in this chapter, a fundamental characteristic of an option-free bond (that is, a bond that is not callable, putable, or convertible) is that its price changes in the opposite direction from the change in yield. This behavior follows from the fact that the price of a bond is equal to the present value of its cash flow.

Table 18-1 illustrates this property for four hypothetical bonds: a 9% coupon bond with 5 years to maturity, a 9% coupon bond with 20 years to maturity, a 5% coupon bond with 5 years to maturity, and a 5% coupon bond with 20 years to maturity. The price for each bond in the table is computed using equation (18.7).

The graph of the price/yield relationship for any of these bonds would exhibit the shape shown in Figure 18-1. Notice that the shape of this relationship for any option-free bond is not linear, but rather is convex. Keep in mind that the price/yield relationship that we discussed is appropriate only at a given point in the life of the bond.

PRICE VOLATILITY PROPERTIES

Although the prices of all (option-free) bonds move in the opposite direction of the change in yields, neither dollar price changes nor percentage price changes are the same for all bonds, as shown for the four hypothetical bonds in Table 18-2. The top panel of the table shows the dollar price change and the bottom panel the percentage price change for various changes in the yield assuming that initially all four bonds are priced to yield 9%.

Note from Table 18-2 that for a given bond the absolute dollar price change and the absolute percentage price change are not the same for an equal increase and decrease in the yield, except for very small changes in the yield. Even for a small change in yield, the absolute dollar price change is less symmetric than the absolute percentage price change. In general, the dollar price increase and the percentage price increase when the yield declines are greater than the dollar price decrease and percentage price decrease when the yield increases.

TABLE 18-1 Price/Yield Relationship for Four Hypothetical Bonds

Yield	Price at given yield*			
	9%/5-yr	9%/20-yr	5%/5-yr	5%/20-yr
6.00%	112.7953	134.6722	95.7349	88.4426
7.00	108.3166	121.3551	91.6834	78.6449
8.00	104.0554	109.8964	87.8337	70.3108
8.50	102.0027	104.7693	85.9809	66.6148
8.90	100.3966	100.9267	84.5322	63.8593
8.99	100.0396	100.0921	84.2102	63.2626
9.00	100.0000	100.0000	84.1746	63.1968
9.01	99.9604	99.9081	84.1389	63.1311
9.10	99.6053	99.0865	83.8187	62.5445
9.50	98.0459	95.5592	82.4132	60.0332
10.00	96.1391	91.4205	80.6957	57.1023
11.00	92.4624	83.9539	77.3871	51.8616
12.00	88.9599	77.4306	74.2397	47.3380

*Par = 100

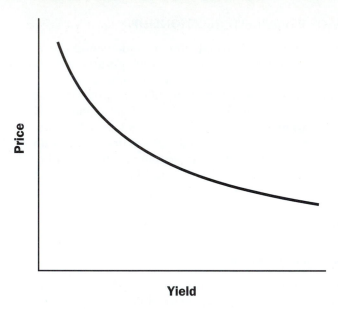

FIGURE 18-1 Shape of the Price/Yield Relationship for an Option-Free Bond

These two observations—that the absolute and percentage price change are not equal for all bonds, and that the absolute and percentage price change are asymmetric for equal changes in yield—are due to the characteristics of bonds that determine the shape of the price/yield relationship depicted in Figure 18-1. Later in this section we will provide an explanation for the second observation. First we look at the particular characteristics of a bond that affect its price volatility.

CHARACTERISTICS OF A BOND THAT AFFECT PRICE VOLATILITY

Two characteristics of a bond provide the primary determinants of its price volatility: coupon and term to maturity. First, we look at price volatility in terms of percentage price change for a change in yields. For a given term to maturity and initial market yield, percentage price volatility is greater the lower the coupon rate. This property can be seen by comparing the 9% and 5% coupon bonds with the same maturity (lower panel of Table 18-2). The second characteristic of a bond that affects its price volatility is its term to maturity. For a given coupon rate and initial yield, the longer the term to maturity, the greater the price volatility, in terms of percentage price change.[5] Note this relationship in the lower panel of Table 18-2 by comparing the 5-year bonds to the 20-year bonds with the same coupon.

Now we can ask if the same properties hold when volatility is measured in terms of dollar price change rather than percentage price change. The upper panel of Table 18-2 demonstrates that, holding all other factors constant, the dollar price change is greater, the longer the term to maturity. However, the first characteristic concerning the effect of the coupon rate does not hold when volatility is measured in terms of dollar price change instead of percentage price change. In terms of dollar price change, for a given maturity and initial market yield, the lower the coupon rate, the smaller the dollar price change.

MEASURE OF PRICE VOLATILITY: DURATION

Now we know that coupon and maturity affect a security's price volatility when yield changes, and that the level of interest rates affect price volatility. What is needed is a measure that encompasses these three factors that affect a security's price volatility

---

[5] Certain exceptions apply to certain deep-discount, long-term *coupon* bonds.

TABLE 18-2   Instantaneous Dollar and Percentage Price Changes for Four Hypothetical Bonds

Bonds priced initially to yield 9%:

9% coupon, 5 years to maturity, price = 100.0000
9% coupon, 20 years to maturity, price = 100.0000
5% coupon, 5 years to maturity, price = 84.1746
5% coupon, 20 years to maturity, price = 63.1968

Yield changes to	Change in basis points	Dollar price change per $100 par			
		9%/5-yr	9%/20-yr	5%/5-yr	5%/20-yr
6.00%	−300	12.7953	34.6722	11.5603	25.2458
7.00	−200	8.3166	21.3551	7.5088	15.4481
8.00	−100	4.0554	9.8964	3.6591	7.1140
8.50	−50	2.0027	4.7693	1.8063	3.4180
8.90	−10	0.3966	0.9267	0.3576	0.6625
8.99	−1	0.0396	0.0921	0.0356	0.0658
9.01	1	−0.3960	−0.0919	−0.0357	−0.0657
9.10	10	−0.3947	−0.9135	−0.3559	−0.6523
9.50	50	−1.9541	−4.4408	−1.7614	−3.1636
10.00	100	−3.8609	−8.5795	−3.4789	−6.0945
11.00	200	−7.5376	−16.0461	−6.7875	−11.3352
12.00	300	−11.0401	−22.5694	−9.9349	−15.8588

Yield changes to	Change in basis points	Percentage price change			
		9%/5-yr	9%/20-yr	5%/5-yr	5%/20-yr
6.00%	−300	12.80%	34.67%	13.73%	39.95
7.00	−200	8.32	21.36	9.92	24.44
8.00	−100	4.06	9.90	4.35	11.26
8.50	−50	2.00	4.77	2.15	5.41
8.90	−10	0.40	0.93	0.42	1.05
8.99	−1	0.04	0.09	0.04	0.10
9.01	1	−0.04	−0.09	−0.04	−0.10
9.10	10	−0.40	−0.91	−0.42	−1.03
9.50	50	−1.95	−4.44	−2.09	−5.01
10.00	100	−3.86	−8.58	−4.13	−9.64
11.00	200	−7.54	−16.05	−8.06	−17.94
12.00	300	−11.04	−22.57	−11.89	−25.09

when yields change. The most obvious way to measure the price sensitivity of a security to changes in interest rates is to change rates by a small number of basis points and calculate how the price or value of the security will change.

To make these calculations, we use the following notation.

Δy = change in the yield of a security (in decimal form)
V_0 = initial value or price of a security (per $100 par value)
V_- = the estimated value of a security per $100 of par value if the yield is decreased by Δy
V_+ = the estimated value of a security per $100 of par value if the yield is increased by Δy

Two key points to keep in mind are important to our discussion. First, the change in yield is the same change in yield for all maturities. This assumption is commonly referred to as a **parallel yield curve shift assumption**. Thus, the foregoing discussion about the price sensitivity of a security to interest rate changes is limited to parallel shifts in the yield curve. Other measures allow for an analysis of how the yield curve may shift in a nonparallel fashion, but those measures are beyond the scope of this book.[6]

Second, the notation refers to the estimated value of the security. This value is obtained from a valuation model. Earlier in this chapter we explained the fundamental principles of bond valuation and showed how a basic (i.e., option-free) bond is valued. But certain bonds are much more complicated to value because of their embedded options, which must be incorporated into a valuation model. Consequently, the resulting measure of the price sensitivity of a security to interest rate changes is only as good as the valuation model employed to obtain the estimated value of the security.

Now let's focus on the measure of interest. We want to determine the percentage change in the price of a security when interest rates change by a small number of basis points. Using a given decline in yield (Δy), the percentage price is obtained as follows:

$$\frac{V_- - V_0}{V_0}$$

The numerator shows the difference in the security's value after the decline in yield and the denominator shows the initial value. The percentage change in price per basis point decrease in interest rates is found by dividing the percentage price change by the number of basis points. Since the number of basis points is equal to Δy times 100, the percentage price change per basis point decrease is

$$\frac{V_- - V_0}{V_0(\Delta y)100}$$

Similarly, the percentage change in price per basis point change for an increase in yield of Δy is

$$\frac{V_0 - V_+}{V_0(\Delta y)100}$$

The average percentage price change per basis point change in yield can be calculated as follows:

$$\frac{1}{2}\left[\frac{V_- - V_0}{V_0(\Delta y)100} + \frac{V_0 - V_+}{V_0(\Delta y)100}\right]$$

or equivalently,

$$\frac{V_- - V_+}{2V_0(\Delta y)100}$$

The approximate percentage price change for a 100 basis point change in yield is found by multiplying the previous formula by 100. The name popularly used to refer to the approximate percentage price change is **duration**. Thus,

$$\text{Duration} = \frac{V_- - V_+}{2V_0\Delta y} \qquad \textbf{(18.10)}$$

---

[6] For a discussion of these measures, see Frank J. Fabozzi, *Duration, Convexity, and Other Bond Risk Measures* (New Hope, PA: Frank J. Fabozzi Associates, 1999).

To illustrate the duration calculation given by equation (18.10), consider the following option-free bond: a 9% coupon, 5-year bond trading to yield 9%. The initial price or value (V_0), as shown in Table 18-1, is 100. Suppose the yield changes 50 basis points. If the yield decreases to 8.5%, the value of this bond (V_-), as shown in Table 18-1, would be 102.0027. If the yield increases to 9.5%, the value of this bond (V_+) would be 98.0459. Thus,

$$\Delta_y = 0.005$$
$$V_0 = 100$$
$$V_- = 102.0027$$
$$V_+ = 98.0459$$

Substituting these values into the duration formula given by equation (18.10):

$$\text{Duration} = \frac{102.0027 - 98.0459}{2(100)(0.005)} = 3.96$$

The durations for the four bonds shown in Table 18-1 appear here, assuming the initial yield of 9% and changing the yield by 50 basis points:

Coupon	Maturity	Duration
9%	5 years	3.96
9%	20 years	9.21
5%	5 years	4.24
5%	20 years	10.40

Two characteristics affect the duration of a bond and therefore its price volatility. First, duration for a coupon bond is less than its maturity. For a zero-coupon bond, the duration is equal to its maturity. For bonds with the same maturity and selling at the same yield, the lower the coupon rate, the greater are a bond's duration and price sensitivity. Second, for two bonds with the same coupon rate and selling at the same yield, the longer the maturity, the larger are the duration and price sensitivity.[7] These properties are consistent with our earlier observations with respect to Table 18-2.

Using Duration to Approximate the Percentage Price Change   Our objective is to use duration to approximate how the price of a security changes when interest rates change. Mathematically, the relationship between duration and the approximate price change is as follows:

$$\text{Approximate percentage price change} = -\text{Duration }(\Delta y)100 \qquad \textbf{(18.11)}$$

To illustrate the relationship, consider the 5%, 20-year bond selling at 63.1968 to yield 9%. The duration is 10.40. Suppose yields increase instantaneously from 9.00% to 9.10%. The yield change is +0.001 (0.091 − 0.090); then

$$-10.40(+0.001)100 = -1.04\%$$

Notice from the lower panel of Table 18-2 that the actual percentage price change is −1.03%.

Similarly, if yields decrease instantaneously from 9.00% to 8.90% (a yield decrease of 0.001), the formula indicates that the percentage change in price would be +1.04%. From the lower panel of Table 18-2, the actual percentage price change would be +1.05%. This example illustrates that for small changes in yield, duration provides a good approximation of the percentage price change.

---

[7]   This property does not necessarily hold for long-maturity deep-discount coupon bonds.

Instead of a small change in yield, let's assume that yields increase by 200 basis points, from 9% to 11% (a yield change of 0.02 from 0.09 to 0.11). The percentage change in price estimated using duration would be:

$$-10.40\big(+0.02\big)100 = -20.80\%$$

How good is this approximation? As can be seen from the lower panel of Table 18-2, the actual percentage change in price is only −18.94%. Moreover, if the yield decreases by 200 basis points, from 9% to 7%, the approximate percentage price change based on duration would be +20.80%, compared to an actual percentage price change of +24.44%. Not only is the approximation off, but we also can see that duration estimates a symmetric percentage change in price, which, as we pointed out earlier, is not a property of the price/yield relationship for an option-free bond.

The bottom line is that duration provides only an approximation of the percentage price change when yields change. The approximation is good for a small change in yield. For a large change in yields, the approximation is not as good. Shortly we will see how another measure can be introduced to improve the approximation.

Interpretation of Duration   A useful interpretation of duration can be obtained by substituting 100 basis points ($\Delta y = 0.01$) into equation (18.11) and ignoring the sign of the price change. The percentage price change would then be:

$$\text{Duration}\,\big(0.01\big)100 = \text{Duration}$$

Thus, duration can be interpreted as the approximate percentage price change for a 100 basis point change in yields. For example, a bond with a duration of 4.8 will change by approximately 4.8% for a 100 basis point parallel shift in the yield curve. For a 50 basis point change in the yield, the bond's price will change by approximately 2.4%; for a 25 basis point parallel shift in the yield curve, 1.2%, and so on. Institutional investors adjust the duration of a portfolio to increase (decrease) their interest rate risk exposure if interest rates are expected to fall (rise).

Dollar Duration   If duration measures the percentage price change, then **dollar duration** of a bond measures the dollar price change. The dollar duration can be easily obtained given the bond's price. For example, if the duration of a bond is 5 and its price is 90, its price will change by approximately $4.5 (5% times $90) for a 100 basis point change in yield. Thus, the dollar price change, or dollar duration, is $4.5 for a 100 basis change in yield.

Macaulay Duration and Modified Duration   A more formal way of deriving the duration of **option-free bonds** and the relationship between the percentage price change and the change in yield uses elementary calculus.

We begin with equation (18.7), which shows the price of an option-free bond selling to yield *y*. Using elementary calculus, one can obtain the change of the price to a change in yield by taking the first derivative of equation (18.7). Then the percentage price change can be obtained by dividing by the price. Finally, by multiplying by the change in yield, the following is obtained:

$$\frac{\Delta P}{P} = -\left[\frac{1}{\big(1+y\big)}\right]D\big(\Delta y\big) \qquad\qquad \textbf{(18.12)}$$

where

P = price
ΔP = change in price
y = yield
Δy = change in yield

and

$$D = \frac{\dfrac{(1)C}{(1+y)} + \dfrac{(2)C}{(1+y)^2} + \dfrac{(3)C}{(1+y)^3} + \cdots + \dfrac{(n)(C+M)}{(1+y)^n}}{P} \quad \textbf{(18.13)}$$

Notice that equation (18.12), derived using calculus, says the same thing as equation (18.11). It shows a linear relationship between some measure, D, and the change in yield. Now, what is D as shown by equation (18.13)? D in equation (18.13) is called **Macaulay duration**. It is named in honor of Frederick Macaulay who used this measure in a study published in 1938.[8] Notice that Macaulay duration is a weighted-average term to maturity of the components of a bond's cash flows, in which the time of receipt of each payment is weighted by the present value of that payment. The denominator is the sum of the weights, which is precisely the price of the bond.

In Table 18-3, the calculation of the Macaulay duration for the 9% coupon, 5-year bond selling to yield 9% is shown. For this bond, the Macaulay duration is 4.13.

If one divides D, Macaulay duration, by $(1 + y)$, the resulting measure is called **modified duration**. That is

$$\text{Modified duration} = \frac{\text{Macaulay duration}}{(1+y)}$$

The value for y in the preceding formula must recognize that the cash flows are in 6-month periods. So, if the yield is 9%, then y in the formula is 4.5%. For our 9% coupon, 5-year bond selling to yield 9%, the modified duration is calculated as follows:

$$\text{Macaulay duration} \left(\text{from Table } 18\text{-}3\right) = 4.13$$

$$y = 0.09/2 = 0.045$$

$$\text{Modified duration} = \frac{4.13}{(1.045)} = 3.95$$

Notice that the modified duration for this bond agrees with the duration calculated earlier using the duration formula given by equation (18.10). (The slight difference of 3.95 versus 3.96 is due to rounding error.)

Moreover, inserting the modified duration into equation (18.12), we get

$$\frac{\Delta P}{P} = -\text{Modified duration} \left(\Delta y\right) \quad \textbf{(18.14)}$$

---

[8]   Frederick R. Macaulay, *Some Theoretical Problems Suggested by the Movement of Interest Rates, Bond Yields, and Stock Prices in the U.S. Since 1856* (National Bureau of Economic Research, New York, 1938). Hicks used the same measure in his study of the properties of cash flows that made the ratio of their values invariant with respect to changes in interest. He called his measure "average maturity." See John R. Hicks, *Value and Capital*, 2nd ed. (Oxford: Clarendon Press, 1946). In a study of the impact of a rise in interest rates on the banking system, Samuelson used a similar concept, which he called the "average time period" of the cash flow. See Paul A. Samuelson, "The Effects of Interest Rate Increases on the Banking System," *American Economic Review* (March 1945), pp. 16–27.

TABLE 18-3   Calculation of Macaulay Duration for a 9%, 5-Year Bond Selling at Par

Formula for Macaulay duration:

$$\dfrac{\dfrac{(1)C}{(1+y)}+\dfrac{(2)C}{(1+y)^2}+\dfrac{(3)C}{(1+y)^3}+\ldots+\dfrac{(n)(C+M)}{(1+y)^n}}{P}$$

Information about bond per $100 par:
Annual coupon = 0.09 × $100 = $9.00
Yield to maturity = 0.09
Number of years to maturity = 5 years
Price = P = 100

Values adjusting for semiannual payments:
C = $9.00/2 = $4.5
y = 0.9/2 = .045
n = 5 × 2 = 10

t	C	$\dfrac{C}{(1.045)^t}$	$t \times \dfrac{C}{(1.045)^t}$
1	$ 4.5	4.306220	4.30622
2	4.5	4.120785	8.24156
3	4.5	3.943335	11.83000
4	4.5	3.773526	15.09410
5	4.5	3.611030	18.05514
6	4.5	3.455531	20.73318
7	4.5	3.306728	23.14709
8	4.5	3.164333	25.31466
9	4.5	3.028070	27.25262
10	104.5	67.290443	672.90442
Total		100.000000	826.87899

$$\dfrac{(1)C}{(1+y)}+\dfrac{(2)C}{(1+y)^2}+\dfrac{(3)C}{(1+y)^3}+\ldots+\dfrac{(n)(C+M)}{(1+y)^n} = 826.87899$$

Macaulay duration in 6-month periods: $\dfrac{826.87899}{100} = 8.27$

Macaulay duration in years: $\dfrac{8.27}{2} = 4.13$

From equation (18.14) one can easily see the relationship between duration and the approximate percentage price change when yields change as given by equation (18.11).

So, we see that by computing duration using equation (18.10) or by first calculating Macaulay duration using equation (18.13) and then obtaining modified duration gets us to the same value. Vendors of analytical services used by investors do not calculate Macaulay duration and then calculate modified duration. Rather, equation (18.10) is used.

Misconception About Duration   Unfortunately, market participants often confuse the main purpose of duration by constantly referring to it as either (1) some measure of the weighted average life of a bond, or (2) the first derivative of the price of a bond, because of the original use of duration and derivation of duration. We did see that, in fact, Macaulay duration is some temporal measure of the cash flows and that Macaulay (and modified) duration is derived by taking the first derivative. So, what is wrong with either interpretation?

The problem is not so much the interpretation as it is the misuse of duration when interpreted as a temporal measure. Our interpretation provided earlier was that duration is the approximate percentage change in price for a 100 basis point change in yields. When interpreting duration as some type of temporal measure (i.e., years) or as a first derivative, it offers no real meaning for a market participant who uses duration to control the interest rate risk exposure of a portfolio or a financial institution. Three reasons can be given.

First, in applying the first derivative to equation (18.7) to obtain Macaulay duration, the assumption is that when yield changes, the cash flow of the bond does not change. This assumption arises because equation (18.7) applies to the price of an option-free bond with fixed cash flows. However, as we see as we develop our understanding of the wide range of debt obligations, the cash flows of certain fixed income securities change as yields in the market change. Examples are callable and putable bonds and mortgage-backed and certain types of asset-backed securities. These securities are said to have **embedded options**, that is, an option whereby the investor or issuer can change the cash flows such that when yields change the cash flows can be expected to change. The derivation of Macaulay duration does not allow for cash flows to change.

Modified duration suffers from the same problem. Thus, modified duration can be interpreted only as the approximate percentage in the price of bond for a 100 basis point change in yield assuming that when yields change the cash flows do *not* change. This measure is fine for securities that do not have embedded options.

In contrast to modified duration, a measure that does consider how changes in yield will affect the cash flows and therefore price when yields change is **effective duration**. This measure, also called **option-adjusted duration**, is found by using equation (18.10). What it requires is a model that allows one to compute the new price of the security when yields change. We do not discuss these more complex models in this book. But what is important to note is that they are not simple equations such as equation (18.7) from which one can take the first derivative. Rather, they use binomial trees (such as was described in Chapter 15 for valuing stock options) or Monte Carlo simulation.

Second, using Macaulay duration or modified duration for complex securities leads some to believe that they can avoid the issue of being able to value such securities. In order to obtain the duration of a complex security using equation (18.10), the formula cannot be applied if a good estimate of what the price will be if yields change cannot be obtained. Equation (18.10) stresses the need to revalue a bond, taking into consideration the effect of a change in the cash flow due to a change in yield. Macaulay duration ignores changes in cash flow and hides the need to revalue the bond.

Finally, the temporal meaning is misleading in terms of years. If one relies on this interpretation of duration, it will be difficult to understand why a bond with a maturity of 20 years can have a duration greater than 20. For example, in Chapter 26 we will discuss collateralized mortgage obligation (CMO) bond classes. Certain CMO bond classes have a greater duration than the underlying mortgage loans. That is, a CMO bond class can have a duration of 50 while the underlining mortgage loans from which the CMO is created can have a maturity of 30 years. Also, some CMO bond classes have a negative duration.

CONVEXITY

Notice that the duration measure indicates that regardless of whether the yield increases or decreases, the approximate percentage price change is the same. However, this result does not agree with the properties of a bond's price volatility. As can be seen from Table 18-2, for small changes in yield the percentage price change will be the same for an increase or decrease in yield. However, for large changes in yield, the same is not true. It suggests that duration is only a good approximation of the percentage price change for a small change in yield.

Consider once again the 9% coupon, 20-year bond selling to yield 9% with a duration of 9.21. If yields increase instantaneously by 10 basis points (from 9% to 9.1%), then, using duration, the approximate percentage price change would be −0.92% (−9.2% divided by 10, remembering that duration is the percentage price change for a 100 basis point change in yield). Notice from the second panel of Table 18-2 that the actual percentage price change is −0.91%. Similarly, if the yield decreases instantaneously by 10 basis points (from 9.00% to 8.90%), then the percentage change in price would be +0.92%. From the second panel of Table 18-3, the actual percentage price change would be +0.93%. These results illustrate that for small changes in yield, duration does an excellent job of approximating the percentage price change.

Instead of a small change in yield, let's assume that yields increase by 200 basis points, from 9% to 11%. The approximate percentage change is −18.42% (−9.21% times 2). As can be seen from the second panel of Table 18-2, the actual percentage change in price is only −16.05%. Moreover, if the yield decreased by 200 basis points from 9% to 7%, the approximate percentage price change based on duration would be +18.42%, compared to an actual percentage price change of +21.36%. Thus, the approximation is not as good for a 200 basis point change in yield.

Duration is in fact a first approximation for a small change in yield. The approximation can be improved by using a second approximation. This approximation is referred to as a bond's **convexity**. The use of this term in the industry is unfortunate because the term *convexity* is also used to describe the shape or curvature of the price/yield relationship, as explained earlier in this chapter. The convexity measure of a security is the approximate change in price that is not explained by duration.

The following relationship is used to estimate the approximate percentage change in the price of a security not explained by duration:

$$\text{Approximate percentage price change not explained by duration} = Con(\Delta y)^2 \qquad \textbf{(18.15)}$$

where

$$Con = \frac{V_+ + V_- - 2V_0}{2V_0(\Delta y)^2} \qquad \textbf{(18.16)}$$

and V_+, V_-, V_0, and Δy are the same as in the duration formula given by equation (18.10).

We illustrate convexity with our hypothetical 9% coupon, 20-year bond selling to yield 9%, for a 200 basis point change in yield. We know from Table 18-1 that

$V_0 = 100$ (the initial price when yield is 9%)
$V_- = 121.3551$ (the price if yield is decreased to 7%)
$V_+ = 83.9539$ (the price when yield is increased to 11%)

We also know that $\Delta y = +0.02$ (a 200 basis point increase in yield in decimal form). Substituting these values into equation (18.16), we get

$$Con = \frac{121.3551 + 83.9539 - 2(100)}{2(100)(+0.02)^2} = 66.36$$

Substituting into equation (18.15), we get

Approximate percentage change in price not explained
by duration $= 66.36(+0.02)^2 = 0.0265 = 2.65\%$

Note that for a 200 basis point decrease in yield, the same value of 2.65% is obtained. By substituting $(-0.02)^2$ into equations (18.15) and (18.16), the results will be the same.

To get the approximate percentage price change we simply add the two approximations. That is, the approximate percentage change for a given change in yield is:

Approximate percentage price change due to duration
+ Approximate percentage price change not explained by duration

Again, we use the 9% coupon bond maturing in 20 years and selling to yield 9% to demonstrate. If the yield increases from 9% to 11%, we know that the approximate percentage price change due to duration is −18.42%. We just determined the approximate percentage price change not explained by duration is 2.65%. Therefore,

Approximate percentage price change $= -18.42\% + 2.65\% = -15.77\%$

Compare this value to the one in Table 18-2, which shows the actual percentage price change is −16.05%. Thus, using duration and taking into account convexity does a better job of estimating the percentage change.

For a 200 basis point decrease in yield from 9% to 7%, we know that the approximate percentage price change using duration is 18.42% and the approximate percentage price change not explained by duration is 2.65%. Therefore,

Approximate percentage price change $= 18.42\% + 2.65\% = 21.07\%$

From Table 18-2 we can see that the actual percentage price change is 21.36%. Again, duration combined with convexity does a better job of estimating the actual percentage price change.

Modified Convexity and Effective Convexity   The prices used in equation (18.16) to calculate *Con* can be obtained by either assuming that when the yield changes the expected cash flows do not change or they do change. In the former case, the resulting convexity is referred to as **modified convexity**. Actually, in the industry, convexity is not qualified by the adjective "modified." Thus, in practice the term *convexity* typically means the cash flows are assumed not to change when yields change. **Effective convexity**, or **option-adjusted convexity**, in contrast, gives recognition that the cash flows do change when yields change. This same distinction is made for modified duration and effective duration.

As with duration, a significant difference between the calculated modified convexity and effective convexity could apply to bonds with embedded options. In fact, for all option-free bonds, the approximate percentage price change not explained by duration results in a positive value and such securities are said to have **positive convexity**. For securities with embedded options, the approximate percentage price change not explained by duration can be either positive or negative. When it is negative, a security is said to exhibit **negative convexity**.

Summary

The cash flow from a bond consists of periodic coupon payments (semiannual payments in the United States) and the repayment of the principal. The value of a bond is the present value of the cash flow it provides until maturity. The yield to maturity measure is used as an index to compare the rate of return of instruments having different cash flows and different maturities. Because the yield to maturity assumes that the investor will hold the bond to the maturity date, and that all cash flows can be reinvested at the calculated yield to maturity, it has limited value in determining the relative value of two bonds with different maturities over some investment horizon. The risk that cash flows will have to be reinvested at an interest rate lower than the calculated yield to maturity is called reinvestment risk. The risk that a bond will have to be sold at a price less than the purchase price is called interest rate risk, or price risk.

A bond's price changes over time for several reasons. First, the level of interest rates in the economy may change. Second, a bond selling at a price above par decreases in price as its maturity date approaches if interest rates in the economy do not change; the price of a bond selling below par increases if interest rates in the economy do not change. For non-U.S. Treasury securities, two additional reasons explain why a bond's price may change: a change in the yield spread between Treasury and non-Treasury securities, or a change in the perceived credit quality of the issuer.

Finally, we explored the sensitivity of bond prices to changes in interest rates. A graph of the relationship between price and yield for any option-free bond takes a convex shape. Not all bonds change by the same percentage or dollar amount if interest rates change. Two characteristics of a bond that affect its price volatility and therefore its interest rate risk exposure are maturity and coupon rate. For a given yield and coupon rate, the longer the maturity, the greater the price volatility. Although exceptions occur, for a given yield and maturity, price volatility is greater, the lower the coupon rate.

A measure of price volatility that relates coupon and maturity is duration. Duration is interpreted as the approximate percentage price change of a bond for a 100 basis point change in interest rates. Dollar duration measures the dollar price change when interest rates change. The best way to think about duration is as a measure of price sensitivity rather than some weighted time measure. The duration of any bond can be determined by changing the bond's yield up and down by a small number of basis points and looking at how its price would change.

Convexity is another measure of price volatility to be used in conjunction with duration to improve the estimate for price volatility for large changes in interest rates.

In the next chapter we continue our study of the theory of the determinants of bond prices and long-term interest rates, focusing on the relationship between interest rates on bonds of the same issuer (the U.S. government) but with different maturities.

Key Terms

- Balloon payment
- Bond equivalent yield
- Bullet maturity
- Convexity
- Coupon
- Coupon rate
- Dollar duration
- Duration
- Effective convexity
- Effective duration
- Embedded option
- Face value
- Interest rate risk
- Macaulay duration
- Maturity value

- Modified convexity
- Modified duration
- Negative convexity
- Option-adjusted convexity
- Option-adjusted duration

- Option-free bonds
- Par value
- Par value relation
- Parallel yield curve shift assumption
- Positive convexity

- Price risk
- Reinvestment risk
- Yield to maturity
- Zero-coupon instruments

Questions ▪▪

1. Determine the value of the following risk-free debt instrument, which promises to make the respective payments when the appropriate annual rates are as shown in the last column.

Year	Cash Payment	Appropriate Annual Rate
1	$15,000	8.0%
2	17,000	8.5
3	20,000	9.0
4	21,000	9.5

2. For each of the following, calculate the price per $1,000 of par value assuming semiannual coupon payments.

Bond	Coupon Rate	Years to Maturity	Required Yield
A	8%	9	7%
B	9	20	9
C	6	15	10
D	0	14	8

3. What is the maximum price of a bond?
4. Consider a bond selling at par ($100) with a coupon rate of 6% and 10 years to maturity.
   a. What is the price of this bond if the required yield is 15%?
   b. What is the price of this bond if the required yield increases from 15% to 16%, and by what percentage did the price of this bond change?
   c. What is the price of this bond if the required yield is 5%?
   d. What is the price of this bond if the required yield increases from 5% to 6%, and by what percentage did the price of this bond change?
   e. From your answers to parts (b) and (d) what can you say about the relative price volatility of a bond in high compared to low interest rate environments?
5. Suppose you purchased a debt obligation 3 years ago at its par value of $100,000. The market price of this debt obligation today is $90,000. What are some of the reasons why the price of this debt obligation could have declined since you purchased it 3 years ago?
6. What is meant by the "yield to maturity" of a bond?
7. What is meant by the yield to maturity calculated on a bond-equivalent basis?
8. a. Show the cash flows for the following four bonds, each of which has a par value of $1,000 and pays interest semiannually.

Bond	Coupon Rate	Years to Maturity	Price
W	7%	5	$884.20
X	8	7	948.90
Y	9	4	967.70
Z	10	10	456.39

b. Calculate the yield to maturity for the four bonds.

9. A portfolio manager is considering buying two bonds. Bond A matures in 3 years and has a coupon rate of 10% payable semiannually. Bond B, of the same credit quality, matures in 10 years and has a coupon rate of 12% payable semiannually. Both bonds are priced at par.
   a. Suppose the portfolio manager plans to hold the bond that is purchased for 3 years. Which would be the best bond for the portfolio manager to purchase?
   b. Suppose the portfolio manager plans to hold the bond that is purchased for 6 years instead of 3 years. In this case, which would be the best bond for the portfolio manager to purchase?
   c. Suppose that the portfolio manager is managing the assets of a life insurance company that issued a 5-year guaranteed investment contract (GIC). The interest rate that the life insurance company agreed to pay is 9% on a semi-annual basis. Which of the two bonds should the portfolio manager purchase to assure that the GIC payments will be satisfied and that a profit will be generated by the life insurance company?

10. What is meant by reinvestment risk when purchasing a bond?

11. Can you tell from the following information which of the three bonds will have the greatest price volatility, assuming each is trading to offer the same yield to maturity?

Bond	Coupon Rate	Maturity
X	8%	9 years
Y	10	11
Z	11	12

12. Calculate the requested measures for bonds A and B (assume each bond pays interest semiannually):

	A	B
Coupon	8%	9%
Yield to maturity	8%	8%
Maturity (in years)	2	5
Par	100.00	100.00
Price	100.000	104.055

   a. Calculate the duration for the two bonds by changing the yield up and down 25 basis points.
   b. Calculate the duration for the two bonds by changing the yield up and down by 10 basis points.
   c. Compare your answers to parts (a) and (b).
   d. Calculate the Macaulay duration for the two bonds.
   e. Calculate the modified duration for the two bonds.
   f. Compare the modified duration for the two bonds computed in parts (e) and (a).

13. For bonds A and B in the previous question:
   a. Calculate the actual price of the bonds for a 100 basis point increase in yield.
   b. Using duration, estimate the price of the bonds for a 100 basis point increase in yield.
   c. Using both duration and convexity, estimate the price of the bonds for a 100 basis point increase in yield.
   d. Comment on the accuracy of your results in parts (b) and (c), and state why one approximation is closer to the actual price than the other.
   e. Without working through calculations, indicate whether the duration of the two bonds would be higher or lower if the yield to maturity is 10% rather than 8%.

14. Which of the following bonds will have the larger price change for a 50 basis point change in yield?

Bond	Duration	Price
E	7	50
F	5	100

15. What is the difference between modified duration and effective duration?

16. What is assumed about how the yield curve changes when using duration?

17. An investor is discussing the duration of a highly complex bond with his broker. The broker tells the investor that the duration of this bond is negative 5. The investor is confused about the negative value and tells the broker that the figure must be in error because the duration is always positive because it is some type of weighted average of time of the cash flows. Comment.

18. As a portfolio manager, you present a report to a client. The report indicates the duration of each security in the portfolio. One of the securities has a maturity of 15 years but a duration of 25. The client believes that the report contains an error because she believes that the duration cannot be greater than the security's maturity. What would be your response to this client?

19. A strategy called immunization is used by institutional investors to protect a portfolio against an adverse change in interest rates. Basically this strategy seeks to offset interest rate risk and reinvestment risk. Why do these two risks offset each other to a certain extent when interest rates change?

CHAPTER 19

The Term Structure of Interest Rates

Learning Objectives

After reading this chapter you will understand:

◆ what is meant by the term structure of interest rates.

◆ what the yield curve is.

◆ the different shapes the term structure can take.

◆ what is meant by a spot rate and a spot rate curve.

◆ how a theoretical spot rate curve can be determined from the Treasury yield curve.

◆ what is meant by an implicit forward rate and how it can be calculated.

◆ how long-term rates are related to the current short-term rate and short-term forward rates.

◆ the different theories about the determinants of the shape of the term structure: pure expectations theory, the liquidity theory, the preferred habitat theory, and the market segmentation theory.

◆ the risks associated with investing in bonds when interest rates change—price risk and reinvestment risk.

In this chapter, we extend the theories and principles of the last chapter to the relationship between the yield on a bond and its maturity. Since the maturity of a bond is referred to as its *term to maturity* or simply *term*, the relationship between yield and maturity is referred to as the **term structure of interest rates**. We also explain the various theories about the determinations of the term structure of interest rates.

◆ THE YIELD CURVE AND THE TERM STRUCTURE

The graphic that depicts the relationship between the yield on bonds of the same credit quality but different maturities is known as the **yield curve**. Market participants tend to construct yield curves from observations of prices and yields in the Treasury market. Two reasons account for this tendency. First, Treasury securities are free of default risk, and differences in creditworthiness do not affect yield estimates. Second, as the largest and most active bond market, the Treasury market offers the fewest problems of illiquidty or infrequent trading. Figure 19-1 shows the shape of three hypothetical Treasury yield curves observed from time to time in the United States. However, as noted in the previous chapter, new benchmarks are being considered by market par-

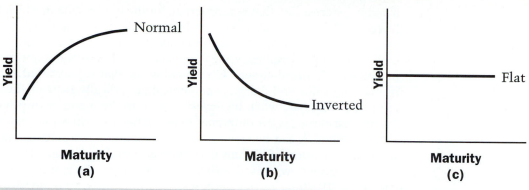

FIGURE 19-1   Three Hypothetical Yield Curves

ticipants because of the dwindling supply of U.S. Treasury securities. Nevertheless, the principles set forth in this chapter apply to any other benchmark selected.

From a practical viewpoint, as we explained in the previous chapter, the Treasury yield curve functions mainly as a benchmark for pricing bonds and setting yields in many other sectors of the debt market—bank loans, mortgages, corporate debt, and international bonds. More recently market participants have come to realize that the traditionally constructed Treasury yield curve is an unsatisfactory measure of the relationship between required yield and maturity. The key reason is that securities with the same maturity may actually provide different yields. As we will explain, this phenomenon reflects the role and impact of differences in the bonds' coupon rates. Hence, it is necessary to develop more accurate and reliable estimates of the Treasury yield curve. In what follows, we will show the problems posed by traditional approaches to the Treasury yield curve, and offer an innovative and increasingly popular approach to building a yield curve. The approach consists of identifying yields that apply to zero-coupon bonds and, therefore, eliminates the problem of nonuniqueness in the yield-maturity relationship.

USING THE YIELD CURVE TO PRICE A BOND

As we explained in Chapter 10, the price of any financial asset is the present value of its cash flow. However, in our illustrations and our discussion to this point in the book, we have assumed that one interest rate should be used to discount all cash flows from a financial asset. In the previous chapter, we indicated that the appropriate interest rate is the yield on a Treasury security with the same maturity as the financial asset, plus an appropriate yield premium or spread.

As just noted, however, there is a problem with using the Treasury yield curve to determine the appropriate yield at which to discount the cash flow of a bond. To illustrate this problem, consider the following two hypothetical 5-year Treasury bonds, A and B. The difference between these two Treasury bonds is the coupon rate, which is 12% for A and 3% for B. The cash flow for these two bonds per $100 of par value for the 10 6-month periods to maturity would be:

Period	Cash Flow for A	Cash Flow for B
1-9	$ 6.00	$ 1.50
10	106.00	101.50

Because of the different cash flow patterns, it is not appropriate to use the same interest rate to discount all cash flows. Instead, each cash flow should be discounted at a unique interest rate that is appropriate for the time period in which the cash flow will be received. But what should be the interest rate for each period?

The correct way to think about bonds A and B is not as bonds but as packages of cash flows. More specifically, they are packages of zero-coupon instruments. As noted in Chapter 10, a **zero-coupon instrument** is one that is purchased at an amount below its maturity value and that pays no interest periodically. Instead, the interest is earned at the maturity date when the investor receives the maturity or principal value. Thus, the interest earned is the difference between the maturity value and the price paid. For example, bond A can be viewed as 10 zero-coupon instruments: one with a maturity value of $6 maturing 6 months from now; a second with a maturity value of $6 maturing 1 year from now; a third with a maturity value of $6 maturing 1.5 years from now, and so on. The final zero-coupon instrument matures 10 6-month periods from now and has a maturity value of $106.

Likewise, bond B can be viewed as 10 zero-coupon instruments: one with a maturity value of $1.50 maturing 6 months from now; one with a maturity value of $1.50 maturing 1 year from now; one with a maturity value of $1.50 maturing 1.5 years from now, and so on. The final zero-coupon instrument matures 10 6-month periods from now and has a maturity value of $101.50. Obviously, in the case of each coupon bond, the value or price of the bond is equal to the total value of its component zero-coupon instruments.

In general, any bond can be viewed as a package of zero-coupon instruments. That is, each zero-coupon instrument in the package has a maturity equal to its coupon payment date or, in the case of the principal, the maturity date. The value of the bond should equal the value of all the component zero-coupon instruments. If this does not hold, it is possible for a market participant to generate riskless profits. Because no one can pass up riskless and certain profits, the market must drive these two prices to equality, and our discussion here assumes that equality.

To determine the value of each zero-coupon instrument, it is necessary to know the yield on a zero-coupon Treasury with that same maturity. This yield is called the **spot rate**, and the graphical depiction of the relationship between the spot rate and its maturity is called the **spot rate curve**. Later we will see how to derive this curve from theoretical considerations of the yields of the actually traded Treasury securities. Such a curve is called a *theoretical spot rate curve*.

CONSTRUCTING THE THEORETICAL SPOT RATE CURVE

In this section, we explain how the theoretical spot rate curve is constructed from the yield curve that is based on the observed yields of Treasury bills and Treasury coupon securities. The process of creating a theoretical spot rate curve in this way is called **bootstrapping**.[1] To explain this process, we'll use the data for the hypothetical price,

---

[1] In practice, the Treasury securities that are used to construct the theoretical spot rate curve are the most recently auctioned Treasury securities of a given maturity. Such issues are referred to as the *on-the-run Treasury issues*. As we will explain in Chapter 21, there are actual zero-coupon Treasury securities with a maturity greater than 1 year that are outstanding in the market. These securities are not issued by the U.S. Treasury but are created by certain market participants from actual coupon Treasury securities. It would seem logical that the observed yield on zero-coupon Treasury securities can be used to construct an actual spot rate curve, but there are problems with this approach. First, the liquidity of these securities is not as great as that of the coupon Treasury market. Second, there are maturity sectors of the zero-coupon Treasury market that attract specific investors who may be willing to trade off yield in exchange for an attractive feature associated with that particular maturity sector, thereby distorting the term structure relationship.

TABLE 19-1   Maturity and Yield to Maturity for 20 Hypothetical Treasury Securities

Maturity (years)	Coupon Rate	Yield to Maturity	Price
0.50	0.0000	0.0800	$ 96.15
1.00	0.0000	0.0830	92.19
1.50	0.0850	0.0890	99.45
2.00	0.0900	0.0920	99.64
2.50	0.1100	0.0940	103.49
3.00	0.0950	0.0970	99.49
3.50	0.1000	0.1000	100.00
4.00	0.1000	0.1040	98.72
4.50	0.1150	0.1060	103.16
5.00	0.0875	0.1080	92.24
5.50	0.1050	0.1090	98.38
6.00	0.1100	0.1120	99.14
6.50	0.0850	0.1140	86.94
7.00	0.0825	0.1160	84.24
7.50	0.1100	0.1180	96.09
8.00	0.0650	0.1190	72.62
8.50	0.0875	0.1200	82.97
9.00	0.1300	0.1220	104.30
9.50	0.1150	0.1240	95.06
10.00	0.1250	0.1250	100.00

annualized yield (yield to maturity), and maturity of the 20 Treasury securities shown in Table 19-1. (In practice, all the coupon rates are estimated so that the price of each bond is par.)

Throughout the analysis and illustrations to come, it is important to remember that the basic principle underlying bootstrapping is that the value of the Treasury coupon security should be equal to the value of the package of zero-coupon Treasury securities that duplicates the coupon bond's cash flow.

Consider the 6-month Treasury bill in Table 19-1. As we explained in the previous chapter, a Treasury bill is a zero-coupon instrument. Therefore, its annualized yield of 8% is equal to the spot rate. Similarly, for the 1-year Treasury, the cited yield of 8.3% is the 1-year spot rate. Given these two spot rates, we can compute the spot rate for a theoretical 1.5-year zero-coupon Treasury. The price of a theoretical 1.5-year zero-coupon Treasury should equal the present value of the three cash flows from an actual 1.5-year coupon Treasury, where the yield used for discounting is the spot rate corresponding to the cash flow. Using $100 as par, the cash flow for the 1.5 year Treasury with the 8.5% coupon rate is:

$$0.5 \text{ years } 0.085 \times \$100 \times 0.5 = \$4.25$$
$$1.0 \text{ years } 0.085 \times \$100 \times 0.5 = \$4.25$$
$$1.5 \text{ years } 0.085 \times \$100 \times 0.5 + 100 = \$104.25$$

The present value of the cash flow is then:

$$\frac{4.25}{\left(1 + z_1\right)^1} + \frac{4.25}{\left(1 + z_2\right)^2} + \frac{104.25}{\left(1 + z_3\right)^3}$$

where

z_1 = one-half the annualized 6-month theoretical spot rate
z_2 = one-half the 1-year theoretical spot rate
z_3 = one-half the 1.5-year theoretical spot rate

Since the 6-month spot rate and 1-year spot rate are 8.0% and 8.3%, respectively, we know these facts:

$$z_1 = 0.04 \text{ and } z_2 = 0.0415$$

We can compute the present value of the 1.5-year coupon Treasury security as:

$$\frac{4.25}{(1.0400)^1} + \frac{4.25}{(1.0415)^2} + \frac{104.25}{(1+z_3)^3}$$

Since the price of the 1.5-year coupon Treasury security (from Table 19-1) is $99.45, the following relationship between market price and the present value of the cash flow must hold:

$$99.45 = \frac{4.25}{(1.0400)^1} + \frac{4.25}{(1.0415)^2} + \frac{104.25}{(1+z_3)^3}$$

We can solve for the theoretical 1.5-year spot rate as follows:

$$99.45 = 4.08654 + 3.91805 + \frac{104.25}{(1+z_3)^3}$$

$$91.44541 = \frac{104.25}{(1+z_3)^3}$$

$$(1+z_3)^3 = 1.140024$$

$$z_3 = 0.04465$$

Doubling this yield, we obtain the bond equivalent yield of 0.0893 or 8.93%, which is the theoretical 1.5-year spot rate. That rate is the rate that the market would apply to a 1.5-year zero-coupon Treasury security if, in fact, such a security existed.

Given the theoretical 1.5-year spot rate, we can obtain the theoretical 2-year spot rate. The cash flow for the 2-year coupon Treasury in Table 19-1 is:

0.5 years $0.090 \times \$100 \times 0.5 = \$4.50$
1.0 years $0.090 \times \$100 \times 0.5 = \$4.50$
1.5 years $0.090 \times \$100 \times 0.5 = \$4.50$
2.0 years $0.090 \times \$100 \times 0.5 + 100 = \$104.50$

The present value of the cash flow is then:

$$\frac{4.50}{(1+z_1)^1} + \frac{4.50}{(1+z_2)^2} + \frac{4.50}{(1+z_3)^3} + \frac{104.50}{(1+z_4)^4}$$

where z_4 is one-half the 2-year theoretical spot rate. Since the 6-month spot rate, 1-year spot rate, and 1.5-year spot rate are 8.0%, 8.3%, and 8.93%, respectively, then:

$$z_1 = 0.04, \; z_2 = 0.0415 \text{ and } z_3 = 0.04465$$

Therefore, the present value of the 2-year Treasury security is:

$$\frac{4.50}{\left(1.0400\right)^1} + \frac{4.50}{\left(1.0415\right)^2} + \frac{4.50}{\left(1.04465\right)^3} + \frac{104.50}{\left(1+z_4\right)^4}$$

Since the price of the 2-year coupon Treasury security is \$99.64, the following relationship must hold:

$$99.64 = \frac{4.50}{\left(1.0400\right)^1} + \frac{4.50}{\left(1.0415\right)^2} + \frac{4.50}{\left(1.04465\right)^3} + \frac{104.50}{\left(1+z_4\right)^4}$$

We can solve for the theoretical 2-year spot rate as follows:

$$99.64 = 4.32692 + 4.14853 + 3.94730 + \frac{104.25}{\left(1+z_4\right)^4}$$

$$87.21725 = \frac{104.50}{\left(1+z_4\right)^4}$$

$$\left(1+z_4\right)^4 = 1.198158$$

$$z_4 = 0.046235$$

Doubling this yield, we obtain the theoretical 2-year spot rate bond-equivalent yield of 9.247%.

One can follow this approach sequentially to derive the theoretical 2.5-year spot rate from the calculated values of z_1, z_2, z_3, and z_4 (the 6-month, 1-year, 1.5-year, and 2-year rates), and the price and coupon of the bond with a maturity of 2.5 years. Furthermore, one could derive theoretical spot rates for the remaining 15 half-yearly rates. The spot rates thus obtained are shown in Table 19-2. They represent the term structure of interest rates for maturities up to 10 years, at the particular time to which the bond price quotations refer.

Column 2 of Table 19-2 reproduces the calculated yield to maturity for the coupon issue listed in Table 19-1. A comparison of this column with the last column giving the yield to maturity of a zero-coupon bond is instructive, for it confirms that bonds of the same maturity may have different yields to maturity. That is, the yield of bonds of the same credit quality does not depend on their maturity alone. Although the two columns do not change much at the beginning, they diverge more after the third year, and by the ninth year the zero-coupon yield is nearly 100 basis points higher than that of the same maturity with a coupon of 13% and selling at a premium.

USING SPOT RATES TO VALUE A BOND

Given the spot rates, the theoretical value of a bond can be calculated by discounting a cash flow for a given period by the corresponding spot rate for that period. This is illustrated in Table 19-3.

The bond in our illustration is a 10-year, 10% coupon Treasury bond. The second column of Table 19-2 shows the cash flow per \$100 of par value for a 10% coupon bond. The third column shows the theoretical spot rates. The fourth column is simply one half of the annual spot rate of the previous column. The last column shows the present value of the cash flow in the second column when discounted at the semiannual spot rate. The value of this bond is the total present value, \$85.35477.

TABLE 19-2   Theoretical Spot Rates

Maturity (years)	Yield to Maturity	Theoretical Spot Rate
0.50	0.0800	0.08000
1.00	0.0830	0.08300
1.50	0.0890	0.08930
2.00	0.0920	0.09247
2.50	0.0940	0.09468
3.00	0.0970	0.09787
3.50	0.1000	0.10129
4.00	0.1040	0.10592
4.50	0.1060	0.10850
5.00	0.1080	0.11021
5.50	0.1090	0.11175
6.00	0.1120	0.11584
6.50	0.1140	0.11744
7.00	0.1160	0.11991
7.50	0.1180	0.12405
8.00	0.1190	0.12278
8.50	0.1200	0.12546
9.00	0.1220	0.13152
9.50	0.1240	0.13377
10.00	0.1250	0.13623

TABLE 19-3   Illustration of How to Value a 10-Year, 10% Treasury Bond Using Spot Rates

Maturity (years)	Cash Flow	Spot Rate	Semiannual Spot Rate	Present Value
0.5	5	0.08000	0.04000	4.8077
1.0	5	0.08300	0.04150	4.6095
1.5	5	0.08930	0.04465	4.3859
2.0	5	0.09247	0.04624	4.1730
2.5	5	0.09468	0.04734	3.9676
3.0	5	0.09787	0.04894	3.7539
3.5	5	0.10129	0.05065	3.5382
4.0	5	0.10592	0.05296	3.3088
4.5	5	0.10850	0.05425	3.1080
5.0	5	0.11021	0.05511	2.9242
5.5	5	0.11175	0.05588	2.7494
6.0	5	0.11584	0.05792	2.5441
6.5	5	0.11744	0.05872	2.3813
7.0	5	0.11991	0.05996	2.2128
7.5	5	0.12405	0.06203	2.0274
8.0	5	0.12278	0.06139	1.9274
8.5	5	0.12546	0.06273	1.7774
9.0	5	0.13152	0.06576	1.5889
9.5	5	0.13377	0.06689	1.4613
10.0	105	0.13623	0.06812	28.1079
Total				85.35477

◆ FORWARD RATES

Thus far we have seen that from the Treasury yield curve we can extrapolate the theoretical spot rates. In addition, we can extrapolate what some market participants refer to as the *market's consensus of future interest rates*. To see the importance of knowing the market's consensus for future interest rates, consider the following two investment alternatives for an investor who has a 1-year investment horizon:

Alternative 1: Investor buys a 1-year instrument.
Alternative 2: Investor buys a 6-month instrument and when it matures
in 6 months the investor buys another 6-month instrument.

With Alternative 1, the investor will realize the 1-year spot rate and that rate is known with certainty. In contrast, with Alternative 2, the investor will realize the 6-month spot rate, but the 6-month rate 6 months from now is unknown. Therefore, for Alternative 2, the rate that will be earned over 1 year is not known with certainty, which is illustrated in Figure 19-2.

Suppose that this investor expected that 6 months from now the 6-month rate will be higher than it is today. The investor might then feel Alternative 2 would be the better investment. However, this expectation is not necessarily true. To understand why and to appreciate the need to understand why it is necessary to know what the market's consensus of future interest rates is, let's continue with our illustration.

The investor will be indifferent to the two alternatives if they produce the same total dollars over the 1-year investment horizon. Given the 1-year spot rate, there is some rate on a 6-month instrument 6 months from now that will make the investor indifferent between the two alternatives. We will denote that rate by f.

The value of f can be readily determined given the 1-year spot rate and the 6-month spot rate. If an investor placed $100 in a 1-year instrument (Alternative 1), the total dollars that will be generated at the end of 1 year is:

$$\text{Total dollars at the end of year for Alternative 1} = \$100\,(1 + z_2)^2$$

where z_2 is the 1-year spot rate. (Remember we are working in 6-month periods, so the subscript 2 represents two 6-month periods, or 1 year.)

The proceeds from investing at the 6-month spot rate will generate the following total dollars at the end of 6 months:

$$\text{Total dollars at the end of 6 months for Alternative 2} = \$100\,(1 + z_1)$$

where z_1 is the 6-month spot rate. If this amount is reinvested at the 6-month rate 6 months from now, which we denoted f, then the total dollars at the end of 1 year would be:

$$\text{Total dollars at the end of year for Alternative 2} = \$100\,(1 + z_1)(1 + f)$$

FIGURE 19-2 Two Alternative 1-Year Investments

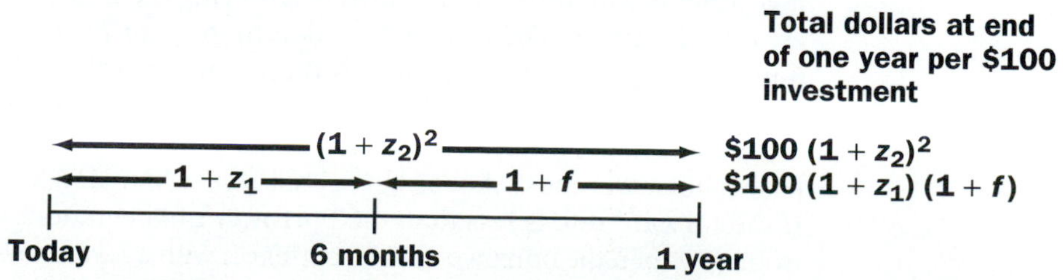

The investor will be indifferent between the two alternatives if the total dollars are the same. Setting the two equations for the total dollars at the end of 1 year for the two alternatives equal we get:

$$\$100 = \left(1 + z_2\right)^2 = \$100 = \left(1 + z_1\right)\left(1 + f\right)$$

Solving the preceding equation for f, we get

$$f = \frac{\left(1 + z_2\right)^2}{\left(1 + z_1\right)} - 1$$

Doubling f gives the bond-equivalent yield for the 6-month rate 6 months from now that we are interested in.

We can illustrate the calculation of f using the theoretical spot rates shown in Table 19-2. From that table, we know that:

6-month spot rate = 0.080, therefore z_1 = 0.0400
1-year spot rate = 0.083, therefore z_2 = 0.0415

Substituting into the formula, we have:

$$f = \frac{\left(1.0415\right)^2}{\left(1.0400\right)} - 1$$

$$= 0.043$$

Therefore, the forward rate on a 6-month security, quoted on a bond-equivalent basis, is 8.6% (0.043 × 2).

Here is how we use this rate of 8.6%. If the 6-month rate 6 months from now is less than 8.6%, then the total dollars at the end of 1 year would be higher by investing in the 1-year instrument (Alternative 1). If the 6-month rate 6 months from now is greater than 8.6%, then the total dollars at the end of 1 year would be higher by investing in the 6-month instrument and reinvesting the proceeds 6 months from now at the 6-month rate at the time (Alternative 2). Of course, if the 6-month rate 6 months from now is 8.6%, the two alternatives give the same total dollars at the end of 1 year.

Now that we have the rate f in which we are interested and we know how that rate can be used, let's return to the question we posed at the outset. From Table 19-2, the 6-month spot rate is 8%. Suppose that the investor expects that 6 months from now, the 6-month rate will be 8.2%. That is, the investor expects that the 6-month rate will be higher than its current level. Should the investor select Alternative 2 because the 6-month rate 6 months from now is expected to be higher? The answer is no. As we explained in the previous paragraph, if the rate is less than 8.6%, then Alternative 1 is the better alternative. Because this investor expects a rate of 8.2%, then he or she should select Alternative 1 despite the fact that he or she expects the 6-month rate to be higher than it is today.

This result is somewhat surprising for some investors. But the reason why is that the market prices its expectations of future interest rates into the rates offered on investments with different maturities. Knowing the market's consensus of future interest rates is critical. The rate that we determined for f is the market's consensus for the 6-month rate 6 months from now. A future interest rate calculated from either the spot rates or the yield curve is called a **forward rate** or an **implied forward rate**.

Similarly, borrowers need to understand what a forward rate is. For example, suppose a borrower must choose between a 1-year loan and a series of two 6-month loans. If the forward rate is less than the borrower's expectations of 6-month rates 6 months from now, then the borrower will be better off with a 1-year loan. If, instead, the borrower's expectations are that 6-month rates 6 months from now will be less than the forward rate, the borrower will be better off by choosing a series of two 6-month loans.

The forward rate consists of two elements. The first is when in the future the rate begins. The second is the length of time for the rate. For example the 2-year forward rate 3 years from now means a rate 3 years from now for a length of 2 years. The notation used for a forward rate, *f*, will have two subscripts—one before *f* and one after *f* as shown:

$$_t f_m$$

The subscript before *f* is *t* and is the length of time that the rate applies. The subscript after *f* is *m* and is when the forward rate begins. That is,

the length of time of the forward rate *f* when the forward rate begins

Remember our time periods are still 6-month periods. Given the preceding notation, here is what the following mean:

Notation	Interpretation for the forward rate
$_1f_{12}$	6-month (one-period) forward rate beginning 6 years (12 periods) from now
$_2f_8$	1-year (two-period) forward rate beginning 4 years (8 periods) from now
$_6f_4$	3-year (six-period) forward rate beginning 2 years (4 periods) from now
$_8f_{10}$	4-year (eight period) forward rate beginning 5 years (10 periods) from now

It can be demonstrated that the formula to compute any forward rate is

$$_t f_m = \left[\frac{\left(1 + z_{m+t}\right)^{m+t}}{\left(1 + z_m\right)^m} \right]^{1/t} - 1$$

Notice that if *t* is equal to 1, the formula reduces to the one-period (6-month) forward rate.

To illustrate, for the spot rates shown in Table 19-2, suppose that an investor wants to know the 2-year forward rate 3 years from now. In terms of the notation, *t* is equal to 4 and *m* is equal to 6. Substituting for *t* and *m* into the equation for the forward rate we have

$$_4 f_6 = \left[\frac{\left(1 + z_{6+4}\right)^{6+4}}{\left(1 + z_6\right)^6} \right]^{1/4} - 1$$

It means that the following spot rates are needed: z_6 (the 3-year spot rate) and z_{10} (the 5-year spot rate). From Table 19-3 we know

$$z_6 \left(\text{the 3 - year spot rate}\right) = 9.9787\% / 2 = 4.894\% = 0.04894$$

$$z_{10} \left(\text{the 5 - year spot rate}\right) = 13.623\% / 2 = 6.812\% = 0.06812$$

then

$$_4 f_6 = \left[\frac{\left(1.06812\right)^{10}}{\left(1.04894\right)^6} \right]^{1/4} - 1 = 0.09755 = 9.755\%$$

Therefore, $_4f_6$ is equal to 9.755%, and doubling this rate gives 19.510%, the forward rate on a bond-equivalent basis.

We can verify this result. Investing $100 for 10 periods at the semiannual spot rate of 6.812% will produce the following value:

$$\$100(1.06812)^{10} = \$193.286$$

By investing $100 for six periods at 4.894% and reinvesting the proceeds for four periods at the forward rate of 9.755% gives the same value:

$$\$100(1.04894)^6 (1.09755)^4 = \$193.286$$

RELATIONSHIP BETWEEN SPOT RATES AND SHORT-TERM FORWARD RATES

Suppose an investor purchases a 5-year, zero-coupon Treasury security for $58.48 with a maturity value of $100. The investor could instead buy a 6-month Treasury bill and reinvest the proceeds every 6 months for 5 years. The number of dollars that will be realized will depend on the 6-month forward rates. Suppose that the investor can actually reinvest the proceeds maturing every 6 months at the implied 6-month forward rates. Let us see how many dollars would accumulate at the end of 5 years. The implied 6-month forward rates were calculated for the yield curve given in Table 19-2. Letting f_t denote the 6-month forward rate beginning t 6-month periods from now, then the semiannual implied forward rates using the spot rates shown in Table 19-2 are:

$$f_1 = 0.043000 \qquad f_2 = 0.050980 \qquad f_3 = 0.051005 \qquad f_4 = 0.051770$$
$$f_5 = 0.056945 \qquad f_6 = 0.060965 \qquad f_7 = 0.069310 \qquad f_8 = 0.064625$$
$$f_9 = 0.062830$$

By investing the $58.48 at the 6-month spot rate of 4% (8% on a bond-equivalent basis) and reinvesting at the foregoing forward rates, the number of dollars accumulated at the end of 5 years would be:

$$\$58.48(1.04)(1.043)(1.05098)(1.051005)(1.05177)(1.056945)$$
$$(1.060965)(1.069310)(1.064625)(1.06283) = \$100$$

Therefore, we see that if the implied forward rates are realized, the $58.48 investment will produce the same number of dollars as an investment in a 5-year, zero-coupon Treasury security at the 5-year spot rate. From this illustration, we can see that the 5-year spot rate is related to the current 6-month spot rate and the implied 6-month forward rates.

In general, the relationship between a t-period spot rate, the current 6-month spot rate, and the implied 6-month forward rates is as follows:

$$z_t = \left[(1 + z_1)(1 + f_1)(1 + f_2)(1 + f_3) \ldots (1 + f_{t-1})\right]^{1/t} - 1$$

To illustrate how to use this equation, look at how the 5-year (10-period) spot rate is related to the 6-month forward rates. Substituting into the preceding equation the relevant forward rates just given and the one-period spot rate of 4% (one-half the 8% annual spot rate), we obtain

$$z_{10} = \left[(1.04)(1.043)(1.05098)(1.051005)(1.05177)(1.056945)\right.$$
$$\left.(1.060965)(1.069310)(1.064625)(1.06283)\right]^{1/10} - 1$$
$$= 5.51\%$$

Doubling 5.51% gives an annual spot rate of 11.02%, which agrees with the spot rate given in Table 19-2.

FORWARD RATE AS A HEDGEABLE RATE

A natural question about forward rates is how well they do at predicting future interest rates. Studies demonstrate that forward rates do not do a good job in predicting future interest rates.[2] Then, why the big deal about understanding forward rates? The reason, as we demonstrated in our illustration of how to select between two alternative investments, is that the forward rates indicate how an investor's expectations must differ from the market consensus in order to make the correct decision.

In our illustration, the 6-month forward rate may not be realized, which is irrelevant. The fact is that the 6-month forward rate indicated to the investor that if expectations about the 6-month rate 6 months from now are less than 8.6%, the investor would be better off with Alternative 1.

For this reason, as well as others explained later, some market participants prefer not to talk about forward rates as being market consensus rates. Instead, they refer to forward rates as being **hedgeable rates**. For example, by buying the 1-year security, the investor was able to hedge the 6-month rate 6 months from now.

DETERMINANTS OF THE SHAPE OF THE TERM STRUCTURE

If we plot the term structure—the yield to maturity, or the spot rate, at successive maturities against maturity—what is it likely to look like? Figure 19-1 shows three shapes that appeared with some frequency over time. Panel A shows an upward-sloping yield curve; that is, yield rises steadily as maturity increases. This shape is commonly referred to as a normal or positive yield curve. Panel B shows a downward-sloping or inverted yield curve, where yields decline as maturity increases. Finally, panel C shows a flat yield curve.

Two major theories evolved to account for these observed shapes of the yield curve: the *expectations theory* and the *market segmentation theory*.

Several forms of the expectations theory include the *pure expectations theory,* the *liquidity theory,* and the *preferred habitat theory.* All share a hypothesis about the behavior of short-term forward rates and also assume that the forward rates in current long-term contracts are closely related to the market's expectations about future short-term rates. These three theories differ, however, on whether other factors also affect forward rates, and how. The pure expectations theory postulates that no systematic factors other than expected future short-term rates affect forward rates; the liquidity theory and the preferred habitat theory assert other factors are involved. Accordingly, the last two forms of the expectations theory are sometimes referred to as **biased expectations theories**. Figure 19-3 depicts the relationship between these three theories.

THE PURE EXPECTATIONS THEORY

According to the **pure expectations theory**, the forward rates exclusively represent the expected rates. Thus, the entire term structure at a given time reflects the market's current expectations of the family of future short-term rates. Under this view, a rising term structure, as in Panel A of Figure 19-1, must indicate that the market expects short-term rates to rise throughout the relevant future. Similarly, a flat term structure reflects an expectation that future short-term rates will be mostly constant, while a falling term structure must reflect an expectation that future short rates will decline steadily.

---

2   Eugene F. Fama, "Forward Rates as Predictors of Future Spot Rates," *Journal of Financial Economics* 3, no. 4 (1976), pp. 361–77.

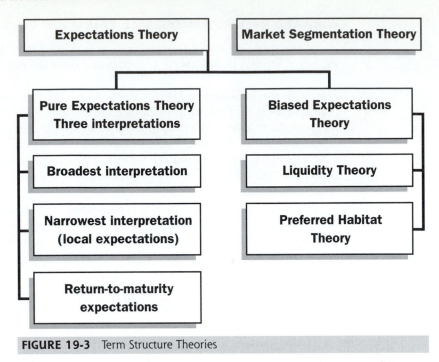

FIGURE 19-3 Term Structure Theories

Source: Frank J. Fabozzi, *Valuation of Fixed Income Securities and Derivatives* (New Hope, PA: Frank J. Fabozzi Associates, 1995), p. 49.

We can illustrate this theory by considering how an expectation of a rising short-term future rate would affect the behavior of various market participants, so as to result in a rising yield curve. Assume an initially flat term structure, and suppose that economic news subsequently leads market participants to expect interest rates to rise.

1. Those market participants interested in a long-term investment would not want to buy long-term bonds because they would expect the yield structure to rise sooner or later, resulting in a price decline for the bonds and a capital loss on the long-term bonds purchased. Instead, they would want to invest in short-term debt obligations until the rise in yield occurred, permitting them to reinvest their funds at the higher yield.

2. Speculators expecting rising rates would anticipate a decline in the price of long-term bonds and, therefore, would want to sell any long-term bonds they own and possibly to "short sell" some they do not now own.[3] (Should interest rates rise as expected, the price of longer-term bonds will fall. If the speculator sold these bonds short and can then purchase them at a lower price to cover the short sale, a profit is earned.) The proceeds received from the selling of long-term debt issues the speculators now hold or the shorting of longer-term bonds will be invested in short-term debt obligations.

3. Borrowers wishing to acquire long-term funds would be pulled toward borrowing now, in the long end of the market, by the expectation that borrowing at a later time would be more expensive.

All these responses would tend either to lower the net demand for, or to increase the supply of, long-maturity bonds, and two responses would increase demand for short-term obligations. Clearing of the market would require a rise in long-term yields

---

[3] Short selling means selling a security that is not owned but borrowed. The process for selling stocks short is described in Chapter 6.

in relation to short-term yields; that is, these actions by investors, speculators, and borrowers would tilt the term structure upward until it is consistent with expectations of higher future interest rates. By analogous reasoning, an unexpected event leading to the expectation of lower future rates will result in the yield curve sloping downward.

Unfortunately, the pure expectations theory suffers from one shortcoming, which, qualitatively, is quite serious. It neglects the risks inherent in investing in bonds and like instruments. If forward rates were perfect predictors of future interest rates, then the future prices of bonds would be known with certainty. The return over any investment period would be certain and independent of the maturity of the instrument initially acquired and of the time at which the investor needed to liquidate the instrument. However, with uncertainty about future interest rates and hence about future prices of bonds, these instruments become risky investments in the sense that the return over some investment horizon is unknown.

Similarly, from a borrower or issuer's perspective, the cost of borrowing for any required period of financing would be certain and independent of the maturity of the instrument initially sold if the rate at which the borrower must refinance debt in the future is known. But with uncertainty about future interest rates, the cost of borrowing is uncertain if the borrower must refinance at some time over the periods in which the funds are initially needed.

In the following section, we examine more closely the sources and types of risk that the pure expectations theory ignores.

Risks Associated with Bond Investment   Two risks cause uncertainty about the return over some investment horizon. The first is the uncertainty about the price of the bond at the end of the investment horizon. For example, an investor who plans to invest for 5 years might consider the following three investment alternatives: (1) invest in a 5-year bond and hold it for 5 years; (2) invest in a 12-year bond and sell it at the end of 5 years; and (3) invest in a 30-year bond and sell it at the end of 5 years. The return that will be realized for the second and third alternatives is not known because the price of each long-term bond at the end of 5 years is not known. In the case of the 12-year bond, the price will depend on the yield on 7-year debt securities 5 years from now; and the price of the 30-year bond will depend on the yield on 25-year bonds 5 years from now. Because forward rates implicit in the current term structure for a future 12-year bond and a future 25-year bond are not perfect predictors of the actual future rates, the price for both bonds 5 years from now remains uncertain.

The risk that the price of the bond will be lower than currently expected at the end of the investment horizon is called **price risk**. An important feature of price risk is that it is greater, the longer the maturity of the bond. The reason should be familiar from our discussion in Chapter 18, and it is that the longer the maturity, the greater the price volatility of a bond when yields rise. Thus, investors are exposed to price risk when they invest in a bond that will be sold prior to the bond's maturity date.

The second risk has to do with uncertainty about the rate at which the proceeds from a bond that matures prior to the maturity date can be reinvested until the maturity date. For example, an investor who plans to invest for 5 years might consider the following three alternative investments: (1) invest in a 5-year bond and hold it for 5 years; (2) invest in a 6-month instrument and, when it matures, reinvest the proceeds in 6-month instruments over the entire 5-year investment horizon; and (3) invest in a 2-year bond and, when it matures, reinvest the proceeds in a 3-year bond. The risk in the second and third alternatives is that the return over the 5-year investment horizon is unknown because rates at which the proceeds can be reinvested until maturity are unknown. This risk is referred to as **reinvestment risk**.

Interpretations of the Pure Expectations Theory Several interpretations of the pure expectations theory have been put forth by economists. These interpretations are not exact equivalents, nor are they consistent with each other, in large part because they offer different treatments of the two risks associated with realizing a return that we have just explained.[4]

The broadest interpretation of the pure expectations theory suggests that investors expect the return for any investment horizon to be the same, regardless of the maturity strategy selected.[5] For example, consider an investor with a 5-year investment horizon. According to this theory, it makes no difference if a 5-year, 12-year, or 30-year bond is purchased and held for 5 years because the investor expects the return from all three bonds to be the same over 5 years. A major criticism of this broad interpretation of the theory is that, because of price risk associated with investing in bonds with a maturity greater than the investment horizon, the expected returns from these three different bond investments should differ in significant ways.[6]

A second interpretation, referred to as the *local expectations* form of the pure expectations theory, suggests that the return will be the same over a short-term investment horizon starting today. For example, if an investor has a 6-month investment horizon, buying a 5-year, 10-year, or 20-year bond will produce the same 6-month return. Studies demonstrate that the local expectations formulation, which is narrow in scope, is the only one of the interpretations of the pure expectations theory that can be sustained in equilibrium. [7]

The third and final interpretation of the pure expectations theory suggests that the return that an investor will realize by rolling over short-term bonds to some investment horizon will be the same as holding a zero-coupon bond with a maturity identical to the investment horizon. (A zero-coupon bond has no reinvestment risk, so future interest rates over the investment horizon do not affect the return.) This variant is called the *return-to-maturity expectations* interpretation.

For example, let's once again assume that an investor has a 5-year investment horizon. By buying a 5-year zero-coupon bond and holding it to maturity, the investor's return is the difference between the maturity value and the price of the bond, all divided by the price of the bond. According to return-to-maturity expectations, the same return will be realized by buying a 6-month instrument and rolling it over for 5 years. At this time, the validity of this interpretation is subject to considerable doubt.

THE LIQUIDITY THEORY

We explained that the drawback of the pure expectations theory is that it does not consider the risks associated with investing in bonds. Nonetheless, we have just shown that risk is indeed involved in holding a long-term bond for one period, and that risk increases with the bond's maturity because maturity and price volatility are directly related.

Given this uncertainty, and the reasonable consideration that investors typically do not like uncertainty, some economists and financial analysts suggest a different theory. This theory states that investors will hold longer-term maturities if they are offered a long-term rate higher than the average of expected future rates by a risk premium that is positively related to the term to maturity.[8] Put differently, the forward rates should

---

[4] These formulations are summarized by John Cox, Jonathan Ingersoll, Jr., and Stephen Ross, "A Re-Examination of Traditional Hypotheses About the Term Structure of Interest Rates," *Journal of Finance* (September 1981), pp. 769–99.

[5] F. Lutz, "The Structure of Interest Rates," *Quarterly Journal of Economics* (1940–41), pp. 36–63.

[6] Cox, Ingersoll, and Ross, "A Re-Examination of Traditional Hypotheses," pp. 774–5.

[7] Ibid.

[8] John R. Hicks, *Value and Capital,* 2nd ed. (London: Oxford University Press, 1946), pp. 141–5.

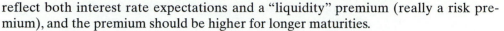

reflect both interest rate expectations and a "liquidity" premium (really a risk premium), and the premium should be higher for longer maturities.

According to this theory, which is called the **liquidity theory of the term structure**, the implicit forward rates will not be an unbiased estimate of the market's expectations of future interest rates because they embody a liquidity premium. Thus, an upward-sloping yield curve may reflect expectations that future interest rates either (1) will rise, or (2) will be flat or even fall, but with a liquidity premium increasing fast enough with maturity so as to produce an upward-sloping yield curve.

THE PREFERRED HABITAT THEORY

Another theory, known as the **preferred habitat theory**, also adopts the view that the term structure reflects the expectation of the future path of interest rates as well as a risk premium. However, the habitat theory rejects the assertion that the risk premium must rise uniformly with maturity.[9] Proponents of the habitat theory say that the latter conclusion could be accepted if all investors intend to liquidate their investment at the first possible date, while all borrowers are eager to borrow long, but that assumption can be rejected for a number of reasons.

In the first place, it is obvious that many investors wish to carry resources forward for appreciable periods of time—to buy a house, for example, or to provide for retirement. Such investors are concerned with the amount available at the appropriate time, and not the path by which that goal is reached. Hence, risk aversion dictates that they should prefer an instrument with a maturity matching the period for which they wish to invest over shorter-term investment vehicles. If these investors buy a shorter instrument, they will bear reinvestment risk—the risk of a fall in the interest rates available for reinvesting proceeds of the shorter instrument. Investors can avoid that risk only by locking in the current long rate through a long-term contract. Similarly, if they buy an instrument with maturity longer than the time they wish to invest for, they will bear the risk of a loss in the price of the asset (price risk) when liquidating it before its maturity; because of a rise in interest rates. Entirely analogous considerations apply to borrowers; prudence and safety call for borrowing for a maturity by matching the length of time for which funds are required.

In the second place, a lot of the demand for and supply of securities these days comes from financial intermediaries, which have liabilities with specified maturities. These institutions seek to match as closely as possible the maturity of their liabilities with the cash flow of a portfolio of assets. In constructing such a portfolio, a financial institution will restrict its investments to certain maturity sectors.

To illustrate this preference for maturity sectors, consider a life insurance company that issued a 5-year guaranteed investment contract.[10] The insurance company will not want to invest in 6-month instruments because of the associated reinvestment risk. As another example, assume a thrift borrowed funds at a fixed rate for 1 year with the proceeds from the issuance of a 1-year certificate of deposit. The thrift is exposed to price (or interest rate) risk if the borrowed funds are invested in a bond with 20 years to maturity. Clearly, then, either of these institutions faces some kind of risk if it invests outside its preferred maturity sector.

The preferred habitat theory asserts that, to the extent that the demand and supply of funds in a given maturity range do not match, some lenders and borrowers will be induced to shift to maturities showing the opposite imbalances. However, they need to

---

[9] Franco Modigliani and Richard Sutch, "Innovation in Interest Rate Policy." *American Economic Review* (May 1966), pp. 178–97.

[10] See Chapter 4 for a discussion of guaranteed investment contracts.

be compensated by an appropriate risk premium whose magnitude reflects the extent of aversion to either price or reinvestment risk.

Thus, this theory proposes that the shape of the yield curve is determined by both expectations of future interest rates and a risk premium, positive or negative, to induce market participants to shift out of their preferred habitat. Clearly, according to this theory, yield curves sloping up, down, flat, or humped are all possible.

MARKET SEGMENTATION THEORY

The **market segmentation theory** also recognizes that investors' preferred habitats dictate saving and investment flows. This theory also proposes that the major reason for the shape of the yield curve lies in asset/liability management constraints (either regulatory or self-imposed) and/or creditors (borrowers) restricting their lending (financing) to specific maturity sectors.[11] However, the market segmentation theory differs from the preferred habitat theory in that it assumes that neither investors nor borrowers are willing to shift from one maturity sector to another to take advantage of opportunities arising from differences between expectations and forward rates.

Thus, for the segmentation theory, the shape of the yield curve is determined by supply of and demand for securities within each maturity sector. This formulation seems untenable because it presupposes the prevalence of absolute risk aversion, while the evidence does not support that proposition. Thus, market participants must be expected to shift away from their habitat when sufficiently large discrepancies occur between market and expected rates. This potential shifting ensures that the differences between market and expected rates will not grow too large, and this consideration leads back to the preferred habitat theory.

Summary

The relationship between yield and maturity is referred to as the term structure of interest rates. The graphical depiction of the relationship between the yield on bonds of the same credit quality but different maturities is known as the yield curve. Historically the yield on Treasury securities is the benchmark rate used for the yield on nongovernment bonds. Consequently, the most commonly constructed yield curve is the Treasury yield curve.

A problem arises with using the Treasury yield curve to determine the one yield at which to discount all the cash payments of any bond. Each cash flow within a bond's total pattern of cash flows should be discounted at a unique interest rate that is applicable to the time period when the cash flow is to be received. Any bond can be viewed as a package of zero-coupon instruments, so its value should equal the value of all the component zero-coupon instruments. The rate on a zero-coupon bond is called the spot rate. The theoretical spot rate curve for Treasury securities can be estimated from the Treasury yield curve using a methodology known as bootstrapping.

Under certain assumptions, the market's expectation of future interest rates can be extrapolated from the theoretical Treasury spot rate curve. The resulting forward rate is called the implicit forward rate. The spot rate is related to the current 6-month spot rate and the implicit 6-month forward rates. A knowledge of the forward rates implicit in the current long-term rate is relevant in formulating both investment strategies and borrowing policies.

Several theories have been proposed about the determination of the term structure. The pure expectations theory hypothesizes that the one-period forward rates simply rep-

[11] This theory was suggested in J. M. Culbertson, "The Term Structure of Interest Rates," *Quarterly Journal of Economics* (November 1957), pp. 489–504.

resent the market's expectations of future actual rates. Thus, the long-term spot rate would itself be explained fully by the market expectations of future short rates. The term structure might then be rising, falling, or flat, according to whether the market expects rising, falling, or unchanged short-term rates. This formulation fails to recognize the risks associated with investing in bonds—price risk and reinvestment risk—when investors buy bonds whose maturity is different from the time for which they plan to hold the bond.

The fact of price risk in investing in long-term bonds, and that it increases with maturity, gives rise to an alternative liquidity theory of the term structure. According to this theory, forward rates are the sum of expected future rates and a risk premium that increases for more and more distant future rates and, hence, rises with the maturity of a bond. This formulation has shortcomings because it presupposes that all lenders want to lend short and all borrowers want to borrow long. If so, long borrowers must offer lenders a premium, rising with maturity, to accept the risk of going long. But in reality both lenders and borrowers vary substantially in their maturity preferences. Each market participant can eliminate risk, not by borrowing or lending short, but by lending (or borrowing) for a period coinciding with their preferred habitat. But, at the same time, agents would presumably be willing to depart from their preferred habitat by the inducement of a risk premium.

Accordingly, the third version of the expectations theory—namely, the preferred habitat theory—suggests, like the liquidity theory, that forward rates are the sum of a component reflecting expected future rates and a risk premium. However, the premium will not rise continuously with maturity but will materialize in any maturity neighborhood where supply exceeds demand. A negative premium or discount would be expected if supply exceeds demand.

One final theory explains the shape of the term structure by the concept of market segmentation. In common with the preferred habitat theory, it recognizes that participants in the bond market have maturity preferences. However, it postulates that these preferences are absolute and cannot be overcome by the expectation of a higher return from a different maturity, no matter how large. Each maturity is therefore a separate market, and the interest rate in every such market is determined by the given demand and supply. Thus, the interest rate at any maturity is totally unrelated to expectations of future rates. This formulation is of doubtful use because it implies highly irrational, implausible, and counterfactual behavior.

Key Terms

- Biased expectations theories
- Bootstrapping
- Forward rate
- Hedgeable rates
- Implied forward rate
- Liquidity theory of the term structure
- Market segmentation theory
- Preferred habitat theory
- Price risk
- Pure expectations theory
- Reinvestment risk
- Spot rate
- Spot rate curve
- Term structure of interest rates
- Yield curve
- Zero-coupon instrument

Questions

1. a. What is a yield curve?
   b. Why is the Treasury yield curve closely watched by market participants?
2. What is meant by a spot rate?
3. Explain why it is inappropriate to use one yield to discount all the cash flows of a financial asset.
4. Explain why a financial asset can be viewed as a package of zero-coupon instruments.

5. Why is it important for lenders and borrowers to have a knowledge of forward rates?
6. How are spot rates related to forward rates?
7. You are a financial consultant. At various times you hear the following comments on interest rates from clients. How would you respond to each comment?
   a. "The yield curve is upward sloping today. This suggests that the market consensus is that interest rates are expected to increase in the future."
   b. "I can't make any sense out of today's term structure. For short-term yields (up to 3 years), the spot rates increase with maturity; for maturities greater than 3 years but less than 8 years, the spot rates decline with maturity; and for maturities greater than 8 years the spot rates are virtually the same for each maturity. There is simply no theory that explains a term structure with this shape."
   c. "When I want to determine the market's consensus of future interest rates, I calculate the implicit forward rates."
8. You observe the following Treasury yield curve (all yields are shown on a bond-equivalent basis):

Year	Yield to maturity	Spot rate
0.5	5.25%	5.25%
1.0	5.50	5.50
1.5	5.75	5.76
2.0	6.00	?
2.5	6.25	?
3.0	6.50	?
3.5	6.75	?
4.0	7.00	?
4.5	7.25	?
5.0	7.50	?
5.5	7.75	7.97
6.0	8.00	8.27
6.5	8.25	8.59
7.0	8.50	8.92
7.5	8.75	9.25
8.0	9.00	9.61
8.5	9.25	9.97
9.0	9.50	10.36
9.5	9.75	10.77
10.0	10.00	11.20

All the securities maturing from 1.5 years on are selling at par. The 6-month and 1-year securities are zero-coupon instruments.
   a. Calculate the missing spot rates.
   b. What should the price of the 6-year Treasury security be?
   c. What is the implicit 6-month forward rate starting in the sixth year?
9. You observe the following Treasury yield curve (all yields are shown on a bond-equivalent basis):

Year	Yield to maturity	Spot Rate
0.5	10.00%	10.00%
1.0	9.75	9.75
1.5	9.50	9.48
2.0	9.25	9.22
2.5	9.00	8.95

Year	Yield to maturity	Spot Rate
3.0	8.75	8.68
3.5	8.50	8.41
4.0	8.25	8.14
4.5	8.00	7.86
5.0	7.75	7.58
5.5	7.50	7.30
6.0	7.25	7.02
6.5	7.00	6.74
7.0	6.75	6.46
7.5	6.50	6.18
8.0	6.25	5.90
8.5	6.00	5.62
9.0	5.75	5.35
9.5	5.50	?
10.0	5.25	?

All the securities maturing from 1.5 years on are selling at par. The 6-month and 1-year securities are zero-coupon instruments.
a. Calculate the missing spot rates.
b. What should the price of the 4-year Treasury security be?

10. Using the theoretical spot rates in Table 19-2, calculate the theoretical value of a 7%, 6-year Treasury bond.

11. a. Using the theoretical spot rates in Table 19-2, calculate the 2-year forward rate 4 years from now.
   b. Verify the answer by assuming an investment of $100 is invested for 6 years.

12. Explain the role that forward rates play in making investment decisions.

13. "Forward rates are poor predictors of the actual futures rates that are realized. Consequently, they are of little value to an investor." Explain why you agree or disagree with this statement.

14. An investor is considering two alternative investments. The first alternative is to invest in an instrument that matures in 2 years. The second alternative is to invest in an instrument that matures in 1 year and at the end of 1 year, reinvest the proceeds in a 1-year instrument. The investor believes that 1-year interest rates 1 year from now will be higher than they are today and, therefore, is leaning in favor of the second alternative. What would you recommend to this investor?

15. What is the common hypothesis about the behavior of short-term forward rates shared by the various forms of the expectations theory?

16. What are the types of risks associated with investing in bonds, and how do these two risks affect the pure expectations theory?

17. Give three interpretations of the pure expectations theory.

18. What are the two biased expectations theories about the term structure of interest rates?

19. What are the underlying hypotheses of the two biased expectations theories of interest rates?

CHAPTER 20

Money Markets

Learning Objectives

After reading this chapter you will understand:

◆ what the money market is.

◆ what a Treasury bill is.

◆ what commercial paper is and why it is issued.

◆ the types of issuers and major buyers of commercial paper.

◆ the credit ratings of commercial paper and why they are important.

◆ the difference between directly placed and dealer-placed commercial paper.

◆ what a bankers acceptance is and how it is created.

◆ what a certificate of deposit is and the different types of certificates of deposit.

◆ what a repurchase agreement is and how it can be used to finance a security position.

◆ the factors that influence the interest rate on repurchase agreements.

◆ what the federal funds market is.

In this section of the book we turn our attention to debt securities—instruments that obligate the debtor to make a contractually fixed series of payments, generally in nominal dollars, up to some terminal maturity date. This chapter focuses on debt instruments that at the time of issuance have a maturity of 1 year or less. These instruments are referred to as **money market instruments**, and the market they trade in is called the **money market**. It is in this market where (1) governments, government agencies, corporations, and municipal governments borrow money on a short-term basis, and (2) investors with funds to invest for a short term can invest.

The assets traded in the money market include Treasury bills, commercial paper, medium-term notes, bankers acceptances, short-term federal agency securities, short-term municipal obligations, certificates of deposit, repurchase agreements, and federal funds.[1] The U.S. Department of the Treasury borrows short term by issuing Treasury bills. Both financial and nonfinancial corporations issue commercial paper. Obligations of one type of financial corporation, depository institutions (banks and savings and loan associations), include certificates of deposit, bankers acceptances, and federal funds borrowing. Repurchase agreements provide the most common mechanism for entities to borrow funds using securities as collateral.

---

[1] The money market has also been extended to include securities with an original maturity in excess of 1 year but which now have a maturity of 1 year or less.

In this chapter we discuss Treasury bills, commercial paper, bankers acceptances, certificates of deposit, repurchase agreements, and federal funds. Short-term municipal securities are discussed in Chapter 23; medium-term notes are reserved for Chapter 22. Medium-term notes are corporate debt instruments with maturities ranging from 9 months to 30 years. In Chapters 24 through 27 we deal with debt instruments with longer-term maturities.

◆ TREASURY BILLS

Treasury securities are issued by the U.S. Department of the Treasury and backed by the full faith and credit of the U.S. government. As a result, market participants perceive Treasury securities to carry no risk of default.

The U.S. Treasury issues three types of securities: bills, notes, and bonds. At issuance, bills mature in 1 year or less, notes more than 2 years but no more than 10 years, and bonds more than 10 years. In the next chapter we cover Treasury securities in greater detail, but here we limit our discussion of Treasury securities to bills because they fall into the category of money market instruments, that is, instruments with 1 year or less to maturity. These securities are called **Treasury bills** and are issued on a regular basis with initial maturities of 4 weeks, 13 weeks, and 26 weeks. The latter two bills are more popularly referred to as the 3-month and 6-month Treasury bills, respectively.[2] We describe the auction process for the issuance of Treasury bills in the next chapter.

A Treasury bill is a discount security. Such securities do not make periodic interest payments. The security holder receives interest instead at the maturity date, when the amount received is the face value (maturity value or par value), which is larger than the purchase price. For example, suppose an investor purchases a 6-month Treasury bill with a face value of $100,000 for $96,000. By holding the bill until the maturity date, the investor receives $100,000; the difference of $4,000 between the proceeds received at maturity and the amount paid to purchase the bill represents the interest. Treasury bills are only one example of a number of money market instruments that are **discount securities**.

The market for Treasury bills is the most liquid market in the world. Interest on Treasury bills is exempt from state and local income taxes.

BID AND OFFER QUOTES ON TREASURY BILLS

Bids and offers on Treasury bills are quoted in a special way. Unlike bonds that pay coupon interest, Treasury bills are quoted on a bank discount basis, not on a price basis. The yield on a bank discount basis is computed as follows:

$$Y_D = \frac{D}{F} \times \frac{360}{t}$$

where
$\quad Y_D$ = yield on a bank discount basis (expressed as a decimal)
$\quad D$ = dollar discount, which is equal to the difference between the face value and the price
$\quad F$ = face value
$\quad t$ = number of days remaining to maturity

---

[2] Because of holidays, at issuance the number of days to maturity for 4-week, 3-month, and 6-month Treasury bills differ based on the number of holidays in the period. For example, a 3-month Treasury bill can have 90 or 91 days to maturity.

As an example, a Treasury bill with 100 days to maturity, a face value of $100,000, and selling for $97,569 would be quoted at 8.75% on a bank discount basis:

$$D = \$100,000 - \$97,569 = \$2,431$$

Therefore

$$Y_D = \frac{\$2,431}{\$100,000} \times \frac{360}{100} = 8.75\%$$

Given the yield on a bank discount basis, the price of a Treasury bill is found by first solving the formula for Y_D for the dollar discount (D), as follows:

$$D = Y_D \times F\left(\frac{t}{360}\right)$$

The price is then

$$\text{Price} = F - D$$

or equivalently,

$$\text{Price} = F\left[1 - Y_D\left(\frac{t}{360}\right)\right]$$

For our 100-day Treasury bill with a face value of $100,000, if the yield on a bank discount basis is quoted as 8.75%, D is equal to

$$D = 0.0875 \times \$100,000 \times \frac{100}{360} = \$2,431$$

Therefore

$$\text{Price} = \$100,000 - \$2,431 = \$97,569$$

The quoted yield on a bank discount basis is not a meaningful measure of the return from holding a Treasury bill for two reasons. First, the measure is based on a face value investment rather than on the actual dollar amount invested. Second, the yield is annualized according to a 360-day rather than 365-day year, making it difficult to compare Treasury bill yields with Treasury notes and bonds, which pay interest on a 365-day basis. The use of 360 days for a year is a money market convention for some money market instruments, however. Despite its shortcomings as a measure of return, it is the method dealers adopted to quote Treasury bills. Many dealer quote sheets and some reporting services provide two other yield measures that attempt to make the quoted yield comparable to that for a coupon bond and other money market instruments.

The measure that seeks to make the Treasury bill quote comparable to Treasury notes and bonds is called the bond equivalent yield, which we explained in Chapter 18. The **CD equivalent yield** (also called the **money market equivalent yield**) makes the quoted yield on a Treasury bill more comparable to yield quotations on other money market instruments that pay interest on a 360-day basis. It does so by taking into consideration the price of the Treasury bill rather than its face value. The formula for the CD equivalent yield is:

$$\text{CD equivalent yield} = \frac{360 Y_D}{360 - t(Y_D)}$$

As an illustration, consider once again the hypothetical 100-day Treasury bill with a face value of $100,000 selling for $97,569, and offering a yield on a bank discount basis of 8.75%. The CD-equivalent yield is

$$\frac{360(.0875)}{360 - 100(.0875)} = 8.97\%$$

THE PRIMARY MARKET FOR TREASURY BILLS

Treasury securities typically are issued on an auction basis according to regular cycles for specific maturities. Three-month and 6-month Treasury bills are auctioned every Monday. The amounts to be auctioned are ordinarily announced the previous Tuesday afternoon. The 4-week bill is auctioned every Tuesday. When the Treasury is temporarily short of cash, it issues cash management bills. The maturities of cash management bills coincide with the length of time that the Treasury anticipates the shortfall of funds.

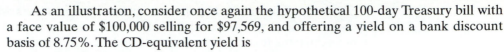

◆ COMMERCIAL PAPER

Commercial paper is a short-term unsecured promissory note issued in the open market that represents the obligation of the issuing corporation. The issuance of commercial paper is an alternative to bank borrowing for large corporations (nonfinancial and financial) with strong credit ratings.

The original purpose of commercial paper was to provide short-term funds for seasonal and working capital needs, but companies use this instrument for other purposes. It is used quite often for bridge financing. For example, suppose that a corporation needs long-term funds to build a plant or acquire equipment. Rather than raising long-term funds immediately, the corporation may elect to postpone the offering until more favorable capital market conditions prevail. The funds raised by issuing commercial paper are used until longer-term securities are sold. Interestingly, commercial paper sometimes acts as bridge financing to finance corporate takeovers.

In the United States, the maturity of commercial paper is typically less than 270 days, with the most maturing in less than 90 days. Several reasons explain this pattern of maturities. First, the Securities Act of 1933 requires that securities be registered with the SEC. Special provisions in the 1933 Act exempt commercial paper from registration as long as the maturity does not exceed 270 days. Hence, to avoid the costs associated with registering issues with the SEC, firms rarely issue commercial paper with maturities exceeding 270 days. Another consideration in determining the maturity is whether the commercial paper would be eligible collateral for a bank borrowing from the Federal Reserve Bank's discount window. In order to be eligible, the maturity of the paper may not exceed 90 days. Because eligible paper trades at a lower cost than paper that is not eligible, firms prefer to issue paper whose maturity does not exceed 90 days.

To pay off holders of maturing paper, issuers generally use the proceeds obtained by selling new commercial paper. This process is often described as rolling over short-term paper. The risk that the investor in commercial paper faces is that the issuer will be unable to sell new paper at maturity. As a safeguard against this rollover risk, commercial paper is typically backed by unused bank credit lines. The commitment fee the bank charges for providing a credit line increases the effective cost of issuing commercial paper.

Investors in commercial paper are institutional investors. Money market mutual funds purchase roughly one-third of all the commercial paper issued. Pension funds, commercial bank trust departments, state and local governments, and nonfinancial corporations seeking short-term investments purchase the balance.

Little secondary trading of commercial paper takes place. Typically, an investor in commercial paper is an entity that plans to hold it until maturity, which is understandable because an investor can purchase commercial paper in a direct transaction with the issuer, who sells paper with the specific maturity the investor desires.

ISSUERS OF COMMERCIAL PAPER

Corporate issuers of commercial paper can be divided into financial companies and non-financial companies. Financial companies are the major issuers of commercial paper.

Three types of financial companies include captive finance companies, bank-related finance companies, and independent finance companies. Captive finance companies are subsidiaries of equipment manufacturing companies. Their primary purpose is to secure financing for the customers of the parent company. For example, the three major U.S. automobile manufacturers have captive finance companies: General Motors Acceptance Corporation (GMAC), Ford Credit, and Chrysler Financial. GMAC is by far the largest issuer of commercial paper in the United States. Furthermore, a bank holding company may have a subsidiary finance company that provides loans to enable individuals and businesses to acquire a wide range of products. Independent finance companies are not subsidiaries of equipment manufacturing firms or bank holding companies.

The issuers of commercial paper typically have high credit ratings. Smaller and less well-known companies with lower credit ratings have been able to issue paper, however, by means of credit support from a firm with a high credit rating (such paper is called credit-supported commercial paper) or by collateralizing the issue with high-quality assets (such paper is called asset-backed commercial paper). An example of credit-supported commercial paper is one supported by a letter of credit. The terms of a letter of credit specify that the bank issuing the letter guarantees that the bank will pay off the paper when it comes due, if the issuer fails to do so. The bank will charge a fee for the letter of credit. From the issuer's perspective, the fee enables it to enter the commercial paper market and thereby obtain funding at a lower cost than that of bank borrowing. Commercial paper issued with this credit enhancement is referred to as LOC paper. The credit enhancement may also take the form of a surety bond from an insurance company.[3]

Both domestic and foreign corporations issue commercial paper in the United States. Commercial paper issued by foreign entities is called **Yankee commercial paper**.

In Chapter 17 we discuss organizations that evaluate the credit risk of entities issuing debt obligations and assign a letter rating based on the likelihood of default. These organizations are Moody's Investors Service, Standard & Poor's, and Fitch. The ratings assigned to commercial paper are shown in Table 20-1.

Commercial paper may be issued in either a discount form or in interest-bearing form. In a discount form, the investor buys the paper at less than the face value and when it matures receives the face value. The difference between the face value and the purchase price is the interest. It is the same form as Treasury bills. When the paper is issued in interest-bearing form, it is purchased from the issuer at face value and a specified interest rate. At maturity the investor receives the face value plus the accrued

---

[3] A surety bond is a policy written by an insurance company to protect another party against loss on violation of a contract.

TABLE 20-1   Commercial Paper Ratings

Category	Commercial Rating Company		
	Fitch	Moody's	S&P
Higher/A Prime	F-1+		A-1+
	F-1	P-1	A-1
Lower/A Prime	F-2	P-2	A-2
	F-3	P-3	A-3
Speculative Below Prime	F-5	NP (not prime)	B
			C
Defaulted	D	NP (not prime)	D

interest based on the specified interest rate. As with Treasury bills, yields are quoted on a discounted basis.

DIRECTLY PLACED VERSUS DEALER-PLACED PAPER

Commercial paper is classified as either direct paper or dealer-placed paper. **Directly placed paper** is sold by the issuing firm directly to investors without the help of an agent or an intermediary. (An issuer may set up its own dealer firm to handle sales.) A majority of the issuers of direct paper are financial companies. These entities require continuous funds in order to provide loans to customers. As a result, they find it cost-effective to establish a salesforce to sell their commercial paper directly to investors. An institutional investor can obtain information about the rates posted for issuers on Bloomberg Financial Markets, Telerate/Bridge, Reuters, and the Internet (available at www.cpmarket.com).[4]

General Electric Capital Corporation (GE Capital) is an example of a direct issuer, having issued commercial paper for 50 years. GE Capital is the principal financial services arm of General Electric Company and is now the largest and most active direct issuer in the United States, with commercial paper outstanding in excess of $70 billion.[5] (It is also the largest issuer in the Eurocommercial paper market, discussed later.) Corporate Treasury unit of GE Capital manages the commercial paper programs of General Electric Company, GE Capital Services, GE Capital, and other GE-related programs. These programs include the following as of June 30, 2001:

Issuer	Program Size (billion)	Ratings	
		S&P	Moody's
General Electric Capital Corporation	$66.6	A-1+	P-1
General Electric Capital Services, Inc.	6.7	A-1+	P-1
General Electric Company	—	A-1+	P-1

The paper is marketed directly to institutional investors on a continuous basis by Corporate Treasury or through GECC Capital Markets Group, Inc. (an NASD registered broker-dealer). The minimum investment is $100,000 for transactions of 7 days or more and $500,000 for 1–6 days.

---

[4] www.cpmarket.com is the first Internet, browser-based portal for commercial paper transaction.
[5] See www.gedirectcp.com/cpdirect.

Dealer-placed commercial paper requires the services of an agent to sell an issuer's paper. The agent distributes the paper on a best efforts underwriting basis. (For more on best efforts underwriting, see Chapter 6) by commercial banks and securities houses.)

TIER 1 AND TIER 2 PAPER

A major investor in commercial paper is money market mutual funds. However, the SEC imposes restrictions on money market mutual funds. Specifically, Rule 2a-7 of the Investment Company Act of 1940 limits the credit risk exposure of money market mutual funds by restricting their investments to "eligible" paper. Eligibility is defined in terms of the credit ratings shown in Table 20-1. To be eligible paper, the issue must carry one of the two highest ratings ("1" or "2") from at least two of the nationally recognized statistical ratings agencies. Tier 1 paper is defined as eligible paper that is rated "1" by at least two of the rating agencies; Tier 2 paper security is defined as eligible paper that is not a Tier 1 security.

Money market funds may hold no more than 5% of their assets in the Tier 1 paper of any individual issuer and no more than 1% of their assets in the Tier 2 paper of any individual issuer. Furthermore, holdings of Tier 2 paper may not represent more than 5% of the fund's assets.

THE SECONDARY MARKET

Despite the fact that the commercial paper market is larger than markets for other money market instruments, secondary trading activity is much smaller. The typical investor in commercial paper plans to hold it until maturity, given that an investor can purchase commercial paper with the specific maturity desired. Should an investor's economic circumstances change, causing a need to sell the paper, it can be sold back to the dealer or, in the case of directly placed paper, the issuer will repurchase it.

YIELDS ON COMMERCIAL PAPER

The yield offered on commercial paper tracks that of other money market instruments. The commercial paper rate is higher than that on Treasury bills for the same maturity based on three reasons. First, the investor in commercial paper is exposed to credit risk. Second, interest earned from investing in Treasury bills is exempt from state and local income taxes; as a result, commercial paper has to offer a higher yield to offset this tax advantage. Finally, commercial paper is less liquid than Treasury bills. The liquidity premium demanded is probably small, however, because investors typically follow a buy-and-hold strategy with commercial paper and so are less concerned with liquidity.

NON-U.S. COMMERCIAL PAPER MARKETS

Other countries develop their own commercial paper markets for companies domiciled in the country and for foreign companies. For example, in Japan commercial paper can be issued by Japanese corporations in its domestic market and yen-dominated commercial paper can be issued by non-Japanese entities. The latter commercial paper is referred to as **Samurai commercial paper**.

Eurocommercial paper is issued and placed outside the jurisdiction of the currency of denomination. U.S. commercial paper and Eurocommercial paper differ with respect to the characteristics of the paper and the structure of the market. First, commercial paper issued in the United States usually has a maturity of less than 270 days, with the most common maturity ranging from 30 to 50 days or less. The maturity of Eurocommercial paper can be considerably longer. Second, although an issuer in the United States must have unused bank credit lines, it is possible to issue commercial paper without such backing in the Eurocommercial paper market. Third, in the United States commercial paper can be directly placed or dealer placed, but Eurocommercial paper is almost always dealer placed. The fourth distinction is that numerous dealers participate in the Eurocommercial paper market, while only a few dealers dominate the market in the United States. Finally, because of the longer maturity of Eurocommercial paper, it is traded more often in the secondary market than U.S. commercial paper. Investors in commercial paper in the United States typically buy and hold to maturity, and the secondary market is thin and illiquid.

◆ LARGE-DENOMINATION NEGOTIABLE CERTIFICATES OF DEPOSIT

A certificate of deposit (CD) is a financial asset issued by a bank or thrift that indicates a specified sum of money deposited at the issuing depository institution. Banks and thrifts issue CDs to raise funds for financing their business activities. A CD bears a maturity date and a specified interest rate, and can be issued in any denomination. CDs issued by banks are insured by the Federal Deposit Insurance Corporation but only for amounts up to $100,000. CDs are not subject to any limit on the maximum maturity, but by Federal Reserve regulations CDs cannot have a maturity of less than 7 days.

A CD may be nonnegotiable or negotiable. In the former case, the initial depositor must wait until the maturity date of the CD to obtain the funds. If the depositor chooses to withdraw funds prior to the maturity date, an early withdrawal penalty is imposed. In contrast, a negotiable CD allows the initial depositor (or any subsequent owner of the CD) to sell the CD in the open market prior to the maturity date.

Negotiable CDs were introduced in the early 1960s. At that time the interest rate banks could pay on various types of deposits was subject to ceilings administered by the Federal Reserve (except for demand deposits defined as deposits of less than 1 month that by law could pay no interest). For complex historical reasons, these ceiling rates started low, rose with maturity, and remained below market rates up to some fairly long maturity. Before introduction of the negotiable CD, those with money to invest for, say, 1 month had no incentive to deposit it with a bank, for they would get a below-market rate unless they were prepared to tie up their capital for a much longer period of time. When negotiable CDs came along, investors could buy a 3-month or longer negotiable CD yielding a market interest rate, and recoup all or more than the investment (depending on market conditions) by selling it in the market.

This innovation helped banks increase the amount of funds raised in the money market, a position that had languished in the earlier postwar period. It also motivated competition among banks, ushering in a new era. Now, two types of negotiable CDs are available. The first is the large-denomination CD, usually issued in denominations of $1 million or more. This type is the negotiable CDs whose history we just described.

In 1982, Merrill Lynch entered the retail CD business by opening up a primary and secondary market in small-denomination (less than $100,000) CDs, the second type. Even though it made the CDs of its numerous banking and savings institution clients available to retail customers, Merrill Lynch also gave these customers the negotiability enjoyed by institutional investors by standing ready to buy back the CDs prior to maturity. Today, several retail-oriented brokerage firms offer CDs that are salable in a secondary market. Our focus in this chapter, though, is on the large-denomination negotiable CD, and we refer to them simply as CDs throughout the chapter.

The largest group of CD investors is investment companies, and money market funds make up the bulk of them. Far behind are banks and bank trust departments, followed by municipal entities and corporations.

CD ISSUERS

CDs can be classified into four categories, according to the issuing institution. First are CDs issued by domestic banks. Second are CDs denominated in U.S. dollars but issued outside the United States. These CDs are called Eurodollar CDs, or Euro CDs. A third category of CD is the Yankee CD, a CD denominated in U.S. dollars and issued by a foreign bank with a branch in the United States. Finally, thrift CDs are issued by savings and loan associations and savings banks.

Money center banks and large regional banks are the primary issuers of domestic CDs. Most CDs are issued with a maturity of less than 1 year. Those issued with a maturity greater than 1 year are called *term CDs*.

Unlike Treasury bills, commercial paper, and bankers acceptances (discussed later), yields on domestic CDs are quoted on an interest-bearing basis. CDs with a maturity of 1 year or less pay interest at maturity. For purposes of calculating interest, a year is treated as having 360 days. Term CDs issued in the United States normally pay interest semiannually, again with a year taken as 360 days.

With a floating-rate CD (FRCD), its interest rate changes periodically in accordance with a predetermined formula that indicates the spread (or margin) above some index at which the rate will reset periodically. FRCDs reset the coupon daily, weekly, monthly, quarterly, or semiannually. Typically FRCDs have maturities from 18 months to 5 years.

Euro CDs are U.S. dollar-denominated CDs issued primarily in London by U.S., Canadian, European, and Japanese banks.

The yields posted on CDs vary depending on three factors: (1) the credit rating of the issuing bank; (2) the maturity of the CD; and (3) the supply and demand for CDs. With respect to the third factor, banks and thrifts issue CDs as part of their liability management strategy, so the supply of CDs will be driven by the demand for bank loans and the cost of alternative sources of capital to fund these loans. Moreover, bank loan demand depends on the cost of alternative funding sources such as commercial paper. When loan demand is weak, CD rates decline. When demand is strong, the rates rise. The effect of maturity depends on the shape of the yield curve, a topic we covered in Chapter 19.

Credit risk is becoming more of an issue. At one time domestic CDs issued by money center banks traded on a no-name basis. Recent financial crises in the banking industry, however, caused investors to take a closer look at issuing banks. Prime CDs (those issued by high-rated domestic banks) trade at a lower yield than nonprime CDs (those issued by lower-rated domestic banks). Because of investors' unfamiliarity with foreign banks, generally Yankee CDs trade at a higher yield than domestic CDs.

Euro CDs offer a higher yield than domestic CDs for three reasons. First, the Federal Reserve imposes reserve requirements on CDs issued by U.S. banks that do not apply to issuers of Euro CDs. The reserve requirement effectively raises the cost of funds to the issuing bank because it cannot invest all the proceeds it receives from the issuance of a CD, and the amount that must be kept as reserves will not earn a return for the bank. Because it earns less on funds raised by selling domestic CDs, the domestic issuing bank pays less on its domestic CD than a Euro CD. Second, the bank issuing the CD must pay an insurance premium to the FDIC, which again raises the cost of funds. Finally, Euro CDs are dollar obligations payable by an entity operating under a foreign jurisdiction, exposing the holders to a risk (referred to as sovereign risk) that their claim may not be enforced by the foreign jurisdiction. As a result, a portion of the spread between the yield offered on Euro CDs and domestic CDs reflects what can be termed a *sovereign risk premium.* This premium varies with the degree of confidence in the international banking system.

CD yields are higher than yields on Treasury securities of the same maturity. The spread is due mainly to the credit risk that a CD investor is exposed to and the fact that CDs offer less liquidity. The spread due to credit risk varies with both economic conditions and confidence in the banking system, increasing during a "flight to quality" (which means investors shift their funds in significant amounts to debt of high quality or little risk), or a crisis in the banking system.

At one time, more than 30 dealers made markets in CDs. The presence of that many dealers provided good liquidity to the market. Today, fewer dealers are interested in making markets in CDs, and the market can be characterized as an illiquid one.

◆ BANKERS ACCEPTANCES

Simply put, a **bankers acceptance** is a vehicle created to facilitate commercial trade transactions. The instrument is called a bankers acceptance because a bank accepts the ultimate responsibility to repay a loan to its holder. The use of bankers acceptances to finance a commercial transaction is referred to as acceptance financing.

The transactions in which bankers acceptances are created include (1) the importing of goods into the United States; (2) the exporting of goods from the United States to foreign entities; (3) the storing and shipping of goods between two foreign countries where neither the importer nor the exporter is a U.S. firm;[6] and (4) the storing and shipping of goods between two entities in the United States. As demonstrated in the following illustration, maturities are typically arranged to cover the time required to ship and dispose of the goods being financed.

Bankers acceptances are sold on a discounted basis just as Treasury bills and commercial paper. To calculate the rate to be charged the customer for issuing a bankers acceptance, a bank determines the rate for which it can sell its bankers acceptance in the open market. To this rate it adds a commission.

ILLUSTRATION OF THE CREATION OF A BANKERS ACCEPTANCE

The best way to explain the creation of a bankers acceptance is by an illustration. Several entities are involved in our transaction:

- Car Imports Corporation of American (Car Imports), a firm in New Jersey that sells automobiles
- Germany Fast Autos Inc. (GFA), a manufacturer of automobiles in Germany
- First Hoboken Bank (Hoboken Bank), a commercial bank in Hoboken, New Jersey
- West Berlin National Bank (Berlin Bank), a bank in Germany
- High-Caliber Money Market Fund, a mutual fund in the United States that invests in money market instruments

Car Imports and GFA are considering a commercial transaction. Car Imports wants to import 15 cars manufactured by GFA. GFA is concerned with the ability of Car Imports to make payment on the 15 cars when they are received.

Acceptance financing is suggested as a means for facilitating the transaction. Car Imports offers $300,000 for the 15 cars. The terms of the sale stipulate payment to be made to GFA 60 days after it ships the 15 cars to Car Imports. GFA determines whether it is willing to accept the $300,000. In considering the offering price, GFA must calculate the present value of the $300,000, because it will not be receiving payment until 60 days after shipment. Suppose that GFA agrees to these terms.

---

[6] Bankers acceptances created from these transactions are called third-country acceptances.

Car Imports arranges with its bank, Hoboken Bank, to issue a letter of credit. The letter of credit indicates that Hoboken Bank will make good on the payment of $300,000 that Car Imports must make to GFA 60 days after shipment. The letter of credit, or time draft, will be sent by Hoboken Bank to GFA's bank, Berlin Bank. Upon receipt of the letter of credit, Berlin Bank will notify GFA, which will then ship the 15 cars. After the cars are shipped, GFA presents the shipping documents to Berlin Bank and receives the present value of $300,000. GFA is now out of the picture.

Berlin Bank presents the time draft and the shipping documents to Hoboken Bank. The latter will then stamp "accepted" on the time draft. By doing so, Hoboken Bank creates a bankers acceptance and agrees to pay the holder of the bankers acceptance $300,000 at the maturity date. Car Imports receives the shipping documents so that it can procure the 15 cars once it signs a note or some other type of financing arrangement with Hoboken Bank.

At this point, the holder of the bankers acceptance is the Berlin Bank. It has two choices. It can continue to hold the bankers acceptance as an investment in its loan portfolio, or it can request that Hoboken Bank make a payment of the present value of $300,000. Let's assume that Berlin Bank requests payment of the present value of $300,000.

Now the holder of the bankers acceptance is Hoboken Bank. It has two choices: retain the bankers acceptance as an investment as part of its loan portfolio, or sell it to an investor. Suppose that Hoboken Bank chooses the latter, and that High-Caliber Money Market Fund is seeking a high-quality investment with the same maturity as that of the bankers acceptance. Hoboken Bank sells the bankers acceptance to the money market fund at the present value of $300,000. Rather than sell the instrument directly to an investor, Hoboken Bank could sell it to a dealer, who would then resell it to an investor such as a money market fund. In either case, at the maturity date, the money market fund presents the bankers acceptance to Hoboken Bank, receiving $300,000, which the bank in turn recovers from Car Imports.

ACCEPTING BANKS

Banks that create bankers acceptances are called **accepting banks**. Bankers acceptances can be distributed through a dealer market, which involves 15 to 20 large firms, most of whom are headquartered in New York City. The larger regional banks maintain their own salesforces to sell the bankers acceptances they create but will use dealers to distribute those they cannot sell.

Eligible Bankers Acceptance   An accepting bank that decides to retain a bankers acceptance in its portfolio may be able to use it as collateral for a loan at the discount window of the Federal Reserve. The reason we say "may" is because, to be used as collateral, bankers acceptances must meet certain eligibility requirements established by the Federal Reserve. One requirement for eligibility is maturity, which with a few exceptions cannot exceed 6 months. Although the other requirements for eligibility are too detailed to review here, the basic principle is simple.[7] The bankers acceptance should be financing a self-liquidating commercial transaction.

Eligibility is also important because the Federal Reserve imposes a reserve requirement on funds raised via bankers acceptances that are ineligible. Bankers acceptances sold by an accepting bank are potential liabilities of the bank, but no

---

[7]   The eligibility requirement are described in Jean M. Hahr and William C. Melton, "Bankers Acceptances," *Quarterly Review,* Federal Reserve Bank of New York (Summer 1981).

reserve requirements are imposed for eligible bankers acceptances. Consequently, most bankers acceptances satisfy the various eligibility criteria. Finally, the Federal Reserve also imposes a limit on the amount of eligible bankers acceptances that may be issued by a bank.

CREDIT RISK

Investing in bankers acceptances exposes the investor to credit risk that neither the borrower nor the accepting bank will be able to pay the principal due at the maturity date. The market interest rates that acceptances offer investors reflect this risk because bankers acceptances have higher yields than risk-free Treasury bills. A yield may also include a premium for relative illiquidity. The yield on a bankers acceptance has such a premium because its secondary market is far less developed than that of a Treasury bill. Hence, the spread between bankers acceptance rates and Treasury bill rates represents a combined reward to investors for bearing the higher risk and relative illiquidity of the acceptance. That spread is not constant over time. The change in the spread reveals shifting investor valuation of the risk and illiquidity differences between the assets.

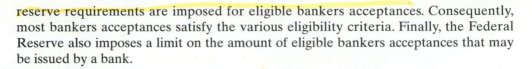

◆ REPURCHASE AGREEMENTS

A **repurchase agreement** is the sale of a security with a commitment by the seller to buy the security back from the purchaser at a specified price at a designated future date. Basically, a repurchase agreement is a collaterized loan, where the collateral is a security. The collateral in a repo can be money market instruments, Treasury securities, federal agency securities, mortgage-backed securities, or asset-backed securities.

The agreement is best explained with an illustration. Suppose a securities dealer purchases $10 million of a particular bond. Where does the dealer obtain the funds to finance that position? Of course, the dealer can finance the position with its own funds or by borrowing from a bank. Typically, however, the dealer uses the repurchase agreement or **repo market** to obtain financing. In the repo market the dealer can use the $10 million of the bond as collateral for a loan. The term of the loan and the interest rate that the dealer agrees to pay (the "repo rate") are specified. When the term of the loan is 1 day, it is called an "overnight repo;" a loan for more than 1 day is called a "term repo."

The transaction is referred to as a repurchase agreement because it calls for the sale of the security and its repurchase at a future date. Both the sale price and the purchase price are specified in the agreement. The difference between the purchase (repurchase) price and the sale price is the dollar interest cost of the loan.

In our illustration the dealer needs to finance $10 million par value of the bond that it purchased and plans to hold overnight. Suppose that a customer of the dealer has excess funds of $10 million.[8] The dealer would agree to deliver ("sell") $10 million of the bond to the customer for an amount determined by the repo rate and buy ("repurchase") the same bond from the customer for $10 million the next day. Suppose that the overnight repo rate is 6.5%. Then (as explained on the next page), the dealer would agree to deliver the bond for $9,998,195 and repurchase the same bond for $10 million the next day. The $1,805 difference between the sale price of $9,998,195 and the repurchase price of $10 million is the dollar interest on the financing. From the customer's perspective, the agreement is called a "reverse repo."

---

[8]   The customer might be a municipality with tax receipts it has just collected and no immediate need to disburse the funds.

The following formula is used to calculate the dollar interest on a repo transaction:

$$\text{Dollar interest} = \text{Dollar principal} \times \text{Repo rate} \times \frac{\text{Repo term}}{360}$$

Notice that the interest is computed on a 360-day basis. In our example, at a repo rate of 6.5% and a repo term of 1 day (overnight), the dollar interest is $1,805:

$$\$9,998,195 \times 0.065 \times \frac{1}{360} = \$1,805$$

The advantage to the dealer of using the repo market for borrowing on a short-term basis is that the rate is less than the cost of bank financing. We explain why later in this section. From the customer's perspective, the repo market offers an attractive yield on a short-term secured transaction that is highly liquid.

The example illustrates financing a dealer's long position in the repo market, but dealers can also use the market to cover a short position. For example, suppose a government dealer sold $10 million of Treasury securities 2 weeks ago and must now cover the position—that is, deliver the securities. The dealer can do a reverse repo (agree to buy the securities and sell them back). Of course, the dealer eventually would have to buy the Treasury security in the market in order to cover its short position.

A good deal of Wall Street jargon describes repo transactions. To understand it, remember that one party is lending money and accepting security as collateral for the loan; the other party is borrowing money and giving collateral to borrow money. When someone lends securities in order to receive cash (i.e., borrows money), that party is said to be "reversing out" securities. A party that lends money with the security as collateral is said to be "reversing in" securities. The expressions "to repo securities" and "to do repo" are also used. The former means that someone is going to finance securities using the security as collateral; the latter means that the party is going to invest in a repo. Finally, the expressions "selling collateral" and "buying collateral" are used to describe a party financing a security with a repo on the one hand, and lending on the basis of collateral on the other.

CREDIT RISKS

Despite the high-quality collateral typically underlying a repo transaction, both parties to the transaction are exposed to credit risk. The failure of a few small government securities dealer firms involving repo transactions in the 1980s made market participants more cautious about the creditworthiness of the counterparty to a repo.[9]

Why does credit risk occur in a repo transaction? Consider our initial example in which the dealer used $10 million of government securities as collateral to borrow. If the dealer cannot repurchase the government securities, the customer may keep the collateral; if interest rates on government securities increases subsequent to the repo transaction, however, the market value of the government securities declines, and the customer owns securities with a market value less than the amount it loaned to the dealer. If the market value of the security rises instead, the dealer firm will be concerned with the return of the collateral, which then has a market value higher than the loan.

Repos are now more carefully structured to reduce credit risk exposure. The amount loaned is less than the market value of the security used as collateral, which provides the lender with some cushion should the market value of the security decline. The amount by which the market value of the security used as collateral exceeds the

---

[9] Failed firms include Drysdale Government Securities, Lion Capital, RTD Securities, Inc., Belvill Bressler & Schulman, Inc., and ESM Government Securities, Inc.

value of the loan is called "margin" or "haircut." The amount of margin is generally between 1% and 3%. For borrowers of lower creditworthiness and/or when less liquid securities are used as collateral, the margin might be 10% or more.

Another practice to limit credit risk is to mark the collateral to market on a regular basis. Recall that the practice of marking to market, which we first discussed when we explained futures contracts in Chapter 10, means recording the value of a position at its market value. When market value changes by a certain percentage, the repo position is adjusted accordingly. Suppose that a dealer firm borrows $20 million using collateral with a market value of $20.4 million—the margin is 2%. Suppose further that the market value of the collateral drops to $20.1 million. A repo agreement can specify either a margin call, or repricing of the repo. In the case of a margin call, the dealer firm is required to put up additional collateral with a market value of $300,000 in order to bring the margin up to $400,000. If repricing is agreed upon, the principal amount of the repo will be changed from $20 million to $19.7 million (the market value of $20.1 million divided by 1.02). The dealer would then send the customer $300,000.

One concern in structuring a repo is delivery of the collateral to the lender. The most obvious procedure is for the borrower to deliver the collateral to the lender. At the end of the repo term, the lender returns the collateral to the borrower in exchange for the principal and interest payment. This procedure may be too costly, though, particularly for short-term repos, because of the costs associated with delivering the collateral. The cost of delivery would be factored into the transaction by a lower repo rate offered by the borrower. The risk of the lender not taking possession of the collateral is that the borrower may sell the security or use the same security as collateral for a repo with another party.

As an alternative to delivering the collateral, the lender may agree to allow the borrower to hold the security in a segregated customer account. Of course, the lender still faces the risk that the borrower uses the collateral fraudulently by offering it as collateral for another repo transaction.

Another method is for the borrower to deliver the collateral to the lender's custodial account at the borrower's clearing bank. The custodian then takes possession of the collateral, which it holds on behalf of the lender. This practice reduces the cost of delivery because it is merely a transfer within the borrower's clearing bank. If, for example, a dealer enters into an overnight repo with Customer A, the next day the collateral is transferred back to the dealer. The dealer can then enter into a repo with Customer B for, say, 5 days without having to redeliver the collateral. The clearing bank simply establishes a custodian account for Customer B and holds the collateral in that account. This called a tri-party agreement.

PARTICIPANTS IN THE MARKET

Because it is used by dealer firms (investment banking firms and money center banks acting as dealers) to finance positions and cover short positions, the repo market represents one of the largest sectors of the money market. Financial and nonfinancial firms participate in the market as both sellers and buyers, depending on the circumstances they face. Thrifts and commercial banks are typically net sellers of collateral (i.e., net borrowers of funds); money market funds, bank trust departments, municipalities, and corporations are typically net buyers of collateral (i.e., providers of funds).

Even though dealer firms use the repo market as the primary means for financing inventory and covering short positions, they also use the repo market to run a **matched book** by taking on repos and reverse repos with the same maturity. A dealer firm uses a matched book to capture the spread at which it enters into the repo and reverse repo agreements. For example, suppose that a dealer firm enters into a term repo of 10 days with a money market fund and a reverse repo with a thrift for 10 days in which the collateral is identical. In this transaction the dealer firm borrows funds from the money market fund and lends money to the thrift. If the rate on the repo is 7.5% and the rate on the reverse repo is 7.55%, the dealer firm borrows at 7.5% and lends at 7.55%, locking in a spread of 0.05% (five basis points).

Another participant is the **repo broker**. To understand the role of the repo broker, suppose that a dealer firm shorts $50 million of a security. It then surveys its regular customers to determine whether it can borrow via a reverse repo the security it shorted. Suppose that it cannot find a customer willing to do a repo transaction (repo from the customer's point of view, reverse repo from the dealer's). At that point, the dealer firm uses the services of a repo broker. When the collateral is difficult to acquire, it is said to be a "hot" or "special" issue.

The Federal Reserve is also involved in the repo market. The Fed influences short-term interest rates through its open market operations, that is, by the outright purchase or sale of government securities. This practice is not commonly followed by the Fed, however. Instead it uses the repo market to implement monetary policy by purchasing or selling collateral. By buying collateral (i.e., lending funds), the Fed injects money into the financial markets, thereby exerting downward pressure on short-term interest rates. When the Fed buys collateral for its own account, it is called a "system repo." The Fed also buys collateral on behalf of foreign central banks in repo transactions referred to as "customer repos." It is primarily through system repos that the Fed attempts to influence short-term rates. By selling securities for its own account, the Fed drains money from the financial markets, thereby exerting upward pressure on short-term interest rates. This transaction is called a matched sale.

Note the language used to describe the transactions of the Fed in the repo market. When the Fed lends funds based on collateral, we call it a system or customer repo, not a reverse repo. Borrowing funds using collateral is called a matched sale, not a repo. The jargon is confusing, which is why we used the terms *buying collateral* and *selling collateral* to describe what parties in the market are doing.

DETERMINANTS OF THE REPO RATE

Repo rates vary from transaction to transaction depending on the following factors.

- *Quality*. The higher the credit quality and liquidity of the collateral, the lower is the repo rate.
- *Term of the repo*. The effect of the term of the repo on the rate depends on the shape of the yield curve.
- *Delivery requirement*. As noted earlier, if delivery of the collateral to the lender is required, the repo rate will be lower. If the collateral can be deposited with the bank of the borrower, a higher repo rate is paid.
- *Availability of collateral*. The more difficult it is to obtain the collateral, the lower the repo rate. To understand why, remember that the borrower (or equivalently the seller of the collateral) has a security that is a hot or special issue. The party that needs the collateral will be willing to lend funds at a lower repo rate in order to obtain the collateral.

Although these factors determine the repo rate on a particular transaction, the federal funds rate determines the general level of repo rates. The repo rate will be below the federal funds rate because a repo involves collateralized borrowing, while a federal funds transaction is unsecured borrowing.

The last market we discuss here is the federal funds market. The rate determined in this market influences the rate paid on all the other money market instruments described in this chapter.

As we explained in Chapter 3, depository institutions (commercial banks and thrifts) are required to maintain reserves. The reserves are deposits at their district Federal Reserve Bank, which are called federal funds. The level of the reserves that a bank must maintain is based on its average daily deposits over the previous 14 days.

No interest is earned on federal funds. Consequently, a depository institution that maintains federal funds in excess of the amount required incurs an opportunity cost—the loss of interest income that could be earned on the excess reserves. At the same time, some depository institutions find themselves with fewer federal funds than the amount required. Typically, smaller banks have excess reserves, while money center banks short of reserves must make up the shortfall. Banks maintain federal funds desks whose managers are responsible for the bank's federal funds position.

One way that banks with less than the required reserves can bring reserves to the required level is to enter into a repo with a nonbank customer. An alternative is for the bank to borrow federal funds from a bank with excess reserves. The market in which federal funds are bought (borrowed) by banks that need these funds, and sold (lent) by banks with excess federal funds is called the federal funds market. Commercial banks are by far the largest investors in federal funds.

The equilibrium interest rate as determined by the supply and demand for federal funds is the federal funds rate. The federal funds rate and the repo rate are tied together because both are a means for a bank to borrow. The federal funds rate is higher because the lending of federal funds is done on an unsecured basis, which differs from the repo, in which the lender has a security as collateral. The spread between the two rates varies depending on market conditions; typically the spread is about 25 basis points.

The term of most federal funds transactions is overnight, but some longer-term transactions range from 1 week to 6 months. Trading typically takes place directly between the buyer and seller—usually between a large bank and one of its correspondent banks. Some federal funds transactions require the use of a broker.

Summary

Money market instruments are debt obligations that at issuance have a maturity of 1 year or less. Treasury securities with a maturity of 1 year or less when they are issued are called Treasury bills. Treasury bills are issued at a discount from their face value. The interest the investor earns is the difference between the face value received at the maturity date and the price paid to purchase the Treasury bill. Bids and offers on Treasury bills are quoted on a bank discount basis.

Commercial paper is a short-term unsecured promissory note issued in the open market that represents the obligation of the issuing entity. Generally, commercial paper maturity is less than 90 days. Financial and nonfinancial corporations issue commercial paper, with the majority issued by the former. Directly placed paper is sold by the issuing firm directly to investors without using an agent as an intermediary. For dealer-placed commercial paper, the issuer uses the services of an agent to sell its paper. Commercial paper markets exist outside the United States. Eurocommercial paper is paper issued and placed outside the jurisdiction of the currency of denomination.

Certificates of deposit are issued by banks and thrifts to raise funds for financing their business activities. Unlike other bank deposits, CDs are negotiable in the secondary market. CDs can be classified into four types: domestic CDs, Eurodollar CDs (or Euro CDs), Yankee CDs, and thrift CDs. Unlike Treasury bills, commercial paper, and bankers acceptances, yields on domestic CDs are quoted on an interest-bearing basis. A floating-rate CD is one whose coupon interest rate changes periodically in accordance with a predetermined formula.

A bankers' acceptance is a vehicle created to facilitate commercial trade transactions, particularly international transactions. The name, *bankers acceptance,* arises because a bank accepts the responsibility to repay a loan to the holder of the vehicle created in a commercial transaction in case the debtor fails to perform. Bankers acceptances are sold on a discounted basis as are Treasury bills and commercial paper.

A repurchase agreement is a lending transaction in which the borrower uses a security as collateral for the borrowing. The transaction is referred to as a repurchase agreement because it specifies the sale of a security and its subsequent repurchase at a future date. The difference between the purchase (repurchase) price and the sale price is the dollar interest cost of the loan. An overnight repo is for 1 day; a loan for more than 1 day is called a term repo. The collateral in a repo may be a Treasury security, money market instrument, federal agency security, or mortgage-backed security. The parties to a repo are exposed to credit risk, limited by margin and mark-to-market practices included in a repo agreement. Dealers use the repo market to finance positions and cover short positions, and to run a matched book so that they can earn spread income. The Fed uses the repo market to implement monetary policy. Factors that determine the repo rate are the federal funds rate, the quality of the collateral, the term of the repo, the delivery requirement, and the availability of the collateral.

In the federal funds market, depository institutions borrow (buy) and sell (lend) excess reserves held in the form of deposits in a Federal Reserve bank. The federal funds rate, which is the rate at which all money market interest rates are anchored, is determined in this market. The federal funds rate is higher than the repo rate because borrowing done in the federal funds market is unsecured borrowing. The fed funds rate is often a target of the Fed's monetary policy, so it can exhibit a considerable amount of volatility or change in level over time.

Key Terms ■

- Accepting banks
- Bankers acceptance
- CD equivalent yield
- Commercial paper
- Dealer-placed commercial paper
- Directly placed paper
- Discount securities
- Eurocommercial paper
- Matched book
- Money market
- Money market equivalent yield
- Money market instruments
- Repo broker
- Repo market
- Repurchase agreement
- Samurai commercial paper
- Treasury bills
- Yankee commercial paper

Questions ■

1. Suppose that the price of a Treasury bill with 90 days to maturity and a $1 million face value is $980,000.
   a. What is the yield on a bank discount basis?
   b. Why is the yield on a bank discount basis not a meaningful measure of the return from holding a Treasury bill?
2. Suppose the bid and ask yields for a Treasury bill maturing on some day are quoted by a dealer as 3.91% and 3.89%, respectively. Shouldn't the bid yield be

less than the ask yield, because the bid yield indicates how much the dealer is willing to pay, and the ask yield is what the dealer is willing to sell the Treasury bill for?

3. The Treasury issues Treasury bills with what maturities?

4. Why is commercial paper an alternative to short-term bank borrowing for a corporation?

5. a. Why does commercial paper have a maturity of less than 270 days?
   b. Why does paper typically have a maturity of less than 90 days?

6. What is the difference between directly placed paper and dealer-placed paper?

7. What is Tier 1 and Tier 2 commercial paper?

8. What does the yield spread between commercial paper and Treasury bills of the same maturity reflect?

9. How does Eurocommercial paper differ from commercial paper issued in the United States?

10. a. Why is a bank that creates a bankers acceptance referred to as an accepting bank?
    b. Why is the "eligibility" of a bankers acceptance important?

11. How does a bank determine the rate it will charge its customer for issuing a bankers acceptance?

12. How can a repurchase agreement be used by a dealer firm to finance a long position in a bond?

13. One party in a repo transaction is said to "buy collateral," the other party to "sell collateral." Why?

14. Why would the lender of funds in a repo transaction be exposed to credit risk?

15. What is meant by a repo dealer running a "matched book"?

16. When a shortage of a specific security occurs in a repo transaction, will the repo rate increase or decrease?

17. a. What is a system repo?
    b. What is a customer repo?

18. In a repo transaction, what is meant by a "haircut"?

19. Suppose the dollar principal in a repo transaction is $40 million and the repo rate is 5%.
    a. What is the dollar interest if the term of the repo is 1 day?
    b. What is the dollar interest if the term of the repo is 5 days?

20. a. What is the federal funds market?
    b. Which rate should be higher: the overnight repo rate or the overnight federal funds rate?

Treasury and Agency Securities Markets

21

Learning Objectives

After reading this chapter you will understand:

- ◆ the importance of the Treasury market.
- ◆ the different types of Treasury coupon securities.
- ◆ the operation of the primary market for Treasury securities.
- ◆ the role of government dealers and government brokers.
- ◆ the secondary market for Treasury securities.
- ◆ how Treasury securities are quoted in the secondary market.
- ◆ how government dealers use the repurchase agreement market.
- ◆ the zero-coupon Treasury securities market.
- ◆ how the government securities market is regulated.
- ◆ the difference between government-sponsored enterprises and federally related institutions.
- ◆ functions of government-sponsored enterprises that issue securities.
- ◆ non-U.S. government bond markets.

Market participants view Treasury securities as having no credit risk because they are issued by the U.S. Treasury and backed by the full faith and credit of the U.S. government. As explained in Chapter 17, historically, interest rates on Treasury securities provided the benchmark interest rates throughout the U.S. economy. However, since the late 1990s, the declining deficit of the U.S. government caused a reduction in U.S. Treasury issuance of long-term securities and the pursuit of a policy of buying back longer-term securities. As a result, even though U.S. Treasury securities still play a prominent role in financial markets, a current search is on for a sector of the bond market that might take over the role of Treasury securities as the benchmark. We mentioned in Chapter 17 three candidates. In this chapter, we discuss the Treasury coupon securities market and the market for U.S. agency securities. It is, in fact, the yields on securities of U.S. agencies (more specifically, government-sponsored enterprises) that seek to become the new benchmark interest rates. At the end of this chapter, we discuss non-U.S. government bond markets.

◆ **TREASURY SECURITIES**[1]

Two factors account for the prominent role of U.S Treasury securities: volume (in terms of dollars outstanding) and liquidity. The U.S. Treasury is the largest single issuer of debt in the world. The large volume of total debt and the large size of any single issue contribute to making the Treasury market the most active and hence the most liquid market in the world. The spread between bid and ask prices is considerably narrower than in other sectors of the bond market, and most issues can be traded easily. Many issues in the corporate and municipal markets are illiquid by contrast and cannot be traded readily. The U.S. Treasury is concerned with the liquidity, integrity, and efficiency of the Treasury market because these market attributes are essential for the federal government to borrow at the lowest possible cost and for the effective execution of monetary policy by the Federal Reserve System via its open market operations.

Treasury securities are available in book-entry form at the Federal Reserve Bank, which means that the investor receives only a receipt as evidence of ownership instead of an engraved certificate. An advantage of book-entry is ease in transferring ownership of the security. Interest income from Treasury securities is subject to federal income taxes but is exempt from state and local income taxes.

TYPES OF TREASURY SECURITIES

Two categories of government securities are discount and coupon securities. The fundamental difference between the two types lies in the form of the stream of payments that the holder receives, which is reflected in turn in the prices at which the securities are issued. **Coupon securities** pay interest every 6 months, plus principal at maturity. **Discount securities** pay only a contractually fixed amount at maturity, called maturity value or face value. Discount instruments are issued below maturity value, and return to the investor the difference between issue price and maturity value.

Current Treasury practice is to issue all securities with maturities of 1 year or less as discount securities. These securities are called *Treasury bills*. We discussed Treasury bills in Chapter 20. All securities with maturities of 2 years or longer are issued as coupon securities. Treasury coupon securities issued with original maturities between 2 and 10 years are called **Treasury notes**; those with original maturities greater than 10 years are called **Treasury bonds**. Although this distinction separates Treasury notes from bonds, in this chapter we refer to both as simply Treasury bonds.

Treasury Inflation Protection Securities On January 29, 1997, the U.S. Treasury issued for the first time Treasury securities that adjust for inflation. These securities are popularly referred to as **Treasury inflation protection securities (TIPS)**. (The Treasury refers to these securities as Treasury inflation indexed securities, or TIIS.) The Treasury issues TIPS that are notes and bonds. TIPS work as follows. The coupon rate on an issue is set at a fixed rate. That rate is determined via the auction process described later in this section. The coupon rate is called the "real rate" because it is the rate that the investor ultimately earns above the inflation rate. The inflation index that the government decides to use for the inflation adjustment is the nonseasonally adjusted U.S. City Average All Items Consumer Price Index for All Urban Consumers (CPI-U).

---

1 Portions of this section are adapted from Chapter 3 in Frank J. Fabozzi, *Bond Portfolio Management* (New Hope, PA: Frank J. Fabozzi Associates, 2001) and in other published writings by Frank J. Fabozzi.

The adjustment for inflation is as follows. The principal on which the Treasury Department will base both the dollar amount of the coupon payment and the maturity value is adjusted semiannually. It is called the inflation-adjusted principal. For example, suppose that the coupon rate for a TIPS is 3.5% and the annual inflation rate is 3%. Suppose further that an investor purchases on January 1, $100,000 of par value (principal) of this issue. The semiannual inflation rate is 1.5% (3% divided by 2). The inflation-adjusted principal at the end of the first 6-month period is found by multiplying the original par value by the semiannual inflation rate. In our example, the inflation-adjusted principal at the end of the first 6-month period is $101,500. This inflation-adjusted principal provides the basis for computing the coupon interest for the first 6-month period. The coupon payment is then 1.75% (one-half the real rate of 3.5%) multiplied by the inflation-adjusted principal at the coupon payment date ($101,500). The coupon payment is therefore $1,776.25

Let us look at the next 6 months. The inflation-adjusted principal at the beginning of the period is $101,500. Suppose that the semiannual inflation rate for the second 6-month period is 1%. Then the inflation-adjusted principal at the end of the second 6-month period is the inflation-adjusted principal at the beginning of the six-month period ($101,500) increased by the semiannual inflation rate (1%). The adjustment to the principal is $1,015 (1% times $101,500). So, the inflation-adjusted principal at the end of the second 6-month period (December 31 in our example) is $102,515 ($101,500 + $1,015). The coupon interest that will be paid to the investor at the second coupon payment date is found by multiplying the inflation-adjusted principal on the coupon payment date ($102,515) by one-half the real rate (i.e., one-half of 3.5%). That is, the coupon payment will be $1,794.01

As can be seen, part of the adjustment for inflation comes in the coupon payment because it is based on the inflation-adjusted principal. However, the U.S. government decided to tax the adjustment each year. This feature reduces the attractiveness of TIPS as an investment in the accounts of tax-paying entities.

Because of the possibility of disinflation (i.e., price declines), the inflation-adjusted principal at maturity may turn out to be less than the initial par value. However, the Treasury structured TIPS to be redeemable at the greater of the inflation-adjusted principal and the initial par value.

An inflation-adjusted principal must be calculated for a settlement date. The inflation-adjusted principal is defined in terms of an index ratio, which is the ratio of the reference CPI for the settlement date to the reference CPI for the issue date. The reference CPI is calculated with a 3-month lag. For example, the reference CPI for May 1 is the CPI-U reported in February. The U.S. Treasury publishes and makes available on its Web site (www.publicdebt.treas.gov) a daily index ratio for an issue.

THE PRIMARY MARKET

The U.S. Treasury issues its new securities in the primary market.

Auction Cycles   The U.S. Treasury determines the procedure for auctioning new Treasury securities, when to auction them, and what maturities to issue. Occasionally, it makes changes in the auction cycles and the maturity of the issues auctioned. For coupon securities, it holds monthly 2-year note and 5-year note auctions, and quarterly auctions for the 10-year note (the "refunding" auction).

On the announcement day, the Treasury publishes the amount of each issue to be auctioned, the auction date, and maturities to be issued. Occasionally an outstanding issue is "reopened" (that is, the amount of an outstanding note is increased) at an auction instead of auctioning a new issue. In recent years, the U.S. Treasury has reopened the 10-year note several times.

Determination of the Results of an Auction   The auction for Treasury securities is conducted on a competitive bidding basis. Competitive bids must be submitted on a yield basis. Noncompetitive tenders may also be submitted for up to $1 million face amount. Such tenders are based only on quantity, not yield.

The auction results are determined by first deducting the total noncompetitive tenders and nonpublic purchases (such as purchases by the Federal Reserve itself) from the total securities being auctioned. The remainder is the amount to be awarded to the competitive bidders. The bids are then arranged from the lowest-yield bid to the highest-yield bid, which is equivalent to arranging the bids from the highest price to the lowest price. Starting from the lowest-yield bid, all competitive bids are accepted until the amount to be distributed to the competitive bidders is completely allocated. The highest yield accepted by the Treasury is referred to as the **stop yield**, and bidders at that yield are awarded a percentage of their total tender offer. Bidders higher in yield than the stop yield are not distributed any of the new issue. Such bidders are said to have "missed" or were "shut out."

At what yield is a winning bidder awarded the security? All U.S. Treasury auctions are single-price auctions. In a single-price auction, all bidders are awarded securities at the highest yield of accepted competitive tenders (i.e., the stop yield). This type of auction is called a "Dutch auction." Historically, the Treasury auctioned securities through multiple-price auctions. With multiple-price auctions, the Treasury still accepted the lowest-yielding bids up to the yield required to sell the amount offered (less the amount of noncompetitive bids), but accepted bids were awarded at the particular yields bid, rather than at the stop yield. In September 1992, the Treasury started conducting single-price auctions for the 2- and 5-year notes. In November 1998, the Treasury adopted the single-price method for all auctions.

Competitive bids must typically be submitted by 1:00 P.M. eastern time on the day of the auction. Noncompetitive bids must typically be submitted by noon on the day of the auction. The results of the auction are announced within an hour following the 1:00 P.M. auction deadline. When the results of the auction are announced, the Treasury provides the following information: the stop yield, the associated price, the proportion of securities awarded to those investors who bid exactly the stop yield, the quantity of noncompetitive tenders, the median yield bid, and the bid-to-cover ratio. The **bid-to-cover ratio** is the ratio of the total par amount of competitive and noncompetitive bids by the public divided by the total par amount of the securities awarded to the public. Some market observers consider this ratio to be an indicator of the bidding interest and, consequently, some barometer of the success of the auction. The higher the bid-to-cover ratio, the greater is the success of the auction.

Figure 21-1 shows the August 1, 2001, announcement by the U.S. Treasury of the August 2001 quarterly auctioning of three Treasury coupon securities: $4\frac{3}{4}$-year notes, a 10-year note, and a 29.5-year bond. Notice that the $4\frac{3}{4}$ note and the 29.5-year bond are reopening of securities that were originally a 5-year note (issued in May 2001) and 30-year bond (issued in February 2001), respectively. For this reason, the coupon rate was provided for each issue. The 10-year note was an initial offering so the coupon rate was to be determined by the auction process.

Figure 21-2 shows the results of the 10-year note auction. Note the following:

- The high yield or stop yield was 5.078%, the yield at which all winning bidders were awarded securities.
- The coupon rate on the issue was set at 5%.
- Given the yield of 5.078%, a coupon rate of 5%, and a maturity of 10 years, the price that all winning bidders paid was $99.394 (per $100 par value).

OFFICE OF PUBLIC AFFAIRS • 1500 PENNSYLVANIA AVENUE, N.W. • WASHINGTON, D.C. • 20220 • (202) 622-2960

FOR RELEASE WHEN AUTHORIZED AT PRESS CONFERENCE CONTACT: Office of Financing
August 1, 2001   202/691-3550

TREASURY AUGUST QUARTERLY FINANCING

The Treasury will auction $11,000 million of 4-3/4-year 4-5/8% notes, $11,000 million of 10-year notes, and $5,000 million of 29-1/2-year 5-3/8% bonds to refund $11,885 million of publicly held securities maturing August 15, 2001, and to raise about $15,115 million of new cash.

In addition to the public holdings, Federal Reserve Banks hold $2,207 million of the maturing securities for their own accounts, which may be refunded by issuing additional amounts of the new securities.

Up to $1,000 million in noncompetitive bids from Foreign and International Monetary Authority (FIMA) accounts bidding through the Federal Reserve Bank of New York will be included within the offering amount of each auction. These noncompetitive bids will have a limit of $200 million per account and will be accepted in the order of smallest to largest, up to the aggregate award limit of $1,000 million.

TreasuryDirect customers requested that we reinvest their maturing holdings of approximately $37 million into the 4-3/4-year note, $11 million into the 10-year note, and $1 million into the 29-1/2-year bond.

All of the auctions being announced today will be conducted in the single-price auction format. All competitive and noncompetitive awards will be at the highest yield of accepted competitive tenders. The allocation percentage applied to bids awarded at the highest yield will be rounded up to the next hundredth of a whole percentage point, e.g., 17.13%.

NOTE: The net long position reporting threshold amount for *only* the 29-1/2-year bond is $1 billion.

All of the securities being offered today are eligible for the STRIPS program.

This offering of Treasury securities is governed by the terms and conditions set forth in the Uniform Offering Circular for the Sale and Issue of Marketable Book-Entry Treasury Bills, Notes, and Bonds (31 CFR Part 356, as amended).

Details about the notes and bond are given in the attached offering highlights.

oOo

Attachment

For press releases, speeches, public schedules and official biographies, call our 24-hour fax line at (202) 622-2040

FIGURE 21-1 U.S. Treasury Securities Auction Announcement

HIGHLIGHTS OF TREASURY OFFERINGS TO THE PUBLIC
AUGUST 2001 QUARTERLY FINANCING

August 1, 2001

Offering Amount	$11,000 million	$11,000 million	$5,000 million
Public Offering	Offering amount less the amount awarded to FIMA accounts		

Description of Offering:

Term and type of security	4-3/4-year notes (reopening)	10-year notes	29-1/2-year bonds (reopening)
Series	E-2006	C-2011	Bonds of February 2031
CUSIP number	912827 6X 5	912827 7B 2	912810 FP 8
Auction date	August 7, 2001	August 8, 2001	August 9, 2001
Issue date	August 15, 2001	August 15, 2001	August 15, 2001
Dated date	May 15, 2001	August 15, 2001	February 15, 2001
Maturity date	May 15, 2006	August 15, 2011	February 15, 2031
Interest rate	4-5/8%	Determined based on the highest accepted competitive bid	5-3/8%
Amount currently outstanding	$16,181 million	Not applicable	$10,887 million
Yield	Determined at auction	Determined at auction	Determined at auction
Interest payment dates	November 15 and May 15	February 15 and August 15	February 15 and August 15
Minimum bid amount and multiples	$1,000	$1,000	$1,000
Accrued interest payable by investor	$11.56250 per $1,000 (from May 15 to August 15, 2001)	None	None
Premium or discount	Determined at auction	Determined at auction	Determined at auction

STRIPS Information:

Minimum amount required	$1,000	$1,000	$1,000
Corpus CUSIP number	912820 GG 6	912820 GL 5	912803 CK 7
Due date(s) and CUSIP number(s) for additional TINT(s)	Not applicable	Not applicable	Not applicable

The following rules apply to all securities mentioned above:

Submission of Bids:

Noncompetitive bids: Accepted in full up to $5,000,000 at the highest accepted yield.

Foreign and International Monetary Authority (FIMA) bids: Noncompetitive bids submitted through the Federal Reserve Banks as agents for FIMA accounts. Accepted in order of size from smallest to largest with no more than $200 million awarded per account. The total noncompetitive amount awarded to Federal Reserve Banks as agents for FIMA accounts will not exceed $1,000 million. A single bid that would cause the limit to be exceeded will be partially accepted in the amount that brings the aggregate award total to the $1,000 million limit. However, if there are two or more bids of equal amounts that would cause the the limit to be exceeded, each will be prorated to avoid exceeding the limit.

Competitive bids:

(1) Must be expressed as a yield with three decimals, e.g., 7.123%.

(2) Net long position for each bidder must be reported when the sum of the total bid amount, at all yields, and the net long position is $2 billion or greater for each of the notes and $1 billion or greater for the bond.

(3) Net long position must be determined as of one half-hour prior to the closing time for receipt of competitive tenders.

Maximum Recognized Bid at a Single Yield: 35% of public offering

Maximum Award: 35% of public offering

Receipt of Tenders: Noncompetitive tenders: Prior to 12:00 noon eastern daylight saving time on auction day

Competitive tenders: Prior to 1:00 p.m. eastern daylight saving time on auction day

Payment Terms: By charge to a funds account at a Federal Reserve Bank on issue date, or payment of full par amount with tender. TreasuryDirect customers can use the Pay Direct feature which authorizes a charge to their account of record at their financial institution on issue date.

FIGURE 21-1 (Continued)

Source: www.publicdebt.treas.gov.

PUBLIC DEBT NEWS

Department of the Treasury • Bureau of the Public Debt • Washington, DC 20239

TREASURY SECURITY AUCTION RESULTS
BUREAU OF THE PUBLIC DEBT - WASHINGTON DC

FOR IMMEDIATE RELEASE   CONTACT: Office of Financing
August 08, 2001   202-691-3550

RESULTS OF TREASURY'S AUCTION OF 10-YEAR NOTES

Interest Rate: 5%   Issue Date: August 15, 2001
Series: C-2011   Dated Date: August 15, 2001
CUSIP No: 9128277B2   Maturity Date: August 15, 2011

High Yield: 5.078%   Price: 99.394

All noncompetitive and successful competitive bidders were awarded
securities at the high yield. Tenders at the high yield were
allotted 63.72%. All tenders at lower yields were accepted in full.

AMOUNTS TENDERED AND ACCEPTED (in thousands)

Tender Type	Tendered	Accepted
Competitive	$ 31,244,345	$ 10,892,363
Noncompetitive	107,692	107,692
SUBTOTAL	31,352,037	11,000,055 1/
Federal Reserve	1,043,030	1,043,030
TOTAL	$ 32,395,067	$ 12,043,085

Median yield 5.070%: 50% of the amount of accepted competitive tenders
was tendered at or below that rate. Low yield 5.030%: 5% of the amount
of accepted competitive tenders was tendered at or below that rate.

BID-TO-COVER RATIO = 31,352,037 / 11,000,055 = 2.85
NO FIMA NONCOMPETITIVE BIDS WERE TENDERED IN TODAY'S AUCTION. THE STRIPS
MINIMUM IS $1,000.

1/ Awards to TREASURY DIRECT = $69,605,000

FIGURE 21-2   Results of Treasury Auction for 10-Year Notes

Source: www.publicdebt.treas.gov.

- For those bidders who bid the high yield of 5.078, they were allocated 63.7% of the amount that they bid.
- Because the total amount of bids by both competitive and noncompetitive bidders was $31,352,037,000 and the total amount awarded was $11,000,055,000, the bid-to-cover ratio was 2.85 ($31,352,037,000/$11,000,055,000).

Figure 21-3 shows the auction results for the 20.5-year Treasury bond. Recall that this was a reopened issue. Its coupon rate was already set at $5\frac{3}{8}$%. The high yield or stop yield was 5.520%. Given a coupon rate of $5\frac{3}{8}$%, a yield of 5.520%, and a maturity of 29.5 years, the price that winning bidders paid was $97.900 (per $100 of par value).

Primary Dealers   Any firm can deal in government securities, but in implementing its open market operations, the Federal Reserve deals directly only with dealers designated as **primary** or **recognized dealers**. Basically, the Federal Reserve wants to be sure that firms requesting status as primary dealers have adequate capital relative to positions assumed in Treasury securities and do a reasonable amount of volume in Treasury securities. Table 21-1 lists the primary government dealers as of October 31, 2001.

PUBLIC DEBT NEWS

Department of the Treasury • Bureau of the Public Debt • Washington, DC 20239

```
                    TREASURY SECURITY AUCTION RESULTS
                 BUREAU OF THE PUBLIC DEBT - WASHINGTON DC

 FOR IMMEDIATE RELEASE                    CONTACT:    Office of Financing
 August 09, 2001                                      202-691-3550

              RESULTS OF TREASURY'S AUCTION OF 29-1/2-YEAR BONDS

    This issue is a reopening of a bond originally issued February 15, 2001.

 Interest Rate:  5 3/8%                Issue Date:      August 15, 2001
 Series:                              Dated Date:      August 15, 2001
 CUSIP No:       912810FP8             Maturity Date:   February 15, 2031
 STRIPS Minimum: $1,000

             High Yield:   5.520%    Price:  97.900

    All noncompetitive and successful competitive bidders were awarded
 securities at the high yield.  Tenders at the high yield were
 allotted   7.10%.  All tenders at lower yields were accepted in full.

             AMOUNTS TENDERED AND ACCEPTED (in thousands)

     Tender Type                   Tendered             Accepted
     -----------                -----------------    -----------------
     Competitive            $       10,772,512    $        4,967,684
     Noncompetitive                     32,343                32,343
                                -----------------    -----------------
       SUBTOTAL                     10,804,855             5,000,027 1/

     Federal Reserve                   540,230               540,230
                                -----------------    -----------------
     TOTAL                  $       11,345,085    $        5,540,257

    Median yield   5.472%:  50% of the amount of accepted competitive tenders
 was tendered at or below that rate.  Low yield   5.400%:   5% of the amount
 of accepted competitive tenders was tendered at or below that rate.

 BID-TO-COVER RATIO = 10,804,855 / 5,000,027 = 2.16
 NO FIMA NONCOMPETITIVE BIDS WERE TENDERED IN TODAY'S AUCTION.

 1/ Awards to TREASURY DIRECT = $21,301,000
```

FIGURE 21-3   Results of Treasury Auction for 29.5-Year Bonds

Source: www.publicdebt.treas.gov.

When a firm requests status as a primary dealer, the Federal Reserve requests first that the applying firm informally report its positions and trading volume. If these are acceptable to the Federal Reserve, it gives the firm status as a **reporting dealer**. This means that the firm will be put on the Federal Reserve's regular reporting list. After the firm serves for some time as a reporting dealer, the Federal Reserve will make it a primary dealer if it is convinced that the firm will continue to meet the criteria established.

Submission of Bids   Until 1991, primary dealers and large commercial banks that were not primary dealers submitted bids for their own account and for their customers. Others who wished to participate in the auction process could only submit competitive bids for their own account, not their customers. Consequently, a broker/dealer in government securities that was not a primary dealer could not submit a competitive bid on behalf of its customers. Moreover, unlike primary dealers, nonprimary dealers had to make large cash deposits or provide guarantees to ensure that they could fulfill their obligation to purchase the securities for which they bid.

> **TABLE 21-1   Primary Government Securities Dealers Reporting to the Federal Reserve Bank of New York**
>
> ABN AMRO Incorporated
> BNP Paribas Securities Corp.
> Banc of American Securities LLC
> Banc One Capital Markets, Inc.
> Barclays Capital Inc.
> Bear, Stearns & Co., Inc.
> BMO Nesbitt Burns Securities Inc.
> CIBC World Markets Corp.
> Credit Suisse First Boston Corporation
> Daiwa Securities America Inc.
> Deutsche Banc Alex. Brown Inc.
> Dresdner Kleinwort Wasterstein Securities
> Fuji Securities Inc.
> Goldman, Sachs & Co.
> Greenwich Capital Markets, Inc.
> HSBC Securities (USA) Inc.
> J. P. Morgan Securities
> Lehman Brothers, Inc.
> Merrill Lynch Government Securities Inc.
> Morgan Stanley & Co. Incorporated
> Nomura Securities International, Inc.
> Salomon Smith Barney Inc.
> UBS Warburg LLC.
> Zions First National Bank

Source: Securities Reports Division, Federal Reserve Bank of New York, October 31, 2001. An updated list of primary dealers is available at www.ny.frb.org/pihome/news/opnmktops/.

Well-publicized violations of the auction process by Salomon Brothers in the summer of 1991 forced Treasury officials to more closely scrutinize the activities of primary dealers and also reconsider the procedure by which Treasury securities are auctioned.[2] Specifically, the Treasury announced that it would allow qualified broker/dealers to bid for their customers at Treasury auctions. If a qualified broker/dealer establishes a payment link with the Federal Reserve system, no deposit or guarantee would be required. Moreover, the auction would no longer be handled by the submission of hand-delivered sealed bids to the Federal Reserve. The new computerized auction system can be electronically accessed by qualified broker/dealers.

THE SECONDARY MARKET

The secondary market for Treasury securities is an over-the-counter market where a group of U.S government securities dealers offer continuous bid and ask prices on outstanding Treasuries for a virtual 24-hour trading of Treasury securities.[3] The three primary

---

[2] Salomon Brothers admitted that it repeatedly violated a restriction that limited the amount that any one firm could purchase at the Treasury auction. The firm also admitted that it submitted unauthorized bids for some of its customers.

[3] Some trading of Treasury coupon securities does occur on the New York Stock Exchange, but the volume of these exchange-traded transactions is small when compared to over-the-counter transactions.

trading locations are New York, London, and Tokyo. The normal settlement period for Treasury securities is the business day after the transaction day ("next day" settlement).

The most recently auctioned issue is referred to as the *on-the-run issue* or the *current issue.* For example, in May 1999, the on-the-run 30-year Treasury issue was the 5.25s of 2/15/2029. Securities that are replaced by the on-the-run issue are called *off-the-run issues.* For example, prior to the issuance of the 5.25s of 2/15/2029, the on-the-run 30-year Treasury issue was the 5.25s of 11/15/2028 which in May 1999 became an off-the-run issue. At a given point in time, more than one off-the-run issue may offer approximately the same remaining maturity as the on-the-run issue. Issues replaced by several on-the-run issues are said to be "well off-the-run issues." For example, in May 1999, the 30-year 6.5% coupon issued in November 1996 and due in May 2026 was a well off-the-run issue.

Despite the huge volume of trading in the secondary market for government securities, the reporting of trades (i.e., the transparency of the market) is nowhere at the level of that for common stocks. However, the reporting of government securities transactions made some major strides since 1991. These developments came from the private sector. The most prominent example is GovPX. This firm, created in 1991 by primary dealers and interdealer brokers in the government securities market, provides 24-hour, worldwide distribution of government securities information as transacted by market participants through interdealer brokers. (It boasts 50,000 global users.) The information reported by GovPX is the price and size of the best bid and best offer, total volume (aggregate daily volume per issue and total volume), and current repo rates and volume (intraday update) for repo transactions. The information reported by this firm is distributed worldwide through Bloomberg Financial Markets, Reuters, and Bridge.

When-Issued Market Treasury securities are traded prior to the time they are issued by the Treasury. This component of the Treasury secondary market is called the **when-issued market**, or **wi market**. When-issued trading for both bills and coupon securities extends from the day the auction is announced until the issue day.

Repo Market In the previous chapter we discussed the repo market and how market participants can use that market to finance positions or to cover short positions. The repo market is critical for the key functioning of the government securities market.

Government Brokers Treasury dealers trade with the investing public and with other dealer firms. When they trade with each other, it is through intermediaries known as **interdealer brokers**. The brokers include BrokerTec, eSpeed, Garban-Intercapital, Hilliard Farber, and Tullett & Tokyo Liberty. These five firms service the primary government dealers and a dozen or so other large government dealers aspiring to be primary dealers.

Dealers use interdealer brokers because of the speed and efficiency with which trades can be accomplished. Interdealer brokers do not trade for their own account, and they keep the names of the dealers involved in trades confidential. The quotes provided on the government dealer screens represent prices in the "inside" or "interdealer" market. Historically, primary dealers resisted attempts to allow the general public to have access to them. However, as a result of government pressure, GovPX Inc. was formed to provide greater public disclosure. GovPX is a joint venture of five of the six interdealer brokers and the primary dealers in which information on best bids and offers, size, and trade price are distributed via Bloomberg, Reuters, and Knight-Ridder. In addition, some dealers have developed an electronic trading system that allows trading between them and investors via Bloomberg. One example is Deutsche Morgan Grenfell's AutoBond System.

Buybacks In January 2000, the Treasury Department began a program of redeeming outstanding unmatured Treasury securities by purchasing them in the secondary market through reverse auctions referred to as the Treasury's **buyback program**. The Treasury typically announces the buyback of an outstanding issue on the third and fourth Wednesdays of each month. The reverse auction is conducted the next day.

REGULATION OF THE SECONDARY MARKET

The Government Securities Act of 1986 (GSA) was the first legislation that provided federal regulation of the government securities market. The objective of the GSA was to protect investors and to ensure the maintenance of a fair, honest, and liquid government securities market. Specifically, the GSA gave the U.S. Treasury authority to establish rules relating to (1) transactions that involve government securities by government securities broker/dealers and (2) custodial holdings of government securities by depository institutions.

In early 1992, a framework for surveillance and enforcement of secondary market trading of government securities and related products (i.e., the when-issued market, the futures market, and the repo market) was provided by the Working Group for Treasury Market Surveillance (WorkingGroup). The WorkingGroup consisted of the Securities and Exchange Commission (SEC), the Department of the Treasury, Federal Reserve Bank of New York (FRBNY), the Commodity Futures Trading Commission, and the Board of Governors of the Federal Reserve.

The distribution of responsibilities as set forth by the WorkingGroup was as follows. The FRBNY was given the primary responsibility for day-to-day surveillance of the Treasury securities market. More specifically, this activity is carried out by the staff in the Markets Group at the FRBNY. The SEC is responsible for monitoring suspicious price/yield and volume movements and overall market conditions. In accomplishing its duty, the SEC relies on the FRBNY to collect and analyze dealer position data, as well as other market information that will help the SEC identify whether a particular price/yield or volume observed may be an indication of fraudulent or manipulative activity. In performing its analysis, the Markets Group staff of the FRBNY contacts the appropriate parties for an explanation of their overall trading strategies. The FRBNY then distributes the results of its investigation and analysis to the agencies in the WorkingGroup which, in turn, decides whether further inquiries are necessary. If a further investigation is warranted, it is undertaken by the SEC and, if a violation is uncovered, the SEC prosecutes the parties involved.

The Government Securities Act Amendments of 1993 (GSAA) enhanced specified large position rules and requires that all government securities brokers and dealers furnish to the SEC, on request, records (automated or manual) of government securities transactions. This information includes the date and time of execution of trades. The implementation of the large position rules played a critical role in allowing regulators to carry out their surveillance and enforcement responsibilities in the government securities market. Figure 21-4 provides a sample large position report. The GSA also deals with the transparency of the government securities markets. Specifically, it requires the SEC to monitor and report on efforts undertaken in the private sector to improve the timely public dissemination and availability of information concerning government securities transactions and quotations.

The GSAA directed the Secretary of the Treasury, the SEC, and the Board of Governors of the Federal Reserve System to evaluate certain rules for government securities. The agencies did in fact undertake a joint study and that study was submitted to Congress on March 26, 1998. The study concluded:

> We believe the GSAA addressed the major concerns facing the government securities market and believe that there are no significant issues that would warrant seeking additional regulatory authority at the present time.[4]

---

[4] *Joint Study of the Regulatory System for Government Securities*, p. 19.

Appendix B to Part 420—Sample Large Position Report
Formula for Determining a Reportable Position
($ Amounts in Millions at Par Value as of Trade Date)

Security Being Reported: _____

Date For Which Information is Being Reported: _____

1. Net Trading Position $_____

 (Total of cash/immediate net settled positions; net when-issued positions; net forward positions, including next day settling; net futures contracts that require delivery of the specific security; and net holdings of STRIPS principal components of the security.)

2. Gross Financing Position   + $_____

(Total of securities received through reverse repos (including forward settling reverse repos), bonds borrowed, collateral for financial derivative transactions and for other securities transactions which total may be reduced by the optional exclusion described in §§ 420.2(c).)

3. Net Fails Position   + $_____

(Fails to receive less fails to deliver. If equal to or less than zero, report 0.)

4. TOTAL REPORTABLE POSITION   = $_____

Memorandum: Report one total which includes the gross par amounts of securities delivered through repurchase agreements, securities loaned, and as collateral for financial derivatives and other securities transactions. Not to be included in item #2 (Gross Financing Position) as reported above.

$_____

Administrative Information to be Provided in the Report

Name of Reporting Entity:
Address of Principal Place of Business:
Name and Address of the Designated Filing Entity:
Treasury Security Reported on:
CUSIP Number:
Date or Dates for Which Information Is Being Reported:
Date Report Submitted:
Name and Telephone Number of Person to Contact Regarding Information Reported:

Name and Position of Authorized Individual Submitting this Report (Chief Compliance Officer; Chief Legal Officer; Chief Financial Officer; Chief Operating Officer; Chief Executive Officer: or Managing Partner or Equivalent of the Designated Filing Entity Authorized to Sign Such Report on Behalf of the Entity):

Statement of Certification: "By signing below, I certify that the information contained in this report with regard to the designated filing entity is accurate and complete. Further, after reasonable inquiry and to the best of my knowledge and belief, I certify: (i) that the information contained in this report with regard to any other aggregating entities is accurate and complete; and (ii) that the reporting entity, including all aggregating entities, is in compliance with the requirements of 17 CFR Part 420."

Signature of Authorized Person Named Above:
_____

Source: Federal Reserve Bank of New York.

FIGURE 21-4   Sample Large Position Report

STRIPPED TREASURY SECURITIES

The Treasury does not issue zero-coupon notes or bonds. In August 1982, however, both Merrill Lynch and Salomon Brothers created synthetic zero-coupon Treasury receipts. Merrill Lynch marketed its Treasury receipts as Treasury Income Growth Receipts (TIGRs); Salomon Brothers marketed its as Certificates of Accrual on Treasury Securities (CATS). The procedure was to purchase Treasury bonds and deposit them in a bank custody account. The firms then issued (that is, sold) receipts representing an ownership interest in each coupon payment on the underlying Treasury bond in the account and a receipt for ownership of the underlying Treasury bond's maturity value. This process of separating each coupon payment, as well as the principal (called the **corpus**), and selling securities against them is referred to as **coupon stripping**. Although the receipts created from the coupon-stripping process are not issued by the U.S. Treasury, the underlying bond deposited in the bank custody account is a debt obligation of the U.S. Treasury, so the cash flow from the underlying security is certain.

To illustrate the process, suppose $100 million of a Treasury bond with a 10-year maturity and a coupon rate of 10% is purchased to create zero-coupon Treasury securities. The cash flow from this Treasury bond is 20 semiannual payments of $5 million each ($100 million times 0.10 divided by two) and the repayment of principal (corpus) of $100 million 10 years from now. This Treasury bond is deposited in a bank custody account. Receipts are then issued, each with a different single payment claim on the bank custody account. For this bond the Treasury must make 21 different payments. For each of these payments, a receipt representing a single payment claim is issued, which is effectively a zero-coupon bond. The amount of the maturity value for a receipt on a particular payment, whether coupon or corpus, depends on the amount of the payment to be made by the Treasury on the underlying Treasury bond. In our example, 20 coupon receipts each have a maturity value of $5 million, and one receipt, the corpus, has a maturity value of $100 million. The maturity dates for the receipts coincide with the corresponding payment dates by the Treasury, as illustrated in Figure 21-5.

Other investment banking firms followed suit by creating their own receipts.[5] They all are referred to as **trademark zero-coupon Treasury securities** because they are associated with particular firms.[6] Receipts of one firm were rarely traded by competing dealers, so the secondary market was not liquid for any one trademark. Moreover, the investor was exposed to the risk—as small as it may be—that the custodian bank may go bankrupt.

To broaden the market and improve liquidity of these receipts, a group of primary dealers in the government market agreed to issue generic receipts that would not be directly associated with any of the participating dealers. These generic receipts are referred to as Treasury receipts (TRs). Rather than representing a share of the trust as the trademarks do, TRs represent ownership of a Treasury security. A common problem with both trademark and generic receipts was that settlement required physical delivery, which is often cumbersome and inefficient.

In February 1985, the Treasury announced its Separate Trading of Registered Interest and Principal of Securities (STRIPS) program to facilitate the stripping of designated Treasury securities. Specifically, all new Treasury bonds and all new Treasury notes with maturities of 10 years and longer are eligible. The zero coupon Treasury securities created under the STRIPS program are direct obligations of the U.S. government. Moreover, the securities clear through the Federal Reserve's book-entry system. Creation of the STRIPS program ended the origination of trademarks and generic receipts.

---

[5] Lehman Brothers offered Lehman Investment Opportunities Notes (LIONs); E. F. Hutton offered Treasury Bond Receipts (TBRs); and Dean Witter Reynolds offered Easy Growth Treasury Receipts (ETRs). There were also GATORs, COUGARs, and—you'll like this one—DOGS (Dibs on Government Securities).

[6] They are also called "animal products" for obvious reasons.

Dealer purchases $100 million par of a 10%, 10-year Treasury security

Security

Par: $100 million
Coupon: 10%, semiannual
Maturity: 10 years

Cash flow

| Coupon: $5 million Receipt in: 6 months | Coupon: $5 million Receipt in: 1 year | Coupon: $5 million Receipt in: 1.5 years | … | Coupon: $5 million Receipt in: 10 years | Maturity value: $100 million Receipt in: 10 years |

Zero-coupon Treasury securities created

| Maturity value: $5 million Maturity: 6 months | Maturity value: $5 million Maturity: 1 year | Maturity value: $5 million Maturity: 1.5 years | … | Maturity value: $5 million Maturity: 10 years | Maturity value: $100 million Maturity: 10 years |

FIGURE 21-5 Coupon Stripping: Creating Zero-Coupon Treasury Securities

Today, stripped Treasury securities are simply referred to as **Treasury strips**. On dealer quote sheets and vendor screens they are identified by whether the cash flow is created from the coupon (denoted "ci"), principal from a Treasury bond (denoted "bp"), or principal from a Treasury note (denoted "np"). Strips created from coupon payments are called **coupon strips**, and those created from the principal are called **principal strips**. The reason why a distinction is made between coupon strips and the principal strips has to do with the tax treatment by non-U.S. entities.

A disadvantage of a taxable entity investing in Treasury strips is that accrued interest is taxed each year even though interest is not paid. Thus, these instruments are negative cash flow instruments until the maturity date. They have negative cash flow since tax payments on interest earned but not received in cash must be made. One reason for distinguishing between strips created from the principal and coupon is that some foreign buyers have a preference for the strips created from the principal (i.e., the principal strips). This preference is due to the tax treatment of the interest in their home country. Some country's tax laws treat the interest as a capital gain if the principal strip is purchased. The capital gain receives a preferential tax treatment (i.e., lower tax rate) compared to ordinary income.

COUPON STRIPPING AND THE THEORETICAL VALUE OF TREASURY SECURITIES

Financial theory tells us that the theoretical value of a Treasury security should be equal to the present value of the cash flow where each cash flow is discounted at the appropriate theoretical spot rate. We review this theory in Chapter 19. What we do not do in that chapter, however, is demonstrate what economic force will assure that the actual market price of a Treasury security will not depart significantly from its theoretical value. We were not able to do that in Chapter 19 because we had not yet introduced stripped Treasury securities. Given our discussion of these instruments, we can now demonstrate the economic force that will move the actual price of a Treasury security toward its theoretical value.

To demonstrate, we use the Treasury yield curve as represented by the 20 hypothetical Treasury securities given in Table 19-1 in Chapter 19. The longest-maturity bond given in that table is the 10-year, 12.5% coupon issue selling at par and, therefore, with a yield maturity of 12.5%. Suppose that a government dealer buys a 14%, 10-year Treasury security. Because it is a 10-year security, using the yield for 10-year instruments, 12.5% given in Table 19-1, would suggest that this issue should sell to offer a yield of 12.5%. Table 21–2 shows the price of a 14%, 10-year Treasury issue if it is selling in the market to yield 12.5%. The present value of the cash flows when discounted at 12.5% is $108.4305 per $100 of par value.

Suppose that this issue is selling at that price. A government dealer can purchase that issue and strip it. The stripped Treasury securities should offer approximately the theoretical spot rate. Table 19-2 shows the theoretical spot rates. Table 21-3 shows the theoretical value of the 14% coupon issue if the cash flows are discounted at the theoretical spot rates. The theoretical value is $108.7889 per $100 par value. Thus, if a dealer purchased this issue for $108.4305, stripped it, and subsequently resold the zero-coupon instruments created at about the theoretical spot rates, the dealer would generate $108.7889 per $100 par value. This amount would result in an arbitrage profit of $0.3584 per $100 of par value. The only way to eliminate this arbitrage profit is for this security to sell for approximately $108.7889—its theoretical value as determined by the theoretical spot rates.

TABLE 21-2 Price of a 10-Year, 14% Coupon Treasury Based on the 10-Year Yield of 12.5%

Maturity	Cash Flow Per $100 Par	Required Yield of 0.125	Semiannual Yield	Present Value
0.5	$ 7	0.125	0.0625	$ 6.5882
1.0	7	0.125	0.0625	6.2007
1.5	7	0.125	0.0625	5.8359
2.0	7	0.125	0.0625	5.4927
2.5	7	0.125	0.0625	5.1696
3.0	7	0.125	0.0625	4.8655
3.5	7	0.125	0.0625	4.5793
4.0	7	0.125	0.0625	4.3099
4.5	7	0.125	0.0625	4.0564
5.0	7	0.125	0.0625	3.8178
5.5	7	0.125	0.0625	3.5932
6.0	7	0.125	0.0625	3.3818
6.5	7	0.125	0.0625	3.1829
7.0	7	0.125	0.0625	2.9957
7.5	7	0.125	0.0625	2.8194
8.0	7	0.125	0.0625	2.6536
8.5	7	0.125	0.0625	2.4975
9.0	7	0.125	0.0625	2.3506
9.5	7	0.125	0.0625	2.2123
10.0	107	0.125	0.0625	31.8277
Total				$108.4305

Table 21-3   Theoretical Value of a 10-Year, 14% Coupon Treasury Based on the Theoretical Spot Rate

Maturity	Cash Flow Per $100 Par	Spot Rate	Semiannual Spot Rate	Present Value
0.5	$ 7	0.08000	0.04000	$ 6.7308
1.0	7	0.08300	0.04150	6.4533
1.5	7	0.08930	0.04465	6.1402
2.0	7	0.09247	0.04624	5.8423
2.5	7	0.09468	0.04734	5.5547
3.0	7	0.09787	0.04894	5.2554
3.5	7	0.10129	0.05065	4.9534
4.0	7	0.10592	0.05296	4.6324
4.5	7	0.10850	0.05425	4.3512
5.0	7	0.11021	0.05511	4.0939
5.5	7	0.11175	0.05588	3.8491
6.0	7	0.11584	0.05792	3.5618
6.5	7	0.11744	0.05872	3.3338
7.0	7	0.11991	0.05996	3.0979
7.5	7	0.12405	0.06203	2.8384
8.0	7	0.12278	0.06139	2.6983
8.5	7	0.12546	0.06273	2.4883
9.0	7	0.13152	0.06576	2.2245
9.5	7	0.13377	0.06689	2.0458
10.0	$107	0.13623	0.06812	28.6433
Total				$108.7889

Reconstitution   In this instance, coupon stripping shows that the sum of the parts is greater than the whole. Consider instead a 10-year, 14% coupon Treasury in which the coupon rate is 10%. In Chapter 19, we show that the theoretical value for that issue based on the spot rates would be $85.35477. If the cash flows are instead discounted at the 12.5% yield for 10-year Treasury securities, it can be shown that the price would be $85.9491. Thus, if the market price was $85.9491 when the theoretical value based on spot rates indicated a value of $85.35477, a dealer would not want to strip this issue. The proceeds received by selling the zero-coupon instruments created would be less than the cost of purchasing the issue.

What can a dealer (or any other entity) do in this instance when the security is undervalued (i.e., less than its theoretical value) in the market? The U.S. Treasury allows STRIPS (both interest strips and principal strips) to be reassembled or "reconstituted" into a fully constituted security. To do so, the entity that seeks to reconstitute a security must obtain the appropriate principal component and all unmatured interest components for the security being reconstituted. This process is called **reconstitution**.

So, in our illustration a dealer can purchase in the market a package of zero-coupon stripped Treasury securities such that the cash flow of the package of securities replicates the cash flow of the mispriced coupon Treasury security. By doing so, the dealer will realize a yield higher than the yield on the coupon Treasury security. By buying 20 zero-coupon bonds with maturity values identical to the cash flow for the 10%, 10-year Treasury, the dealer is effectively purchasing a 10-year Treasury coupon security at a cost of $85.35477 instead of $85.9491.

It is the process of coupon stripping and reconstituting that forces the price of a Treasury security to trade near its theoretical value based on spot rates.

Federal agency securities can be classified by the type of issuer: those issued by federally related institutions and those issued by government-sponsored enterprises.

Federally related institutions (also referred to as **government-owned agencies**) are arms of the federal government and generally do not issue securities directly in the marketplace. The major issues have been the Tennessee Valley Authority (TVA) and the Government National Mortgage Association (Ginnie Mae). All federally related institutions are exempt from SEC registration. With the exception of securities of the TVA and the Private Export Funding Corporation, the securities are backed by the full faith and credit of the U.S. government.

Government-sponsored enterprises (GSEs) are privately owned, publicly chartered entities. They were created by Congress to reduce the cost of capital for certain borrowing sectors of the economy deemed to be important enough to warrant assistance. The entities in these privileged sectors include farmers, homeowners, and students. Government-sponsored enterprises issue securities directly in the marketplace.

Today six GSEs issue securities: Federal Farm Credit System, Federal Home Loan Bank System, Federal National Mortgage Association (Fannie Mae), Federal Home Loan Bank Corporation (Freddie Mac), The Federal Agricultural Mortgage Corporation (Farmer Mac), and Student Loan Marketing Association (Sallie Mae). The Federal Farm Credit Bank System is responsible for the credit market in the agricultural sector of the economy. The Federal Home Loan Bank, Freddie Mac, and Fannie Mae are responsible for providing credit to the housing sectors. Farmer Mac provides a secondary market for first mortgage agricultural real estate loans. It was created by Congress in 1998 to improve the availability of mortgage credit to farmers, ranchers, and rural homeowners, businesses, and communities. Sallie Mae provides funds to support higher education. With the exception of the securities issued by the Farm Credit Financial Assistance Corporation, GSE securities are not backed by the full faith and credit of the U.S. government, as is the case with Treasury and federally related securities. Consequently, investors purchasing GSEs are exposed to credit risk.

The securities issued by GSEs are one of two types: debentures and mortgage-backed/asset-backed securities. Debentures do not have any specific collateral backing the bond. The ability to repay bondholders depends on the ability of the issuing GSE to generate sufficient cash flows to satisfy the obligation. The other type of security issued is a security backed by specific pools or either mortgage loans or other types of loan. These securities are called mortgage-backed securities or asset-backed securities. We will discuss these securities in Chapters 26 and 27.

Here we describe the debentures issued by three GSEs: Fannie Mae and Freddie Mac, and the Federal Home Loan Banks.[8] These two GSEs are frequent issuers of debentures and therefore have developed regular programs for securities that they issue. Both are hoping that their securities appeal to investors as a substitute for Treasury securities and thereby take the place of U.S. Treasury securities as the benchmark interest rates in the United States.

Fannie Mae issues short-term debentures, benchmark bills, discount notes, medium-term notes, benchmark notes, benchmark bonds, callable benchmark notes, and global bonds. We will discuss medium-term notes in Chapter 22. Short-term debentures have maturities of 1 year or less and pay interest semiannually. They may be non-

7   Portions of this section are adapted from Frank J. Fabozzi, *Bond Portfolio Management* (New Hope, PA: Frank J. Fabozzi Associates, 2001), Chapter 3.
8   For a further discussion of federal agency securities, see Frank J. Fabozzi and George P. Kegler, "Federal Agency Securities," *The Handbook of Financial Instruments* (New York: John Wiley & Sons, 2002), Chapter 9.

callable or have a callable feature. A call feature allows the issuer to pay off an issue prior to the stated maturity date. (We will discuss this feature in Chapter 22). Benchmark bills and discount notes are issued at a discount from their maturity value and have maturities of 360 days or less. Benchmark notes are large issues ($2 to $5 billion in initial size) of 5-year to 10-year maturity and are noncallable. Fannie Mae expects either to issue a new benchmark note monthly or to reopen a current issue according to a published issuance calendar. Benchmark bonds are large ($2 to $4 billion initial size), 30-year maturity issues that are issued or reopened twice a year. Both benchmark notes and bonds are eligible for stripping; that is, the issue can be stripped in the same way that Treasury securities are stripped.

Freddie Mac issues reference bills, discount notes, medium-term notes, reference notes, callable reference bonds, callable reference notes, and global bonds. Reference bills and discount notes are issued with maturities of 1 year or less. Reference notes and callable reference notes have maturities of 2 to 10 years and are the equivalent to Fannie Mae's benchmark notes and callable benchmark notes. Freddie Mac will issue and/or reopen reference bills, reference notes, and 30-year reference bonds according to a published issuance calendar. Initial reference note sizes will be $3 to $6 billion, with $2 billion minimum reopenings and initial reference bonds sizes of $2 billion with $1 billion minimum reopenings. Freddie Mac reference notes and reference bonds are eligible for stripping.

The Federal Home Loan Banks (FHLB) issues discount notes and medium-term notes. The FHLB established its benchmark securities program, which is called the Tap Issue Program, in the summer of 1999. The program reopens coupon securities of four common maturities up to twice a day for 3 months. The securities are sold via a competitive auction.

◆ A LOOK AT NON-U.S. GOVERNMENT BOND MARKETS

The U.S. bond market is the largest government bond market in the world, although that may change in the future if the U.S. deficit declines. The structure of the government securities market of other countries follows that of the United States. Primary dealers are involved in the auction process and in the secondary markets. Government authorities generally allow government securities to be stripped. Market participants use the repo market to finance positions and cover short positions.

Major government bond markets outside the United States include those of Japan, Germany, France, United Kingdom, Italy, Spain, Belgium, Holland, Sweden, and Denmark. The yields on German government bonds are viewed as benchmark interest rates in Europe.

TYPES OF SECURITIES ISSUED

Most central governments issue fixed-rate coupon bonds just as issued by the U.S. Department of the Treasury. Non-U.S. central governments also offer bonds with other characteristics. For example, the British government, whose bonds are referred to as gilts, offer bonds called convertibles. These gilts have short maturities that give the holder the option to convert into a specified amount of a longer-maturity gilt (or more than one gilt) for a number of years. The British government also offers index-linked gilts. These gilts have coupons and final redemption amounts linked to the General Index of Retail Price (RPI), an index that is released each month by the Central Statistical Office. Index-linked gilts have low coupons, 2% to 2.5%, which, in effect, reflect the real rate of return. Maturities of index-linked gilts vary from short term to 2024.

Other central governments offer bonds linked to inflation. For example, in 1991, the Canadian government issued its first issue of real return bonds ($700 million, due in 2021). The issue was priced to yield a real return equal to 4.25%. The Australian government has small amounts of index-linked Treasury bonds that have either interest payments or capital linked to the Australian Consumer Price Index. Interest-indexed securities pay a fixed coupon every 6 months plus an arrears adjustment that amounts to the increase in the CPI. Capital-indexed securities also pay a fixed coupon (usually 4%) with the increase in the CPI added to the capital value of the bond and paid on maturity.

METHODS OF DISTRIBUTION

Four methods of distribution are most often used by the central governments in issuing government bonds: the regular auction calendar/Dutch-style system, the regular calendar auction/minimum-price offering, the ad hoc auction system, and the tap system.

In the **regular auction calendar/Dutch-style system**, winning bidders are allocated securities at the yield (price) they bid. At one time, this distribution method was used.

In the **regular calendar auction/minimum-price offering system**, a regular calendar of offerings is followed. The winners and the amount they receive are determined in the same manner as in the regular calendar auction/Dutch-style system. However, the price (yield) at which winning bidders are awarded the securities is different. Rather than awarding winning bidders at the yield (price) they bid, all winning bidders are awarded securities at the highest yield accepted by the government (i.e., the stop yield). As noted earlier, U.S. Treasury securities are issued using this auction system, which we referred to as the single-price auction. The regular calendar auction/minimum-price offering method is used in Germany and France.

In the **ad hoc auction system**, governments announce auctions when prevailing market conditions appear favorable. It is only at the time of the auction that the amount to be auctioned and the maturity of the security to be offered are announced. It is one of the methods used by the Bank of England in distributing British government bonds. An ad hoc auction system offers two advantages over a regular calendar auction from the issuing government's perspective. First, a regular calendar auction introduces greater market volatility than an ad hoc auction, because yields tend to rise as the announced auction date approaches and then fall afterward. Second, a regular calendar auction reduces flexibility in raising funds. After the election of the Conservative Party in England in 1992, the yields on British government bonds dropped significantly. The Bank of England used that window to obtain almost a third of the government's funding needs for fiscal year 1992–1993 in just the first 2 months of its fiscal year.

In a **tap system**, additional bonds of a previously outstanding bond issue are auctioned. The government announces periodically that it is adding this new supply. The tap system has been used in the United Kingdom and the Netherlands, as well as in the United States for the 10-year note.

Summary

The U.S. Treasury market is closely watched by all participants in the financial markets because interest rates on Treasury securities are the benchmark interest rates throughout the world. The Treasury issues three type of securities: bills, notes, and bonds. Treasury bills have a maturity of 1 year or less, are sold at a discount from par, and do not make periodic interest payments. Treasury notes and bonds are coupon securities. The two types of Treasury coupon securities are fixed coupon rate securities and inflation protection securities.

Treasury securities are issued on a competitive bid auction basis, according to a regular auction cycle. The auction process relies on the participation of the primary government securities dealers, with which the Federal Reserve deals directly. Revisions to the auction process has allowed greater participation by eligible nonprimary dealers.

The secondary market for Treasury securities is an over-the-counter market, where dealers trade with the general investing public and with other dealers. In the secondary market, Treasury bills are quoted on a bank discount basis; Treasury coupon securities are quoted on a price basis. Government brokers are used by primary dealers to trade among themselves. Pressure has been placed on primary dealers to provide greater access to prices of Treasury securities.

Although the Treasury does not issue zero-coupon Treasury securities, government dealers have created these instruments synthetically by a process called coupon stripping. Zero-coupon Treasury securities include trademarks. Treasury receipts, and STRIPS. Creation of the first two types of zero-coupon Treasury securities has ceased: STRIPS now dominate the market. The ability to strip Treasury coupon securities and reconstitute stripped Treasury securities forces the market price of a Treasury security to sell at a price close to its theoretical value based on theoretical spot rates.

Government-sponsored enterprise securities and federally related institution securities comprise the federal agency securities market. The former are privately owned, publicly chartered entities created to reduce the cost of borrowing for certain sectors of the economy. Federally related institutions are arms of the federal government whose debt is guaranteed by the U.S. government. While government-sponsored enterprises issue their own securities, federally related institutions obtain all or part of their financing by borrowing from the Federal Financing Bank.

The U.S. government bond market is the largest in the world, followed by the Japanese, Italian, and German government bond markets. Some central governments offer bonds indexed to the country's inflation. Four methods of distribution used by the central governments in issuing bonds include the regular auction calendar/Dutch-style system, the regular calendar auction/minimum-price offering, the ad hoc auction system, and the tap system.

Key Terms

- Ad hoc auction system
- Bid-to-cover ratio
- Buyback program
- Corpus
- Coupon securities
- Coupon stripping
- Coupon strips
- Discount securities
- Federally related institution
- Government-owned agencies
- Government-sponsored enterprises (GSEs)
- Interdealer broker
- Primary dealer
- Principal strips
- Recognized dealer
- Reconstitution
- Regular auction calendar/Dutch-style system
- Regular calendar auction/minimum-price offering system
- Reporting dealer
- Stop yield
- Tap system
- Trademark zero-coupon treasury securities
- Treasury bonds
- Treasury inflation protection securities (TIPS)
- Treasury notes
- Treasury strips
- When-issued (or wi) market

Questions

1. Why do government dealers use government brokers?
2. Suppose a portfolio manager purchases $1 million of par value of a Treasury inflation protection security. The real rate (determined at the auction) is 3.2%.

a. Assume that at the end of the first 6 months the CPI-U is 3.6% (annual rate). Compute (i) the inflation adjustment to principal at the end of the first 6 months, (ii) the inflation-adjusted principal at the end of the first 6 months, and (iii) the coupon payment made to the investor at the end of the first 6 months.

b. Assume that at the end of the second 6 months the CPI-U is 4.0% (annual rate). Compute (i) the inflation adjustment to principal at the end of the second 6 months, (ii) the inflation-adjusted principal at the end of the second 6 months, and (iii) the coupon payment made to the investor at the end of the second 6 months.

3. a. What is the measure of the rate of inflation selected by the U.S. Treasury for determining the inflation adjustment for Treasury inflation protection securities?

b. Suppose that deflation over the life of a Treasury inflation protection security results in an inflation-adjusted principal at the maturity date that is less than the initial par value. How much will the U.S. Treasury pay at the maturity date to redeem the principal?

c. Why is it necessary for the U.S. Treasury to report a daily index ratio for each TIPS issue?

4. a. Does the U.S. Department of the Treasury use a single-price or multiple-price auction in the issuance of Treasury coupon securities?

b. How is the yield of winning bidders determined in a Treasury auction?

5. a. What is the difference between a STRIP, a trademark Treasury zero-coupon security, and a Treasury receipt?

b. What is the most common type of Treasury zero-coupon security?

6. What economic mechanism forces the actual market price of a Treasury security toward its theoretical value based on theoretical spot rates?

7. a. Based on a yield to maturity of 12.5% for 10-year Treasury securities, demonstrate that the price of a 13% coupon, 10-year Treasury would be $102.8102 per $100 par value if all cash flows are discounted at 12.5%.

b. Based on the theoretical spot rates in Table 21-3, show that the theoretical value would be $102.9304 per $100 par value.

c. Explain why the market price for this Treasury security would trade close to its theoretical value.

8. Consider the following Treasury auction and results:

Total to be issued = $9.00 billion
Noncompetitive bids = $3.44 billion
Total competitive bids received:

Amount ($ billions)	Bid (yield%)
$0.20	7.55% (lowest yield/highest price)
0.26	7.56
0.33	7.57
0.57	7.58
0.79	7.59
0.96	7.60
1.25	7.61
1.52	7.62 (stop or largest yield/stop or lowest price)
2.00	7.63
1.12	7.64
1.10	7.65
No bids above 7.65%	

    a. How much is available to be awarded to competitive bidders?

    b. What is the stop yield?

    c. Which bidders will be awarded securities?

    d. At what yield will a winning bidder be awarded securities?

    e. If a bidder bid for $10 million at the stop yield, how much will be awarded to that bidder?

    f. What is the bid-to-cover ratio for this auction?

9. The results of the September 26, 2001, Treasury auction for the 2-year note was as follows:

High yield = 2.869%

Coupon rate on issue = 2.75%

Amounts Tendered and Accepted (in thousands)

Tender Type	Tendered	Accepted
Competitive	$40,262,145	$16,080,820
Noncompetitive	919,267	919,267

    a. At what yield were winning bidders awarded the securities that they bid for?

    b. Were the securities issued at par value, above par value, or below par value?

    c. What was the bid-to-cover ratio?

10. In the reopening of a Treasury issue, the coupon rate is already specified. Explain why.

11. What is GovPX?

12. The following quote is from the *Joint Study of the Regulatory System for Government Securities*, a joint report of the Department of the Treasury, the SEC, and the Federal Reserve Board, published in March 1998:

> Members of the FRBNY Markets Group staff monitor the condition of the government securities market generally and analyze trading in the Treasury securities market in particular for indications of potential disruption or questionable trader behavior. They monitor quantitative indicators such as relative cash-market values, pressure on particular issues in the financing market (i.e., "specials" rates), transaction volumes and position reports provided by the primary dealers. They also gather commentary from traders, market researchers, and newswire services. They occasionally hear claims of potentially questionable trader behavior, in response to which they follow up with calls to the trader in question or his or her managers, obtain information about their activities, and pass this information along to other members of the Working Group for discussion and possible investigation by market regulators.

Explain how the monitoring of "quantitative indicators such as relative cash-market values, pressure on particular issues in the financing market (i.e., "specials" rates), transaction volumes, and position reports provided by the primary dealers" by the FRBNY Markets Group staff can help identify potential fraudulent or manipulative practices.

13. The following quote is from the *Joint Study of the Regulatory System for Government Securities,* a joint report of the Department of the Treasury, the SEC, and the Federal Reserve Board, published in March 1998:

> Treasury's large position rules have also enhanced surveillance and enforcement in the government securities market by providing regulators with relatively quick access to information about price anomalies and concentrations of positions in Treasury securities

Explain why.

14. What is the difference between a government-sponsored enterprise and a federally related institution?
15. Are government-sponsored enterprise securities backed by the full faith and credit of the U.S. government?
16. What is the difference between an agency debenture and an agency mortgage-backed security?
17. a. What are reference notes and benchmark notes?
    b. What government-sponsored enterprises are seeking to have the rates that they offer viewed as the benchmark interest rates in the U.S. financial market?
18. a. The interest rates on what European country's government bond market is viewed as the benchmark rates in Europe?
    b. What is a gilt?
19. What are the different methods for the issuance of government securities throughout the world?

CHAPTER

22

Corporate Senior Instruments Markets: I

Learning Objectives

After reading this chapter you will understand:

◆ the various financing alternatives available to corporations.

◆ the different forms of credit risk: default risk, credit spread risk, and downgrade risk.

◆ the importance of credit ratings.

◆ what a medium-term note is.

◆ what a syndicated loan is.

◆ the two different ways a syndicated loan can be sold: assignment and participation.

◆ the basic terms of a loan agreement.

◆ what a lease financing transaction is.

◆ the difference between a single-investor lease and a leveraged lease.

Corporate senior instruments are financial obligations of a corporation that have priority over its common stock in the case of bankruptcy. They include debt obligations and preferred stock. The market for corporate debt obligations can be classified into six sectors: (1) commercial paper market, (2) medium-term note market, (3) bank loan market, (4) equipment leasing market, (5) bond market, and (6) asset-backed securities market. In Chapter 20 we covered commercial paper. In this chapter we discuss medium-term note, bank loan, and equipment leasing sectors. In the next chapter we cover the corporate bond market, as well as preferred stock. Asset-backed securities are taken up in Chapter 27.

Securities such as commercial paper, medium-term notes, and bonds represent alternatives to bank loans for companies needing to raise funds. The issuance of securities in the international market has increased substantially since the 1980s, in stark contrast to the bank borrowing trend. This phenomenon of borrower preference for issuing securities over borrowing directly from banks is referred to as the securitization of capital markets. The term *securitization* is actually used in two ways. It is in the broader sense that we use it here. In the more narrow sense, the term *securitization,* more specifically, *asset securitization,* describes the process of pooling loans and issuing securities backed by these loans. We introduced asset securitization in Chapter 2.

■ **441** ■

Unlike investing in a U.S. Treasury security, an investor who lends funds to a corporation by purchasing its debt obligation is exposed to *credit risk.* But what is credit risk? Traditionally credit risk is defined as the risk that the borrower will fail to satisfy the terms of the obligation with respect to the timely payment of interest and repayment of the amount borrowed. This form of credit risk is called *default risk.*

In addition to default risk, other risks are associated with the investment in debt securities that are also components of credit risk. Even in the absence of default, the investor is concerned that the market value of a debt instrument will decline in value and/or the relative price performance of that instrument will be worse compared to other debt obligations. As explained in Chapter 17, the yield on a corporate debt instrument is made up of two components: (1) the yield on a similar maturity Treasury issue, and (2) a premium to compensate for the risks associated with the debt instrument that do not exist in a Treasury issue, referred to as a *spread.* The part of the risk premium or spread attributable to credit risk is called the **credit spread**.

The price performance of a non-Treasury debt obligation and its return over some investment horizon depend on how the credit spread changes. If the credit spread increases—investors say that the spread has "widened"—the market price of the debt obligation will decline. The risk that an issuer's debt obligation will decline due to an increase in the credit spread is called **credit spread risk**.

Professional money managers analyze an issuer's financial information and the specifications of the debt instrument itself in order to estimate the ability of the issuer to live up to its future contractual obligations. This activity is known as **credit analysis**. Some large institutional investors have their own credit analysis department but most individual and institutional investors do not conduct such analytical studies. Instead, they rely primarily on commercial rating companies that perform credit analysis and express their conclusions by a system of ratings. As we explained in Chapter 17, the three commercial rating companies are Standard & Poor's Corporation, Moody's Investors Service, Inc., and Fitch.

Once a rating is assigned to a corporate debt instrument, it can be changed based on subsequent economic and financial developments. An improvement in the credit quality of an issue or issuer is rewarded with a better credit rating, referred to as an **upgrade**, a deterioration in the credit quality of an issue or issuer is penalized by the assignment of an inferior credit rating, referred to as a **downgrade**. An unanticipated downgrading of an issue or issuer increases the credit spread sought by the market, resulting in a decline in the price of the issuer of the issuer's debt obligation. This risk is referred to as **downgrade risk**.

The credit-rating companies play a key role in the functioning of debt markets. Investors take great comfort in knowing that the rating companies monitor the creditworthiness of issuers and keep the investing public informed of their findings. One would expect that other countries would have organizations that provide a similar function. However, only since the mid 1970s have credit-rating companies appeared in other countries. For example, in Japan it was not until 1977 that a formal corporate bond-rating system was introduced. The original system for rating corporate bonds that was introduced in Japan in 1959 was based solely on the size of the issue.[1]

---

[1] Edward W. Karp and Akira Koike, "The Japanese Corporate Bond Market," Chapter 11 in Frank J. Fabozzi (ed.), *The Japanese Bond Markets* (Chicago: Probus Publishing, 1990), p. 377.

◆ **MEDIUM-TERM NOTES**

A **medium-term note (MTN)** is a corporate debt instrument, with the unique characteristic that notes are offered continuously to investors by an agent of the issuer. Investors can select from several maturity ranges: 9 months to 1 year, more than 1 year to 18 months, more than 18 months to 2 years, and so on up to 30 years. Medium-term notes are registered with the Securities and Exchange Commission under Rule 415 (the shelf registration rule), which gives a corporation the maximum flexibility for issuing securities on a continuous basis.[2]

The term *medium-term note* to describe this corporate debt instrument is misleading. Traditionally, the term *note* or *medium term* was used to refer to debt issues with a maturity greater than 1 year but less than 15 years. Certainly, this characteristic is stretched for MTNs, since they have been sold with maturities from 9 months to 30 years, and even longer. For example, in July 1993, Walt Disney Corporation issued a security with a 100-year maturity off its medium-term note shelf registration.

General Motors Acceptance Corporation first used medium-term notes in 1972 to fund automobile loans with maturities of 5 years or less. The purpose of the MTN was to fill the funding gap between commercial paper and long-term bonds. It is for this reason that they are referred to as "medium term." The medium-term notes were issued directly to investors without the use of an agent. Only a few corporations issued MTNs in the 1970s. About $800 million of MTNs were outstanding by 1981.

The modern-day medium-term note was pioneered by Merrill Lynch in 1981. The first medium-term note issuer was Ford Motor Credit Company. By 1983, GMAC and Chrysler Financial used Merrill Lynch as an agent to issue medium-term notes. Merrill Lynch and other investment banking firms committed funds to make a secondary market for MTNs, thereby improving liquidity. In 1982, Rule 415 was adopted, making it easier for issuers to sell registered securities on a continuous basis. The public offering of MTNs by U.S. corporations between 1983 through 1998 increased from $5.5 billion in 1983 to $150 billion in 1998. From only 12 issuers of MTNs in 1983, the number increased to 94 U.S. corporations issuing MTNs in 1998. At that time, the MTNs of more than 451 corporations were outstanding.[3]

The growth of the domestic medium-term note market and its importance as a funding source can be seen by comparing it to the amount of intermediate and long-term corporate debt issued. The ratio of outstanding MTNs to the amount of outstanding public corporate debt (MTNs plus public corporate bonds) was 9% in 1989 and 41% in 1999. For financial firms and nonfinancial firms the share in 1999 was 57% and 12%, respectively.

Euro medium-term notes are those issued in the Euromarket. The market began in 1987. Euro medium-term notes are issued by sovereign issuers (i.e., governments and governmental agencies), nonfinancial corporations, and financial institutions.

Borrowers have flexibility in designing MTNs to satisfy their own needs. They can issue fixed- or floating-rate debt. The coupon payments can be denominated in U.S dollars or in a foreign currency. In the next chapter we describe corporate bonds and the various security structures, sometimes used by MTN issuers.

When the treasurer of a corporation contemplates an offering of either MTNs or corporate bonds, two factors affect the decision. The most obvious is the cost of the funds

---

[2]   The shelf registration rule is explained in Chapter 6.
[3]   Data about medium-term note issuance by corporations are provided on the Federal Reserve Bank Web site: www.federalreserve/releases/medterm.

raised after consideration of registration and distribution costs. This cost is referred to as the **all-in-cost of funds**. The second is the flexibility afforded to the issuer in structuring the offering. The growth in the MTN market is evidence of the relative advantage of MTNs with respect cost and flexibility for some offerings. However, some corporations raise funds by issuing both bonds and MTNs, which would indicate that no absolute advantage can be gained in all instances and market environments.

MTNs are rated by the nationally recognized rating companies. About 99% of all MTNs issued receive an investment-grade rating at the time of issuance.

THE PRIMARY MARKET

Medium-term notes differ from corporate bonds in the manner in which they are distributed to investors when initially sold. Although some investment-grade corporate bond issues are sold on a best efforts basis, typically they are underwritten by investment bankers. The traditional method of distribution for MTNs is on a best efforts basis by either an investment banking firm or other broker/dealers acting as agents. Another difference between corporate bonds and MTNs when they are offered is that MTNs are usually sold in relatively small amounts on a continuous or an intermittent basis, while corporate bonds are sold in large, discrete offerings.

A corporation that wants an MTN program will file a shelf registration with the SEC for the offering of securities. The SEC registration for MTN offerings is between $100 and $1 billion, but once the total is sold, the issuer can file another shelf registration.[4] The registration includes a list of the investment banking firms, usually two to four, with which the corporation arranged to act as agents to distribute the MTNs. The large New York-based investment banking firms dominate the distribution market for MTNs.

The issuer then posts rates over a range of maturities: for example, 9 months to 1 year, 1 year to 18 months, 18 months to 2 years, and annually thereafter. Table 22-1 provides an example of an offering rate schedule for a medium-term note program. Usually, an issuer will post rates as a spread over a Treasury security of comparable maturity. For example, in the 2- to 3-year maturity range, the offering rate is 35 basis points over the 2-year Treasury. Since the 2-year Treasury is shown in the table at 4%, the offering rate is 4.35%. Rates will not be posted for maturity ranges that the issuer does not desire to sell. For example, in Table 22-1 the issuer does not wish to sell MTNs with a maturity of less than 2 years.

The agents then make the offering rate schedule available to their investor base interested in MTNs. An investor interested in the offering contacts the agent. In turn, the agent contacts the issuer to confirm the terms of the transaction. Because the maturity range in the offering rate schedule does not specify a specific maturity date, the investor can choose the final maturity subject to approval by the issuer. The minimum size an investor can purchase of an MTN offering typically ranges from $1 million to $25 million.

The rate offering schedule can be changed at any time by the issuer either in response to changing market conditions or because the issuer raised the desired amount of funds at a given maturity. In the latter case, the issuer can either not post a rate for that maturity range or lower the rate.

STRUCTURED MTNS

It is common today for issuers of MTNs to couple their offerings with transactions in the derivative markets (options, futures/forwards, swaps, caps, and floors) so as to create debt obligations with more interesting risk/return features than are available in the

---

4 Leland F. Crabbe, "Medium-Term Notes," in Frank J. Fabozzi (ed.), *Then Handbook of Fixed Income Securities*, 6th ed. (New York: McGraw Hill, 2001), Chapter 12.

TABLE 22-1   An Offering Rate Schedule for a Medium-Term Note Program

	Medium-Term Notes		Treasury Securities	
Maturity Range	**Yield (percent)**	**Yield Spread of MTN over Treasury Securities (basis points)**	**Maturity**	**Yield (percent)**
9 months to 12 months	*	*	9 months	3.35
12 months to 18 months	*	*	12 months	3.50
18 months to 2 years	*	*	18 months	3.80
2 years to 5 years	4.35	35	2 years	4.00
3 years to 4 years	5.05	55	3 years	4.50
4 years to 5 years	5.60	60	4 years	5.00
5 years to 6 years	6.05	60	5 years	5.45
6 years to 7 years	6.10	40	6 years	5.70
7 years to 8 years	6.30	40	7 years	5.90
8 years to 9 years	6.45	40	8 years	6.05
9 years to 10 years	6.60	40	10 years	6.20
10 years	6.70	40	10 years	6.30

*No rate posted.

Source: Leland E. Crabbe. "The Anatomy of the Medium-Term Note Market." *Federal Reserve Bulletin* (August 1993), p. 753.

corporate bond market. Specifically, an issue can have a floating rate over all or part of the life of the security and the coupon reset formula can be based on a benchmark interest rate, equity index or individual stock price, a foreign exchange rate, or a commodity index. Some MTNs even offer coupon reset formulas that vary inversely with a benchmark interest rate; that is, if the benchmark interest rate increases (decreases), the coupon rate decreases (increases). Debt instruments with this coupon characteristic are called **inverse floating-rate securities**.

MTNs created when the issuer simultaneously transacts in the derivative markets are called **structured notes**. It is estimated today that new-issue volume of structured notes is 20% to 30% of new-issuance volume. The most common derivative instrument used in creating structured notes is a swap—a derivative instrument that we discuss in Chapter 12.

◆ BANK LOANS

As an alternative to the issuance of securities, a corporation can raise funds by borrowing from a bank.[5] A corporation may use any of five sourcing alternatives: (1) a domestic bank in the corporation's home country; (2) a subsidiary of a foreign bank established in the corporation's home country; (3) a foreign bank domiciled in a country where the corporation does business; (4) a subsidiary of a domestic bank established in a country where the corporation does business; or (5) an offshore or Eurobank. Loans made by offshore banks are referred to as **Eurocurrency loans**.[6]

---

[5] Bank debt is widely used as the senior financing for a leveraged buyout, acquisition, or recapitalization. These are collectively referred to as *highly leveraged transactions* or HLTs.

[6] A loan can be denominated in a variety of currencies. Loans denominated in U.S. dollars are called *Eurodollar loans*.

SYNDICATED BANK LOANS

A **syndicated bank loan** is one in which a group (or syndicate) of banks provides funds to the borrower. The need for a group of banks arises because the amount sought by a borrower may be too large for any one bank to be exposed to the credit risk of that borrower. Therefore, the syndicated bank loan is used by borrowers who seek to raise a large amount of funds in the loan market rather than through the issuance of securities.

These bank loans are called **senior bank loans** because of their priority position over subordinated lenders (bondholders) with respect to repayment of interest and principal. The interest rate on a syndicated bank loan is a rate that **floats**, which means that the loan rate is based on some reference rate. The loan rate is periodically reset at the reference rate plus a spread. The reference rate is typically the London interbank offered rate (LIBOR), although it could be the prime rate (that is, the rate that a bank charges its most creditworthy customers) or the rate on certificates of deposits. The term of the loan is fixed. A syndicated loan is typically structured so that it is amortized according to a predetermined schedule, and repayment of principal begins after a specified number of years (typically not longer than 5 or 6 years). Structures in which no repayment of the principal is made until the maturity date can be arranged and are referred to as **bullet loans**.

A syndicated loan is arranged by either a bank or a securities house. The arranger then lines up the syndicate. Each bank in the syndicate provides the funds for which it has committed. The banks in the syndicate have the right to sell their parts of the loan subsequently to other banks.

Syndicated loans are distributed by two methods: assignment or participation. Each method has its relative advantages and disadvantages, with the method of assignment the more desirable of the two.

The holder of a loan who is interested in selling a portion can do so by passing the interest in the loan by the **method of assignment**. In this procedure, the seller transfers all rights completely to the holder of the assignment, now called the **assignee**. The assignee is said to have **privity of contract** with the borrower. Because of the clear path between the borrower and assignee, assignment is the more desirable choice of transfer and ownership.

A **participation** involves a holder of a loan "participating out" a portion of the holding in that particular loan. The holder of the participation does not become a party to the loan agreement, and has a relationship not with the borrower but with the seller of the participation. Unlike an assignment, a participation does not confer privity of contract on the holder of the participation, although the holder of the participation has the right to vote on certain legal matters concerning amendments to the loan agreement. These matters include changes regarding maturity, interest rate, and issues concerning the loan collateral. Because syndicated loans can be sold in this manner, they are marketable.

In response to the large amount of bank loans issued and their strong credit protection, some commercial banks and securities houses are more willing to commit capital and resources to facilitate trading as broker/dealers. Also, these senior bank loans can be securitized through the same innovations discussed in Chapter 2 for the securitization of loans and discussed further in Chapter 27.[7] Further development of the senior bank loan market will no doubt eventually erode the once important distinction between a security and a loan: A security has long been seen as a marketable financial asset, while a loan has not been marketable. Interestingly, the trading of these loans is not limited to *performing loans,* which are loans whose borrowers are fulfilling contractual commitments. A market also exists for the trading of nonperforming loans—loans in which the borrowers have defaulted.

---

[7] For a discussion of the trading and securitization of senior bank loans, see John H. Carlson and Frank J. Fabozzi (eds.), *The Trading and Securitization of Senior Bank Loans* (Chicago: Probus Publishing, 1992).

LEASE FINANCING

The market for lease financing is a segment of the larger market for equipment financing. Any type of equipment that can be purchased with borrowed funds can also be leased. Our interest here is in the leasing of equipment that can be classified as a big-ticket item (that is, equipment costing more than $5 million). Included in this group are commercial aircraft, large ships, large quantities of production equipment, and energy facilities. A special type of leasing arrangement, known as a leveraged lease, is used in financing such equipment.

Leasing works as follows. The potential equipment user, called the **lessee** first selects the equipment and the dealer or manufacturer from whom the equipment will be purchased. The lessee negotiates such aspects of the transaction as the purchase price, specifications, warranties, and delivery date. When the lessee accepts the terms of the deal, another party, such as a bank or finance company, buys the equipment from the dealer or manufacturer and leases it to the lessee. This party is called the **lessor**. The lease is so arranged that the lessor realizes the tax benefits associated with the ownership of the leased equipment.

Basically, leasing is a vehicle by which tax benefits can be transferred from the user of the equipment (the lessee), who may not have the capacity to take advantage of the tax benefits associated with equipment ownership (such as depreciation and any tax credits), to another entity who can utilize them (the lessor). In exchange for these tax benefits, a lessor provides lower-cost financing to the lessee than the lessee could get by purchasing the equipment with borrowed funds. Such leases are referred to as **tax-oriented leases**.

The two ways in which a lessor can finance the purchase of the equipment are, first, to provide all the financing from its own funds and therefore be at risk for 100% of the funds used to purchase the equipment. Such leasing arrangements are referred to as **single-investor** or **direct leases**. Essentially, such leases are two-party agreements (the lessee and the lessor). The second way is for the lessor to use only a portion of its own funds to purchase the equipment, and to borrow the balance from a bank or group of banks. This type of leasing arrangement is called a **leveraged lease**. The three parties to a leveraged lease agreement include the lessee, the lessor, and the lender. The leveraged lease arrangement allows the lessor to realize all the tax benefits from owning the equipment and the tax benefits from borrowing funds—deductible interest payments—while putting up only a portion of its own funds to purchase the equipment. Therefore, leveraged leasing is commonly used in financing big-ticket items.

In a leveraged lease transaction, it is necessary for a party to arrange for the equity and the debt portions of the funding involved. The same party can arrange both. The equity portion is typically provided by one or more institutional investors. The debt portion is arranged with a bank. Because leveraged lease transactions are for large-ticket items, the bank debt is typically arranged as a syndicated bank loan. For example, the financing of aircraft is normally accomplished through leveraged lease financing.

Summary

Corporate senior instruments include debt obligations and preferred stock. Holders of these obligations take priority over holders of a corporation's common stock in the case of bankruptcy. In this chapter we discuss four sectors of this market: the commercial paper market, the medium-term note market, the Euronote market, and the bank loan market.

Investors typically do not perform their own analysis of the issuer's creditworthiness. Instead, they rely on a system of credit ratings developed by commercial rating companies. The companies in the United States that rate corporate debt in terms of the likelihood of default are Moody's Investor Service, Standard & Poor's Corporation, and Fitch.

Medium-term notes are corporate debt obligations offered on a continuous basis. The maturities range from 9 months to 30 years and provide a financing alternative with maturities between those of commercial paper and long-term bonds.

Bank loans represent an alternative to the issuance of securities. In a syndicated bank loan, a group of banks provides funds to the borrower. Senior bank loans are now marketable, more actively traded, and can be securitized.

Leasing is a form of bank borrowing. Basically leasing is a vehicle by which tax benefits can be transferred from the user of the equipment (the lessee), who may not have the capacity to utilize the tax benefits associated with equipment ownership, to another entity who can utilize them. A single-investor lease is a two-party agreement involving the lessee and the lessor. In a leveraged lease, the lessor uses only a portion of its own funds to purchase the equipment and borrows the balance from a bank or group of banks.

Key Terms

- All-in-cost of funds
- Assignee
- Bullet loans
- Credit analysis
- Credit spread
- Credit spread risk
- Direct lease
- Downgrade
- Downgrade risk
- Euro medium-term note
- Eurocurrency loans
- Floats
- Inverse floating-rate securities
- Lessee
- Lessor
- Leveraged lease
- Medium-term note (MTN)
- Method of assignment
- Participation
- Privity of contract
- Senior bank loan
- Single-investor lease
- Structured notes
- Syndicated bank loan
- Tax-oriented lease
- Upgrade

Questions

1. What are the different forms of credit risk?
2. What role do rating companies play in financial markets?
3. What is meant by a creditor or quality spread?
4. What is a medium-term note?
5. What determines the yield that will be offered on a medium-term note?
6. What is a Euro medium-term note?
7. What is a structured note?
8. a. What is a syndicated bank loan?
   b. What is the reference rate typically used for a syndicated bank loan?
   c. What is the difference between an amortized bank loan and a bullet bank loan?
9. Explain the two ways in which a bank can sell its position in a syndicated loan.
10. a. For a lease financing transaction, who are the lessee and the lessor?
    b. Who is entitled to the tax benefits, and what are those tax benefits?
    c. If a manufacturing corporation has no taxable income, is it likely to buy equipment or lease equipment? Why?
11. What is the difference between a single-investor lease and a leveraged lease?

23

Corporate Senior Instruments Markets: II

Learning Objectives

After reading this chapter you will understand:

◆ the key provisions of a corporate bond issue.

◆ the risks associated with investing in corporate bonds.

◆ what a callable bond is.

◆ bonds with special features and why they are issued.

◆ the high-yield or junk bond sector of the corporate bond market.

◆ the purpose for which junk bond issuers use bond proceeds.

◆ the different type of bond structures used in the junk bond market.

◆ the Eurobond market and the different types of bond structures issued.

◆ the difference between preferred stock, corporate debt, and common stock.

◆ the difference between the various types of preferred stock: fixed-rate, adjustable-rate, and auction and remarketed preferred stock.

◆ the basic provisions in the Bankruptcy Reform Act of 1978.

◆ the difference between a liquidation and a reorganization.

◆ the principle of absolute priority in a bankruptcy.

In this chapter, we continue coverage of corporate senior instruments, focusing on corporate bonds and preferred stock. Preferred stock is classified as a senior instrument in that holders of these securities take priority over common stockholders in the case of bankruptcy. We conclude this chapter with a discussion of corporate bankruptcy.

◆ CORPORATE BONDS

Corporate bonds are classified by the type of issuer. The four general classifications used by bond information services are (1) utilities, (2) transportations, (3) industrials, and (4) banks and finance companies. Finer breakdowns are often made to create more homogeneous groupings. For example, utilities are subdivided into electric power companies, gas distribution companies, water companies, and communication companies. Transportations are further divided into airlines, railroads, and trucking companies. Industrials are the catchall class, and the most heterogeneous of the groupings with respect to investment characteristics. Industrials include all kinds of manufacturing, merchandising, and service companies. In recent years, industrials raised the largest amount in the corporate bond market, followed by financial institutions and then utilities.[1] The largest investor group is life insurance companies, followed by pension funds, public and private. Historically, these institutional investors hold more than half of outstanding corporate bonds. The balance is held by households, foreign investors, depository institutions, nonlife insurance companies, and mutual funds and securities brokers/dealers.

BASIC FEATURES OF A CORPORATE BOND ISSUE

The essential features of a corporate bond are relatively simple. The corporate issuer promises to pay a specified percentage of par value (known as the coupon payments) on designated dates, and to repay par or principal value of the bond at maturity. Failure to pay either principal or interest when due constitutes legal default, and court proceedings can be instituted to enforce the contract. Bondholders, as creditors, have a prior legal claim over common and preferred stockholders as to both income and assets of the corporation for the principal and interest due them.

The promises of corporate bond issuers and the rights of investors who buy them are set forth in great detail in contracts called **bond indentures**. If bondholders were handed the complete indenture, they would have trouble understanding its language, and even greater difficulty in determining at a particular time whether the corporate issuer were keeping all its promises. These problems are solved for the most part by bringing in a corporate trustee as a third party to the contract. The indenture is made out to the corporate trustee as a representative of the interests of bondholders; that is, the trustee acts in a fiduciary capacity for investors who own the bond issue. A corporate trustee is a bond or trust company with a corporate trust department and officers who are experts in performing the functions of a trustee.

A bond's indenture clearly outlines three important aspects: its maturity, its security, and its provisions for retirement.

Maturity of Bonds   Most corporate bonds are **term bonds**, that is, they run for a term of years, then become due and payable. Term bonds are often referred to as **bullet-maturity**, or simply, **bullet bonds**. Any amount of the liability not paid off prior to maturity must be paid off at that time. The bond's term may be long or short. Generally, obligations due less than 10 years from the date of issue are called **notes**.[2]

Most corporate borrowings take the form of **bonds** due in 20 to 30 years. Term bonds may be retired by payment at final maturity or retired prior to maturity if provided for in the indenture. Some corporate bond issues are so arranged that specified principal amounts become due on specified dates prior to maturity. Such issues are called **serial bonds**. Equipment trust certificates (discussed later) are structured as serial bonds.

---

[1] *Moody's Bond Survey*, selected, year-end issues.

[2] From our discussion of the various debt instruments in the previous chapter, it can be seen that the word *notes* is used to describe a variety of instruments—medium-term notes and Euronotes. The use of the term *notes* here is as a market convention distinguishing notes and bonds on the basis of the number of years to maturity at the time the security is issued.

Security for Bonds   Either real property (using a mortgage) or personal property may be pledged to offer security beyond that of the general credit standing of the issuer. A **mortgage bond** grants the bondholders a lien against the pledged assets. A **lien** is a legal right to sell mortgaged property to satisfy unpaid obligations to bondholders. In practice, foreclosure and sale of mortgaged property are unusual. If a default occurs, usually a financial reorganization of the issuer makes the provision for settlement of the debt to bondholders. The mortgage lien is important, though, because it gives the mortgage bondholders a strong bargaining position relative to other creditors in determining the terms of a reorganization.

Some companies do not own fixed assets or other real property, and so have nothing on which they can give a mortgage lien to secure bondholders. Instead, these firms own securities of other companies and, thus, are **holding companies**. The firms whose shares are owned are **subsidiaries**. To satisfy the desire of bondholders for security, the holding companies pledge stocks, notes, bonds, or whatever other kind of financial instruments they own. These assets are termed **collateral** (or personal property), and bonds secured by such assets are called **collateral trust bonds**.

Many years ago the railway companies developed a way of financing the purchase of cars and locomotives, called **rolling stock**, that enabled them to borrow at just about the lowest rates in the corporate bond market. Railway rolling stock for a long time was regarded by investors as excellent security for debt. The equipment is sufficiently standardized that it can be used by one railway as well as another. And of course it can readily be moved from the tracks of one railroad to those of another. Therefore, generally a good market exists for lease or sale of cars and locomotives. The railroads take advantage of these characteristics of rolling stock by developing a legal arrangement for giving investors a legal claim on it that is different from, and generally superior to, a mortgage lien.

The legal arrangement in this situation is one that vests legal title to railway equipment in a trustee. When a railway company orders some cars and locomotives from a manufacturer, the manufacturer transfers legal title to the equipment to a trustee. The trustee, in turn, leases the equipment to the railroad, and at the same time sells **equipment trust certificates** to obtain the funds to pay the manufacturer. The trustee collects lease payments from the railroad and uses these receipts to pay interest and principal on the certificates. The principal is therefore paid off on specified dates, a provision that makes a certificate different from a term bond.

The general idea of the equipment trust arrangement is also used by companies engaged in providing other kinds of transportation. For example, trucking companies finance the purchase of huge fleets of trucks in the same manner; airlines use this kind of financing to purchase transport planes; and international oil companies use this financing method to buy huge tankers.

A **debenture bond** is not secured by a specific pledge of property, which does not mean that this type of bond has no claim on property of issuers or on their earnings. Debenture bondholders hold the claim of general creditors on all assets of the issuer not pledged specifically to secure other debt. Also, holders of debentures can claim pledged assets to the extent that these assets have value greater than necessary to satisfy secured creditors. A **subordinated debenture bond** is an issue that ranks after secured debt, after debenture bonds, and often after some general creditors in its claim on assets and earnings.

The type of corporate security issued determines the cost to the issuer. For a given corporation, mortgage bonds will cost less than debenture bonds; debenture bonds will cost less than subordinated debenture bonds.

A **guaranteed bond** is an obligation guaranteed by another entity. The safety of a guaranteed bond depends upon the financial capability of the guarantor to satisfy the terms of the guarantee, as well as the financial capability of the issuer. The terms of the guarantee may call for the guarantor to guarantee the payment of interest and/or repayment of the principal.

It is important to recognize that a superior legal status will not prevent bond-holders from suffering financial loss when the issuer's ability to generate cash flow adequate to pay its obligations is seriously eroded.

Provisions for Paying Off Bonds   Most corporate issues contain a call provision allowing the issuer an option to buy back all or part of the issue prior to maturity. Some issues carry a sinking fund provision, which specifies that the issuer must retire a predetermined amount of the issue periodically.[3]

An important question in negotiating the terms of a new bond issue is whether the issuer shall have the right to redeem the *entire amount* of bonds outstanding on a date before maturity. Issuers generally want this right because they recognize that at some time in the future the general level of interest rates may fall sufficiently below the issue's coupon rate, so that redeeming the issue and replacing it with another issue carrying a lower coupon rate would be attractive. For reasons discussed later in this chapter, this right represents a disadvantage to the bondholder.

The usual practice is a provision that denies the issuer the right to redeem bonds during the first 5 to 10 years following the date of issue with proceeds received from the sale of lower-cost debt obligations that have an equal or superior rank to the debt to be redeemed. This type of redemption is called **refunding**. Even though most long-term issues carry these refunding restrictions, they may be immediately callable, in whole or in part, if the source of funds is something other than money raised with debt of a lower interest. Under such a provision, acceptable sources include cash flow from operations, proceeds from a common stock sale, or funds from the sale of property.

Investors often confuse refunding protection with call protection. Call protection is much more comprehensive because it prohibits the early redemption of the bond *for any reason.* Refunding restrictions, by contrast, provide protection only against the one type of redemption already mentioned.

As a rule, corporate bonds are callable at a premium above par. Generally, the amount of the premium declines as the bond approaches maturity and often reaches zero after a number of years following issuance. The initial amount of the premium may be as much as 1 year's coupon interest, or as little as the coupon interest for half of a year.

If the issuer has the choice to retire all or part of an issue prior to maturity, the buyer of the bond takes the chance that the issue will be called away at a disadvantageous time. This risk is referred to as **call risk**, or **timing risk**. Call provisions present two disadvantages from the investor's perspective. First, as explained in Chapter 18, a decline in interest rates in the economy increases the price of a debt instrument, although in the case of a callable bond, the price increase is somewhat limited. If and when interest rates decline far enough below the coupon rate to make call an immediate or prospective danger, the market value of the callable bond will not rise as much as that of noncallable issues that are similar in all other respects. Second, when a bond issue is called as a result of a decline in interest rates, the investor must reinvest the proceeds received at a lower interest rate (unless the investor chooses debt of greater risk).

Corporate bond indentures may require the issuer to retire a specified portion of an issue each year. This sinking fund provision for the repayment of the debt may be

---

[3]   For a more detailed explanation of corporate call provisions, see Richard S. Wilson and Frank J. Fabozzi, *Corporate Bonds: Structures & Analysis* (New Hope, PA: Frank J. Fabozzi Associates, 1996).

designed to liquidate all of a bond issue by the maturity date, or it may call for the liquidation of only a part of the total by the end of the term. If only a part of the outstanding bond is paid before retirement, the remainder is called a **balloon maturity**. The purpose of the sinking fund provision is to reduce credit risk. Generally, the issuer may satisfy the sinking fund requirement by either (1) making a cash payment of the face amount of the bonds to be retired to the corporate trustee, who then calls the bonds for redemption using a lottery, or (2) delivering to the trustee bonds with a total face value equal to the amount that must be retired from bonds purchased in the open market.

BONDS WITH SPECIAL FEATURES

Prior to the 1970s, securities issued in the U.S. bond market had a simple structure. They had a fixed coupon rate and a fixed maturity date. The only option available to the issuer was the right to call all or part of the issue prior to the stated maturity date. The historically high interest rates that prevailed in the United States in the late 1970s and early 1980s, and the volatile interest rates since the 1970s, prompted introduction of new structures or the increased use of existing structures with special features that made issues more attractive to both borrowers and investors. Various bond structures are reviewed here.

Convertible and Exchangeable Bonds   The conversion provision in a corporate bond issue grants the bondholder the right to convert the bond to a predetermined number of shares of common stock of the issuer. A **convertible bond** is therefore a corporate bond with a call option to buy the common stock of the issuer. An **exchangeable bond** grants the bondholder the right to exchange the bonds for the common stock of a firm *other* than the issuer of the bond. For example, Ford Motor Credit exchangeable bonds are exchangeable for the common stock of its parent company, Ford Motor Company.

Issues of Debt with Warrants   Warrants may be attached as a part of a bond issue. A **warrant** grants the holder the right to purchase a designated security at a specified price from the issuer of the bond. A warrant is simply a call option. It may permit the holder to purchase the common stock of the issuer of the debt or the common stock of a firm other than the issuer's. Or, the warrant may grant the holder the right to purchase a debt obligation of the issuer. Generally, warrants can be detached from the bond and sold separately. Typically, in exercising the warrant, an investor may choose either to pay cash or to offer the debt, to be valued at par, that was part of the offering. A major difference between warrants and either convertible or exchangeable bonds is that an investor exercising the option provided by the latter must turn the bond in to the issuer.

Putable Bonds   A putable bond grants the bondholder the right to sell the issue back to the issuer at par value on designated dates. The advantage to the bondholder is that if interest rates rise after the issue date, thereby reducing the market value of the bond, the bondholder can sell the bond back to the issuer for par.

Zero-Coupon Bonds   Zero-coupon bonds are, just as the name implies, bonds without coupon payments or a stated interest rate. In the Treasury market, the U.S. government does not issue zero-coupon bonds. Dealers strip issues and create these bonds from the cash flow of a coupon Treasury bond. Corporations, however, can and do issue zero-coupon bonds. The first such public offering was in the spring of 1981. The attractiveness of a zero-coupon bond from the investor's perspective is that the investor who holds the bond to the maturity date will realize a predetermined return on the bond, unlike a coupon bond where the actual return realized, if the bond is held to maturity, depends on the rate at which coupon payments can be reinvested.

Floating-Rate Securities The coupon interest on floating-rate securities is reset periodically to follow changes in the level of some predetermined benchmark rate. For example, the coupon rate may be reset every 6 months to a rate equal to a spread of 100 basis points over the 6-month Treasury bill rate.

Floating-rate securities are attractive to some institutional investors because they allow the purchase of an asset with an income stream that closely matches the floating nature of the income of specific liabilities. Certain floating-rate instruments are viewed by some investors as a passive substitute for short-term investments, particularly that part of a short-term portfolio that is more or less consistently maintained at certain minimum levels. Thus, floating-rate securities save on the costs of constantly rolling over short-term securities as they reach maturity.

Why do corporations issue floating-rate securities? Closer matching of their income flows from variable-rate assets with floating-rate liabilities is of major importance, especially with lenders such as banks, thrifts, and finance companies. Issuers can fix or lock in a spread between the cost of borrowed funds and the rate at which those funds are loaned out. Another reason might be to avoid uncertainties associated with what could be an unreceptive market at some future date. The issuer can tap a new source for intermediate- to long-term funds at short-term rates, thereby making fewer trips to the marketplace and avoiding related issuance costs.

Also, in the presence of inflation, a floating-rate security (rolled over, if needed) may have a lower interest cost than a fixed-rate, long-term security. The reason is that, with inflation, the long rate may incorporate a substantial premium against the uncertainty of future inflation and interest rates. Finally, as we noted in our Chapter 12 discussion of the innovative world of swaps, an issuer may find that it can issue a floating-rate security and convert payments into a fixed-rate stream through an interest rate swap agreement. An issuer will elect this approach if the cost of issuing a floating-rate security and then using an interest rate swap results in a lower cost than simply issuing a fixed-rate security.

Other features may be included in a floating-rate issue. For example, many floating-rate issues include a put option. Some issues are exchangeable either automatically at a certain date (often 5 years after issuance) or at the option of the issuer into fixed-rate securities. A few issues are convertible into the common stock of the issuer. Some floating-rate issues have a ceiling or maximum interest rate for the coupon rate; some have a floor or minimum interest rate for the coupon rate.

CORPORATE BOND CREDIT RATINGS

Market participants typically do not conduct their own credit analysis of a debt obligation. Instead, they rely primarily on nationally recognized rating companies that perform credit analysis and issue their conclusions in the form of ratings. The rating systems of the three nationally recognized rating companies—Moody's Investors Service, Standard & Poor's Corporation, and Fitch—use similar symbols, as shown in Table 23-1.

Rating Systems In all systems the term *high grade* means low credit risk, or conversely, high probability of future payments. The highest-grade bonds are designated by Moody's by the symbol Aaa, and by the other two rating systems by the symbol AAA. The next highest grade is denoted by the symbol Aa (Moody's) or AA (the other two rating systems); for the third grade all rating systems use A. The next three grades are Baa or BBB, Ba or BB, and B, respectively, followed by the C grades. Moody's uses 1, 2, or 3 to provide a narrower credit quality breakdown within each class, and the other rating companies use plus and minus signs for the same purpose.

TABLE 23-1   Summary of Corporate Bond Rating Systems and Symbols

Moody's	S&P	Fitch	Brief Definition
Investment grade—High creditworthiness			
Aaa	AAA	AAA	Exceptional, prime, maximum safety
Aa1	AA+	AA+	
Aa2	AA	AA	Very high grade, high quality
Aa3	AA−	AA−	
A1	A+	A+	
A2	A	A	Upper medium grade
A3	A−	A−	
Baa1	BBB+	BBB+	
Baa2	BBB	BBB	Lower medium grade
Baa3	BBB−	BBB−	
Distinctly speculative—Low creditworthiness			
Ba1	BB	BB+	
Ba2	BB	BB	Low grade, speculative
Ba3	BB−	BB−	
B1	B+	B+	
B2	B	B	Highly speculative
B3	B−	B−	
Predominantly speculative—Substantial risk in default			
	CCC+		
Caa	CCC	CCC	Substantial risk, in poor standing
	CCC−		
Ca	CC	CC	May be in default, extremely speculative
C	C	C	Even more speculative
	C1		C1 = Income bonds—no interest is being paid
		DDD	Default
		DD	
D	D		

Source: Richard S. Wilson and Frank J. Fabozzi, *Corporate Bonds: Structures & Analysis* (New Hope, PA: Frank J. Fabozzi Associates, 1996).

Bonds rated triple A (AAA or Aaa) are said to be *prime,* double A (AA or Aa) are of high quality; single A issues are called *upper medium grade,* and triple B are *medium grade.* Lower-rated bonds are said to have speculative elements or be distinctly speculative.

Bond issues assigned a rating in the top four categories are referred to as *investment-grade bonds.* Issues that carry a rating below the top four categories are referred to as *noninvestment-grade bonds,* or more popularly as *high-yield bonds* or *junk bonds.* Thus, the corporate bond market can be divided into two sectors: the investment-grade and noninvestment-grade markets.

Ratings of bonds change over time. Issuers are upgraded when their likelihood of default as assessed by the rating company improves and downgraded when their likelihood of default as assessed by the rating company deteriorates. The rating companies publish the issues that they are reviewing for possible rating changes. The lists are called *credit watch lists.*

To see how ratings change over time, the rating agencies periodically publish this information in the form of a table. This table is called a **rating transition matrix**.

Investors find the table useful to assess potential downgrades and upgrades. A rating transition matrix is available for different transition periods. Table 23-2 shows a hypothetical rating transition matrix for a 1-year period. The first column shows the ratings at the start of the year and the first row shows the rating at the end of the year. To interpret the numbers, look at the cell where the rating at the beginning of the year is AA and the rating at the end of the year is AA. This cell represents the percentage of issues rated AA at the beginning of the year that did not change their rating over the year, that is, experienced no downgrades or upgrades. As can be seen, 92.75% of the issues rated AA at the start of the year were rated AA at the end of the year. Now look at the cell where the rating at the beginning of the year is AA and at the end of the year is A. This shows the percentage of issues rated AA at the beginning of the year that were downgraded to A by the end of the year. In our hypothetical 1-year rating transition matrix, this percentage is 5.07%. One can view this figure as a probability. It is the probability that an issue rated AA will be downgraded to A by the end of the year. A rating transition matrix also shows the potential for upgrades. Again, in Table 23-2, issues rated AA at the beginning of the year have a chance of being AAA rated at the end of the year.

In general, the probability of a downgrade is much higher than for an upgrade for investment-grade bonds. Also, the longer the transition period, the lower the probability that an issuer will retain its original rating. A 1-year rating transition matrix will have a lower probability of a downgrade for a particular rating than a 5-year rating transition mix for that same rating.

Occasionally, the ability of an issuer to make interest and principal payments is seriously and unexpectedly changed by (1) a natural or industrial accident or some regulatory change, or (2) a takeover or corporate restructuring. These risks are referred to generically as **event risks**. Two examples of the first type of event risk are a change in the accounting treatment of loan losses for commercial banks and the cancellation of nuclear plants by public utilities.

An example of the second type of event risk is the takeover in 1988 of RJR Nabisco for $25 billion through a financing technique known as a **leveraged buyout (LBO)**. The new company took on a substantial amount of debt to finance the acquisition of the firm.[4] In the case of RJR Nabisco, the debt and equity after the leveraged buyout were $29.9 billion and $1.2 billion, respectively. Because of the need to service a larger amount of debt, the company's credit rating was reduced. RJR Nabisco's credit

TABLE 23-2 Hypothetical 1-Year Rating Transition Matrix

Rating at Start of Year	Rating at End of Year								
	AAA	AA	A	BBB	BB	B	CCC	D	Total
AAA	93.20	6.00	0.60	0.12	0.08	0.00	0.00	0.00	100
AA	1.60	92.75	5.07	0.36	0.11	0.07	0.03	0.01	100
A	0.18	2.65	91.91	4.80	0.37	0.02	0.02	0.05	100
BBB	0.04	0.30	5.20	87.70	5.70	0.70	0.16	0.20	100
BB	0.03	0.11	0.61	6.80	81.65	7.10	2.60	1.10	100
B	0.01	0.09	0.55	0.88	7.90	75.67	8.70	6.20	100
CCC	0.00	0.01	0.31	0.84	2.30	8.10	62.54	25.90	100

[4] For a discussion of event risk associated with takeovers, see N. R. Vijayarghavan and Randy Snook, "Takeover Event Risk and Corporate Bond Portfolio Management," in Frank J. Fabozzi (ed.), *Advances and Innovations in Bond and Mortgage Markets* (Chicago: Probus Publishing, 1989).

rating as assigned by Moody's dropped from A1 to B3. As a result, investors demanded a higher credit spread because of this new capital structure with a greater proportion of debt. The yield spread to a benchmark Treasury rate increased from about 100 basis points to 350 basis points.

Factors Considered in Assigning Ratings   In conducting its examination, the rating agencies consider the four Cs of credit—character, capacity, collateral, and covenants. The first of the Cs stands for **character** of management, the foundation of sound credit. Character includes the ethical reputation as well as the business qualifications and operating record of the board of directors, management, and executives responsible for the use of borrowed funds and repayment of those funds. The next C is **capacity** or the ability of an issuer to repay its obligations. The third C, collateral, is not only assets pledged to secure the debt, but also the quality and value of those unpledged assets controlled by the issuer. In both aspects the collateral is capable of supplying additional aid, comfort, and support to the debt and the debt holder. Assets form the basis for the generation of cash flow, which services the debt in good times as well as bad. The final C is for **covenants**, the terms and conditions of the lending agreement. Covenants lay down restrictions on how management operates the company and conducts its financial affairs. Covenants can restrict management's discretion. A default or violation of any covenant may serve as an early warning that enables investors to take positive and corrective action before the situation deteriorates further. Covenants play an important role in minimizing risk to creditors. They help prevent the unconscionable transfer of wealth from debt holders to equity holders.

Character analysis involves the analysis of the quality of management. In discussing the factors it considers in assigning a credit rating, Moody's Investors Service notes the following regarding the quality of management.

> Although difficult to quantify, management quality is one of the most important factors supporting an issuer's credit strength. When the unexpected occurs, it is a management's ability to react appropriately that will sustain the company's performance.[5]

In assessing management quality, the analysts at Moody's, for example, try to understand the business strategies and policies formulated by management. The following factors are considered: (1) strategic direction, (2) financial philosophy, (3) conservatism, (4) track record, (5) succession planning, and (6) control systems.[6]

In assessing the ability of an issuer to pay, an analysis of the financial statements is undertaken. In addition to management quality, the factors examined by Moody's, for example, are (1) industry trends, (2) the regulatory environment, (3) basic operating and competitive position, (4) financial position and sources of liquidity, (5) company structure (including structural subordination and priority of claim), (6) parent company support agreements, and (7) special event risk.[7]

In considering industry trends, the rating agencies look at the vulnerability of the company to economic cycles, the barriers to entry, and the exposure of the company to technological changes. For firms in regulated industries, proposed changes in regulations must be analyzed to assess their impact on future cash flows. At the company level, diversification of the product line and the cost structure are examined in assessing the basic operating position of the firm.

---

[5] "Industrial Company Rating Methodology," *Moody's Investor Service: Global Credit Research* (July 1998), p. 6.

[6] "Industrial Company Rating Methodology," p. 7.

[7] Ibid., p. 3.

The rating agencies must look at the capacity of a firm to obtain additional financing and backup credit facilities. Of the various forms of backup facilities, the strongest forms are contractually binding and do not include provisions that permit the lender to refuse to provide funds. An example of such a provision is one that allows the bank to refuse funding if the bank feels that the borrower's financial condition or operating position has deteriorated significantly. (Such a provision is called a **material adverse change clause**.) Noncontractual facilities such as lines of credit that make it easy for a bank to refuse funding should be of concern to the rating agency. The rating agency also examines the quality of the bank providing the backup facility. Other sources of liquidity for a company may be third-party guarantees, the most common being a contractual agreement with its parent company. When such a financial guarantee exists, the analyst must undertake a credit analysis of the parent company.

As explained earlier, a corporate debt obligation can be secured or unsecured. In our discussion of creditor rights in a bankruptcy later in this chapter, we see that in the case of a liquidation, proceeds from a bankruptcy are distributed to creditors based on the absolute priority rule. However, in the case of a reorganization, the absolute priority rule rarely holds. That is, an unsecured creditor may receive distributions for the entire amount of his or her claim and common stockholders may receive something, while a secured creditor may receive only a portion of its claim. The reason is that a reorganization requires approval of all the parties. Consequently, secured creditors are willing to negotiate with both unsecured creditors and stockholders in order to obtain approval of the plan of reorganization.

The question is, then, what does a secured position mean in the case of a reorganization if the absolute priority rule is not followed in a reorganization? The claim position of a secured creditor is important in terms of the negotiation process. However, because absolute priority is not followed and the final distribution in a reorganization depends on the bargaining ability of the parties, some analysts place less emphasis on collateral compared to other factors and covenants.

Covenants deal with limitations and restrictions on the borrower's activities. Affirmative covenants call upon the debtor to make promises to do certain things. Negative covenants require the borrower not to take certain actions. Negative covenants are usually negotiated between the borrower and the lender or their agents. Borrowers want the least restrictive loan agreement available, while lenders should want the most restrictive, consistent with sound business practices. But lenders should try not to restrain borrowers from accepted business activities and conduct. A borrower might be willing to include additional restrictions (up to a point) if it can get a lower interest rate on the debt obligation. When borrowers seek to weaken restrictions in their favor, they are often willing to pay more interest or give other consideration.

HIGH-YIELD SECTOR

As already noted, high-yield bonds are issues with a credit rating below triple B. Bond issues in this sector of the market may have been rated investment grade at the time of issuance and have been downgraded subsequently to noninvestment grade, or they may have been rated noninvestment grade at the time of issuance, called *orignal-issue, high-yield bonds*.

Downgraded bonds fall into two groups: (1) issues downgraded because the issuer voluntarily significantly increased its debt as a result of a leveraged buyout or a recapitalization, and (2) issues downgraded for other reasons. The latter issues are commonly referred to as **fallen angels**.

The modern high-yield market began in the late 1970s. Due to the market's dramatic successes (such as the $15 billion leveraged buyout of Metromedia by John Kluge in 1984 and Kolberg Kravis Roberts & Company's 1986 LBO of Beatrice, a company with many well-known brand names), the media began to report stories helping to pique investors' appetites. The market's early growth was dominated by a single investment bank, Drexel Burnham Lambert, and it was not until the mid-1980s that this firm began to experience serious competition from other investment banks, namely, Merrill Lynch, Morgan Stanley, and First Boston.

The Role of High-Yield Bonds in Corporate Finance   The introduction of original-issue, high-yield bonds proved to be an important financial innovation with wide impact throughout the financial system. A common view held that high default risk bonds would not be attractive to the investing public, at least at interest rates that would be acceptable to the borrower. The view rested on the skewed nature of the outcomes offered by the instrument: The maximum return that an investor may obtain is capped by the coupon and face value, but the loss could be as large as the principal invested. It was the merit of Drexel Burnham Lambert, and particularly of Michael Milken of that firm, to disprove that view as evidenced by the explosive growth of that market.

Before development of the high-yield market, U.S. corporations that could not issue securities in the public debt market would borrow from commercial banks or finance companies on a short-term to intermediate-term basis or would be shut off from credit. With the advent of the high-yield bond structure, financing shifted from commercial banks to the public market. One study estimated that about two-thirds of the $90 to $100 billion of the high-yield bonds issued represents simply a replacement of commercial bank borrowing. The same study concluded that high-yield bonds are "no more a threat to the stability of the financial system than the bank debt itself was."[8]

In essence, the high-yield bond market shifts the risk from commercial banks to the investing public in general. Several advantages occur with such a shift. First, when commercial banks lend to high credit risk borrowers, that risk is accepted indirectly by all U.S. citizens, who may not wish to accept the risk. The reason is that the commercial bank liabilities are backed by the Federal Deposit Insurance Company. If high credit risk corporations default on their loans, causing an FDIC bailout, all taxpayers eventually may have to pay. The liabilities of other investors (excluding thrifts that have invested in high-yield bonds) are not backed by the U.S. government (and, therefore, not by U.S. citizens). The risks of this investing are accepted by the specific investor group willing to accept them.

The second advantage is that commercial bank loans are typically short-term, floating-rate loans, which make debt financing less attractive to corporations. High-yield bond issues give corporations the opportunity to issue long-term, fixed rate debt. Third, commercial banks set interest rates based on their credit analysis. When high-yield bonds are traded in a public market, the investing public establishes the interest rate. Finally, the high-yield market opens the possibility of funding for some firms that previously had no means to it.

Corporate bond issuers use the proceeds from a bond sale for a number of purposes, including working capital, expansion of facilities, refinancing of outstanding debt, and financing takeovers (mergers and acquisitions). In the case of noninvestment-grade bonds, it is the use of the proceeds to finance takeovers (particularly hostile takeovers) that aroused public concern over the excessive use of debt by U.S. corporations.[9]

---

[8]   November 1986 speech by John Paulus, chief economist at Morgan Stanley, at a conference sponsored by *Citizens for a Sound Economy.*
[9]   In a hostile takeover the targeted firm's management resists the merger or acquisition.

High-Yield Bond Structures   In the early years of the high-yield market, all the issues followed a conventional structure; that is, the issues paid a fixed coupon rate and were term bonds. Today, however, more complex bond structures occupy the junk bond area, particularly for bonds issued for LBO financing and recapitalizations producing higher debt.

In an LBO or a recapitalization, the heavy interest payment burden that the corporation assumes places severe cash flow constraints on the firm. To reduce this burden, firms involved in LBOs and recapitalizations issue bonds with deferred coupon structures that permit the issuer to avoid using cash to make interest payments for a period of 3 to 7 years. Three types of deferred coupon structures include (1) deferred-interest bonds, (2) step-up bonds, and (3) payment-in-kind bonds.

Deferred-interest bonds are the most coupon type of **deferred coupon structure**. These bonds sell at a deep discount and do not pay interest for an initial period, typically for 3 to 7 years. (Because no interest is paid for an initial period, these bonds are sometimes referred to as zero-coupon bonds.) **Step-up bonds** do pay coupon interest, but the coupon rate is low for an initial period and then increases ("steps up") to a higher coupon rate. Finally, **payment-in-kind (PIK) bonds** give the issuer an option to pay cash at a coupon payment date or give the bondholder a similar bond (i.e., a bond with the same coupon rate and a par value equal to the amount of the coupon payment that would have been paid). The period during which the issuer can make this choice varies from 5 to 10 years.

SECONDARY MARKET

The two secondary corporate bond markets are the exchange market (New York Stock Exchange and American Stock Exchange) and the over-the-counter (OTC) market. Almost all trading volume takes place in the OTC market, which is the market used by institutional investors and professional money managers.

Here is how corporate bond trading by institutional investors works today in the over-the-counter market. An institutional investor may want to buy a specific corporate bond with certain characteristics, or an institutional investor may have a specific corporate bond in its portfolio. The portfolio manager contacts brokers at several different brokerage firms to inquire about prices (to buy or sell, whatever the case may be). The broker obtains prices from its trading desk. These prices depend on the inventory of that corporate bond that the trading desk has. Thus, the institutional investor must search for the corporate bonds that he or she is interested in buying or selling.

The over-the-counter market relies on a commitment of capital from bond dealers' trading desks to make a market in corporate bonds by carrying inventory of corporate bonds. In general, capital allocation by dealer desks has been declining. For example, in 1988, of the $200 billion outstanding in the high-yield corporate bond sector, dealer capital as a percentage of that was 1%. Ten years later, the high-yield corporate bond sector was $572 billion, and the dealer capital was at 0.6%. This shift suggests that even though the size of the high-yield corporate bond market tripled, capital that was used to service that sector by the dealer community nearly halved.

The concern in the corporate bond market is on the transparency of prices and trades. The Nasdaq's Fixed Income Pricing System (FIPS) is an electronic trading system for disseminating price quotes and reporting trades for high-yield corporate bonds. FIPS began operations in April 1994. However, FIPS is not really a reporting system per se. It reports to the Securities and Exchange Commission and Nasdaq, but those prices don't go anywhere. The self-regulatory organizations abrogated the control of the bond market to the dealer community, and the dealers do not want those prices out, which is the reason they are not out, preventing the transparency of high-yield bond prices to the investment community.

In recent years several electronic trading systems developed via the Internet. Online bond trading Web sites sponsored by Wall Street firms emerged along with independent bond trading Web sites. Electronic trading could carve a niche for itself by enabling investors to transact more efficiently. The major advantage to a broker/dealer is that the dealer can show its bond inventory to its customers and representatives efficiently. Instead of a customer calling a trading desk to find prices for a bond that meets certain criteria, the customer can do the query himself or herself. Thus, the broker/dealer can do more trades without having to add people to trading desks. Customers get better pricing as they see more inventory and can choose the best prices. It is much more efficient to check a computer monitor for different quotes on a particular bond than to call several broker/dealers.

The liquidity of corporate bonds varies from issue to issue. The bonds of large firms, usually sold to the public in large amounts, can have a high degree of liquidity. However, the issues of smaller, less well-known firms may be quite illiquid.

EUROBOND MARKET

The Eurobond sector of the global bond market includes bonds with several distinguishing features.

1. They are underwritten by an international syndicate.
2. At issuance they are offered simultaneously to investors in a number of countries.
3. They are issued outside the jurisdiction of any single country.
4. They are in unregistered form.

Although Eurobonds are typically listed on a national stock exchange (the most common are the Luxembourg, London, or Zurich exchanges), the bulk of all trading is in the over-the-counter market. Firms list these bonds purely to circumvent restrictions imposed on some institutional investors that are prohibited from purchasing securities not listed on an exchange. Some of the stronger issuers privately place their debt with international institutional investors.

Borrowers in the Eurobond market include nonfinancial corporations, banks, sovereign governments, entities whose debt is guaranteed by a sovereign government, provinces, municipalities, cities, and supranational entities such as the World Bank. The major issuer group is nonfinancial corporations, followed by banks. Traditionally, the main currency used in Eurobond offerings has been the U.S. dollar, although the share of Eurobond offerings denominated in U.S. dollars has been declining.

The Eurobond market is characterized by new and innovative bond structures to accommodate particular needs of issuers and investors throughout the world. Some issues, of course, are the "plain vanilla," fixed-rate coupon bonds, referred to as **Euro straights**. Because they are issued on an unsecured basis, they are usually the debt of high-quality entities.

Coupon payments on Eurobonds are made annually, rather than semiannually. Bond issues may also be zero-coupon issues, deferred-coupon issues, and step-up issues. Some of the innovative issues in this market are **dual-currency issues**: They pay coupon interest in one currency but the principal in a different currency. For example, the coupon interest payments can be made in Swiss francs, while the principal may be paid in U.S. dollars.

Some Eurobonds are convertible or exchangeable, and bonds with attached warrants represent a large part of the market. Most warrants on Eurobonds are detachable from the bond with which they originally came to market; the bondholder may detach the warrant from the bond and sell it separately.

The warrants on Eurobonds vary: Some are equity warrants, others are debt warrants, and still others may be currency warrants. An equity warrant permits the warrant owner to buy the common stock of the issuer at a specified price. A debt warrant entitles the warrant owner to buy additional bonds from the issuer at the same price and yield as the host bond. The debt warrant owner benefits if interest rates decline because the warrant allows the owner to purchase a bond with a higher coupon than the same issuer would offer. A currency warrant permits the warrant owner to exchange one currency for another at a set price (that is, a fixed exchange rate). This feature protects the bondholder against a depreciation of the foreign currency in which the bond's cash flows are denominated. Finally, we also note that some warrants are gold warrants and allow the warrant holder to purchase gold from the bond issuer at a prespecified price.

Eurobonds make use of a wide variety of floating-rate structures. Almost all the floating-rate notes are denominated in U.S. dollars, and non-U.S. banks are the major issuers of these bonds. The coupon rate on a floating-rate note is some stated margin over the London interbank offered rate (LIBOR), the bid on LIBOR (referred to as LIBID), or the arithmetic average of LIBOR and LIBID (referred to as LIMEAN). Many floating-rate issues provide for either a minimum rate (or floor) that the coupon rate cannot fall below or a maximum rate (or cap) that the coupon rate cannot exceed. An issue with both a floor and a cap it said to be **collared**. Some floating-rate issues grant the borrower the right to convert the floating coupon rate into a fixed coupon rate at some time. Some issues, referred to as **drop-lock bonds**, automatically convert the floating coupon rate into a fixed coupon rate under certain circumstances.

◆ PREFERRED STOCK

Preferred stock is a class of stock, not a debt instrument, but it shares characteristics of both common stock and debt. Like the holder of common stock, the preferred stockholder is entitled to dividends. Unlike those on common stock, however, preferred dividends are a specified percentage of par or face value.[10] The percentage is called the dividend rate; it need not be fixed, but may float over the life of the issue.

Failure to make preferred stock dividend payments cannot force the issuer into bankruptcy. Should the issuer not make the preferred stock dividend payment, usually paid quarterly, one of two things can happen, depending on the terms of the issue. First, the dividend payment can accrue until it is fully paid. Preferred stock with this feature is called **cumulative preferred stock**. If a dividend payment is missed and the security-holder must forgo the payment, the preferred stock is said to be **noncumulative preferred stock**. Second, the failure to make dividend payments may result in the imposition of certain restrictions on management. For example, if dividend payments are in arrears, preferred stockholders might be granted voting rights.

Preferred stock differs from debt in a major way: The current tax code for corporations treats payments made to preferred stockholders as a distribution of earnings and not as tax-deductible expenses, which is how the tax code views interest payments. Although this difference in tax status raises the after-tax cost of funds for a corporation issuing preferred stock rather than borrowing, another factor in the tax code reduces the cost differential. A provision in the tax code exempts 70% of qualified dividends from federal income taxation, if the recipient is a qualified corporation.

---

[10] Almost all preferred stock limits the security holder to the specified amount. Historically, some issues entitled the preferred stockholder to participate in earnings distribution beyond the specified amount (based on some formula). Preferred stock with this feature is referred to as participating preferred stock.

For example, if Corporation A owns the preferred stock of Corporation B, then only $30 of each $100 that A receives in dividends from B will be taxed at A's marginal tax rate. The purpose of this provision is to mitigate the effect of the double taxation of corporate earnings. Two implications arise out of this tax treatment of preferred stock dividends. First, the major buyers of preferred stock are corporations seeking tax-advantaged investments. Second, the cost of preferred stock issuance is lower than it would be in the absence of the tax provision, because the tax benefits are passed through to the issuer by the willingness of buyers to accept a lower dividend rate.

Preferred stock, particularly cumulative preferred stock, shares some important similarities with debt: (1) The issuer promises fixed cash payments to preferred stockholders; and (2) preferred stockholders take priority over common stockholders with respect to dividend payments and the distribution of assets in the case of bankruptcy. (The position of noncumulative preferred stock is considerably weaker.) Because of this second feature, preferred stock is called a senior corporate instrument—it is senior to common stock. Note, however, that preferred stock is classified as equity on corporate balance sheets.

Almost all preferred stock comes with a sinking fund provision, and some preferred stock is convertible into common stock. Preferred stock may be issued without a maturity date, which is called **perpetual preferred stock**.

The preferred stock is a relatively small part of the financial system. Historically, utilities have been the major issuers of preferred stock, accounting for more than half of each year's issuance. Since 1985, major issuers are the financially oriented companies—finance companies, banks, thrifts, and insurance companies.

The same commercial companies that assign ratings to corporate bond issues also rate preferred stock issues.

The three types of preferred stock are (1) fixed-rate preferred stock, (2) adjustable-rate preferred stock, and (3) auction and remarketed preferred stock. Before 1982, all publicly issued preferred stock was fixed-rate preferred stock. In May 1982, the first adjustable-rate preferred stock issue was sold in the public market.[11]

ADJUSTABLE-RATE PREFERRED STOCK

The dividend rate on an adjustable-rate preferred stock (ARPS) is fixed quarterly and based on a predetermined spread from the highest of three points on the Treasury yield curve.[12] The predetermined spread is called the **dividend reset spread**. The motivation for linking the dividend rate to the highest of the three points on the Treasury yield curve is to provide the investor with protection against unfavorable shifts in the yield curve.

Most ARPS is perpetual, with a floor and ceiling imposed on the dividend rate. Because most ARPS is not putable, it can trade below par if, after issuance, the spread demanded by the market to reflect the issuer's credit risk is greater than the dividend reset spread.

The major issuers of ARPS have been bank holding companies for two reasons. First, floating-rate obligations provide a better liability match, given the floating-rate

[11] Private placement of ARPS occurred as early as 1978—illustrating how an innovation is first developed in this market. For historical background on the development of the ARPS market, see Richard S. Wilson, "Adjustable Rate Preferred Stocks," in Frank J. Fabozzi (ed.), *Floating Rate Instruments: Characteristics, Valuation and Portfolio Strategies* (Chicago: Probus Publishing, 1986), Chapter 3.

[12] The Treasury yield curve is described in Chapter 19. The three points on the yield curve (called the benchmark rate) to which the dividend reset spread is either added or subtracted are the highest of: (1) the 3-month Treasury bill rate; (2) the 2-year constant maturity rate; or (3) a 10-year or 30-year constant maturity rate. The Treasury constant maturity rate is reported in the Federal Reserve Report H.15(519). It is based on the closing market bid yields on actively traded Treasury securities.

nature of bank assets. Second, bank holding companies seek to strengthen their capital positions, and regulators permit bank holding companies to count perpetual preferred stock as part of their primary capital. Issuing ARPS provides not only better asset/liability match, but also allows bank holding companies to improve primary capital without having to issue common stock.

AUCTION AND REMARKETED PREFERRED STOCK

The popularity of ARPS declined when instruments began to trade below their par value, because the dividend reset rate is determined at the time of issuance, not by market forces. In 1984, a new type of preferred stock, **auction preferred stock (APS)**, was designed to overcome this problem, particularly for corporate treasurers who sought tax-advantaged short-term instruments to invest excess funds.[13] The dividend rate on APS is set periodically, as with ARPS, but it is established through an auction process.[14] Participants in the auction consist of current holders and potential buyers. The dividend rate that participants are willing to accept reflects current market conditions.

In the case of **remarketed preferred stock (RP)**, the dividend rate is determined periodically by a remarketing agent who resets the dividend rate so that any preferred stock can be tendered at par and be resold (remarketed) at the original offering price. An investor has the choice of dividend resets every 7 days or every 49 days.

Since 1985, APS and RP have become the dominant type of preferred stock issued.

◆ BANKRUPTCY AND CREDITOR RIGHTS

In this chapter and the previous one, we discussed senior corporate securities. By *senior* we mean that the holder of the security takes priority over the equity owners in the case of bankruptcy of a corporation. And, as explained, certain creditors have priority over other creditors. In this section, we provide an overview of the bankruptcy process and then look at what actually happens to creditors in bankruptcies.

THE BANKRUPTCY PROCESS

The law governing bankruptcy in the United States is the Bankruptcy Reform Act of 1978. The act sets forth the rules for a corporation to be either liquidated or reorganized. The **liquidation** of a corporation means that all the assets will be distributed to the holders of claims on the corporation and no corporate entity will survive. In a **reorganization**, a new corporate entity will result. Some holders of claims against the bankrupt corporation receive cash in exchange for their claims, others may receive new securities in the corporation that results from the reorganization, and others may receive a combination of both cash and new securities in the resulting corporation.

Another purpose of the bankruptcy act is to give a corporation time to decide whether to reorganize or liquidate, and then the necessary time to formulate a plan to accomplish either decision. The time is allowed because when a corporation files for bankruptcy, the act grants the corporation protection from creditors who seek to collect their claims. The petition for bankruptcy can be filed either by the company itself, in which case it is called a **voluntary bankruptcy**, or by its creditors, in which case it is called an **involuntary bankruptcy**.

---

[13] Each investment bank developed its own trademark name for APS. The instrument developed by Shearson Lehman/American Express was called Money Market Preferred (MMP). Salomon Brothers called it Dutch Auction Rate Transferable Securities (DARTS).

[14] The auction process is described in Richard S. Wilson, "Money Market Preferred Stock," in Frank J. Fabozzi (ed.), *Floating Rate Instruments*, Chapter 4, pp. 85–88.

A company that files for protection under the bankruptcy act generally becomes a "debtor in possession" and continues to operate its business under the supervision of the court.

The bankruptcy act is comprised of 15 chapters, each chapter covering a particular type of bankruptcy. Of particular interest are Chapter 7 and Chapter 11 bankruptcies. Chapter 7 deals with the liquidation of a company; Chapter 11 deals with the reorganization of a company.

ABSOLUTE PRIORITY: THEORY AND PRACTICE

When a company is liquidated, creditors receive distribution based on the absolute priority rule to the extent assets are available. The **absolute priority rule** is the principle that senior creditors are paid in full before junior creditors are paid anything. For secured creditors and unsecured creditors, the absolute priority rule guarantees their seniority to equity holders.

In liquidations, the absolute priority rule generally holds. In contrast, a good body of literature argues that in reorganizations, strict absolute priority is not upheld by the courts or the SEC.[15] Studies of actual reorganizations under Chapter 11 find that the violation of absolute priority is the rule rather than the exception.[16]

Failure of the courts to follow strict absolute priority creates implications for the capital structure decision, (that is, choice between debt and equity) of a firm. The view by financial economists that the firm is effectively owned by the creditors who sold the shareholders a call option on the firm's assets is not sustainable if the stockholders are not viewed as residual claimants.[17]

Several hypotheses have been suggested as to why in a reorganization the distribution made to claim holders diverges from that required by the absolute priority principle. The **incentive hypothesis** argues that the longer the negotiation process among the parties, the greater the bankruptcy costs and the smaller the amount to be distributed to all parties. In a reorganization, a committee representing the various claim holders is appointed with the purpose of formulating a plan of reorganization. To be accepted, a plan of reorganization must be approved by at least two-thirds of the amount and a majority of the number of claims voting, and at least two-thirds of the outstanding shares of each class of interests. Consequently, a lengthy bargaining process is expected. The longer the negotiation process among the parties, the more likely that the company will be operated in a manner not in the best interest of the creditors and, as a result, the smaller the amount to be distributed to all parties. Because all impaired classes, including equity holders, generally must approve the plan of reorganization, creditors often convince equity holders to accept the plan by offering to distribute some value to them.

The **recontracting process hypothesis** argues that the violation of absolute priority reflects a recontracting process between stockholders and senior creditors that gives

---

[15] See for example, William H. Meckling, "Financial Markets, Default, and Bankruptcy," *Law and Contemporary Problems* 41 (1977), pp. 124–77; Merton H. Miller, "The Wealth Transfers of Bankruptcy: Some Illustrative Examples," *Law and Contemporary Problems* 41 (1977), pp. 39–46; Jerold B. Warner, "Bankruptcy, Absolute Priority, and the Pricing of Risky Debt Claims," *Journal of Financial Economics* 4 (1977), pp. 239–76; and Thomas H. Jackson, "Of Liquidation, Continuation, and Delay: An Analysis of Bankruptcy Policy and Nonbankruptcy Rules," *American Bankruptcy Law Journal* 60 (1986), pp. 399–428.

[16] See Julian R. Franks and Walter N. Torous, "An Empirical Investigation of U.S. Firms in Reorganization," *Journal of Finance* (July 1989), pp. 747–69; Lawrence A. Weiss, "Bankruptcy Resolution: Direct Costs and Violation of Priority of Claims," *Journal of Financial Economics* (1990), pp. 285–314; and Frank J. Fabozzi, Jane Tripp Howe, Takashi Makabe, and Toshihide Sudo, "Recent Evidence on the Distribution Patterns in Chapter 11 Reorganizations," *Journal of Fixed Income* (Spring 1993), pp. 6–23.

[17] Fischer Black and Myron Scholes, "The Pricing of Options and Corporate Liabilities," *Journal of Political Economy* 81 (1973), pp. 637–54. Also, in the derivation of the pricing of risky debt, Robert Merton assumes that absolute priority holds; see Robert Merton, "The Pricing of Corporate Debt: The Risk Structure of Interest Rates," *Journal of Finance* 29 (1974), pp. 449–70.

recognition to the ability of management to preserve value on behalf of stockholders.[18] According to the **stockholders' influence on reorganization plan hypothesis**, creditors are less informed about the true economic operating conditions of the firm than is management. Because the distribution to creditors in the plan of reorganization is based on the valuation by the firm, creditors without perfect information suffer the loss.[19] According to Wruck, managers generally have a better understanding than creditors or stockholders about a firm's internal operations, while creditors and stockholders can have better information about industry trends. Management may therefore use its superior knowledge to present the data in a manner that reinforces its position.[20]

The essence of the **strategic bargaining process hypothesis** is that the increasing complexity of firms that declare bankruptcy accentuates the negotiating process and results in an even higher incidence of violation of the absolute priority rule. The likely outcome is further supported by the increased number of official committees in the reorganization process as well as the increased number of financial and legal advisors.

Some argue that creditors receive a higher value in reorganization than they would in liquidation, in part because of the costs associated with liquidation.[21] Finally, the lack of symmetry in the tax system (negative taxes are not permitted, although loss deductions may be carried forward) results in situations in which the only way to use all current loss deductions is to merge.[22] The tax system may encourage continuance or merger and discourage bankruptcy.

Consequently, while investors in the debt of a corporation may feel that they have priority over the equity owners and priority over other classes of debtors, the actual outcome of a bankruptcy may be far different from what the terms of the debt agreement state.

Fabozzi, Howe, Makabe, and Sudo examined the extent of violation of the absolute priority rule among three broad groups—secured creditors, unsecured creditors, and equity holders—and among various types of debt and equity securities. They also provided evidence on which asset class bears the cost of violations of absolute priority, and an initial estimate of total distributed value relative to liquidation value. Their findings suggest that unsecured creditors bear a disproportionate cost of reorganization, and that more senior unsecured creditors may bear a disproportionate cost relative to the junior unsecured creditors, while equity holders often benefit from violations of absolute priority.

◆ DEFAULT AND RECOVERY STATISTICS

A good deal of published research by both rating agencies and academicians deals with default rates.[23] From an investment perspective, default rates by themselves are not of paramount significance: It is perfectly possible for a portfolio of corporate bonds to suffer defaults and to outperform Treasuries at the same time, provided the yield spread of the portfolio is sufficiently high to offset the losses from default.

[18] Douglas G. Baird and Thomas H. Jackson, "Bargaining After the Fall and the Contours of the Absolute Priority Rule," *University of Chicago Law Review* 55 (1988), pp. 738–89.
[19] L. A. Bebchuk, "A New Approach to Corporate Reorganizations," *Harvard Law Review* 101 (1988), pp. 775–804.
[20] Karen Hooper Wruck, "Financial Distress, Reorganization, and Organizational Efficiency," *Journal of Financial Economics* 27 (1990), pp. 419–44.
[21] Michael C. Jensen, "Eclipse of the Public Corporation," *Harvard Business Review* 89 (1989), pp. 61–62; and Wruck, "Financial Distress, Reorganization, and Organizational Efficiency."
[22] J. I. Bulow and J. B. Shoven, "The Bankruptcy Decision," *Bell Journal of Economics* (1978). For a further discussion of the importance of net operating losses and the current tax law, see Fabozzi *et al.*, "Recent Evidence on the Distribution Patterns in Chapter 11 Reorganizations."
[23] See, for example, Edward I. Altman, "Measuring Corporate Bond Mortality and Performance," *Journal of Finance* (September 1989), pp. 909–22; Edward I. Altman, "Research Update: Mortality Rates and

Furthermore, because holders of defaulted bonds typically recover a percentage of the face amount of their investment, the **default loss rate** can be substantially lower than the default rate. The default loss rate is defined as follows:

$$\text{Default loss rate} = \text{Default rate} \times (100\% - \text{Recovery rate})$$

For instance, a default rate of 5% and a recovery rate of 30% means a default loss rate of only 3.5% (5% × 70%). Therefore, focusing exclusively on default rates merely highlights the worst possible outcome that a diversified portfolio of corporate bonds would suffer, assuming all defaulted bonds would be totally worthless.

First, let's look at what research reveals about the default rate experience of corporate bonds. We begin with a discussion of the experience for high-yield corporate bonds because what will be apparent are various ways to define default rates as clearly illustrated by these studies of high-yield corporate bonds.

In their 1987 study, Altman and Nammacher found that the annual default rate for low-rated corporate debt was 2.15%, a figure that Altman since updated to 2.40%. Drexel Burnham Lambert's (DBL) estimates also show default rates of about 2.40% per year. Asquith, Mullins, and Wolff, however, found that nearly one out of every three high-yield corporate bonds defaults. The large discrepancy arises because the researchers use three different definitions of "default rate"; even if applied to the same universe of bonds (which they are not), all three results could be valid simultaneously.[24]

Altman and Nammacher define the default rate as the par value of all high-yield bonds that defaulted in a given calendar year, divided by the total par value outstanding during the year. Their estimates (2.15% and 2.40%) are simple averages of the annual default rates over a number of years. DBL look the cumulative dollar value of all defaulted high-yield bonds, divided by the cumulative dollar value of all high-yield issuance, and further divided by the weighted average number of years outstanding to obtain an average annual default rate. Asquith, Mullins, and Wolff use a cumulative default statistic. For all bonds issued in a given year, the default rate is the total par value of defaulted issues as of the date of their study, divided by the total par amount originally issued to obtain a cumulative default rate. Their result (that about one in three high-yield bonds default) is not normalized by the number of years outstanding.

Although all three measures provide useful indicators of bond default propensity, they are not directly comparable. Even when restated on an annualized basis, they do not all measure the same quantity. The default statistics from all studies, however, are surprisingly similar once cumulative rates are annualized.

Losses, Bond Rating Drift," unpublished study prepared for a workshop sponsored by Merrill Lynch Merchant Banking Group, High Yield Sales and Trading (1989); Edward I. Altman and Scott A. Nammacher, *Investing in Junk Bonds* (New York: John Wiley, 1987); Paul Asquith, David W. Mullins, Jr., and Eric D. Wolff, "Original Issue High-Yield Bonds: Aging Analysis of Defaults, Exchanges, and Calls," *Journal of Finance* (September 1989), pp. 923–52; Marshall Blume and Donald Keim, "Risk and Return Characteristics of Lower-Grade Bonds 1977–1987," working paper (8-89), Rodney L. White Center for Financial Research, Wharton School, University of Pennsylvania (1989); Marshall Blume and Donald Keim, "Realized Returns and Defaults on Lower-Grade Bonds," Rodney L. White Center for Financial Research, Wharton School, University of Pennsylvania (1989); Bond Investors Association, "Bond Investors Association Issues Definitive Corporate Default Statistics," press release dated August 15, 1989; Gregory T. Hradsky and Robert D. Long, "High-Yield Default Losses and the Return Performance of Bankrupt Debt," *Financial Analysts Journal* (July/August 1989), pp. 38–49; "Historical Default Rates of Corporate Bond Issuers 1970–1988," *Moody's Special Report* (July 1989); "High-Yield Bond Default Rates, Standard & Poor's *Creditweek* (August 7, 1989), pp. 21–23; David Wyss, Christopher Probyn, and Robert de Angelis, "The Impact of Recession on High-Yield Bonds," (Washington, D.C.: Alliance for Capital Access, 1989); and the 1984–1989 issues of *High Yield Market Report: Financing America's Futures* (New York and Beverly Hills: Drexel Burnham Lambert, Inc.).

[24] As a parallel, we know that the mortality rate in the United States is currently less than 1% per year, but we also know that 100% of humans (eventually) die.

Altman and Kishore find that the arithmetic average default rate for the period 1971 to 1997 was 2.6% and the weighted average default rate (i.e., weighted by the par value of the amount outstanding for each year) was 3.3%. In contrast, the arithmetic average default rate for all corporate bonds (i.e., investment grade and high-yield issues) for the period 1971 to 1997 was 0.53% and the weighted average default rate was 0.66%.[25]

Next let's look at the historical recovery rates realized by investors in all corporate bonds as reported by Altman and Kishore. They find that for the period 1978 to 1997 the average recovery rate was $40.55 per $100 par value, or 40.55% of par value. Several studies confirm that the recovery rate is closely related to the bond's seniority. Altman and Kishore computed the weighted average recovery rate for 777 bond issues that defaulted between 1978 and 1997 for the following bond classes: (1) senior secured, (2) senior unsecured, (3) senior subordinated, (4) subordinated, and (5) discount and zero coupon. The recovery rate for senior-secured bonds averaged 59% of par value, compared with 49% for senior-unsecured, 35% for senior-subordinated, and 32% for subordinated bonds.[26]

Summary

Corporate bonds are debts obligating a corporation to pay periodic interest with full repayment at maturity. The promises of the corporate bond issuer and the rights of the investors are set forth in the bond indenture. Provisions to be specified include call and sinking fund provisions.

Security for bonds may be real or personal property. Debenture bonds are not secured by a specific pledge of property. Subordinated debenture bonds are issues that rank after secured debt, after debenture bonds, and often after some general creditors in their claim on assets and earnings.

Special corporate bond features include convertible and exchangeable bonds, units of debt with warrants, putable bonds, zero-coupon bonds, and floating-rate securities. Junk bonds or high-yield bonds are issues with quality ratings below triple B. The introduction of several complex bond structures in the junk bond area, particularly bonds issued for LBO financing and recapitalizations producing higher levels of debt to equity occurred in recent years. These bonds include deferred-coupon bonds (deferred-interest bonds, step-up bonds, and payment-in-kind bonds) and extendable reset bonds.

Many innovative bond structures introduced in the Eurobond market include dual-currency issues and various types of convertible bonds and bonds with warrants. A warrant permits its owner to enter into another financial transaction with the issuer if the owner will benefit as a result of exercising. The floating-rate sector of the Eurobond market is dominated by U.S. dollar-denominated issues.

Preferred stock is a class of stock with the characteristics of both common stock and debt. Because a special provision in the tax code allows taxation of only a portion of dividends when they are received by a corporation, the major buyers of preferred stock are corporations. Three types of preferred stock besides the traditional fixed-rate preferred stock include adjustable-rate preferred stock, auction preferred stock, and remarketed preferred stock.

[25] See Exhibits 1 and 5 in Edward I. Altman and Vellore M. Kishore, "Defaults and Returns on High-Yield Bonds," in Frank J. Fabozzi (ed.), *The Handbook of Corporate Debt Instruments* (New Hope, PA: Frank J. Fabozzi Associates, 1998), Chapter 14.
[26] See Exhibit 8 in Altman and Kishore, "Defaults and Returns on High-Yield Bonds."

The Bankruptcy Reform Act of 1978 governs the bankruptcy process in the United States. Chapter 7 of the bankruptcy act deals with the liquidation of a company. Chapter 11 deals with the reorganization of a company. Creditors receive distributions based on the absolute priority rule to the extent assets are available, meaning that senior creditors are paid in full before junior creditors are paid anything. Generally, this rule holds in the case of liquidations. In contrast, the absolute priority rule is typically violated in a reorganization.

Focusing on default rates on corporate bonds does not provide sufficient insight into the risks of investing in corporate bonds. An investor must look at both the default rate and the recovery rate. The default loss rate is defined as the product of the default rate and (1 – recovery rate). Several different methods can be used to compute default rates. Studies of recovery rates indicate that about 41% of par value is recovered and that recovery rates depend on seniority.

Key Terms

- Absolute priority rule
- Auction preferred stock (APS)
- Balloon maturity
- Bond indentures
- Bonds
- Bullet bonds
- Bullet-maturity bonds
- Call risk
- Capacity
- Character
- Collared
- Collateral
- Collateral trust bonds
- Convertible bond
- Covenants
- Cumulative preferred stock
- Debenture bond
- Default loss rate
- Deferred coupon structure
- Deferred-interest bonds

- Dividend reset spread
- Drop-lock bonds
- Dual-currency issues
- Equipment trust certificates
- Euro straights
- Event risk
- Exchangeable bond
- Fallen angels
- Guaranteed bond
- Holding companies
- Incentive hypothesis
- Involuntary bankruptcy
- Leveraged buyout (LBO)
- Lien
- Liquidation
- Material adverse change clause
- Mortgage bond
- Noncumulative preferred stock
- Notes
- Payment-in-kind (PIK) bonds

- Perpetual preferred stock
- Rating transition matrix
- Recontracting process hypothesis
- Refunding
- Remarketed preferred stock (RPS)
- Reorganization
- Rolling stock
- Serial bonds
- Sinking fund
- Step-up bonds
- Stockholders' influence on reorganization plan hypothesis
- Strategic bargaining process hypothesis
- Subordinated debenture bond
- Subsidiaries
- Term bonds
- Timing risk
- Voluntary bankruptcy
- Warrant

Questions

1. a. What are the disadvantages of investing in a callable bond?
    b. What is the advantage to the issuer of issuing a callable bond?
    c. What is the difference between a noncallable bond and a nonrefundable bond?
2. a. What is a sinking fund requirement in a bond issue?
    b. "A sinking fund provision in a bond issue benefits the investor." Do you agree with this statement?
3. What is a:
    a. Serial bond?
    b. Mortgage bond?
    c. Equipment trust certificate?
    d. Collateral bond?
4. What is the difference between a convertible bond and an exchangeable bond?

5. Explain why you agree or disagree with this statement: "Zero-coupon corporate bonds are created in the same way as in the Treasury market—by stripping coupon bonds."

6. a. What is event risk?
   b. Give two examples of event risk.

7. What is meant by a rating transition matrix?

8. What is the difference between a fallen angel and an original-issue, high-yield bond?

9. Indicate why you agree or disagree with the following statement: "Today, the proceeds from most original-issue, high-yield bonds are used for leveraged buyouts and recapitalizations."

10. a. What is a Eurobond?
    b. How often is the coupon payment on a Eurobond made?
    c. Name the two currencies most often used to denominate Eurobonds.

11. What is a dual-currency bond?

12. a. Explain what an institutional investor will do to purchase or sell a corporate bond.
    b. What has happened to the commitment of capital of dealer firms to the high-yield corporate bond market in recent years?

13. a. Why are corporate treasurers the main buyers of preferred stock?
    b. What was the reason for the popularity of auction and remarketed preferred stock?

14. a. What is the difference between a liquidation and a reorganization?
    b. What is the difference between a Chapter 7 and Chapter 11 bankruptcy filing?
    c. What is meant by a debtor-in-possession?

15. a. What is meant by the principle of absolute priority?
    b. Comment on this statement: "An investor who purchases the mortgage bonds of a corporation knows that, should the corporation become bankrupt, mortgage bondholders will be paid in full before the common stockholders receive any proceeds."

16. Give three reasons to explain why absolute priority might be violated in a reorganization.

17. Why is insight limited when focusing only on default rates?

18. If the default rate is 5% and the recovery rate is 60%, what is the default loss rate?

CHAPTER 24

Municipal Securities Markets

Learning Objectives

After reading this chapter you will understand:

◆ who buys municipal securities and why the securities are attractive investments to these buyers.

◆ the types of municipal securities and why they are issued.

◆ the risks unique to investment in municipal securities.

◆ the primary and secondary markets for municipal securities.

◆ the yield relationship between municipal securities and taxable bonds.

◆ the yield relationships among municipal securities within the municipal market.

◆ the degree of regulation of the municipal securities market.

In this chapter, we discuss municipal securities and the market in which they trade. Municipal securities are issued by state and local governments and by entities that they establish. All states issue municipal securities. Local governments include cities and counties. Political subdivisions of municipalities that issue securities include school districts and special districts for fire prevention, water, sewer, and other purposes. Public agencies or instrumentalities include authorities and commissions.

The attractiveness of municipal securities is due to their tax treatment at the federal income tax level. Most municipal securities are tax exempt, which means that interest on municipal bonds is exempt from federal income taxation. The exemption applies to interest income, not capital gains. The exemption may or may not extend to the state and local levels. Each state has its own rule as to how interest on municipal securities is taxed.[1] While most municipal bonds outstanding are tax exempt, some issues are taxable at the federal level.

Municipal securities are issued for various purposes. Short-term notes typically are sold in anticipation of the receipt of funds from taxes or proceeds from the sale of a bond issue, for example. The proceeds from the sale of short-term notes permit the issuing municipality to cover seasonal and temporary imbalances between outlays for expenditures and tax inflows. Municipalities issue long-term bonds as the principal means for financing both (1) long-term capital projects such as the construction of

---

[1] The tax treatment at the state level will be one of the following: (1) exemption on interest from all municipal securities, (2) taxation of interest from all municipal securities, (3) exemption of interest from municipal securities where the issuer is in the state but taxation of interest where the issuer is out of the state.

schools, bridges, roads, and airports, and (2) long-term budget deficits that arise from current operations.

The number of municipal bond issuers is remarkable. One broker/dealer's estimate places the total at 60,055. Also, Bloomberg Financial Markets' database contains 55,000 active issuers. Even more noteworthy is the number of different issues. Interactive Data, a company that provides pricing information for institutional investors, claims that it quotes daily prices for more than 1.2 million individual issues in its database. Bloomberg's database contains 1.7 million issues with complete description pages.

◆ TYPES AND FEATURES OF MUNICIPAL SECURITIES[2]

The two basic types of municipal security structures are tax-backed debt and revenue bonds. Other securities share characteristics of tax-backed debt and revenue bonds.

TAX-BACKED DEBT

Tax-backed debt obligations are instruments issued by states, counties, special districts, cities, towns, and school districts and secured by some form of tax revenue. Tax-backed debt includes general obligation debt, appropriation-backed obligations, and debt obligations supported by public credit enhancement programs.

General Obligation Debt   The broadest type of tax-backed debt is **general obligation debt**. The two types of general obligation pledges are unlimited and limited. An unlimited tax general obligation debt is the stronger form of general obligation pledge because it is secured by the issuer's unlimited taxing power. Tax revenue sources include corporate and individual income taxes, sales taxes, and property taxes. Unlimited tax general obligation debt is said to be secured by the full faith and credit of the issuer. A limited tax general obligation debt is a limited tax pledge because of a statutory limit on the tax rates the issuer may levy to service the debt.

Certain general obligation bonds are secured not only by the issuer's general taxing powers to create revenues accumulated in a general fund but also by certain identified fees, grants, and special charges, which provide additional revenues from outside the general fund. Such bonds are known as double-barreled in security because of the dual nature of the revenue sources. For example, the debt obligations issued by special purpose service systems may be secured by a pledge of property taxes, a pledge of special fees/operating revenue from the service provided, or a pledge of both property taxes and special fees/operating revenues. In the last case, they are double-barreled.

Appropriation-Backed Obligations   Agencies or authorities of several states issue bonds that carry a potential state liability for making up shortfalls in the issuing entity's obligation. The appropriation of funds from the state's general tax revenue must be approved by the state legislature. However, the state's pledge is not binding. Debt obligations with this nonbinding pledge of tax revenue are called **moral obligation bonds**. Because a moral obligation bond requires legislative approval to appropriate the funds, it is classified as an appropriation-backed obligation. The purpose of the moral obligation pledge is to enhance the creditworthiness of the issuing entity.

---

[2]   For a further discussion of these securities, see Frank J. Fabozzi, *Fixed Income Securities* (New Hope, PA: Frank J. Fabozzi Associates, 1998), Chapter 5.

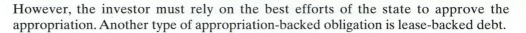

However, the investor must rely on the best efforts of the state to approve the appropriation. Another type of appropriation-backed obligation is lease-backed debt.

Debt Obligations Supported by Public Credit Enhancement Programs   Even though a moral obligation is a form of credit enhancement provided by a state, it is not a legally enforceable or legally binding obligation of the state. Some entities issue debt that carries some form of public credit enhancement that is legally enforceable. This type of enhancement occurs when the state or a federal agency guarantees or takes on an obligation to automatically withhold and deploy state aid to pay any defaulted debt service by the issuing entity. Typically, the latter form of public credit enhancement is used for debt obligations of a state's school systems.

Some examples of state credit enhancement programs include Virginia's bond guarantee program that authorizes the government to withhold state aid payments to a municipality and divert those funds to pay principal and interest to a municipality's general obligation holders in the event of a default. South Carolina's constitution requires mandatory withholding of state aid by the state treasurer if a school district is not capable of meeting its general obligation debt. Texas created the Permanent School Fund to guarantee the timely payment of principal and interest of the debt obligations of qualified school districts. The fund's income is obtained from land and mineral rights owned by the state of Texas.

REVENUE BONDS

The second basic type of security structure is found in a revenue bond. Such bonds are issued for either project or enterprise financings where the bond issuers pledge to the bondholders the revenues generated by the operating projects financed. A feasibility study is performed before the endeavor is undertaken to determine whether it will be self-supporting.

Examples of revenue bonds include airport revenue bonds, college and university revenue bonds, hospital revenue bonds, single-family mortgage revenue bonds, multi-family revenue bonds, public power revenue bonds, resource recovery revenue bonds, seaport revenue bonds, sports complex and convention center revenue bonds, student loan revenue bonds, toll road and gas tax revenue bonds, and water revenue bonds.

HYBRID AND SPECIAL BOND STRUCTURES

Some municipal securities create special security structures that share characteristics of tax-backed debt and revenue bonds. They include insured bonds, prefunded bonds, and structured/asset-based bonds.

Insured Bonds   Insured bonds, in addition to being secured by the issuer's revenue, are also backed by insurance policies written by commercial insurance companies. Insurance on a municipal bond is an agreement by an insurance company to pay the bondholder any bond principal and/or coupon interest due on a stated maturity date that is not paid by the bond issuer. Once issued, this municipal bond insurance usually extends for the term of the bond issue, and it cannot be canceled by the insurance company.

Prefunded Bonds   Although originally issued as either revenue or general obligation bonds, municipals are sometimes prefunded and called prefunded municipal bonds. (They are also called *refunded bonds.*) A prefunding usually occurs when the original bonds are escrowed or collateralized by direct obligations guaranteed by the U.S. government.[3] A portfolio of securities guaranteed by the U.S. government is placed in a trust. The portfolio is assembled such that the cash flows from the securities match the obligations that the issuer must pay. For example, suppose that a municipality has a 7% $100 million issue with 12 years remaining to maturity. The municipality's obligation is to make payments of $3.5 million every 6 months for the next 12 years and $100 million 12 years from now. If the issuer wants to prerefund this issue, it purchases a portfolio of U.S. government obligations with cash flows of $3.5 million every 6 months for the next 12 years and $100 million 12 years from now.

Once this portfolio of securities whose cash flows match those of the municipality's obligation is in place, the prerefunded bonds are no longer secured as either general obligation or revenue bonds. The bonds are now supported by cash flows from the portfolio or securities held in an escrow fund. Such bonds, if escrowed with securities guaranteed by the U.S. government, have little, if any, credit risk. They are the safest municipal bonds available.

The escrow fund for a prerefunded municipal bond can be structured so that the bonds to be refunded are to be called at the first possible call date or a subsequent call date established in the original bond indenture. Although prerefunded bonds are usually retired at their first or subsequent call date, some are structured to match the debt obligation to the maturity date. Such bonds are known as **escrowed-to-maturity bonds**.

Asset-Backed Bonds   In recent years, states and local governments began issuing bonds where the debt service is to be paid from so-called "dedicated" revenues such as sales taxes, tobacco settlement payments, fees, and penalty payments. These structures mimic the asset-backed bonds that are discussed in Chapter 27. Asset-backed bonds are also referred to as *dedicated revenue bonds* and *structured bonds*.

MUNICIPAL NOTES

Municipal securities issued for periods up to three years are considered to be short term in nature. These include **tax anticipation notes (TANs)**, **revenue anticipation notes (RANs)**, **grant anticipation notes (GANs)**, and **bond anticipation notes (BANs)**.

TANs, RANs, GANs, and BANs are temporary borrowings by states, local governments, and special jurisdictions. Usually, notes are issued for a period of 12 months, although it is not uncommon for notes to be issued for periods as short as 3 months or as long as 3 years. TANs and RANs (also known as TRANs) are issued in anticipation of the collection of taxes or other expected revenues. The purpose of these borrowings is to even out irregular flows into the treasuries of the issuing entity. BANs are issued in anticipation of the sale of long-term bonds.

REDEMPTION FEATURES

Municipal bonds are issued with one of two debt retirement structures or a combination of both. Either a bond has a serial maturity structure or a term maturity structure. A **serial maturity structure** requires a portion of the debt obligation to be retired each year. A **term maturity structure** provides for the debt obligation to be repaid at the end of the bond's planned life. Usually, term bond maturities range from 20 to 40 years.

---

[3]   Because the interest rate that a municipality must pay on borrowed funds is less than the interest rate paid by the U.S. government, in the absence of any restrictions in the tax code, a municipal issuer can realize a tax arbitrage by issuing a bond and immediately investing the proceeds in a U.S. government security. Tax rules may prevent such arbitrage in some cases. Should a municipal issuer violate the tax arbitrage rules, the issue will be ruled to be taxable. If subsequent to the issuance of a bond, however, interest rates decline so that the issuer will find it advantageous to call the bond, the establishment of the escrow fund will not violate the tax arbitrage rules.

With such bonds sinking fund provisions often call for partial and systematic retirement of the debt on a set schedule that begins 5 or 10 years before the time of maturity. Another provision that permits the early redemption of a term bond is the call privilege, which allows the issuer, under certain and well-specified circumstances, to pay off the debt prior to the scheduled maturity. Sinking fund and call provisions are noted features of corporate debt, discussed in Chapter 23.

◆ MUNICIPAL BOND RATINGS

Although municipal bonds have long been considered second in safety only to U.S. Treasury securities, today new concerns surround the credit risks of many municipal bonds.[4]

The first concern came out of the New York City billion-dollar financial crisis in 1975. On February 25, 1975, the state of New York's Urban Development Corporation defaulted on a $100 million note issue that was the obligation of New York City. Many market participants were convinced that the state of New York would not allow the issue to default. Although New York City was able later to obtain a $140 million revolving credit from banks to cure the default, lenders became concerned that the city would face difficulties in repaying its accumulated debt, which stood at $14 billion on March 31, 1975.[5] This financial crisis sent a loud and clear warning to market participants: Despite supposedly ironclad protection for the bondholder, when issuers such as large cities have severe financial difficulties, the financial stakes of public employee unions, vendors, and community groups may be dominant forces in balancing budgets. This reality was reinforced by the federal bankruptcy law taking effect in October 1979, which makes it easier for the issuer of a municipal security to go into bankruptcy.

The second reason for concern about the credit risk of municipal securities is the proliferation in this market of innovative financing techniques to secure new bond issues. In addition to the established general obligation bonds and revenue bonds, new and more innovative, and legally untested, security mechanisms do not require voters' approval. What distinguishes these newer bonds from the more traditional general obligation and revenue bonds is that they lack any history of court decisions or other case law that firmly establishes the rights of the bondholders and the obligations of the issuers. It is not possible to determine in advance the probable legal outcome if the newer financing mechanisms were to be challenged in court. The importance of this uncertainty is illustrated most dramatically by the bonds of the Washington Public Power Supply System (WPPSS) where bondholder rights to certain revenues were not upheld by the highest court in the state of Washington.

More recently, municipal bond investors grew increasingly concerned with those who manage the investment funds of municipalities as a result of the collapse of the Orange County (California) Investment Pool, which lost $1.7 billion due to a poorly conceived investment strategy by Robert L. Citron, the county treasurer. Citron followed a strategy that resulted in a leveraged position in securities that benefited if interest rates declined. Basically, he used the repurchase agreement, but instead of

---

4   For a history of defaults of municipal bonds, see Sylvan G. Feldstein and Frank J. Fabozzi, *The Dow Jones-Irwin Guide to Municipal Bonds* (Homewood, IL: Dow Jones-Irwin, 1987), Chapter 2.

5   Securities and Exchange Commissions Staff Report on *Transactions in Securities of the City of New York* (Washington, DC: U.S. Government Printing Office, 1977), p. 2. The reasons for the New York City financial crisis are documented in Donna E. Shalala and Carol Bellamy, "A State Saves a City: The New York Case," *Duke Law Journal* (January 1976), pp. 1119–26.

using it as a short-term investment vehicle, he used it to create leverage via a reverse repurchase agreement. The loss resulting from this strategy, as well as investments in instructured notes, resulted in the bankruptcy of Orange County. To date, it is the largest municipal failure in U.S. history.[6]

Many institutional investors in the municipal bond market rely on their own in-house municipal credit analysts for determining the creditworthiness of a municipal issue; other investors rely on the three nationally recognized rating companies. The assigned rating system is the same as that used for corporate bonds that we discussed in Chapter 23.

To evaluate general obligation bonds, the commercial rating companies assess information in four basic categories. The first category includes information on the issuer's debt structure and overall debt burden. The second category relates to the issuer's ability and political discipline to maintain sound budgetary policy. The focus of attention here usually is on the issuer's general operating funds and whether it has maintained balanced budgets over 3 to 5 years. The third category involves determining the specific local taxes and intergovernmental revenues available to the issuer, as well as obtaining historical information both on tax collection rates, which are important when looking at property tax levies, and the dependence of local budgets on specific revenue sources. The fourth and last category of information necessary to the credit analysis is an assessment of the issuer's overall socioeconomic environment. The determinations to be made here include trends of local employment distribution and composition, population growth, real estate property valuation, and personal income, among other economic factors.

Although numerous security structures can be used for revenue bonds, the underlying principle in rating is whether the project being financed will generate sufficient cash flow to satisfy the obligation due bondholders.

◆ TAX RISKS ASSOCIATED WITH INVESTING IN MUNICIPAL SECURITIES

Tax-exempt municipal securities buyers are exposed to two types of tax risk. The first is the risk that the federal income tax rate will be reduced. The higher the marginal tax rate is, the more valuable the tax-exemption feature will be. As the marginal tax rate declines, so does the price of a tax-exempt municipal security. Proposals to reduce the marginal tax rate result in less demand for municipal securities and, as a result, a decline in their price. This drop in demand occurred most recently in 1995 when proposals of a flat tax in which the tax rate would be less than the prevailing rate were being debated.

The second type of tax risk is that a municipal bond issued as a tax-exempt issue may eventually be declared by the Internal Revenue Service to be taxable. Many municipal revenue bonds have elaborate security structures that could be subject to future adverse Congressional action and IRS interpretation. A loss of the tax-exemption feature will cause the municipal bond to decline in value in order to provide a yield comparable to similar taxable bonds. An example of this risk is the following situation: In June 1980, the Battery Park City Authority sold $97.315 million in notes, which at the time of issuance seemed to be exempt from federal income taxation. In November 1980, however, the IRS held that interest on these notes was not exempt. The legal question was not settled until September 1981, when the authority and the IRS signed a formal agreement resolving the matter so as to make the interest on the notes tax-exempt.

---

[6] For an excellent account of the Orange County bankruptcy, see Philipe Jorian, *Big Bets Gone Bad* (New York: Academic Press, 1995).

◆ THE PRIMARY MARKET

A substantial number of municipal obligations are brought to market each week. A state or local government can market its new issue by offering bonds publicly to the investing community or by placing them privately with a small group of investors. When a public offering is selected, the issue usually is underwritten by investment bankers and/or municipal bond departments of commercial banks. Public offerings may be marketed by either competitive bidding or direct negotiations with underwriters. In a competitive process, the bidder submitting the highest bid price for the security gets the right to market the debt to investors.[7]

Most states mandate that general obligation issues be marketed through competitive bidding, but generally it is not necessary for revenue bonds. Usually, state and local governments require a competitive sale to be announced in a recognized financial publication, such as *The Bond Buyer*, which is a trade publication for the municipal bond industry. *The Bond Buyer* also provides information on upcoming competitive sales and most negotiated sales, as well as the results of previous weeks. However the debt is marketed, the municipal unit prepares an **official statement** describing its financial situation and the terms of the issue. These terms include the call and sinking fund provisions.

◆ THE SECONDARY MARKET

Municipal bonds are traded in the over-the-counter market supported by municipal bond dealers across the country. Markets for the debts of smaller issuers (referred to as **local credits**) are maintained by regional brokerage firms, local banks, and by some of the larger Wall Street firms. Markets for the bonds of larger issuers (referred to as **general names**) are supported by the larger brokerage firms and banks, many of whom have investment banking relationships with these issuers. Some brokers serve as intermediaries in the sale of large blocks of municipal bonds among dealers and large institutional investors. Beginning in 2000, bonds in the secondary market as well as some new issue competitive and negotiated issues began to be auctioned and sold over the Internet by large and small broker/dealers to institutional and individual investors.

In the municipal bond market, an odd lot of bonds is $25,000 or less in par value for retail investors. For institutions, anything below $100,000 in par value is considered an odd lot. Dealer spreads depend on several factors. For the retail investor, the spread can range from as low as one-quarter of one point ($12.50 per $5,000 par value) on large blocks of actively traded bonds to four points ($200 per $5,000 of par value) for odd-lot sales of an inactive issue. For institutional investors, the dealer spread rarely exceeds one-half of one point ($25 per $5,000 of par value).

The convention for both corporate and Treasury bonds is to quote prices as a percentage of par value with 100 equal to par. Municipal bonds, however, generally are traded and quoted in terms of yield (yield to maturity or yield to call). The price of the bond in this case is called a basis price. The exception is certain long-maturity revenue bonds. A bond traded and quoted in dollar prices (actually, as a percentage of par value) is called a dollar bond.

Actual price and trade information for specific municipal bonds is available on a daily basis at no charge at www.investinginbonds.com. It is the homepage of the Bond

---

[7] See Chapter 16 for more information about underwriting.

Market Association. The trade information provided is from the Municipal Securities Rulemaking Board and Standard & Poor's J. J. Kenny. The original source of the trades reported are transactions between dealer to dealer and dealer to institutional customer and retail (individual investor).

◆ YIELDS ON MUNICIPAL BONDS

Because of the tax-exempt feature of municipal bonds, the yield on municipal bonds is less than that on Treasuries with the same maturity. Table 24-1 shows this relationship on August 16, 1999, for AAA-rated general obligation bonds. The difference in yield between tax-exempt securities and Treasury securities is typically measured not in basis points but in percentage terms. More specifically, it is measured as the percentage of the yield on a money security relative to a comparable Treasury security, as reported in Table 24-1.

The yield ratio changes over time. The higher the tax rate is, the more attractive the tax-exempt feature and the lower the yield ratio. The yield ratio for 10-year AAA general obligation bonds and 10-year Treasury securities varied in the 1990s from a low of 0.72 on September 30, 1994, to a high of 0.94 on September 30, 1998.

In the municipal bond market, several benchmark curves exist. In general, a benchmark yield curve is constructed for AAA-rated state general obligation.

In the Treasury and corporate bond markets, it is not unusual to find at different times shapes for the yield curve described in Chapter 19. In general, the municipal yield curve is positively sloped. For a brief period, the municipal yield curve became inverted. In fact, during the period when the Treasury yield curve was inverted, the municipal yield curve maintained its upward-sloping shape. Prior to 1986 the municipal yield curve was consistently steeper than the Treasury yield curve as measured by the spread between the 30-year and 1-year issues. Between 1986 and 1990, the steepness was comparable. In 1991, the municipal yield curve because steeper than the Treasury yield curve.

TABLE 24-1	Yield Ratio for AAA General Obligation Municipal Bonds to U.S. Treasuries on the Same Maturity on August 16, 1999		
Maturity	*Yield on AAA General Obligation*	*Yield on U.S. Treasury*	*Yield Ratio*
3 months	3.29%	4.93%	0.67
6 months	3.43	5.21	0.66
1 year	3.56	5.55	0.64
2 years	4.03	5.78	0.70
3 years	4.23	5.84	0.72
4 years	4.37	6.00	0.73
5 years	4.46	5.87	0.76
7 years	4.66	6.20	0.75
10 years	4.95	5.99	0.83
15 years	5.33	6.39	0.83
20 years	5.50	6.47	0.85
30 years	5.55	6.26	0.89

Source: Bloomberg Financial Markets.

◆ REGULATION OF THE MUNICIPAL SECURITIES MARKET[8]

Congress specifically exempted municipal securities from both the registration requirements of the Securities Act of 1933 and the periodic reporting requirements of the Securities Exchange Act of 1934. Antifraud provisions apply nevertheless to offerings of, or dealings in, municipal securities.

The reasons for the exemption afforded municipal securities appear to relate to (1) a desire for harmonious and cooperative relations among the various levels of government in the United States; (2) the absence of recurrent abuses in transactions involving municipal securities; (3) the greater level of sophistication of investors in this segment of the securities markets (the market was long dominated by institutional investors); and (4) the occurrence of few defaults by municipal issuers. Consequently, between the enactment of federal securities acts in the early 1930s and the early 1970s, the municipal securities market was relatively free from federal regulation.

In the early 1970s, however, circumstances changed. As incomes rose, individual investors began to participate in the municipal securities market to a much greater extent, and public concern over selling practices was expressed with greater frequency. Moreover, the financial problems of some municipal issuers, notably New York City, made market participants aware of the potential for municipal issuers to experience severe financial difficulties approaching bankruptcy levels.

Congress passed the Securities Act Amendment of 1975 to broaden federal regulation in the market for municipal debt. This legislation brought brokers/dealers in the municipal securities market, including banks that underwrite and trade municipal securities, under the regulatory umbrella of the Securities Exchange Act of 1934. The legislation mandated also that the SEC establish a 15-member Municipal Securities Rulemaking Board (MSRB) as an independent, self-regulatory agency whose primary responsibility is to develop rules governing the activities of banks, brokers, and dealers in municipal securities. Rules adopted by the MSRB must be approved by the SEC. The MSRB has no enforcement or inspection authority. That authority is vested with the SEC, the National Association of Securities Dealers, and certain regulatory banking agencies such as the Federal Reserve Bank.

The Securities Act Amendment of 1975 does not require municipal issuers to comply with the registration requirements of the 1933 Act or the periodic reporting requirement of the 1934 Act, despite several legislative proposals to mandate such financial disclosure. Even in the absence of federal legislation dealing with the regulation of financial disclosure, however, underwriters began insisting upon greater disclosure as it became apparent that the SEC was exercising stricter application of the antifraud provisions. Moreover, underwriters recognized the need for improved disclosure to sell municipal securities to an investing public that had become much more concerned about the credit risk of municipal issuers.

On June 28, 1989, the SEC formally approved the first bond disclosure rule, effective January 1, 1990. Although the disclosure rule contains several exemptions, in general it applies to new issue municipal securities offerings of $1 million or more.

---

[8] Parts of this section are drawn from Thomas F. Mitchell, "Disclosure and the Municipal Bond Industry," Chapter 40, and Nancy H. Wojtas, "The SEC and Investor Safeguards," Chapter 42 in Frank J. Fabozzi, Sylvan G. Feldstein, Irving M. Pollack, and Frank Zarb (eds.), *The Municipal Bond Handbook: Volume I* (Homewood, IL: Dow Jones-Irwin, 1983).

Summary

Municipal securities are issued by state and local governments and their authorities, with the interest on most issues exempt from federal income taxes. The primary investors in these securities are households (which includes mutual funds), commercial banks, and property and casualty insurance companies.

Both tax-exempt and taxable municipal securities are available. "Tax-exempt" means that interest on a municipal security is exempt from federal income taxation; most municipal securities issued are tax-exempt.

The two basic types of municipal security structures are tax-backed debt and revenue bonds. Tax-backed debt obligations are instruments issued by states, counties, special districts, cities, towns, and school districts that are secured by some form of tax revenue. Tax-backed debt includes general obligation debt (the broadest type of tax backed debt), appropriation-backed obligations, and debt obligations supported by public credit enhancement programs. A general obligation bond is said to be double-barreled when it is secured not only by the issuer's general taxing powers to create revenues accumulated in a general fund but also by certain identified fees, grants, and special charges, which provide additional revenues from outside the general fund. Revenue bonds are issued for enterprise financings secured by the revenues generated by the completed projects themselves, or for general public-purpose financings in which the issuers pledge to the bondholders the tax and revenue resources that were previously part of the general fund.

Insured bonds, in addition to being secured by the issuer's revenue, are backed by insurance policies written by commercial insurance companies. Prerefunded bonds are no longer secured as either general obligation or revenue bonds but are supported by a portfolio of securities held in an escrow fund. If escrowed with securities guaranteed by the U.S. government, refunded bonds are the safest municipal bonds available. A prerefunded municipal bond is one in which the escrow fund is structured so that the bonds are to be called at the first possible call date or a subsequent call date established in the original bond indenture. Municipal securities structured as asset-backed securities are backed by "dedicated" revenues such as sales taxes, tobacco settlement payments, fees, and penalty payments.

Municipal notes are issued for shorter periods (1 to 3 years) than municipal bonds. Municipal bonds may be retired with a serial maturity structure, a term maturity structure, or a combination of both. Investing in municipal securities exposes investors to credit risk and tax risk.

Key Terms

- Bond anticipation notes (BANs)
- Escrowed-to-maturity bonds
- General names
- General obligation debt
- Grant anticipation notes (GANs)
- Local credits
- Moral obligation bonds
- Official statement
- Prerefunded municipal bonds
- Refunded bonds
- Revenue anticipation notes (RANs)
- Serial maturity structure
- Tax anticipation notes (TANs)
- Tax-backed debt obligation
- Term maturity structure

Questions

1. Explain why you agree or disagree with the following statement: "All municipal bonds are exempt from federal income taxes."
2. a. Who are the three major investors in municipal securities?

  b. What aspect of their situation and what feature of these bonds attract these investors to this market?
 3. If it is expected that Congress will change the tax law so as to increase marginal tax rates, what do you think will happen to the price of municipal bonds?
 4. What is the major difference between a tax-backed debt and a revenue bond?
 5. What is the difference between a limited and unlimited general obligation bond?
 6. a. Why are more municipal bonds insured today than in 1970?
    b. In your view, would the typical AAA-rated municipal bond be insured?
 7. "A moral obligation bond is a form of a limited general obligation bond." Explain why you agree or disagree with this statement.
 8. a. What is a prefunded bond?
    b. Identify two reasons why an issuing municipality would want to prefund an outstanding bond.
 9. Why does a properly structured prefunded municipal bond have no credit risk?
10. In recent years, municipalities have begun to issue asset-backed securities. What are the revenues of these securities backed by?
11. For years, observers and analysts of the debt market believed that municipal securities were free of any risk of default. Why do most people now believe that municipal debt can carry a substantial amount of credit or default risk?
12. Because many people know that interest payments on municipal debt generally are exempt from taxation by the federal government, they would undoubtedly be surprised by the term tax risk investing in municipal bonds. Can you explain this term, and state why an astute investor should always be aware of this risk when buying municipal bonds?
13. How does the shape of the Treasury yield curve compare to that of the municipal yield curve?
14. Why isn't the Treasury yield curve used as a benchmark in measuring yield spreads between different sectors of the municipal bond market?

CHAPTER 25

The Mortgage Market

Learning Objectives

After reading this chapter you will understand:

◆ what a mortgage is.

◆ the difference between a residential mortgage loan and a commercial mortgage loan.

◆ who the major originators of residential mortgages are.

◆ the mortgage origination process.

◆ the borrower and property characteristics considered by a lender in evaluating the credit risk of an applicant for a mortgage loan.

◆ the risks associated with the origination process for residential mortgage loans.

◆ what the servicing of a residential mortgage loan involves.

◆ the fixed-rate, level-payment, fully amortized mortgage instrument (for traditional mortgage), and its cash flow characteristics.

◆ what a prepayment is.

◆ what a prepayment penalty mortgage is.

◆ deficiencies of the traditional mortgage: mismatch and tilt problems.

◆ alternative mortgage instruments, their cash flow characteristics, and how they correct for the deficiencies of the traditional mortgage instrument.

◆ risks associated with investing in mortgages.

◆ the significance of prepayment risk.

◆ the features of a commercial mortgage loan and provisions for protecting the lender against prepayment risk.

◆ the measures used to assess the credit risk of a commercial mortgage loan.

The mortgage market is a collection of markets that includes a primary (or origination) market and a secondary market where mortgages trade. We look in this chapter at the market participants (mortgage originators and investors) and the risks they face. We also review the various types of mortgage instruments. We discuss the development of the current secondary mortgage market in the next chapter, when we explain the securitization of mortgage loans. We postpone the discussion because development of the secondary market is tied to development of the market for instruments backed by mortgage loans (that is, mortgage-backed securities).

◆ WHAT IS A MORTGAGE?

By definition, a mortgage is a pledge of property to secure payment of a debt. Typically, property refers to real estate, which is often in the form of a house; the debt is the loan given to the buyer of the house by a lender. Thus, a mortgage might be a pledge of a house to secure payment of a loan. If a homeowner (the **mortgagor**) fails to pay the lender (the **mortgagee**), the lender has the right to foreclose the loan and seize the property in order to ensure that it is repaid.

When the loan is based solely on the credit of the borrower and on the collateral for the mortgage, the mortgage is said to be a **conventional mortgage**. The lender also may take out mortgage insurance to provide a guarantee for the fulfillment of the borrower's obligations. Three forms of mortgage insurance are guaranteed by the U.S. government if the borrower can qualify: Federal Housing Administration (FHA), Veterans Administration (VA), and Rural Housing Service (RHS) insurance. Private mortgage insurers include Mortgage Guaranty Insurance Company, and PMI Mortgage Insurance Company (owned by Sears, Roebuck). The cost of mortgage insurance is paid to the guarantor by the mortgage originator but passed along to the borrower in the form of higher mortgage payments.

The types of real estate properties that can be mortgaged are divided into two broad categories: single-family (one- to four-family) residential and commercial properties. The former category includes houses, condominiums, cooperatives, and apartments. Commercial properties are income-producing properties: multifamily properties (i.e., apartment buildings), office buildings, industrial properties (including warehouses), shopping centers, hotels, and health-care facilities (e.g., senior housing care facilities).

Our primary focus in this chapter is on mortgage loans for residential property. At the end of this chapter we discuss commercial mortgage loans.

◆ MORTGAGE ORIGINATION

The original lender is called the **mortgage originator**. The principal originators of residential mortgage loans are thrifts, commercial banks, and mortgage bankers. Other private mortgage originators are life insurance companies and, to a much lesser extent, pension funds.

Mortgage originators may generate income from mortgage activity in one or more ways. First, they typically charge an **origination fee**. This fee is expressed in terms of points, where each point represents 1% of the borrowed funds. For example, an origination fee of two points on a $100,000 mortgage loan is $2,000. Originators also may charge application fees and certain processing fees. The second source of revenue is the profit that might be generated from selling a mortgage at a higher price than it originally cost. This profit is called **secondary market profit**. If mortgage rates rise, an originator realizes a loss when the mortgages are sold in the secondary market.

Although technically the sources of revenue attributable to the origination function are origination fees and secondary marketing profits, two other potential sources may provide revenues. First, mortgage originators may service the mortgages they originate, for which they obtain a **servicing fee**. Servicing of the mortgage involves collecting monthly payments from mortgagors and forwarding proceeds to owners of the loan, sending payment notices to mortgagors, reminding mortgagors when payments are overdue, maintaining records of mortgage balances, furnishing tax information to mortgagors, administering an escrow account for real estate taxes and insurance purposes, and, if necessary, initiating foreclosure proceedings. The servicing fee is a fixed percentage of the outstanding mortgage balance, typically 50 basis points to 100 basis points per year. The mortgage originator may sell the servicing of the mortgage to another party who would then receive the servicing fee. Second, the mortgage originator may hold the mortgage in its investment portfolio.

Historically, regulatory and tax considerations encouraged thrifts to invest in mortgages, and, until quite recently, they tried to keep mortgages in their portfolios. However, both because of mismatching maturities (their liabilities being short term and mortgage loans being long term), and because of reduced tax benefits resulting from the 1986 tax act, banks and thrifts tend to sell a good portion of what they originate and to become increasingly dependent on the fees generated from originating and servicing mortgages.

Mortgage banking refers to the activity of originating mortgages. As already explained, banks and thrifts undertake mortgage banking. However, companies not associated with a bank or thrift are also involved in mortgage banking. These mortgage bankers, unlike banks and thrifts, typically do not invest in the mortgages that they originate. Instead, they derive their income from the origination fees. Commercial banks derive their income from all three sources, but no regulatory benefits accrue to them from investing in mortgages or mortgage-backed securities.

THE MORTGAGE ORIGINATION PROCESS

Someone who wants to borrow funds to purchase a home applies for a loan from a mortgage originator. The potential homeowner completes an application form, which provides financial information about the applicant, and pays an application fee; then the mortgage originator performs a credit evaluation of the applicant. The two primary factors in determining whether the funds will be loaned are the (1) **payment-to-income (PTI) ratio**, and (2) the **loan-to-value (LTV) ratio**. The first is the ratio of monthly payments to monthly income, which measures the ability of the applicant to make monthly payments (both mortgage and real estate tax payments). The lower this ratio is, the greater the likelihood is that the applicant will be able to meet the required payments.

The difference between the purchase price of the property and the amount borrowed is the borrower's down payment. The LTV is the ratio of the amount of the loan to the market (or appraised) value of the property. The lower this ratio is, the greater the protection for the lender is if the applicant defaults on the payments and the lender must repossess and sell the property. For example, if an applicant wants to borrow $150,000 on property with an appraised value of $200,000, the LTV is 75%. Suppose the applicant subsequently defaults on the mortgage. The lender can then repossess the property and sell it to recover the amount owed. But the amount that will be received by the lender depends on the market value of the property. In our example, even if conditions in the housing market are weak, the lender will still be able to recover the proceeds loaned, if the value of the property declines by $50,000. Suppose, instead, that the applicant wanted to borrow $180,000 for the same property. The LTV would then be 90%. If the lender had to sell the property because the applicant defaults, the LTV offers less protection for the lender.

If the lender decides to lend the funds, it sends a **commitment letter** to the applicant. This letter commits the lender to provide funds to the applicant. The length of time of the commitment varies between 30 and 60 days. At the time of the commitment letter, the lender will require that the applicant pay a commitment fee. It is important to understand that the commitment letter obligates the lender—not the applicant—to perform. The commitment fee that the applicant pays is lost if the applicant decides not to purchase the property or uses an alternative source of funds to purchase the property. Thus, the commitment letter states that, for a fee, the applicant has the right but not the obligation to require the lender to provide funds at a certain interest rate and on certain terms.

At the time the application is submitted, the mortgage originator will give the applicant a choice among various types of mortgages. Basically, the choice is between a **fixed-rate mortgage** or an **adjustable-rate mortgage (ARM)**. In the case of a fixed-rate mortgage, the lender typically gives the applicant a choice as to when the interest rate on the mortgage will be determined. The three choices may be: (1) at the time the loan application is submitted; (2) at the time a commitment letter is issued to the borrower; or (3) at the closing date (the date that the property is purchased). These choices granted the applicant—the right to decide whether to close on the property and the right to select when to set the interest rate—expose the mortgage originator to certain risks, against which the originator will protect itself.

Mortgage originators can either (1) hold the mortgage in their portfolio; (2) sell the mortgage to an investor that wishes to hold the mortgage in its portfolio or that will place the mortgage in a pool of mortgages to be used as collateral for the issuance of a security; or (3) use the mortgage themselves as collateral for the issuance of a security. When a mortgage is used as collateral for the issuance of a security, the mortgage is said to be **securitized**. We discuss the process of securitizing loans in Chapter 4. In the next chapter, we will discuss the securitization of mortgage loans.

When a mortgage originator intends to sell the mortgage, it will obtain a commitment from the potential investor (buyer). Two federally sponsored agencies and several private companies buy mortgages. These agencies and private companies pool these mortgages and sell them to investors and therefore are called **conduits**.

Two agencies, the Federal Home Loan Mortgage Corporation and the Federal National Mortgage Association, purchase only **conforming mortgages**—that is, a mortgage loan that meets the agency underwriting standards to be included in a pool of mortgages underlying a security that they guarantee. Three underwriting standards established by these agencies in order to qualify as a conforming mortgage are (1) a maximum PTI; (2) a maximum LTV; and (3) a maximum loan amount. If an applicant does not satisfy the underwriting standards, the mortgage is called a **nonconforming mortgage**.[1] The mortgages acquired by the agency may be held as a portfolio investment or securitized.

Examples of private conduits are Residential Funding Corporation, GE Capital Mortgage Services, Countrywide, and Prudential Home Mortgage. Both conforming and nonconforming mortgages are purchased.

Nonconforming mortgages do not necessarily have greater credit risk. For example, an individual with an annual income of $500,000 may apply for a mortgage loan of $200,000 on real estate that she wants to purchase for $1 million. This mortgage would be nonconforming because the amount of the mortgage exceeds the limit currently established for a conforming mortgage, yet the individual's income can easily accommodate the monthly mortgage payments. Moreover, the lender's risk exposure is minimal in loaning $200,000 against collateral of $1 million.

The mortgage rate that the originator sets on the loan depends on the mortgage rate required by the investor who plans to purchase the mortgage. At any time, different mortgage rates apply to delivery at different future times (30 days, 60 days, or 90 days).

---

[1] Loans that exceed the maximum loan amount and therefore do not qualify as conforming mortgages are called *jumbo loans.*

THE RISKS ASSOCIATED WITH MORTGAGE ORIGINATION

The loan applications being processed and the commitments made by a mortgage originator together are called its **pipeline**. **Pipeline risk** refers to the risks associated with originating mortgages. This risk has two components: price risk and fallout risk.

Price risk refers to the adverse effects on the value of the pipeline if mortgage rates rise. If mortgage rates rise, and the mortgage originator has made commitments at a lower mortgage rate, it either must sell the mortgages when they close at a value below the funds loaned to homeowners, or retain the mortgages as a portfolio investment earning a below-market mortgage rate. The mortgage originator faces the same risk for mortgage applications in the pipeline where the applicant elected to fix the rate at the time the application is submitted.

Fallout risk is the risk that applicants or those who were issued commitment letters will not close (complete the transaction by purchasing the property with funds borrowed from the mortgage originator). The chief reason that potential borrowers may cancel their commitment or withdraw their mortgage application is that mortgage rates decline sufficiently and make it economical to seek an alternative source of funds. Fallout risk is the result of the mortgage originator giving the potential borrower the right but not the obligation to close (that is, the right to cancel the agreement). Reasons other than a decline in mortgage rates may also cause a potential borrower to fall out of the pipeline, such as an unfavorable property inspection report, or the purchase was predicated on a change in employment that did not occur.

Mortgage originators have several alternatives to protect themselves against pipeline risk. To protect against price risk, the originator could get a commitment from the agency or the private conduit to whom the mortgage originator plans to sell the mortgage.[2] This sort of commitment is effectively a forward contract, a contract described in Chapter 29. The mortgage originator agrees to deliver a mortgage at a future date, and another party (either one of the agencies or a private conduit) agrees to buy the mortgage at that time at a predetermined price (or mortgage rate).

Consider what happens, however, if mortgage rates decline, and potential borrowers elect to cancel the agreement. The mortgage originator agreed to deliver a mortgage with a specified mortgage rate. If the potential borrower does not close, the mortgage originator cannot back out of its commitment to deliver the mortgage to the agency or private conduit. As a result, the mortgage originator realizes a loss—it must deliver a mortgage at a higher mortgage rate in a lower mortgage rate environment.

Mortgage originators can protect themselves against this fallout risk by entering into an agreement with an agency or private conduit for optional rather than mandatory delivery of the mortgage. In such an agreement, the mortgage originator is effectively buying an option that gives it the right, but not the obligation, to deliver a mortgage. The agency or private conduit sold that option to the mortgage originator and, therefore, charges a fee for allowing optional delivery.

◆ TYPES OF MORTGAGE DESIGNS

Between the mid-1930s and the early 1970s, only one type of mortgage loan was available in the United States: the fixed-rate, level-payment, fully amortized mortgage. The deficiencies of this mortgage design, commonly referred to as the **traditional mortgage**, led to the introduction of new mortgage designs.

---

[2] This commitment that the mortgage originator obtains to protect itself should not be confused with the commitment that the mortgage originator gives to the potential borrower.

FIXED-RATE, LEVEL-PAYMENT, FULLY AMORTIZED MORTGAGES

The basic idea behind the design of the traditional mortgage is that the borrower pays interest and repays principal in equal installments over an agreed-upon period of time, called the maturity or term of the mortgage. Thus, at the end of the term, the loan has been fully amortized—no mortgage balance remains. The interest rate is generally above the risk-free rate because of servicing costs, default risk that is present despite the collateral, and some further risks as discussed later. The frequency of payment is typically monthly, and the prevailing term of the mortgage is 15 to 30 years.

Cash Flow Characteristics of the Traditional Mortgage   Each monthly mortgage payment for a level-payment, fixed-rate mortgage is due on the first of each month and consists of:

1. Interest of $\frac{1}{12}$ of the fixed annual interest rate times the amount of the outstanding mortgage balance at the beginning of the previous month
2. A repayment of a portion of the outstanding mortgage balance (principal).

The difference between the monthly mortgage payment and the portion of the payment that represents interest equals the amount that is applied to reduce the outstanding mortgage balance. The monthly mortgage payment is designed so that after the last scheduled monthly payment of the loan is made, the amount of the outstanding mortgage balance is zero (that is, the mortgage is fully repaid).

As an illustration of a level-payment, fixed-rate mortgage, consider a 30-year (360-month), $100,000 mortgage with a 9.5% mortgage rate. The monthly mortgage payment would be $840.85. Table 25-1 shows for selected months how each monthly mortgage payment is divided between interest and repayment of principal. At the beginning of Month 1, the mortgage balance is $100,000, the amount of the original loan. The mortgage payment for Month 1 includes interest on the $100,000 borrowed for the month. As the interest rate is 9.5%, the monthly interest rate is 0.0079167.

A borrower can also make principal repayments prior to the scheduled date. A monthly principal repayment that is in excess of the scheduled principal repayment is called a **prepayment**. Typically, there is no penalty imposed on the borrower for prepaying. Thus, the cash flow of a mortgage consists of (1) interest, (2) regularly scheduled principal repayments, and (3) prepayments.

Deficiencies of the Traditional Mortgage   The problems with the traditional mortgage design are readily apparent. In the presence of high and variable inflation, this mortgage design suffers from two basic and serious shortcomings: the *mismatch problem* and the *tilt problem*.

Savings and loan associations faced the mismatch problem during most of the post–World War II period because mortgages—a long-term asset—were financed largely by depository institutions that obtain their funds through deposits that are primarily, if not entirely, of a short-term nature. These institutions engaged inevitably in a higher speculative activity: borrowing short and lending long; that is, they mismatched the maturity of the assets (mortgages) and the liabilities raised to fund those assets. Speculation of this sort proves a losing proposition if interest rates rise, as is bound to happen in the presence of significant inflation. The institution may be earning the contractual rate, but to attract the deposits needed to finance the loan, it must pay the current higher market rate. Considering that the intermediation margin or spread is modest—some 100 to 200 basis points—it will not take much inflation or rise in interest rates before an institution runs into a loss.

Another way to describe the mismatch problem is in terms of the balance sheet rather than the income statement. The difference between lending and borrowing rates will cause the lending institution to become technically insolvent, in the sense that the

Table 25-1   Amortization Schedule for a Level-Payment, Fixed-Rate Mortgage

Mortgage loan: $100,000
Mortgage rate: 9.5%
Monthly payment: $840.85
Term of loan: 30 years (360 months)

Month	Beginning Mortgage Balance	Monthly Mortgage Payment	Interest for Month	Principal Repayment	Ending Mortgage Balance
1	$100,000.00	$840.85	$791.67	$ 49.19	$99,950.81
2	99,950.81	840.85	791.28	49.58	99,901.24
3	99,901.24	840.85	790.88	49.97	99,851.27
4	99,851.27	840.85	790.49	50.37	99,800.90
5	99,800.90	840.85	790.09	50.76	99,750.14
6	99,750.14	840.85	789.69	51.17	99,698.97
7	99,698.97	840.85	789.28	51.57	99,647.40
8	99,647.40	840.85	788.88	51.98	99,596.42
9	99,595.42	840.85	788.45	52.39	99,543.03
10	99,543.03	840.85	788.05	52.81	99,490.23
...	...	...	...	...	...
...	...	...	...	...	...
...	...	...	...	...	...
98	99,862.54	840.85	735.16	105.69	92,756.85
99	92,756.85	840.85	734.33	106.53	92,650.32
100	92,640.32	840.85	733.48	107.37	92,542.95
101	92,542.95	840.85	732.63	108.22	92,434.72
102	92,434.72	840.85	731.77	109.08	92,325.64
103	92,325.64	840.85	730.91	109.94	92,215.70
104	92,215.70	840.85	730.04	110.81	92,104.89
105	92,104.89	840.85	729.16	111.69	91,993.20
106	91,993.20	840.85	728.28	112.57	91,880.62
...	...	...	...	...	...
...	...	...	...	...	...
...	...	...	...	...	...
209	74,177.40	840.85	587.24	253.62	73,923.78
210	73,923.78	840.85	585.23	255.62	73,668.16
211	73,668.16	840.85	583.21	257.65	73,410.51
212	73,410.51	840.85	581.17	259.69	73,150.82
...	...	...	...	...	...
...	...	...	...	...	...
...	...	...	...	...	...
354	5,703.93	840.85	45.16	795.70	4,908.23
355	4,908.23	840.85	38.86	802.00	4,106.24
356	4,106.24	840.85	35.21	808.35	3,297.89
357	3,297.89	840.85	26.11	814.75	2,483.14
358	2,483.14	840.85	19.66	821.20	1,661.95
359	1,661.95	840.85	13.16	827.70	834.25
360	834.25	840.85	6.60	834.26	0.00

market value of its assets will be insufficient to cover its liabilities. The reason is because the institution's liabilities are related to the face value of its mortgage assets, but the market value of these assets falls below the face value of the mortgage loan. For these reasons, both losses and technical insolvencies occurred on a large scale after the late 1960s, especially in the 1970s and early 1980s.

One obvious way to resolve this problem is for the institution that primarily finances fixed-rate mortgages to lengthen its liabilities through term deposits or analogous instruments. Actually, this approach was used only modestly during recent years. In fact, it is doubtful that it could go far in addressing the problem, for what made S&Ls so popular is unquestionably the higher liquid, riskless nature of their deposits. If they were allowed to finance mortgages only by long-term deposits, we might expect a substantial decline in the volume of funds available to them for mortgage financing. A second alternative is to design a different sort of mortgage.

The tilt problem refers to what happens to the real burden of mortgage payments over the life of the mortgage as a result of inflation. If the general price level rises, the real value of the mortgage payments will decline over time. If a homeowner's real income rises over time, coupled with a decline in the real value of the mortgage payments, the burden of the mortgage payments declines over time. Thus, the mortgage obligation represents a greater burden in real terms for the homeowner in the initial years. In other words, the real burden is "tilted" to the initial years, which discourages people from purchasing a home in their early earning years. The tilt problem is behind the development of other types of mortgage instruments.

ADJUSTABLE-RATE MORTGAGES

One way to resolve the mismatch problem is to redesign the traditional mortgage so as to produce an asset whose return would match the short-term market rates, thus better matching the cost of the liabilities. One considerably popular instrument that satisfies these requirements is the so-called *adjustable-rate mortgage.*

Characteristics of the Adjustable-Rate Mortgage   The adjustable-rate mortgage (ARM) calls for resetting the interest rate periodically, in accordance with some appropriately chosen index that reflects short-term market rates. This mortgage represents an approach applied to many other instruments, such as bank loans, especially in the Eurodollar market. By using a short-term rate as the index, S&Ls can more closely match their returns to their cost of funds. An instrument earning the market rate could be expected to remain close to par whether interest rates rise or fall, thus avoiding the problems of technical insolvency that plague the S&Ls relying on the traditional mortgage. Note also that, with high and variable rates of inflation, an adjustable-rate, in principle, reduces risk for the borrower—reduced inflation generally is accompanied by a fall in interest rates, which benefits borrowers with an adjustable-rate contract.

The adjustable-rate contracts currently popular in the United States call for resetting the interest rate either every month, six months, year, 2 years, or 3 years. The interest rate at the reset date is equal to a benchmark index plus a spread. The spread is between 100 and 200 basis points.

The two most popular indexes are the 1-year Treasury rate and the 11th District Cost of Funds. The latter index is a calculation based on the monthly weighted average interest cost for liabilities of the thrifts in the 11th Federal Home Loan Bank Board District.[3] This district includes the states of California, Arizona, and Nevada.

---

[3]   The cost of funds is calculated by first computing the monthly interest expenses for all thrifts included in the 11th District. The interest expenses are summed and then divided by the average of the beginning and ending monthly balance.

Lenders like ARMs because they shift interest rate risk from the lender to the borrower. To be sure, the risk resulting from falling rates tends to be shifted from the borrower to the lender, but then this risk is borne by the lenders anyway, at least in part, because of the borrower's prepayment option. Thrifts accordingly prefer to hold ARMs in their portfolios rather than fixed-rate mortgages such as the traditional mortgage, because ARMs provide a better matching with their liabilities. Liabilities are closely tied to the calculated cost of funds index, therefore thrifts prefer ARMs benchmarked to the 11th District Cost of Funds.

The basic ARM resets periodically and includes no other terms that affect the monthly mortgage payment.[4] Typically, the mortgage rate is affected by other terms, including periodic caps and lifetime rate caps and floors. Periodic caps limit the amount that the interest rate may increase or decrease at the reset date. The periodic rate cap is expressed in percentage points. Most ARMs have an upper limit on the mortgage rate that can be charged over the life of the loan. This lifetime loan cap is expressed in terms of the initial rate; the most common lifetime cap is 5% to 6%. For example, if the initial mortgage rate is 7% and the lifetime cap is 5%, the maximum interest rate that the lender can charge over the life of the loan is 12%. Many ARMs also have a lower limit (floor) on the interest rate that can be charged over the life of the loan.

Balloon/Reset Mortgages Another type of adjustable-rate mortgage is the balloon/reset mortgage. The primary difference between a balloon/reset mortgage design and the basic ARM is that the mortgage rate is reset less frequently.

Although new to the U.S. mortgage market, the balloon/reset mortgage has long been used in Canada, where it is referred to as a **rollover mortgage**. In this mortgage design, the borrower is given long-term financing by the lender, but at specified future dates the contract rate is renegotiated. Thus, the lender provides long-term funds for what is effectively short-term borrowing, how short depends on the frequency of the renegotiation period. Effectively, it is a short-term balloon loan in which the lender agrees to provide financing for the remainder of the term of the mortgage. The balloon payment is the original amount borrowed less the amount amortized.

The Federal Home Loan Bank Board attempted to introduce this mortgage design in January 1980, when it proposed a prototype rollover mortgage design. The prototype called for the contract rate to be renegotiated every 3 to 5 years (with the specific time period determined at the time the mortgage is originated), with a maximum contract rate change of 50 basis points for each year in the renegotiation period (for example, 150 basis points if renegotiated every 3 years and 250 basis points if every 5 years), and the lender guaranteeing to provide new financing. Several proposals gave suggestions as to how the new contract rate should be determined.

Although many hailed the rollover mortgage as an important step in alleviating the mismatch problem that thrifts face, it did not catch on until 1990. Now called **balloon/reset mortgages**, or simply **balloon mortgages**, these mortgages are the focal points of purchase programs of two government-sponsored entities, Fannie Mae and Freddie Mac. Freddie Mac's 30-year balloon/resets, for example, can have either a renegotiation period of 5 years ("30-due-in-5" FRMs) or 7 years ("30-due-in-7" FRMs). If certain conditions are met, Freddie Mac guarantees the extension of the loan. The contract rate set by Freddie Mac is based on its 30-year, single-family, fixed-rate, 60-day-delivery, mortgage rate. If the borrower elects to extend the mortgage, a $250 processing fee is charged.

Assessment of Adjustable-Rate Mortgages On the whole, the adjustable-rate mortgage and its variants have the merit of providing a manageable solution to the problem of the mismatch of maturities. To borrowers, these mortgages reduce the risk

---

[4] Some ARMs, called *convertible ARMs,* can be converted into fixed-rate mortgages.

associated with uncertain inflation. Unfortunately, the merits of the ARM have been significantly impaired by arbitrary and misguided regulatory rules, particularly interest rate caps. These caps, meant to protect the borrower, might make sense if rates were set unilaterally by the lender, but they do not make sense when they are tied to an objective market rate, or to the cost of funds to the lending institution. Furthermore, we know that an increase in nominal rates tends to accompany any appreciable rise in inflation, in which case the borrower, in general, can afford to pay the higher interest rate while it lasts.

The main effect of caps is to increase the risk of inflation to intermediary lenders who have no way of putting a cap on the rate they have to pay. Nor is a lower cap adequate compensation, because borrowers have the right to repay. Of course, some of the expected loss will tend to be recouped by a higher spread, and thus finally unloaded on some borrowers; even so, it would be best to leave the matter of caps to private bargaining.

Unfortunately, regulators still do not grasp these simple principles. Nor do they understand that in many cases the consumer generally pays for "consumer protection" in the form of higher rates or other less favorable terms. Finally, the adjustable-rate mortgage is not a satisfactory answer to inflation-swollen interest rates because it does not address the tilt problem. And the tilt problem remains in effect because, in these mortgages, the payments are still based on a nominal rather than a real interest rate.

MORTGAGE DESIGNS THAT DEAL WITH INFLATION

The traditional mortgage was designed so that the borrower would repay the debt in constant nominal installments. This form of repayment would seem highly desirable from the debtor's point of view, as long as inflation is zero or small, because a level nominal repayment rate in that case implies a level real rate of repayment. But during significant inflation, the traditional mortgage turns into a malfunctioning, undesirable vehicle for home financing. The reason is not, as frequently supposed, that inflation increases interest rates. To be sure, with a 5% rate of inflation we would expect nominal interest rates to rise by roughly 500 basis points. But this rise does not, per se, make the lender any better off or the borrower any worse off, because the increase is offset by inflation losses and gains, leaving the real rate largely unchanged. The higher interest rate is, by and large, compensated for by the erosion of the principal in terms of purchasing power. (In nominal terms, the higher rate is offset by the rise in the value of the property.)

The problem is not addressed by the adjustable-rate mortgage. It uses a nominal interest rate comparable to the fixed-rate mortgage. In particular, the critical early payment will be roughly as high as with a traditional mortgage. Actually, one can show that the adjustable rate is, in some ways, even worse for borrowers than the traditional mortgage. It starts with a rate as high as the traditional mortgage independent of inflation, and makes a substantial jump every time the interest rate is adjusted and the payment shifts from one nominal level to another—even though the rate of payment is level as long as the interest rate does not change.

Can the tilt problem be remedied? It is clear that in principle a solution must involve reducing the interest rate used in the early payments and recouping later. Three mortgage designs (with many variants) offered to solve the tilt problem include the *graduated-payment mortgage*, the *price-level-adjusted mortgage*, and the *dual-rate mortgage*. A discussion of these mortgage designs is beyond the scope of this chapter.[5]

---

[5] For more details about these mortgage designs, see Frank J. Fabozzi, Franco Modigliani, Frank J. Jones, and Michael Ferr, *Foundation of Financial Markets and Institutions,* 3rd ed. (Upper Saddle River, NJ: Prentice Hall, 2002), Chapter 23.

OTHER MORTGAGE DESIGNS[6]

Other mortgage designs are available to meet the unique needs of some borrowers. Lenders also make loans to borrowers with blemished credit, reduced documentation with nonstandard specifications, and even loans that require less down payment than previously, or do not need any down payment at all. To address the distinctive needs of various mortgagors in the changing mortgage market, lenders offer such specialized programs as high-LTV, Alt-A, and subprime loans, which are discussed in this section.

Prepayment Penalty Mortgages   As explained previously in this chapter, the majority of mortgages outstanding do not penalize the borrower from prepaying any part or all of the outstanding mortgage balance. However, in recent years mortgage originators have originated **prepayment penalty mortgages (PPMs)**.

The laws and regulations governing the imposition of prepayment penalties are established at the federal and state levels.[7] Usually, the applicable laws for fixed-rate mortgages are specified at the state level. Some states do not permit prepayment penalties on fixed-rate mortgages with a first lien. Other states do permit prepayment penalties but restrict the type of penalty. For some mortgage designs, such as adjustable-rate and balloon mortgages, federal laws override state laws.

The basic structure of a PPM includes a specified time period during which prepayments are not permitted except for the sale of the mortgaged property. This time period is called the **lockout period**. Typically, this period is either 3 years or 5 years. Depending on the structure, a certain amount of prepayments can be made during the lockout period without the imposition of a prepayment penalty. The common prepayment penalty structure is one that allows partial prepayments up to 20% of the original loan amount in any consecutive 12-month period without a prepayment penalty. When a prepayment penalty is imposed, it typically takes the following form:[8]

- For a 3-year lockout period, the prepayment penalty is the lesser of 2% of any prepayment amount within 3 years that is greater than 20% of the original mortgage, or 6 months of interest on the portion of the prepayment amount that exceeds 20% of the original principal balance.
- For a 5-year lockout period, the prepayment penalty is 6 months' interest on any prepayment amount in the first 5 years that is greater than 20% of the original principal balance.

For example, suppose that a borrower with a PPM with a mortgage rate of 8.5%, original principal balance of $150,000, and a lockout period of 5 years refinances within the first 5 years and prepays the entire balance. The prepayment penalty will be 6 months of interest on the amount prepaid in excess of 20% of the original principal balance. Since 80% of the original principal balance of $150,000 is $120,000 and interest for 1 year at 8.5% is $10,200 (8.5% times $120,000). The prepayment penalty is 6-months' interest: $5,100.

The motivation for the PPM is that it reduces prepayment risk (discussed later in this chapter) for the lender during the lockout period. It does so by effectively making

---

[6]   Portions of the discussion in this section draw from Anand K. Bhattacharya, Frank J. Fabozzi, and S. Esther Chang, "Overview of the Mortgage Market," in Frank J. Fabozzi (ed.), *The Handbook of Mortgage-Backed Securities,* 5th ed. (New York: McGraw-Hill, 2001), Chapter 1.

[7]   For a discussion of these laws and regulations, see Anand K. Bhattacharya and Paul C. Wang, "Prepayment Penalty MBS," in Frank J. Fabozzi (ed.), *The Handbook of Mortgage-Backed Securities,* 5th ed. (New York: McGraw-Hill, 2001). The information in this section draws from that chapter.

[8]   The prepayment penalty structures are explained in Bhattacharya and Wang, "Prepayment Penalty MBS," op. cit.

it more costly for the borrower to prepay. In exchange for this reduction in prepayment risk, the lender will offer a mortgage rate that is lower than an otherwise comparable mortgage loan without a prepayment penalty.

Growing-Equity Mortgage   A variation of the GPM that avoids negative amortization is the **growing-equity mortgage (GEM)**, which has a fixed-rate mortgage whose monthly mortgage payments increase over time. Rather, the higher monthly mortgage payments serve to pay down the principal faster and shorten the term of the mortgage. For example, a 30-year, $100,000 GEM loan with a contract rate of 9.5% might call for an initial monthly payment of $840.85. However, the GEM payment would gradually increase, and the GEM might be fully paid in only 15 years.

Thus, a GEM effectively shortens the life of a mortgage. The advantage of this mortgage design for the borrower is that because it has a shorter life than a level-payment mortgage, in an upward-sloping yield curve environment a lender will be willing to provide a lower mortgage rate than for a level-payment mortgage. As the borrower's income grows over time, the borrower can afford to make the higher payments that lead to the shorter life for the mortgage.

Reverse Mortgages   **Reverse mortgages** are designed for senior home owners who want to convert their home equity into cash. Fannie Mae, for instance, offers two types of reverse mortgages for senior borrowers. The Home Keeper Mortgage is an adjustable-rate conventional reverse mortgage for borrowers who are at least 62 years of age, who either own the home outright, or have a low amount of unpaid principle balance. The maximum amount that can be borrowed is based upon the homeowner's age, the property's value, and the interest rate. The borrower does not have to repay the loan until he or she no longer occupies the home as a principal residence, and cannot be forced to sell or vacate the home to pay off the loan as long as the property is maintained. The other type of reverse mortgage, Home Keeper for Home Purchase, enables senior borrowers to buy a new home with a combination of personal funds and calculated amount of reverse mortgage that is based upon the borrower's age, number of borrowers, the adjusted property value, and the equity share option chosen.

High-LTV Loans   Traditionally for a conventional, conforming loan, borrowers typically were required to make a down payment of 20% when qualifying for a mortgage. However, today a mortgagor with good credit has the option of making a lesser down or no down payment, resulting in loans with higher LTVs. Hence, these mortgage loans are called **high-LTV loans**. For borrowers interested in conventional, nonconforming loans, programs available for 103% LTV require no down payment because 100% of the home's price, as well as an additional 3% for closing costs, can be financed into the mortgage.

Alt-A Loans   **Alt-A loans** are made to borrowers whose qualifying mortgage characteristics do not meet the conforming underwriting criteria established by the government-sponsored enterprises that we will discuss in the next chapter. For instance, the borrower may be self-employed and may not be able to provide all the necessary documentation for income verification. In such respects, Alt-A loans allow reduced or alternate forms of documentation to qualify the loan. An Alt-A loan borrower, however, should not be confused with borrowers with blemished credits. The typical Alt-A borrower has an excellent credit rating—referred to as an "A" rating, and hence the loan is referred to as an Alt-A loan—which is especially important to the originator because the credit quality of the borrower must compensate for the lack of other necessary documentation. What is appealing to borrowers about the Alt-A program is the flexibility that the program offers in terms of documentation, and they will pay a premium for the privilege. Typically, rates on Alt-A loans range between 75 to 125 basis points above the rate on otherwise comparable standard mortgage rates.

Subprime Loans   Borrowers who apply for **subprime loans** vary from those who have or had credit problems due to difficulties in repayment of debt brought on by an adverse event, such as job loss or medical emergencies, to those who continue to mismanage their debt and finances. The distinguishing feature of a subprime mortgage is that the potential universe of subprime mortgagors can be divided into various risk grades, ranging from A through D. The risk gradation is a function of past credit history and the magnitude of credit blemishes existing in the history. Additionally, some of the higher grades in this loan category are labeled as "fallen angels" to indicate the fact that the creditworthiness of such borrowers was hampered by a life event, such as job loss or illness. Because such borrowers tend to have lower credit scores and pose greater credit risk, subprime mortgages command a pricing premium over standard mortgages.

◆ COMMERCIAL MORTGAGE LOANS

Commercial mortgage loans are loans for income-producing properties. These properties include multifamily properties (i.e., apartment buildings), office buildings, industrial properties (including warehouses), shopping centers, hotels, and health-care facilities (e.g., senior housing care facilities).

Unlike residential mortgage loans where the lender relies on the ability of the borrower to repay and has recourse to the borrower if the payment terms are not satisfied, commercial mortgage loans are **nonrecourse loans**. The lender can only look to the income-producing property backing the loan for interest and principal repayment. In case of a default, the lender looks to the proceeds from the sale of the property for repayment and has no recourse to the borrower for any unpaid balance. The lender therefore must evaluate each property using measures appropriate for assessing credit risk.

MEASURES USED IN EVALUATING THE CREDIT RISK OF COMMERCIAL MORTGAGE LOANS

Regardless of the property type, the two key indicators of the potential credit performance are the debt-to-service coverage ratio and the loan-to-value ratio. The **debt-to-service coverage (DSC) ratio** is the ratio of property's net operating income (NOI) divided by the debt service. The NOI is defined as the rental income reduced by cash operating expenses (adjusted for a replacement reserve). A ratio greater than 1 means that the cash flow from the property is sufficient to cover debt servicing. The higher the ratio is, the more likely it is that the borrower will be able to meet debt servicing from the property's cash flow.

PREPAYMENT PROTECTION FOR LENDERS

We discussed earlier the prepayment risk of mortgage loans and that for residential mortgages prepayments are typically penalty-free (the typical residential mortgage loan). For a commercial mortgage loan, prepayment (or call) protection is provided. It can take one of the following forms: (1) prepayment lockout, (2) defeasance, (3) prepayment penalty points, or (4) yield maintenance charges.

A **prepayment lockout** is a contractual agreement that prohibits any prepayments during a specified period of time, called the lockout period. The lockout period at

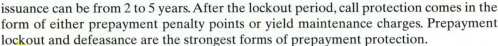

issuance can be from 2 to 5 years. After the lockout period, call protection comes in the form of either prepayment penalty points or yield maintenance charges. Prepayment lockout and defeasance are the strongest forms of prepayment protection.

With **defeasance**, rather than prepaying a loan, the borrower provides sufficient funds for the servicer to invest in a portfolio of Treasury securities that replicates the cash flows that would exist in the absence of prepayments. Unlike the other call protection provisions discussed next, no distribution is made to the bondholders when the defeasance takes place. Moreover, the substitution of the cash flow of a Treasury portfolio for that of the borrower improves the credit quality of the loan.

Prepayment penalty points are predetermined penalties that must be paid by the borrower if the borrower wishes to refinance. For example, 5-4-3-2-1 is a common prepayment penalty point structure. That is, if the borrower wishes to prepay during the first year, he or she must pay a 5% penalty for a total of $105 rather than $100 (which is the norm in the residential market). Likewise, during the second year, a 4% penalty would apply, and so on. Today, prepayment penalty points are not common in newly originated commercial mortgage loans. Instead, the next form of call protection discussed, yield maintenance charges, is more commonly used.

A **yield maintenance charge**, in its simplest terms, is designed to make the lender indifferent as to the timing of prepayments. The yield maintenance charge, also called the **make whole charge**, makes it uneconomical for the borrower to refinance solely to get a lower mortgage rate. The simplest and most restrictive form of yield maintenance charge ("Treasury flat yield maintenance") penalizes the borrower based on the difference between the mortgage coupon and the prevailing Treasury rate.

◆ INVESTMENT RISKS

The principal investors in mortgage loans include thrifts and commercial banks. Pension funds and life insurance companies also invest in these loans, but their ownership is small compared to that of the banks and thrifts.

Investors face four main risks by investing in mortgage loans: (1) credit risk, (2) liquidity risk, (3) price risk, and (4) prepayment risk.

CREDIT RISK

Credit risk is the risk that the home owner/borrower will default. For FHA-, VA-, and FmHA-insured mortgages, this risk is minimal. For privately insured mortgages, the risk can be gauged by the credit rating of the private insurance company that has insured the mortgage. For conventional mortgages, the credit risk depends on the borrower. The LTV provides a useful measure of the risk of loss of principal in case of default. When LTV is high, default is more likely because the borrower has little equity in the property.

LIQUIDITY RISK

Although a secondary market exists for mortgage loans, which we discuss in the next chapter, the fact is that bid-ask spreads are large compared to other debt instruments. That is, mortgage loans tend to be rather illiquid because they are large and indivisible.

PRICE RISK

As explained in Chapter 18, the price of a fixed income instrument moves in an opposite direction from market interest rates. Thus, a rise in interest rates decreases the price of a mortgage loan.

PREPAYMENTS AND CASH FLOW UNCERTAINTY

Payments made in excess of the scheduled principal repayments are called *prepayments*. Prepayments occur for one of several reasons. First, home owners prepay the entire mortgage when they sell their house for any number of reasons that require moving. Second, the borrower has the right to pay off all or part of the mortgage balance at any time. Effectively, those who invest in mortgages grant the borrower an option to prepay the mortgage, and the debtor experiences incentive to do so as the interest rate in the mortgage market falls below the mortgage rate that the borrower is paying. Third, if home owners cannot meet their mortgage obligations, the property is repossessed and sold, with the proceeds from the sale used to pay the lender in the case of a conventional mortgage. For an insured mortgage, the insurer will pay off the mortgage balance. Finally, if property is destroyed by fire, or another insured catastrophe occurs, the insurance proceeds are used to pay off the mortgage.

The effect of the prepayment right is that the cash flow from a mortgage is not known with certainty. This uncertainty is true not only for level-payment, fixed-rate mortgages but also for all the mortgages we discussed in this chapter.

Summary ●

The types of real estate properties that can be mortgaged are single-family residential and commercial properties. Single-family residential properties include one- to four-family dwellings. Commercial properties are income-producing properties.

The major originators of residential mortgage loans are thrifts, banks, and mortgage bankers. The risks associated with originating mortgages (pipeline risk) include price risk and fallout risk.

The traditional type of mortgage, characterized by a fixed-rate, level (nominal) payment, and full amortization, performed well in the first years of the postwar period, becoming the dominant vehicle for house financing. But this design showed drawbacks in the presence of high and variable inflation. First, traditional mortgages were financed mainly by depository institutions with short-term funds, even though a mortgage is a long-term instrument; this mismatch of maturities proved catastrophic when short-term rates rose sharply, leading to widespread insolvency of S&Ls, the major lenders. Second, in the presence of inflation-driven high interest rates, mortgage repayment in real terms is no longer level, but instead starts high and ends low, shutting off many would-be borrowers.

Two remedies in use in the United States are the adjustable-rate mortgage (ARM) and the graduated-payment mortgage (GPM). The first addresses the mismatch problem, and the second (imperfectly) the tilt problem; neither addresses both. Two other solutions, the price-level-adjusted mortgage (PLAM) and the dual-rate mortgage (DRM), fairly effectively address both problems, but neither of these instruments has yet been adopted on a large scale in the United States.

Several types of mortgage designs are offered to borrowers with features that make them more appealing to specific borrower groups with special needs or objectives, including growing-equity mortgages, reverse mortgages, and loans to borrowers with blemished credit (subprime mortgages), reduced documentation with nonstandard specifications (Alt-A mortgages), and loans that require less down payment than a standard mortgage loan or no down payment at all (high-LTV mortgages).

Although prepayments—mortgage payments that exceed the amount that is due—can typically be made by the borrower without a penalty, in recent years prepayment penalty mortgages have been offered.

Uncertainty associated with investing in any of these mortgages comes from prepayments, which affect their cash flow. This uncertainty is called prepayment risk. Investors in mortgages also face marketability risk and price risk, and may be exposed to credit risk.

Commercial mortgage loans are for income-producing properties including multi-family properties (i.e., apartment buildings), office buildings, industrial properties (including warehouses), shopping centers, hotels, and health-care facilities (e.g., senior housing care facilities). Commercial mortgage loans are nonrecourse loans, meaning that the lender can only look to the income-producing property backing the loan for interest and principal repayment. The two key indicators of the potential credit performance of commercial property are the debt-to-service coverage ratio and the loan-to-value ratio. Various provisions in a commercial mortgage loan protect the lender against prepayments.

Key Terms ■

- Adjustable-rate mortgage (ARM)
- Alt-A loan
- Balloon mortgage
- Balloon/reset mortgage
- Commercial mortgage loan
- Commitment letter
- Conduits
- Conforming mortgage
- Conventional mortgage
- Debt-to-service coverage (DSC) ratio
- Defeasance
- Fallout risk
- Fixed-rate mortgage
- Growing-equity mortgage

- High-LTV loan
- Loan-to-value (LTV) ratio
- Lockout period
- Make whole charge
- Mortgage banking
- Mortgage originator
- Mortgagee
- Mortgagor
- Nonconforming mortgages
- Nonrecourse loan
- Origination fee
- Payment-to-income (PTI) ratio
- Pipeline
- Pipeline risk

- Prepayment lockout
- Prepayment penalty mortgage (PPM)
- Prepayment penalty points
- Prepayment
- Price risk
- Reverse mortgages
- Rollover mortgage
- Secondary market profit
- Securitized
- Servicing fee
- Subprime loans
- Traditional mortgage
- Yield maintenance charge

Questions ■

1. What are the sources of revenue arising from mortgage origination?
2. What are the risks associated with the mortgage origination process?
3. What are the two primary factors in determining whether funds will be loaned to an applicant for a residential mortgage loan?
4. What can mortgage originators do with a loan after originating it?
5. Explain why in a fixed-rate, level-payment mortgage the amount of the mortgage payment applied to interest declines over time, while the amount applied to the repayment of principal increases.
6. Consider the following fixed-rate, level-payment mortgage:

> maturity = 360 months
> amount borrowed = $100,000
> annual mortgage rate = 10%
> monthly mortgage payment = $877.57

    a. Construct an amortization schedule for the first 10 months.
    b. What will the mortgage balance be at the end of the 360th month?

7. Why is the interest rate on a mortgage loan not necessarily the same as the interest rate that the investor receives?

8. a. Why is the cash flow of a residential mortgage loan unknown?
   b. In what sense does the investor in a residential mortgage loan grant the borrower (home owner) a call option?

9. If the borrower prepays a residential mortgage loan, what is the prepayment penalty?

10. a. What features of an adjustable-rate mortgage will affect its cash flow?
    b. What are the two categories of benchmark indexes used in adjustable-rate mortgages?

11. With respect to a default by the borrower, how does a residential mortgage loan differ from a commercial mortgage loan?

12. What types of provisions are usually included in a commercial loan to protect the lender against prepayment risk?

13. Why is the debt-to-service coverage ratio used to assess the credit risk of a commercial mortgage loan?

CHAPTER 26

The Market for Mortgage-Backed Securities

Learning Objectives

After reading this chapter you will understand:

◆ the development of the current mortgage market, and the role of public and private conduits.

◆ the agency pass-through market.

◆ the nonagency pass-through market.

◆ the investment characteristics of mortgage pass-through securities.

◆ the importance of prepayments.

◆ why a collateralized mortgage obligation is created.

◆ how different types of collateralized mortgage obligation bond classes are created.

◆ the investment characteristics of stripped mortgage-backed securities.

◆ the features of a commercial mortgage-backed security and the types of deals.

Our major focus in this chapter is on the market for securities created from residential mortgage loans. The basic mortgage-backed security is the mortgage pass-through security. From this security, derivative mortgaged-backed securities are created: collateralized mortgage obligations and stripped mortgage-backed securities. We begin by describing how the process of securitizing mortgages resulted in the strong secondary mortgage market that exists today. At the end of the chapter, we discuss mortgage-backed securities backed by commercial mortgage loans.

◆ DEVELOPMENT OF THE SECONDARY MORTGAGE MARKET

The driving force in the development of a strong secondary market for residential mortgage loans was a financial innovation that involves the packaging (or "pooling") of mortgages and the issuance of securities collateralized by these mortgages. As we explained in Chapter 2, this system, called *asset securitization,* is radically different from the traditional system for financing the acquisition of assets, which calls for one financial intermediary, such as a commercial bank, thrift, or insurance company, to (1) originate a loan; (2) retain the loan in its portfolio of assets, thereby accepting the credit risk associated with the loan; (3) service the loan by collecting payments and providing tax or other information to the borrower; and (4) obtain funds from the public with which to finance its assets (except for the small amount representing the institution's equity).

With asset securitization more than one institution may be involved in lending capital. In the case of mortgage activities, a lending scenario can look like this: (1) A thrift or commercial bank can originate a mortgage loan; (2) the thrift or commercial bank can sell its mortgages to an investment banking firm that creates a security backed by the pool of mortgages; (3) the investment banker can obtain credit risk insurance for the pool of mortgages from a private insurance company; (4) the investment banker can sell the right to service the loans to another thrift or a company specializing in servicing mortgages; and (5) the investment banking firm can sell the securities to individuals and institutional investors. Besides the original bank or thrift, participants include an investment bank, an insurance company, another thrift, an individual, and other institutional investors. The bank or thrift in this case does not have to absorb the credit risk, service the mortgage, or provide the funding.

FOUNDATIONS OF THE MORTGAGE MARKET

The foundations for the secondary mortgage market can be traced back to the Great Depression and the legislation that followed. Congress's response to the Depression and its effects on financial markets was to establish several public purpose agencies. The Federal Reserve provided increased liquidity for commercial banks through the Federal Reserve discount window. Liquidity for thrifts was provided by the creation of the Federal Home Loan Banks (FHLBs), which were granted the right to borrow from the Treasury.

Another creation of Congress, the Federal Housing Administration (FHA), addressed the problems presented by the mortgages used at that time. This government agency developed and promoted the fixed-rate, level-payment, fully amortized mortgage. The FHA also reduced credit risk for investors by offering insurance against mortgage defaults. Not all mortgages could be insured, however—the mortgage applicant had to satisfy FHA underwriting standards, which made the FHA the first to standardize mortgage terms. Although we may take standardization for granted today, it is the basis for the development of a secondary mortgage market. In 1944, the Veterans Administration began insuring qualified mortgages.

But who was going to invest in these mortgages? Thrifts could do so, especially with the inducement provided by several tax and regulatory advantages. But the investment would be illiquid in the absence of a market for trading mortgages. Congress thought of that, too. It created another government-sponsored agency, the Federal National Mortgage Association (FNMA). This agency, popularly known as Fannie Mae, was charged with the responsibility to create a liquid secondary market for FHA- and VA-insured mortgages, which it tried to accomplish by buying mortgages. Fannie Mae needed a funding source in case it faced a liquidity squeeze. Congress provided it by giving Fannie Mae a credit line with the Treasury.

Despite the creation of Fannie Mae, the secondary mortgage market did not develop to any significant extent. During periods of tight money, Fannie Mae could do little to mitigate the housing crisis. In 1968, Congress divided Fannie Mae into two organizations: (1) the current Fannie Mae, and (2) the Government National Mortgage Association, popularly known as Ginnie Mae. Ginnie Mae's function is to use the "full faith and credit of the U.S. government" to support the FHA and VA mortgage market. Two years later, in 1970, Congress authorized Fannie Mae to purchase conventional mortgage loans (that is, those not insured by the FHA or VA) and created the Federal Home Loan Mortgage Corporation (popularly known as Freddie Mac) to provide support for FHA/VA-insured mortgages and conventional mortgages.

SECURITIZATION OF MORTGAGES

Ginnie Mae accomplished its objective by guaranteeing securities issued by private entities who pooled mortgages together and then used these mortgages as collateral for the security sold. Freddie Mac and Fannie Mae purchased mortgages, pooled these mortgages, and issued securities using the pool of mortgages as collateral. The securities created are called *mortgage pass-through securities.* They are purchased by many types of investors (domestic and foreign) who previously shunned investment in the mortgage market.

In the 1980s, private issuers of mortgage pass-through securities who did not use the backing of the three agencies but instead some form of private credit enhancement began issuing pass-through securities backed by conventional family mortgages and commercial real estate mortgages.

◆ MORTGAGE PASS-THROUGH SECURITIES

As we noted in the previous chapter, investing in mortgages exposes the investor to default risk, price risk, liquidity risk, and prepayment risk. A more efficient investment technique is to invest in a **mortgage pass-through security,** a security created when one or more holders of mortgages form a collection (pool) of mortgages and sell shares or participation certificates in the pool. A pool may consist of several thousand mortgages or only a few. The first mortgage pass-through security was created in 1968. Risk-averse investors prefer investing in a pool to investing in a single mortgage, partly because a mortgage pass-through security is considerably more liquid than an individual mortgage.

When a mortgage is included in a pool of mortgages that is used as collateral for a mortgage pass-through security, the mortgage is said to be **securitized.** More than one-third of mortgages for one- to four-family houses have been securitized. Only 25% of conventional mortgages are securitized, but 85% of FHA/VA-insured mortgages are. Fewer than 10% of multifamily unit mortgages find their way into a mortgage pool backing a mortgage pass-through security.

CASH FLOW CHARACTERISTICS

The cash flow of a mortgage pass-through security depends on the cash flow of the underlying mortgages. As explained in the previous chapter, the cash flow consists of monthly mortgage payments representing interest, the scheduled repayment of principal, and any prepayments.

Payments are made to security holders each month. The amounts and the timing of the cash flow from the pool of mortgages and the cash flow passed through to investors, however, are not identical. The monthly cash flow for a pass-through security is less than the monthly cash flow of the underlying mortgages by an amount equal to servicing and other fees. The other fees are those charged by the issuer or guarantor of the pass-through security for guaranteeing the issue (discussed later).[1]

The timing of the cash flow also differs. The monthly mortgage payment is due from each mortgagor on the first day of each month, but a delay affects the passing through of the corresponding monthly cash flow to the security holders. The length of the delay varies by the type of pass-through security.

Figure 26-1 illustrates the process of creating a mortgage pass-through security.

---

[1]   Actually, the servicer pays the guarantee fee to the issuer or guarantor.

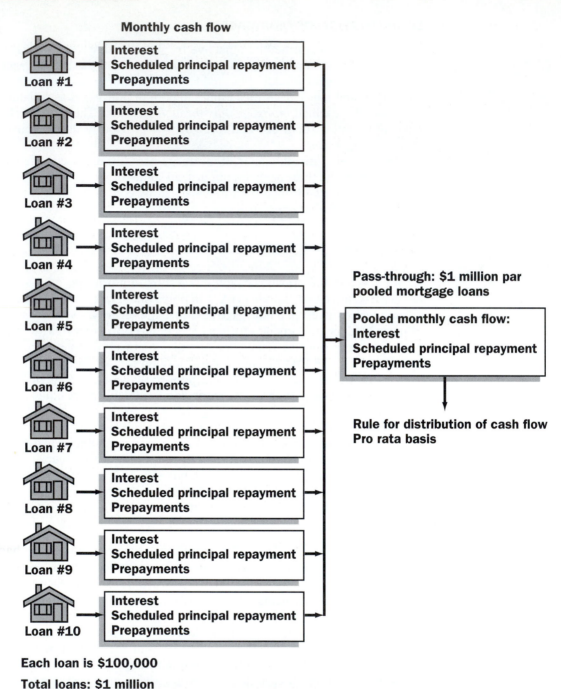

Monthly cash flow

Loan #1 → Interest / Scheduled principal repayment / Prepayments

Loan #2 → Interest / Scheduled principal repayment / Prepayments

Loan #3 → Interest / Scheduled principal repayment / Prepayments

Loan #4 → Interest / Scheduled principal repayment / Prepayments

Loan #5 → Interest / Scheduled principal repayment / Prepayments

Loan #6 → Interest / Scheduled principal repayment / Prepayments

Loan #7 → Interest / Scheduled principal repayment / Prepayments

Loan #8 → Interest / Scheduled principal repayment / Prepayments

Loan #9 → Interest / Scheduled principal repayment / Prepayments

Loan #10 → Interest / Scheduled principal repayment / Prepayments

Pass-through: $1 million par pooled mortgage loans

Pooled monthly cash flow:
Interest
Scheduled principal repayment
Prepayments

Rule for distribution of cash flow
Pro rata basis

Each loan is $100,000

Total loans: $1 million

FIGURE 26-1 Illustration of Creation of a Mortgage Pass-Through Security

ISSUERS OF MORTGAGE PASS-THROUGH SECURITIES

The three major types of pass-through securities are guaranteed by the agencies created by Congress to increase the supply of capital to the residential mortgage market and to provide support for an active secondary market: Government National Mortgage Association (Ginnie Mae), Federal Home Loan Mortgage Corporation (Freddie Mac), and Federal National Mortgage Association (Fannie Mae).

Although Fannie Mae and Freddie Mac are commonly referred to as *agencies* of the U.S. government, in fact both are corporate instrumentalities of the government. Their stock trades on the New York Stock Exchange, making them effectively quasi-private corporations. They do not receive a government subsidy or appropriation, and are taxed like any other corporation. Fannie Mae and Freddie Mac are more appropriately referred to as **government-sponsored enterprises**. Their guarantee does not carry the full faith and credit of the U.S. government. Ginnie Mae, by contrast, is a federally related institution because it is part of the Department of Housing and Urban Development. Its guarantee, therefore, carries the full faith and credit of the U.S. government.

The securities associated with these three entities are known as **agency pass-through securities**. About 98% of all pass-through securities are agency pass-through securities. The balance of mortgage pass-through securities are privately issued. These securities are called **nonagency mortgage pass-through securities**. Although the major portion of pass-throughs issues have residential mortgages as their collateral, pass-throughs collateralized by mortgages on commercial property also have been issued.

GOVERNMENT NATIONAL MORTGAGE ASSOCIATION

Ginnie Mae's mortgage-backed securities represent the largest proportion of mortgage pass-through securities outstanding. They are guaranteed by the full faith and credit of the U.S. government with respect to timely payment of both interest and principal. That is, the interest and principal are paid when due even if mortgagors fail to make their monthly mortgage payment.

Although Ginnie Mae provides the guarantee, it is not the issuer. Pass-through securities are issued by lenders it approves, such as thrifts, commercial banks, and mortgage bankers. These lenders receive approval only if the underlying mortgages satisfy the underwriting standards established by Ginnie Mae. When it guarantees securities issued by approved lenders, Ginnie Mae permits these lenders to convert illiquid individual mortgages into liquid securities backed by the U.S. government. In the process, Ginnie Mae accomplishes its goal to supply funds to the residential mortgage market and provide an active secondary market. For the guarantee, Ginnie Mae receives a fee, called the **guaranteeing fee**.

The security guaranteed by Ginnie Mae is called a **mortgage-backed security (MBS)**. These securities are sold in minimum denominations of $25,000 and in increments of $5,000 thereafter. The first MBS was issued in 1968. Only mortgages insured or guaranteed by either the Federal Housing Administration, the Veterans Administration, or the Farmers Home Administration can be included in a mortgage pool guaranteed by Ginnie Mae.

FEDERAL HOME LOAN MORTGAGE CORPORATION

The second largest category of agency pass-through securities contains those issued by the Federal Home Loan Mortgage Corporation (FHLMC). The security issued by Freddie Mac is called a **participation certificate (PC)**. The first PCs were issued in 1971.

Most of the pools of mortgages underlying Freddie Mac participation certificates consist of conventional mortgages, although participation certificates with underlying pools consisting of FHA-insured and VA-guaranteed mortgages have been issued. All new participation certificates issued guarantee the timely payment of both interest and principal. There are outstanding Freddie Mac participation certificates that guarantee only the timely payment of interest. The scheduled principal is passed through as it is collected, with Freddie Mac guaranteeing only that the scheduled payment will be made no later than 1 year after it is due. A Freddie Mac guarantee is not a guarantee by the U.S. government. Most market participants, though, view Freddie Mac participation certificates as similar in creditworthiness to Ginnie Mae pass-throughs, which are fully guaranteed by the U.S. government.

Freddie Mac creates PCs from two programs: the Cash Program and the Guarantor/ Swap Program. The underlying loans for both programs are conventional mortgages (i.e., mortgages not backed by a government agency). Conventional regular PCs are issued under the Cash Program. In this program, the mortgages that back the PC include individual conventional one- to four-family mortgage loans that Freddie Mac purchases from mortgage obligators, pools, and sells. Under the Conventional Guarantor/Swap Program, Freddie Mac allows originators to swap pooled mortgages for PCs in those same pools. For example, a thrift may have $50 million of mortgages. It can swap these mortgages for a Freddie Mac PC whose underlying mortgage pool is the $50 million mortgage pool the thrift swapped for the PC.

Both programs provide capital to the residential mortgage market and foster a secondary mortgage market. The Guarantor/Swap Program was designed specifically to provide liquidity to the troubled thrift industry. It allows thrifts to swap mortgages trading below par (because mortgage rates are lower than the current mortgage rate) without recognizing an accounting loss for financial reporting purposes. The PC that the thrift gets in exchange for the mortgage pool can then be either (1) held as an investment; (2) used as collateral for either short-term or long-term borrowing; or (3) sold. The Guarantor/Swap program has been a huge success and is one of the reasons for the significant growth of the amount of PCs issued.

In the fall of 1990, Freddie Mac introduced its Gold PC, which it issues in both its Cash Program and Guarantor/Swap Program. The Gold PC is the only type of pass-through it will issue in the future. Gold PCs are guaranteed with respect to timely payment of both interest and principal.

FEDERAL NATIONAL MORTGAGE ASSOCIATION

Although it was created by Congress in 1938, the Federal National Mortgage Association (FNMA), in its current form, is the newest player in the agency pass-through securities market. Fannie Mae was charged by Congress with promoting a secondary market for conventional and FHA/VA single- and multifamily mortgages. To meet that obligation, since 1972 it purchased those mortgages and held them as investments. Not until 1981 did Fannie Mae pool these mortgages and issue its first mortgage pass-through securities, called *mortgage-backed securities* (MBS). These pass-throughs are guaranteed with respect to the timely payment of both interest and principal. Like Freddie Mac participation certificates, Fannie Mae mortgage-backed securities are not obligations of the U.S. government. Fannie Mae also has a swap program similar to that of Freddie Mac. It provides liquidity to mortgage originators such as thrifts.

NONAGENCY PASS-THROUGH SECURITIES

The mortgages that the agencies could purchase or guarantee in securitized form are restricted to conforming mortgages—those that meet their underwriting standards related to the maximum size of the loan and the maximum ratio of the amount of the loan to the market value of the mortgaged property, for example. A nonconforming mortgage on the other hand fails to satisfy the underwriting standard. Mortgage loans greater than the maximum permissible loan size are referred to as *jumbo loans*. Even though Congress periodically increases the maximum amount of the loan that may be included in pass-throughs guaranteed by the three agencies, the loan size is still often below the typical average cost of a home in certain geographical areas.

The agencies cannot affect the liquidity of nonconforming mortgages such as jumbo mortgages. This sector of the mortgage market is securitized by the private sector, without government guarantee.

Privately issued—that is, *nonagency*—pass-throughs were first issued in 1977 by the Bank of America, but faced many impediments to widespread acceptance. The government wanted to see the private sector market develop, not only to improve its liquidity, but also because it was concerned about the huge potential liability of the U.S. government, should the agencies have to make good on their guarantee in the event of massive home owner defaults. One of the objectives of the Presidential Commission on Housing, established in mid-1981, was to recommend a number of private-sector alternatives.

The commission's report in April 1982 recommended the privatization of Fannie Mae and Freddie Mac and the development of private-sector alternatives to the two government-sponsored enterprises. The commission identified three major problems to be solved before an efficient private-sector market could be developed. First, private pass-throughs were being crowded out by agency issues. Second, private issuers faced federal and state laws or regulations that either limited the demand for private label products, or resulted in security structures that were not cost-efficient for issuers. Moreover, these restrictions were without economic justification. For example, federal or state regulators would not permit such securities to be treated as qualified investments for the institutions they regulated. Tax rules regarding how a transaction must be structured in order to qualify as a nontaxable conduit resulted in needlessly expensive security structures. Finally, private issues lacked standardization, a deficiency that limited liquidity.

The development of the nonagency pass-through market resulted from government intervention in an attempt to foster the growth of this sector, as well as initiatives undertaken by the private sector to structure pass-throughs to enhance their credit quality.

Government Intervention   Several legislative acts and regulatory changes helped foster the development of the nonagency mortgage-backed securities market. The Secondary Mortgage Market Enhancement Act of 1984 (SMMEA) included provisions to improve the marketability of mortgage-related securities earning a double-A quality rating or better from one of the nationally recognized commercial rating companies. More specifically, SMMEA made such securities legal investments for federally chartered banks and thrifts. These investments are referred to as **SMMEA-qualified securities**.

This legislation also made SMMEA-qualified securities permissible investments for state-regulated financial institutions (depository institutions and insurance companies), which are permitted to invest in Treasury securities or federal agency securities. This action opened the door to enormous pools of investment capital. The SMMEA granted individual states the right to override this particular provision of the act by October 1991. As many states exercised their prerogative and overrode this provision of the act, they reduced funds from the entities they regulate that could invest in the private-sector market. The Department of Labor, which has the responsibility of regulating pension funds, has since made nonagency pass-throughs acceptable assets for pension plans.

The peculiarities of creating pass-throughs made it difficult for issuers to comply with SEC registration regulations. The SEC, for example, requires that a prospectus provide pertinent information about the underlying pool of mortgages. In the creation of mortgage-backed securities, however, issuers sell the securities while assembling the underlying pool of mortgage loans. Thus, the final pool would be unknown at the time of registration and could not be indicated in the prospectus. SEC regulations prevented the registration of these **blind pools** and refused to allow such underwriting on a shelf registration basis (Rule 415). Issuers also had to contend with the periodic reporting requirements after a mortgage-backed security was issued. None of these actions was required for agency mortgage-backed securities, because such securities are exempt from SEC registration. All these factors—the increased cost associated with the inability to time issuances through shelf registration, the lost flexibility to assemble pools prior to the offering, and the ongoing reporting requirements—made private issuance unattractive and impeded development of the private label pass-through market.

Recognizing these disincentives, the SEC significantly modified the requirements for private pass-through issuers in 1983 by permitting the registration of securities backed by blind pools, as long as the issuer commits to obtain a specified quality rating and provides sufficient information about the potential pool in the prospectus. When the final pool is assembled, that information must be sent to investors. Private mortgage-backed security issuers can now also qualify for shelf registration, and the periodic reporting requirements are less stringent than for corporate issuers.

The Tax Reform Act of 1986 also made the structuring of private mortgage-related securities less costly from a tax perspective. The 1986 Act expanded the types of structures that could be issued, and exempted from seperate taxation the legal entity that distributes the cash flow if cetain conditions are satisfied. Finally, brokers and dealers could use agency pass-throughs as collateral for margin transactions. Prior to 1983, private pass-throughs were not marginable. In January 1983, the Federal Reserve Board amended Regulation T to allow the same margin requirements as for over-the-counter nonconvertible bonds.

The Issuers   Nonagency pass-throughs are issued by conduits of (1) commercial banks, (2) investment banking firms, and (3) entities not associated with either commercial banks or investment banking firms. The following are some of the issuers of nonagency pass-through securities: Countrywide, Residential Funding Corporation, Citicorp/Citibank Housing, Chase Mortgage Finance, Prudential Home, Saxon Mortgage, and GE Capital Mortgage.

In addition, the Resolution Trust Corporation (RTC) acted as an important issuer in this market. The RTC used the mortgages it acquired by taking over S&Ls to create mortgage pass-through securities. Even though the RTC was a government entity, an investor in the securities issued by this entity was not protected against credit risk by the U.S. government.

Credit Enhancement   Unlike agency pass-through securities, nonagency mortgage pass-through securities are rated. Often they are supported by credit enhancements so that they can obtain a high rating. Most nonagency mortgage pass-through securities have a rating of at least double A. The development of private credit enhancement is the key to the success of this market and, indeed, the key to the development of all asset securitization. Credit enhancement may take the form of (1) corporate guarantees, (2) pool insurance from a mortgage insurance company, (3) a bank letter of credit, or (4) senior/subordinated interests.

In the case of a corporate guarantee, the issuer of a conventional pass-through uses its own credit rating to back the security. Under the second approach to credit enhancement, a mortgage pool policy is obtained to cover defaults up to a specified amount. The rating of the mortgage insurance company that writes the policy must be equal to or higher than the rating that the issuer seeks for the pass-through security. For example, if an issuer seeks a double-A rating for the pass-through, it cannot obtain a pool insurance policy from a single-A rated mortgage insurance company. The cost of a letter of credit is relatively high because of the limited number of financial institutions willing to issue such guarantees, and therefore this form of credit enhancement is not common.

The fourth approach to credit enhancement is the senior/subordinated structure, also known as the A/B pass-through. In this structure, a mortgage pool is partitioned into senior certificates and subordinated certificates. The senior certificate holder has priority on the cash flow from the underlying collateral. It is the senior certificates that are rated and sold to investors as conventional pass-throughs. The subordinated certificates absorb the default risk. The amount of subordinated certificates relative to senior certificates that a mortgage pool is divided into will determine its credit rating. The greater the portion of subordinated certificates relative to senior certificates, the higher the credit rating that can be obtained.[2]

We discuss these credit enhancements in more detail in the next chapter where we cover asset-backed securities.

PREPAYMENT RISKS ASSOCIATED WITH PASS-THROUGH SECURITIES

An investor who owns pass-through securities does not know what the cash flow will be because cash flow depends on prepayments. The risk associated with prepayments is called *prepayment risk.*

To understand prepayment risk, suppose an investor buys a 10% coupon Ginnie Mae at a time when the mortgage rates are 10%. Let's consider what will happen to prepayments if mortgage rates decline to, say, 6%. Two adverse consequences occur. First, as we explained in Chapter 18, the price of an option-free bond such as a Treasury bond will rise. In the case of a pass-through security, the rise in price will not be as large as that of an option-free bond, because a fall in interest rates will increase the probability that the market rate will fall below the rate the borrower is paying. This fall in rates gives the borrower an incentive to prepay the loan and refinance the debt at a lower rate. To the extent that this happens, the security holder will be repaid not at a price incorporating the premium but at par value. The holder risks capital loss, which reflects the fact that the anticipated reimbursements at par will not yield the initial cash flow.

The adverse consequences when mortgage rates decline are the same as those faced by holders of callable corporate and municipal bonds. As in the case of those instruments, the upside price potential of a pass-through security is truncated because of prepayments. This result should not be surprising because a mortgage loan effectively grants the borrower the right to call the loan at par value. The adverse consequence when mortgage rates decline is referred to as **contraction risk**.

Now let's look at what happens if mortgage rates rise to 15%. The price of the pass-through, like the price of any bond, will decline. But again it will decline more because the higher rates will tend to slow down the rate of prepayment, in effect increasing the amount invested at the coupon rate, which is lower than the market rate. Prepayments will slow down because home owners will not refinance or partially prepay their mortgages when mortgage rates are higher than the contractual rate of 10%. Of course, it is just the time when investors want prepayments to speed up so that they can reinvest the prepayments at the higher market interest rate. This adverse consequence of rising mortgage rates is called **extension risk**.

Therefore, prepayment risk encompasses contraction risk and extension risk. Prepayment risk makes pass-throughs unattractive for certain financial institutions to hold from an asset/liability perspective. Let's look at why particular institutional investors may find pass-throughs unattractive.

1. Thrifts and commercial banks, as we explained in Chapter 3, want to lock in a spread over their cost of funds. Their funds are raised on a short-term basis. If they invest in fixed-rate pass-through securities, they mismatch because a pass-through

---

[2]   For a more detailed description of this structure, see Frank J. Fabozzi and Chuck Ramsey, *Collateralized Mortgage Obligations: Structures and Analysis*, 3rd ed. (New Hope, PA: Frank J. Fabozzi Associates, 1998), Chapter 8.

is a longer-term security. In particular, depository institutions are exposed to extension risk when they invest in pass-through securities.

2. To satisfy certain obligations of insurance companies, pass-through securities may be unattractive. More specifically, consider a life insurance company that has issued a 4-year GIC. The uncertainty about the cash flow from a pass-through security, and the likelihood that slow prepayments will result in the instrument being long term, make it an unappealing investment vehicle for such accounts. In such instances, a pass-through security exposes the insurance company to extension risk.

3. Consider a pension fund that wants to fund a 15-year liability. Buying a pass-through security exposes the pension fund to the risk that prepayments will speed up and that the maturity of the investment will shorten to considerably less than 15 years. Prepayments speed up when interest rates decline, thereby forcing reinvestment of the prepaid amounts at a lower interest rate. In this case, the pension fund is open to contraction risk.

We can see that some institutional investors are concerned with extension risk and others with contraction risk when they purchase a pass-through security. Altering the cash flow of a pass-through so as to reduce the contraction risk and extension risk for institutional investors is explained later in this chapter when we cover collateralized mortgage obligations.

PREPAYMENT CONVENTIONS

The only way to project a cash flow is to make some assumption about the prepayment rate over the life of the underlying mortgage pool. The prepayment rate assumed is called the **prepayment speed** or, simply, **speed**.

Conditional Prepayment Rate The **conditional prepayment rate (CPR)** assumes that some fraction of the remaining principal in the pool is prepaid each year for the remaining term of the mortgage. The prepayment rate assumed for a pool is based on the characteristics of the pool (including its historical prepayment experience) and the current and expected future economic environment. It is referred to as a *conditional* rate because it is conditional on the remaining mortgage balance.

The CPR is an annual prepayment rate. To estimate monthly prepayments, the CPR must be converted into a monthly prepayment rate, commonly referred to as the **single-monthly mortality rate (SMM)**. The following formula can be used to determine the SMM for a given CPR:

$$\text{SMM} = 1 - \left(1 - \text{CPR}\right)^{1/12} \tag{26.1}$$

Suppose that the CPR used to estimate prepayments is 6%. The corresponding SMM is

$$\text{SMM} = 1 - \left(1 - 0.06\right)^{1/12}$$
$$= 1 - \left(0.94\right)^{0.08333} = 0.005143$$

An SMM of $w\%$ means that approximately $w\%$ of the remaining mortgage balance at the beginning of the month, less the scheduled principal payment, will prepay that month. That is,

$$\text{Prepayment for month } t = \text{SMM} \times (\text{Beginning mortgage balance for month } t - \text{Scheduled principal payment for month } t) \tag{26.2}$$

For example, suppose that an investor owns a pass-through in which the remaining mortgage balance at the beginning of some month is $290 million. Assuming that the SMM is 0.5143% and the scheduled principal payment is $3 million, the estimated prepayment for the month is:

$$0.005143 \times \left(\$290,000,000 - \$3,000,000 \right) = \$1,476,041$$

PSA Benchmark   The Public Securities Association (PSA) prepayment benchmark is expressed as a monthly series of annual prepayment rates. The PSA benchmark assumes that prepayment rates are low for newly originated mortgages and then speed up as the mortgages become seasoned.

The PSA benchmark assumes the following CPRs for 30-year mortgages:

1. A CPR of 0.2% for the first month, increased by 0.2% per year per month for the next 30 months when it reaches 6% per year
2. A 6% CPR for the remaining years

This benchmark, referred to as ***100% PSA*** or simply ***100 PSA***, is graphically depicted in Figure 26-2. Mathematically, 100 PSA can be expressed as follows:

$$\text{If } t \leq 30, \text{ then CPR } = 6\%\left(t \ / \ 30\right)$$

$$\text{If } t > 30, \text{ then CPR } = 6\%$$

where t is the number of months since the mortgage originated.

Slower or faster speeds are then referred to as some percentage of PSA. For example, 50 PSA means one-half the CPR of the PSA benchmark prepayment rate; 150 PSA means one-and-a-half times the CPR of the PSA benchmark prepayment rate; 300 PSA means three times the CPR of the benchmark prepayment rate. A prepayment rate of 0 PSA means that no prepayments are assumed.

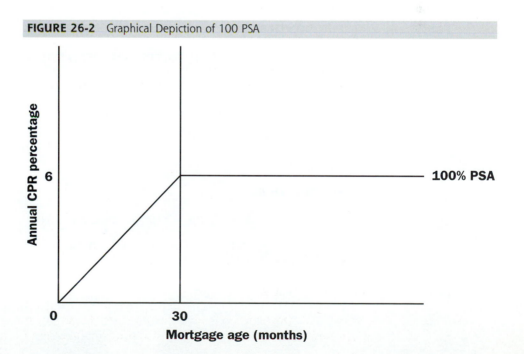

FIGURE 26-2   Graphical Depiction of 100 PSA

The CPR is converted to an SMM using equation (26.1). For example, the SMMs for month 5, month 20, and months 31 through 360 assuming 100 PSA are calculated as follows:

FOR MONTH 5:

$$CPR = 6\%\left(5 / 30\right) = 1\% = 0.01$$

$$SMM = 1 - \left(1 - 0.01\right)^{1/12}$$

$$= 1 - \left(0.99\right)^{0.083333} = 0.000837$$

FOR MONTH 20:

$$CPR = 6\%\left(20 / 30\right) = 1\% = 0.01$$

$$SMM = 1 - \left(1 - 0.04\right)^{1/12}$$

$$= 1 - \left(0.96\right)^{0.083333} = 0.003396$$

FOR MONTHS 31 TO 360:

$$CPR = 6\%$$

$$SMM = 1 - \left(1 - 0.06\right)^{1/12}$$

$$= 1 - \left(0.9835\right)^{0.083333} = 0.001386$$

The SMMs for month 5, month 20, and months 31 through 360 assuming 165 PSA are computed as follows:

FOR MONTH 5:

$$CPR = 6\%\left(5 / 30\right) = 1\% = 0.01$$

$$165\ PSA = 1.65\left(0.01\right) = 0.0165$$

$$SMM = 1 - \left(1 - 0.0165\right)^{1/12}$$

$$= 1 - \left(0.9835\right)^{0.083333} = 0.001386$$

FOR MONTH 20:

$$CPR = 6\%\left(20 / 30\right) = 4\% = 0.04$$

$$165\ PSA = 1.65\left(0.04\right) = 0.066$$

$$SMM = 1 - \left(1 - 0.066\right)^{1/12}$$

$$= 1 - \left(0.934\right)^{0.083333} = 0.005674$$

FOR MONTHS 31 TO 360:

$$CPR = 6\%$$

$$165\,PSA = 1.65(0.06) = 0.099$$

$$SMM = 1 - (1 - 0.099)^{1/12}$$

$$= 1 - (0.901)^{0.083333} = 0.00865$$

Notice that the SMM assuming 165 PSA is not just 1.65 times the SMM assuming 100 PSA. It is the CPR that is a multiple of the CPR assuming 100 PSA.

Illustration of Monthly Cash Flow Construction   We now show how to construct a monthly cash flow for a hypothetical pass-through given a PSA assumption. For the purpose of this illustration, the underlying mortgages for this hypothetical pass-through are assumed to be fixed-rate, level-payment mortgages and the pass-through rate is assumed to be 7.5%. Furthermore, it is assumed that the weighted average maturity (WAM) of the pool of mortgages is 357 months.[3]

Table 26-1 shows the cash flow for selected months assuming 100 PSA. The cash flow breaks down into three components: (1) interest (based on the pass-through rate), (2) the regularly scheduled principal repayment, and (3) prepayments based on 100 PSA.

Let's walk through Table 26-1 column by column.

Column 1: This indicates the month.

Column 2: The outstanding mortgage balance at the beginning of the month equals the outstanding balance at the beginning of the previous month reduced by the total principal payment in the previous month.

Column 3: The SMM for 100 PSA changes, based on the assumptions for the CPR. Two things should be noted in this column. First, for month 1, the SMM is for a pass-through that has been seasoned 3 months; that is, the CPR is 0.8% because the WAM is 357. Second, from month 27 on, the SMM is 0.00514, which corresponds to a CPR of 6%.

Column 4: The total monthly mortgage payment declines over time as prepayments reduce the mortgage balance outstanding. A formula determines what the monthly balance will be for each month given prepayments.[4]

Column 5: The monthly interest paid to the pass-through investor is determined by multiplying the outstanding mortgage balance at the beginning of the month by the pass-through rate of 7.5% and dividing by 12.

Column 6: The regularly scheduled principal repayment is the difference between the total monthly mortgage payment (the amount shown in column 4) and the gross coupon interest for the month. The gross coupon interest is 8.125% multiplied by the outstanding mortgage balance at the beginning of the month, then divided by 12.

Column 7: The prepayment for the month is found by using equation (26.2). So, for example, in month 100, the beginning mortgage balance is $231,249,776, the

[3] It is necessary to calculate a WAM for a pool of mortgages because not all the mortgages have the same number of months remaining to maturity.
[4] The formula is presented in Frank J. Fabozzi, *Fixed Income Mathematics: Analytical and Statistical Techniques* (Chicago: Probus Publishing, 1993), Chapter 20.

TABLE 26-1 Monthly Cash Flow for a $400 Million, 7.5% Pass-Through Rate (with a WAC of 8.125% and a WAM of 357 months assuming 100 PSA)

Month	Outstanding Balance	SMM	Mortgage Payment	Net Interest	Scheduled Principal	Prepayment	Total Principal	Total Cash Flow
1	$400,000,000	0.00067	$2,975,868	$2,500,000	$267,535	$ 267,470	$ 535,005	$3,035,005
2	399,464,995	0.00084	2,973,877	2,496,656	269,166	334,198	603,364	3,100,020
3	398,861,631	0.00101	2,971,387	2,492,885	270,762	400,800	671,562	3,164,447
4	398,190,069	0.00117	2,968,399	2,488,688	272,321	467,243	739,564	3,228,252
5	397,450,505	0.00134	2,964,914	2,484,066	273,843	533,493	807,335	3,291,401
6	396,643,170	0.00151	2,960,931	2,479,020	275,327	599,514	874,841	3,353,860
7	395,768,329	0.00168	2,956,453	2,473,552	276,772	665,273	942,045	3,415,597
8	394,826,284	0.00185	2,951,480	2,467,664	278,177	730,736	1,008,913	3,476,577
9	393,817,371	0.00202	2,946,013	2,461,359	279,542	795,869	1,075,410	3,536,769
10	392,741,961	0.00219	2,940,056	2,454,637	280,865	860,637	1,141,502	3,596,140
11	391,600,459	0.00236	2,933,608	2,447,503	282,147	925,008	1,207,155	3,654,658
12	390,393,304	0.00254	2,926,674	2,439,958	283,386	988,948	1,272,333	3,712,291
13	389,120,971	0.00271	2,919,254	2,432,006	284,581	1,052,423	1,337,004	3,769,010
14	387,783,966	0.00288	2,911,353	2,423,650	285,733	1,115,402	1,401,134	3,824,784
15	386,382,832	0.00305	2,902,973	2,414,893	286,839	1,177,851	1,464,690	3,879,583
16	384,918,142	0.00322	2,894,117	2,405,738	287,900	1,239,739	1,527,639	3,933,378
17	383,390,502	0.00340	2,884,789	2,396,191	288,915	1,301,033	1,589,949	3,986,139
18	381,800,553	0.00357	2,874,992	2,386,253	289,884	1,361,703	1,651,587	4,037,840
19	380,148,966	0.00374	2,864,730	2,375,931	290,805	1,421,717	1,712,522	4,088,453
20	378,436,444	0.00392	2,854,008	2,365,228	291,678	1,481,046	1,772,724	4,137,952
21	376,663,720	0.00409	2,842,830	2,354,148	292,503	1,539,658	1,832,161	4,186,309
22	374,831,559	0.00427	2,831,201	2,342,697	293,279	1,597,525	1,890,804	4,233,501
23	372,940,755	0.00444	2,819,125	2,330,880	294,005	1,654,618	1,948,623	4,279,503
24	370,992,132	0.00462	2,806,607	2,318,701	294,681	1,710,908	2,005,589	4,324,290
25	368,986,543	0.00479	2,793,654	2,306,166	295,307	1,766,368	2,061,675	4,367,841
26	366,924,868	0.00497	2,780,270	2,293,280	295,883	1,820,970	2,116,852	4,410,133
27	364,808,016	0.00514	2,766,461	2,280,050	296,406	1,874,688	2,171,094	4,451,144
28	362,636,921	0.00514	2,752,233	2,266,481	296,879	1,863,519	2,160,398	4,426,879
29	360,476,523	0.00514	2,738,078	2,252,978	297,351	1,852,406	2,149,578	4,402,736
30	358,326,766	0.00514	2,723,996	2,239,542	297,825	1,841,347	2,139,173	4,378,715
100	231,249,776	0.00514	1,898,682	1,445,311	332,928	1,187,608	1,520,537	2,965,848
101	229,729,239	0.00514	1,888,917	1,435,808	333,459	1,179,785	1,513,244	2,949,052
102	228,215,995	0.00514	1,879,202	1,426,350	333,990	1,172,000	1,505,990	2,932,340
103	226,710,004	0.00514	1,869,538	1,416,938	334,522	1,164,252	1,498,774	2,915,712
104	225,211,230	0.00514	1,859,923	1,407,570	335,055	1,156,541	1,491,596	2,899,166
105	223,719,634	0.00514	1,850,357	1,398,248	335,589	1,148,867	1,484,456	2,882,703
200	109,791,339	0.00514	1,133,751	686,196	390,372	562,651	953,023	1,639,219
201	108,838,316	0.00514	1,127,920	680,239	390,994	557,746	948,740	1,628,980
202	107,889,576	0.00514	1,122,119	674,310	391,617	552,863	944,480	1,618,790
203	106,945,096	0.00514	1,116,348	668,407	392,241	548,003	940,243	1,608,650
204	106,004,852	0.00514	1,110,607	662,530	392,866	543,164	936,029	1,598,560
205	105,068,823	0.00514	1,104,895	656,680	393,491	538,347	931,838	1,588,518
300	32,383,611	0.00514	676,991	202,398	457,727	164,195	621,923	824,320
301	31,761,689	0.00514	673,510	198,511	458,457	160,993	619,449	817,960
302	31,142,239	0.00514	670,046	194,639	459,187	157,803	616,990	811,629

(continued)

TABLE 26-1   (cont.)

303	30,525,249	0.00514	666,600	190,783	459,918	154,626	614,545	805,328
304	29,910,704	0.00514	663,171	186,942	460,651	151,462	612,113	799,055
305	29,298,591	0.00514	659,761	183,116	461,385	148,310	609,695	792,811
350	4,060,411	0.00514	523,138	25,378	495,645	18,334	513,979	539,356
351	3,546,432	0.00514	520,447	22,165	496,435	15,686	512,121	534,286
352	3,034,311	0.00514	517,770	18,964	497,226	13,048	510,274	529,238
353	2,524,037	0.00514	515,107	15,775	498,018	10,420	508,437	524,213
354	2,015,600	0.00514	512,458	12,597	498,811	7,801	506,612	519,209
355	1,508,988	0.00514	509,823	9,431	499,606	5,191	504,797	514,228
356	1,004,191	0.00514	507,201	6,276	500,401	2,591	502,992	509,269
357	501,199	0.00514	504,592	3,132	$501,199	0	501,199	504,331

scheduled principal payment is $332,298, and the SMM at 100 PSA is 0.00514301 (only 0.00514 is shown in the table to save space), so the prepayment is:

$$0.00514301(\$231,249,776 - \$332,928) = \$1,187,608$$

Column 8: The total principal payment combines the scheduled principal payment and the prepayment amount from columns (6) and (7).

Column 9: The projected monthly cash flow for this pass-through is the sum of the interest paid to the pass-through investor in column (5) and the total principal payments for the month in column (8).

Table 26-2 shows selected monthly cash flows for the same pass-through assuming 165 PSA.

AVERAGE LIFE

The stated maturity of a mortgage pass-through security is an inappropriate measure of the security's life because of prepayments. Instead, market participants commonly use the security's average life. The **average life** of a mortgage-backed security is the average time to receipt of principal payments (scheduled principal payments and projected prepayments), weighted by the amount of principal expected. Mathematically, the average life is expressed as follows:

$$\text{Average life} = \sum_{t=1}^{T} \frac{t \times \text{Principal received at time } t}{12 \left(\text{Total principal} \right)}$$

where T is the number of months.

The average life of a pass-through depends on the PSA prepayment assumption. To see this, the average life follows for different prepayment speeds for the pass-through we used to illustrate the cash flow for 100 PSA and 165 PSA in Table 26-1 and Table 26-2:

PSA speed	50	100	165	200	300	400	500	600	700
Average life	15.11	11.66	8.76	7.68	5.63	4.44	3.68	3.16	2.78

TABLE 26-2 Monthly Cash Flow for a $400 Million, 7.5% Pass-Through Rate (with a WAC of 8.125% and a WAM of 357 months assuming 165 PSA)

Month	Outstanding Balance	SMM	Mortgage Payment	Net Interest	Scheduled Principal	Prepay-ment	Total Principal	Total Cash Flow
1	$400,000,000	0.00111	$2,975,868	$2,500,000	$267,535	$442,389	$709,923	$3,209,923
2	399,290,077	0.00139	2,972,575	2,495,563	269,048	552,847	821,896	3,317,459
3	398,468,181	0.00167	2,968,456	2,490,426	270,495	663,065	933,560	3,423,986
4	397,534,621	0.00195	2,963,513	2,484,591	271,873	772,949	1,044,822	3,529,413
5	396,489,799	0.00223	2,957,747	2,478,061	273,181	882,405	1,155,586	3,633,647
6	395,334,213	0.00251	2,951,160	2,470,839	274,418	991,341	1,265,759	3,736,598
7	394,068,454	0.00279	2,943,755	2,462,928	275,583	1,099,664	1,375,246	3,838,174
8	392,693,208	0.00308	2,935,534	2,454,333	276,674	1,207,280	1,483,954	3,938,287
9	391,209,254	0.00336	2,926,503	2,445,058	277,690	1,314,099	1,591,789	4,036,847
10	389,617,464	0.00365	2,916,666	2,435,109	278,631	1,420,029	1,698,659	4,133,769
11	387,918,805	0.00393	2,906,028	2,424,493	279,494	1,524,979	1,804,473	4,228,965
12	386,114,332	0.00422	2,894,595	2,413,215	280,280	1,628,859	1,909,139	4,322,353
13	384,205,194	0.00451	2,882,375	2,401,282	280,986	1,731,581	2,012,567	4,413,850
14	382,192,626	0.00480	2,869,375	2,388,704	281,613	1,833,058	2,114,670	4,503,374
15	380,077,956	0.00509	2,855,603	2,375,487	282,159	1,933,203	2,215,361	4,590,848
16	377,862,595	0.00538	2,841,068	2,361,641	282,623	2,031,931	2,314,554	4,676,195
17	375,548,041	0.00567	2,825,779	2,347,175	283,006	2,129,159	2,412,164	4,759,339
18	373,135,877	0.00597	2,809,746	2,332,099	283,305	2,224,805	2,508,110	4,840,210
19	370,627,766	0.00626	2,792,980	2,316,424	283,521	2,318,790	2,602,312	4,918,735
20	368,025,455	0.00656	2,775,493	2,300,159	283,654	2,411,036	2,694,690	4,994,849
21	365,330,765	0.00685	2,757,296	2,283,317	283,702	2,501,466	2,785,169	5,068,486
22	362,545,596	0.00715	2,738,402	2,265,910	283,666	2,590,008	2,873,674	5,139,584
23	359,671,922	0.00745	2,718,823	2,247,950	283,545	2,676,588	2,960,133	5,208,083
24	356,711,789	0.00775	2,698,575	2,229,449	283,338	2,761,139	3,044,477	5,273,926
25	353,667,312	0.00805	2,677,670	2,210,421	283,047	2,843,593	3,126,640	5,337,061
26	350,540,672	0.00835	2,656,123	2,190,879	282,671	2,923,885	3,206,556	5,397,435
27	347,334,116	0.00865	2,633,950	2,170,838	282,209	3,001,955	3,284,164	5,455,022
28	344,049,952	0.00865	2,611,167	2,150,312	281,662	2,973,553	3,255,215	5,405,527
29	340,794,737	0.00865	2,588,581	2,129,967	281,116	2,945,400	3,226,516	5,356,483
30	337,568,221	0.00865	2,566,190	2,109,801	280,572	2,917,496	3,198,067	5,307,869
100	170,142,350	0.00865	1,396,958	1,063,390	244,953	1,469,591	1,714,544	2,777,933
101	168,427,806	0.00865	1,384,875	1,052,674	244,478	1,454,765	1,699,243	2,751,916
102	166,728,563	0.00865	1,372,896	1,042,054	244,004	1,440,071	1,684,075	2,726,128
103	165,044,489	0.00865	1,361,020	1,031,528	243,531	1,425,508	1,669,039	2,700,567
104	163,375,450	0.00865	1,349,248	1,021,097	243,060	1,411,075	1,654,134	2,675,231
105	161,721,315	0.00865	1,337,577	1,010,758	242,589	1,396,771	1,639,359	2,650,118
200	56,746,664	0.00865	585,990	354,667	201,767	489,106	690,874	1,045,540
201	56,055,790	0.00865	580,921	350,349	201,377	483,134	684,510	1,034,859
202	55,371,280	0.00865	575,896	346,070	200,986	477,216	678,202	1,024,273
203	54,693,077	0.00865	570,915	341,832	200,597	471,353	671,950	1,013,782
204	54,021,127	0.00865	565,976	337,632	200,208	465,544	665,752	1,003,384
205	53,355,375	0.00865	561,081	333,471	199,820	459,789	659,609	993,080
300	11,758,141	0.00865	245,808	73,488	166,196	100,269	266,456	339,953
301	11,491,677	0.00865	243,682	71,823	165,874	97,967	263,841	335,664
302	11,227,836	0.00865	241,574	70,174	165,552	95,687	261,240	331,414

(continued)

TABLE 26-2   (cont.)

303	10,966,596	0.00865	239,485	68,541	165,232	93,430	258,662	327,203
304	10,707,934	0.00865	237,413	66,925	164,912	91,196	256,107	323,032
305	10,451,827	0.00865	235,360	65,324	164,592	88,983	253,575	318,899
350	1,235,674	0.00865	159,202	7,723	150,836	9,384	160,220	167,943
351	1,075,454	0.00865	157,825	6,722	150,544	8,000	158,544	165,266
352	916,910	0.00865	156,460	5,731	150,252	6,631	156,883	162,614
353	760,027	0.00865	155,107	4,750	149,961	5,277	155,238	159,988
354	604,789	0.00865	153,765	3,780	149,670	3,937	153,607	157,387
355	451,182	0.00865	152,435	2,820	149,380	2,611	151,991	154,811
356	299,191	0.00865	151,117	1,870	149,091	1,298	150,398	152,259
357	148,802	0.00865	149,809	930	$148,802	0	148,802	149,732

◆ COLLATERALIZED MORTGAGE OBLIGATIONS

Some institutional investors are concerned with extension risk and others with contraction risk when they invest in a pass-through. This problem can be mitigated by redirecting the cash flows of mortgage pass-through securities to different bond classes, called **tranches**, so as to create securities that have different exposure to prepayment risk and, therefore, risk/return patterns different from the pass-through securities from which the tranches were created.

When the cash flows of pools of mortgage pass-through securities are redistributed to different bond classes, the resulting securities are called **collateralized mortgage obligations (CMO)**. The creation of a CMO cannot eliminate prepayment risk; it can only distribute the various forms of this risk among different classes of bondholders. The CMO's major financial innovation is that the securities created more closely satisfy the asset/liability needs of institutional investors and thus broaden the appeal of mortgage-backed products to traditional bond investors.

Rather than list the different types of tranches that can be created in a CMO structure, we show how the tranches can be created as an illustration of financial engineering. Although many different types of CMOs have been created, we only look at three of the key innovations in the CMO market: sequential-pay tranches, accrual tranches, and planned amortization class bonds. Two other important tranches that are not illustrated here are the floating-rate tranche and inverse floating-rate tranche.

SEQUENTIAL-PAY CMOs

The first CMO was created in 1983 and was structured so that each class of bond would be retired sequentially. Such structures are referred to as **sequential-pay CMOs**. To illustrate a sequential-pay CMO, we discuss CMO-1, a hypothetical deal made up to illustrate the basic features of the structure. The collateral for this hypothetical CMO is a hypothetical pass-through with a total par value of $400 million and the following characteristics: (1) The pass-through coupon rate is 7.5%; (2) the weighted average coupon (WAC) is 8.125%; and (3) the weighted average maturity (WAM) is 357 months. We used this same pass-through earlier in the chapter to describe the cash flow of a pass-through based on some PSA assumptions.

From this $400 million of collateral, four bond classes or tranches are created. Their characteristics are summarized in Table 26-3. The total par value of the four tranches is equal to the par value of the collateral (i.e., the pass-through security). In

TABLE 26-3 CMO-1: A Hypothetical Four-Tranche, Sequential-Pay Structure

Tranche	Par Amount	Coupon Rate
A	$194,500,000	7.5%
B	36,000,000	7.5
C	96,500,000	7.5
D	73,000,000	7.5
Total	$400,000,000	

Payment rules:

1. *For payment of periodic coupon interest:* Disburse periodic coupon interest to each tranche on the basis of the amount of principal outstanding at the beginning of the period.

2. *For disbursement of principal payments:* Disburse principal payments to tranche A until it is completely paid off. After tranche A is completely paid off, disburse principal payments to tranche B until it is completely paid off. After tranche B is completely paid off, disburse principal payments to tranche C until it is completely paid off. After tranche C is completely paid off, disburse principal payments to tranche D until it is completely paid off.

this simple structure, the coupon rate is the same for each tranche and also the same as the coupon rate on the collateral. In reality, the coupon rate typically varies by tranche.

Now remember that a CMO is created by redistributing the cash flow—interest and principal—to the different tranches based on a set of payment rules. The payment rules at the bottom of Table 26-3 describe how the cash flow from the pass-through (i.e., collateral) is to be distributed to the four tranches. Separate rules determine the payment of the coupon interest and the payment of the principal, the principal being the total of the regularly scheduled principal payment and any prepayments.

In CMO-1, each tranche receives periodic coupon interest payments based on the amount of the outstanding balance at the beginning of the month. The disbursement of the principal, however, is made in a special way. A tranche is not entitled to receive principal until the entire principal of the tranche is paid off. More specifically, tranche A receives all the principal payments until the entire principal amount owed to that bond class, $194,500,000, is paid off; then tranche B begins to receive principal and continues to do so until it is paid the entire $36,000,000.

Tranche C then receives principal, and when it is paid off, tranche D starts receiving principal payments.

Although the priority rules for the disbursement of the principal payments are known, the precise amount of the principal in each period is not. This amount depends on the cash flow and, therefore, on the principal payments of the collateral, which will depend on the actual prepayment rate of the collateral. An assumed PSA speed allows the cash flow to be projected. Table 26-2 shows the cash flow (interest, regularly scheduled principal repayment, and prepayments) assuming 165 PSA. Assuming that the collateral does prepay at 165 PSA, the cash flow available to all four tranches in CMO-1 will be precisely the cash flow shown in Table 26-2.

To demonstrate how the priority rules for CMO-1 work, Table 26-4 shows the cash flow for selected months assuming the collateral prepays at 165 PSA. For each tranche, the table shows (1) the balance at the end of the month, (2) the principal paid down (regularly scheduled principal repayment plus prepayments), and (3) interest. In month 1, the cash flow for the collateral consists of principal payment of $709,923 and interest of $2.5 million (0.075 times $400 million divided by 12). The interest payment is distributed to the four tranches based on the amount of the par value outstanding. So, for example, tranche A receives $1,215,625 (0.075 times $194,500,000 divided by 12) of the $2.5 million. The principal, however, is all distributed to tranche A. Therefore, the cash flow for tranche A in month 1 is $1,925,548. The principal balance at the end of month 1 for tranche A is $193,790,076 (the original principal balance of $194,500,000 less the principal payment of $709,923). No principal payment is distributed to the three other tranches because a principal balance is still outstanding for tranche A. This scenario will be true for months 2 through 80.

After month 81, the principal balance will be zero for tranche A. For the collateral, the cash flow in month 81 is $3,318,521, consisting of a principal payment of $2,032,196 and interest of $1,286,325. At the beginning of month 81 (end of month 80), the principal balance for tranche A is $311,926. Therefore, $311,926 of the $2,032,196 of the principal payment from the collateral will be disbursed to tranche A. After this payment is

TABLE 26-4 Monthly Cash Flow for Selected Months for CMO-1 Assuming 165 PSA

Month	Tranche A Balance	Principal	Interest	Tranche B Balance	Principal	Interest
1	$194,500,000	$ 709,923	$1,215,625	$36,000,000	$0	$225,000
2	193,790,077	821,896	1,211,188	36,000,000	0	255,000
3	192,968,181	933,560	1,206,051	36,000,000	0	225,000
4	192,034,621	1,044,822	1,200,216	36,000,000	0	225,000
5	190,989,799	1,155,586	1,193,686	36,000,000	0	225,000
6	189,834,213	1,265,759	1,186,464	36,000,000	0	225,000
7	188,568,454	1,375,246	1,178,553	36,000,000	0	225,000
8	187,193,208	1,483,954	1,169,958	36,000,000	0	225,000
9	185,709,254	1,591,789	1,160,683	36,000,000	0	225,000
10	184,117,464	1,698,659	1,150,734	36,000,000	0	225,000
11	182,418,805	1,804,473	1,140,118	36,000,000	0	225,000
12	180,614,332	1,909,139	1,128,840	36,000,000	0	225,000
75	12,893,479	2,143,974	80,584	36,000,000	0	225,000
76	10,749,504	2,124,935	67,184	36,000,000	0	225,000
77	8,624,569	2,106,062	53,904	36,000,000	0	225,000
78	6,518,507	2,087,353	40,741	36,000,000	0	225,000
79	4,431,154	2,068,807	27,695	36,000,000	0	225,000
80	2,362,347	2,050,422	14,765	36,000,000	0	225,000
81	311,926	311,926	1,950	36,000,000	1,720,271	225,000
82	0	0	0	34,279,729	2,014,130	214,248
83	0	0	0	32,265,599	1,996,221	201,660
84	0	0	0	30,269,378	1,978,468	189,184
85	0	0	0	28,290,911	1,960,869	176,818
95	0	0	0	9,449,331	1,793,089	59,058
96	0	0	0	7,656,242	1,777,104	47,852
97	0	0	0	5,879,138	1,761,258	36,745
98	0	0	0	4,117,880	1,745,550	25,737
99	0	0	0	2,372,329	1,729,979	14,827
100	0	0	0	642,350	642,350	4,015
101	0	0	0	0	0	0
102	0	0	0	0	0	0
103	0	0	0	0	0	0
104	0	0	0	0	0	0
105	0	0	0	0	0	0

(continued)

TABLE 26-4 (cont.)

	Tranche C			Tranche D		
Month	*Balance*	*Principal*	*Interest*	*Balance*	*Principal*	*Interest*
1	96,500,000	0	603,125	73,000,000	0	456,250
2	96,500,000	0	603,125	73,000,000	0	456,250
3	95,500,000	0	603,125	73,000,000	0	456,250
4	96,500,000	0	603,125	73,000,000	0	456,250
5	96,500,000	0	603,125	73,000,000	0	456,250
6	96,500,000	0	603,125	73,000,000	0	456,250
7	96,500,000	0	603,125	73,000,000	0	456,250
8	96,500,000	0	603,125	73,000,000	0	456,250
9	96,500,000	0	603,125	73,000,000	0	456,250
10	96,500,000	0	603,125	73,000,000	0	456,250
11	96,500,000	0	603,125	73,000,000	0	456,250
12	96,500,000	0	603,125	73,000,000	0	456,250
95	96,500,000	0	603,125	73,000,000	0	456,250
96	96,500,000	0	603,125	73,000,000	0	456,250
97	96,500,000	0	603,125	73,000,000	0	456,250
98	96,500,000	0	603,125	73,000,000	0	456,250
99	95,500,000	0	603,125	73,000,000	0	456,250
100	96,500,000	1,072,194	603,125	73,000,000	0	456,250
101	95,427,806	1,699,243	596,424	73,000,000	0	456,250
102	93,728,563	1,684,075	585,804	73,000,000	0	456,250
103	92,044,489	1,669,039	575,278	73,000,000	0	456,250
104	90,375,450	1,654,134	564,847	73,000,000	0	456,250
105	88,721,315	1,639,359	554,508	73,000,000	0	456,250
175	3,260,287	869,602	20,377	73,000,000	0	456,250
176	2,390,685	861,673	14,942	73,000,000	0	456,250
177	1,529,013	853,813	9,556	73,000,000	0	456,250
178	675,199	675,199	4,220	73,000,000	170,824	456,250
179	0	0	0	72,829,176	838,300	455,182
180	0	0	0	71,990,876	830,646	449,943
181	0	0	0	71,160,230	823,058	444,751
182	0	0	0	70,337,173	815,536	439,607
183	0	0	0	69,521,637	808,081	434,510
184	0	0	0	68,713,556	800,690	429,460
185	0	0	0	67,912,866	793,365	424,455
350	0	0	0	1,235,674	160,220	7,723
351	0	0	0	1,075,454	158,544	6,722
352	0	0	0	916,910	156,883	5,731
353	0	0	0	760,027	155,238	4,750
354	0	0	0	604,789	153,607	3,780
355	0	0	0	451,182	151,991	2,820
356	0	0	0	299,191	150,389	1,870
357	$0	$0	$0	148,802	$148,802	$930

made, no additional principal payments are made to this tranche as the principal balance is zero. The remaining principal payment from the collateral, $1,720,271, is disbursed to tranche B. According to the assumed prepayment speed of 165 PSA, tranche B then begins receiving principal payments in month 81.

Table 26-4 shows that tranche B is fully paid off by month 100, when tranche C now begins to receive principal payments. Tranche C is not fully paid off until month 178, at which time tranche D begins receiving the remaining principal payments. The maturity (i.e., the time until the principal is fully paid off) for these four tranches assuming 165 PSA would be 81 months for tranche A, 100 months for tranche B, 178 months for tranche C, and 357 months for tranche D.

Let's look at what has been accomplished by creating the CMO. First, as shown earlier in this chapter, the average life for the pass-through is 8.76 years, assuming a prepayment speed of 165 PSA. Table 26-5 reports the average life of the collateral and the four tranches assuming different prepayment speeds. Notice that the four tranches have average lives that are both shorter and longer than the collateral, thereby attracting investors who have a preference for an average life different from that of the collateral.

A major problem remains: The average life for the tranches varies considerably. We see how this issue can be tackled later on. However, some protection is provided for each tranche against prepayment risk. Prioritizing the distribution of principal (i.e., establishing the payment rules for principal) effectively protects the shorter-term tranche A in this structure against extension risk. This protection must come from somewhere, so it comes from the three other tranches. Similarly, tranches C and D provide protection against extension risk for tranches A and B. At the same time, tranches C and D benefit because they are provided protection against contraction risk, the protection coming from tranches A and B.

ACCRUAL BONDS

In CMO-1, the payment rules for interest provide for all tranches to be paid interest each month. In many sequential-pay CMO structures, at least one tranche does not receive current interest. Instead, the interest for that tranche would accrue and be added to the principal balance. Such a bond class is commonly referred to as an **accrual tranche**, or a **Z bond** (because the bond is similar to a zero-coupon bond). The interest that would have been paid to the accrual bond class is then used to speed up paying down the principal balance of earlier bond classes.

TABLE 26-5 Average Life for the Collateral and the Four Tranches of CMO-1

Prepayment Speed (PSA)	Average Life for				
	Collateral	Tranche A	Tranche B	Tranche C	Tranche D
50	15.11	7.48	15.98	21.08	27.24
100	11.66	4.90	10.86	15.78	24.58
165	8.76	3.48	7.49	11.19	20.27
200	7.68	3.05	6.42	9.60	18.11
300	5.63	2.32	4.64	6.81	13.36
400	4.44	1.94	3.70	5.31	10.34
500	3.68	1.69	3.12	4.38	8.35
600	3.16	1.51	2.74	3.75	6.96
700	2.78	1.38	2.47	3.30	5.95

To see this process, consider CMO-2, a hypothetical CMO structure with the same collateral as CMO-1 and with four tranches, each with a coupon rate of 7.5%. The structure is shown in Table 26-6. The difference is in the last tranche, Z, which is an accrual bond.

Let's look at month 1 and compare it to month 1 in Table 26-4 based on 165 PSA. The principal payment from the collateral is $709,923. In CMO-1, this amount is the principal paydown for tranche A. In CMO-2, the interest for tranche Z, $456,250, is not paid to that tranche but instead is used to pay down the principal of tranche A. So, the principal payment to tranche A is $1,166,173, the collateral's principal payment of $709,923 plus the interest of $456,250 that was diverted from tranche Z.

The inclusion of the accrual tranche results in a shortening of the expected final maturity for tranches A, B, and C. The final payout for tranche A is 64 months rather than 81 months, for tranche B it is 77 months rather than 100 months, and for tranche C it is 112 rather than 178 months.

The average lives for tranches A, B, and C are shorter in CMO-2 compared to CMO-1 because of the inclusion of the accrual bond. For example, at 165 PSA, the average lives are as follows:

Structure	Tranche A	Tranche B	Tranche C
CMO-2	2.90	5.86	7.87
CMO-1	3.48	7.49	11.19

The reason for the shortening of the nonaccrual tranches is that the interest that would be paid to the accrual bond is being allocated to the other tranches. Tranche Z in CMO-2 will have a longer average life than tranche D in CMO-1.

Thus, shorter-term tranches and a longer-term tranche are created by including an accrual bond. The accrual bond appeals to investors who are concerned with reinvestment risk. The lack of coupon payments that must be reinvested eliminates reinvestment risk until all the other tranches are paid off.

TABLE 26-6   CMO-2: A Hypothetical Four-Tranche Sequential-Pay Structure with an Accrual Bond Class

Tranche	Par Amount	Coupon Rate
A	$194,500,000	7.5%
B	36,000,000	7.5
C	96,500,000	7.5
Z (Accrual)	73,000,000	7.5
Total	$400,000,000	

Payment rules:

1. *For payment of periodic coupon interest:* Disburse periodic coupon interest to tranches A, B, and C on the basis of the amount of principal outstanding at the beginning of the period. For tranche Z, accrue the interest based on the principal plus accrued interest in the previous period. The interest for tranche Z is to be paid to the earlier tranches as a principal paydown.

2. *For disbursement of principal payments:* Disburse principal payments to tranche A until it is completely paid off. After tranche A is completely paid off, disburse principal payments to tranche B until it is completely paid off. After tranche B is completely paid off, disburse principal payments to tranche C until it is completely paid off. After tranche C is completely paid off, disburse principal payments to tranche Z until the original principal balance plus accrued interest is completely paid off.

PLANNED AMORTIZATION CLASS TRANCHES

Many investors were still concerned about investing in an instrument they continued to perceive as posing significant prepayment risk because of the substantial average life variability despite the innovations designed to reduce prepayment risk. Traditional corporate bond buyers sought a structure with both the characteristics of a corporate bond (either a bullet maturity or a sinking fund type of schedule for principal repayment) and high credit quality. Although CMOs satisfied the second condition, they did not satisfy the first.

In 1987, CMO issuers began issuing bonds with the characteristic that if prepayments are within a specified range, the cash flow pattern is known. The greater predictability of the cash flow for these classes of bonds, referred to as **planned amortization class (PAC) bonds**, occurs because of a principal repayment schedule that must be satisfied. PAC bondholders take priority over all other classes in the CMO issue in receiving principal payments from the underlying collateral. The greater certainty of the cash flow for the PAC bonds comes at the expense of the non-PAC classes, called the **support** or **companion bonds**. These bonds absorb the prepayment risk. Because PAC bonds have protection against both extension risk and contraction risk, they are said to provide *two-sided prepayment protection*.

To illustrate how to create a PAC bond, we use as collateral the $400 million pass-through with a coupon rate of 7.5%, a WAC of 8.125%, and a WAM of 357 months. The second column of Table 26-7 shows the principal payment (regularly scheduled principal repayment plus prepayments) for selected months assuming a prepayment speed of 90 PSA, and the next column shows the principal payments for selected months assuming that the pass-through prepays at 300 PSA.

The last column of Table 26-7 gives the *minimum* principal payment if the collateral speed is 90 PSA or 300 PSA for months 1 to 349. (After month 346, the outstanding principal balance will be paid off if the prepayment speed is between 90 PSA and 300 PSA.) For example, in the first month, the principal payment would be $508,169.52 if the collateral prepays at 90 PSA and $1,075,931.20 if the collateral prepays at 300 PSA. Thus, the minimum principal payment is $508,169.52, as reported in the last column of Table 26-7. In month 103, the minimum principal payment is also the amount if the prepayment speed is 90 PSA, $1,446,761, compared to $1,458,618.04 for 300 PSA. In month 104, however, a prepayment speed of 300 PSA would produce a principal payment of $1,433,539.23, which is less than the principal payment of $1,440,825.55 assuming 90 PSA. So, $1,433,539.23 is reported in the last column of Table 26-7. In fact, from month 104 on, the minimum principal payment is the one that would result assuming a prepayment speed of 300 PSA.

In fact, if the collateral prepays at *any* speed between 90 PSA and 300 PSA, the minimum principal payment would be the amount reported in the last column of Table 26-7. For example, if we had included principal payment figures assuming a prepayment speed of 200 PSA, the minimum principal payment would not change: From month 11 through month 103, the minimum principal payment is that generated from 90 PSA, but from month 104 on, the minimum principal payment is that generated from 300 PSA.

This characteristic of the collateral allows for the creation of a PAC bond, assuming that the collateral prepays over its life at a constant speed between 90 PSA and 300 PSA. A schedule of principal repayments that the PAC bondholders are entitled to receive before any other bond class in the CMO is specified. The monthly schedule of principal repayments is as specified in the last column of Table 26-7, which shows the minimum principal payment. Although collateral prepayment between these two speeds cannot be guaranteed, a PAC bond can be structured to assume that it is.

TABLE 26-7 Monthly Principal Payment for $400 Million, 7.5% Coupon Pass-Through (with an 8.125% WAC and a 357 WAM assuming prepayment rates of 90 PSA and 300 PSA)

Month	At 90% PSA	At 300% PSA	Minimum Principal Payment—The PAC Schedule
1	$ 508,169.52	$1,075,931.20	$ 508,169.52
2	569,843.43	1,279,412.11	569,843.43
3	631,377.11	1,482,194.45	631,377.11
4	692,741.89	1,683,966.17	692,741.89
5	753,909.12	1,884,414.62	753,909.12
6	814,850.22	2,083,227.31	814,850.22
7	875,536.68	2,280,092.68	875,536.68
8	935,940.10	2,474,700.92	935,940.10
9	996,032.19	2,666,744.77	996,032.19
10	1,055,784.82	2,855,920.32	1,055,784.82
11	1,115,170.01	3,041,927.81	1,115,170.01
12	1,174,160.00	3,224,472.44	1,174,160.00
13	1,232,727.22	3,403,265.17	1,232,727.22
14	1,290,844.32	3,578,023.49	1,290,844.32
15	1,348,484.24	3,748,472.23	1,348,484.24
16	1,405,620.17	3,914,344.26	1,405,620.17
17	1,462,225.60	4,075,381.29	1,462,225.60
18	1,518,274.36	4,231,334.57	1,518,274.36
101	1,458,719.34	1,510,072.17	1,458,719.34
102	1,452,725.55	1,484,126.59	1,452,725.55
103	1,446,761.00	1,458,618.04	1,446,761.00
104	1,440,825.55	1,433,539.23	1,433,539.23
105	1,434,919.07	1,408,883.01	1,408,883.01
211	949,482.58	213,309.00	213,309.00
212	946,033.34	209,409.09	209,409.09
213	942,601.99	205,577.05	205,577.05
346	618,684.59	13,269.17	13,269.17
347	617,071.58	12,944.51	12,944.51
348	615,468.65	12,626.21	12,626.21
349	613,875.77	12,314.16	3,432.32
350	612,292.88	12,008.25	0
351	610,719.96	11,708.38	0
352	609,156.96	11,414.42	0
353	607,603.84	11,126.28	0
354	606,060.57	10,843.85	0
355	604,527.09	10,567.02	0
356	603,003.38	10,295.70	0
357	601,489.39	10,029.78	0

TABLE 26-8 CMO-3 CMO Structure with One PAC Bond and One Support Bond

Tranche	Par Amount	Coupon Rate
P (PAC)	$243,800,000	7.5%
S (Support)	156,200,000	7.5% *f·sk·ve(*
Total	$400,000,000	

Payment Rules:

1. *For payment of periodic coupon interest:* Disburse periodic coupon interest to each tranche on the basis of the amount of principal outstanding at the beginning of the period.

2. *For disbursement of principal payments:* Disburse principal payments to tranche P based on its schedule of principal repayments. Tranche P has priority with respect to current and future principal payments to satisfy the schedule. Any excess principal payments in a month over the amount necessary to satisfy the schedule for tranche P are paid to tranche S. When tranche S is completely paid off, all principal payments are to be made to tranche P regardless of the schedule.

Table 26-8 shows a CMO structure, CMO-3, created from the $400 million, 7.5% coupon pass-through with a WAC of 8.125% and a WAM of 357 months.

The two bond classes in this structure are a 7.5% coupon PAC bond created assuming 90 to 300 PSA with par value of $243.8 million, and a support bond with a par value of $156.2 million.

Table 26-9 reports the average life for the PAC bond and the support bond in CMO-3 assuming various *actual* prepayment speeds. Notice that between 90 PSA and 300 PSA, the average life for the PAC bond is stable at 7.26 years. However, at slower or faster PSA speeds, the schedule is broken, and the average life changes, lengthening when the prepayment speed is less than 90 PSA and shortening when it is greater than 300 PSA. Even so, much greater variability characterizes the average life of the support bond, which is substantial.

TABLE 26-9 Average Life for PAC Bond and Support Bond in CMO-3 Assuming Various Prepayment Speeds

Prepayment Rate (PSA)	PAC Bond (P)	Support Bond (S)
0	15.97	27.26
50	9.44	24.00
90	7.26	18.56
100	7.26	18.56
150	7.26	12.57
165	7.26	11.16
200	7.26	8.38
250	7.26	5.37
300	7.26	3.13
350	6.56	2.51
400	5.92	2.17
450	5.38	1.94
500	4.93	1.77
700	3.70	1.37

◆ STRIPPED MORTGAGE-BACKED SECURITIES

Stripped mortgage-backed securities, introduced by Fannie Mae in 1986, are another example of derivative mortgage securities. A mortgage pass-through security divides the cash flow from the underlying pool of mortgages on a pro rata basis to the security holders. A stripped mortgage-backed security is created by altering that distribution of principal and interest from a pro rata distribution to an unequal distribution. As a result, some of the securities created demonstrate a price/yield relationship different from the price/yield relationship of the underlying mortgage pool. Stripped mortgage-backed securities, if properly used, provide a means by which investors can hedge prepayment risk.

The first generation of stripped mortgage-backed securities were partially stripped, and among them were securities issued by Fannie Mae in mid-1986. The Class B stripped mortgage-backed securities were backed by FNMA pass-through securities with a 9% coupon. The mortgage payments from the underlying mortgage pool were distributed to Class B-1 and Class B-2 so that both classes received an equal amount of the principal, but Class B-1 received one-third of the interest payments while Class B-2 received two-thirds.

In a subsequent issue, Fannie Mae distributed the cash flow from the underlying mortgage pool in a far different way. Using FNMA 11% coupon pools, Fannie Mae created Class A-1 and Class A-2. Class A-1 was given 4.95% of the 11% coupon interest, while Class A-2 received the other 6.05%. Class A-1 was given almost all of the principal payments, 99%, while Class A-2 was allotted only 1% of the principal payments.

In early 1987, stripped mortgage-backed securities began to be issued allocating all the interest to one class (called the *interest-only* or IO class) and all the principal to the other class (called the *principal-only* or PO class). The IO class receives no principal payments.

The PO security is purchased at a substantial discount from par value. The yield an investor realizes depends on the speed at which prepayments are made. The faster the prepayments are made, the higher the investor's yield is. For example, suppose a mortgage pool consists of only 30-year mortgages, with $400 million in principal, and that investors can purchase POs backed by this mortgage pool for $175 million. The dollar return on this investment will be $225 million. How quickly that dollar return is recovered by PO investors determines the yield realized. In the extreme case, if all home owners in the underlying mortgage pool decide to prepay their mortgage loans immediately, PO investors will realize the $225 million immediately. At the other extreme, if all home owners decide to remain in their homes for 30 years and make no prepayments, the $225 million will be spread out over 30 years, which would result in a lower yield for PO investors.

The price of a PO security rises when interest rates decline and falls when interest rates rise. This price/interest relationship is typical of all the bonds discussed thus far in this book. A characteristic of a PO is that its price is sensitive to changes in interest rates.

An IO has no par value. In contrast to the PO investor, the IO investor wants prepayments to be slow. The reason is that the IO investor receives interest only on the amount of the principal outstanding. When prepayments are made, less dollar interest will be received as the outstanding principal declines. In fact, if prepayments are too fast, the *IO investor may not recover the amount paid for the IO*. The unique aspect of an IO is that its price changes in the *same* direction as the change in interest rates. Moreover, as in the case of the PO, its price is highly responsive to a change in interest rates.

Because of these price volatility characteristics of stripped mortgage-backed securities, institutional investors use them to control the risk of a portfolio of mortgage-backed securities by creating a risk/return pattern that better fits their needs.

◆ YIELDS ON MORTGAGE-BACKED SECURITIES

Although many of the securities issued in the mortgage-backed securities market carry the explicit or implicit guarantee of the U.S. government, which does not mean that they offer the same yield as U.S. Treasury securities or other government agency securities. The primary reason for a difference in yields lies in the uncertainty of the cash flow of a mortgage-backed security and the exposure to prepayment risk. This risk arises because the investor grants the home owner/borrower the right to prepay a loan at any time without penalty. Of course, investors require a higher potential yield as compensation for prepayment risk. This situation is not any different from that of an investor who buys a callable corporate bond and seeks compensation for the call risk associated with such a bond. In a CMO structure, classes exposed to less prepayment risk are willing to accept a lower yield than other classes, such as the support bond classes, that are exposed to greater prepayment risk.

The problem of calculating a yield for a mortgage-backed security is a complex one. As explained in Chapter 17, calculating the yield requires a determination of the cash flow. In the case of a mortgage-backed security, the cash flow is not known because of prepayments. To calculate the potential yield, projections of prepayments must be made for a mortgage-backed security. The PSA convention described earlier is used. What is important, however, is recognition that the yield on any mortgage-backed security is based on some assumption about prepayments. For a nonagency mortgage-backed security a projection must be made regarding defaults and recoveries of the mortgages in the underlying pool.

◆ COMMERCIAL MORTGAGE-BACKED SECURITIES

As explained in the previous chapter, the mortgage market is comprised of the residential mortgage market and the commercial mortgage market. Thus far in this chapter, we focused on the securitization of residential mortgage loans. We conclude this chapter with a brief look at securities backed by commercial mortgage loans.

With the exception of some securities backed by a pool of multifamily houses issued by government-sponsored enterprises, commercial mortgage-backed securities have issued by private entities without any implicit or explicit government guarantee. As with nonagency mortgage-backed securities backed by a pool of residential loans, commercial mortgage-backed securities must be credit enhanced.

In the previous chapter, we described how, unlike residential mortgage loans, commercial mortgage loans are nonresource loans. We explained how the debt-to-service coverage ratio and the loan-to-value ratio are used to gauge the credit risk of an individual commercial mortgage loan. When assessing the credit quality of a commercial mortgage-backed security, investors look not only at these two measures for the individual loans in the pool but also at the concentration of loans by property type and by geographical location.

In the previous chapter we reviewed the types of prepayment protection afforded the lender in a commercial mortgage loan, that is, loan-level protection against prepayment risk. For a commercial mortgage-backed security, additional prepayment protection can be provided for some tranches of a deal. This type of call protection available at the deal level is referred to as structural protection and is provided by creating tranches similar to those in a collateralized mortgage obligation. In it, a sequential pay structure for the tranches in a deal allow for the redistribution of prepayment risk.

Today investors use different types of CMBS deals. A *multiproperty single borrower deal* is one where the pool of commercial mortgage loans consists of multiple properties for only one borrower. For example, the pool can include apartment buildings and strip malls owned by one borrower. A *conduit-originated deal* has as its collateral multiproperties with multiple borrowers. Conduits are commercial-lending entities established for the sole purpose of generating collateral to securitize. It is the fastest growing segment of the CMBS market. A special type of conduit deal is a *fusion conduit deal.* In such deals a large loan (greater than $50 million) is included with smaller loans. **Liquidating trusts** (also called **nonperforming trusts**) are deals backed by nonperforming mortgage loans (i.e., loans where the borrowers are in default).

Summary

In this chapter we discussed the market for mortgage-backed securities and the important role that securitization played in the development of the secondary mortgage market. The basic mortgage-backed security is the mortgage pass-through security. The types of mortgage pass-through securities are agency and nonagency pass-through securities. The latter require private credit enhancements in order to receive a high credit rating.

To address the prepayment risk associated with investing in mortgage pass-through securities—contraction risk and extension risk—collateralized mortgage obligations (CMOs) were created. Another derivative mortgage-backed security, the stripped mortgage-backed security, was created for better controlling the risk of a portfolio of mortgage-backed securities.

The market for agency pass-through securities is now the second most liquid long-term fixed income market in the United States, the first being the U.S. Treasury securities market. The greater liquidity, coupled with new mortgage designs and security structures, increased participation by a greater number of nondepository financial institutions. This development, in turn, assured a supply of funds to the mortgage market so that mortgage rates are in line with rates in other sectors of the long-term debt market. Rates in the mortgage market, therefore, more nearly reflect supply and demand in the capital markets rather than the fortunes or misfortunes of the thrifts that historically were primary suppliers of funds to the mortgage market.

Securities backed by a pool of commercial mortgage loans are called commercial mortgage-backed securities. Typically, these securities are issued by private entities that do not have any implicit or explicit government guarantee and therefore require credit enhancements. The tranches in a CMBS deal can be structured to provide additional prepayment protection above and beyond that provided at the loan level. CMBS deals are classified as multiproperty single borrower deals, conduit-originated deals, and liquidating trusts.

Key Terms

- 100 PSA
- 100% PSA
- Accrual tranche
- Agency pass-through securities
- Average life
- Blind pools
- Collateralized mortgage obligation (CMO)
- Companion bonds
- Conditional prepayment rate (CPR)
- Contraction risk
- Extension risk
- Government-sponsored enterprises
- Guaranteeing fee
- Liquidating trust
- Mortgage pass-through security
- Mortgage-backed security (MBS)
- Nonagency mortgage pass-through securities
- Nonperforming trust
- Participation certificate (PC)
- Planned amortization class (PAC) bond
- Prepayment speed

- Securitize
- Sequential-pay CMOs
- Single-monthly mortality rate (SMM)

- SMMEA-qualified securities
- Speed
- Support bond

- Tranches
- Z bond

Questions

1. What is a mortgage pass-through security?
2. Describe the cash flow of a mortgage pass-through security.
3. How does securitization enhance the liquidity of mortgages?
4. a. What are the different types of agency pass-through securities?
   b. Which type of agency pass-through carries the full faith and credit of the U.S. government?
5. a. Who are the issuers of nonagency pass-through securities?
   b. Why must a nonagency CMO be credit enhanced?
6. What is meant by prepayment risk, contraction risk, and extension risk?
7. Why would a pass-through be an unattractive investment for a savings and loan association?
8. What is meant by the average life of a pass-through?
9. Why is an assumed prepayment speed necessary to project the cash flow of a pass-through?
10. A cash flow for a pass-through typically is based on some prepayment benchmark. Describe the benchmark.
11. What does a conditional prepayment rate of 8% mean?
12. What does 250 PSA mean?
13. How does a collateralized mortgage obligation alter the cash flow from mortgages so as to shift the prepayment risk across various classes of bondholders?
14. "By creating a CMO, an issuer eliminates the prepayment risk associated with the underlying mortgages." Do you agree with this statement? Explain.
15. Explain the effect of including an accrual tranche in a CMO structure on the average lives of the sequential-pay structures.
16. What types of investors would be attracted to an accrual bond?
17. What was the motivation for the creation of PAC bonds?
18. Describe how the schedule for a PAC tranche is created.
19. a. In a commercial mortgage-backed securities deal, explain why the investor in a security is provided prepayment protection at the loan level and may be afforded prepayment protection at the deal level.
    b. Why would an investor in a commercial mortgage-backed security be concerned with the concentration of loans by property type and by geographical location?
20. What is the difference between a multiproperty single-borrower commercial mortgage-backed securities deal and a conduit-originated commercial mortgage-backed securities deal?

The Market for Asset-Backed Securities*

27

Learning Objectives

After reading this chapter you will understand:

◆ what an asset-backed security is.

◆ the role of a special purpose vehicle in an asset-backed securities transaction.

◆ the motivation for an entity needing funds to issue an asset-backed security rather than a straight debt issue.

◆ the difference between amortizing assets and nonamortizing assets and why the former may have prepayments.

◆ the difference between an external and internal credit enhancement.

◆ the different types of external and internal credit enhancements.

◆ the difference between a pass-through structure and a pay-through structure.

◆ the cash flow for securities backed by closed-end home equity loans, open-end home equity loans, manufactured housing loans, student loans, SBA loans, and credit card receivables.

◆ the collateral used for a collateralized debt obligation.

◆ the basic structure of a collateralized debt obligation and the types of tranches.

◆ the difference between true securitization and a hybrid securitization.

Even though the securitization of residential mortgage loans is by far the largest type of asset securitized, securities backed by other assets (consumer and business loans and receivables) can also be securitized. The largest sectors of the asset-backed securities market in the United States are securities backed by credit card receivables, auto loans, home equity loans, manufactured housing loans, student loans, Small Business Administration loans, and bond obligations. Because home equity loans and manufactured housing loans are backed by real estate property, the securities backed by them are referred to as **real estate-backed asset-backed securities**. Other asset-backed securities include securities backed by home improvement loans, health-care receivables, agricultural equipment loans, equipment leases, commercial mortgage loans, music royalty receivables, movie royalty receivables, and municipal parking ticket receivables. The list continues to expand. Moreover, asset-backed securities are

---

* This chapter is adapted from material written by Frank J. Fabozzi and published in several books by Frank J. Fabozzi Associates on the topic.

not limited to the U.S. market. Many countries develop asset-backed securities backed by a wide range of loans and receivables.

In this chapter, we discuss the basic features of asset-backed securities. These products are used by both corporations, federal agencies, and municipalities to raise funds. The issuer must structure the transaction so as to deal with both credit risk and prepayment risk. We begin with the motivation for a corporation to use an asset-backed security rather than a straight corporate bond offering. The same rationale applies to other entities such as federal agencies and municipalities in deciding whether to issue a traditional bond or an asset-backed security.

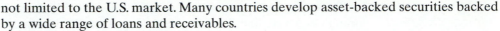

◆ MOTIVATION FOR ISSUING AN ASSET-BACKED SECURITY

For a corporation, an asset-backed security provides an alternative means for raising funds, rather than issuing a straight corporate bond. Why doesn't a corporation simply issue a corporate bond or medium-term note rather than an asset-backed security? To understand why, consider a triple BBB-rated corporation that manufactures construction equipment. We refer to this corporation as XYZ Corp. Some of its sales are for cash, and others are on an installment sales basis. The installment sales are assets on the balance sheet of XYZ Corp. shown as "installment sales receivables."

Suppose XYZ Corp. wants to raise $75 million. If it issues a corporate bond, for example, XYZ Corp.'s funding cost would be whatever the benchmark Treasury yield is, plus a yield for BBB issuers. Suppose, instead, that XYZ Corp. has installment sales receivables that are more than $75 million. XYZ Corp. can use the installment sales receivables as collateral for a bond issue. What will its funding cost be? It will probably be the same as if it issued a corporate bond. The reason is that if XYZ Corp. defaults on any of its obligation, creditors go after all of its assets, including the installment sales receivables.

However, suppose that XYZ Corp. can create another corporation or legal entity and sell the installment sales receivables to that entity. We refer to this entity as SPV Corp. If the transaction is done properly, SPV Corp. owns the installment sales receivables, not XYZ Corp. Therefore, if XYZ Corp. is forced into bankruptcy, its creditors cannot go after the installment sales receivables because they are owned by SPV Corp. What are the implications?

Suppose that SPV Corp. sells securities backed by the installment sales receivables. Now creditors evaluate the credit risk associated with collecting the receivables independent of the credit rating of XYZ Corp. What credit rating will be received for the securities issued by SPV Corp.? Whatever SPV Corp. wants the rating to be! It may seem strange that the issuer (SPV Corp.) can get any rating it wants, but that is the case. The reason is that SPV Corp. will show the characteristics of the collateral for the security (i.e., the installment sales receivables) to a rating agency. It turn, the rating agency will evaluate the credit quality of the collateral and inform the issuer what must be done to obtain specific ratings.

More specifically, the issuer will be asked to "credit enhance" the securities. We review the various forms of credit enhancement later. Basically, the rating agencies look at the potential losses from the pool of installment sales receivables and make a determination of how much credit enhancement is needed for it to issue a specific rating. The higher the credit rating sought by the issuer, the greater the credit enhancement is. Thus, XYZ Corp., which is BBB rated, can obtain funding using its installment sales receivables as collateral to obtain a better credit rating for the securities issued. In fact, with enough credit enhancement it can issue a AAA-rated security.

The key to a corporation issuing a security with a higher credit rating than the corporation's own credit rating is the SPV Corp. Actually, this legal entity that a corporation sells the assets to is called a **special purpose vehicle (SPV)** or **special purpose corporation**. It plays a critical role in the ability to create a security—an asset-backed security—that separates the assets used as collateral from the corporation that is seeking financing.

Why doesn't a corporation always seek the highest credit rating (AAA) for its securities backed by collateral? The answer is that credit enhancement does not come without a cost. As described later, the company requires credit enhancement mechanisms, which increase the costs associated with a securitized borrowing via an asset-backed security. So, when seeking a higher rating, the corporation must monitor the trade-off between the additional cost of credit enhancing the security versus the reduction in funding cost by issuing a security with a higher credit rating.

Additionally, if bankruptcy occurs, a bankruptcy judge could potentially decide that the assets of the special purpose vehicle are assets that the creditors of the corporation seeking financing (XYZ Corp. in our example) may go after. It is an important but unresolved legal issue in the United States that legal experts argue is unlikely to occur. A legal opinion addressing this issue appears in the prospectus of an asset-backed security. For this reason, special purpose vehicles in the United States are referred to as "bankruptcy remote" entities.

◆ FEATURES OF AN ASSET-BACKED SECURITY

Before we discuss the major types of asset-backed securities, let's first look at the general features of the underlying collateral and the structure.

AMORTIZING VERSUS NONAMORTIZING ASSETS

The collateral for an asset-backed security can be classified as either amortizing or nonamortizing assets. Amortizing assets are loans in which the borrower's periodic payment consists of scheduled principal and interest payments over the life of the loan. The schedule for the repayment of the principal is called an **amortization schedule**. The standard residential mortgage loan falls into this category. Auto loans and certain types of home equity loans (specifically, closed-end home equity loans discussed later in this chapter) are amortizing assets. Any excess payment over the scheduled principal payment is called a *prepayment*. Prepayments can be made to pay off the entire balance or a partial prepayment, called a *curtailment*.

In contrast to amortizing assets, nonamortizing assets do not have a schedule for the periodic payments that the individual borrower must make. Instead, a nonamortizing asset is one in which the borrower must make a minimum periodic payment. If that payment is less than the interest on the outstanding loan balance, the shortfall is added to the outstanding loan balance. If the periodic payment is greater than the interest on the outstanding loan balance, then the difference is applied to the reduction of the outstanding loan balance. No schedule of principal payments (i.e., no amortization schedule) applies to a nonamortizing asset. Consequently, the concept of a prepayment does not apply. Credit card receivables and certain types of home equity loans described later in this chapter are examples of nonamortizing assets.

For an amortizing asset, projection of the cash flows requires projecting prepayments. One factor that may affect prepayments is the prevailing level of interest rates relative to the interest rate on the loan. In projecting prepayments it is critical to determine the extent to which borrowers take advantage of a decline in interest rates below the loan rate in order to refinance the loan.

As with nonagency mortgage-backed securities described in the previous chapter, modeling defaults for the collateral is critical in estimating the cash flows of an asset-backed security. Proceeds recovered in the event of a default of a loan prior to the scheduled principal repayment date of an amortizing asset represent a prepayment and are referred to as an **involuntary prepayment**. Projecting prepayments for amortizing assets requires an assumption of the default rate and the recovery rate. For a non-amortizing asset, although the concept of a prepayment does not exist, a projection of defaults is still necessary to project how much will be recovered and when.

The analysis of prepayments can be performed on a pool level or a loan level. In pool-level analysis, it is assumed that all loans comprising the collateral are identical. For an amortizing asset, the amortization schedule is based on the **gross weighted average coupon (GWAC)** and weighted average maturity (WAM) for that single loan. Pool-level analysis is appropriate where the underlying loans are homogeneous. Loan-level analysis involves amortizing each loan (or group of homogenous loans).

The maturity of an asset-backed security is not a meaningful parameter. Instead, the average life of the security is calculated. This measure was introduced in the previous chapter when we discussed agency pass-through securities.

FIXED RATE VERSUS FLOATING RATE

Asset-backed securities are either fixed rate or floating rate. Floating-rate asset-backed securities are typically created where the underlying pool of loans or receivables pay a floating rate. The most common are securities backed by credit card receivables, home equity line of credit receivables, closed-end home equity loans with an adjustable rate, student loans, Small Business Administration loans, and trade receivables. As demonstrated in the previous chapter, fixed-rate loans also can be used to create a structure containing one or more floating-rate tranches. For example, closed-end home equity loans with a fixed rate can be pooled to create a structure with floating-rate tranches.

CREDIT ENHANCEMENTS

All asset-backed securities are **credit enhanced**, which means that support is provided for one or more of the bondholders in the structure. Credit enhancement levels are determined relative to a specific rating desired by the issuer for a security by each rating agency. Specifically, an investor in an AAA-rated security expects to have "minimal," that is to say, virtually no chance of losing any principal due to defaults. For example, a rating agency may require credit enhancement equal to four times expected losses to obtain a AAA rating or three times expected losses to obtain a AA rating. The amount of credit enhancement necessary depends on rating agency requirements.

The two general types of credit enhancement structures are external and internal. We describe each type here.

External Credit Enhancements   External credit enhancements come in the form of third-party guarantees that provide for protection against losses up to a specified level, for example, 10%. This third-party protection is referred to as **first loss protection** because it provides protection against losses before the internal credit enhancements, discussed later, are drawn upon to provide protection. The most common forms of external credit enhancements are

- A corporate guarantee
- A letter of credit from a bank
- Bond insurance.

Typically, external credit enhancements is not used as the primary protection but to supplement other forms of credit enhancement. For example, suppose that a $300 million asset-backed securities deal is issued, and the sponsor (i.e., effectively the seller of the securities) agrees to guarantee $10 million. Then, if losses exceed $10 million, the sponsor is not responsible for the excess over $10 million. Bond insurance provides the same function as in municipal bond structures. However, in the case of asset-backed securities, the insurance covers only up to a specified amount of the loss.

An asset-backed security with external credit support is subject to the credit risk of the third-party guarantor. Should the third-party guarantor be downgraded, the issue itself could be subject to downgrade even if the structure is performing as expected. This practice is based on the "weak link" test followed by rating agencies. According to this test, when evaluating a proposed structure, credit quality of the issue is only as good as the weakest link in credit enhancement regardless of the quality of underlying loans.

Internal Credit Enhancements Internal credit enhancements come in more complicated forms than external credit enhancements. The most common form of internal credit enhancements are reserve funds, overcollaterization, and senior/subordinated structures.

Reserve funds come in two forms: cash reserve funds and excess servicing spread accounts. **Cash reserve funds** are straight deposits of cash generated from issuance proceeds. In this case, part of the underwriting profits from the deal are deposited into a fund that typically invests in money market instruments. Cash reserve funds are most often used in conjunction with external credit enhancements.

Excess servicing spread accounts involve the allocation of excess spread or cash into a separate reserve account after paying out the net coupon, servicing fee, and all other expenses on a monthly basis. For example, suppose that:

1. Gross weighted average coupon (gross WAC) is 8.00% (the interest rate paid by the borrowers).
2. Servicing and other fees are 0.25%.
3. Net weighted average coupon (net WAC) is 7.25% (The rate that is paid to all the tranches in the structure).

So, for this hypothetical deal, 8.00% is available to make payments to the tranches, to cover servicing fees and to cover other fees. Of that amount, 0.25% is paid for servicing and other fees, and 7.25% is paid to the tranches. Therefore, only 7.50% must be paid out, leaving 0.50% (8.00% – 7.50%). This 0.50% or 50 basis points is called the excess spread. This amount is placed in a reserve account—the excess servicing spread account—which gradually increases and can be used to pay for possible future losses.

Overcollateralization works as follows: The total par value of the tranches is the liability of the structure. So, if a structure has two tranches with a par value of $200 million, then that is the amount of the liability. The amount of the collateral backing the structure must be at least equal to the amount of the liability. If the amount of the collateral exceeds the amount of the liability of the structure, the deal is said to be overcollaterized. The amount of overcollaterization represents a form of internal credit enhancement because it can be used to absorb losses. For example, if the liability of the structure is $200 million and the collateral's value is $214 million, then the structure is overcollaterized by $14 million. Thus, the first $14 million of losses will not result in a loss to any of the tranches.

The most popular form of credit enhancement is the **senior/subordinated structure**. This structure contains a senior tranche and at least one junior or subordinated tranche. For example, suppose a deal has $300 million as collateral (i.e., a pool of loans or receivables). The structure may look as follows:

Senior tranche	$280 million
Subordinated tranche	$20 million

The first $20 million of losses are absorbed by the subordinated tranche. The structure may have more than one subordinated tranche. For example, the structure could be as follows:

Senior tranche	$280 million
Subordinated tranche 1	$15 million
Subordinated tranche 2	$5 million

In this structure, the subordinate tranches 1 and 2 are called the **nonsenior tranches**. The senior tranche still has protection up to $20 million as in the previous structure with only one subordinated tranche. In the second structure, the first $5 million of losses is absorbed by the subordinated tranche 2. Hence, this tranche is referred to as the first loss tranche. Subordinated tranche 1 has protection of up to $5 million in losses, the protection provided by the first loss tranche.

The basic concern in the senior/subordinated structure is that while the subordinated tranches provide a certain level of credit protection for the senior tranche at the closing of the deal, the level of protection changes over time due to prepayments. The objective after the deal closes is to distribute any prepayments such that the credit protection for the senior tranche does not deteriorate over time.

In real estate-related asset-backed securities, as well as nonagency mortgage-backed securities, a well-developed mechanism is used to address this concern called the **shifting interest mechanism**. Here is how it works. The percentage of the mortgage balance of the subordinated tranche to that of the mortgage balance for the entire deal is called the level of subordination or the subordinate interest. The higher the percentage is, the greater the level of protection is for the senior tranches. The subordinate interest changes after the deal is closed due to prepayments; that is, the subordinate interest shifts (hence the term *shifting interest*). The purpose of a shifting interest mechanism is to allocate prepayments so that the subordinate interest is maintained at an acceptable level to protect the senior tranche. In effect, by paying down the senior tranche more quickly, the amount of subordination is maintained at the desired level.

PASS-THROUGH VERSUS PAY-THROUGH STRUCTURES

In the previous chapter, we saw how a mortgage pass-through security is created. A pool of mortgage loans is used as collateral, and certificates (securities) are issued with each certificate entitled to a pro rata share of the cash flow from the pool of mortgage loans. So, if a $100 million mortgage pool is the collateral for a pass-through security and 10,000 certificates are issued, then the holder of one certificate is entitled to 1/10,000 of the cash flow from the collateral.

The same type of structure, a pass-through structure, can be used for an asset-backed security deal. Each certificate holder is entitled to a pro rata share of the cash flow from the underlying pool of loans or receivables. For example, consider the following asset-backed security structure:

Senior tranche	$280 million	10,000 certificates issued
Subordinated tranche	$ 20 million	1,000 certificates issued

Each certificate holder of the senior tranche is entitled to receive 1/10,000 of the cash flow to be paid to the senior tranche from the collateral. Each certificate holder of the subordinated tranche is entitled to receive 1/1,000 of the cash flow to be paid to the subordinated tranche from the collateral.

In the previous chapter, we saw how a pass-through security can be used to create a collateralized mortgage obligation (CMO) in which pass-through securities are pooled and used as collateral for a CMO. Another name for a CMO structure is a pay-through structure. In the case of an asset-backed security, the loans are either pooled and issued as a pass-through security or as a pay-through security. Unlike in the agency mortgage-backed securities market, a pass-through is not created first, and then the pass-through is used to create a pay-through security.

In a pay-through structure, the senior tranches can be simple sequential-pays, just as we described for CMOs in the previous chapter. Or, there could be a PAC structure with, say, senior tranche 1 being a short average life PAC, senior tranche 2 being a long average life PAC tranche, and two senior tranches that are support tranches.

It is important to emphasize that the senior/subordinated structure is a mechanism for redistributing credit risk from the senior tranche to the subordinated tranches and is referred to as credit tranching. When the senior tranche is carved up into tranches with different exposures to prepayment risk in a pay-through structure, prepayment risk can be transferred among the senior tranches as in a nonagency CMO. This categorization is referred to as prepayment tranching or **time tranching**.

◆ MAJOR SECTORS OF THE ABS MARKET

As noted at the outset of this chapter, the collateral used for creating asset-backed securities (ABS) is continually expanding. Here we provide a summary of some of the major sectors of the ABS market.

HOME EQUITY LOANS

A **home equity loan (HEL)** is a loan backed by residential property. At one time, the loan was typically a second lien on property that was already pledged to secure a first lien. In some cases, the lien was a third lien. In recent years, the character of a home equity loan has changed. Today, a home equity loan is often a first lien on property where the borrower has either an impaired credit history and/or the payment-to-income ratio is too high for the loan to qualify as a conforming loan for securitization by Ginnie Mae, Fannie Mae, or Freddie Mac. Typically, the borrower used a home equity loan to consolidate consumer debt using the current home as collateral rather than to obtain funds to purchase a new home.

Home equity loans can either be closed-end or open-end. Most home equity deals are backed by closed-end HELs. A closed-end HEL is structured the same way as a fully amortizing residential mortgage loan. That is, it has a fixed maturity and the payments are structured to fully amortize the loan by the maturity date.

Both fixed-rate and variable-rate closed-end HELs are available. Typically, variable-rate loans have a reference rate of 6-month LIBOR as well as periodic caps and lifetime caps. (A periodic cap limits the change in the mortgage rate from the previous time the mortgage rate was reset; a lifetime cap sets a maximum that the mortgage rate can ever be for the loan.) The cash flow of a pool of closed-end HELs is comprised of interest, regularly scheduled principal repayments, and prepayments, just as with mortgage-backed securities. Thus, it is necessary to have a prepayment model and a default model to forecast cash flows. The prepayment speed is measured in terms of a conditional prepayment rate (CPR).

Borrower characteristics and the seasoning process must be kept in mind when trying to assess prepayments for a particular deal. In the prospectus of an offering, a base case prepayment assumption is made: the initial speed and the amount of time until the collateral is expected to be seasoned. Thus, the prepayment benchmark is issuer specific. The benchmark speed in the prospectus is called the **prospectus prepayment curve (PPC)**. As with the PSA benchmark described in the previous chapter, slower or faster prepayments speeds are a multiple of the PPC.

Typically, home equity loan–backed securities are securitized by both closed-end fixed-rate and adjustable-rate (or variable-rate) HELs. The securities backed by the latter are called **HEL floaters**. The reference rate of the underlying loans typically is 6-month LIBOR. The cash flow of these loans is affected by periodic and lifetime caps on the loan rate.

Institutional investors that seek securities that better match their floating-rate funding costs are attracted to securities that offer a floating-rate coupon. To increase the attractiveness of home equity loan-backed securities to such investors, the securities typically have been created in which the reference rate is 1-month LIBOR. Because of (1) the mismatch between the reference rate on the underlying loans and that of the HEL floater, and (2) the periodic and life caps of the underlying loans, the coupon rate for the HEL floater is capped. Unlike a typical floater, which has a cap that is fixed throughout the security's life, the effective periodic and lifetime cap of a HEL floater is variable. The effective cap, referred to as the **available funds cap**, depends on the amount of funds generated by the net coupon on the principal, less any fees.

Let's look at one issue, Advanta Mortgage Loan Trust 1995-2 issued in June 1995. At the offering, this issue had approximately $122 million closed-end HELs. Its 1,192 HELs consisted of 727 fixed-rate loans and 465 variable-rate loans. Its five classes (A-1, A-2, A-3, A-4, and A-5) and a residual are summarized here:

Class	Par Amount	Pass-Through Coupon Rate
A-1	$ 9,229,000	7.30%
A-2	30,330,000	6.60
A-3	16,455,000	6.85
A-4	9,081,000	Floating rate
A-5	56,917,000	Floating rate

The collateral is divided into group I and group II. The 727 fixed-rate loans are included in group I and support Classes A-1, A-2, A-3, and A-4 certificates. The 465 variable-rate loans are in group II and support Class A-5.

MANUFACTURED HOUSING–BACKED SECURITIES

Manufactured housing–backed securities are backed by loans for manufactured homes. In contrast to site-built homes, manufactured homes are built at a factory and then transported to a manufactured home community or private land. The loan can be either a mortgage loan (for both the land and the mobile home) or a consumer retail installment loan.

Manufactured housing–backed securities are issued by Ginnie Mae and private entities. The former securities are guaranteed by the full faith and credit of the U.S. government. The manufactured home loans that are collateral for the securities issues and guaranteed by Ginnie Mae are loans guaranteed by the Federal Housing Administration (FHA) or Veterans Administration (VA). Loans not backed by the FHA or VA are called conventional loans. Manufactured housing–backed securities backed by such loans are called conventional manufactured housing–backed securities. These securities are issued by private entities.

The typical loan for a manufactured home is 15 years to 20 years. The loan repayment is structured to fully amortize the amount borrowed. Therefore, as with residential mortgage loans and HELs, the cash flow consists of net interest, regularly scheduled principal, and prepayments. However, prepayments are more stable for manufactured housing-backed securities because they are not sensitive to refinancing for several reasons. First, the loan balances are typically small so no significant dollar savings result from refinancing. Second, the rate of depreciation of mobile homes may be such that in the earlier years, depreciation is greater than the amount of the loan paid off, which makes it difficult to refinance the loan. Finally, borrowers are typically of lower credit quality and therefore find it difficult to obtain funds to refinance.

As with residential mortgage loans and HELs, prepayments on manufactured housing–backed securities are measured in terms of CPR.

The payment structure is the same as with nonagency mortgage-backed securities and home equity loan–backed securities. For example, consider the Green Tree Manufactured Housing Contract Trust 1995-3 issue. The four classes in this $502.1 million issue are A-1, M-1, B-1, and B-2. Class A-1 is the senior class, Classes M-1, B-1, and B-2 are the subordinated or junior classes. The priority of payments is as follows: First payments are made to Class A-1, then to Class M-1, then to Class B-1, and then finally Class B-2. The losses, however, are realized in reverse order, that is, B-2, B-1, M-1, and finally A-1.

AUTO LOAN–BACKED SECURITIES

Auto loan–backed securities are issued by the following:

- The financial subsidiaries of auto manufacturers (domestic and foreign)
- Commercial banks
- Independent finance companies and small financial institutions specializing in auto loans

Auto loans can range in maturity from 3 years to 6 years.

The cash flow for auto–backed securities consists of regularly scheduled monthly loan payments (interest and scheduled principal repayments) and any prepayments. For securities backed by auto loans, prepayments result from (1) sales and trade-ins requiring full payoff of the loan, (2) repossession and subsequent resale of the automobile, (3) loss or destruction of the vehicle, (4) payoff of the loan with cash to save on the interest cost, and (5) refinancing of the loan at a lower interest cost. Although refinancings may be a major reason for prepayments of mortgage loans, they are of minor importance for automobile loans. Moreover, the interest rates for the automobile loans underlying some deals are substantially below market rates because they are offered by manufacturers as part of a sales promotion.

Prepayments for auto loan–backed securities are measured in terms of the **absolute prepayment speed (ABS)**. The ABS is the monthly prepayment expressed as a percentage of the original collateral amount. As explained in the previous chapter, the SMM (monthly CPR) expresses prepayments based on the prior month's balance.

Some auto loan–backed deals are pass-through structures and pay-through structures. This typical pass-through structure contains a senior tranche and a subordinate tranche. Another class is an interest-only. Whereas more deals are structured as pass-throughs, this structure is typically used for smaller deals. Larger deals usually have a pay-through structure.

STUDENT LOAN ASSET–BACKED SECURITIES

Student loans are made to cover college costs (undergraduate, graduate, and professional programs such as medical and law school) and tuition for a wide range of vocational and trade schools. **Student loan asset-backed securities**, popularly referred to as **SLABS** have similar structural features as other asset-backed securities already discussed.

The student loans most commonly securitized are those made under the Federal Family Education Loan Program (FFELP). Under this program, the government makes loans to a student via private lenders. The decision by private lenders to extend a loan to a student is not based on the applicant's ability to repay the loan. If a default of a loan occurs and the loan has been properly serviced, then the government will guarantee up to 98% of the principal plus accrued interest.

Loans that are not part of a government guarantee program are called **alternative loans**. These loans are basically consumer loans, and the lender's decision to extend an alternative loan will be based on the ability of the applicant to repay the loan. Alternative loans can be securitized.

Congress created Fannie Mae and Freddie Mac to provide liquidity in the mortgage market by allowing these government-sponsored enterprises to buy mortgage loans in the secondary market. Congress created the Student Loan Marketing Association (nicknamed "Sallie Mae") as a government-sponsored enterprise to purchase student loans in the secondary market and to securitize pools of student loans. Since its first issuance in 1995, Sallie Mae has been the major issuer of SLABS, and its issues are viewed as the benchmark issues. Other entities that issue SLABS are either traditional corporate entities (e.g., the Money Store and PNC Bank) or nonprofit organizations (Michigan Higher Education Loan Authority and the California Educational Facilities Authority). The SLABS of the latter typically are issued as tax-exempt securities and therefore trade in the municipal market. In recent years, several not-for-profit entities changed their charter and applied for "for profit" treatment.

Let's first look at the cash flow for the student loans themselves. Different types of student loans under the FFELP include subsidized and unsubsidized Stafford loans, Parental Loans for Undergraduate Students (PLUS), and Supplemental Loans to Students (SLS). These loans involve three periods with respect to the borrower's payments: deferment period, grace period, and loan repayment period. Typically, student loans work as follows. While a student is in school, the deferment period, no payments are made by the student on the loan. Upon leaving school, the student is extended a grace period of usually 6 months when no payments on the loan must be made. After this period, payments are made on the loan by the borrower.

Prior to July 1, 1998, the reference rate for student loans originated under FFELP was the 3-month Treasury bill rate plus a margin of either 250 basis points (during the deferment and grace periods) or 310 basis points (during the repayment period). Since July 1, 1998, the Higher Education Act changed the reference rate to the 10-year Treasury note. Specifically, the interest rate is the 10-year Treasury note rate plus 100 basis points. The spread over the reference rate varies with the cycle period for the loan.

Typically, non-Sallie Mae issues have been LIBOR-based floaters. Sallie Mae issues provide an indirect government guarantee. Sallie Mae typically issues SLABS indexed to the 3-month Treasury bill rate. However, late in the second quarter of 1999, Sallie Mae issued bonds in which the buyer of the 2-year average life tranche could choose between receiving either LIBOR plus 8 basis points or the 3-month Treasury bill rate plus 87 basis points. Funds caps are available in SLABS because of the different reference rates for the loans and the securities.

Prepayments typically occur due to defaults or loan consolidation. Even without any loss of principal to the investor when defaults occur, the investor is still exposed to contraction risk. It is the risk that the investor must reinvest the proceeds at a lower spread and in the case of a bond purchased at a premium, the premium will be lost. Studies show student loan prepayments are insensitive to the level of interest rates. Consolidations of a loan occurs when the student who has loans over several years combines them into a single loan. The proceeds from the consolidation are distributed to the original lender and, in turn, distributed to the bondholders.

SBA LOAN–BACKED SECURITIES

The Small Business Association (SBA) is an agency of the U.S. government empowered to guarantee loans made by approved SBA lenders to qualified borrowers. The loans are backed by the full faith and credit of the government. Most of SBA loans are variable-rate loans where the reference rate is the prime rate. The rate on the loan is reset monthly on the first of the month or quarterly on the first of January, April, July, and October. SBA regulations specify the maximum coupon allowable in the secondary market. Newly originated loans have maturities between 5 and 25 years.

The Small Business Secondary Market Improvement Act passed in 1984 permitted the pooling of SBA loans. When pooled, the underlying loans must have similar terms and features. The maturities typically used for pooling loans are 7, 10, 15, 20, and 25 years. Loans without caps are not pooled with loans that have caps.

Most variable-rate SBA loans make monthly payments consisting of interest and principal repayment. The amount of the monthly payment for an individual loan is determined as follows. Given the coupon formula of the prime rate plus the loan's quoted margin, the interest rate is determined for each loan. Given the interest rate, a level payment amortization schedule is determined. It is this level payment that is paid for the next month until the coupon rate is reset.

The monthly cash flow that the investor in a SBA-backed security receives consists of the following:

- The coupon interest based on the coupon rate set for the period
- The scheduled principal repayment (i.e., scheduled amortization)
- Prepayments

Prepayments for SBA-backed securities are measured in terms of CPR. Voluntary prepayments can be made by the borrower without any penalty. Several factors contribute to the prepayment speed of a pool of SBA loans. A factor affecting prepayments is the maturity date of the loan; the fastest speeds on SBA loans and pools occur for shorter maturities. The purpose of the loan also affects prepayments. Some loans are made for working capital purposes and others to finance real estate construction or acquisition. SBA pools with maturities of 10 years or less made for working capital purposes tend to prepay at the fastest speed. In contrast, loans backed by real estate with long maturities tend to prepay at a slow speed. All other factors constant, pools with capped loans tend to prepay more slowly than pools of uncapped loans.

CREDIT CARD RECEIVABLE-BACKED SECURITIES

Credit card receivable-backed securities are backed by credit card receivables. Credit cards are issued by:

- Banks (e.g., Visa and MasterCard)
- Retailers (e.g., JCPenney and Sears)
- Travel and entertainment companies (e.g., American Express)

Credit card deals are structured as a **master trust**. With a master trust the issuer can sell several series from the same trust. For example, consider the following two deals: Sears Credit Account Master Trust II, Series 1995-4, and Standard Credit Card Master Trust I, Series 1995-A.

Sears offers several open-end revolving credit plans. From these various plans, Sears generates a portfolio of receivables. As of July 1995, the master trust comprised $4 billion of principal receivables. These receivables were randomly selected from the entire portfolio of receivables of Sears Roebuck and Company. About 38% of the accounts had credit limits of $1,999 and about 61% were seasoned at least 5 years. All series issued from this Master Trust II share in the cash flow from the pool of receivables that were randomly selected. Information about the specific accounts in the pool selected for Master Trust II was not disclosed; however, because of the random selection process, an investor might expect that the composition did not differ significantly from the entire portfolio of receivables. Each time a new series of securities is issued, more receivables are randomly selected to be added to the trust. The Sears Credit Account Master Trust II, Series 1995-4 was the sixth of a series issued by Group One of Sears Credit Account Master Trust II. Two classes of certificates were offered to the public: Class A Master Trust Certificates and Class B Master Trust Certificates. The principal for the former was $500 million and for the latter $22.5 million.

The Standard Credit Card Master Trust I is a Citibank master trust. The master trust as of May 22, 1995, was comprised of 20,092,662 accounts with principal receivables of approximately $24.3 billion and approximately $290.8 million of finance charge receivables. The average credit limit was $3,282 and the average principal balance of the accounts was $1,210. About 69% of the accounts were seasoned more than 2 years. The SCCMTI Series 1995A is the twenty-second in a series issued by Group One of Standard Credit Card Master Trust I and is a Euro issue. Only one certificate was offered to the public—$300 million of Floating Rate Class A Credit Card Participation Certificates.

The 10 largest Master Trusts as of March 1999 were (1) MBNA Master Trust II, (2) Citibank, (3) First USA, (4) Discover, (5) Chase, (6) First Chicago, (7) AT&T Universal, (8) Sears Master Trust II, (9) Capital One, and (10) Fleet/Advanta.

Cash Flow   For a pool of credit card receivables, the cash flow consists of finance charges collected, fees, and principal. Finance charges collected represent the periodic interest the credit card borrower is charged based on the unpaid balance after the grace period. Fees include late payment fees and any annual membership fees.

Interest to security holders is paid periodically (e.g., monthly, quarterly, or semiannually). The interest rate may be fixed or floating; roughly half of the securities are floaters. The floating rate is uncapped.

A credit card receivable-backed security is a nonamortizing security. For a specified period of time, referred to as the **lockout period** or **revolving period**, the principal payments made by credit card borrowers comprising the pool are retained by the trustee and reinvested in additional receivables to maintain the size of the pool. The lockout period can vary from 18 months to 10 years. So, during the lockout period, the cash flow that is paid out to security holders is based on finance charges collected and fees.

After the lockout period, the principal is no longer reinvested but paid to investors. This period is referred to as the **principal amortization period**, and the various types of structures are described later.

Performance of the Portfolio of Receivables   Several concepts must be understood in order to assess the performance of the portfolio of receivables and the ability of the issuer to meet its interest obligation and repay principal as scheduled.

We begin with the concept of the **gross portfolio yield**. This yield includes finance charges collected and fees. Charge-offs represent the accounts charged off as uncollectible. Net portfolio yield is equal to gross portfolio minus charge-offs. The net portfolio yield is important because it is from this yield that the bondholders will be paid. So, for example, if the average yield (WAC) that must be paid to the various tranches in the structure is 5% and the net portfolio yield for the month is only 4.5%, the risk is that the bondholder obligations will not be satisfied.

Delinquencies are the percentages of receivables that are past due for a specified number of months, usually 30, 60,and 90 days. They are considered an indicator of potential future charge-offs.

The monthly payment rate (MPR) expresses the monthly payment (which includes finance charges, fees, and any principal repayment) of a credit card receivable portfolio as a percentage of credit card debt outstanding in the previous month. For example, suppose a $500 million credit card receivable portfolio in January realized $50 million of payments in February. The MPR would then be 10% ($50 million divided by $500 million).

The MPR is important for two reasons. First, if the MPR reaches an extremely low level, extension risk may be realized with respect to the principal payments on the bonds. Second, if the MPR is very low, cash flows may be insufficient to pay off principal. It is one event that could trigger early amortization of the principal (described next).

At issuance, portfolio yield, charge-offs, delinquency, and MPR information are provided in the prospectus. Information about portfolio performance is then available from various sources.

Early Amortization Triggers   Certain provisions in credit card receivable-backed securities require early amortization of the principal if certain events occur. Such provisions, which are referred to as either **early amortization** or **rapid amortization**, are included to safeguard the credit quality of the issue. The only way that the principal cash flows can be altered is by the triggering of the early amortization provision.

Typically, early amortization allows for the rapid return of principal in the event that the 3-month average excess spread earned on the receivables falls to zero or less. When early amortization occurs, the credit card tranches are retired sequentially (i.e., first the AAA-rated bond then the AA-rated bond, etc.) by paying the principal payments made by the credit card borrowers to the investors instead of using them to purchase more receivables. The length of time until the return of principal is largely a function of the monthly payment rate. For example, supposed that a AAA tranche is 82% of the overall deal. If the monthly payment rate is 11%, then the AAA tranche would return principal over a 7.5-month period (82%/11%). An 18% monthly payment rate would return principal over a 4.5-month period (82%/18%).

COLLATERIZED DEBT OBLIGATIONS

A **collateralized debt obligation (CDO)** is an asset-backed security backed by a diversified pool of one or more of the following types of debt obligations:

- U.S. domestic high-yield corporate bonds
- U.S. domestic bank loans
- Emerging market bonds
- Special situation loans and distressed debt
- Foreign bank loans

When the underlying pool of debt obligations are bond-type instruments (high-yield corporate and emerging market bonds), a CDO is referred to as a **collateralized**

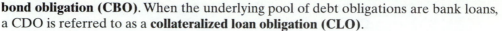

bond obligation (CBO). When the underlying pool of debt obligations are bank loans, a CDO is referred to as a **collateralized loan obligation (CLO)**.

In a CDO structure, an asset manager is responsible for managing the portfolio of debt obligations. There are restrictions imposed as to what the asset manager may do and certain tests that must be satisfied for the tranches in the CDO to maintain the credit rating assigned at the time of issuance. We discuss some of these requirements later.

The funds to purchase the underlying assets (i.e., the bonds and loans) are obtained from the issuance of debt obligations. These debt obligations are referred to as tranches. The tranches are:

- Senior tranches
- Mezzanine tranches
- Subordinate/equity tranche

A rating is sought for all but the subordinate/equity tranche. For the senior tranches, at least an A rating is typically sought. For the mezzanine tranches, a rating of BBB but no less than B is sought. Because the subordinate/equity tranche receives the residual cash flow, no rating is sought for this tranche.

The ability of the asset manager to make the interest payments to the tranches and pay off the tranches as they mature depends on the performance of the underlying assets. The proceeds to meet the obligations to the CDO tranches (interest and principal repayment) can come from (1) coupon interest payments of the underlying assets, (2) maturing assets in the underlying pools, and (3) sale of assets in the underlying pool.

In a typical structure, one or more of the tranches is a floating-rate security. With the exception of deals backed by bank loans, which pay a floating rate, the asset manager invests in fixed-rate bonds. Paying tranche investors a floating rate and investing in assets with a fixed rate presents a problem. To deal with this problem, the asset manager uses derivative instruments to be able to convert fixed-rate payments from the assets into floating-rate payments. In particular, interest rate swaps are used. This instrument allows the market participant to swap fixed-rate payments for floating-rate payments, or vice versa. Because of the mismatch between the nature of the cash flows of the debt obligations in which the asset manager invests and the floating-rate liability of any of the tranches, the asset manager must use an interest rate swap. A rating agency requires the use of swaps to eliminate this mismatch.

CDOs are categorized based on the motivation of the sponsor of the transaction. If the motivation of the sponsor is to earn the spread between the yield offered on the debt obligations in the underlying pool and the payments made to the various tranches in the structure, then the transaction is referred to as an **arbitrage transaction**. If the motivation of the sponsor is to remove debt instruments (primarily loans) from its balance sheet, then the transaction is referred to as a **balance sheet transaction**. Sponsors of balance sheet transactions are typically financial institutions such as banks seeking to reduce their capital requirements by removing loans due to their higher risk-based requirements.

The focus in this chapter is on arbitrage transactions. Arbitrage transactions can be divided into two types depending on where the primary source of the proceeds from the underlying assets are to come from to satisfy the obligation to the tranches. If the primary source is the interest and maturing principal from the underlying assets, then the transaction is referred to as a **cash flow transaction**. If instead the proceeds to meet the obligations depend heavily on the total return generated from the portfolio, then the transaction is referred to as a **market value transaction**.

Next we discuss the economics of arbitrage transactions and then explain cash flow and market value transactions.

Arbitrage Transactions The key as to whether it is economic to create an arbitrage CDO is whether a structure that offers a competitive return for the subordinate/equity tranche is available.

To understand how the subordinate/equity tranche generates cash flows, consider the following basic $100 million CDO structure with the coupon rate to be offered at the time of issuance as shown:

Tranche	Par Value	Coupon Rate
Senior	$80,000,000	LIBOR + 70 basis points
Mezzanine	$10,000,000	Treasury rate + 200 basis points
Subordinate/Equity	$10,000,000	

Suppose that the collateral consists of bonds that all mature in 10 years and the coupon rate for every bond is the 10-year Treasury rate plus 400 basis points. The asset manager enters into an interest rate swap agreement with another party with a notional amount or notional principal of $80 million in which it agrees to do the following:

- Pay a fixed rate each year equal to the 10-year Treasury rate plus 100 basis points
- Receive LIBOR

As explained in Chapter 29, an interest rate agreement is simply an agreement to periodically exchange interest payments. The payments are benchmarked off a notional amount. This amount is not exchanged between the two parties. Rather it is used simply to determine the dollar interest payment of each party, which is all we need to know about an interest rate swap in order to understand the economics of an arbitrage transaction. Keep in mind, the goal is to show how the subordinate/equity tranche can be expected to generate a return.

Let's assume that the 10-year Treasury rate at the time the CDO is issued is 7%. Now we can walk through the cash flows for each year. Look first at the collateral. The collateral pays interest each year (assuming no defaults) equal to the 10-year Treasury rate of 7% plus 400 basis points. So the interest is

$$11\% \times \$100,000,000 = \$11,000,000$$

Now let's determine the interest that must be paid to the senior and mezzanine tranches. For the senior tranche the interest payment will be

$$\$80,000,000 \times \left(\text{LIBOR} + 70 \text{ bp}\right)$$

The coupon rate for the mezzanine tranche is 7% plus 200 basis points. So, the coupon rate is 9% and the interest is

$$9\% \times \$10,000,000 = \$900,000$$

Finally, let's look at the interest rate swap. In this agreement, the asset manager agrees to pay some third party (the swap counterparty) each year 7% (the 10-year Treasury rate) plus 100 basis points, or 8%. But 8% of what? As already explained, in an interest rate swap, payments are based on a notional amount. In our illustration, the notional amount is $80 million. The reason the asset manager selected the $80 million was because it is the amount of principal for the senior tranche. So, the asset manager pays to the swap counterparty.

$$8\% \times \$80,000,000 = \$6,400,000$$

The interest payment received from the swap counterparty is LIBOR based on a notional amount of $80 million. That is,

$$\$80,000,000 \times \text{LIBOR}$$

Now we can put this all together. Let's look at the interest coming into the CDO:

Interest from collateral	$11,000,000
Interest from swap counterparty	$80,000 × LIBOR
Total interest received	$11,000,000 + ($80,000,000 × LIBOR)

The interest to be paid out to the senior and mezzanine tranches and to the swap counterparty include:

Interest to senior tranche	$80,000,000 × (LIBOR + 70bp)
Interest to mezzanine tranche	$900,000
Interest to swap counterparty	$6,400,000
Total interest paid	$7,300,000 + $80,000,000 × (LIBOR + 70 bp)

Netting the interest payments coming in and going out we have:

Total interest received	$11,000,000 + ($80,000,000 × LIBOR)
Total interest paid	$7,300,000 + [$80,000,000 × (LIBOR + 70 bp)]
Net interest	$3,700,000 − ($80,000,000 × 70 bp)

Since 70 basis points times $80 million is $560,000, the net interest remaining is $3,700,000 − $56,000 = $3,140,000. From this amount any fees (including the asset management fee) must be paid. The balance is then the amount available to pay the subordinate/equity tranche. Suppose that these fees are $634,000. Then the cash flow available to the subordinate/equity tranche is $2.5 million. If the tranche has a par value of $10 million and is assumed to be sold at par, the return is 25%.

Obviously, some simplifying assumptions have been made. For example, it is assumed that there are no defaults. It is assumed that all of the issues purchased by the asset manager are noncallable and therefore the coupon rate would not decline because issues are called. Moreover, as explained, after some period the asset manager must begin repaying principal to the senior and mezzanine tranches. Consequently, the interest swap must be structured to take into account principal repayment because the entire amount of the senior tranche is not outstanding for the life of the collateral. Despite the simplifying assumptions, the illustration does demonstrate the basic economics of the CDO, the need for the use of an interest rate swap, and how the subordinate/equity tranche realizes a return.

Cash Flow Structures   In a cash flow structure, the objective of the asset manager is to generate cash flow for the senior and mezzanine tranches without the active trading of bonds. Because the cash flows from the structure are designed to accomplish the objective for each tranche, restrictions are imposed on the asset managers. The asset manager is not free to buy and sell bonds. The conditions for disposing of issues held are specified and are usually driven by credit risk management. Also, in assembling the portfolio, the asset manager must meet certain requirements set forth by the rating agency or agencies that rate the deal.

Three periods are relevant. The first is the **ramp up period** following the closing date of the transaction during which the manager begins investing the proceeds from the sale of the debt obligations issued. This period usually lasts from 1 to 2 years. The **reinvestment period** or revolving period is when principal proceeds are reinvested and is usually for 5 or more years. In the final period, the portfolio assets are sold and the debt holders are paid off.

Income is derived from interest income from the underlying assets and capital appreciation. The income is then used as follows: Fee payments are first made to the trustee and administrators and then to the senior asset managers. Once these fees are paid, then the senior tranches are paid their interest. At this point, before any other payments are made, certain tests must be passed. These tests are called coverage tests. If the coverage tests are passed then interest is paid to the mezzanine tranches. Once the mezzanine tranches are paid, interest is paid to the subordinate/equity tranche.

In contrast, if the coverage tests are not passed then payments are made so as to protect the senior tranches. The remaining income after paying the fees and senior tranche interest is used to redeem the senior tranches (i.e., pay off principal) until the coverage tests are brought into compliance. If the senior tranches are paid off fully because the coverage tests are not brought into compliance, then any remaining income is used to redeem the mezzanine tranches. Any remaining income is then used to redeem the subordinate/equity tranche.

The principal cash flow is distributed as follows after the payment of the fees to the trustees, administrators, and senior managers. Any shortfall in interest paid to the senior tranches is made up from principal proceeds. Assuming that the coverage tests are satisfied, during the reinvestment period the principal is reinvested. After the reinvestment period or if the coverage tests are failed, the principal cash flow is used to pay down the senior tranches until the coverage tests are satisfied. If all the senior tranches are paid down, then the mezzanine tranches are paid off, and then the subordinate/equity tranche is paid off.

The asset manager must monitor the collateral to ensure that certain tests are being met. The two types of tests imposed by rating agencies include quality tests and coverage tests.

In rating a transaction, the rating agencies are concerned with the diversity of the assets and apply **quality tests** to measure diversity levels. An asset manager may not undertake a trade that violates any of the quality tests. Quality tests include (1) a minimum asset diversity score, (2) a minimum weighted average rating, and (3) maturity restrictions. Moreover, for CDOs in which the collateral is emerging market bonds, certain countries or regions impose restrictions on the concentration of bond issuers.

Market Value Transactions   As with a cash flow transaction, market value transactions contain debt tranches and an equity tranche. However, because it is a market value transaction, the asset manager must sell assets in the underlying pool in order to generate proceeds for interest and repayment of maturing tranches. A careful monitoring of the assets and their price volatility is accomplished through frequent marking to market of the assets.

Because a market value transaction relies on the activities of the asset manager to generate capital appreciation and enhanced return to meet the obligations of the tranches in the structure, greater flexibility is granted to the asset manager with respect to some activities compared to a cash flow transaction. For example, while in a cash flow transaction the capital structure is fixed, in a market value transaction the asset manager is permitted to utilize additional leverage after the closing of the transaction. However, the structural covenants imposed on the asset manager in a market value transaction are based on the market value of the underlying assets, not their par value as in the case of cash flow transactions.

Let's illustrate the structure with the hypothetical transaction shown in Table 27.1 The first column shows the capital structure in the transaction. The capital structure includes a senior facility, senior notes, senior/subordinated notes, subordinate notes, and equity. The senior facility is a floating-rate revolving loan. The second column shows the capital structure at the closing date.

During the ramp-up period, the asset manager obtains additional funding based on the target leverage. The additional leverage is provided from the senior borrowing facility

TABLE 27-1   Illustration of a Hypothetical Market Value Transaction ($ millions)

Capital Structure	At Closing Date	Fully Ramped Up
Senior facility	$ 0	$364
Senior note	40	160
Senior/subordinated notes	80	80
Subordinates notes	40	40
Equity	8	160

and additional amount provided by senior notes. Additional equity is also injected. The last column indicates the capital structure when the transaction is fully ramped up.

The order of priority of the payments in the capital structure is as follows: Fees are paid first for trustees, administrators, and managers. After these fees are paid, the senior facility and the senior notes are paid. The two classes in the capital structure are treated *pari passu* (i.e., equal in their rights to their claim on cash proceeds from the underlying assets). That is, their payments are prorated should a shortfall occur. If the senior facility or senior notes are amortizing, they would have the next priority on the cash proceeds from the underlying assets with respect to the payment of the principal due. The senior-subordinated notes would be paid, followed by the subordinated notes.

After all the debt obligations are satisfied in full and if permissible, the equity investors are paid. Typically, incentive fees are also paid to management based on performance. Usually, a target return for the equity investors is established at the inception of the transaction. Management is then permitted to share on some prorated basis once the target return is achieved.

A deal can be terminated early if certain events of default occur. These events basically relate to conditions that would materially adversely impact the performance of the underlying assets. Such events include (1) the failure to comply with certain convenants, (2) failure to meet payments (interest and/or principal) of senior debt obligations, (3) bankruptcy of the issuing entity of the CDO, and (4) departure of the portfolio management team if an acceptable replacement is not found.

◆ CREDIT CONSIDERATION FOR A CORPORATE BOND VERSUS AN ASSET-BACKED SECURITY

We conclude this chapter with a look at how the rating of an asset-backed security transaction differs from that of a corporate bond issue. To understand the difference, it is important to appreciate how the cash flow that must be generated differs for an asset-backed security transaction and a corporate bond issue.

In a corporate bond issue, management through its operations must undertake the necessary activities that will produce revenues and collect revenues. Management incurs costs in creating products and services. These costs include management compensation, employees' salaries, the costs of raw materials, and financial costs. Consequently, in evaluating the credit risk of a corporate bond issue, a rating agency examines these factors.

In contrast, in an asset-backed security transaction, some assets (loans or receivables) are to be collected and distributed to bondholders. No operating or business risks such as the competitive environment or existence of control systems are needed to assess the cash flow. What is important is the quality of the collateral in generating the cash flow needed to make interest and principal payments. The greater predictability of the cash flow in an asset-backed security transaction due to the absence of operational risks distinguishes it from a corporate bond issue.

In a "true" asset-backed security transaction, the role of the servicer is to simply collect the cash flow. No active management with respect to the collateral is necessary as is the case with operating a corporation to generate cash flow to pay bondholders. Standard & Poor's defines a "true" asset-backed security transaction (which it refers to as a "true securitization") as follows:

> In a true securitization, repayment is not dependent on the ability of the servicer to replenish the pool with new collateral or to perform more than routine administrative functions.

For some asset-backed security transactions the role of the servicer is more than administrative. Where the role is more than administrative, Standard & Poor's, for example, refers to such transactions as hybrid transactions. Such transactions have elements of an asset-backed security transaction and a corporation performing a service. According to Standard & Poor's:

> In a hybrid transaction, the role of the servicer is akin to that of a business manager. The hybrid servicer performs not only administrative duties, as in a true securitization, but also . . . [other] services that are needed to generate cash flow for debt service.

Moreover, Standard & Poor's notes that:

> Unlike a true securitization, where the servicer is a fungible entity replaceable with few, if any, consequences to the transaction, bondholders depend on the expertise of the hybrid servicer for repayment. . . . Not coincidentally, these are the same attributes that form the basis of a corporate rating of the hybrid servicer. They also explain the rating linkage between the securitization and its hybrid servicer.

Standard & Poor's provides an illustration of the distinction between a true asset-backed securitization transaction and one requiring a more active role for the servicer. Consider a railcar company that has several hundred leases and the leases are with a pool of diversified highly rated companies. Suppose that each lease is for 10 years, and it is the responsibility of the customers—not the railcar company—to perform the necessary maintenance on the leased railcars. If these leases back an asset-backed security transaction and the term of the transaction is 10 years, then the role of the servicer is minimal. Because the leases are for 10 years and the securities issued are for 10 years, the servicer is just collecting the lease payments and distributing them to the holders of the securities. In such a transaction, it is possible for this issue to obtain a high investment-grade rating as a true asset-backed security transaction.

Suppose we change the assumptions as follows. The securities issued are for 25 years, not 10 years. Also, assume that the railcar company, not the customers, are responsible for the servicing. Now the role of the servicer changes. The servicer will be responsible for finding new companies to re-lease the railcars to when the original leases terminate in 10 years. This re-leasing is necessary because the securities issued have a maturity of 25 years but the original leases only cover payments to security holders for the first 10 years. The re-leasing of the railcars is required for the last 15 years. The servicer under this new set of assumptions is also responsible for the maintenance of the railcars leased. Thus, the servicer must be capable of maintaining the railcars or have ongoing arrangements with one or more companies with the ability to perform such maintenance.

How do rating agencies evaluate hybrid transactions? These transactions will be rated both in terms of a standard methodology for rating an asset-backed security transaction and using a "quasi-corporate approach" (in the words of Standard & Poor's) which involves an analysis of the servicer. The relative weight of the evaluations in assigning a rating to an asset-backed security transaction depends on the involvement of the servicer. The more important the role of the servicer, the more weight will be assigned to the quasi-corporate approach analysis.

Summary

Asset-backed securities are backed by a pool of loans or receivables. Throughout the world, the types of loans and receivables that are being used as collateral for an asset-backed security continues to grow. The motivation for issuers to issue an asset-backed security rather than a traditional debt obligation is based on the opportunity to reduce funding cost by separating the credit rating of the issuer from the credit quality of the pool of loans or receivables. The separation of the pool of assets from the issuer is accomplished by means of a special purpose vehicle or special purpose corporation.

In obtaining a credit rating for an asset-backed security, the rating agencies require that the issue be credit enhanced; the higher the credit rating sought, the greater the credit enhancement needed. Two general types of credit enhancement structures are external and internal. External credit enhancements come in the form of third-party guarantees that provide for first loss protection against losses up to a specified level. The most common forms of external credit enhancements are (1) a corporate guarantee, (2) a letter of credit, and (3) bond insurance. The most common forms of internal credit enhancements are reserve funds and senior/subordinated structures. The creation of a senior-subordinated structure is a means of credit tranching, or reallocating credit risk from one tranche to another. When the senior tranche is carved up to create several senior tranches with different exposures to prepayment risk, the structure is referred to as a pay-through security.

Fundamentally, because of the absence of operational risk an asset-backed security transaction generally has greater certainty about the cash flow than a corporate bond issue. A true asset-backed security transaction involves minimal involvement by the servicer beyond administrative functions. In a hybrid asset-backed security transaction, the service has more than an administrative function; the greater the importance of the service, the more the transaction should be evaluated as a quasi-corporate entity.

The collateral for an asset-backed security can be either amortizing assets (e.g., auto loans and closed-end home equity loans) or nonamortizing assets, (e.g., credit card receivables). For amortizing assets, projection of the cash flow requires projecting prepayments. For nonamortizing assets, prepayments by an individual borrower do not apply since there is no schedule of principal repayments. One factor that may affect prepayments is the prevailing level of interest rates relative to the interest rate on the loan. Since a default is a prepayment (an involuntary prepayment), prepayment modeling for an asset-backed security backed by amortizing assets requires a model for projecting the amount that will be recovered and when it will be recovered.

The collateral for a home equity loan is typically a first lien on residential property, and the loan fails to satisfy the underwriting standards for inclusion in a loan pool of Ginnie Mae, Fannie Mae, or Freddie Mac. Typically, a home equity loan is used by a borrower to consolidate consumer debt using the current home as collateral rather than to obtain funds to purchase a new home. Home equity loans can be either closed-end (i.e., structured the same way as a fully amortizing residential mortgage loan) or open-end (i.e., homeowner given a credit line). The monthly cash flow for a home equity loan–backed security backed by closed-end HELs consists of (1) net interest, (2) regularly scheduled principal payments, and (3) prepayments.

Manufactured housing–backed securities are backed by loans on manufactured homes (i.e., homes built at a factory and then transported to a site). Manufactured housing–backed securities are issued by Ginnie Mae and private entities, the former being guaranteed by the full faith and credit of the U.S. government. A manufactured housing loan's cash flow consists of net interest, regularly scheduled principal, and prepayments. Prepayments are more stable for manufactured housing-backed securities because they are not sensitive to refinancing.

Auto loan–backed securities are issued by the financial subsidiaries of auto manufacturers, commercial banks, independent finance companies, and small financial institutions specializing in auto loans. The cash flow for auto loan–backed securities consists of regularly scheduled monthly loan payments (interest and scheduled principal repayments) and any prepayments. Prepayments on auto loans are not sensitive to interest rates. Prepayments on auto loan–backed securities are measured in terms of the absolute prepayment rate (denoted ABS), which measures monthly prepayments relative to the original collateral amount.

SLABS are asset-backed securities backed by student loans. The student loans most commonly securitized are made under the Federal Family Education Loan Program (FFELP), whereby the government makes loans to students via private lenders and the government guarantees up to 98% of the principal plus accrued interest. Alternative loans are student loans that are not part of a government guarantee program and are basically consumer loans. In contrast to government-guaranteed loans, the lender's decision to extend an alternative loan is based on the ability of the applicant to repay the loan. Student loans involve three periods with respect to the borrower's payments: deferment period, grace period, and loan repayment period. Prepayments typically occur due to defaults or a loan consolidation (i.e., a loan to consolidate loans over several years into a single loan). Issuers of SLABs include the Student Loan Marketing Association (Sallie Mae, a government-sponsored enterprise), traditional corporate entities, and nonprofit organizations.

Small Business Administration (SBA) loans are backed by the full faith and credit of the U.S. government. Most SBA loans are variable-rate loans where the reference rate is the prime rate with monthly payments consisting of interest and principal repayment. Prepayments for SBA-backed securities are measured in terms of CPR. Voluntary prepayments can be made by the SBA borrower without any penalty.

Credit card receivable-backed securities are backed by credit card receivables for credit cards issued by banks, retailers, and travel and entertainment companies. Credit card deals are structured as a master trust. For a pool of credit card receivables, the cash flow consists of finance charges collected, fees, and principal. The principal repayment of a credit card receivable-backed security is not amortized; instead, during the lockout period, the principal payments made by credit card borrowers are retained by the trustee and reinvested in additional receivables and after the lockout period (the principal-amortization period), the principal received by the trustee is no longer reinvested but paid to investors. Certain provisions in credit card receivable-backed securities require early amortization of the principal if certain events occur.

A collateralized debt obligation is an asset-backed security backed by a diversified pool of debt obligations (high-yield corporate bonds, domestic bank loans, emerging market bonds, and special situation loans and distressed debt). A collateralized bond obligation is a CDO in which the underlying pool of debt obligations consists of bond-type instruments (high-yield corporate and emerging market bonds). A collateralized loan obligation is a CDO in which the underlying pool of debt obligations consists of bank loans. In a CDO, an asset manager takes responsibility for managing the portfolio of debt obligations. The tranches in a CDO include senior tranches, mezzanine tranches, and subordinate/equity tranches. The senior and mezzanine tranches are rated and the subordinate/equity tranches is unrated. The proceeds to meet the obligations to the CDO tranches (interest and principal repayment) can come from (1) coupon interest payments of the underlying assets, (2) maturing assets in the underlying pools, and (3) sale of assets in the underlying pool.

CDOs are categorized based on the motivation of the sponsor of the transaction — arbitrage and balance sheet transactions. The motivation in an arbitrage transaction is for the sponsor to earn the spread between the yield offered on the debt obligations in the underlying pool and the payments made to the various tranches in the structure. In a balance sheet transaction, the motivation of the sponsor is to remove debt instruments (primarily loans) from its balance sheet. The key as to whether it is economic to create an arbitrage transaction depends on whether a structure offers a competitive return for the subordinate/equity tranche. Arbitrage transactions can be divided into two types depending on where the primary source of the proceeds from the underlying assets are to come from to satisfy the obligation to the tranches. In a cash flow transaction the primary source is the interest and maturing principal from the underlying assets; in a market value transaction, the proceeds to meet the obligations depend heavily on the total return generated from the portfolio. In market value structures the focus is on monitoring of the assets and their price volatility by the frequent marking to market of the assets.

Key Terms

- Absolute Prepayment Speed (ABS)
- Alternative loans
- Amortization schedule
- Arbitrage transaction
- Available funds cap
- Balance sheet transaction
- Cash flow transaction
- Cash reserve funds
- Collateralized bond obligation (CBO)
- Collateralized debt obligation (CDO)
- Collateralized loan obligation (CLO)
- Credit enhanced
- Early amortization

- Effective cap speed (ABS)
- Excess servicing spread accounts
- First loss protection
- Gross portfolio yield
- Gross weighted average coupon (GWAC)
- HEL floaters
- Home equity loan (HEL)
- Involuntary prepayment
- Lockout period
- Market value transaction
- Master trust
- Nonsenior tranches
- Overcollateralization
- Prepayment tranching
- Principal amortization period

- Prospectus prepayment curve (PPC)
- Quality tests
- Ramp up period
- Rapid amortization
- Real estate-backed asset-backed securities
- Reinvestment period
- Revolving period
- Senior/subordinated structure
- Shifting interest mechanims
- Special purpose corporation
- Special purpose vehicle (SPV)
- Student loan asset-backed securities (SLABS)
- Time tranching

Questions

1. A financial corporation with a BBB rating has a consumer loan portfolio. An investment banker suggested that this corporation consider issuing an asset-backed security where the collateral for the security is the consumer loan portfolio. What would be the advantage of issuing an asset-backed security rather than a straight offering of corporate bonds?
2. What is the role played by a special purpose vehicle in an asset-backed security structure?

3. a. What are the various forms of external credit enhancement for an asset-backed security?

   b. What is the disadvantage of using an external credit enhancement in an asset-backed security structure?

4. Suppose that the collateral for an asset-backed securities structure has a gross weighted average coupon of 8.6%. The servicing fee is 50 basis points. The tranches issued have a weighted average coupon rate of 7.1%. What is the excess servicing spread?

5. Suppose that the structure for an asset-backed security transaction is as follows:

Senior tranche	$220 million
Subordinated tranche 1	$ 50 million
Subordinated tranche 2	$ 30 million

   and that the value of the collateral for the structure is $320 million. Subordinated tranche 2 is the first loss tranche.

   a. How much is the overcollateralization in this structure?

   b. What is the amount of the loss for each tranche if losses due to defaults over the life of the structure total $15 million?

   c. What is the amount of the loss for each tranche is losses due to defaults over the life of the structure total $35 million?

   d. What is the amount of the loss for each tranche if losses due to defaults over the life of the structure total $85 million?

   e. What is the amount of the loss for each tranche if losses due to defaults over the life of the structure total $110 million?

6. What is the difference between a pass-through structure and a pay-through structure?

7. An asset-backed security has been credit enhanced with a letter of credit from a bank with a single A credit rating. If it is the only form of credit enhancement, explain why this issue is unlikely to receive a AAA credit rating.

8. Why would it be critical for insurance companies that offer bond insurance for asset-backed security transactions to maintain a AAA credit rating?

9. What is the difference between a cash reserve fund and an excess servicing spread account?

10. a. Explain why a senior-subordinated structure is a form of internal credit enhancement.

    b. Explain the need for a shifting interest mechanism in a senior-subordinated structure when the underlying assets are subject to prepayments.

11. Indicate whether you agree or disagree with the following statement: "Typically, closed-end home equity loans are loan to borrowers of the highest credit quality."

12. a. What are the components of the cash flow for a home equity loan–backed security and manufactured housing-backed security?

    b. What are the reasons why prepayments due to refinancing are not significant for manufactured housing loans?

13. a. What are the components of the cash flow for an auto loan–backed security?

    b. How important are prepayments due to refinancing for auto loans?

14. For a student loan–backed security, what is the difference between the deferment period and the grace period?

15. a. What are the components of the cash flow for a Small Business Administration–backed security?

    b. What reference rate is used for setting the coupon interest, and how often is the coupon rate reset?

16. a. What is the cash flow for a credit card receivable-backed security during the lockout or revolving period?

b. How is the principal received from credit card borrowers handled during the lockout or revolving period?

17. a. What is meant by the monthly payment rate for a credit card deal?
    b. What is the significance of the monthly payment rate?
    c. How is the net portfolio yield determined for a credit card deal?

18. Explain why you agree or disagree with the following statement: "The asset manager for a CBO is free to actively manage the portfolio without any constraints."

19. In a collateralized debt obligation based on arbitrage, what determines whether a deal will be created?

20. What is the motivation for a balance sheet collateralized debt obligation?

21. Consider the following basic $200 million CDO structure with the coupon rate to be offered at the time of issuance as shown:

Tranche	Par Value	Coupon Rate
Senior	$160,000,000	LIBOR + 50 basis points
Mezzanine	$ 20,000,000	Treasury rate + 200 basis points
Subordinated/Equity	$ 20,000,000	

Assume the following:

- The collateral consists of bonds that all mature in 10 years.
- The coupon rate for every bond is the 10-Treasury rate plus 200 basis points.
- The asset manager enters into an interest rate swap agreement with another party with a notional amount of $160 million.
- In the interest rate swap the manager agrees to pay a fixed rate each year equal to the 10-year Treasury rate plus 100 basis points and receive LIBOR.

a. What is the potential return for the subordinated/equity tranche assuming no defaults?
b. Why will the actual return be less than the return computed?

22. What is the significance of the coverage tests in a collateralized debt obligation?

23. a. Some asset-backed security transactions may be characterized as "true securitizations," while others may be more properly classified as "hybrid transactions." What is the distinguishing feature of a "true securitization" and a "hybrid transaction"?
    b. How is the credit quality of a "hybrid transaction" evaluated?

24. Explain whether you would consider a collateralized bond obligation a true securitization or a hybrid securitization.

Exchange-Traded Interest Rate Futures and Options

Learning Objectives

After reading this chapter you will understand:

◆ the features of interest rate futures contracts.

◆ features of the Treasury bill, Eurodollar CD, Treasury bond, Treasury note, and agency note futures contracts.

◆ the delivery options embedded in the Treasury bond and note futures and agency futures contract and their impact on the futures price.

◆ the features of interest rate options contracts.

◆ what futures options are, their trading mechanics, and the reasons for their popularity.

◆ the empirical evidence on the pricing efficiency of futures options.

◆ the limitations of applying the Black-Scholes option-pricing model to options on fixed-income securities.

◆ an overview of more appropriate models for pricing interest rate options.

◆ applications of interest rate futures and options by institutional money managers and borrowers.

This chapter and the next describe derivative contracts or instruments that investors and issuers can use to control interest rate risk. Basically, the underlying economic variable for these derivative contracts is some interest rate. The derivative contract either is based directly on an interest rate, or it based indirectly on an interest rate by making a debt obligation the underlying instrument for the contract. In this chapter we describe three derivative contracts to control interest rate risk: interest rate futures, interest rate options, and options on future. We cover portfolio strategies using these contracts, unique features for pricing them, and considerations of pricing efficiency.

Futures contracts are products created by exchanges. Options on futures, a derivative product that we introduce in this chapter, are also created by exchanges. Options, however, can be exchange-traded products or OTC options. Most market participants rely almost exclusively on exchange-traded products in the case of options on common stocks and options on stock indexes; however, institutional investors and issuers make greater use of the over-the-counter options market to create tailor-made contracts to control interest rate risk. In the next chapter we will discuss OTC options when we focus on customized interest rate risk control instruments.

◆ **INTEREST RATE FUTURES CONTRACTS**

In October 1975, the Chicago Board of Trade (CBOT) pioneered trading in a futures contract based on a fixed-income instrument—Government National Mortgage Association certificates. Three months later, the International Monetary Market (IMM) of the Chicago Mercantile Exchange began trading futures contracts based on 13-week Treasury bills. Other exchanges soon followed with their own interest rate futures contracts.

FEATURES OF ACTIVELY TRADED CONTRACTS

Interest rate futures contracts can be classified by the maturity of their underlying security. Short-term interest rate futures contracts have an underlying security that matures in less than 1 year. The maturity of the underlying security of long-term futures contracts exceeds 1 year. Examples of the former are the futures contracts in which the underlying is a 3-month Treasury bill, a 3-month Eurodollar certificate of deposit, 1-month LIBOR, and 30-day federal funds. All of these contracts are traded on the Chicago Mercantile Exchange. Examples of long-term futures are contracts in which the underlying is a Treasury bond, a Treasury note, or an agency security. The more actively traded contracts traded in the United States are described here. Interest rate futures contracts are also traded in other countries.

Treasury Bill Futures   Treasury bill futures and Eurodollar futures contracts are futures whose underlying instrument is a short-term debt obligation. The Treasury bill futures contract, which is traded on the IMM, is based on a 13-week (3-month) Treasury bill with a face value of $1 million. More specifically, the seller of a Treasury bill futures contract agrees to deliver to the buyer at the settlement date a Treasury bill with 13 weeks remaining to maturity and a face value of $1 million. The Treasury bill delivered can be newly issued or seasoned. The futures price is the price at which the Treasury bill will be sold by the short and purchased by the buyer. For example, a 9-month Treasury bill futures contract requires that 9 months from now the short deliver to the long $1 million face value of a Treasury bill with 13 weeks remaining to maturity. The Treasury bill could be a newly issued 13-week Treasury bill or a Treasury bill that was issued 1 year prior to the settlement date and therefore at the settlement has only 13 weeks remaining to maturity.

As we explain in Chapter 21, Treasury bills are quoted in the cash market in terms of an annualized yield on a bank discount basis, where:

$$Y_D = \frac{D}{F} \times \frac{360}{t}$$

where

$\quad Y_D$ = annualized yield on a bank discount basis (expressed as a decimal)
$\quad D$ = dollar discount, which is equal to the difference between the face
$\qquad$ value and the price of a bill maturing in t days
$\quad F$ = face value
$\quad t$ = number of days remaining to maturity

The dollar discount *(D)* is found by:

$$D = Y_D \times F \times \frac{t}{360}$$

In contrast, the Treasury bill futures contract is not quoted directly in terms of yield but instead on an index basis that is related to the yield on a bank discount basis as follows:

$$\text{Index price} = 100 - \left(Y_D \times 100\right)$$

For example, if Y_D is 8%, the index price is: $100 - (0.08 \times 100) = 92$.

It will be seen that the **index price** of an instrument differs from its actual price because it is the price of an instrument with the same annual yield but maturing in a year. The primary purpose of this convention is that all instruments with the same annual yield have the same price, regardless of maturity. Conversely, instruments with the same price have the same yield to maturity and bank discount basis, which clearly facilitates comparison of annual yields across maturities.

Given the price of the futures contract, the futures yield on a bank discount basis for the futures contract is determined as follows:

$$Y_D = \frac{100 - \text{Index price}}{100}$$

To see how this equation works, suppose that the index price for a Treasury bill futures contract is 92.52. The futures yield on a bank discount basis for this Treasury bill futures contract is:

$$Y_D = \frac{100 - 92.52}{100} = 0.0748 \text{ or } 7.48\%$$

The price that the buyer of a futures contract must pay the seller at the settlement date is called the **invoice price**. In the case of the Treasury bill futures contract, the invoice price that the buyer of $1 million face value of 13-week Treasury bills must pay at settlement is found by first computing the dollar discount, as follows:

$$D = Y_D \times \$1,000,000 \times \frac{t}{360}$$

where t is either 90 or 91 days. Typically, the number of days to maturity of a 13-week Treasury bill is 91 days.

The invoice price is then

$$\text{Invoice price} = \$1,000,000 - D$$

For example, for the Treasury bill futures contract with an index price of 92.52 (and a yield on a bank discount basis of 7.48%), the dollar discount for the 13-week Treasury bill to be delivered with 91 days to maturity is

$$D = 0.0748 \times \$1,000,000 \times \frac{91}{360} = \$18,907.78$$

The invoice price is

$$\$1,000,000 - \$18,907.78 = \$981,092.22$$

The minimum index price fluctuation or "tick" for this futures contract is 0.01. A change of 0.01 for the minimum index price translates into a change in the yield on a bank discount basis of one basis point (0.0001). The change in the value of one basis point will change the dollar discount, and therefore the invoice price, by

$$0.0001 \times \$1,000,000 \times \frac{t}{360}$$

For a 13-week Treasury bill with 91 days to maturity, the change in the dollar discount is

$$0.0001 \times \$1,000,000 \times \frac{91}{360} = \$25.28$$

For a 13-week Treasury bill with 90 days to maturity, the change in the dollar discount would be $25. Despite the fact that a 13-week Treasury bill typically has 91 days to maturity, market participants commonly refer to the value of a basis point for this futures contract as $25.

Eurodollar CD Futures   Eurodollar certificates of deposit (CDs) are denominated in dollars but represent the liabilities of banks outside the United States. The contracts are traded on both the International Monetary Market of the Chicago Mercantile Exchange and the London International Financial Futures Exchange. The rate paid on Eurodollar CDs is the London interbank offered rate (LIBOR).

The 3-month Eurodollar CD is the underlying instrument for the Eurodollar CD futures contract. As with the Treasury bill futures contract, this contract is for $1 million of face value and is traded on an index-price basis. The index-price basis in which the contract is quoted is equal to 100 minus the annualized futures LIBOR. For example, a Eurodollar CD futures price of 94.00 means a futures 3-month LIBOR of 6%.

The minimum price fluctuation (tick) for this contract is 0.01 (or 0.0001 in terms of LIBOR). It means that the price value of a basis point for this contract is $25, found as follows. The simple interest on $1 million for 90 days is equal to

$$\$1,000,000 \times \left(\text{LIBOR} \times 90 / 360 \right)$$

If LIBOR changes by one basis point (0.0001), then

$$\$1,000,000 \times \left(0.0001 \times 90 / 360 \right) = \$25$$

The Eurodollar CD futures contract is a cash settlement contract. That is, the parties settle in cash for the value of a Eurodollar CD based on LIBOR at the settlement date. The Eurodollar CD futures contract is one of the most heavily traded futures contracts in the world. It is frequently used to trade the short end of the yield curve, and many hedgers have found this contract to be the best hedging vehicle for a wide range of hedging situations.

Treasury Bond Futures   The underlying instrument for a Treasury bond futures contract is $100,000 par value of a hypothetical 20-year, 6% coupon bond. The futures price is quoted in terms of par being 100. Quotes are in 32nds of 1%. Thus a quote for a Treasury bond futures contract of 97-16 means 97 and 16/32nds, or 97.50. So, if a buyer and seller agree on a futures price of 97-16, the buyer agrees to accept delivery of the hypothetical underlying Treasury bond and pay 97.50% of par value, and the seller agrees to accept 97.50% of par value. Since the par value is $100,000, the futures price that the buyer and seller agree to pay for this hypothetical Treasury bond is $97,500.

The minimum price fluctuation for the Treasury bond futures contract is a 32nd of 1%. The dollar value of a 32nd for a $100,000 par value (the par value for the underlying Treasury bond) is $31.25. Thus, the minimum price fluctuation is $31.25 for this contract.

We have been referring to the underlying as a hypothetical Treasury bond. That reference does not mean that the contract is a cash settlement contract, as is the case with stock index futures described in Chapter 16. The seller of Treasury bond futures who decides to make delivery rather than liquidate the position by buying back the contract prior to the settlement date must deliver some Treasury bond. But what Treasury bond? The Chicago Board of Trade allows the seller to deliver one of several

Treasury bonds that the CBOT declares is acceptable for delivery. The specific bonds that the seller may deliver are published by the CBOT prior to the initial trading of a futures contract with a specific settlement date.

Table 28-1 shows the Treasury issues that the seller could have selected from to deliver to the buyer of the June 2002 futures contract as of August 30, 2001. The CBOT makes its determination of the Treasury issues that are acceptable for delivery from all outstanding Treasury issues that meet the following criteria: an issue must have at least 15 years to maturity from the date of delivery, if not callable; in the case of callable bonds, the issue must not be callable for at least 15 years from the first day of the delivery month. Note that Table 28-1 shows the eligible issues as of August 30, 2001. If the Department of the Treasury issues new Treasury bonds between August 30, 2001, and the settlement of the June 2002 futures, those issues will be eligible for delivery.

TABLE 28-1 Eligible Treasury Bonds (as of August 31, 2001) and Corresponding Conversion Factors for Settlement in June 2002

Coupon	Issue Date	Maturity Date	Conversion Factor
5 1/4	11/16/98	11/15/28	0.9014
5 1/4	02/16/99	02/15/29	0.9011
5 3/8	02/15/01	02/15/31	0.9152
5 1/2	08/17/98	08/15/28	0.9346
6	02/15/96	02/15/26	1.0000
6 1/8	11/17/97	11/15/27	1.0160
6 1/8	08/16/99	08/15/29	1.0166
6 1/4	08/16/93	08/15/23	1.0296
6 1/4	02/15/00	05/15/30	1.0335
6 3/8	08/15/97	08/15/27	1.0482
6 1/2	11/15/96	11/15/26	1.0633
6 5/8	02/18/97	02/15/27	1.0797
6 3/4	08/15/96	08/15/26	1.0948
6 7/8	08/15/95	08/15/25	1.1084
7 1/8	02/16/93	02/15/23	1.1317
7 1/4	08/17/92	08/15/22	1.1445
7 1/2	08/15/94	11/15/24	1.1828
7 5/8	11/15/92	11/15/22	1.1889
7 5/8	02/15/95	02/15/25	1.1992
7 7/8	02/15/91	02/15/21	1.2078
8	11/15/91	11/15/21	1.2264
8 1/8	08/15/89	08/15/19	1.2245
8 1/8	05/15/91	05/15/21	1.2371
8 1/8	08/15/91	08/15/21	1.2390
8 1/2	02/15/90	02/15/20	1.2686
8 3/4	05/15/90	05/15/20	1.2977
8 3/4	08/15/90	08/15/20	1.3002
8 7/8	08/15/87	08/15/17	1.2818
8 7/8	02/15/89	02/15/19	1.2985
9	11/22/88	11/15/18	1.3085
9 1/8	05/15/88	05/15/18	1.3154

Source: Chicago Board of Trade.

The delivery process for the Treasury bond futures contract makes the contract interesting. At the settlement date, the seller of a futures contract (the short) is required to deliver to the buyer (the long) $100,000 par value of a 6%, 20-year Treasury bond. Because no such bond exists, the seller must choose from one of the acceptable deliverable Treasury bonds that the CBOT has specified. Suppose the seller is entitled to deliver $100,000 of a 4%, 20-year Treasury bond to settle the futures contract. The value of this bond, of course, is less than the value of a 6%, 20-year bond. Delivery of a 4%, 20-year would be unfair to the buyer of the futures contract who contracted to receive $100,000 of a 6%, 20-year Treasury bond. Alternatively, suppose the seller delivers $100,000 of a 10%, 20-year Treasury bond. The value of a 10%, 20-year Treasury bond is greater than that of a 6%, 20-year bond, which would be a disadvantage to the seller.

How can this problem be resolved? To make delivery equitable to both parties, the CBOT introduced **conversion factors** for determining the invoice price of each acceptable deliverable Treasury issue against the Treasury bond futures contract. The conversion factor is determined by the CBOT before a contract with a specific settlement date begins trading. Table 28-1 shows for each of the acceptable Treasury issues the corresponding conversion factor.[1] The conversion factor is constant throughout the trading period of the futures contract. The short must notify the long of the actual bond that will be delivered one day before the delivery date.

The invoice price for the Treasury bond futures contract is the futures price plus accrued interest. However, as just noted, the seller can deliver one of several acceptable Treasury issues, and to make delivery fair to both parties, the invoice price must be adjusted based on the actual Treasury issue delivered. The conversion factors are used to adjust the invoice price. The invoice price is

$$\text{Invoice price} = \text{Contract size} \times \text{Futures contract settlement price} \times \text{Conversion factor} + \text{Accrued interest}$$

Suppose the Treasury bond futures contract settles at 94-08 and that the short elects to deliver a Treasury bond issue with a conversion factor of 1.20. The futures contract settlement price of 94-08 means 94.25% of par value. As the contract size is $100,000, the invoice price the buyer pays the seller is

$$\$100,000 \times 0.9425 \times 1.20 + \text{Accrued interest} = \$113,100 + \text{Accrued interest}$$

In selecting the issue to be delivered, the short will select from all the deliverable issues the one that is cheapest to deliver. This issue is referred to as the **cheapest-to-deliver issue** and it plays a key role in the pricing of a futures contract. The cheapest-to-deliver issue is determined by participants in the market as follows. For each of the acceptable Treasury issues from which the seller can select, the seller calculates the return that can be earned by buying that issue and delivering it at the settlement date. Note that the seller can calculate the return based on the known price of the Treasury issue now and the futures price agreed to for delivery of the issue. The return so calculated is called the **implied repo rate**. The cheapest-to-deliver issue is then the one issue among all acceptable Treasury issues with the highest implied repo rate because it is the issue that would give the seller of the futures contract the highest return by buying and then delivering the issue, as depicted in Figure 28-1.

In addition to the choice of which acceptable Treasury issue to deliver—sometimes referred to as the **quality option** or **swap option**—the short position has two more options granted under CBOT delivery guidelines. The short position is permitted to

---

[1]   The conversion factor is based on the price that a deliverable bond would sell for at the beginning of the delivery month if it were to yield 6%.

Implied repo state: Rate of return by buying an acceptable Treasury issue, shorting the Treasury bond futures, and delivering the issue at the settlement date.

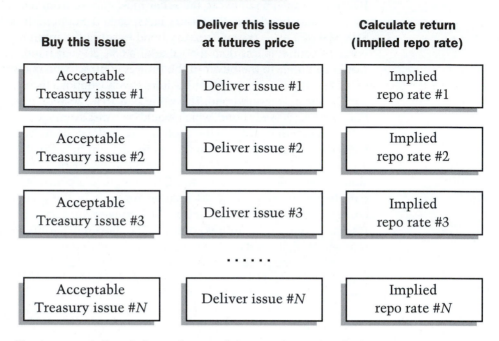

Cheapest-to-deliver is issue that produces maximum implied repo rate

FIGURE 28-1 Determination of Cheapest-to-Deliver Issue Based on the Implied Repo Rate

decide when in the delivery month the delivery will actually take place, which is called the **timing option**. The other option is the right of the short position to give notice of intent to deliver up to 8:00 P.M. Chicago time after the closing of the exchange (3:15 P.M. Chicago time) on the date when the futures settlement price has been fixed. This option is referred to as the **wild card option**. The quality option, the timing option, and the wild card option (in sum referred to as the **delivery options**), mean that the long position can never be sure of which Treasury bond will be delivered or when it will be delivered. The delivery options are summarized in Table 28-2.

The contract specification for the Treasury bond futures has been used in other countries to design a futures contract on their government bond.

Treasury Note Futures The three Treasury note futures contracts are 10-year, 5-year, and 2-year. All three contracts are modeled after the Treasury bond futures contract and are traded on the CBOT. The underlying instrument for the 10-year Treasury note futures contract is $100,000 par value of a hypothetical 10-year, 6% Treasury note.

TABLE 28-2 Delivery Options Granted to the Short (seller) of a CBOT Treasury Bond Futures Contract

Delivery Option	*Description*
Quality or swap option	Choice of which acceptable Treasury issue to deliver
Timing option	Choice of when in delivery month to deliver
Wild card option	Choice to deliver after the closing price of the futures contract is determined

Several acceptable Treasury issues may be delivered by the short. An issue is acceptable if the maturity is not less than 6.5 years and not greater than 10 years from the first day of the delivery month. Delivery options are granted to the short position. For the 5-year Treasury note futures contract, the underlying is $100,000 par value of a 6% notional coupon U.S. Treasury note that satisfies the following conditions: (1) an original maturity of not more than 5 years and 3 months, (2) a remaining maturity no greater than 5 years and 3 months, and (3) a remaining maturity not less than 4 years and 2 months. The underlying for the 2-year Treasury note futures contract is $200,000 par value of a 6% notional coupon U.S. Treasury note with a remaining maturity of not more than 2 years and not less than 1 year and 9 months. Moreover, the original maturity of the note delivered to satisfy the 2-year futures cannot be more than 5 years and 3 months.

Agency Note Futures Contract   As explained in Chapter 21, agencies, specifically, Fannie Mae and Freddie Mac, stepped in to issue debenture securities that they hope will become the benchmark interest rates in the financial market. As a result of the anticipated important role of agency securities for becoming the benchmark yields that reflect spread risk, the CBOT and the Chicago Mercantile Exchange (CME) began trading in 2000 futures contracts in which the underlying is a Fannie Mae or Freddie Mac agency debenture security.

The underlying for the CBOT 10-year agency note futures contract is a Fannie Mae benchmark note or Freddie Mac reference note having a par value of $100,000 and a notional coupon of 6%. As with the Treasury futures contract, more than one issue is deliverable. For an issue to be deliverable it must be (1) a noncallable Fannie Mae benchmark note or Freddie Mac reference note maturing at least 6.5 years but not more than 10.25 years (original maturity) from the first day of the delivery month, (2) have an original issuance of at least $3 billion, and (3) pay semiannual fixed coupons. The contract delivery months are March, June, September, and December. As with the Treasury futures contract a conversion factor applies to each eligible issue. Table 28-3 shows the issues eligible to satisfy the June 2002 contract and the corresponding conversion factor for each issue. Because many issues are deliverable,

TABLE 28-3	Fannie Mae Benchmark and Freddie Mac Reference Issues (acceptable as of September 17, 2001, for delivery to satisfy the 10-Year CBOT agency contract of June 2002)			
Issuer	*Coupon*	*Settlement Date*	*Maturity Date*	*Conversion Factor*
Fannie Mae	5 1/4	01/11/99	01/15/09	0.9601
Fannie Mae	5 1/2	03/26/01	03/15/11	0.9662
Fannie Mae	6	05/25/01	05/15/11	0.9999
Fannie Mae	6 3/8	06/08/99	06/15/09	1.0212
Fannie Mae	6 5/8	09/01/99	09/15/09	1.0362
Fannie Mae	6 5/8	11/03/00	11/15/10	1.0401
Fannie Mae	7 1/8	06/09/00	06/15/10	1.0707
Fannie Mae	7 1/4	01/14/00	01/15/10	1.0746
Freddie Mac	5 5/8	03/15/01	03/15/11	0.9747
Freddie Mac	5 3/4	03/12/99	03/15/09	0.9862
Freddie Mac	6	06/15/01	06/15/11	1.0000
Freddie Mac	6 5/8	09/16/99	09/15/09	1.0362
Freddie Mac	6 7/8	09/22/00	09/15/10	1.0562
Freddie Mac	7	03/24/00	03/15/10	1.0611

Source: Chicago Board of Trade.

one issue is the cheapest-to-deliver issue. This issue is found in exactly the same way as with the Treasury futures contract.

The 10-year agency note futures contract of the CME is similar to that of the CBOT, but has a notional coupon of 6.5% instead of 6%. For an issue to be deliverable, the CME requires that its original maturity is 10 years and that it does not mature for a period of at least 6.5 years from the date of delivery.

The CBOT and the CME also have a 5-year agency note futures contract. Again, the CBOT's underlying is a 6% notional coupon and the CME's is a 6.5% notional coupon.

PRICING OF INTEREST RATE FUTURES CONTRACTS

In Chapter 10, we explained how the price of a futures contract can be determined based on arbitrage arguments. (Recall the cash-and-carry trade and the reverse cash-and-carry trade.) We showed that the theoretical futures price depends on the cash market price, the financing cost, and the cash yield on the underlying instrument. In the case of stock index futures, the cash yield on the underlying instrument is the expected stream of cash dividends earned until the settlement date. For interest rate futures, the cash yield is the coupon interest earned until the settlement date, not the yield to maturity. Therefore, for an interest rate futures contract, the theoretical futures price is

$$\text{Futures price} = \text{Cash market price} + \text{Cash market price} \times (\text{Financing cost} - \text{Cash yield on bond}) \quad \textbf{(28.1)}$$

The futures price can trade at a discount or a premium to the cash price, depending on whether the cost of carry ("carry" for short) is positive (i.e., the cash yield on the bond is greater than the financing cost) or negative (i.e., the cash yield on the bond is less than the financing cost). In the case of interest rate futures, the financing cost is determined by rates at the short end of the yield curve. The cash yields for Treasury bonds and Treasury notes will be determined by yields at the long-term and intermediate term-maturity sectors of the yield curve, respectively. Therefore, the shape of the yield curve determines carry and, in turn, whether the futures price trades at a premium, at a discount, or equal to the cash market price. This relationship is summarized in Table 28-4.

The shape of the yield curve also influences when the short will choose to deliver (i.e., exercise the timing option). If carry is positive, it will be beneficial for the short to delay delivery until the last permissible settlement date. If carry is negative, the short will deliver on the first permissible settlement date.

To derive the theoretical futures price in Chapter 10 using the arbitrage argument, several assumptions had to be made; we explained the implications of these assumptions for the divergence between the actual futures price and the theoretical futures price for any futures contract. In Chapter 16, we highlighted the limitations as applied to stock index futures. Here we will do the same for interest rate futures.

Interim Cash Flows In Chapter 10, we explained that the model assumes no interim cash flows due to variation margin or coupon interest payments but that they can be incorporated. The unique aspect of interest rate futures is that if interest rates rise, the short will receive margin as the futures price decreases; the margin can then be reinvested

TABLE 28-4 Effect of Shape of Yield Curve on Futures Price

Shape of Yield Curve	*Carry*	*Futures Price*
Normal	Positive	Sell at a discount to cash price
Inverted	Negative	Sell at a premium to cash price
Flat	Zero	Be equal to the cash price

at a higher interest rate. If interest rates fall, variation margin must be financed by the short, but because interest rates declined, it can be financed at a lower cost. Thus the advantage seems to go to the short as interest rates change. Correspondingly, a disadvantage goes to the long.

Deliverable Bond Is Not Known   The arbitrage arguments used to derive equation (28.1) assumed that only one instrument is deliverable. But the futures contracts on Treasury bonds and Treasury notes are designed to allow the short the choice of delivering one of a number of deliverable issues (the quality or swap option). Because more than one issue may be deliverable, market participants track the price of each deliverable bond and determine which bond is the cheapest to deliver. The futures price will then trade in relation to the cheapest-to-deliver issue.

Although an issue may be the cheapest to deliver at the time a position in the futures contract is taken, the short takes a risk that it may not be the cheapest to deliver after that time. A change in the cheapest-to-deliver issue can dramatically alter the futures price.

What are the implications of the quality (swap) option on the futures price? Because the swap option is an option granted by the long to the short, the long will want to pay less for the futures contract than indicated by equation (28.1). Therefore, as a result of the quality option, the theoretical futures price as given by equation (28.1) must be adjusted as follows:

$$
\begin{aligned}
\text{Futures price} = {} & \text{Cash market price} + \text{Cash market price} \\
& \times (\text{Financing cost} - \text{Cash yield on bond}) \qquad \textbf{(28.2)} \\
& - \text{Value of quality option}
\end{aligned}
$$

Market participants employ theoretical models in attempting to estimate the fair value of the quality option. These models are beyond the scope of this chapter.

Delivery Date Is Not Known   In the pricing model based on arbitrage arguments, a known delivery date is assumed. For Treasury bond and note futures contracts, the short has a timing and wild card option, so the long does not know when the securities will be delivered. The effect of the timing and wild card options on the theoretical futures price is the same as with the quality option. These delivery options should result in a theoretical futures price that is lower than the one suggested in equations (28.1) and (28.2), as shown here:

$$
\begin{aligned}
\text{Futures price} = {} & \text{Cash market price} + \text{Cash market price} \\
& \times (\text{Financing cost} - \text{Cash yield on bond}) \qquad \textbf{(28.3)} \\
& - \text{Value of quality option} - \text{Value of wild card option}
\end{aligned}
$$

Or alternatively,

$$
\begin{aligned}
\text{Futures price} = {} & \text{Cash market price} + \text{Cash market price} \\
& \times (\text{Financing cost} - \text{Cash yield on bond}) \qquad \textbf{(28.4)} \\
& - \text{Delivery options}
\end{aligned}
$$

Market participants attempt to value the delivery option in order to apply equation (28.4).

Deliverable Is Not a Basket of Securities   The municipal index futures contract is a cash settlement contract based on a basket of securities. The difficulty in arbitraging this futures contract is that it is too expensive to buy or sell every bond included in the index. Instead, as we explained in Chapter 16 in our discussion of the pricing of stock index futures, a portfolio containing a smaller number of bonds may be constructed to "track" the index. The arbitrage, however, is no longer risk-free because of tracking-error risk.

PRICING EFFICIENCY OF INTEREST RATE FUTURES

When interest rate futures began trading, some market observers noted that futures prices for Treasury bonds were less than their theoretical price, leading earlier observers to conclude that the market was inefficient. Yet researchers quickly pointed out that divergence between actual and theoretical futures prices is due to the delivery options granted to the short as discussed earlier.[2] The empirical question then becomes: What is the value of these options?

In two separate studies Kane and Marcus examine the value of the quality option and the wild card option.[3] Using a simulation approach to analyze these two delivery options, they find that each has a significant influence on the price of Treasury bond futures, each option reduces the value of the futures contract by roughly $0.20 (based on a futures price of $72). Michael Hemler finds that the quality option has somewhat less of an effect for Treasury bond futures contracts.[4]

APPLICATIONS OF INTEREST RATE FUTURES

We now describe six ways in which market participants can employ interest rate futures.

1. To speculate on the movement of interest rates.
2. To control the interest rate risk of a portfolio (alter duration).
3. To hedge against adverse interest rate movements.
4. To enhance returns when futures are mispriced.
5. To allocate funds between stocks and bonds.
6. To provide portfolio insurance (dynamic hedging).

Speculating on the Movement of Interest Rates The price of a futures contract moves in the opposite direction from interest rates: When rates rise (fall), the futures price will fall (rise). An investor who wants to speculate that interest rates will rise (fall) can sell (buy) interest rate futures. Before interest rate futures were available, investors who wanted to speculate on interest rates did so with the long-term Treasury bond: shorting it if they expected interest rates to rise, and buying it if they expected interest rates to fall. Three advantages can be gained through using interest rate futures instead of the cash markets (trading long-term Treasuries themselves). First, transactions costs are lower for futures compared to cash markets. Second, margin requirements are lower for futures than for Treasury securities; using futures thus permits greater leverage. Finally, it is easier to sell short in the futures market than in the Treasuries market. We repeat here what we said when we discussed the use of stock index futures to speculate on stock price movements; however, making speculation easier for investors is not the function of interest rate futures contracts.

Controlling the Interest Rate Risk of a Portfolio Stock index futures can be used to change the market risk of a diversified stock portfolio, that is, to alter the beta of a portfolio. Likewise, interest rate futures can be used to alter the interest rate sensitivity

[2] See Gerald D. Gay and Steven Manaster, "The Quality Option Implicit in Futures Contracts," *Journal of Financial Economics* (September 1984), pp. 353–70; and "Implicit Delivery Options and Optimal Delivery Strategies for Financial Futures Contracts," *Journal of Financial Economics* (May 1986), pp. 41–72.

[3] Alex Kane and Alan Marcus, "The Quality Option in the Treasury Bond Futures Market: An Empirical Assessment," *Journal of Futures Markets* (Summer 1986), pp. 231–48, and "Valuation and Optimal Exercise of the Wild Card Option in the Treasury Bond Futures Market," *Journal of Finance* (March 1986), pp. 195–207.

[4] Michael J. Hemler, "The Quality Delivery Option in Treasury Bond Futures Contracts," doctoral dissertation, Graduate School of Business, University of Chicago, March 1988.

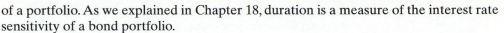

of a portfolio. As we explained in Chapter 18, duration is a measure of the interest rate sensitivity of a bond portfolio.

Investment managers with strong expectations about the direction of the future course of interest rates will adjust the durations of their portfolios so as to capitalize on their expectations. Specifically, if a manager expects rates to increase, the duration will be shortened; if interest rates are expected to decrease, the duration will be lengthened. Even though investment managers can alter the durations of their portfolios with cash market instruments, a quick and inexpensive means for doing so (on either a temporary or permanent basis) is to use futures contracts.

Hedging Against Adverse Interest Rate Movements Interest rate futures can be used to hedge against adverse interest rate movements by locking in either a price or an interest rate. Because in most applications the bond or the rate to be hedged is not identical to the bond or the rate underlying the futures contract, hedging with interest rate futures involves cross-hedging. The following are some examples of hedging with interest rate futures.

1. Suppose that a pension fund manager knows that bonds must be liquidated in 40 days to make a $5 million payment to the beneficiaries of the pension funds. If interest rates rise in 40 days, more bonds will have to be liquidated to realize $5 million. The pension fund manager can hedge by selling bonds in the futures market to lock in a selling price. This example is a sell or short hedge.[5]

2. A pension fund manager may use a long hedge when substantial cash contributions are expected and the pension fund manager is concerned that interest rates may fall. Also, a money manager who knows that bonds are maturing in the near future and who expects that interest rates will fall can employ a long hedge. In both cases, interest rate futures are used to hedge against a fall in interest rates that would cause cash flows to be invested at an interest rate lower than current rates.

3. Suppose a corporation plans to sell long-term bonds 2 months from now. To protect itself against a rise in interest rates, the corporation can sell interest rate futures now.

4. A thrift or commercial bank can hedge its costs of funds by locking in a rate using the Eurodollar CD futures contract.[6]

5. Suppose a corporation plans to see commercial paper 1 month from now. Treasury bill futures or Eurodollar CD futures can be used to lock in a commercial paper rate.[7]

6. Investment banking firms can use interest rate futures to protect both the value of positions held by their trading desks and positions assumed by underwriting bonds. An example of the latter is a 1979 Salomon Brothers underwriting of $1 billion of IBM bonds. To protect itself against a rise in interest rates, which would reduce the value of the IBM bonds, Salomon Brothers sold (shorted) Treasury

[5] For evidence of the effectiveness of hedging corporate bonds with interest rate futures, see Joanne Hill and Thomas Schneeweis, "Risk Reduction Potential of Financial Futures for Corporate Bond Positions," in Gerald Gay and Robert W. Kolb (eds.), *Interest Rate Futures: Concepts and Issues* (Richmond, VA: Dame, 1982), pp. 307–23. For an illustration of hedging a corporate bond with Treasury futures, see Mark Pitts and Frank J. Fabozzi, *Interest Rate Futures and Options* (Chicago: Probus Publishing, 1989), Chapter 9. For evidence on the effectiveness of hedging municipal bonds with the municipal bond index futures contract, see Richard Bookstaber and Hal Heaton, "On the Hedging Performance of the New Municipal Bond Futures Contract," in Frank J. Fabozzi and T. Dessa Garlicki (eds.), *Advances in Bond Analysis and Portfolio Strategies* (Chicago: Probus Publishing, 1987).

[6] See Michael Smirlock, "An Analysis of Hedging Certificates of Deposit with Interest Rate Futures: Bank and Contract Specific Evidence," in *Advances in Futures and Options Research*, Vol. 2, Part B (1986), pp. 153–70.

[7] For an illustration, see Pitts and Fabozzi, *Interest Rate Futures and Options*, Chapter 9.

futures. In October 1979, interest rates rose following an announcement by the Federal Reserve Board that it was allowing interest rates more flexibility to move. Although the value of the IBM bonds held by Salomon Brothers declined in value, so did the Treasury bond futures contracts; but because Salomon Brothers sold these futures it realized a gain, reducing the loss on the IBM bonds it underwrote.

Enhancing Returns When Futures Are Mispriced   In Chapter 16 we explained that institutional investors look for the mispricing of stock index futures to create arbitrage profits and thereby enhance portfolio returns. We referred to this strategy as index arbitrage because it involves a stock index. If interest rate futures are mispriced even after considering the pricing problems we discussed earlier, institutional investors can enhance returns in the same way that they do in equities.

Allocating Funds Between Stocks and Bonds   A pension sponsor may wish to alter the composition of the pension's funds between stocks and bonds, that is, change its asset allocation. Suppose that a pension sponsor wants to shift a $1 billion fund from its current allocation of $500 million in stocks and $500 million in bonds to $300 million in stocks and $700 million in bonds. This shift can be made directly by selling $200 million of stocks and buying a like amount of bonds. The costs associated with shifting funds in this manner are (1) the transactions costs with respect to commissions and bid-ask spreads, (2) the market impact costs, and (3) the disruption of the activities of the money managers employed by the pension sponsor.

An alternative course of action is to use interest rate futures and stock index futures. Assume the pension sponsor wants to shift $200 million from stocks to bonds. Buying an appropriate number of interest rate futures and selling an appropriate number of stock index futures can achieve the desired exposure to stocks and bonds. Futures positions can be maintained or slowly liquidated as funds invested in the cash markets are actually shifted. The advantages of using financial futures contracts are (1) transactions costs are lower, (2) market impact costs are avoided or reduced by allowing the sponsor time to buy and sell securities in the cash market, and (3) activities of the money managers employed by the pension sponsor are not disrupted.[8]

Portfolio Insurance (Dynamic Hedging)   In Chapter 16, we explained that a put option on a portfolio can be created synthetically with a portfolio of Treasury bills and stock index futures. This strategy requires rebalancing, or dynamic hedging, of the portfolios. Although dynamic hedging is employed more commonly in the case of stock portfolios, bond portfolio managers have shown some interest in this strategy.[9]

◆ EXCHANGE-TRADED INTEREST RATE OPTIONS

Interest rate options can be written on cash instruments or futures. At one time, several exchange-traded option contracts had a debt instrument as their underlying instrument. This type of contract is referred to as **options on physicals.** The most liquid exchange-

[8] See Roger Clarke, "Asset Allocation Using Futures," in Robert Arnott and Frank J. Fabozzi (eds.), *Asset Allocation* (Chicago: Probus Publishing, 1988), Chapter 16, and Mark Zurak and Ravi Dattatreya, "Asset Allocation Using Futures Contracts," in Frank J. Fabozzi and Gregory Kipnis (eds.), *The Handbook of Stock Index Futures and Options* (Homewood, IL: Probus Publishing, 1988), Chapter 20.

[9] For an explanation and illustration of portfolio insurance for fixed-income portfolios, see Colin Negrych and Dexter Senft, "Portfolio Insurance Using Synthetic Puts—The Reasons, Rewards, and Risk," in Frank J. Fabozzi (ed.), *The Handbook of Fixed Income Options* (Chicago: Probus Publishing, 1989), Chapter 12; or Erol Hakanoglu, Robert Kopprasch, and Emmanuel Roman, "Portfolio Insurance in the Fixed Income Market," in Frank J. Fabozzi (ed.), *Fixed Income Portfolio Strategies* (Chicago: Probus Publishing, 1989), Chapter 11.

traded option on a fixed-income security at the time of this writing is an option on Treasury bonds traded on the Chicago Board Options Exchange. For reasons explained later, options on futures have been far more popular than options on physicals.

EXCHANGE-TRADED FUTURES OPTIONS

An **option on futures** contract, commonly referred to as a **futures option,** gives the buyer the right to buy from or sell to the writer a designated futures contract at a designated price at any time during the life of the option. If the futures option is a call option, the buyer has the right to purchase one designated futures contract at the exercise price; that is, the buyer has the right to acquire a long futures position in the designated futures contract. If the buyer exercises the call option, the writer (seller) acquires a corresponding short position in the futures contract.

A put option on a futures contract grants the buyer the right to sell one designated futures contract to the writer at the exercise price; that is, the option buyer has the right to acquire a short position in the designated futures contract. If the put option is exercised, the writer acquires a corresponding long position in the designated futures contract. Futures options are available on all the interest rate futures contracts reviewed in the previous section.

Mechanics of Trading Futures Options   As the parties to the futures option realize a position in a futures contract when the option is exercised, the question is: What will the futures price be? That is, at what price will the long be required to pay for the instrument underlying the futures contract, and at what price will the short be required to sell the instrument underlying the futures contract?

Upon exercise, the futures price for the futures contract will be set equal to the exercise price. The position of the two parties is then immediately marked-to-market based on the then-current futures price. Thus, the futures position of the two parties will be at the prevailing futures price. At the same time, the option buyer receives from the option seller the economic benefit from exercising. In the case of a call futures option, the option writer must pay the difference between the current futures price and the exercise price to the buyer of the option. In the case of a put futures option, the option writer must pay the option buyer the difference between the exercise price and the current futures price.

For example, suppose an investor buys a call option on some futures contract in which the exercise price is 85. Assume also that the futures price is 95 and that the buyer exercises the call option. Upon exercise, the call buyer is given a long position in the futures contract at 85 and the call writer is assigned the corresponding short position in the futures contract at 85. The futures position of the buyer and the writer is immediately marked-to-market by the exchange. Since the prevailing futures price is 95 and the exercise price is 85, the long futures position (the position of the call buyer) realizes a gain of 10 while the short futures position (the position of the call writer) realizes a loss of 10. The call writer pays the exchange 10 and the call buyer receives from the exchange 10. The call buyer who now has a long futures position at 95 can either liquidate the futures position at 95 or maintain a long futures position. If the former course of action is taken, the call buyer sells a futures contract at the prevailing futures price of 95. No gain or loss results from liquidating the position. Overall, the call buyer realizes a gain of 10. A call buyer who elects to hold the long futures position will face the same risk and reward of holding such a position. But the call buyer still realized a gain of 10 from the exercise of the call option.

Suppose instead that the futures option is a put rather than a call, and the current futures price is 60 rather than 95. Then if the buyer of this put option exercises it, the buyer would have a short position in the futures contract at 85; the option writer would have a long position in the futures contract at 85. The exchange then marks the position to market at the then-current futures price of 60, resulting in a gain to the put buyer of 25 and a loss to the put writer of the same amount. The put buyer who now has a short futures position at 60 can either liquidate the short futures position by buying a futures contract at the prevailing futures price of 60 or maintain the short futures position. In either case the put buyer realizes a gain of 25 from exercising the put option. Table 28-5 summarizes the position of the buyer and seller of a futures option.

The buyer of a futures option is not subject to margin requirements once the option price has been paid in full. Because the option price is the maximum amount that the buyer can lose, regardless of how adverse the price movement of the underlying instrument, margin is not needed.

Because the writer (seller) of an option agrees to accept all of the risk (and none of the reward) of the position in the underlying instrument, the writer (seller) is required to deposit not only the margin required on the interest rate futures contract position if it is the underlying instrument, but, with certain exceptions, also the option price received for writing the option. In addition, as prices adversely affect the writer's position, the writer would be required to deposit variation margin as it is marked-to-market.

The price of a futures option is quoted in 64ths of 1% of par value. For example, a price of 24 means 24/64ths of 1% of par value. Because the par value of a Treasury bond futures contract is $100,000, an option price of 24 means

$$\left[\left(24 \, / \, 64\right) \, / \, 100\right] \times \$100,000 = \$375$$

In general, the price of a futures option quoted at Q is equal to

$$\text{Option price} = \left[\left(Q \, / \, 64\right) \, / \, 100\right] \times \$100,000$$

Popularity of Futures Options   Three reasons explain why futures options on fixed income securities have largely supplanted options on physicals as the options vehicle used by institutional investors.[10] First, unlike options on fixed income securities, futures options on Treasury coupon futures do not require payments for accrued interest. Consequently, when a futures option is exercised, the call buyer and the put writer need not compensate the other party for accrued interest.

Second, futures options are believed to be "cleaner" instruments because of the reduced likelihood of delivery squeezes. Market participants who must deliver an

TABLE 28-5   Futures Options

Type	Buyer has the right to and then has	If exercised, the seller then has . . .	and the seller pays the buyer . . .
Call	Purchase one futures contract @ the strike price a long futures position	a short futures position	Current futures price − Strike price
Put	Sell one futures contract @ the strike price a short futures position	a long futures position	Strike price − Current futures price

---

[10]   Laurie Goodman, "Introduction to Debt Options," in Frank J. Fabozzi (ed.), *Winning the Interest Rate Game: A Guide to Debt Options* (Chicago, IL: Probus Publishing, 1985), Chapter 1, pp. 13–14.

instrument are concerned that at the time of delivery the instrument to be delivered will be in short supply, resulting in a higher price to acquire the instrument. As the deliverable supply of futures contracts is more than adequate for futures options currently traded, traders face little concern about a delivery squeeze.

Finally, in order to price any option, it is imperative to know at all times the price of the underlying instrument. In the bond market, current prices are not as easily available as price information on the futures contract.

APPLICATIONS OF INTEREST RATE OPTIONS

No new strategies for using interest rate options are available beyond what we explained in Chapter 11, 15, and 16. An institutional investor can use interest rate options to speculate on fixed income security price movements based on expectations of interest rate movements. Because a call option increases in price if interest rates decline, an investor can buy call options if he or she expects interest rates to move in that direction. Alternatively, because the writer of a put option will benefit if the price increases, an investor who expects interest rates to fall can write put options. Purchasing put options and/or selling call options would be appropriate for an investor who expects interest rates to rise. Remember that unlike speculation in interest rate futures, interest rate options limit downside risk while reducing upside potential by the amount of the option price.

Hedging Against Adverse Interest Rate Movements   Interest rate options can be used to hedge against adverse interest rate movements but still benefit from a favorable interest rate movement by setting a floor or ceiling on a rate. We use the illustrations given earlier for interest rate futures to explain how this hedge works and to compare the outcomes using futures and options.

1. Suppose that a pension fund manager knows that bonds must be liquidated in 40 days to make a $5 million payment to the beneficiaries of the pension fund. If interest rates rise in 40 days, more bonds will have to be liquidated to realize $5 million. The hedger buys put options. Should interest rates rise, the value of the bonds to be sold declines, but the put options purchased rise in value. If the transaction is properly structured, the gain on the put options offsets the loss on the bonds. The cost of the safety bought by this strategy equals the option price paid. If, instead, interest rates decline, the value of the bonds rises. The pension fund manager does not exercise the put option. A gain equal to the rise in the bond value minus the put option price is realized. As we explained in Chapter 15, a strategy of buying put options on securities held in a portfolio is called a protective put buying strategy.

2. Suppose a pension fund manager knows that substantial cash contributions will flow into the fund and is concerned that interest rates may fall. Or, suppose a money manager knows that bonds are maturing in the near future and expects interest rates to fall. In both cases, proceeds will be reinvested at a lower interest rate. Call options can be purchased in this situation. Should interest rates fall, the call options increase in value, offsetting the loss in interest income that results when the proceeds must be invested at a lower interest rate. The cost of this hedge strategy is the call option price. Should interest rates rise instead, the proceeds can be invested at a higher rate. The benefits of the higher rate are reduced by the cost of the call option, which expires worthless.

3. Suppose a corporation plans to issue long-term bonds two months from now. To protect itself against a rise in interest rates, the corporation can buy put options. If interest rates rise, the interest cost of the bonds issued 2 months from now will be

higher, but the put option will have increased in value. Buying an appropriate number of put options yields a gain on the put options sufficient to offset the higher interest costs of the bond issue. Again, the cost of this strategy is the price of the put options. Should interest rates decline instead, the corporation benefits from a lower interest cost when the bonds are issued—a benefit reduced by the cost of the put options.

4. Suppose a thrift or commercial bank wants to make sure that the cost of its funds will not exceed a certain level. It can do so by buying put options on Eurodollar CD futures.

5. Suppose a corporation plans to sell commercial paper 1 month from now. Buying put options on Treasury bill futures or Eurodollar CD futures lets the corporation set a ceiling on its commercial paper interest cost.

Allocating Funds between Stocks and Bonds   A pension sponsor may wish to alter the composition of the pension funds between stocks and bonds. Stock index options and interest rate options can be used rather than transacting in the cash market.[11]

OPTION-PRICING MODELS

In Chapters 11 and 15, we discussed two models popularly used for valuing options: the Black-Scholes model and the binomial model. Some problems arise when using these models to price an option on a bond. To illustrate the problems with the Black-Scholes option-pricing model if applied to the pricing of interest rate options, consider a 3-month European call option on a 3-year zero-coupon bond.[12] The maturity value of the underlying bond is $100, and the strike price is $120. Suppose further that the current price of the bond is $75.13, the 3-year risk-free rate is 10% annually, and expected price volatility is 4%. What would be the fair value for this option? Do you really need an option-pricing model to determine the value of this option?

Think about it. This zero-coupon bond is never priced above $100 because $100 is the maturity value. As the strike price is $120, the option will never be exercised; its value is therefore zero. If you can get anyone to buy such an option, any price you obtain will be free money. Yet an option buyer armed with the Black-Scholes option pricing model inputs the variables we assumed and come up with a value for this option of $5.60! Why is the Black-Scholes model off by so much? The answer comes out of its underlying assumptions (see Table 28-6).

TABLE 28-6   Limitations of Applying the Black-Scholes Stock Option-Pricing Model to Price Interest Rate Options

Assumptions	*Fixed Income Realities*
The price of the underlying has some possibility of rising to any price.	A bond has a maximum price and any higher price assumes a negative interest rate is possible.
Short-term rates remain constant.	Changes in short-term rates cause bond prices to change.
Volatility (variance of price is constant over the life of the option	Bond price volatility decreases as the bond approaches maturity.

11   For an explanation and illustration, see Ravi Dattatreya, "Asset Allocation Using Futures and Options," in Frank J. Fabozzi (ed), *The Handbook of Fixed Income Securities*, 3rd ed. (Homewood, IL: BusinessOne Irwin, 1991), Chapter 50.

12   This example is given in Lawrence J. Dyer and David P. Jacob, "Guide to Fixed Income Option Pricing Models," in Frank J. Fabozzi (ed.), *The Handbook of Fixed Income Options*, pp. 81–2.

Three assumptions of the Black-Scholes model limit its use in pricing options on interest rate instruments. First, the probability distribution for the prices assumed by the Black-Scholes option pricing model permits some probability—no matter how small—that the price can take on any positive value. However, in the case of a zero-coupon bond, the price cannot take on a value above $100. In the case of a coupon bond, we know that the price cannot exceed the sum of the coupon payments plus the maturity value. For example, for a 5-year, 10% coupon bond with a maturity value of $100, the price cannot be greater than $150 (five coupon payments of $10 plus the maturity value of $100). Thus, unlike stock prices, bond prices have a maximum value. The only way that a bond's price can exceed the maximum value is if negative interest rates are permitted. Such rates are not likely, so any probability distribution for prices assumed by an option pricing model that permits bond prices to be higher than the maximum bond value could generate nonsensical option prices. The Black-Scholes model does allow bond prices to exceed the maximum bond value (or, equivalently, allows negative interest rates). It is one of the reasons why we can get a senseless option price for the 3-month European call option on the 3-year zero-coupon bond.

The second assumption of the Black-Scholes option pricing model is that the short-term interest rate is constant over the life of the option. Yet the price of an interest rate option changes as interest rates change. A change in the short-term interest rate changes the rates along the yield curve. Therefore, to assume that the short-term rate will be constant is inappropriate for interest rate options. The third assumption is that the variance of prices is constant over the life of the option. Recall from Chapter 18 that as a bond moves closer to maturity its price volatility declines. Therefore, the assumption that price variance is constant over the life of the option is inappropriate.

In addition to illustrating the problem of using the Black-Scholes model to price interest rate options, we can also show that the binomial option-pricing model based on the price distribution of the underlying bond suffers from the same problems. A way around the problem of negative interest rates is to use a binomial option-pricing model based on the distribution of interest rates rather than prices, and construct the binomial tree.[13] Once a binomial interest rate tree is constructed, it can be converted into a binomial price tree by using the interest rates on the tree to determine the price of the bond. Then we follow the standard procedure for calculating the option price by working backward from the value of the call option at the expiration date.

The binomial option pricing model based on yields is superior to models based on prices, but it still has a theoretical drawback. All option-pricing models to be theoretically valid must satisfy the put-call parity relationship explained in Chapter 11. The problem with the binomial model based on yields is that it does not satisfy this relationship. It violates the relationship by failing to take into consideration the yield curve, thereby allowing arbitrage opportunities.

The most elaborate models that take the yield curve into consideration and as a result do not permit arbitrage opportunities are called **yield curve option-pricing models** or **arbitrage-free option-pricing models**. These models can incorporate different

---

[13] For example, in constructing the binomial tree based on interest rates, the following formula can be used:

If yield increases:	If yield decreases:
$Y_{t+1} = Y_t e^{+s}$	$Y_{t+1} = Y_t e^{-s}$

where

Y_{t+1} = yield to maturity in time period $t + 1$

Y_t = yield to maturity in time period t

s = expected interest rate volatility

volatility assumptions along the yield curve. The most popular model employed by dealer firms is the Black-Derman-Toy model.[14]

PRICING EFFICIENCY OF THE OPTIONS MARKETS

In our review of the pricing efficiency of the common stock options market, we explained two types of tests: (1) tests based on violations of boundary conditions and put-call parity, and (2) tests based on an option-pricing model. Researchers have studied options on interest rate futures in both categories.

Jordan and Seale employed a large transactions database (21,402 observations) for Treasury bond futures and futures options to test for both the lower boundary condition and put-call parity.[15] The time period studied is October 5, 1982 (when futures options began trading), through March 26, 1985. They found that actual prices conformed closely to the theoretical prices specified by the lower boundary and put-call parity. The deviations from put-call parity found were not sufficiently large to be exploitable by even the lowest-cost traders. Therefore, the findings of Jordan and Seale provided virtually no evidence for rejecting the hypothesis that the market is efficient.

Merville and Overdahl empirically examined the mispricing bias and market efficiency for call options on Treasury bond futures from December 1982 through June 1985, using several options-pricing models.[16] They found that the pricing efficiency of call options improved only marginally with the inception of futures option trading. According to their option-pricing model, in-the-money options tended to be underpriced and at- and out-of-the-money options tended to be overpriced. These results, however, may be due simply to the lack of a good theoretical model to price the options.

Summary ●

In this chapter we reviewed the markets for interest rate futures and options contracts. Currently traded interest rate futures contracts include Treasury bill futures, Eurodollar CD futures, Treasury bond and note futures, and agency futures. Interest rate futures are also traded on foreign exchanges where the underlying fixed income security is foreign debt.

The Treasury bond and note futures contracts give the short several delivery options—quality or swap option, timing option, and wild card option. All three delivery options reduce the futures price below the theoretical futures price suggested by the standard arbitrage model.

The CBOT and the CME trade futures contracts on the 10-year and 5-year agency note and the underlying instrument for these contracts is one Fannie Mae benchmark note or Freddie Mac reference note. As with the Treasury futures contract, a cheapest-to-deliver issue for the agency note futures contract can be determined.

---

[14] Fischer Black, Emanuel Derman, and William Toy, "A One-Factor Model of Interest Rates and Its Application to Treasury Bond Options," *Financial Analysts Journal* (January/February 1990), pp. 24–32.

[15] James V. Jordan and William E. Seale, "Transactions Data Tests of Minimum Prices and Put-Call Parity for Treasury Bond Futures Options," *Advances in Futures and Options Research,* Vol. 1, Part A, 1986, pp. 63–87.

[16] Larry J. Merville and James A. Overdahl, "An Empirical Examination of the T-Bond Futures (Call) Options Markets Under Conditions of Constant and Changing Variance Rates," *Advances in Futures and Options Research,* vol. 1, Part A (1986), pp. 89–118.

Interest rate futures can be used by institutional investors to speculate on interest rate movements, to control a bond portfolio's exposure to interest rate changes (altering duration), to enhance returns when futures are mispriced, to allocate funds between stocks and bonds (in combination with stock index futures), and to create synthetic put options (portfolio insurance or dynamic hedging). The most popular use of interest rate futures by institutional money managers and corporate financial managers is for hedging—locking in an interest rate or a price.

Interest rate options include options on fixed income securities and options on interest rate futures contracts. The latter, more commonly called futures options, are the preferred vehicle for implementing investment strategies. Strategies using interest rate options include speculating on interest rate movements and hedging.

The assumptions underlying the Black-Scholes pricing models and the binomial model based on prices limit their application to options on fixed income instruments. The binomial option pricing model based on yields is a better model, but it still suffers from the problem that it does not satisfy the put-call parity relationship. More sophisticated models called yield curve or arbitrage-free pricing models overcome this drawback by incorporating the yield curve into the pricing model.

Key Terms

- Arbitrage-free option-pricing models
- Cheapest-to-deliver issue
- Conversion factors
- Delivery options
- Futures options

- Implied repo rate
- Index price
- Invoice price
- Options on futures
- Options on physicals
- Quality option

- Swap option
- Timing option
- Wild card option
- Yield curve option-pricing models

Questions

1. a. What is the underlying instrument for the Treasury bill futures contract?
   b. If the futures price of a Treasury bill futures contract is 93.5, what is the futures yield on a bank discount basis?
   c. What is the invoice price at the settlement date for a Treasury bill futures contract if the futures price is 93.10?
2. a. What is the underlying instrument for the Eurodollar CD futures contract?
   b. If the index price of a Eurodollar CD futures contract is 92.40, what is the annualized futures LIBOR?
3. What is the underlying instrument for an agency futures contract?
4. What does it mean if the cost of carry is positive for a Treasury bond futures contract?
5. How do you think the cost of carry affects the decision of the short as to when in the delivery month the short will elect to deliver?
6. What is the underlying instrument for the Treasury bond futures contract?
7. What are the delivery options granted to the seller of the Treasury bond futures contract?
8. a. What is the purpose of the conversion factors for the U.S. Treasury bond futures contract?
   b. Are the conversion factors changed once a contract with a specific settlement date begins trading?
9. How is the theoretical futures price of a Treasury bond futures contract affected by the delivery options granted to the short?

10. Suppose that the conversion factor for a particular Treasury bond that is acceptable for delivery in a Treasury bond futures contract is 0.85 and that the futures price settles at 105. Assume also that the accrued interest for this Treasury bond is 4. What is the invoice price if the seller delivers this Treasury bond at the settlement date?

11. What is the implied repo rate?

12. Explain why the implied repo rate is important in determining the cheapest-to-deliver issue?

13. As the corporate treasurer of a major corporation, you envision that the firm will have to borrow $125 million in 3 months' time.
    a. How could you use a Treasury bond futures contract to hedge against increased interest rates over the next quarter?
    b. Why might this approach not work as a perfect hedge?

14. What are the difficulties in pricing the municipal bond futures contract?

15. An investor owns a call option on bond X with a strike price of 100. The coupon rate on bond X is 9% and has 10 years to maturity. The call option expires today at a time when bond X is selling to yield 8%. Should the investor exercise the call option?

16. What is the difference between an option on a bond and an option on a bond futures contract?

17. If the price of a futures option is quoted at 32, what is the option price in dollars per contract?

18. Why are exchange-traded futures options more poplar than exchange-traded options on physicals?

19. Suppose an investor buys a call option on some futures contract in which the exercise price is 90. Assume also that the current futures price is 95 and that the buyer exercises the option.
    a. How much must the option writer pay the option buyer?
    b. What is the resulting futures position for the option buyer and option writer?

20. Suppose an investor buys a put option on some futures contract in which the exercise price is 92. Assume also that the current futures price is 88 and that the buyer exercises the option.
    a. How much must the option writer pay the option buyer?
    b. What is the resulting futures position for the option buyer and option writer?

21. An investor wants to protect against a rise in the market yield on a Treasury bond. Should the investor purchase a put option or a call option to obtain protection?

22. Respond to the questions following each of these excerpts from an article entitled "It's Boom Time for Bond Options as Interest-Rate Hedges Bloom," published in the November 8, 1990, issue of *The Wall Street Journal*.

    > *"The threat of a large interest-rate swing in either direction is driving people to options to hedge their portfolios of long-term Treasury bonds and medium-term Treasury notes," said Steven Northern, who manages fixed-income mutual funds for Massachusetts Financial Services Co. in Boston.*

    a. Why would a large interest rate swing in either direction encourage people to hedge?

    > *If the market moves against an option purchaser, the option expires worthless, and all the investor has lost is the relatively low purchase price, or "premium," of the option.*

    b. Comment on the accuracy of this statement.

    > *Futures contracts also can be used to hedge portfolios, but they cost more, and there isn't any limit on the amount of losses they could produce before an investor bails out.*

  c. Comment on the accuracy of this statement.

> *Mr. Northern said Massachusetts Financial has been trading actively in bond and note put options. "The concept is simple," he said. "If you're concerned about interest rates but don't want to alter the nature of what you own in a fixed-income portfolio, you can just buy puts."*

  d. Why might put options be a preferable means of altering the nature of a fixed income portfolio?

23. What arguments would be given by those who feel that Black-Scholes model does not apply in pricing interest rate options?

24. Suppose that you are offered the following call option on a zero-coupon bond with a maturity value of 100, 2 years to expiration, and strike price of 100.25.
  a. Explain why the value of this option would be zero.
  b. Given the assumptions that (1) the current price of the underlying zero-coupon bond is 83.96, (2) the expected price volatility is 10%, and (3) the risk-free rate is 6%, calculate the theoretical value for this call option using the Black-Scholes option-pricing model. (See Chapter 15 for the formula.) Comment on your findings.

CHAPTER 29

OTC Interest Rate and Credit Derivative Markets

Learning Objectives

After reading this chapter you will understand:

- the types of over-the-counter interest rate options.
- why over-the-counter interest rate options are used by market participants.
- what a compound option is and its use.
- what a forward rate agreement is and its use.
- how an interest rate swap can be used by institutional investors and corporate borrowers.
- why the interest rate swap market has grown so rapidly.
- how the swap rate is determined.
- how to value an interest rate swap.
- the various types of interest rate swaps and reasons for their development.
- what an option on a swap is, and how it can be used.
- what an interest rate agreement (cap or floor) is, and how these agreements can be used by institutional investors and corporate borrowers.
- the relationship between an interest rate agreement and options.
- how an interest rate collar can be created.
- the different types of credit risk: default risk, credit spread risk, and downgrade risk.
- the basic feature of credit derivatives: credit options, credit forward contracts, and credit swaps.

In Chapter 28 we discussed exchange-traded interest rate futures and options and how they can be used to control interest rate risk. Commercial banks and investment banks also customize for their clients interest rate contracts useful for controlling risk or for taking positions in markets. These contracts include interest rate options, forward rate agreements, interest rate swaps and options on swaps, interest rate agreements (caps and floors) and options on these agreements, and compound options. In this chapter we review each of them and explain how they can be used by borrowers and institutional investors. All of these contracts are accompanied by counterparty risk. Although interest rate derivatives can be used to control for changes in the level

■ **574** ■

of interest rates, they do not protect against changes in credit spreads. At the end of this chapter we describe derivative instruments that can be used to control for credit risk. These instruments are called credit derivatives.

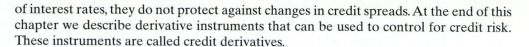

◆ **OVER-THE-COUNTER INTEREST RATE OPTIONS**

Institutional investors who want to purchase an option on a specific Treasury security or a Ginnie Mae pass-through can do so on an over-the-counter basis. Some government and mortgage-backed securities dealers make a market in options on specific securities.

Over-the-counter (or dealer) options typically are purchased by institutional investors who want to hedge the risk associated with a specific security. For example, a thrift may be interested in hedging its position in a specific mortgage pass-through security. Typically, the maturity of the option coincides with the time period over which the buyer of the option wants to hedge, so the buyer is typically not concerned with the option's liquidity.

Besides these basic OTC options on fixed income securities, more complex options were referred to as "exotic options" in Chapter 11. Two examples are the alternative option and the outperformance option. In our discussion of equity derivative products in Chapter 16, we explained how these two options can be used by managers of equity portfolios. They can also be used by managers of bond portfolios in betting on the better of two performing sectors of the bond market (alternative options) or the relative performance of two sectors of the bond market (outperformance options).

An option whose payoff depends on the spread between two sectors of the bond market such as between Treasuries and double-A corporates can be used by corporate treasurers to reduce risk. For example, consider a corporation that plans to sell bonds in two months. The rate that the corporate issuer will pay in two months is the Treasury rate plus the spread to Treasuries. If the corporate treasurer is satisfied with the spread but not the Treasury rate, the firm can buy an option on the spread.

A common OTC option between two sectors of the market is an option on the yield curve. Here a sector is defined as the maturity sector. The reason for the popularity of yield curve options is that the performance of many institutional investors is affected by a change in the shape of the yield curve.

COMPOUND OR SPLIT-FEE OPTIONS

A **compound** or **split-fee option** is an option to purchase an option. We can explain the elements of a compound option by using a long call option on a long put option. This compound option gives the buyer of the option the right but not the obligation to require the writer of the compound option to sell the buyer a put option. The compound option would specify the following terms:

1. The day on which the buyer of the compound option has the choice of either requiring the writer of the option to sell the buyer a put option or allowing the option to expire, which is called the **extension date**.
2. The strike price and the expiration date of the put option that the buyer acquires from the writer, which is called the **notification date**.

The payment that the buyer makes to acquire the compound option is called the **front fee**. If the buyer exercises the call option in order to acquire the put option, a second payment is made to the writer of the option. That payment is called the **back fee**.

An option that allows the option buyer to purchase a put option is called a **caput**. A **cacall** grants the option buyer the right to purchase a call option.

Compound options are most commonly used by mortgage originators to hedge pipeline risk.[1] They can also be used in any situation when the asset/liability manager needs additional time to gather information about the need to purchase an option.

◆ FORWARD RATE AGREEMENT

A **forward rate agreement (FRA)** is a customized agreement between two parties (one of whom is a dealer firm—a commercial bank or investment banking firm) where the two parties agree at a specified future date to exchange an amount of money based on a reference interest rate and a notional principal amount.

To illustrate an FRA, suppose that Industrial Products Company and an investment bank enter into the following 3-month FRA whose notional principal amount is $10 million: If 1-year LIBOR 3 months from now exceeds 9%, the investment banking firm must pay the Industrial Products Company an amount determined by the formula (1-year LIBOR 3 months from now − 0.09) × $10,000,000.

For example, if 1-year LIBOR 3 months from now is 12%, Industrial Products Company receives: (0.12 − 0.09) × $10,000,000 = $300,000. If 1-year LIBOR 3 months from now is less than 9%, Industrial Products Company must pay the investment banking firm an amount based on the same formula.

Borrowers and investors can use FRAs to hedge against adverse interest rate risk by locking in a rate. To see how a borrower can use an FRA, consider the preceding hypothetical FRA. Suppose that the management of Industrial Products Company plans 3 months from now to borrow $10 million for 1 year. The firm can borrow funds at some spread over 1-year LIBOR, which is currently 9%. The risk that the firm faces is that 3 months from now 1-year LIBOR will be greater than 9%. Suppose further that management wishes to eliminate the risk of a rise in 1-year LIBOR by locking in a rate of 9%. By entering into the hypothetical FRA, the management of Industrial Products Company has done so. Should 1-year LIBOR rise above 9% 3 months from now, under the terms of the FRA the investment banking firm is obligated to make up the difference. If 1-year LIBOR 3 months from now is below 9%, the Industrial Products Company does not benefit from the lower rate because it must pay the investment banking firm an amount such that the effective cost of borrowing is 9%.

◆ INTEREST RATE SWAPS

As explained in Chapter 12, an interest rate swap is an agreement whereby two parties (called counterparties) agree to exchange periodic interest payments. The dollar amount of the interest payments exchanged is based on the notional amount. The dollar amount each counterparty pays to the other is the agreed-upon periodic interest rate multiplied by the notional amount. The only dollars that are exchanged between the parties are the interest payments, not the notional principal amount. In the most common type of swap, one party agrees to pay the other party fixed interest payments at designated dates for the life of the contract. The other party agrees to make interest rate payments that float with some reference rate and is referred to as the floating-rate payer.

The reference rates that are commonly used for the floating rate in an interest rate swap are those on various money market instruments: Treasury bills, London interbank

---

[1] Pipeline risk is discussed in Chapter 26. For a discussion of how compound options can be used to hedge pipeline risk, see Anand K. Bhattacharya, "Compound Options on Mortgage-Backed Securities," in *The Handbook of Fixed-Income Options* (Chicago, Probus Publishing, 1989), Chapter 22.

offered rate (LIBOR), commercial paper, bankers acceptances, certificates of deposit, federal funds rate, and prime rate.

INTERPRETATION OF A SWAP

In Chapter 12, we explained that a swap can be viewed as a package of forward contracts. In another important interpretation of a swap it can be viewed as a package of cash market instruments. To understand why an interest rate swap can be interpreted as a package of cash market instruments, consider an investor who enters into a transaction to do the following:

- Buy a $50 million par of a 5-year floating-rate bond that pays 6-month LIBOR every 6 months.
- Finance the purchase by borrowing $50 million for 5 years at a 10% annual interest rate paid every 6 months.

The cash flows for this transaction are set forth in Table 29-1. The second column of the table shows the cash flow from purchasing the 5-year floating-rate bond. It starts with a $50 million cash outlay and then 10 cash inflows. The amount of the cash inflows is uncertain because they depend on future LIBOR. The next column shows the cash flow from borrowing $50 million on a fixed-rate basis. The fourth column shows the net cash flow from the entire transaction. As the last column indicates, no initial cash flow (no cash inflow or cash outlay) is required. In all ten 6-month periods, the net position results in a cash inflow of LIBOR and a cash outlay of $2.5 million. This net position, however, is identical to the position of a fixed-rate payer/floating-rate receiver.

It can be seen from the net cash flow in Table 29-1 that a fixed-rate payer has a cash market position that is equivalent to a long position in a floating-rate bond and a short position in a fixed-rate bond—the short position being the equivalent of borrowing by issuing a fixed-rate bond.

What about the position of a floating-rate payer? It can be easily demonstrated that the position of a floating-rate payer is equivalent to purchasing a fixed-rate bond and financing that purchase at a floating rate, where the floating rate is the reference

TABLE 29-1   Cash Flow for Purchase of a 5-Year Floating-Rate Bond Financed by Borrowing on a Fixed-Rate Basis (Cash flow in millions of dollars)

Six-Month Period	Floating-Rate Bond	Borrowing Cost	Net	
0	$-$50	+$50.0	$0	
1	$+(LIBOR_1/2 \times 50$	-2.5	$+(LIBOR_1/2) \times 50$	-2.5
2	$+(LIBOR_2/2) \times 50$	-2.5	$+(LIBOR_2/2) \times 50$	-2.5
3	$+(LIBOR_3/2) \times 50$	-2.5	$+(LIBOR_3/2) \times 50$	-2.5
4	$+(LIBOR_4/2) \times 50$	-2.5	$+(LIBOR_4/2) \times 50$	-2.5
5	$+(LIBOR_5/2) \times 50$	-2.5	$+(LIBOR_5/2) \times 50$	-2.5
6	$+(LIBOR_6/2) \times 50$	-2.5	$+(LIBOR_6/2) \times 50$	-2.5
7	$+(LIBOR_7/2) \times 50$	-2.5	$+(LIBOR_7/2) \times 50$	-2.5
8	$+(LIBOR_8/2) \times 50$	-2.5	$+(LIBOR_8/2) \times 50$	-2.5
9	$+(LIBOR_9/2) \times 50$	-2.5	$+(LIBOR_9/2) \times 50$	-2.5
10	$+(LIBOR_{10}/2) \times 50 + 50$	-52.5	$+(LIBOR_{10}/2 \times 50$	-2.5

Note: The subscript for LIBOR indicates 6-month LIBOR as per the terms of the floating-rate bond at time t.

interest rate for the swap. That is, the position of a floating-rate payer is equivalent to a long position in a fixed-rate bond and a short position in a floating-rate bond.

APPLICATIONS

In Chapter 12, we provided a simple illustration of how a depository institution can use an interest rate swap to alter the cash-flow character of assets or liabilities from a fixed-rate basis to a floating-rate basis, or vice versa. We provide two illustrations of applications here.

Illustration 1   In the first illustration we look at how an interest rate swap can be used to alter the cash-flow characteristics of an institution's assets so as to provide a better match between assets and liabilities. The two institutions are a commercial bank and a life insurance company.

Suppose a bank has a portfolio consisting of 5-year term commercial loans with a fixed interest rate. The principal value of the portfolio is $50 million, and the interest rate on all the loans in the portfolio is 10%. The loans are interest-only loans; interest is paid semiannually, and the principal is paid at the end of 5 years. That is, assuming no default on the loans, the cash flow from the loan portfolio is $2.5 million every 6 months for the next 5 years and $50 million at the end of 5 years. To fund its loan portfolio, assume that the bank is relying on the issuance of 6-month certificates of deposit. The interest rate that the bank plans to pay on its 6-month CDs is the 6-month Treasury bill rate plus 40 basis points.

The risk that the bank faces is that the 6-month Treasury bill rate will be 9.6% or greater. To understand why, remember that the bank is earning 10% annually on its commercial loan portfolio. If the 6-month Treasury bill rate is 9.6%, it will have to pay 9.6% plus 40 basis points to depositors for 6-month funds, or 10%, and earns no spread income. Worse, if the 6-month Treasury bill rate rises above 9.6%, it will result in a loss; that is, the cost of funds will exceed the interest rate earned on the loan portfolio. The bank's objective is to lock in a spread over the cost of its funds.

The other party in the interest rate swap illustration is a life insurance company that has committed itself to pay a 9% rate for the next 5 years on a guaranteed investment contract (GIC) it issued. The amount of the GIC is $50 million. Suppose that the life insurance company has the opportunity to invest $50 million in what it considers an attractive 5-year floating-rate instrument in a private-placement transaction. The interest rate on this instrument is the 6-month Treasury bill rate plus 160 basis points. The coupon rate is set every 6 months.

The risk that the life insurance company faces is that the 6-month interest rate will fall so that it will not earn enough to realize a spread over the 9% rate that it has guaranteed to the GIC holders. If the 6-month Treasury bill falls to 7.4% or less, no spread income will be generated. To understand why, suppose that the 6-month Treasury bill rate at the date the floating-rate instrument resets its coupon is 7.4%. Then the coupon rate for the next 6 months will be 9% (7.4% plus 160 basis points). Because the life insurance company agreed to pay 9% on the GIC policy, there will be no spread income. Should the 6-month Treasury bill rate fall below 7.4%, a loss will result.

We can summarize the asset/liability problem of the bank and life insurance company as follows. The bank loaned long term and borrowed short term; if the 6-month Treasury bill rate rises, spread income declines. The life insurance company effectively loans short term and borrows long term; if the 6-month Treasury bill rate falls, spread income declines.

Now suppose that an intermediary offers a 5-year interest rate swap with a notional amount of $50 million to both the bank and the life insurance company. The terms offered to the bank are as follows:

- Every 6 months the bank will pay 10% (annual rate) to the intermediary.
- Every 6 months the intermediary will pay the 6-month Treasury bill rate plus 155 basis points to the bank.

The terms offered to the insurance company are as follows:

- Every 6 months the life insurance company will pay the 6-month Treasury bill rate plus 160 basis points per year to the intermediary.
- Every 6 months the intermediary will pay the bank 10% (annual rate).

What has this interest rate contract done for each entity? We will first consider the bank. For every 6-month period for the life of the swap agreement, the interest rate spread for the bank will be as follows.

Annual Interest Rate Received	
From commercial loan portfolio = 10%	
From interest rate swap	= 6-month T-bill rate + 155 b.p.
Total	= 11.55% + 6-month T-bill rate
Annual Interest Rate Paid	
To CD depositors	= 6-month T-bill rate + 40 b.p.
On interest rate swap	= 10%
Total	= 10.40% + 6-month T-bill rate
Outcome	
To be received	= 11.55% + 6-month T-bill rate
To be paid	= 10.40% + 6-month T-bill rate
Spread income	= 1.15%, or 115 b.p.

Thus, regardless of what happens to the 6-month Treasury bill rate, the bank locks in a spread of 115 basis points.

Now we will look at the effect of the interest rate swap on the life insurance company as follows.

Annual Interest Rate Received	
From floating-rate instrument = 6-month T-bill rate + 160 b.p.	
From interest rate swap	= 10%
Total	= 11.6% + 6-month T-bill rate
Annual Interest Rate Paid	
To GIC policyholders	= 9%
On interest rate swap	= 6-month T-bill rate + 160 b.p.
Total	= 10.6% + 6-month T-bill rate
Outcome	
To be received	= 11.6% + 6-month T-bill rate
To be paid	= 10.6% + 6-month T-bill rate
Spread income	= 1.0%, or 100 b.p.

Regardless of what happens to the 6-month Treasury bill rate, the life insurance company locks in a spread of 100 basis points.

The interest rate swap allows each party to accomplish its asset/liability objective of locking in a spread.[2] It permits the two financial institutions to alter the cash-flow characteristics of its assets: from fixed to floating in the case of the bank, and from floating to fixed in the case of the life insurance company. This type of transaction is referred to as an **asset swap**. Alternatively, the bank and the life insurance company could have used the swap market to change the cash-flow nature of their liabilities. Such a swap is called a **liability swap**. Although in our illustration we used a bank, an interest rate swap obviously would be appropriate for savings and loan associations that borrow short term (i.e., on a floating-rate basis) and lend long term (i.e., on fixed-rate mortgages).

Of course the two institutions could have chosen other ways to accomplish the same thing. The bank might refuse to make fixed-rate commercial loans. If borrowers could find other sources willing to lend on a fixed-rate basis, though, the bank has lost these customers. The life insurance company might refuse to purchase a floating-rate instrument. But suppose that the terms offered on the private-placement instrument were more attractive than what would have been offered on a comparable credit-risk floating rate instrument, and that by using the swap market the life insurance company can earn a yield higher than if it invests directly in a 5-year fixed-rate security. For example, suppose the life insurance company can invest in a comparable credit-risk 5-year fixed-rate security with a yield of 9.8%. Assuming that it commits itself to a GIC with a 9% rate, it would result in spread income of 80 basis points—less than the 100-basis-point spread income it achieved by purchasing the floating-rate instrument and entering into the swap.

Consequently, not only can an interest rate swap be used to change the risk of a transaction by changing the cash flow characteristics of assets or liabilities, but under certain circumstances, it also can be used to enhance returns. Obviously, it depends on the existence of market imperfections.

Before we leave this illustration, look back at the floating-rate payments that the life insurance company makes to the intermediary and the floating-rate payments that the intermediary makes to the bank. The life insurance company pays the 6-month Treasury bill rate plus 160 basis points, but the intermediary pays the bank the 6-month Treasury bill rate plus only 155 basis points. The five-basis point difference represents the fee to the intermediary for the services of intermediation.

Illustration 2 Our second illustration considers two U.S. entities: a triple-A-rated commercial bank, and a triple-B-rated nonfinancial corporation. Each wants to raise $100 million for 10 years. The bank wants to raise floating-rate funds, while the nonfinancial corporation wants to raise fixed-rate funds. The interest rates available to the two entities in the U.S. bond market are as follows. For the bank: Floating rate = 6-month LIBOR + 30 b.p. For the nonfinancial corporation: Fixed rate = 12%.

Assume instead that both entities could issue securities in the Eurodollar bond market. The buyers in this market are typically non-U.S. investors. The criteria used by these investors to assess the default risk of bonds historically have been different from those used in the United States. Suppose that the following terms are available in the Eurodollar bond market for 10-year securities for these two entities. For the bank: Fixed rate = 10.5%. For the nonfinancial corporation: Floating rate = 6-month LIBOR + 80 b.p.

Notice that we indicate the terms that the bank could obtain on fixed-rate financing and that the nonfinancial corporation could obtain on floating-rate securities. You

---

[2] Whether the size of the spread is adequate is not an issue in this illustration.

will see why we did this shortly. First, we summarize the situation for the two entities in the U.S. domestic and Eurodollar bond markets, as shown here.

Floating-Rate Securities Entity	*Bond Market*	*Rate*
Bank	U.S. domestic	6-month LIBOR + 30 b.p.
Nonfinancial corp.	Eurodollar	6-month LIBOR + 80 b.p.
		Quality spread = 50 b.p.

Fixed-Rate Securities Entity	*Bond Market*	*Rate*
Bank	Eurodollar	10.5%
Nonfinancial corp.	U.S. domestic	12.0%
		Quality spread = 150 b.p.

Notice that the quality spread for floating-rate securities (50 basis points) is narrower than the quality spread for fixed-rate securities (150 basis points). This provides an opportunity for both entities to reduce the cost of raising funds. To see how, suppose each entity issued securities in the Eurodollar bond market, and then simultaneously entered into a 10-year interest rate swap with a $100 million notional principal amount offered by an intermediary. The rates available to each entity in this swap are as follows. For the bank: Pay floating rate of 6-month LIBOR + 70 b.p.; receive fixed rate of 11.3%. For the nonfinancial corp.: Pay fixed rate = 11.3%; receive floating rate = 6-month LIBOR + 45 b.p.

The cost of the issue for the bank would then be as follows.

Interest Paid	
On fixed-rate Eurodollar bonds issued	= 10.5%
On interest rate swap	= 6-month + 70 b.p.
Total	= 11.2% + 6-month LIBOR

Interest Received	
On interest rate swap	= 11.3%

Net Cost:	
Interest paid	= 11.2% + 6-month LIBOR
Interest received	= 11.3%
Total	= 6-month LIBOR − 10 b.p.

The cost of the issue for the nonfinancial corporation would then be as follows.

Interest Paid	
On floating-rate Eurodollar bonds issued	= 6-month LIBOR + 80 b.p.
On interest rate swap	= 11.3%
Total	= 12.1% + 6-month LIBOR

Interest Received	
On interest rate swap	= 6-month LIBOR + 45 b.p.

Net Cost	
Interest paid	= 12.1% + 6-month LIBOR
Interest received	= 6-month LIBOR + 45 b.p.
Total	= 11.65%

The transactions are diagrammed in Figure 29-1. By issuing securities in the Eurodollar bond market and using the interest rate swap, both entities are able to reduce their cost of issuing securities. The bank was able to issue floating-rate securities for 6-month LIBOR minus 10 basis points rather than issue floating-rate securities in the U.S. domestic bond market for 6-month LIBOR plus 30 basis points, thereby saving 40 basis points. The nonfinancial corporation saved 35 basis points (11.65% versus 12%) by issuing floating-rate bonds in the Eurodollar bond market and using the interest rate swap.

The point of this illustration is that if differences in quality spreads exist in different sectors of the bond markets, borrowers can use the interest rate swap to arbitrage the inconsistency. Whether they do exist is another question, which we will address next.

Finally, we shall look once again at the intermediary in this transaction. The intermediary pays a floating rate of 6-month LIBOR plus 45 basis points to the nonfinancial corporation, and receives 6-month LIBOR plus 70 basis points, realizing 25 basis points for its intermediary services.

DEVELOPMENT OF THE INTEREST RATE SWAP MARKET

The interest rate swap was first developed in late 1981. By 1987, the market had grown to more than $500 billion (in terms of notional principal amount). What is behind this rapid growth? As our two illustrations demonstrated, an interest rate swap is a quick way for institutional investors and corporate borrowers to change the nature of assets and liabilities or to exploit any perceived capital market imperfection.

Initial motivation for the interest rate swap market was borrower exploitation of what were perceived to be "credit arbitrage" opportunities because of differences between the quality spread between lower- and higher-rated credits in the U.S. and Eurodollar bond fixed-rate markets and the same spread in these two floating-rate markets. Note that our second illustration assumes a spread of 50 basis points in the

FIGURE 29-1 Diagram of Interest Rate Swap for Illustration 2

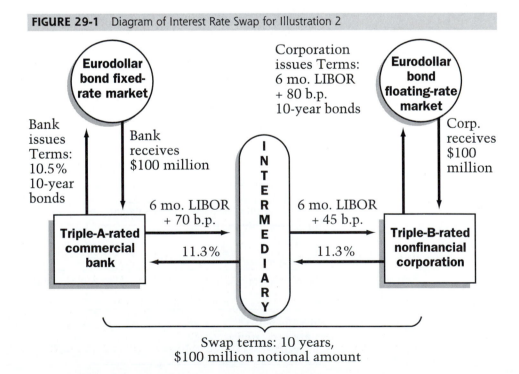

floating-rate markets and 150 basis points in the fixed-rate markets. Publications by dealer firms[3] and academic research have suggested this credit arbitrage motivation.[4]

Basically, the argument for swaps was based on a well-known economic principle of comparative advantage in international economics. The argument in the case of swaps is that even though a high-credit-rated issuer could borrow at a lower cost in both the fixed-rate and floating-rate markets (that is, have an absolute advantage in both), it will have a comparative advantage relative to a lower-credit-rated issuer in one of the markets (and a comparative disadvantage to the other). Under these conditions, each borrower could benefit from issuing securities in the market in which it has a comparative advantage and then swapping obligations for the desired type of financing. The swap market was the vehicle for swapping obligations.

Several observers challenged the notion that credit arbitrage exists. It should be evident that the comparative advantage argument, while based on arbitrage, is not based on the existence of an irrational mispricing, but on assumptions of equilibrium in segmented markets. If two completely separate markets are each perfectly competitive unto themselves, but set different prices for risk, a transactor in both markets simultaneously sees an imperfectly competitive market and can make money. Those who challenge the credit-arbitrage notion argue that the differences in quality spreads in the fixed-rate and floating-rate markets represent differences in the risks that lenders face in these two markets. For example, the interest rate for a floating-rate note effectively represents a short-term interest rate. The quality spread on floating-rate notes therefore represents a spread in the short-term market. In contrast, the quality spread on fixed-rate medium- and long-term notes represents the spread in that maturity sector. Quality spreads do not have to be the same.[5]

Despite arguments that credit-arbitrage opportunities are rare in reasonably efficient international capital markets, and that, even if they did exist, they would be eliminated quickly by arbitrage, the number of interest rate swap transactions has grown substantially. Another explanation is suggested in a May 1984 contribution sponsored by Citicorp that appeared in *Euromoney*:

> The nature of swaps is that they arbitrage market imperfections. As with any arbitrage opportunity, the more it is exploited, the smaller it becomes.
>
> But some of the causes of market imperfections are unlikely to disappear quickly. For example, insurance companies in many countries are constrained to invest mainly in instruments that are domestic in that country. That requirement will tend to favour domestic issuers artificially, and is unlikely to be changed overnight. And even in the world's most liquid markets there are arbitrage opportunities. They are small and exist only briefly. But they exist nevertheless.[6]

As this opinion demonstrates, as early as 1984 it was argued that the difference in quality spreads in the two markets may be attributable to differences in regulations in two countries. Similarly, differences in tax treatment across countries also create

---

[3] See, for example, a January 1986 Salomon Brothers publication: T. Lipsky and S. Elhalaski, "Swap-Driven Primary Issuance in the International Bond Market."

[4] See, for example, James Bicksler and Andrew Chen, "An Economic Analysis of Interest Rate Swaps," *Journal of Finance* (July 1986), pp. 645–55.

[5] Two researchers demonstrate that differences in quality spreads between the fixed-rate and floating-rate markets are consistent with option-pricing theory. See Ian Cooper and Antonio Mello, "Default Spreads in the Fixed and in the Floating Rate Markets: A Contingent Claims Approach," *Advances in Futures and Options Research*, 3 (1988), pp. 269–90.

[6] "Swap Financing Techniques: A Citicorp Guide," Special Sponsored Section, *Euromoney* (May 1984), pp. S1–S7.

market imperfections that can be exploited using swaps.[7] Thus, swaps can be used for regulatory or tax arbitrage.

Rather than relying exclusively on an arbitrage argument, one study suggests that the swap market grew because it allowed borrowers to raise a type of financing that was not possible prior to the introduction of interest rate swaps.[8] To explain this argument, we look at the instruments available to borrowers prior to the introduction of interest rate swaps. They include (1) long-term fixed-rate instruments, (2) long-term floating-rate instruments, and (3) short-term debt. The interest rate for a borrower is composed of the risk-free rate for the relevant maturity plus a credit spread. Consider borrowers with the following expectations:

- Borrower *A* believes that the risk-free rate will rise in the future, and its credit will weaken. This borrower will want to borrow long term with a fixed rate to lock in the prevailing risk-free rate and credit spread.
- Borrower *B* believes that the risk-free rate will fall in the future, but that its credit will weaken. In this case, the borrower will prefer to issue a long-term floating-rate instrument in order to lock in the credit spread, but at the same time to take advantage of an anticipated decline in the risk-free rate.
- Borrower *C* believes that the risk-free rate will fall in the future, but that its credit will strengthen in the future. The instrument of choice for this borrower is short-term floating debt, because its cost of funds in the future will be lower due to the expected decline in the risk-free rate and the lower credit spread that will be imposed by the market.
- Borrower *D* believes that the risk-free rate will rise in the future, and that its credit will strengthen in the future. This borrower would want to fix the risk-free rate but let the credit spread float. Which instrument will this borrower prefer to issue? None of the three instruments already listed can be used by this borrower to take advantage of its expectations.

Borrower *D* can use an interest rate swap, however, to fix the risk-free rate for the term of the swap but allow the credit spread to float.[9] In essence, this particular reason for the growth of interest rate swap market is based on asymmetric information. That is, the borrower possesses information (or a belief) that the market does not possess—namely, that the borrower's credit will improve.

Finally, another argument suggested for the growth of the interest rate swap market is the increased volatility of interest rates that led borrowers and lenders to hedge or manage their exposure. Even though risk/return characteristics can be replicated by a package of forward contracts, interest rate forward contracts are not as liquid as interest rate swaps. And entering into or liquidating swap transactions has been facilitated by the standardization of documentation published by the International Swap Dealers Association in early 1987. Moreover, a swap to hedge or manage a position costs less than a package of interest rate forward contracts.

---

[7] This applies even more so to currency swaps, which we discuss in Chapter 30. Several examples of how swaps can be used to exploit differences in taxes are given in Clifford W. Smith, Charles W. Smithson, and Lee MacDonald Wakeman, "The Evolving Market for Swaps," *Midland Corporate Finance Journal* (Winter 1986), pp. 20–32.

[8] Marcelle Arak, Arturo Estrella, Laurie Goodman, and Andrew Silver, "Interest Rate Swaps: An Alternative Explanation," *Financial Management* (Summer 1988), pp. 12–8.

[9] For an explanation of how this can be done, see Eileen Baecher and Laurie S. Goodman, *The Goldman Sachs Guide to Hedging Corporate Debt Issuance* (New York: Goldman Sachs & Co., 1988).

ROLE OF THE INTERMEDIARY

The role of the intermediary in an interest rate swap sheds some light on the evolution of the market. Intermediaries in these transactions have been commercial banks and investment banks, who in the early stages of the market sought out end-users of swaps. They found in their client bases those entities that needed the swap to accomplish a funding or investing objective, and they matched the two entities. In essence, the intermediary in this type of transaction performed the function of a broker.

The only time that the intermediary would take the opposite side of a swap (that is, would act as a principal) was to balance out the transaction. For example, if an intermediary had two clients that were willing to do a swap but one wanted the notional principal amount to be $100 million while the other wanted it to be $85 million, the intermediary might become the counterparty to the extent of $15 million. That is, the intermediary would warehouse or take a position as a principal to the transaction to make up the $15 million difference between client objectives. To protect itself against an adverse interest rate movement, the intermediary would hedge its position.

Another problem in an interest rate swap remains to be addressed. The parties to the swaps we described had to be concerned that the other party would default on its obligation. Although a default would not mean any principal was lost because the notional principal had not been exchanged, it would mean that the objective for which the swap was entered into would be impaired. As the early transactions involved a higher- and a lower-credit-rated entity, the former would be concerned with the potential for default of the latter. To reduce the risk of default, many early swap transactions required that the lower-credit-rated entity obtain a guarantee from a highly rated commercial bank.

As the frequency and the size of the transactions increased, many intermediaries became comfortable with the transactions and became principals instead of acting as brokers. As long as an intermediary had one entity willing to do a swap, the intermediary was willing to be the counterparty. Consequently, interest rate swaps became part of an intermediary's inventory of product positions. Advances in quantitative techniques and futures products for hedging complex positions such as swaps made the protection of large inventory positions feasible.

Yet another reason encouraged intermediaries to become principals rather than brokers in swaps. As more intermediaries entered the swap market, bid-ask spreads on swaps declined sharply. To make money in the swaps market, intermediaries had to do a sufficient volume of business, which could be done only if an intermediary had (1) an extensive client base willing to use swaps, and (2) a large inventory of swaps. This situation necessitated that intermediaries act as principals. For example, a survey by *Euromoney* asked 150 multinationals and supranationals to identify the characteristics that make a swap house efficient.[10] The results indicated that the speed at which a swap could be arranged for a client was the most important criterion. That speed depends on client base and inventory. The same survey also revealed clients to be less interested in brokered deals than in transactions in which the intermediary is a principal.

Consequently, we can describe the development of the swap market as one that originated to exploit real or perceived imperfections in the capital market, but that evolved into a transactionally efficient market for accomplishing asset/liability objectives.

---

[10] Special Supplement on Swaps, *Euromoney* (July 1987), p. 14.

TERMINOLOGY, CONVENTIONS, AND MARKET QUOTES

We explained the basics of a swap, its applications, and development of the swap market. Here we review some of the terminology used in this market and explain how swaps are quoted.

The date that the counterparties commit to the swap is called the **trade date**. The date that the swap begins accruing interest is called the **effective date**, while the date that the swap stops accruing interest is called the **maturity date**.

Our illustrations assume that the timing of the cash flows for both the fixed-rate payer and floating-rate payer will be the same, but it is rarely the case in a swap. In fact, an agreement may call for the fixed-rate payer to make payments annually but the floating-rate payer to make payments more frequently (semiannually or quarterly). Also, the way interest accrues on each leg of the transaction differs, because several day-count conventions apply in the fixed-income markets.

The terminology used to describe the position of a party in the swap markets combines cash market jargon and futures jargon, given that a swap position can be interpreted as a position in a package of cash market instruments or a package of futures/forward positions. As we have said, the counterparty to an interest rate swap is either a fixed-rate payer or floating-rate payer. A number of ways are used to describe these positions.[11]

THE FIXED-RATE PAYER:

- Pays fixed rate in the swap.
- Receives floating in the swap.
- Is short the bond market.
- Has bought a swap.
- Is long a swap.
- Has established the price sensitivities of a longer-term liability and a floating-rate asset.

THE FLOATING-RATE PAYER:

- Pays floating rate in the swap.
- Receives fixed in the swap.
- Is long the bond market.
- Has sold a swap.
- Is short a swap.
- Has established the price sensitivities of a longer-term asset and a floating-rate liability.

The first two expressions to describe the position of a fixed-rate payer and floating-rate payer are self-explanatory. To understand why the fixed-rate payer is viewed as short the bond market and the floating-rate payer is viewed as long the bond market, consider what happens when interest rates change. Those who borrow on a fixed-rate basis will benefit if interest rates rise because they have locked in a lower interest rate. But those who have a short bond position will also benefit if interest rates rise. Thus, a fixed-rate payer can be said to be "short the bond market." A floating-rate payer benefits if interest rates fall. Because a long position in a bond benefits if interest rates fall, terminology describing a floating-rate payer as "long the bond market" has been adopted.

[11] Robert F. Kopprasch, John Macfarlane, Daniel R. Ross, and Janet Showers, "The Interest Rate Swap Market: Yield Mathematics, Terminology, and Conventions," in Frank J. Fabozzi and Irving M. Pollack (eds.), *The Handbook of Fixed Income Securities* (Homewood, IL: Dow Jones-Irwin, 1987), Chapter 58.

The convention that has evolved for quoting swaps levels is that a swap dealer sets the floating rate equal to the reference rate and then quotes the fixed rate that will apply. For example, suppose that the reference is 3-month LIBOR and the swap is for 10 years. The fixed-rate that applies is the 10-year Treasury yield plus a spread. The spread is called the **swap spread**. The fixed-rate payer/floating-rate receiver would pay the 10-year Treasury yield plus the swap spread and receive the floating rate. The fixed-rate receiver/floating-rate payer would receive the 10-year Treasury yield plus the swap spread and pay the floating rate.

A dealer would quote a bid and an offer. To illustrate this convention, suppose a 10-year swap is offered by a dealer when the 10-year Treasury yield is 8.35%. The floating rate is 3-month LIBOR. Suppose the dealer quotes the swap at "40–50." The swap spread when the dealer is paying the fixed rate is 40 basis points, but the swap spread when the dealer is receiving the fixed rate is 50. Consequently

1. The dealer is willing to enter into a swap in which it pays the floating-rate flat (i.e., without a spread) and receives the Treasury yield of 8.35% plus 50 basis points.
2. The dealer is willing to enter into a swap in which it pays the Treasury yield of 8.35% plus 40 basis points and receives the floating rate.

CALCULATION OF THE SWAP RATE

At the initiation of an interest rate swap, the counterparties agree to exchange future interest rate payments and no upfront payments by either party are made. The swap terms must be such that the present values for the cash flows of the payments to be made by the counterparties are equal. It is equivalent to saying that the present value of the cash flows of payments to be received by the counterparties must be equal. The equivalence of the cash flows is the principle in calculating the swap rate.

For the fixed-rate side, once a swap rate is determined, the payments of the fixed-rate payer are known. However, the floating rate payments are not known because they depend on the value of the reference rate at the reset dates. For a LIBOR-based swap, the Eurodollar CD futures contract (discussed in Chapter 27) can be used to establish the forward (or future) rate for 3-month LIBOR. Given the cash flow based on the forward rate for 3-month LIBOR, the swap rate is the interest rate that will make the present value of the payments on the fixed-rate side equal to the payments on the floating-rate side.

The next question is what interest rate should be used to discount the payments. As explained in Chapter 18, the appropriate rate to discount any cash flow is the theoretical spot rate. Each cash flow should be discounted at a unique discount rate. Where do we get the theoretical spot rates? Recall from Chapter 18 that spot rates can be obtained from forward rates. It is the same 3-month LIBOR forward rates derived from the Eurodollar CD futures contract that can be used to obtain the theoretical spot rates.

We illustrate the procedure with an example.[12] Consider the following terms for our swap.

- The swap starts today, January 1 of year 1 (swap settlement date).
- The floating-rate payments are made quarterly based on "actual/360."
- The reference rate is 3-month LIBOR.
- The notional amount of the swap is $100 million.
- The term of the swap is 3 years.

---

[12] This illustration is taken from Frank J. Fabozzi, *Fixed Income Analysis for the Chartered Financial Analyst Program* (New Hope, PA: Frank J. Fabozzi Associates, 2000), pp. 609–21.

The quarterly floating-rate payments are based on an "actual/360" day count convention. This convention means that 360 days are assumed in a year and that in computing the interest for the quarter the actual number of days in the quarter are used. The floating-rate payment is set at the beginning of the quarter but paid at the end of the quarter; that is, the floating-rate payments are made in arrears.

Suppose that today 3-month LIBOR is 4.05%. Let's look at what the fixed-rate payer will receive on March 31 of year 1—the date when the first quarterly swap payment is made. The investor has no uncertainty about what the floating-rate payment will be. In general, the floating-rate payment is determined as follows:

$$\text{Notional amount} \times \left(3\text{-month LIBOR}\right) \times \frac{\text{Days in period}}{360}$$

In our illustration, assuming a non–leap year, the number of days from January 1 of year 1 to March 31 of year 1 (the first quarter) is 90. If 3-month LIBOR is 4.05%, then the fixed-rate payer will receive a floating-rate payment on March 31 of year 1 equal to

$$\$100,000,000 \times 0.0405 \times \frac{90}{360} = \$1,012,500$$

Now the difficulty is in determining the floating-rate payment after the first quarterly payment, that is the 3-year swap requires 12 quarterly floating-rate payments. So, while the first quarterly payment is known, the next 11 are not. However, the next 11 floating-rate payments can be hedged by using a futures contract. Specifically, the futures contract used to hedge the future floating-rate payments in a swap whose reference rate is 3-month LIBOR is the Eurodollar CD futures contract. We discussed this contract in Chapter 28, and we show how these floating-rate payments are computed using this contract.

We begin with the next quarterly payment—from April 1 of year 1 to June 30 of year 1. This quarter has 91 days. The floating-rate payment will be determined by 3-month LIBOR on April 1 of year 1 and paid on June 30 of year 1. A 3-month Eurodollar CD futures contract settles on June 30 of year 1. That futures contract provides the rate that can be locked in for 3-month LIBOR on April 1 of year 1. For example, if the futures price for the 3-month Eurodollar CD futures contract that settles on June 30 of year 1 is 95.85, then as already explained, the 3-month Eurodollar futures rate is 4.15%. We refer to that rate for 3-month LIBOR as the "forward rate." Therefore, if the fixed-rate payer bought 100 of these 3-month Eurodollar CD futures contracts on January 1 of year 1 (the inception of the swap) that settle on June 30 of year 1, then the payment that will be locked in for the quarter (April to June 30 of year 1) is

$$\$100,000,000 \times 0.0415 \times \frac{91}{360} = \$1,049,028$$

(Note that each futures contract is for $1 million and hence 100 contracts have a notional amount of $100 million.) Similarly, the Eurodollar CD futures contract can be used to lock in a floating-rate payment for each of the next 10 quarters. It is important to emphasize that the reference rate at the beginning of period t determines the floating-rate that will be paid for the period. However, the floating-rate payment is not made until the end of period t.

Table 29-2 shows this payment timing for the 3-year swap. Shown in column (1) is when the quarter begins and in column (2) when the quarter ends. The payment received at the end of the first quarter (March 31 of year 1) is $1,012,500, the known floating-rate payment as explained earlier. It is the only payment that is known. The information used to compute the first payment is in column (4) which shows the current 3-month LIBOR (4.05%). The payment is shown in the last column, column (8).

TABLE 29-2   Floating Cash Flow Based on Initial LIBOR and Eurodollar CD Futures

(1) Quarter Starts	(2) Quarter Ends	(3) Days in Quarter	(4) Current 3-Month LIBOR	(5) Eurodollar Futures Price	(6) Futures Rate	(7) Period = End of Quarter	(8) Floating Cash Flow at End of Quarter
Jan 1 year 1	March 31 year 1	90	4.05%			1	$1,012,500
Apr 1 year 1	June 30 year 1	91		$95.85	4.15%	2	1,049,028
July 1 year 1	Sept 30 year 1	92		95.45	4.55	3	1,162,778
Oct 1 year 1	Dec 31 year 1	92		95.28	4.72	4	1,206,222
Jan 1 year 2	Mar 31 year 2	90		95.10	4.90	5	1,225,000
Apr 1 year 2	June 30 year 2	91		94.97	5.03	6	1,271,472
July 1 year 2	Sept 30 year 2	92		94.85	5.15	7	1,316,111
Oct 1 year 2	Dec 31 year 2	92		94.75	5.25	8	1,341,667
Jan 1 year 3	Mar 31 year 3	90		94.60	5.40	9	1,350,000
Apr 1 year 3	June 30 year 3	91		94.50	5.50	10	1,390,278
July 1 year 3	Sept 30 year 3	92		94.35	5.65	11	1,443,889
Oct 1 year 3	Dec 31 year 3	92		94.24	5.76	12	1,472,000

Notice that column (7) numbers the quarters from 1 through 12. Look at the heading for column (7). It identifies each quarter in terms of the end of the quarter. This practice is important because we will eventually be discounting the payments (cash flows). We must take care to understand when each payment is to be exchanged in order to properly discount. So, for the first payment of $1,012,500 it is going to be received at the end of quarter 1. When we refer to the time period for any payment, the reference is to the end of the quarter. So, the fifth payment of $1,225,000 would be identified as the payment for period 5, where period 5 means that it will be exchanged at the end of the fifth quarter.

Now let's turn to the fixed-rate payments. The swap will specify the frequency of settlement for these payments. The frequency need not be the same as the floating-rate payments. For example, in the 3-year swap we used to illustrate the calculation of the floating-rate payments, the frequency is quarterly. The frequency of the fixed-rate payments could be semiannual rather than quarterly.

In our illustration we assume that the frequency of settlement is quarterly for the fixed-rate payments, the same as with the floating-rate payments. The day count convention is the same as for the floating-rate payment, "actual/360." The equation for determining the dollar amount of the fixed-rate payment for the period is:

$$\text{Notional amount} \times \left(\text{Swap rate}\right) \times \frac{\text{Days in period}}{360}$$

It is the same equation as for determining the floating-rate payment except that the swap rate is used instead of the reference rate (3-month LIBOR in our illustration).

For example, suppose that the swap rate is 4.98% and the quarter has 90 days. Then the fixed-rate payment for the quarter is

$$\$100,000,000 \times 0.0498 \times \frac{90}{360} = \$1,245,000$$

Table 29-3 shows the fixed-rate payments based on an assumed swap rate of 4.9875%. (Later we see how the swap rate is determined.) The first three columns of the exhibit show the same information as in Table 29-2—the beginning and end of the quarter and the number of days in the quarter. Column (4) simply uses the notation for

TABLE 29-3 Fixed-Rate Payments Assuming a Swap Rate of 4.9875%

Quarter Starts	Quarter Ends	Days in Quarter	Period = End of Quarter	Fixed-Rate Payment If Swap Rate Assumed at 4.9875%
Jan 1 year 1	Mar 31 year 1	90	1	$1,246,875
Apr 1 year 1	June 30 year 1	91	2	1,260,729
July 1 year 1	Sept 30 year 1	92	3	1,274,583
Oct 1 year 1	Dec 31 year 1	92	4	1,274,583
Jan 1 year 2	Mar 31 year 2	90	5	1,246,875
Apr 1 year 2	June 30 year 2	91	6	1,260,729
July 1 year 2	Sept 30 year 2	92	7	1,274,583
Oct 1 year 2	Dec 31 year 2	92	8	1,274,583
Jan 1 year 3	Mar 31 year 3	90	9	1,246,875
Apr 1 year 3	June 30 year 3	91	10	1,260,729
July 1 year 3	Sept 30 year 3	92	11	1,274,583
Oct 1 year 3	Dec 31 year 3	92	12	1,274,583

the period. That is, period 1 means the end of the first quarter, period 2 means the end of the second quarter, and so on. Column (5) shows the fixed value payments for each period based on a swap rate of 4.9875%.

Given the swap payments, we can demonstrate how to compute the swap rate. At the initiation of an interest rate swap, the counterparties are agreeing to exchange future payments and no upfront payments by either party are made. The swap terms must be such that the present value of the payments to be made by the counterparties must be at least equal to the present value of the payments that will be received. In fact, to eliminate arbitrage opportunities, the present value of the payments made by a party will be equal to the present value of the payments received by that same party. The equivalence (or no arbitrage) of the present value of the payments is the key principle in calculating the swap rate.

Because we must calculate the present value of the payments, let's show how it is done. As explained earlier, we must be careful about how we compute the present value of payments. In particular, we must carefully specify (1) the timing of the payment, and (2) the interest rates that should be used to discount the payments. We already addressed the first issue. In constructing the exhibit for the payments, we indicated that the payments are at the end of the quarter. So, we denoted the timing of the payments with respect to the end of the quarter.

What interest rates should be used for discounting? Every cash flow should be discounted at its own discount rate using a spot rate. So, if we discounted a cash flow of $1 using the spot rate for period t, the present value would be:

$$\text{Present value of \$1 to be received in } t \text{ period} = \frac{\$1}{\left(1 + \text{Spot rate for period } t\right)^t}$$

As explained in Chapter 19, forward rates are derived from spot rates so that if we discounted a cash flow using forward rates rather than a spot rate, we would come up with the same value. That is, the present value of $1 to be received in period t can be rewritten as

$$\text{Present value of \$1 to be received in period } t = \frac{\$1}{\left(1 + \text{Forward rate for period 1}\right)\left(1 + \text{Forward rate for period 2}\right)\dots\left(1 + \text{Forward rate for period } t\right)}$$

We refer to the present value of $1 to be received in period t as the **forward discount factor**. In our calculations involving swaps, we compute the forward discount factor for a period using the forward rates. These same forward rates are used to compute the floating-rate payments. Specifically, those obtained from the Eurodollar CD futures contract. We must make just one more adjustment. We must adjust the forward rates used in the formula for the number of days in the period (i.e., the quarter in our illustrations) in the same way that we made this adjustment to obtain the payments. Specifically, the forward rate for a period, which we refer to as the **period forward rate**, is computed using the following equation:

$$\text{Period forward rate} = \text{Annual forward rate} \times \left(\frac{\text{Days in period}}{360} \right)$$

For example, look at Table 29-2. The annual forward rate for period 4 is 4.72%. The period forward rate for period 4 is:

$$\text{Period forward rate} = 4.72\% \times \left(\frac{92}{360} \right) = 1.2062\%$$

Column (5) in Table 29-4 shows the annual forward rate for all 12 periods (reproduced from Table 29-2), and column (6) shows the period forward rate for all 12 periods. Note that the period forward rate for period 1 is 90/360 of 4.05%, which is 90/360 of the known rate for 3-month LIBOR.

Also shown in Table 29-4 is the forward discount factor for all 12 periods. These values are shown in the last column. Let's show how the forward discount factor is computed for periods 1, 2, and 3. For period 1, the forward discount factor is

$$\text{Forward discount factor} = \frac{\$1}{\left(1.0125 \right)} = 0.98997649$$

For period 2,

$$\text{Forward discount factor} = \frac{\$1}{\left(1.010125 \right)\left(1.010490 \right)} = 0.97969917$$

TABLE 29-4   Calculating the Forward Discount Factor

(1) Quarter Starts	(2) Quarter Ends	(3) Period = Days in Quarter	(4) End of Quarter	(5) Period Forward Rate	(6) Forward Forward Rate	(7) Discount Factor
Jan 1 year 1	Mar 31 year 1	90	1	4.05%	1.0125%	0.98997649
Apr 1 year 1	June 30 year 1	91	2	4.15	1.0490	0.97969917
July 1 year 1	Sept 30 year 1	92	3	4.55	1.1628	0.96843839
Oct 1 year 1	Dec 31 year 1	92	4	4.72	1.2062	0.95689609
Jan 1 year 2	Mar 31 year 2	90	5	4.90	1.2250	0.94531597
Apr 1 year 2	June 30 year 2	91	6	5.03	1.2715	0.93344745
July 1 year 2	Sept 30 year 2	92	7	5.15	1.3161	0.92132183
Oct 1 year 2	Dec 31 year 2	92	8	5.25	1.3417	0.90912441
Jan 1 year 3	Mar 31 year 3	90	9	5.40	1.3500	0.89701471
Apr 1 year 3	June 30 year 3	91	10	5.50	1.3903	0.88471472
July 1 year 3	Sept 30 year 3	92	11	5.65	1.4439	0.87212224
Oct 1 year 3	Dec 31 year 3	92	12	5.76	1.4720	0.85947083

For period 3,

$$\text{Forward discount factor} = \frac{\$1}{(1.010125)(1.010490)(1.011628)} = 0.96843839$$

Given the floating-rate payment for a period and the forward discount factor for the period, the present value of the payment can be computed. For example, from Table 29-2 we see that the floating-rate payment for period 4 is $1,206,222. From Table 29-4, the forward discount factor for period 4 is 0.95689609. Therefore, the present value of the payment is

$$\text{Present value of period 4 payment} = \$1,206,222 \times 0.95689609 = \$1,154,229$$

Table 29-5 shows the present value for each payment. The total present value of the 12 floating-rate payments is $14,052,917. Thus, the present value of the payments that the fixed-rate payer will receive is $14,052,917 and the present value of the payments that the fixed-rate receiver will make is $14,052,917.

The fixed-rate payer requires that the present value of the fixed-rate payments that must be made based on the swap rate not exceed the $14,052,917 to be received from the floating-rate payments. The fixed-rate receiver requires that the present value of the fixed-rate payments to be received be at least as great as the $14,052,917 that must be paid. It means that both parties require a present value for the fixed-rate payments to be $14,052,917. If that is the case, the present value of the fixed-rate payments is equal to the present value of the floating-rate payments and therefore the value of the swap is zero for both parties at the inception of the swap. The interest rates that should be used to compute the present value of the fixed-rate payments are the same interest rates as those used to discount the floating-rate payments.

Beginning with the basic relationship for no arbitrage to exist:

Present value of floating-rate payments = Present value of fixed-rate payments

TABLE 29-5 Present Value of the Floating-Rate Payments

(1) Quarter Starts	(2) Quarter Ends	(3) Period = End of Quarter	(4) Forward Discount Factor	(5) Floating Cash Flow at End of Quarter	(6) PV of Cash Flow
Jan 1 year 1	Mar 31 year 1	1	0.98997649	$1,012,500	$ 1,002,351
Apr 1 year 1	June 30 year 1	2	0.97969917	1,049,028	1,027,732
July 1 year 1	Sept 30 year 1	3	0.96843839	1,162,778	1,126,079
Oct 1 year 1	Dec 31 year 1	4	0.95689609	1,206,222	1,154,229
Jan 1 year 2	Mar 31 year 2	5	0.94531597	1,225,000	1,158,012
Apr 1 year 2	June 30 year 2	6	0.93344745	1,271,472	1,186,852
July 1 year 2	Sept 30 year 2	7	0.92132183	1,316,111	1,212,562
Oct 1 year 2	Dec 31 year 2	8	0.90912441	1,341,667	1,219,742
Jan 1 year 3	Mar 31 year 3	9	0.89701471	1,350,000	1,210,970
Apr 1 year 3	June 30 year 3	10	0.88471472	1,390,278	1,229,999
July 1 year 3	Sept 30 year 3	11	0.87212224	1,443,889	1,259,248
Oct 1 year 3	Dec 31 year 3	12	0.85947083	1,472,000	1,265,141
				Total	$14,052,917

The formula for the swap rate is derived as follows. The fixed-rate payment for period t is equal to

$$\text{Notional amount} \times \text{Swap rate} \times \frac{\text{Days in period } t}{360}$$

The present value of the fixed-rate payment for period t is found by multiplying the previous expression by the forward discount factor for period t. That is, the present value of the fixed-rate payment for period t is equal to

$$\text{Notional amount} \times \text{Swap rate} \times \frac{\text{Days in period } t}{360}$$
$$\times \text{ Forward discount factor for period } t$$

Summing up the present value of the fixed-rate payment for each period gives the present value of the fixed-rate payments. Letting N be the number of periods in the swap, then the present value of the fixed-rate payments can be expressed as

$$\text{Swap rate} \times \left(\sum_{t=1}^{N} \text{Notational amount} \times \frac{\text{Days in period}}{360} \right.$$
$$\left. \times \text{ Forward discount factor for period } t \right)$$

The condition for no arbitrage is that the present value of the fixed-rate payments as given by the preceding expression is equal to the present value of the floating-rate payments. That is,

$$\text{Swap rate} \times \left(\sum_{t=1}^{N} \text{Notational amount} \times \frac{\text{Days in period } t}{360} \right.$$
$$\left. \times \text{ Forward discount factor for period } t \right) = \text{ Present value of floating - rate payment}$$

Solving for the swap rate gives

$$\text{Swap rate} = \frac{\text{Present value of floating - rate payments}}{\left(\displaystyle\sum_{t=1}^{N} \text{Notional amount} \times \dfrac{\text{Days in period } t}{360} \right.}$$
$$\left. \times \text{ Forward discount factor for period } t \right)$$

Note that all the values to compute the swap rate are known.

Let's apply the formula to determine the swap rate for our 3-year swap. Table 29-6 shows the calculation of the denominator of the formula. The forward discount factor for each period shown in column (5) is obtained from column (4) of Table 29-6. The sum of the last column in Table 29-6 shows that the denominator of the swap rate formula is $281,764,282. We know from Table 29-5 that the present value of the floating-rate payments is $14,052,917. Therefore, the swap rate is

$$\text{Swap rate} = \frac{\$14{,}052{,}917}{\$281{,}764{,}282} = 0.049875 = 4.9875\%$$

Given the swap rate, the swap spread can be determined. For example, for this 3-year swap, the convention is to use the estimated 3-year on-the-run Treasury rate as the benchmark. If the yield on that issue is 4.5875%, the swap spread is 40 basis points (4.9875% − 4.5875%).

TABLE 29-6   Calculating the Denominator for the Swap Rate Formula

(1) Quarter Starts	(2) Quarter Ends	(3) Days in Quarter	(4) Period = End of Quarter	(5) Forward Discount Factor	(6) Days/360	(7) Discount Factor × Days/ 360 × Notional
Jan 1 year 1	Mar 31 year 1	90	1	0.98997649	0.25000000	$ 24,749,412
Apr 1 year 1	June 30 year 1	91	2	0.97969917	0.25277778	24,764,618
July 1 year 1	Sept 30 year 1	92	3	0.96843839	0.25555556	24,748,981
Oct 1 year 1	Dec 31 year 1	92	4	0.95689609	0.25555556	24,454,011
Jan 1 year 2	Mar 31 year 2	90	5	0.94531597	0.25000000	23,632,899
Apr 1 year 2	June 30 year 2	91	6	0.93344745	0.25277778	23,595,477
July 1 year 2	Sept 30 year 2	92	7	0.92132183	0.25555556	23,544,891
Oct 1 year 2	Dec 31 year 2	92	8	0.90912441	0.25555556	23,233,179
Jan 1 year 3	Mar 31 year 3	90	9	0.89701471	0.25000000	22,425,368
Apr 1 year 3	June 30 year 3	91	10	0.88471472	0.25277778	22,363,622
July 1 year 3	Sept 30 year 3	92	11	0.87212224	0.25555556	22,287,568
Oct 1 year 3	Dec 31 year 3	92	12	0.85947083	0.25555556	21,964,255
					Total	$281,764,282

The calculation of the swap rate for all swaps follows the same principle: equating the present value of the fixed-rate payments to that of the floating-rate payments.

VALUING A SWAP

Once the swap transaction is completed, changes in market interest rates change the payments of the floating-rate side of the swap. The value of an interest rate swap is the difference between the present value of the payments of the two sides of the swap. The 3-month LIBOR forward rates from the current Eurodollar CD futures contracts are used to (1) calculate the floating-rate payments, and (2) determine the discount factors at which to calculate the present value of the payments.

To illustrate, consider the 3-year swap used to demonstrate how to calculate the swap rate. Suppose that 1 year later, interest rates change as shown in columns (4) and (6) in Table 29-7. Column (4) shows the current 3-month LIBOR. In column (5) are the Eurodollar CD futures prices for each period. These rates are used to compute the for-

TABLE 29-7   Rates and Floating-Rate Payments 1 Year Later If Rates Increase

(1) Quarter Starts	(2) Quarter Ends	(3) Days in Quarter	(4) Current 3-Month LIBOR	(5) Eurodollar Futures Price	(6) Futures Rate	(7) Period = End of Quarter	(8) Floating Cash Flow at End of Quarter
Jan 1 year 2	Mar 31 year 2	90	5.25%			1	$1,312,500
Apr 1 year 2	June 30 year 2	91		94.27	5.73%	2	1,448,417
July 1 year 2	Sept 30 year 2	92		94.22	5.78	3	1,477,111
Oct 1 year 2	Dec 31 year 2	92		94.00	6.00	4	1,533,333
Jan 1 year 3	Mar 31 year 3	90		93.85	6.15	5	1,537,500
Apr 1 year 3	June 30 year 3	91		93.75	6.25	6	1,579,861
July 1 year 3	Sept 30 year 3	92		93.54	6.46	7	1,650,889
Oct 1 year 3	Dec 31 year 3	92		93.25	6.75	8	1,725,000

TABLE 29-8 Period Forward Rates and Forward Discount Factors 1 Year Later If Rates Increase

(1) Quarter Starts	(2) Quarter Ends	(3) Number of Days in Quarter	(4) Period = End of Quarter	(5) Forward Rate	(6) Period Forward Rate	(7) Forward Discount Factor
Jan 1 year 2	Mar 31 year 2	90	1	5.25%	1.3125%	0.98704503
Apr 1 year 2	June 30 year 2	91	2	5.73	1.4484	0.97295263
July 1 year 2	Sept 30 year 2	92	3	5.78	1.4771	0.95879023
Oct 1 year 2	Dec 31 year 2	92	4	6.00	1.5333	0.94431080
Jan 1 year 3	Mar 31 year 3	90	5	6.15	1.5375	0.93001186
Apr 1 year 3	June 30 year 3	91	6	6.25	1.5799	0.91554749
July 1 year 3	Sept 30 year 3	92	7	6.46	1.6509	0.90067829
Oct 1 year 3	Dec 31 year 3	92	8	6.75	1.7250	0.88540505

ward rates in column (6). Note that the interest rates have increased 1 year later since the rates in Table 29-7 are greater than those in Table 29-2. As in Table 29-2, the current 3-month LIBOR and the forward rates are used to compute the floating-rate payments. These payments are shown in column (8) of Table 29-7.

In Table 29-8, the forward discount factor is computed for each period. The calculation is the same as in Table 29-4 to obtain the forward discount factor for each period. The forward discount factor for each period is shown in the last column of Table 29-8.

In Table 29-9 the forward discount factor (from Table 29-8) and the floating-rate payments (from Table 29-7) are shown. The fixed-rate payments need not be recomputed. They are the payments shown in column (8) of Table 29-3. These fixed-rate payments use the swap rate of 4.9875% and they are reproduced in Table 29-9. Now the

TABLE 29-9 Valuing the Swap 1 Year Later If Rates Increase

(1) Quarter Starts	(2) Quarter Ends	(3) Forward Discount Factor	(4) Floating Cash Flow at End of Quarter	(5) PV of Floating Cash Flow	(6) Fixed Cash Flow at End of Quarter	(7) PV of Fixed Cash Flow
Jan 1 year 2	Mar 31 year 2	0.98704503	$1,312,500	$1,295,497	$1,246,875	$1,230,722
Apr 1 year 2	June 30 year 2	0.97295263	1,448,417	1,409,241	1,260,729	1,226,630
July 1 year 2	Sept 30 year 2	0.95879023	1,477,111	1,416,240	1,274,583	1,222,058
Oct 1 year 2	Dec 31 year 2	0.94431080	1,533,333	1,447,943	1,274,583	1,203,603
Jan 1 year 3	Mar 31 year 3	0.93001186	1,537,500	1,429,893	1,246,875	1,159,609
Apr 1 year 3	June 30 year 3	0.91554749	1,579,861	1,446,438	1,260,729	1,154,257
July 1 year 3	Sept 30 year 3	0.90067829	1,650,889	1,486,920	1,274,583	1,147,990
Oct 1 year 3	Dec 31 year 3	0.88540505	1,725,000	1,527,324	1,274,583	1,128,523
			Total	$11,459,495		$9,473,390

Summary	Fixed-Rate Payer	Fixed-Rate Receiver
PV of payments received	$11,459,495	$ 9,473,390
PV of payments made	9,473,390	11,459,495
Value of swap	1,986,105	−1,986,105

two payment streams must be discounted using the new forward discount factors. As shown at the bottom of Table 29-9, the two present values are as follows:

Present value of floating-rate payments	$11,459,495
Present value of fixed-rate payments	$ 9,473,390

The two present values are not equal and therefore for one party the value of the swap increased and for the other party the value of the swap decreased. Let's look at which party gained and which party lost.

The fixed-rate payer will receive the floating-rate payments. And these payments have a present value of $11,459,495. The present value of the payments that must be made by the fixed-rate payer is $9,473,390. Thus, the swap has a positive value for the fixed-rate payer equal to the difference in the two present values of $1,986,105, which is the value of the swap to the fixed-rate payer. Notice that when interest rates increase (as they did in the illustration analyzed), the fixed-rate payer benefits because the value of the swap increases.

In contrast, the fixed-rate receiver must make payments with a present value of $11,459,495 but will only receive fixed-rate payments with a present value equal to $9,473,390. Thus, the value of the swap for the fixed-rate receiver is −$1,986,105. The fixed-rate receiver is adversely affected by a rise in interest rates because it results in a decline in the value of a swap.

The same valuation principle applies to more complicated swaps that we describe next.

BEYOND THE PLAIN VANILLA SWAP

Thus far we described the plain vanilla or generic interest rate swap. Nongeneric or individualized swaps evolved as a result of the asset/liability needs of borrowers and lenders and include swaps where the notional amount changes in a predetermined way over the life of the swap and swaps in which both counterparties pay a floating rate. Other complex swap structures include options on swaps (called *swaptions*) and swaps where the swap does not begin until some future time (called *forward start swaps*). We discuss all of these swaps next.[13] It may be difficult to fully appreciate the importance of these swap structures as a tool for managing the interest rate risk of a financial institution in this book because of our limited coverage of risk management. What is important to appreciate is that these swap structures are not just "bells and whistles" added to the plain vanilla swap to make them more complicated, but features that managers have found that they need to control interest rate risk.

Varying Notional Amount Swaps   In a generic or plain vanilla swap, the notional amount does not vary over the life of the swap. Thus, it is sometimes referred to as a *bullet swap*. In contrast, for amortizing, accreting, and roller coaster swaps, the notional amount varies over the life of the swap.

An *amortizing swap* is one in which the notional amount decreases in a predetermined way over the life of the swap. Such a swap would be used where the principal of the asset that is being hedged with the swap amortizes over time. For example, in our illustration of the asset/liability problem faced by the bank, the commercial loans are assumed to pay only interest every 6 months and repay principal only at the end of the loan term. However, what if the commercial loan is a typical term loan; that is, suppose

---

[13] See Geoffrey Buetow, Jr. and Frank J. Fabozzi, *Valuation of Interest Rate Swaps and Swaptions* (New Hope, PA: Frank J. Fabozzi Associates, 2001).

it is a loan that amortizes. Or, suppose that it is a typical mortgage loan that amortizes. In such circumstances, the outstanding principal for the loans would decline and the bank would need a swap where the notional amount amortizes in the same way as the loans.

Less common than the amortizing swap are the accreting swap and the roller coaster swap. An **accreting swap** is one in which the notional amount increases in a pre-determined way over time. In a **roller coaster swap**, the notional amount can rise or fall from period to period.

Basis Swaps and Constant Maturity Swaps   The terms of a generic interest rate swap call for the exchange of fixed- and floating-rate payments. In a **basis rate swap**, both parties exchange floating-rate payments based on a different reference rate. As an example, assume a commercial bank has a portfolio of loans in which the lending rate is based on the prime rate, but the bank's cost of funds is based on LIBOR. The risk the bank faces is that the spread between the prime rate and LIBOR will change, which is referred to as **basis risk**. The bank can use a basis rate swap to make floating-rate payments based on the prime rate (because it is the reference rate that determines how much the bank is receiving on the loans) and receive floating-rate payments based on LIBOR (because it is the reference rate that determines the bank's funding cost).

Another popular swap is to have the floating leg tied to a longer-term rate such as the 2-year Treasury note rather than a money market rate. So one of the parties to the swap would pay the 2-year Treasury rate, for example, and the counterparty would pay LIBOR. Such a swap is called a **constant maturity swap**. The reference rate for determining the yield on the constant maturity Treasury in a constant maturity swap is typically the Constant Maturity Treasury (CMT) rate published the Federal Reserve. Consequently, a constant maturity swap tied to the CMT is called a **Constant Maturity Treasury swap**.

Swaptions   The swap structures based on options for interest rate swaps are called **swaptions** and grant the option buyer the right to enter into an interest rate swap at a future date. The time until expiration of the swap, the term of the swap, and the swap rate are specified. The swap rate is the strike rate for the swaption. The swaption has the European-type exercise provision. That is, the option can only be exercised at the option's expiration date.

The two types of swaptions are a payer swaption and a receiver swaption. A **payer swaption** entitles the option buyer to enter into an interest rate swap in which the buyer of the option pays a fixed rate and receives a floating rate. For example, suppose that the strike rate is 7%, the term of the swap is 3 years, and the swaption expires in 2 years. Also assume that it is a European-type exercise provision, which means that the buyer of this swaption at the end of 2 years has the right to enter into a 3-year interest rate swap in which the buyer pays 7% (the swap rate which is equal to the strike rate) and receives the reference rate.

In a **receiver swaption** the buyer of the swaption has the right to enter into an interest rate swap that requires paying a floating rate and receiving a fixed rate. For example, if the strike rate is 6.25%, the swap term is 5 years, and the option expires in 1 year, the buyer of this receiver swaption has the right when the option expires in 1 year (assuming it is a European-type exercise provision) to enter into a 4-year interest rate swap in which the buyer receives a swap rate of 6.25% (i.e., the strike rate) and pays the reference rate.

How is a swaption used? We can see its usefulness in managing interest rate risk if we return to the bank-insurance company example. The bank makes the fixed-rate payments in the interest rate swap (10%) using the interest rate it is earning on the commercial loans (10%). Suppose that the commercial loan borrowers default on their obligations. The bank will then receive from the commercial loans the 10% to make its swap payments. This problem can be addressed at the outset of the initial swap transaction by the bank entering into a swaption that effectively gives it the right to terminate or cancel the swap. That is, the bank will enter into a receiver swaption, receiving fixed-rate payments of 10% so as to offset the fixed rate it is obligated to pay under the initial swap. In fact, the borrowers do not have to fail for the swap to have an adverse impact on the bank. Suppose the commercial loans can be prepaid. Then, the bank has a similar problem. For example, suppose rates on commercial loans decline to 7% and the borrowers prepay. Then the bank would be obligated to make the 10% payments under the terms of the swap. With the proceeds received from the prepayment of the commercial loans, the bank may only be able to invest in similar loans at 7%, for example, a rate that is less than the bank's obligations.

Forward Start Swap A **forward start swap** is a swap wherein the swap does not begin until some future date that is specified in the swap agreement. Thus, the contract designates a beginning date for the swap at some time in the future and a maturity date for the swap. A forward start swap will also specify the swap rate at which the counterparties agree to exchange payments commencing at the start date.

◆ INTEREST RATE AGREEMENTS

In an interest rate agreement between two parties, one party, for an upfront premium, agrees to compensate the other if a designated interest rate, called the reference rate, is different from a predetermined level. When one party agrees to pay the other when the reference rate exceeds a predetermined level, the agreement is referred to as an **interest rate cap** or **ceiling**. The agreement is referred to as an **interest rate floor** when one party agrees to pay the other when the reference rate falls below a predetermined level. The predetermined interest rate level is called the **strike rate**.

The terms of an interest rate agreement include:

1. The reference rate
2. The strike rate that sets the ceiling or floor
3. The length of the agreement
4. The frequency of settlement
5. The notional principal amount

For example, suppose that *C* buys an interest rate cap from *D* with terms as follows:

1. The reference rate is 6-month LIBOR.
2. The strike rate is 8%.
3. The agreement is for 7 years.
4. Settlement is every 6 months.
5. The notional principal amount is $20 million.

Under this agreement, every 6 months for the next 7 years, *D* will pay *C* whenever 6-month LIBOR on the settlement date exceeds 8%. The payment will equal the dollar value of the difference between 6-month LIBOR and 8% times the notional principal amount divided by two. For example, if 6 months from now 6-month LIBOR is 11%, then *D* will pay *C* 3% (11% minus 8%) times $20 million divided by 2, or $300,000. If 6-month LIBOR is 8% or less, *D* does not have to pay anything to *C*.

As an example of an interest rate floor, assume the same terms as the interest rate cap we just illustrated. In this case, if 6-month LIBOR is 11%, *C* receives nothing from

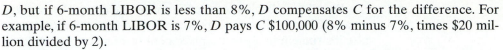

D, but if 6-month LIBOR is less than 8%, *D* compensates *C* for the difference. For example, if 6-month LIBOR is 7%, *D* pays *C* $100,000 (8% minus 7%, times $20 million divided by 2).

Interest rate caps and floors can be combined to create an **interest rate collar**, by buying an interest rate cap and selling an interest rate floor. Some commercial banks and investment banking firms now write options on interest rate agreements for customers. Options on caps are called **captions**; options on floors are called **flotions**.

RISK/RETURN CHARACTERISTICS

In an interest rate agreement, the buyer pays an upfront fee, which represents the maximum amount that the buyer can lose and the maximum amount that the writer of the agreement can gain. The only party required to perform is the writer of the interest rate agreement. The buyer of an interest rate cap benefits if the underlying interest rate rises above the strike rate because the seller (writer) must compensate the buyer. The buyer of an interest rate floor benefits if the interest rate falls below the strike rate, because the seller (writer) must compensate the buyer.

How can we better understand interest rate caps and interest rate floors? In essence these contracts are equivalent to a package of interest rate options. As the buyer benefits if the interest rate rises above the strike rate, an interest rate cap is similar to purchasing a package of put options on a bond or call options on an interest rate; the seller of an interest rate cap has effectively sold a package of options. The buyer of an interest rate floor benefits from a decline in the interest rate below the strike rate. Therefore, the buyer of an interest rate floor has effectively bought a package of call options on a bond or put options on an interest rate from the writer of the option.

Once again, a complex contract can be seen to be a package of basic contracts, or options in the case of interest rate agreements.

APPLICATIONS

To see how interest rate agreements can be used for asset/liability management, consider the problems faced by the commercial bank and the life insurance company we used in the first illustration to demonstrate use of an interest rate swap.[14]

Recall that the bank's objective is to lock in an interest rate spread over its cost of funds. Yet because it borrows short term, its cost of funds is uncertain. The bank may be able to purchase a cap such that the cap rate plus the cost of purchasing the cap is less than the rate it is earning on its fixed-rate commercial loans. If short-term rates decline, the bank does not benefit from the cap, but its cost of funds declines. The cap therefore allows the bank to impose a ceiling on its cost of funds while retaining the opportunity to benefit from a decline in rates, which is consistent with the view of an interest rate cap as simply a package of options.

The bank can reduce the cost of purchasing the cap by selling a floor. In this case, the bank agrees to pay the buyer of the floor if the underlying rate falls below the strike rate. The bank receives a fee for selling the floor, but it has sold off its opportunity to benefit from a decline in rates below the strike rate. By buying a cap and selling a floor, the bank creates a range for its cost of funds—that is, creates a collar.

---

[14] For additional applications in the insurance industry, see David F. Babbel, Peter Bouyoucos, and Robert Stricker, "Capping the Interest Rate Risk in Insurance Products," in Frank J. Fabozzi (ed.), *Fixed Income Portfolio Strategies* (Chicago: Probus Publishing, 1989), Chapter 21. For other applications of interest rate agreements, see Victor J. Haghani and Robert M. Stavis, "Interest Rate Caps and Floors: Tools for Asset/Liability Management," in Frank J. Fabozzi (ed.), *Advances and Innovations in Bond and Mortgage Markets* (Chicago: Probus Publishing, 1989).

Recall the problem of the life insurance company that has guaranteed a 9% rate on a GIC for the next 5 years and is considering the purchase of an attractive floating-rate instrument in a private-placement transaction. The risk that the company faces is that interest rates will fall so that it will not earn enough to realize the 9% guaranteed rate plus a spread. The life insurance company may be able to purchase a floor to set a lower bound on its investment return, yet retain the opportunity to benefit should rates increase. To reduce the cost of purchasing the floor, the life insurance company can sell an interest rate cap. By doing so, however, it gives up the opportunity of benefiting from an increase in the 6-month Treasury bill rate above the strike rate of the interest rate cap.

◆ CREDIT DERIVATIVES

Interest rate derivatives such as Treasury futures contracts, Treasury options, interest rate swaps, caps, and floors can be used to control interest rate risk with respect to changes in the level of interest rates. However, changes in the credit spread must be controlled by investors when investing in non-Treasury securities or by corporations when issuing bonds. The agency note futures contracts discussed in Chapter 28 can be used to partially control the changes in credit spread for corporate bonds. However, the correlation between the credit spread on agency debentures and corporate bonds (both investment grade and noninvestment grade) is not perfect. Moreover, the agency note futures contract is relatively new. (Initial trading began in 2000.) What developed in the over-the-counter or dealer market are derivative instruments that provide protection against credit risk. These products are referred to as **credit derivatives**. The three main types of credit derivatives are credit options, credit forwards, and credit swaps.

TYPES OF CREDIT RISK

An investor who lends funds by purchasing a bond issue is exposed to three types of credit risk: (1) default risk, (2) credit spread risk, and (3) downgrade risk.

Default risk   Traditionally, credit risk is defined as the risk that the issuer will fail to satisfy the terms of the obligation with respect to the timely payment of interest and repayment of the amount borrowed. This form of credit risk is called *default risk*. If a default does occur, it does not mean the investor loses the entire amount invested.

Credit Spread Risk   Even in the absence of default, an investor is concerned that the market value of a bond will decline and/or the price performance of that bond will be worse than that of other bonds against which the investor is compared. To understand, recall that the price of a bond changes in the opposite direction to the change in the yield required by the market. Thus, if yields in the economy increase, the price of a bond declines, and vice versa.

As explained in Chapter 17, the yield on a bond is made up of two components: (1) the yield on a similar default-free bond issue, and (2) a premium above the yield on a default-free bond issue necessary to compensate for the risks associated with the bond. The risk premium is referred to as a *spread*. In the United States, Treasury issues are the benchmark yields because they are believed to be default free, they are highly liquid, and Treasury issues are not callable (with the exception of some old issues). The part of the risk premium or spread attributable to default risk is called the *credit spread*.

The price performance of a non-Treasury bond issue and its return that the investor will realize by holding that issue over some time period will depend on how the credit spread changes. If the credit spread increases—investors say that the spread has "widened"—the market price of the bond issue will decline (assuming Treasury rates have not changed). The risk that an issuer's debt obligation will decline due to an increase in the credit spread is called **credit spread risk**.

This risk exists for an individual issue, for issues in a particular industry or economic sector, and for all non-Treasury issues in the economy. For example, in general during economic recessions investors are concerned that issuers will face a decline in cash flows that would be used to service its bond obligations. As a result, the credit spread tends to widen for non-Treasury issuers and the prices of all such issues throughout the economy will decline.

Downgrade Risk   Some investors seek to allocate funds among different sectors of the bond market to capitalize on anticipated changes in credit spreads. However, an investor investigating the credit quality of an individual issue is concerned with the prospects of the credit spread increasing for that particular issue. Market participants gauge the default risk of an issue by looking at the credit ratings assigned to issues by the rating agencies: Moody's Investors Service, Inc., Standard & Poor's Corporation, and Fitch. Once a credit rating is assigned to a debt obligation, a rating agency monitors the credit quality of the issuer and can reassign a different credit rating. An improvement in the credit quality of an issue or issuer is rewarded with a better credit rating, referred to as an *upgrade;* a deterioration in the credit rating of an issue or issuer is penalized by the assignment of an inferior credit rating, referred to as a downgrade. An unanticipated downgrading of an issue or issuer increases the credit spread and results in a decline in the price of the issue or the issuer's bonds. This risk is referred to as **downgrade risk** and is closely related to credit spread risk.

CREDIT OPTIONS

Credit options come in two types. The first type is a *credit option written on an underlying issue.* For this type of credit option the payout is determined based on whether a default occurs for the underlying issue. The amount of the payout is a fixed amount determined at the time the option is purchased. If a default does not occur by the option's expiration date, no payout occurs.

The same type of credit option—which is basically a "binary option" because it has only two possible payoffs, zero if no default and the predetermined fixed sum if default occurs—can also be written where the payoff is based upon whether the issue is downgraded. Then the payoff is specified by the amount of the loss expected if a downgrade occurs. A credit option can also be written in which a default is defined in broader terms than simply failure to meet an interest or principal payment. For example, the event that triggers a payoff can be defined in terms of whether some financial measure is above or below a certain value. Or a minimum net worth can be specified. Or this form of a credit option can specify that if the issuer's book value falls below $150 million or less then a payoff occurs.

For the second type of credit option, the payoff is determined by the level of the credit spread over a referenced security, typically a Treasury security. The strike is specified in terms of the level of the credit spread. The payoff can specify that if the credit spread for the issue is greater than the strike spread, a payoff occurs. For example, suppose that the referenced issue is a bond of company XYZ. Suppose the current spread is 200 basis points. The strike spread can be specified as 250 basis points, and that if the credit spread by the expiration date exceeds that strike spread, a payoff occurs. Alternatively, the payoff can specify that if the credit spread is less than the strike, a payoff occurs.

The tricky part of the payoff for an option written on a credit spread is the determination of the payoff. Remember that if interest rates in general increase, the price of the issue underlying the option will decline, and vice versa. What the payoff must do is separate the change in the price of the underlying issue due to a change in the general level of rates from the change in the credit spread. This is done by having the payoff based on the difference in the actual credit spread and the strike spread multiplied by a specified notional amount and by a risk factor. For purposes of our discussion, it is not necessary to understand how the risk factor is computed.[15] Instead, let's see how the payoff is determined. The payoff function is determined as follows if the credit option is based on the credit spread being greater than the strike spread.

$$(\text{Credit spread} - \text{Strike spread}) \times \text{Notional amount} \times \text{Risk factor}$$

where the credit spread and the strike spread are expressed in decimal form

For example, suppose that an issue of company XYZ has a strike spread of 250 basis points and that the notional amount of the credit option is $10 million. Suppose also that the risk factor for this issue is 5. If at the expiration date of this option, the credit spread for this issue is 300 basis points, then the payoff is

$$\left(0.030 - 0.025\right) \times \$10,000,000 \times 5 = \$250,000$$

If the credit spread at the expiration date is 250 basis points or less, then no payoff occurs

If the credit spread option had a payoff based on the credit spread narrowing, then the payoff function would be

$$(\text{Strike spread} - \text{Credit spread}) \times \text{Notional amount} \times \text{Risk factor}$$

CREDIT FORWARD CONTRACTS

The underlying for a credit forward contract is the credit spread. The payoff depends on the credit spread at the settlement date of the contract. The payoff is positive (i.e., the party receives cash) if the credit spread moves in favor of the party at the settlement date. The party makes a payment if the credit spread moves against the party at the settlement date.

For example, suppose that an investor has a view that the credit spread will increase (i.e., widen) to more than the current 250 basis points in 1 year for an issue of company XYZ. Then the payoff function for this credit forward contract would be

$$\left(\text{Credit spread at settlement date} - 250\right) \times \text{Notional amount}$$
$$\times \text{Risk factor}$$

Assuming that the notional amount is $10 million and the risk factor is 5, then if the credit spread at the settlement date is 325 basis points, the amount that will be received by the investor is

$$\left(0.035 - 0.025\right) \times \$10,000,000 \times 5 = \$500,000$$

Instead, suppose that the credit spread at the settlement date decreased to 190 basis points, then the investor would have to payout $300,000 as shown:

$$\left(0.019 - 0.025\right) \times \$10,000,000 \times 5 = -\$300,000$$

---

[15] The risk factor is a quantitative measure that is related to the duration of the underlying asset. Duration is discussed in Chapter 18.

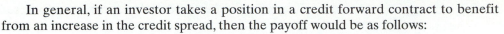

In general, if an investor takes a position in a credit forward contract to benefit from an increase in the credit spread, then the payoff would be as follows:

$$\left(\text{Credit spread at settlement date} - \text{Credit spread in contract}\right)$$

$$\times \text{Notional amount} \times \text{Risk factor}$$

For an investor taking a position that the credit spread will decrease, the payoff is

$$\left(\text{Credit spread in contract} - \text{Credit spread at settlement date}\right)$$

$$\times \text{Notional amount} \times \text{Risk factor}$$

CREDIT SWAPS

The two different types of credit swaps are credit default swaps and total return swaps. **Credit default swaps** are used by an investor to shift credit exposure to a credit protection seller. A **total return swap** is used by an investor to increase credit exposure.

Credit default swaps come in two forms: credit insurance and swapping risky credit payments for certain fixed payments. With **credit insurance**, the buyer pays a fee to enter into a credit default swap. The buyer receives a payment every period for the life of the contract if a referenced credit defaults on a payment. Even though this contract is called a swap, it is basically a package of credit options. Rather than a payment being contingent on an individual referenced credit, the referenced credit can be a portfolio of bonds. The second form of credit default swap is one in which an investor agrees to exchange the total return on a credit risky asset for known periodic payments from the counterparty. The payments are exchanged based on what happens to the value of the credit risky asset. If it declines in value, the investor receives a payment to compensate for the decline in value plus a periodic payment from the counterparty.

With a total return credit swap the investor agrees to pay all cash flows from the referenced asset or assets including the change in the value of the referenced asset or assets. The investor receives in exchange a floating rate plus any depreciation of the referenced asset to the credit swap seller.

Summary

In this chapter we covered over-the-counter interest rate control contracts created by commercial banks and investment banks for their customers. Markets for these instruments grew explosively in the 1980s.

Because of the difficulties of hedging particular bond issues or pass-through securities, many institutions find over-the-counter options more useful than exchange-traded options; these contracts can be customized to meet specific investment goals. Also, exotic options include alternative and out-performance options. A yield curve option is an example of an exotic option. An option that allows a party the right to enter into an option is called a compound or split-fee option. These options are used primarily by mortgage originators to hedge pipeline risk.

An interest rate swap is an agreement specifying that the parties exchange interest payments at designated times. In a typical swap, one party makes fixed-rate payments, and the other will make floating-rate payments, with payments based on the notional amount. Participants in financial markets use interest rate swaps to alter the cash flow characteristics of their assets or liabilities, or to capitalize on perceived capital market inefficiencies.

A number of types of swaps developed to satisfy various needs of market participants includes swaps in which the notional amount varies over the life of the swap (amortizing, accreting, and roller-coaster swaps), swaptions, basis-rate swaps, and forward rate swaps.

An interest rate agreement allows one party for an upfront premium the right to receive compensation from the writer of the agreement if the reference rate is different from the strike rate. An interest rate cap calls for one party to receive a payment if the reference rate is above the strike rate. An interest rate floor lets one party receive a payment if the reference rate is below the strike rate.

An interest rate cap can be used to establish a ceiling on the cost of funding; an interest rate floor can be used to establish a floor return. Buying a cap and selling a floor creates a collar.

Interest rate derivatives can be used to control interest rate risk with respect to changes in the level of interest rates. Credit derivatives can be used to control the credit risk of a security or a portfolio of securities. Credit risk includes three types of risk: (1) the risk that the issuer will default (default risk), (2) the risk that the credit spread will increase (credit spread risk), and (3) the risk that an issue will be downgraded (downgrade risk). The three main types of credit derivatives are credit options, credit forwards, and credit swaps. Credit options include credit options written on an underlying issue and credit spread options. The two different types of credit swaps are credit default swaps and total return swaps. Credit default swaps are used by an investor to shift credit exposure to a credit protection seller while a total return default swap is used by an investor to increase credit exposure.

Key Terms

- Accreting swap
- Asset swap
- Back fee
- Basis rate swap
- Basis risk
- Cacall
- Captions
- Caput
- Compound option
- Constant maturity swap
- Constant Maturity Treasury (CMT) swap
- Credit default swap
- Credit derivatives
- Credit insurance
- Credit spread risk
- Downgrade risk
- Effective date
- Extension date
- Flotions
- Forward discount factor
- Forward rate agreement (FRA)
- Forward start swap
- Front fee
- Interest rate cap
- Interest rate ceiling
- Interest rate collar
- Interest rate floor
- Liability swap
- Maturity date
- Notification date
- Payer swaption
- Period forward rate
- Receiver swaption
- Roller-coaster swap
- Split-fee option
- Strike rate
- Swap spread
- Swaption
- Trade date
- Total return swap

Questions

1. a. What is the motivation for the purchase of an over-the-counter option?
   b. Does it make sense for an investor who wants to speculate on interest rate movements to purchase an over-the-counter option?
2. Why does the buyer and not the seller of an over-the-counter option face counterparty risk?
3. a. What is a yield curve option?
   b. How is the payoff of a yield curve option determined?
4. a. Explain how a compound option works.
   b. We state in this chapter that compound options are most commonly used by mortgage originators to hedge pipeline risk. Why do you think compound options are used to hedge pipeline risk?

5. Suppose that 3 months from now the Summit Manufacturing Company plans to borrow $100 million for 1 year. The interest rate at which Summit Manufacturing expects to borrow is LIBOR plus 100 basis points. Currently, LIBOR is 10%.
   a. What is the funding risk that Summit Manufacturing faces?
   b. Suppose that Summit Manufacturing enters into a 3-month forward rate agreement with an investment banking firm for a notional principal amount of $100 million. Terms of the FRA are as follows: If 1-year LIBOR exceeds 10% 3 months from now, the investment banking firm must pay Summit Manufacturing; if 1-year LIBOR is less than 10% 3 months from now, Summit Manufacturing must pay the investment banking firm. How can this FRA eliminate the risk that you identified in part (a) of this question?

6. The following quotation appeared in an article entitled "Recent Developments in Corporate Finance," published in the August 1990 issue of the *Federal Reserve Bulletin*:

   > *Before the 1980s, it was reasonable in aggregate analysis to characterize commercial paper and bank loans as short-term debt and corporate bonds and mortgages as long-term debt. Such characterizations often were used to gauge corporate exposure to interest rate and liquidity risk, under the assumption that interest rates on short-term debt were variable whereas those on long-term debt were fixed.*
   >
   > *Financial developments and innovations in the past decade have made this classification of debt less useful.*

   a. What financial developments and innovations do you think this article is referring to?
   b. Why have they made the classification between short-term and long-term debt less useful?

7. Why can an interest rate swap be interpreted as a position in two cash market instruments?

8. Consider an interest rate swap with these features: maturity is 5 years, notional amount is $100 million, payments occur every 6 months, the fixed-rate payer pays a rate of 9.05% and receives LIBOR, while the floating-rate payer pays LIBOR and receives 9%. Now, suppose that at a payment date, LIBOR is 6.5%. What is each party's payment and receipt at that date?

9. Suppose a dealer quotes these terms on a 5-year swap: fixed-rate payer to pay 9.5% for LIBOR and floating-rate payer to pay LIBOR for 9.2%.
   a. What is the dealer's bid-ask spread?
   b. How would the dealer quote the terms by reference to the yield on 5-year Treasury notes?

10. a. Why would a depository institution use an interest rate swap?
    b. Why would a corporation that plans to raise funds in the debt market use an interest rate swap?

11. In determining the cash flow for the floating rate side of a LIBOR swap, explain how the cash flow is determined.

12. How is the swap rate calculated?

13. How is the value of a swap determined?

14. Suppose that a life insurance company has issued a 3-year GIC with a fixed rate of 10%. Under what circumstances might it be feasible for the life insurance company to invest the funds in a floating-rate security and enter into a 3-year interest rate swap in which it pays a floating rate and receives a fixed rate?

15. Suppose an S&L buys an interest rate cap that has these terms: the reference rate is the 6-month Treasury bill rate; the cap will last for 5 years; payment is semiannual;

the strike rate is 5.5%; and the notional amount is $10 million. Suppose further that at the end of some 6-month period, the 6-month Treasury bill rate is 6.1%.

    a. What is the amount of the payment that the S&L will receive?

    b. What would the writer of this cap pay if the 6-month Treasury rate were 5.45% instead of 6.1%?

16. How can an interest rate collar be created?

17. What is the relationship between an interest rate agreement and an interest rate option?

18. The following quotes are taken from the January 28, 1991, issue of *Bank Letter*:

> *The surge in the use of derivatives, their lengthening terms and growing complexity all spell greater credit risks for the banks and securities firms that fashion these instruments, according to a recent report by Moody's Investors Service.*
>
>   *The derivatives business includes creating, underwriting, trading and selling instruments including options, swaps, futures, swaptions related to debt and equity securities, commodities and foreign exchange.*
>
>   *Creating "over-the-counter derivatives," with other firms as counterparties also creates new credit risks compared to the use of traded, listed instruments.*

These statements refer to two types of credit risk that banks and investment banking firms face as a result of their activities in the "derivatives business." Explain these two credit risks.

19. A portfolio manager buys a swaption with a strike rate of 6.5% that entitles the portfolio manager to enter into an interest rate swap to pay a fixed rate and receive a floating rate. The term of the swaption is 5 years.

    a. Is this swaption a payer swaption or a receiver swaption? Explain why.

    b. What does the strike rate of 6.5% mean?

20. The manager of a savings and loan association is considering the use of a swap as part of its asset/liability management strategy. The swap would be used to convert the payments of its portfolio of fixed-rate residential mortgage loans into a floating payment.

    a. What is the risk with using a plain vanilla or generic interest rate swap?

    b. Why might a manager consider using an interest rate swap in which the notional amount declines over time?

    c. Why might a manager consider buying a swaption?

21. Suppose that a corporation is considering using an interest rate swap in conjunction with the offering of a floating-rate bond issue. That is, the corporation wants to use the swap to change the funding arrangement from a floating rate to a fixed rate.

    a. Would the corporation enter into a swap in which it pays or receives a fixed rate?

    b. Suppose that the corporation does not plan to issue the bond for 1 year. What type of swap can the firm's management enter into in order to set the terms of the swap today?

22. Consider the following interest rate swap:

- A swap starts today, January 1 of year 1 (swap settlement date).
- The floating-rate payments are made quarterly based on "actual/360."
- The reference rate is 3-month LIBOR.
- The notional amount of the swap is $40 million.
- The term of the swap is 3 years.

    a. Suppose that today 3-month LIBOR is 5.7%. What will the fixed-rate payer for this interest rate swap receive on March 31 of year 1 (assuming that year 1 is not a leap year)?

b. Assume the Eurodollar CD futures price for the next seven quarters is as shown:

Quarter Starts	Quarter Ends	Days in Quarter	Eurodollar CD Futures Price
April 1 year 1	June 30 year 1	91	94.10
July 1 year 1	Sept 30 year 1	92	94.00
Oct 1 year 1	Dec 31 year 1	92	93.70
Jan 1 year 2	Mar 31 year 2	90	93.60
April 1 year 2	June 30 year 2	91	93.50
July 1 year 2	Sept 30 year 2	92	93.20
Oct 1 year 2	Dec 31 year 2	92	93.00

Compute the forward rate for each quarter and the floating-rate payment at the end of each quarter.

c. What is the floating-rate payment at the end of each quarter for this interest rate swap?

23. a. Assume that the swap rate for an interest rate swap is 7% and that the fixed-rate swap payments are made quarterly on an "actual/360 basis." If the notional amount of a 2-year swap is $20 million, what is the fixed-rate payment at the end of each quarter assuming the following number of days in each quarter:

Period Quarter	Days in Quarter
1	92
2	92
3	90
4	91
5	92
6	92
7	90
8	91

b. Assume that the swap in part (a) requires payments semiannually rather than quarterly. What is the semiannual fixed-rate payment every 6 months?

c. Suppose that the notional amount for the 2-year swap is the same in both years. Suppose instead that in year 1 the notional amount is $20 million, but in year 2 the notional amount is $12 million. What is the fixed-rate payment every 6 months?

24. Given the current 3-month LIBOR and the 5 Eurodollar CD futures prices shown in the following table, compute the forward rate and the forward discount factor for each period.

Period	Days in Quarter	Current 3-Month LIBOR	Eurodollar CD Futures Price
1	90	5.90%	
2	91		93.90
3	92		93.70
4	92		93.45
5	90		93.20
6	91		93.14

25. a. Suppose at the inception of a 5-year interest rate swap in which the reference rate is 3-month LIBOR the present value of the floating-rate payments is $16,555,000. The fixed-rate payments are assumed to be semiannual. Assume also that the following is computed for the fixed-rate payments (using the notation in the chapter):

$$\text{Swap rate} \times \sum_{t=1}^{N} \left(\text{Notional amount} \times \frac{\text{Days in period } t}{360} \right.$$

$$\left. \times \text{Forward discount factor for period } t \right) = \$236,500,000$$

What is the swap rate for this swap?
   b. Suppose that the 5-year yield from the on-the-run Treasury yield curve is 6.4%. What is the swap spread?
26. An interest rate swap had an original maturity of 5 years. Today, the swap has 2 years to maturity. The present value of the fixed-rate payments for the remainder of the term of the swap is $910,000. The present value of the floating-rate payments for the remainder of the swap is $710,000.
   a. What is the value of this swap from the perspective of the fixed-rate payer?
   b. What is the value of this swap from the perspective of the fixed-rate receiver?
27. Why is the risk factor used in determining the payoff for an option on a credit spread?
28. The manager of a bond portfolio enters into an option on a credit spread for Company W based on the credit spread of an issuer widening from its current level of 320 basis points. Suppose that the strike spread for the option is 320 basis points and the notional amount is $20 million. Suppose also that the risk factor for this issue is 4.
   a. If at the expiration date of this option the credit spread for this issue of Company W is 400 basis points, what is the dollar amount of the payoff?
   b. If at the expiration date of this option the credit spread for this issue of Company W is 200 basis points, what is the dollar amount of the payoff?
29. A portfolio manager has a view that the credit spread for the bonds of Zen.com will increase (i.e., widen) to more than the current 450 basis points in 1 year. How can the portfolio manager use a credit forward contract to capitalize on this view?
30. Explain how a total return default swap can be used to help an investor increase credit exposure.

CHAPTER 30

The Market for Foreign Exchange and Risk Control Instruments

Learning Objectives

After reading this chapter you will understand:

◆ what is meant by a foreign exchange rate.

◆ the different ways that a foreign exchange rate can be quoted (direct versus indirect).

◆ the conventions for quoting foreign exchange rates.

◆ what foreign exchange risk is.

◆ a cross rate and how to calculate a theoretical cross rate.

◆ what triangular arbitrage is.

◆ the foreign exchange market structure.

◆ what the euro is.

◆ the fundamental determinants of exchange rates: purchasing power parity and interest rate parity.

◆ the different instruments for hedging foreign exchange risk: forwards, futures, options, and swaps.

◆ the limitations of forward and futures contracts for hedging long-dated foreign exchange risk.

◆ how a forward exchange rate is determined and what covered interest arbitrage is.

◆ the basic currency swap structure and the motivation for using currency swaps.

The fundamental fact of international finance is that different countries issue different currencies, and the relative values of those currencies may change quickly, substantially, and without warning. The change, moreover, may either reflect economic developments or be a response to political events that make no economic sense. As a result, the risk that a currency's value may change adversely, which is called **foreign exchange risk** or **currency risk**, is an important consideration for all participants in the international financial markets. Investors who purchase securities denominated in a currency different from their own must worry about the return from those securities

■ 609 ■

after adjusting for changes in the exchange rate. Firms that issue obligations denominated in a foreign currency face the risk of uncertain effective value of the cash payments they owe to investors.

In this chapter, we provide a review of the instruments that can be used to control the risk of an adverse movement in a foreign currency. These instruments include forward contracts, futures contracts, options, and currency swaps. We begin our discussion with a review of the foreign exchange rate market.

◆ FOREIGN EXCHANGE RATES

An **exchange rate** is defined as the amount of one currency that can be exchanged for a unit of another currency. In fact, the exchange rate is the price of one currency in terms of another currency. And, depending on circumstances, one could define either currency as the price for the other. So exchange rates can be quoted "in either direction." For example, the exchange rate between the U.S. dollar and the Swiss franc could be quoted in one of two ways:

1. The amount of U.S. dollars necessary to acquire one Swiss franc, and this is the dollar price of one Swiss franc
2. The number of Swiss francs necessary to acquire one U.S. dollar, or the Swiss franc price of one dollar

EXCHANGE RATE QUOTATION CONVENTIONS

Exchange rate quotations may be either *direct* or *indirect*. The difference depends on identifying one currency as a local currency and the other as a foreign currency. For example, from the perspective of a U.S. participant, the local currency would be U.S. dollars, and any other currency, such as Swiss francs, would be the foreign currency. From the perspective of a Swiss participant, the local currency would be Swiss francs, and other currencies, such as U.S. dollars, the foreign currency. A **direct quote** is the number of units of a local currency exchangeable for one unit of a foreign currency.

An **indirect quote** is the number of units of a foreign currency that can be exchanged for one unit of a local currency. Looking at it from a U.S. participant's perspective, we see that a quote indicating the number of dollars exchangeable for one unit of a foreign currency is a direct quote. An indirect quote from the same participant's perspective would be the number of units of the foreign currency that can be exchanged for one U.S. dollar. Obviously, from the point of view of a non-U.S. participant, the number of U.S. dollars exchangeable for one unit of a non-U.S. currency is an indirect quote; the number of units of a non-U.S. currency exchangeable for a U.S. dollar is a direct quote.

Given a direct quote, we can obtain an indirect quote (which is simply the reciprocal of the direct quote), and vice versa. For example, suppose that on December 22, 2000, a U.S. participant is given a direct quote of 0.6071 U.S. dollars for one Swiss franc. That is, the price of a Swiss franc is $0.6071. The reciprocal of the direct quote is 1.6472, which would be the indirect quote for the U.S. participant; that is, one U.S. dollar can be exchanged for 1.6472 Swiss francs, which is the Swiss price of a dollar.

If the number of units of a foreign currency that can be obtained for one dollar—the price of a dollar in that currency or indirect quotation—rises, the dollar is said to appreciate relative to the currency, and the currency is said to depreciate. Thus, appreciation means a decline in the direct quotation.

FOREIGN EXCHANGE RISK

From the perspective of a U.S. investor, the cash flows of assets denominated in a foreign currency expose the investor to uncertainty as to the actual level of the cash flow measured in U.S. dollars. The actual number of U.S. dollars that the investor eventually gets depends on the exchange rate between the U.S. dollar and the foreign currency at the time the nondollar cash flow is received and exchanged for U.S. dollars. If the foreign currency depreciates (declines in value) relative to the U.S. dollar (that is, the U.S. dollar appreciates), the dollar value of the cash flows will be proportionately less, leading to foreign exchange risk.

Any investor who purchases an asset denominated in a currency that is not the medium of exchange in the investor's country faces foreign exchange risk. For example, a Greek investor who acquires a yen-denominated Japanese bond is exposed to the risk that the Japanese yen will decline in value relative to the Greek drachma.

Foreign exchange risk is a consideration for the issuer, too. Suppose that IBM issues bonds denominated in Japanese yen. IBM's foreign exchange risk is that, at the time the coupon interest payments must be made and the principal repaid, the U.S. dollar will have depreciated relative to the Japanese yen, requiring that IBM pay more dollars to satisfy its obligation.

◆ SPOT MARKET

The **spot exchange rate market** is the market for settlement of a foreign exchange transaction within two business days. (The spot exchange rate is also known as the **cash exchange rate**.) Since the early 1970s, exchange rates among major currencies have been free to float, with market forces determining the relative value of a currency.[1] Thus, each day a currency's price relative to that of another freely floating currency may stay the same, increase, or decrease.

A key factor affecting the expectation of changes in a country's exchange rate with another currency is the relative expected inflation rate of the two countries. Spot exchange rates adjust to compensate for the relative inflation rate. This adjustment reflects the so-called **purchasing power parity** relationship, which posits that the exchange rate—the domestic price of the foreign currency—is proportional to the domestic inflation rate, and inversely proportional to foreign inflation.

Let's look at what happens when the spot exchange rate changes between two currencies. Suppose that on day 1 the spot exchange rate between the U.S. dollar and country X is $0.7966 and on the next day, day 2, it changes to $0.8011. Consequently, on day 1, one currency unit of country X costs $0.7966. On day 2, it costs more U.S. dollars, $0.8011 to buy one currency unit of country X. Thus, the currency unit of country X *appreciated* relative to the U.S. dollar from day 1 to day 2, or, what amounts to the same thing, the U.S. dollar *depreciated* relative to the currency of country X from day 1 to day 2. Suppose further that on day 3 the spot exchange rate for one currency of country X is $0.8000. Relative to day 2, the U.S. dollar appreciated relative to the currency of country X or, equivalently, the currency of country X depreciated relative to the U.S. dollar.

Although quotes can be either direct or indirect, the problem is defining from whose perspective the quote is given. Foreign exchange conventions in fact standardize the

---

[1]   In practice, national monetary authorities can intervene in the foreign market for their currency for a variety of economic reasons, so the current foreign exchange system is sometimes referred to as a "managed" floating-rate system.

ways quotes are given. Because of the importance of the U.S. dollar in the international financial system, currency quotations are all relative to the U.S. dollar. When dealers quote, they either give U.S. dollars per unit of foreign currency (a direct quote from the U.S. perspective) or the number of units of the foreign currency per U.S. dollar (an indirect quote from the U.S. perspective). Quoting in terms of U.S. dollars per unit of foreign currency is called **American terms**, while quoting in terms of the number of units of the foreign currency per U.S. dollar is called **European terms**. The dealer convention is to use European terms in quoting foreign exchange with a few exceptions. The British pound, the Irish pound, the Australian dollar, the New Zealand dollar, and the European currency unit (discussed later) are exceptions that are quoted in American terms.

CROSS RATES

Barring any government restrictions, riskless arbitrage will assure that the exchange rate between two countries will be the same in both countries. The theoretical exchange rate between two countries other than the United States can be inferred from their exchange rates with the U.S. dollar. Rates computed in this way are referred to as **theoretical cross rates**. They would be computed as follows for two countries, X and Y:

$$\frac{\text{Quote in American terms of currency X}}{\text{Quote in American terms of currency Y}}$$

To illustrate, let's calculate the theoretical cross rate between Swiss francs and Japanese yen using the following exchange rates obtained from Yahoo finance on December 22, 2000.[2] The spot exchange rate for the two currencies in American terms is $0.6071 per Swiss franc and $0.008864 per Japanese yen. Then, the number of units of yen (currency Y) per unit of Swiss franc (currency X) is:

$$\frac{\$0.6071}{\$0.008864} = 68.49 \text{ yen per Swiss franc}$$

Taking the reciprocal gives the number of Swiss francs exchangeable for one Japanese yen. In our example, it is 0.0146.

In the real world, it is rare that the theoretical cross rate, as computed from actual dealer dollar exchange rate quotes, will differ from the actual cross rate quoted by dealers. When the discrepancy is large by comparison with the transactions costs of buying and selling the currencies, a riskless arbitrage opportunity arises. Arbitraging to take advantage of cross-rate mispricing is called **triangular arbitrage**, so named because it involves positions in three currencies—the U.S. dollar and the two foreign currencies. The arbitrage keeps actual cross rates in line with theoretical cross rates.

DEALERS

Exchange rates reported in daily periodicals (such as *The Wall Street Journal* and *New York Times*) and services such as Bloomberg Financial Markets and Reuters are indications of the rate at which a foreign currency can be purchased in the spot market. They are the rates for which the dealer is willing to sell foreign exchange. Foreign exchange dealers, however, do not quote one price. Instead, they quote an exchange rate at which they are willing to buy a foreign currency and one at which they are willing to sell a foreign currency. That is, they quote a bid-ask spread. Here are the bid and

---

[2]   www.finance.yahoo.com. The original source for the quote is Reuters.

ask (in terms of the number of the currency to acquire a U.S. dollar) for selected currencies as reported by Reuters on December 24, 2000:

Currency	Bid	Ask	Updated
Japanese yen	112.88	112.93	07:48 GMT/24 DEC 2000
British pound	1.4725	1.4735	07:51 GMT/24 DEC 2000
Swiss franc	1.6440	1.6450	07:48 GMT/24 DEC 2000
Canadian dollar	1.5162	1.5172	07:48 GMT/24 DEC 2000
Hong Kong dollar	7.7985	7.7995	03:01 GMT/23 DEC 2000

Dealers in the foreign exchange market are large international banks and other financial institutions that specialize in making markets in foreign exchange. Commercial banks dominate the market. There is no organized exchange where foreign currency is traded, but dealers are linked by telephone and cable, and by various information transfer services. Consequently, the foreign exchange market can best be described as an interbank over-the-counter market. Most transactions between banks are done through foreign exchange brokers. Brokers are agents that do not take a position in the foreign currencies involved in the transaction. The normal size of a transaction is $1 million or more.

Dealers in the foreign exchange market realize revenue from one or more sources: (1) the bid-ask spread; (2) commissions charged on foreign exchange transactions; and (3) trading profits (appreciation of the currencies that dealers hold a long position in, depreciation of the currencies that they hold a long position in, or appreciation of the currencies that they have a short position in).

THE EURO

The European Union consists of 15 European member countries that engage in European economic and political activities. In February 1992, the Treaty on European Union of 1992 established that monetary union would take place by January 1999. The treaty, also called the Maastricht Treaty because its terms were agreed to at the European Council meeting in Maastricht (Netherlands) in December 1991, called for a single currency and monetary policy for member countries in Europe. Monetary policy was to be administered by the European Central Bank, which we discussed in Chapter 5. The Economic and Monetary Union (EMU) represents the member countries that are part of the European Union that have adopted the single currency and monetary policy.

At the time of the treaty, the single currency was to be the **economic currency unit (ECU)**. It was the most widely used composite currency unit for capital market transactions. It was created in 1979 by the European Economic Community (EEC). The currencies included in the ECU were those of members of the European Monetary System (EMS). The weight of each country's currency is figured according to the relative importance of a country's economic trade and financial sector within the European Economic Community (EEC). Exchange rates between the ECU and those countries not part of the EEC float freely. The exchange rate between countries in the EEC, however, may fluctuate only within a narrow range.

However, at a meeting of the heads of government in Madrid in December 1995, it was agreed that the name of the single currency would be called the **euro**. The reason that the ECU was not selected as the single currency was due to the opinion of Germans that the ECU was perceived to be a weak currency. The countries of the European Union electing to be members of the EMU are subject to a fixed conversion rate against their national currencies and relative to the euro. However, the value of the euro against all other currencies, including member states of the European Union that did not elect to join the EMU, fluctuates according to market conditions.

Members of the EMU are said to be part of "euroland" or the "euro zone" because the euro became the only legal currency. Initially, the member countries maintained their own physical currencies, although they were fixed in value relative to the euro, and the euro had no physical existence. The actual euro currency physically replaced the individual currencies of the participating countries on January 1, 2002. At that time, the relevant authorities of each member country began to withdraw their old national currency from circulation. At the completion of the process, old national currencies can no longer pass as legal tender.

To qualify as a participating country in the EMU requires that a country satisfy certain economic standards. These standards set for fiscal policy were that the annual fiscal deficit could be no more than 3% of the gross disposable product (GDP); and total outstanding government indebtedness could be no more than 60% of GDP. Many other economic, political, and even social requirements for entry apply. Moreover, a provision of the treaty mandated that the voters of a country seeking membership had to approve the joining of the EMU by popular referendum.

These objectives were also, more or less, achieved, and on January 4, 1999 (a Monday, the first business day of the year), the 11 countries shown in Table 30-1 adopted the single currency, the euro. (Greece was selected as a member on June 19, 2000, and joined the common currency on January 1, 2001.) The previous currency for each country and the fixed conversion rate relative to the euro are also shown in the table. The central banks of the 11 participating countries were discontinued and replaced by the European Central Bank.

The birth of the euro on January 4, 1999, was smooth and uneventful in terms of both market volatility and operations. Several notable outcomes resulted from this event. First, despite many skeptics, it worked; it proved viable and fairly stable. Second, it gave birth to a large public and corporate capital market denominated in the euro. With respect to the capital market, the governments of all the participating countries issue their government debt denominated in euros. Thus, the differences in the rate on the government debt are based only on differences in credit risk—because differences in currency risk were eliminated—and are quite small. Table 30-1 provides an estimate of the credit spread, using Germany as a base.

TABLE 30-1 Members of the Economic Monetary Union

Country	Previous Currency	Conversion 1 Euro =	Spread to German 10-Year Yields*
Initial Members:			
Germany	mark	1.95583	—
Finland	markka	5.94573	22 b.p.
Netherlands	guilder	2.20371	17
France	franc	6.55957	16
Spain	peseta	166.386	31
Italy	lire	1936.27	37
Belgium	franc	40.3399	36
Luxembourg	franc	40.3399	—
Austria	schilling	13.7603	31
Ireland	punt	0.787564	26
Portugal	escudo	200.48239	
Subsequent Entrant:			
Greece	drachma	340.750	79

*Source for the spreads is Bloomberg Financial Markets.

On the corporate side, the primary issuance of corporate debt denominated in the euro has become large and liquid. Both European and U.S. investment banks play significant roles in these fundings. The secondary markets in these issues have also become quite liquid.

On September 27, 2000, the group of seven central banks (G-7), composed of U.S., European, and Japanese central banks, conducted a unified currency support intervention to support the euro, the first unified intervention in support of a currency in 2 years. On October 5, 2000, the ECB raised interest rates to support this intervention.

Among the most analyzed aspects of the euro, in addition to its weakness, is who the next participants will be. On September 28, 2000, Denmark voted decisively against joining the EMU. Among the other potential candidates to join are the United Kingdom and Sweden.

◆ INSTRUMENTS FOR HEDGING FOREIGN EXCHANGE RISK

Four instruments are available to borrowers and investors to protect against adverse foreign exchange rate movements: (1) currency forward contracts (2) currency futures contracts (3) currency options and (4) currency swaps.

CURRENCY FORWARD CONTRACTS

Recall that in a forward contract one party agrees to buy the underlying, and another party agrees to sell that same underlying, for a specific price at a designated date in the future. Here we consider forward contracts in which the underlying is foreign exchange.

Most forward contracts have a maturity of less than 2 years. Longer-dated forward contracts have relatively large bid-ask spreads; that is, the size of the bid-ask spread for a given currency increases with the maturity of the contract. Consequently, forward contracts are not attractive for hedging long-dated foreign currency exposure.

As Chapter 10 emphasized, both forward and futures contracts can be used to lock in a certain price, which in this case would be the foreign exchange rate. By locking in a rate and eliminating downside risk, the user foregoes the opportunity to benefit from any advantageous foreign exchange rate movement. Futures contracts, which are creations of an exchange, have certain advantages over forward contracts in many cases, such as stock indexes and Treasury securities. For foreign exchange, by contrast, the forward market is the market of choice, and trading there is much larger than trading on exchanges. However, because the foreign exchange forward market is an inter-bank market, reliable information on the amount of contracts outstanding at any time, or open interest, is not publicly available.

Pricing Currency Forward Contracts   In Chapter 10, we showed the relationship between spot prices and forward prices, and explained how arbitrage ensures that the relationship holds. We now apply similar considerations to the pricing of foreign exchange futures contracts on the basis of the spot exchange rate, using an extended example.

Consider a U.S. investor with a 1-year investment horizon who has two choices:

Alternative 1: Deposit $100,000 in a U.S. bank that pays 7% compounded annually for 1 year.

Alternative 2: Deposit in a bank in country X, the U.S. dollar equivalent of $100,000 in country X's currency that pays 9% compounded annually for 1 year.

The two alternatives and their outcomes 1 year from now are depicted in Figure 30-1. Which is the better alternative? It will be the alternative that produces the most U.S. dollars 1 year from now. Ignoring U.S. and country X taxes on interest income or any other taxes, we need to know two things in order to determine the better alternative: (1) the spot exchange rate between U.S. dollars and country X's currency, and (2) the spot exchange rate 1 year from now between U.S. dollars and country X's currency. The former is know; the latter is not.

We can determine, however, the spot rate 1 year from now between U.S. dollars and country X's currency that will make the investor indifferent between the two alternatives.

Alternative 1: The amount of U.S. dollars available 1 year from now would be $107,000 ($100,000 times 1.07).

Alternative 2: Assume that the spot rate is $0.6558 for one unit of country X's currency at this time. We denote country X's currency as CX. Then, ignoring commissions, $100,000 can be exchanged for CX152,486 ($100,000 divided by 0.6558). The amount of country X's currency available at the end of 1 year would be CX166,210 (CX152,476 times 1.09).

The number of U.S. dollars for which the CX166,210 can be exchanged depends on the exchange rate 1 year from now. Let F denote the exchange rate between these two currencies 1 year from now. Specifically, F denotes the number of U.S. dollars that can

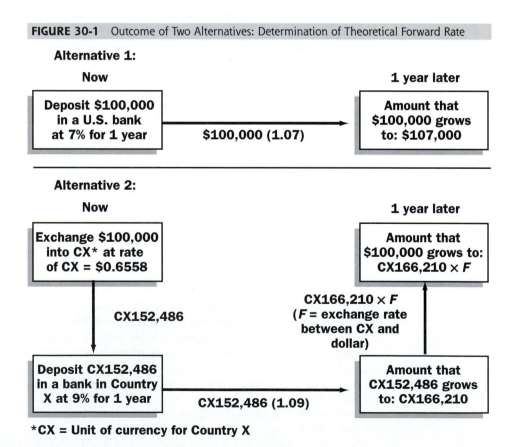

FIGURE 30-1 Outcome of Two Alternatives: Determination of Theoretical Forward Rate

Alternative 1:

Now		1 year later
Deposit $100,000 in a U.S. bank at 7% for 1 year	$100,000 (1.07) →	Amount that $100,000 grows to: $107,000

Alternative 2:

Now		1 year later
Exchange $100,000 into CX* at rate of CX = $0.6558		Amount that $100,000 grows to: CX166,210 × F

CX152,486

CX166,210 × F
(F = exchange rate between CX and dollar)

| Deposit CX152,486 in a bank in Country X at 9% for 1 year | CX152,486 (1.09) → | Amount that CX152,486 grows to: CX166,210 |

*CX = Unit of currency for Country X

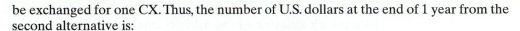

be exchanged for one CX. Thus, the number of U.S. dollars at the end of 1 year from the second alternative is:

$$\text{Amount of U.S. dollars 1 year from now} = \text{CX166,210} \times F$$

The investor will be indifferent between the two alternatives if the number of U.S. dollars is $107,000:

$$\$107,000 = \text{CX166,210} \times F$$

Solving, we find that F is equal to $0.6438. Thus, if 1 year from now the spot exchange rate is $0.6438 for one unit of country X's currency, then the two alternatives will produce the same number of U.S. dollars. If more than $0.6438 can be exchanged for one unit of country X's currency, then the investor receives more than $107,000 at the end of one year. An exchange rate of $0.6500 for one unit of country X's currency, for example, would produce $108,037 (CX166,210 times $0.6500). The opposite is true if less than $0.6438 can be exchanged for one unit of country X's currency. For example, if the future exchange rate is $0.6400, the investor receives $106,374 (CX166,210 times $0.6400).

Let us now look at this situation from the perspective of an investor in country X. Suppose that an investor in country X with a 1-year investment horizon has two alternatives:

Alternative 1: Deposit CX152,486 in a bank in country X that pays 9% compounded annually for 1 year.

Alternative 2: Deposit the equivalent of CX152,486 in U.S. dollars in a U.S. bank that pays 7% compounded annually for 1 year.

Once again, assume that the spot exchange rate is $0.6558 for one unit of country X's currency. The investor in country X will select the alternative that generates the most CX at the end of 1 year. The first alternative would generate CX166,210 (CX152,486 times 1.09). The second alternative requires that CX be exchanged for U.S. dollars at the spot exchange rate at this time. Given the spot exchange rate assumed, CX152,486 can be exchanged for $100,000 (CX152,486 multiplied by $0.6558). At the end of 1 year, the second alternative would generate $107,000 ($100,000 times 1.07). Letting F continue to denote the number of U.S. dollars in country X following alternative 2 will realize the following amount of country X's currency 1 year from now:

$$\text{Amount of country X's currency 1 year from now} = \$107,000 / F$$

The investor will be indifferent between the two alternatives if

$$\$107,000 / F = \text{CX166,210}$$

The equation yields a value for F of $0.6438, the same exchange rate that we found when we sought the exchange rate 1 year from now that would make the U.S. investor indifferent between the two alternatives facing that investor.

Now suppose that a dealer quotes a 1-year forward exchange rate between the two currencies. The 1-year forward exchange rate fixes today the exchange rate 1 year from now. Thus, if the 1-year forward exchange rate quoted is $0.6438 for one unit of country X's currency, investing in the bank in country X will provide no arbitrage opportunity for the U.S. investor. If the 1-year forward rate quoted is more than $0.6438 for one unit of country X's currency, the U.S. investor can arbitrage the situation by selling country X's currency forward (and buying U.S. dollars forward for CX).

To see how this arbitrage opportunity can be exploited, suppose that the 1-year forward exchange rate is $0.6500 for one unit of country X's currency. Also, assume that the borrowing and the lending rates within each currency's country are the same. Suppose that the U.S. investor borrows $100,000 for 1 year at 7% compounded annually and enters into a forward contract agreeing to deliver CX166,210 1 year from now at $0.6500 per CX. That is, 1 year from now the investor is agreeing to deliver CX166,210 in exchange for $108,037 (CX166,210 multiplied by $0.6500).

The $100,000 that was borrowed can be exchanged for CX152,486 at the spot rate of $0.6558 to one unit of country X's currency, which can be invested in country X at 9%. One year from now, the U.S. investor will have CX166,210 from the investment in country X, which can be delivered against the forward contract. The U.S. investor will receive $108,037 and repay $107,000 to satisfy the bank loan, netting $1,037. Assuming that the counterparty to the forward contract does not default, this riskless arbitrage situation results in a $1,037 profit, generated with no initial investment.[3] This riskless profit will prompt many arbitrageurs to follow this strategy and will, obviously, result in the U.S. dollar rising relative to country X's currency in the forward exchange rate market, or possibly some other adjustment.[4]

On the other hand, if the 1-year forward exchange rate quoted is less than $0.6438, an investor in country X can arbitrage the situation by buying CX forward (and by selling U.S. dollars forward). This riskless arbitrage again leads arbitrageurs to act, with the result that the forward exchange rate of U.S. dollars relative to CX falls.[5] The conclusion of this argument is that the 1-year forward exchange rate must be $0.6438, because any other forward exchange rate would result in an arbitrage opportunity for either the U.S. or the investor in country X.

Thus, the spot exchange rate and the interest rates in two countries determine the forward exchange rate of their currencies. The relationship among the spot exchange rate, the interest rates in two countries, and the forward rate is called **interest rate parity**. The parity relationship implies that an investor, by hedging in the forward exchange rate market, realizes the same sure domestic return whether investing domestically or in a foreign country. The arbitrage process that forces interest rate parity is called **covered interest arbitrage**.

Mathematically, interest rate parity between the currencies of two countries, A and B, can be expressed in this way:

Let

I = amount of A's currency to be invested for a time period of length t
S = spot exchange rate: price of foreign currency in terms of domestic currency (units of domestic currency per unit of foreign currency)
F = t-period forward rate: price of foreign currency t periods from now
i_A = interest rate on an investment maturing at time t in country A
i_B = interest rate on an investment maturing at time t in country B

---

[3] An investor in country X could also arbitrage this situation.
[4] Actually, a combination of things may occur when U.S. investors attempt to exploit this situation: (1) The spot exchange rate of U.S. dollars relative to country X's currency will fall as U.S. investors sell dollars and buy CX; (2) U.S. interest rates will rise in the United States as investors borrow in the United States and invest in country X; (3) Country X interest rates will fall as more is invested in country X; and (4) the 1-year forward rate of U.S. dollars relative to CX will fall. In practice, the last will dominate.
[5] A combination of things may occur when country X investors attempt to exploit this situation: (1) The spot exchange rate of U.S. dollars relative to CX will rise as country X investors buy dollars and sell CX; (2) Country X interest rates will fall as more is invested in the United States; and (4) the 1-year forward rate of U.S. dollars relative to CX will rise. In practice, the last will dominate.

Then

$$I\left(1+i_A\right) = \left(I \, / \, S\right)\left(1+i_B\right)F$$

To illustrate, let country A be the United States and country B represent country X. In our example we have:

$$I = \$100,000 \text{ for 1 year}$$
$$S = \$0.6558$$
$$F = \$0.6438$$
$$i_A = 0.07$$
$$i_B = 0.09$$

Then, according to interest rate parity, this relationship holds:

$$\$100,000\left(1.07\right) = \left(\$100,000 \, / \, \$0.6558\right)\left(1.09\right)\left(\$0.6438\right)$$
$$\$107,000 = \$107,005$$

The \$5 difference is due to rounding. Interest rate parity can also be expressed as:

$$\left(1+i_A\right) = \left(F \, / \, S\right)\left(1+i_B\right)$$

Rewriting the equation, we obtain the theoretical forward rate implied by the interest rates and spot exchange rate:

$$F = S\left(\frac{1+i_A}{1+i_B}\right)$$

Although we referred so far to investors, we could use borrowers as well to illustrate interest rate parity. A borrower has the choice of obtaining funds in a domestic or foreign market. Interest rate parity provides that a borrower who hedges in the forward exchange rate market realizes the same domestic borrowing rate whether borrowing domestically or in a foreign country.

To derive the theoretical forward exchange rate using the arbitrage argument, we made several assumptions. When the assumptions are violated, the actual forward exchange rate may deviate from the theoretical forward exchange rate. First, in deriving the theoretical forward exchange rate, we assumed the investor faced no commissions or bid-ask spread when exchanging in the spot market today and at the end of the investment horizon. In practice, investors incur such costs, which cause the actual forward exchange rate to be plus or minus a small amount of the theoretical rate.

Second, we assumed that the borrowing and lending rates in each currency are the same. Dropping this unrealistic assumption eliminates the possibility of a single theoretical forward exchange rate, and instead implies a band around a level reflecting borrowing and lending rates. The actual rate should be within this band.

Third, we ignored taxes. In fact, the divergence between actual and theoretical forward exchange rates can be the result of the different tax structures of the two countries. Finally, we assumed that arbitrageurs could borrow, and invest in another country, as much as they wanted in order to exploit mispricing in the exchange market. It should be noted, however, that any restrictions on foreign investing or borrowing in each country impede arbitrage and may cause a divergence between actual and theoretical forward exchange rates.

Link Between Eurocurrency Market and Forward Prices   In deriving interest rate parity, we looked at the interest rates in both countries. In fact, market participants in most countries look to one interest rate in order to perform covered interest arbitrage, and that is the interest rate in the Eurocurrency market. The **Eurocurrency market** is the name of the unregulated and informal market for bank deposits and bank loans denominated in a currency other than that of the country where the bank initiating the transaction is located. Examples of transactions in the Eurocurrency market are a British bank in London that lends U.S. dollars to a French corporation, and a Japanese corporation that deposits Swiss francs in a German bank. An investor seeking covered interest arbitrage will accomplish it with short-term borrowing and lending in the Eurocurrency market.

The largest sector of the Eurocurrency market involves bank deposits and bank loans in U.S. dollars and is called the Eurodollar market. The seed for the Eurocurrency market was, in fact, the Eurodollar market. As international capital market transactions increased, the market for bank deposits and bank loans in other currencies developed.

CURRENCY FUTURES CONTRACTS

Foreign exchange futures contracts for the major currencies are traded on the International Monetary Market (IMM), a division of the Chicago Mercantile Exchange. The futures contracts traded on the IMM are for the Japanese yen, the German mark, the Canadian dollar, the British pound, the Swiss franc, and the Australian dollar. The amount of each foreign currency that must be delivered for a contract varies by currency. For example, the British pound futures contract calls for delivery of 62,500 pounds, while the Japanese yen futures contract is for delivery of 12.5 million yen. The maturity cycle for currency futures is March, June, September, and December. The longest maturity is 1 year. Consequently, as in the case of a currency forward contract, currency futures do not provide a good vehicle for hedging long-dated foreign exchange risk exposure.

Other exchanges trading currency futures in the United States are the Midamerica Commodity Exchange (a subsidiary of the Chicago Board of Trade) and the Financial Instrument Exchange (a subsidiary of the New York Cotton Exchange). The latter trades a futures contract in which the underlying is a U.S. dollar index. Outside the United States, currency futures are traded on the London International Financial Futures Exchange, the Singapore International Monetary Exchange, the Toronto Futures Exchange, the Sydney Futures Exchange, and the New Zealand Futures Exchange.

CURRENCY OPTION CONTRACTS

In contrast to a forward or futures contract, an option gives the option buyer the opportunity to benefit from favorable exchange rate movements but establishes a maximum loss. The option price is the cost of arranging such a risk/return profile.

The two types of foreign currency options are options on the foreign currency and futures options. The latter are options to enter into foreign exchange futures contracts. (We described the features of futures options in Chapter 28.) Futures options are traded on the IMM, the trading location of the currency futures contracts.

Options on foreign currencies have been traded on the Philadelphia Exchange since 1982. The foreign currencies underlying the options are the same as for the futures. Two sorts of options are traded on the Philadelphia Exchange for each currency: an American-type option and a European-type option. Recall from Chapter 28 that the former permits exercise at any time up to and including the expiration date, while the latter permits exercise only at the expiration date. The number of units of foreign currency underlying each option contract traded on the Philadelphia Exchange is one-half the amount of the futures contract. For example, the Japanese yen option is for 6.25 million yen and the British pound option is for 31,250 pounds. Options on currencies are also traded on the London Stock Exchange and the London International Financial Futures Exchange.

In addition to the organized exchanges, an over-the-counter market exists for options on currencies. Trading in these products is dominated by commercial banks and investment banking firms. As we explained in Chapter 29, over-the-counter options are tailor-made products that accommodate the specific needs of clients. Only options on the major currencies are traded on the organized exchanges. An option on any other currency must be purchased in the over-the-counter market.

The factors that affect the price of any option were discussed in Chapter 28. One key factor is the expected volatility of the underlying over the life of the option. In the case of currency options, the underlying is the foreign currency specified by the option contract. So, the volatility that affects the option's value is the expected volatility of the exchange rate between the two currencies from the present time to the expiration of the option. The strike price also is an exchange rate, and it affects the option's value: the higher the strike price, the lower the value of a call, and the higher the value of a put. Another factor that influences the option price is the relative risk-free interest rate in the two countries.[6]

CURRENCY SWAPS

In Chapter 29, we discussed interest rate swaps—a transaction in which two counter-parties agree to exchange interest payments with no exchange of principal. In a currency swap, both interest and principal are exchanged. The best way to explain a currency swap is with an illustration.

Assume that two companies—a U.S. company and a Swiss company—each seeks to borrow for 10 years in its domestic currency. The U.S. company seeks $100 million U.S. dollar-denominated debt, and the Swiss company seeks debt in the amount of 127 million Swiss francs (SF). For reasons that we explore later, let's suppose that each wants to issue 10-year bonds in the bond market of the other country, and those bonds are denominated in the other country's currency. That is, the U.S. company wants to issue the Swiss franc equivalent of $100 million in Switzerland, and the Swiss company wants to issue the U.S. dollar equivalent of SF 127 million in the United States.

Let's also assume the following:

1. At the time when both companies want to issue their 10-year bonds, the spot exchange rate between U.S. dollars and Swiss francs is one U.S. dollar for 1.27 Swiss francs.
2. The coupon rate that the U.S. company would have to pay on the 10-year, Swiss franc-denominated bonds issued in Switzerland is 6%.
3. The coupon rate that the Swiss company would have to pay on the 10-year, U.S. dollar-denominated bonds issued in the United States is 11%.

By the first assumption, if the U.S. company issues the bonds in Switzerland, it can exchange the SF 127 million for $100 million. By issuing $100 million of bonds in the United States, the Swiss company can exchange the proceeds for SF 127 million. Therefore, both get the amount of financing they seek. Assuming the coupon rates given by the last two assumptions, and assuming for purposes of this illustration that

---

[6]   To understand why, recall the portfolio we created in Chapter 11 to replicate the payoff of a call option on an asset. A portion of the asset is purchased with borrowed funds. In the case of a currency option, it involves purchasing a portion of the foreign currency underlying the option. However, the foreign currency acquired can be invested at a risk-free interest rate in the foreign country. Consequently, the pricing of a currency option is similar to the pricing of an option on an income-earning asset such as a dividend-paying stock or an interest-paying bond. At the same time, the amount that must be set aside to meet the strike price depends on the domestic rate. Thus, the option price, just like interest rate parity, reflects both rates.

coupon payments are made annually, the cash outlays that the companies must make for the next 10 years are summarized as follows:

Year	U.S. Company	Swiss Company
1–10	SF 7,620,000	$11,000,000
10	127,000,000	100,000,000

Each issuer faces the risk that, at the time a payment on its liability must be made, its domestic currency will have depreciated relative to the other currency. Such a depreciation would require a greater outlay of the domestic currency to satisfy the liability. That is, both firms are exposed to foreign exchange risk.

In a currency swap, the two companies issue bonds in the other's bond market and enter into an agreement requiring that:

1. The two parties exchange the proceeds received from the sale of the bonds.
2. The two parties make the coupon payments to service the debt of the other party.
3. At the termination date of the currency swap (which coincides with the maturity of the bonds), both parties agree to exchange the par value of the bonds.

In our illustration, these arrangements result in the following:

1. The U.S. company issues 10-year, 6% coupon bonds with a par value of SF 127 million in Switzerland and gives the proceeds to the Swiss company. At the same time, the Swiss company issues 10-year, 11% bonds with a par value of $100 million in the United States and gives the proceeds to the U.S. company.
2. The U.S. company agrees to service the coupon payments to the Swiss company by paying the $11,000,000 per year for the next 10 years to the Swiss company: the Swiss company agrees to service the coupon payments of the U.S. company by paying SF 7,620,000 for the next 10 years to the U.S. company.
3. At the end of 10 years (the termination date of this currency swap and the maturity of the two bond issues), the U.S. company would pay $100 million to the Swiss company, and the Swiss company would pay SF 127 million to the U.S. company.

This complex agreement is diagrammed in Figure 30-2.

Now let's assess what this transaction accomplishes. Each party received the amount of financing it sought. The U.S. company's coupon payments are in dollars, not Swiss francs; the Swiss company's coupon payments are in Swiss francs, not U.S. dollars. At the termination date, both parties will receive an amount sufficient in their local currency to pay off the holders of their bonds. With the coupon payments and the principal repayment in their local currency, neither party faces foreign exchange risk.

In practice, the two companies would not deal directly with each other. Instead, either a commercial bank or investment banking firm would function as an intermediary (as either a broker or dealer) in the transaction. As a broker, the intermediary simply brings the two parties together, receiving a fee for the service. If instead the intermediary serves as a dealer, it would not only bring the two parties together, but would also guarantee payment to both parties. Thus, if one party were to default, the counterparty would continue to receive its payments from the dealer. Of course, in this arrangement, both parties are concerned with the credit risk of the dealer. When the currency swap market started, transactions were typically brokered. The more prevalent arrangement today is that the intermediary acts as a dealer.

As we explained in Chapter 29, an interest rate swap is nothing more than a package of forward contracts. The same is true for a currency swap; it is simply a package of currency forward contracts.

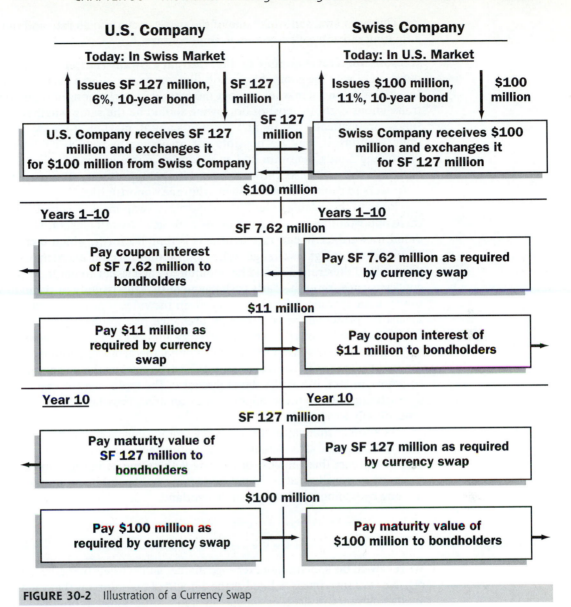

FIGURE 30-2   Illustration of a Currency Swap

Currency Coupon Swap   In our illustration, we assumed that both parties made fixed cash flow payments. Suppose instead that one of the parties sought floating-rate rather than fixed-rate financing. Returning to the same illustration, assume that instead of fixed-rate financing, the Swiss company wanted LIBOR-based financing. In this case, the U.S. company would issue floating-rate bonds in Switzerland. Suppose that it could do so at a rate of LIBOR plus 50 basis points. Because the currency swap would call for the Swiss company to service the coupon payments of the U.S. company, the Swiss company would make annual payments of LIBOR plus 50 basis points. The U.S. company would still make fixed-rate payments in U.S. dollars to service the debt obligation of the Swiss company in the United States. Now, however, the Swiss company would make floating-rate payments (LIBOR plus 50 basis points) in Swiss francs to service the debt obligation of the U.S. company in Switzerland.

Currency swaps in which one of the parties pays a fixed rate and the counterparty a floating rate are called **currency coupon swaps**.

Reasons for Development of the Currency Swap Market Now we turn to the question of why the companies in this illustration may find a currency swap beneficial. In a global financial market without the market imperfections of regulations, taxes, and transactions costs, the cost of borrowing should be the same whether the issuer raises funds domestically or in any foreign capital market. In a world with market imperfections, it may be possible for an issuer to reduce its borrowing cost by borrowing funds denominated in a foreign currency and hedging the associated exchange rate risk, also known as an arbitrage opportunity. The currency swap allows borrowers to capitalize on any such arbitrage opportunities.

Prior to the establishment of the currency swap market, capitalizing on such arbitrage opportunities required use of the currency forward market. The market for long-dated forward exchange rate contracts is thin, however, which increases the cost of eliminating foreign exchange risk. Eliminating foreign exchange risk in our U.S.-Switzerland illustration would have required each issuer to enter 10 currency forward contracts (one for each yearly cash payment that the issuer was committed to make in the foreign currency). The currency swap provides a more transactionally efficient means for protecting against foreign exchange risk when an issuer (or its investment banker) identifies an arbitrage opportunity and seeks to benefit from it.

As the currency swap market developed, the arbitrage opportunities for reduced funding costs that were available in the early days of the swap market became less common. In fact, it was the development of the swap market that reduced arbitrage opportunities. When these opportunities do arise, they last for only a short period of time, usually less than a day.

As another motivation for currency swaps, some companies seek to raise funds in foreign countries as a means of increasing their recognition by foreign investors, despite the fact that the cost of funding is the same as in the United States. The U.S. company in our illustration might be seeking to expand its potential sources of future funding by issuing bonds today in Switzerland.

Summary

We reviewed the spot foreign exchange market and markets for hedging foreign exchange risk. An exchange rate is defined as the amount of one currency that can be exchanged for another currency. A direct exchange rate quote is the domestic price of a foreign currency; an indirect quote is the foreign price of the domestic currency. An investor or issuer whose cash flows are denominated in a foreign currency is exposed to foreign exchange risk.

The spot exchange rate market is the market for settlement of a currency within two business days. In the developed countries, and some of the developing ones, exchange rates are free to float. According to the purchasing power parity relationship, the exchange rate between two countries—the price of the foreign currency in terms of the domestic currency—is proportional to the domestic price level and inversely proportional to the price level in the foreign country. Exchange rates are typically quoted in terms of the U.S. dollar.

The foreign exchange market is an over-the-counter market dominated by large international banks that act as dealers. Foreign exchange dealers quote one price at which they are willing to buy a foreign currency and one at which they are willing to sell a foreign currency. The difference between those prices is one cost a user of the market must pay; another cost is the explicit fee or commission to brokers arranging the purchase or sale of currency.

The Economic and Monetary Union represents the member countries that are part of the European Union and have adopted a single currency and monetary policy. The single currency adopted is the euro. The value of the euro against other currencies will fluctuate according to market conditions.

Currency forward contracts, currency futures contracts, currency options, and currency swaps are four instruments that borrowers and investors can use to protect against adverse foreign exchange rate movements.

Interest rate parity give the relationship among the spot exchange rate, the interest rates in two countries, and the forward rate. The relationship is assured by a covered interest arbitrage. Interest rate parity implies that investors and borrowers who hedge in the forward exchange rate market will realize the same domestic return or face the same domestic borrowing rate whether investing or borrowing domestically or in a foreign country.

In implementing covered interest arbitrage, the relevant interest rates are those in the Eurocurrency market, the market for bank deposits and bank loans denominated in a currency other than that of the country where the bank initiating the transaction is located. The Eurodollar market is the largest sector of this market.

Exchange-traded options on major foreign currencies and futures options on the same currencies trade in the United States. An option on any other currency must be purchased in the over-the-counter market.

A currency swap is effectively a package of currency forward contracts, with the advantage that it allows hedging of long-dated foreign exchange risk and it is more transactionally efficient than futures or forward contracts. Currency swaps are used to arbitrage the increasingly rare opportunities in the global financial market for raising funds at less cost than in the domestic market.

Key Terms

- American terms
- Cash exchange rate
- Covered interest arbitrage
- Currency coupon swaps
- Currency risk
- Direct quote

- Economic currency unit (ECU)
- Euro
- Eurocurrency market
- European terms
- Exchange rate
- Foreign exchange risk

- Indirect quote
- Interest rate parity
- Purchasing power parity
- Spot exchange rate market
- Theoretical cross rates
- Triangular arbitrage

Questions

1. A U.S. life insurance company that buys British government bonds faces foreign exchange risk. Specify the nature of that risk in terms of the company's expected return in U.S. dollars.
2. Explain the difference between a spot exchange rate and a forward exchange rate.
3. These spot foreign exchange rates were reported on December 24, 2000:

	Japanese Yen	British Pound	Canadian Dollar
U.S. Dollars	0.008864	1.477	0.6596

The exchange rates indicate the number of U.S. dollars necessary to purchase one unit of the foreign currency.

a. From the perspective of a U.S. investor, are the preceding foreign exchange rates direct or indirect quotes?

b. How much of each of the foreign currencies is needed to buy one U.S. dollar?

c. Calculate the theoretical cross rates between: (i) the Canadian dollar and the Japanese yen; (ii) the Canadian dollar and the British pound; and (iii) the Japanese yen and the British pound.

4. a. What is the euro?

b. Comment on the following statement: "The exchange rate between the euro and the currencies of all major economic countries is fixed."

c. Comment on the following statement: "The euro was the first choice as the single currency for the Economic and Monetary Union."

5. Explain the meaning of triangular arbitrage, and show how it is related to cross rates.

6. On February 8, 1991, the U.S. dollar/British pound spot rate was U.S. $1.9905 per pound and the U.S. dollar/Japanese yen spot rate was U.S. $0.00779 per yen. The following forward rates were also quoted:

	British Pound	*Japanese Yen*
30 days	1.9908	0.007774
60	1.9597	0.007754
90	1.9337	0.007736

a. Explain what someone who enters into a 30-day forward contract to deliver British pounds is agreeing to do.

b. Explain what someone who enters into a 90-day forward contract to buy Japanese yen is agreeing to do.

c. What can you infer about the relationship between U.S. and British short-term interest rates and U.S. and Japanese short-term interest rates?

7. What is the drawback of using currency forward contracts for hedging long-dated positions?

8. How does covered interest arbitrage relate to interest rate parity?

9. Why are the interest rates in the Eurocurrency market important in covered interest arbitrage?

10. Suppose you know the following items: You can borrow and lend $500,000 at the 1-year interest rate in the United States of 7.5%; in country W both the borrowing and lending rates are 9.2%; the spot exchange rate between the U.S. dollar and country W's currency is now $0.1725 per unit of currency of country W; and the 1-year forward exchange rate is $0.2 per unit of currency of country W.

a. Explain how you could make a profit without risk and without investing any of your own money. (Assume commissions, fees, etc., to be equal to zero.)

b. Aside from assuming commissions, fees, and so on, to be zero, several unrealistic assumptions must be made in answering part (a). What are they?

c. Even if we incorporated realistic considerations regarding commissions and so on, the interest rate and exchange rate numbers in this question would probably produce a profit of some size. Why do you think opportunities like the one in this question are unlikely to come along often in the real world?

11. If the 1-year borrowing and lending rates in Japan were 5%, and 7% in the United States, and if the forward exchange rate between dollars and yen were $0.007576 per yen (i.e., $1 could buy 131.99 yen), then what should the spot exchange rate of dollars for yen be?

12. For which currencies are options and futures traded on organized U.S. exchanges?

13. What is the major difference between a currency swap and an interest rate swap?

14. The following excerpt appeared in the January 14, 1991, issue of *Wall Street Letter*.

The Philadelphia Stock Exchange plans to list the first nondollar denominated options to trade in the United States, according to sources at the exchange. The Phlx will list cross-currency options based on the relationships between the Deutsche mark and the Japanese yen, as well as British pound/yen and pound/mark options, a spokesman confirmed. . . .

The exchange currently lists currency options that are based on the relationship between that currency and the dollar, one Phlx member explained. "If you're not American," he added, "then the dollar doesn't do it for you." The three new cross-currency options should be attractive to the same banks and broker-dealers that currently trade dollar-based currency options, as well as non-U.S. entities that have interests in other currencies.

Cross-currency options are "a very big part of international trade and international capital markets," and are big over-the-counter products, but none currently trades on an exchange. The advantage of exchange-traded options, the Phlx member said, is that "99% of the customers don't have the credit" to trade such a product over-the-counter with a big bank.

a. Explain what the representative of the Phlx means by saying: "If you're not American, then the dollar doesn't do it for you."
b. Why is the credit of customers critical in the over-the-counter market but not for an exchange-traded contract?
c. When the Philadelphia Stock Exchange filed with the SEC to list cross-currency options, the exchange indicated that the demand for this product has been "spawned by recent large fluctuations and dramatic increases in volatility levels for cross-rate options." Why would this increase the demand for cross-currency options?

Index